# Mobil

## Travel Guide®

# MID ATLANTIC

# ACKNOWLEDGMENTS

We gratefully acknowledge the help of our representatives for their efficient and perceptive inspections of the lodging and dining establishments listed, the establishments' proprietors for their cooperation in showing their facilities and providing information about them, and the many users of previous editions who have taken the time to share their experiences. Mobil Travel Guide is also grateful to all the talented writers who contributed entries to this book.

Front and back cover images: ©iStockPhoto.com

All maps: created by Mapping Specialists

ISBN: 9-780841-60860-3          Manufactured in Canada

10 9 8 7 6 5 4 3 2 1

# TABLE OF CONTENTS

**3**

★ **MID ATLANTIC**
★
★
★

# WRITTEN IN THE STARS

Because time is precious and the travel industry is ever-changing, having accurate, reliable travel information at your fingertips has never been more important. With this in mind, Mobil Travel Guide has provided invaluable insight to travelers through its Star Rating system for more than 50 years.

The Mobil Corporation (known as Exxon Mobil Corporation since a 1999 merger) began producing the Mobil Travel Guide books in 1958 following the introduction of the U.S.-interstate highway system in 1956. The first edition covered only five Southwestern states. Since then, our books have become the premier travel guides in North America, covering all 50 states and Canada, and beginning in 2008, international destinations such as Hong Kong and Beijing.

Today, the concept of a "five-star" experience is one that permeates the collective conciousness, but few people realize it's one that originated with Mobil. We created our star rating system to give travelers an easy-to-recognize quality scale for choosing where to stay, dine and spa. Based on an objective process, we make recommendations to our readers that we believe will enhance the quality and value of their travel experiences. Our trusted Mobil One- to Five-Star rating system is the oldest and most respected lodging and restaurant inspection and rating program in North America. Most hoteliers, restaurateurs and industry observers favorably regard the rigor of our inspection program and understand the prestige and benefits that come with receiving a Mobil Star rating.

The Mobil Travel Guide process of rating each establishment includes unannounced inspections, incognito evaluations and a review of unsolicted comments from the general public. We inspect more than 500 attributes at each property we visit, from cleanliness to the condition of the rooms and public spaces, to employee attitude and courtesy. It's a system that rewards those properties that strive for and achieve excellence each year. And the very best properties raise the bar for those that wish to compete with them.

Only facilities that meet Mobil Travel Guide's standards earn the privilege of being listed in the guide. Properties are continuously updated, and deteriorating, poorly managed establishments are removed. We wouldn't recommend that you visit a hotel, restaurant or spa that we wouldn't want to visit ourselves.

★★★★★ The Mobil Five-Star Award indicates that a property is one of the very best in the country and consistently provides gracious and courteous service, superlative quality in its facility and a unique ambience. The lodgings and restaurants at the Mobil Five-Star level consistently continue their commitment to excellence, doing so with grace and perseverance.

★★★★ The Mobil Four-Star Award honors properties for outstanding achievement in overall facility and for providing very strong service levels in all areas. These award winners provide a distinctive experience for the ever-demanding and sophisticated consumer.

★★★ The Mobil Three-Star Award recognizes an excellent property that provides full services and amenities. This category ranges from exceptional hotels with limited services to elegant restaurants with a less formal atmosphere.

★★ The Mobil Two-Star property is a clean and comfortable establishment that has expanded amenities or a distinctive environment. These properties are an excellent place to stay or dine.

★ The Mobil One-Star property is limited in its amenities and services but provides a value experience while meeting travelers' expectations. The properties should be clean, comfortable and convenient.

We do not charge establishments for inclusion in our guides. We have no relationship with any of the businesses and attractions we list and act only as a consumer advocate. We do the investigative legwork so that you won't have to.

Restaurants and hotels—particularly small chains and stand-alone establishments—change management or even go out of business with surprising quickness. Although we make every effort to continuously update information, we recommend that you call ahead to make sure the place you've selected is still open.

**5**

**MID ATLANTIC**

★
★
★
★
☆

# STAR RATINGS

## MOBIL RATED HOTELS

Whether you're looking for the ultimate in luxury or the best bang for your travel buck, we have a hotel recommendation for you. To help you pinpoint properties that meet your needs, Mobil Travel Guide classifies each lodging by type according to the following characteristics.

★★★★★The Mobil Five-Star hotel provides consistently superlative service in an exceptionally distinctive luxury environment. Attention to detail is evident throughout the hotel, resort or inn, from bed linens to staff uniforms.

★★★★The Mobil Four-Star hotel provides a luxury experience with expanded amenities in a distinctive environment. Services may include automatic turndown service, 24-hour room service and valet parking.

★★★The Mobil Three-Star hotel is well appointed, with a full-service restaurant and expanded amenities, such as a fitness center, golf course, tennis courts, 24-hour room service and optional turndown service.

★★The Mobil Two-Star hotel is considered a clean, comfortable and reliable establishment that has expanded amenities, such as a full-service restaurant.

★The Mobil One-Star lodging is a limited-service hotel, motel or inn that is considered a clean, comfortable and reliable establishment.

For every property, we also provide pricing information. The pricing categories break down as follows:

$ = Up to $150

$$ = $151-$250

$$$ = $251-$350

$$$$ = $351 and up

All prices quoted are accurate at the time of publication; however, prices cannot be guaranteed.

# MOBIL RATED RESTAURANTS

Every restaurant in this book has been visited by Mobil Travel Guide's team of experts and comes highly recommended as an outstanding dining experience.

★★★★★The Mobil Five-Star restaurant offers one of few flawless dining experiences in the country. These establishments consistently provide their guests with exceptional food, superlative service, elegant décor and exquisite presentations of each detail surrounding a meal.

★★★★The Mobil Four-Star restaurant provides professional service, distinctive presentations and wonderful food.

★★★The Mobil Three-Star restaurant has good food, warm and skillful service and enjoyable décor.

★★The Mobil Two-Star restaurant serves fresh food in a clean setting with efficient service. Value is considered in this category, as is family friendliness.

★The Mobil One-Star restaurant provides a distinctive experience through culinary specialty, local flair or individual atmosphere.

Because menu prices can fluctuate, we list a pricing category rather than specific prices. The pricing categories are defined as follows, per diner, and assume that you order an appetizer or dessert, an entrée and one drink:

$ = $15 and under

$$ = $16-$35

$$$ = $36-$85

$$$$ = $86 and up

★
★
★
★
★

# MOBIL RATED SPAS

Mobil Travel Guide's spa ratings are based on objective evaluations of hundreds of attributes. About half of these criteria assess basic expectations, such as staff courtesy, the technical proficiency and skill of the employees and whether the facility is clean and maintained properly. Several standards address issues that impact a guest's physical comfort and convenience, as well as the staff's ability to impart a sense of personalized service. Additional criteria measure the spa's ability to create a completely calming ambience.

★★★★★The Mobil Five-Star spa provides consistently superlative service in an exceptionally distinctive luxury environment with extensive amenities. The staff at a Mobil Five-Star spa provides extraordinary service beyond the traditional spa experience, allowing guests to achieve the highest level of relaxation and pampering. These spas offer an extensive array of treatments, often incorporating international themes and products. Attention to detail is evident throughout the spa, from arrival to departure.

★★★★The Mobil Four-Star spa provides a luxurious experience with expanded amenities in an elegant and serene environment. Throughout the spa facility, guests experience personalized service. Amenities might include, but are not limited to, single-sex relaxation rooms where guests wait for their treatments, plunge pools and whirlpools in both men's and women's locker rooms, and an array of treatments, including a selection of massages, body therapies, facials and a variety of salon services.

★★★The Mobil Three-Star spa is physically well appointed and has a full complement of staff.

# INTRODUCTION

If you've been a reader of Mobil Travel Guides, you may have noticed a new look and style in our guidebooks. Since 1958, Mobil Travel Guide has assisted travelers in making smart decisions about where to stay and dine. Fifty-one years later, our mission has not changed: We are committed to our rigorous inspections of hotels, restaurants and, now, spas, to help you cut through all the clutter, and make easy and informed decisions on where you should spend your time and budget. Our team of anonymous inspectors are constantly on the road, sleeping in hotels, eating in restaurants and making spa appointments, evaluating hundreds of standards to determine a property's star rating.

As you read these pages, we hope you get a flavor of the places included in the guides and that you will feel even more inspired to visit and take it all in. We hope you'll experience what it's like to stay in a guest room in the hotels we've rated, taste the food in a restaurant or feel the excitement at an outdoor music venue. We understand the importance of finding the best value when you travel, and making the most of your time. That's why for more than 50 years, Mobil Travel Guide has been the most trusted name in travel.

If any aspect of your accommodation, dining, spa or sightseeing experience motivates you to comment, please contact us at Mobil Travel Guide, 200 W. Madison St., Suite 3950, Chicago, IL 60606, or send an email to info@mobiltravelguide.com Happy travels.

★ MID ATLANTIC

★
★
★
★

# WASHINGTON, D.C.

WHEREVER YOU'RE STANDING IN DOWNTOWN D.C., CHANCES ARE THE WASHINGTON Monument is within sight. By law, no building may be taller than the 12-story monument—but regardless of their physical stature, the rest of D.C.'s buildings cannot be overshadowed. There are world-renowned museums and monuments, first-rate restaurants and shops within quaint neighborhoods, grassy parks and tree-lined streets. And all are just a short ride away on the city's efficient mass-transit system.

Washington was not the first capital of the United States. The city didn't even exist at the time the nation gained its independence in 1789. For a year, the nation's new government met in New York City before relocating to Philadelphia. In 1790, President Washington selected a site for the nation's capital at the junction of the Potomac and Anacostia rivers, 14 miles north of his home in Mount Vernon. Andrew Ellicott surveyed the area, aided by Benjamin Banneker, a free black from Maryland. Using celestial calculations, Banneker, a self-taught astronomer and mathematician, laid out 40 boundary stones at one-mile intervals to mark the city's borders.

President Washington chose Pierre-Charles L'Enfant to plan the new capital. L'Enfant, a French-born architect and urban designer who served in the American Revolutionary Army, created a bold and original plan, one that called for a grid pattern of streets intersected by wide, diagonal avenues. The diagonal avenues would meet at circles, which would anchor the residential neighborhoods. Today, Logan Circle is a clear example where four different thoroughfares converge, including Rhode Island and Vermont avenues. The large open circle sits at the core of a beautiful neighborhood, with many of its residences building up the area soon after the Civil War.

L'Enfant envisioned the Congress House (now the Capitol) situated atop Jenkins Hill, which offered sweeping views of the Potomac River. To the west of Jenkins Hill, L'Enfant planned a 400-foot-wide avenue (now the National Mall) bordered by embassies and cultural institutions. Not everyone was pleased with his plan. Though he had the president's support, L'Enfant faced opposition from some of the district commissioners who had been appointed to oversee the capital city's development. Secretary of State Thomas Jefferson, a noted architect in his own right, disapproved of the plan, but L'Enfant refused to compromise his vision. In 1792, Washington dismissed the genius planner whom he had appointed only a year earlier. In L'Enfant's place, Washington appointed Andrew Ellicott to prepare a map of the city. Along with Benjamin Banneker, Ellicott produced a map of the city that adhered closely to L'Enfant's plan.

L'Enfant sought $95,500 for his services but received less than $4,000. He died in

★ **FUN FACTS** During World War II, to protect the city from possible enemy invasion, antiaircraft guns were placed on top of several government office buildings. One of them accidentally went off and the projectile hit the roof of the Lincoln Monument.

1825, financially destitute and never having received acclaim for his work in planning Washington. He was buried in Maryland, then disinterred and reburied at Arlington National Cemetery in 1909. A marble monument marks the site of his grave.

L'Enfant's visionary plan fostered the growth of the city's eclectic mix of neighborhoods: Capitol Hill, with its 19th-century row houses and brick-lined streets; the National Mall's massive stone monuments, museums and government buildings; Georgetown's quaint shops and restaurants; cosmopolitan Dupont Circle; Adams Morgan, with its bustling nightlife; and Woodley Park's leaf-shaded residential streets.

Thanks to L'Enfant's plan, which identified parks and open spaces as essential elements in urban design, D.C. possesses the sorts of places, as L'Enfant wrote, that may be attractive to the learned and afford diversion to the idle. Pulitzer Prize-winning historian David McCullough has expressed his appreciation of the capital's natural beauty. "In many ways it is our most civilized city," McCullough wrote of Washington. "It accommodates its river, accommodates trees and grass, makes room for nature as other cities don't."

All three branches of the U.S. federal government are based in Washington, D.C., and the number of federal employees commuting into downtown has grown significantly over the years. In 1800, there were 130 federal workers; at the end of the Civil War, there were 7,000; and now there are well over half a million. From politicians on the Hill to lobbyists on K Street to visiting dignitaries, D.C. hosts some of the nation's busiest movers and shakers.

Tourists, too, flock to the nation's capital, visiting their senators and representatives on Capitol Hill, touring the Smithsonian museums along the National Mall, and posing for pictures in front of the Washington Monument and the Lincoln and Jefferson memorials. Sightseeing opportunities abound in this picturesque city. Dining and nightlife options are just as plentiful in neighborhoods such as Georgetown, Dupont Circle, Adams Morgan and the U Street Corridor.

*Information: www.washington.org*

## WHAT TO SEE AND DO
### AFRICAN AMERICAN CIVIL WAR MEMORIAL
*1200 U St. N.W., Washington D.C., 202-667-2667; www.afroamcivilwar.org*
Sculpture pays tribute to the more than 200,000 African-American soldiers who fought in the Civil War. Monday-Friday 10 a.m.-5 p.m., Saturday 10 a.m.-2 p.m.

### AMERICAN RED CROSS MUSEUM
*430 17th St., Washington D.C., 202-303-7066;*
*www.redcross.org/museum/history/visitorinfo.asp*
National headquarters is made up of three buildings bounded by 17th, 18th, D and E streets N.W. The 17th St. building includes marble busts *Faith, Hope* and *Charity* by sculptor Hiram Powers and three original Tiffany stained-glass windows. Tours must be scheduled 72 hours in advance. Wednesday and Fridays 10 a.m. and 2 p.m., Saturdays noon and 2 p.m.

### ANACOSTIA MUSEUM
*1901 Fort Place S.E., Washington D.C., 202-633-4820; www.anacosta.si.edu*
An exhibition and research center for black heritage in the historic Anacostia section of southeast Washington. Changing exhibits. Daily 10 a.m.-5 p.m.

### ANDERSON HOUSE MUSEUM

*2118 Massachusetts Ave. N.W., Washington D.C., 202-785-2040;*
*www.societyofthecincinnati.org*

Revolutionary War museum and national headquarters of the Society of the Cincinnati has portraits by early American artists; 18th-century paintings; 17th-century tapestries; decorative arts of Europe and Asia; and displays of books, medals, swords, silver, glass and china. Tuesday-Saturday 1-4 p.m. Closed New Year's Day, Thanksgiving and Christmas.

### ARENA STAGE

*1101 Sixth St. S.W., Washington D.C., 202-488-3300; www.arena-stage.org*

### ART MUSEUM OF THE AMERICAS, OAS

*201 18th St. N.W., Washington D.C., 202-458-6016; www.museum.oas.org*

Dedicated to Latin American and Caribbean contemporary art; paintings, graphics, sculpture. Tuesday-Sunday 10 a.m.-5 p.m. Admission free. N.W. Washington D.C.

### ARTHUR M. SACKLER GALLERY

*1050 Independence Ave. S.W., Washington D.C., 202-357-2700;*
*www.asia.si.edu*

Changing exhibitions of Asian art, both near- and far-Eastern, from major national and international collections. Permanent collection includes Chinese and South and Southeast Asian art objects presented by Arthur Sackler. Open daily 10 a.m.-5:30 p.m. Closed December 25. Admission free.

### BASILICA OF THE NATIONAL SHRINE OF THE IMMACULATE CONCEPTION

*400 Michigan Ave. N.E., Washington D.C., 202-526-8300; www.nationalshrine.com*

Largest Roman Catholic church in the U.S. and one of the largest in the world. Byzantine and Romanesque architecture; extensive and elaborate collection of mosaics and artwork. Guided tours: Monday-Saturday 9 a.m., 10 a.m., 11 a.m., 1 p.m., 2 p.m. and 3 p.m. Sunday 1:30 p.m., 2:30 p.m. and 3:30 p.m. Carillon concerts: November-March, 7 a.m.-6 p.m.; April-October 7 a.m.-7 p.m.

### BLACK HISTORY RECREATION TRAIL

*1100 Ohio Drive S.W., Washington D.C., 202-619-7222;*
*www.americantrails.org/nationalrecreationtrails/stateNRT/DCnrt.html*

Trail through Washington neighborhoods highlights important sites in African-American history.

### BLAIR-LEE HOUSE

*1651 Pennsylvania Ave. N.W., Washington D.C.; www.blairhouse.org*

Guest house for heads of government and state visiting the U.S. as guests of the president, which dates back to 1824. Not open to the public.

### BLUES ALLEY

*1073 Wisconsin Ave. N.W., Washington D.C., 202-337-4141; www.bluesalley.com*

For nearly 40 years, serious jazz lovers have flocked to this intimate club to hear Dizzy Gillespie, Sarah Vaughan and Maynard Ferguson, among others. Nightly shows run

★
★
★
★

the gamut from vocal and instrumental sounds to solo performers and larger ensembles. Located in an 18th-century brick carriage house in Georgetown, the club has a sophisticated ambience and a Creole-themed-dinner menu. Open 6 p.m.-12:30 a.m.

## BUREAU OF ENGRAVING AND PRINTING

*14th and C St. S.W., Washington D.C., 202-874-2330, 866-874-2330;*
*www.bep.treas.gov*
The tour allows visitors to watch currency being printed. Learn about the latest high-tech steps the Bureau has taken to thwart counterfeiting. You can buy uncut sheets of bills in different denominations as well as shredded cash at the BEP store. Guided tours 9 a.m.-2 p.m. Closed weekends, federal holidays and December 24-January 3.

## THE CAPITOL

*Capitol Hill, Washington D.C., 202-225-6827; www.aoc.gov*
The Capitol has been home to the legislative branch of the U.S. government for more than 200 years. Visitors can take guided tours of several sections, including the beautifully restored Old Supreme Court Chamber and the Old Senate Chamber. The Rotunda, a ceremonial space beneath the soaring dome, is a gallery for paintings and sculptures of historic significance. Below it is the Crypt, built for the remains of George Washington (who asked to be buried at Mount Vernon instead), which is now used for exhibits. Don't miss the National Statuary Hall, where statues of prominent citizens have been donated by all 50 states, and the ornate Brumidi Corridors, named for the Italian artist who designed their murals and many other decorative elements in the Capitol. A state-of-the-art visitor center is currently under construction. Monday-Saturday 9 a.m.-4:30 p.m. Closed Sunday. Tickets for tours are available at the Capitol Guide Service kiosk near the intersection of First Street Southwest and Independence Avenue.

## CAPITOL CITY BREWING COMPANY

*2 Massachusetts Ave. N.E., Washington D.C., 202-842-2337; www.capcitybrew.com*
Shiny copper vats and a large, oval copper bar are the centerpieces of this huge—and hugely popular—brewpub in the beautifully restored 1911 Postal Square Building. Hill staffers and tourists crowd in for made-on-the-premises ales, lagers and pilsners that go down well with warm pretzels and mustard or with whole meals. Monday-Saturday 11 a.m. to midnight, Sunday from noon to midnight.

## CARTER BARRON AMPHITHEATRE

*16 St. and Colorado Ave. N.W., Washington D.C., 202-426-0486;*
*www.nps.gov/rocr/cbarron*
This 4,200-seat outdoor theater in a wooded area is the setting for summer performances of symphonic, folk, pop and jazz music and Shakespearean theater.

## CATHOLIC UNIVERSITY OF AMERICA

*620 Michigan Ave. N.E., Washington D.C., 202-319-5000; www.cua.edu*
This university, established in 1887, is open to all faiths. It has more than 5,510 students. Performances at Hartke Theater (year-round).

**WASHINGTON, D.C.**

★
★
★
★
★

## CHESAPEAKE & OHIO CANAL BOAT RIDES

*1057 Thomas Jefferson St. N.W., Washington D.C., 202-653-5190;*
*www.nps.gov/choh/planyourvisit/publicboatrides.htm*

Narrated one-hour, round-trip canal tours by park rangers in period clothing aboard mule-drawn boats. The ticket office is adjacent. April-October, Wednesday-Sunday.

## CHESAPEAKE & OHIO CANAL TOWPATH

*1057 Thomas Jefferson St. N.W. (Georgetown Visitor Center), Washington D.C.,*
*202-653-5190; www.nps.gov/CHOH*

Biking (or strolling) along the Chesapeake & Ohio Canal towpath is a great way to immerse yourself in history and nature. The canal, which runs 184½ miles between Georgetown and Cumberland, Md., was completed in 1850. Locks, lock houses, aqueducts and other original structures remain. Expect spectacular scenery and all manner of wildlife along the way, including deer, fox and woodpeckers. Fee per cyclist at Great Falls. Georgetown Visitor Center: Saturday-Sunday.

## CHINATOWN

*700 19th St. N.W., Washington D.C.*

Marked by the Chinatown Friendship Archway at seventh and H streets, which is decorated in Chinese architectural styles of Qing and Ming dynasties and is topped with nearly 300 painted dragons.

## CONSTITUTION GARDENS

*900 Ohio Drive S.W., Washington D.C., 202-426-6841; www.nps.gov/coga*

This 50-acre park, with a man-made lake, is also the site of the Signers of the Declaration of Independence Memorial. Open daily.

## CORCORAN GALLERY OF ART

*500 17th St. N.W., Washington D.C., 202-639-1700; www.corcoran.org*

The city's oldest art museum and the largest non-federal one. Known for its strong collection of 19th-century American art (don't miss John Singer Sargent's luminous *Oyster Gatherers of Cancale*) and its support for local artists, the museum also shows important European pieces and contemporary works, including photography, performance art and new media. A glamorous, Frank Gehry-designed addition to the landmark Beaux Arts building is in the works. Wednesday, Friday-Sunday 10 a.m.-5 p.m., Thursday 10 a.m.-9 p.m. Closed Monday and Tuesday.

## DAR HEADQUARTERS

*1776 D St. N.W., Washington D.C., 202-628-1776; www.dar.org*

Includes Memorial Continental Hall and Constitution Hall; DAR Museum Gallery, located in the administration building, has 33 state period rooms; outstanding genealogical research library (fee for nonmembers). Guided tours. Monday-Saturday.

## DECATUR HOUSE MUSEUM

*1610 H St. N.W., Washington D.C., 202-842-0920; www.decaturhouse.org*

Federal townhouse built for naval hero Commodore Stephen Decatur by Benjamin H. Latrobe, second architect of the Capitol. After Decatur's death in 1820, the house was occupied by a succession of American and foreign statesmen, and was a center of political and social life in the city. The ground-floor family rooms reflect Decatur's Federal-period lifestyle. Operated by the National Trust for Historic Preservation. Tuesday-Saturday 10 a.m.-5 p.m., Thursday 10 a.m.-8 p.m., Sunday noon-4 p.m.

## D.C. UNITED (MLS)

*RFK Memorial Stadium, 2400 E. Capitol St. S.W., Washington D.C., 202-587-5000; www.dcunited.com*
Professional soccer team.

## DEPARTMENT OF COMMERCE BUILDING

*1401 Constitution Ave. N.W., Washington D.C.,, 202-482-2000; www.commerce.gov*

## DEPARTMENT OF ENERGY

*1000 Independence Ave. S.W., Washington D.C., 202-586-5575, 800-342-5363; www.energy.gov*
Includes the Interstate Commerce Commission, Constitution Avenue between 12th and 13th streets N.W.; Customs Department, Constitution Avenue between 13th and 14th streets N.W.; and the District Building, Pennsylvania Avenue between 13th and 14th streets N.W., Washington's ornate 1908 city hall.

## DEPARTMENT OF THE INTERIOR

*1849 C St. N.W., Washington D.C., 202-208-3100; www.doi.gov*
(1938) Inside is a museum including exhibits and dioramas depicting the history and activities of the department and its various bureaus. A photo ID is required for admission. (Monday-Friday) Reference library is open to the public.

## DEPARTMENT OF JUSTICE BUILDING

*950 Pennsylvania Ave., Washington D.C., 202-616-3834; www.gsa.gov*
Not open to the public.

## DEPARTMENT OF STATE BUILDING

*2201 C St. N.W., Washington D.C., 202-647-4000; www.dos.gov*
The State Department's diplomatic reception rooms, furnished with 18th-century American furniture and decorative art, are used by the Secretary of State and cabinet members for formal entertaining. Tours (Monday-Friday; closed federal holidays and special events; three- to four-weeks advance reservations; children over 12 years only preferred).

## DEPARTMENT OF THE TREASURY

*1500 Pennsylvania Ave. N.W., Washington D.C., 202-622-0896; www.treasury.gov*
According to legend this Greek Revival building, one of the oldest (built in the mid-1800s) in the city, was built in the middle of Pennsylvania Avenue because Andrew Jackson was tired of endless wrangling over the location and walked out of the White House, planted his cane in the mud and said, "Here." The building has been extensively restored. Saturday mornings 9 a.m., 9:45 a.m., 10:30 a.m. and 11:15 a.m. Admission free.

★
★
★
★

### DUMBARTON OAKS

*1703 32nd St. N.W., Washington D.C., 202-339-6401; www.doaks.org*

These formal, romantic gardens span 16 acres. The mansion has antiques and European art, including El Greco's "The Visitation," galleries of Byzantine art, and a library of rare books on gardening and horticulture. Museum of pre-Columbian artifacts is housed in structure by Philip Johnson. Gardens (closed Mondays). Tuesday-Sunday afternoons. Admission free.

### DUPONT-KALORAMA MUSEUM WALK

*Washington D.C., 202-387-4062; www.dkmuseums.com*

Seven museums joined forces to create an awareness of the area. Information and brochures available.

### EASTERN MARKET

*225 Seventh St. S.E., Washington D.C.; www.easternmarket.net*

Meat, fish and produce are sold. Also antiques, crafts and farmers market on weekends. Tuesday-Sunday.

### EMANCIPATION STATUE

*Lincoln Park, 11th and E. Capitol streets N.E., Washington D.C.*

This bronze work of Thomas Ball depicting Lincoln presenting the Emancipation Proclamation was paid for by voluntary subscriptions from emancipated slaves. It was dedicated on April 14, 1876, the 11th anniversary of Lincoln's assassination. Frederick Douglass was in attendance.

### EMBASSY ROW

*Massachusetts Avenue and 23rd Street N.W., Washington D.C.*

This neighborhood within the city's northwest quadrant is centered around Sheridan Circle and is home to dozens of foreign legations.

### EXPLORERS HALL

*1145 17th St. N.W., Washington D.C., 202-857-7588; www.nationalgeographic.com*

National Geographic Society headquarters. Several traveling exhibits. Daily.

### FEDERAL RESERVE BUILDING

*C and 21st St. N.W., Washington D.C., 202-452-3149; www.federalreserve.gov*

Primarily an office building, but noteworthy for its architecture (it was built in 1937). Rotating art exhibits. Film (20 minutes).

### FEDERAL TRADE COMMISSION BUILDING

*600 Pennsylvania Ave. N.W., Washington D.C., 202-326-2222; www.ftc.gov*

This building dates back to 1938. Monday-Friday.

### FEDERAL TRIANGLE

*Pennsylvania Avenue and 13th Street N.W., Washington D.C.*

The Triangle holds a group of government buildings, nine of which were built for $78 million in the 1930s in modern classic design. The "crown jewel" of the triangle is the Ronald Reagan International Trade Center, located on Pennsylvania Avenue at 13th St. N.W.

## FOLGER SHAKESPEARE LIBRARY

*201 E. Capitol St. S.E., Washington D.C., 202-544-4600; www.folger.edu*

This library, erected in 1932, houses the finest collections of Shakespearean materials in the world, including the 1623 First Folio edition and large holdings of rare books and manuscripts of the English and continental Renaissance. The Great Hall offers year-round exhibits from the Folgers' extensive collection. The Elizabethan Theatre, which was designed to resemble a theater in Shakespeare's day, is the site of the Folger Shakespeare Library's series of museum and performing arts programs, which include literary readings, drama, lectures and education and family programs. Self-guided tours. Guided tours. Monday-Saturday 10 a.m.-5 p.m. Reading room Monday-Friday 8:45 a.m.-4:45 p.m., Saturday 9 a.m.-4:30 p.m.

## FONDO DEL SOL VISUAL ARTS CENTER

*2112 R St. N.W., Washington D.C., 202-483-2777; www.dkmuseums.com*

Dedicated to presenting, promoting and preserving cultures of the Americans, the museum presents exhibitions of contemporary artists and crafters, holds special events and hosts traveling exhibits for museums and other institutions. Tuesday-Saturday 12:30-5:30 p.m.

## FORD'S THEATRE

*511 10th St. N.W., Washington D.C., 202-426-6924; www.fordstheatre.org*

This is the site of Abraham Lincoln's assassination. Ford's became a working theater again in 1968; recent productions have included the play *Inherit the Wind* and a one-man show about George Gershwin. The theater and the museum are now closed for renovations until winter 2009 except for performances (by ticket sale). The Petersen House is still open to the public.

## FORT DUPONT PARK

*1900 Anacostia Drive S.E., Washington D.C., 202-426-7723; www.nps.gov/fodu*

Picnicking, hiking and bicycling in hilly terrain; cultural arts performances in summer. Also films, slides and activities involving natural science; environmental education programs, nature discovery room, Junior Ranger program; garden workshops and programmed activities by reservation. Dawn-dusk.

## FORT DUPONT SPORTS COMPLEX

*3779 Ely Place S.E., Washington D.C., 202-584-5007; www.fdia.org*

Skating, ice hockey (fee); tennis courts, basketball courts, ball fields (daily; free), jogging.

## FORT STEVENS PARK

*13th and Quackenbos streets N.W., Washington D.C., 202-895-6000;*
*www.nps.gov/rocr/ftcircle/stevens.htm*

General Jubal Early and his Confederate troops tried to invade Washington at this spot on July 11-12, 1864. President Lincoln risked his life at the fort during the fighting. Daily.

★
★
★
★
★

### FRANCISCAN MONASTERY

*1400 Quincy St. N.E., Washington D.C., 202-526-6800; www.myfranciscan.org*

Within the church and grounds is the "Holy Land of America"; replicas of sacred Holy Land shrines including the Manger at Bethlehem, the Garden of Gethsemane and the Holy Sepulchre. Also the Grotto at Lourdes and Roman catacombs. Guided tours by the friars. Daily.

### FRANKLIN DELANO ROOSEVELT MEMORIAL

*West Basin Drive, Washington D.C., 202-426-6841; www.nps.gov/fdrm*

This newer memorial, dedicated in 1997, features a series of sculptures depicting the 32nd U.S. President and his wife, Eleanor. Four outdoor rooms represent each of FDR's four presidential terms, which began in the Great Depression and ended at the close of World War II. His "fireside chats" are broadcast throughout the exhibits. Daily 24 hours; interpretive ranger staff onsite 8 a.m.-11:45 p.m.

### FREDERICK DOUGLASS NATIONAL HISTORIC SITE

*1411 W. St. S.E., Washington D.C., 202-426-5961, 800-967-2283; www.nps.gov/frdo*

This 21-room house on nine acres is where Douglass, a former slave who became minister to Haiti and a leading black spokesman, lived from 1877 until his death in 1895; visitor center with film, memorabilia. Mid-April-mid-October, 9 a.m.-5 p.m.; mid-October-mid-April, 9 a.m.-4 p.m. Closed January 1, Thanksgiving and December 25.

★
★
★
★

### FREER GALLERY

*Jefferson Drive at 12th St. S.W., Washington D.C., 202-633-4880; www.asia.si.edu*

Asian art with objects dating from Neolithic period to the early 20th century. Also works by late 19th- and early 20th-century American artists, including a major collection of James McNeill Whistler's work, highlighted by the famous Peacock Room. Next to the Freer is the Smithsonian Institution Building, or "the Castle." Open daily 10 a.m.-5:30 p.m. Closed December 25.

### FRESH FARM MARKET

*20th St. N.W., Washington D.C., 202-362-8889; www.freshfarmmarket.org*

More than 25 local farmers bring in season fruits, vegetables, artisanal cheeses and organic offerings to this weekly market. Daily 9 a.m.-1 p.m.

### GENERAL SERVICES ADMINISTRATION BUILDING

*1800 F St. N.W., Washington D.C.; www.gsa.gov*

This building was originally the Department of Interior when it was built in 1917.

### GEORGE WASHINGTON UNIVERSITY

*2121 First St. N.W., Washington D.C., 202-994-1000; www.gwu.edu*

Theater; art exhibits in Dimock Gallery (Monday-Friday) and University Library.

## GEORGETOWN FLEA MARKET

*1819 35th St. N.W., Washington D.C., 202-775-3532; www.georgetownfleamarket.com*
Offering antique furniture, jewelry, books, rugs, toys, linens and other vintage treasures on Sundays since 1973. (Actress Diane Keaton has been a frequent patron.) About 70 dealers set up booths-year-round; come early for the biggest selection or late for the best bargains. Saturday-Sunday.

## GEORGETOWN UNIVERSITY

*37th and O streets N.W., Washington D.C., 202-687-0100; www.georgetown.edu*
Oldest Catholic college in the U.S., established in 1789. Campus tours Monday-Saturday, by reservation.

## GOVERNMENT PRINTING OFFICE

*732 N. Capitol St. N.W., Washington D.C., 202-512-0000; www.gpo.gov*
Four buildings with 35 acres of floor space where most of the material issued by U.S. government is printed, including production and distribution of the Congressional Record, Federal Register and U.S. passports. (No public tours; for information on the agency, call 202-512-1991.) Office includes the main government bookstore. Nearly 20,000 publications available. Monday-Friday.

## GRAY LINE BUS TOURS

*50 Massachusetts Ave. N.E., Washington D.C., 301-386-8300, 800-862-1400; www.graylinedc.com*
Tours of city and area attractions depart from Union Station.

## HIRSHHORN MUSEUM AND SCULPTURE GARDEN

*Independence Avenue and Seventh Street S.W., Washington D.C., 202-633-4674; www.hirshhorn.si.edu*
The modernity of the paintings and sculptures here—and of the curvy building itself—are a respite for history-sated visitors. Inside is some of the most interesting art produced in the last 100 years: everything from Constantin Brancusi's egg-like *Sleeping Muse I* to Nam June Paik's *Video Flag* made with 70 video monitors. Daily. The lush plaza (7:30 a.m.-5:30 p.m.) and sculpture garden (7:30 a.m.-dusk) also make this an inviting spot. Museum (10 a.m.-5:30 p.m.). Closed December 25.

## HOUSE OFFICE BUILDINGS

*Independence and New Jersey avenues, Washington D.C., 202-224-3121; www.aoc.gov/cc/cobs/index.cfm*
Pedestrian tunnel connects two of the oldest House office buildings with the Capitol.

## HOWARD UNIVERSITY

*2400 Sixth St. N.W., Washington D.C., 202-806-6100; www.howard.edu*
This university dates back to 1867. Main campus: 2400 sixth St. N.W. between W and Harvard streets N.W., West campus: 2900 Van Ness St. N.W., 20008. Three other campuses are in the area. Main campus has a Gallery of Fine Art with a permanent Alain Locke African Collection; changing exhibits September-July, Monday-Friday 9:30 a.m.-5 p.m., Sunday noon-4 p.m.

**WASHINGTON, D.C.**

★
★
★
★
★

### HR-57

*1610 14th St. N.W., Washington D.C., 202-667-3700; www.hr57.org*

This ultra-friendly, bare-bones spot is the performance arm of the Center for the Preservation of Jazz and Blues, a not-for-profit cultural center that named its club after a 1987 House Resolution designating jazz as a rare and valuable national American treasure. Expect to hear well-known and lesser-known artists at the top of their game. Wednesday-Thursday 8:30 p.m.-midnight, Sundays 7-11 p.m.

### THE IMPROV

*1140 Connecticut Ave. N.W., Washington D.C., 202-296-7008; www.dcimprov.com*

The crowd is youngish and the comedy free-flowing here. Onstage talent includes established stars as well as hilarious, original newcomers you may have seen on TV's Comedy Central. Appetizers, sandwiches, beer and wine are available. Daily.

### INTERNATIONAL SPY MUSEUM

*800 F St. N.W., Washington D.C., 202-393-7798, 866-779-6873; www.spymuseum.org*

Opened in 2002, this museum sheds light on the world of international espionage with artifacts including invisible ink, high-tech eavesdropping devices, a through-the-wall camera and a KGB lipstick pistol. Find out how codes were made and broken throughout history, how successful disguises are created and what real-life James Bonds think of the high-stakes game of spying. Daily 10 a.m.-8 p.m.

### ISLAMIC CENTER

*2551 Massachusetts Ave. N.W., Washington D.C., 202-332-8343;*
*www.islamiccenterdc.com*

This mosque has landscaped courtyard, intricate interior mosaics. Daily; no tours during Friday prayer service.

### IWO JIMA STATUE

*Meade Street, Washington D.C.*

Across Theodore Roosevelt Bridge on Arlington Boulevard.

### JOHN F. KENNEDY CENTER FOR THE PERFORMING ARTS

*2700 F St. N.W., Washington D.C., 202-416-8340, 800-444-1324;*
*www.kennedy-center.org*

The home of the National Symphony Orchestra and Washington Opera hosts an impressive array of internationally known artists in dance, theater and music. Opened in 1971 as a memorial to John F. Kennedy, a large bronze bust of the former president graces the Grand Foyer, and paintings, sculptures and other artwork presented by foreign governments are also displayed. Daily.

### JUDICIARY SQUARE

*D and Fourth streets N.W., Washington D.C.*

Two square blocks of judiciary buildings, including five federal and district courts, the U.S. District Court and the U.S. Court of Appeals. At D Street halfway between 4th and 5th streets is the first completed statue of Abraham Lincoln, erected in 1868.

### KENILWORTH AQUATIC GARDENS

*1900 Anacostia Ave. S.E., Washington D.C., 202-426-6905; www.nps.gov*

Water lilies, lotuses and other water plants bloom from mid-May until the frost. Gardens open daily 7 a.m.-4 p.m. Closed Thanksgiving, December 25 and January 1. Guided walks Memorial Day-Labor Day, Saturday-Sunday and holidays, also by appointment.

### KOREAN WAR MEMORIAL

*French Drive S.W. and Independence Avenue, Washington D.C., 202-426-6841;*
*www.nps.gov/kwvm*

This massive sculpture honors the Americans who served in the Korean War, showing 19 soldiers dressed and armed for battle heading toward the American flag, their symbolic goal. The adjacent wall features etched photographs that pay tribute to military support personnel. Daily 8 a.m.-11:45 p.m. Closed December 25.

### LABOR DEPARTMENT

*Francis H. Perkins Building, 200 Constitution Ave. N.W., Washington D.C.,*
*202-693-6613, 866-487-2365; www.dol.gov*

Lobby contains the Labor Hall of Fame, an exhibit depicting labor in the U.S.; the library on the second floor is open to the public. Monday-Friday.

### LAFAYETTE SQUARE

*Pennsylvania Avenue N.W., Washington D.C.*

Statue of Andrew Jackson on horseback in the center was the first Equestrian figure in Washington. One of the park benches was known as Bernard Baruch's office in 1930s and is dedicated to him.

### LIBRARY OF CONGRESS

*101 Independence Ave. S.E., Washington D.C., 202-707-6400; www.loc.gov*

Treasures include a Gutenberg Bible, the first great book printed with movable metal type, and the Giant Bible of Mainz, a 500-year-old illuminated manuscript. Collection includes manuscripts, newspapers, maps, recordings, prints, photographs, posters and more than 30 million books and pamphlets in 60 languages. In the elaborate Jefferson Building is the Great Hall, decorated with murals, mosaics and marble carvings; exhibition halls. In the Madison Building, a 22-minute audiovisual presentation, America's Library, provides a good introduction to the library and its facilities. Monday-Saturday 10 a.m.-5:30 p.m.

### LINCOLN MEMORIAL

*23rd St. N.W., Washington D.C., 202-426-6841; www.nps.gov/linc*

Dedicated in 1922, Daniel Chester French's Abraham Lincoln looks across a reflecting pool to the Washington Monument and the Capitol. Lincoln's Gettysburg Address and Second Inaugural Address are inscribed on the walls of the temple-like structure, which is particularly impressive at night. The 36 columns represent the 36 states in the Union in existence at the time of Lincoln's death. Open daily.

★
★
★
★
☆

## LINCOLN MUSEUM

*511 10th St. N.W., Washington D.C.,, 202-347-4833; www.fordstheatre.org*

Closed for renovations; will reopen in winter 2009.

## MARY MCLEOD BETHUNE MEMORIAL

*1318 Vermont Ave. N.W., Washington D.C.; www.nps.gov/mamc*

Honors the noted educator and advisor to President Lincoln and founder of the National Council of Negro Women. Monday-Saturday 9 a.m.-5 p.m.

## MERIDIAN INTERNATIONAL CENTER

*1624 Crescent Place N.W., Washington D.C., 202-939-5568; www.meridian.org*

Housed in two historic mansions designed by John Russell Pope, the center hosts international exhibits, concerts, lectures and symposia promoting international understanding. Period furnishings, Mortlake tapestry; gardens with linden grove. Wednesday-Sunday 2-5 p.m.

## MARINE BARRACKS

*Eighth and First streets S.E., Washington D.C., 202-433-6060; www.mbw.usmc.mil*

The parade ground, more than two centuries old, is surrounded by handsome and historic structures, including the Commandant's House facing G Street, which is said to be the oldest continuously occupied public building in the city. The parade is open to the public on Friday evenings in summer.

## MARTIN LUTHER KING, JR. MEMORIAL LIBRARY

*901 G St. N.W., Washington D.C., 202-727-0321; www.dclibrary.org*

Main branch of the D.C. public library was designed by architect Mies van der Rohe in 1972. Martin Luther King mural. Books, periodicals, photographs, films, videocassettes, recordings, microfilms, Washingtoniana and the "Washington Star" collection. Library for the visually impaired; librarian for the hearing impaired; black studies division; community information service. Underground parking. Monday-Thursday 9:30 a.m.-9 p.m., Friday-Saturday 9:30 a.m.-5:30 p.m.

## NATIONAL ACADEMY OF SCIENCES

*500 Fifth St. N.W., Washington D.C., 202-337-8566; www.nationalacademies.org*

Established in 1863 to stimulate research and communication among scientists and to advice the federal government in science and technology. A famous 21-foot bronze statue of Albert Einstein by Robert Berks is on the front lawn. Art exhibits and concerts. Schedule varies.

## NATIONAL AIR AND SPACE MUSEUM

*600 Independence Ave. S.W., Washington D.C., 202-633-2563; www.nasm.si.edu*

View the Wright brothers' 1903 Kitty Hawk Flyer, Charles Lindbergh's *Spirit of St. Louis* and the command module *Columbia*, which carried the first men to walk on the moon. In the Apollo to the Moon exhibit, you'll see lunar rocks, spacesuits and John Glenn's squeeze-tube beef stew, among other artifacts. An IMAX theater enables you to view on a huge, five-story-high screen Earth as seen from the space shuttle. And

★
★★
★★★
★★★
☆

don't miss the high-tech shows at the Albert Einstein Planetarium. Daily 10 a.m.-5:30 p.m. Admission free. Closed December 25.

## NATIONAL AQUARIUM

*Department of Commerce Building, 14th St. and Constitution Ave. N.W.,*
*Washington D.C., 202-482-2825; www.nationalaquarium.com*
The nation's oldest public aquarium was established in 1873. It now exhibits more than 1,700 specimens representing approximately 260 species, both freshwater and saltwater. Touch tank; theater. Shark feedings (Monday, Wednesday, Saturday); piranha feedings (Tuesday, Thursday, Sunday). Daily 9 a.m.-5 p.m. Closed Thanksgiving and December 25.

## NATIONAL ARCHIVES

*Constitution Avenue, Washington D.C., 202-501-5205; www.archives.gov*
(1934) The original Declaration of Independence, Bill of Rights and the Constitution; a 1297 version of the Magna Carta and other historic documents, maps and photographs. Guided tours by appointment only. Archives are also available to the public for genealogical and historical research Monday-Saturday. Mid-March-Labor Day, 10 a.m.-7 p.m., Labor Day-mid-March, 10 a.m.-5:30 p.m.

## NATIONAL BUILDING MUSEUM

*401 F St. N.W., Washington D.C., 202-272-2448; www.nbm.org*
Deals with architecture, design, engineering and construction. Permanent exhibits include drawings, blueprints, models, photographs, artifacts and the architectural evolution of Washington's buildings and monuments. The museum's enormous Great Hall is supported by eight of the world's largest Corinthian columns. Group and open tours daily. Monday-Saturday 10 a.m.-5 p.m., Sunday 11 a.m.-5 p.m. Admission free.

## NATIONAL GALLERY OF ART

*Fourth and Constitution avenues N.W., Washington D.C., 202-737-4215;*
*www.nga.gov*
The West Building (1941), designed by John Russell Pope, contains Western European and American art spanning periods between the 13th and 20th centuries: Highlights include the only Leonardo da Vinci painting on display outside of Europe, *Ginevra de' Benci*; a comprehensive collection of Italian paintings and sculpture; major French Impressionists; numerous Rembrandts and examples of the Dutch school; masterpieces from the Mellon, Widener, Kress, Dale and Rosenwald collections; special exhibitions. The East Building (1978), designed by architect I. M. Pei, houses the gallery's growing collection of 20th-century art, including Picasso's *Family of Saltimbanques* and Jackson Pollock's *Lavender Mist*. Daily. Admission free.

## NATIONAL MUSEUM OF AFRICAN ART

*950 Independence Ave. S.W., Washington D.C., 202-633-4600; www.nmafa.si.edu*
Permanent exhibits display masks, musical instruments, sacred objects, ceramics, textiles, household tools and the visual arts of the sub-Sahara. Traveling shows cover even more ground; recent ones have featured colonial-era photography and Ethiopian religious icons. A full schedule of films, musical presentations, lectures and

WASHINGTON, D.C.

★
★
★
★
★

children's events keeps things lively. Daily 10 a.m.-5:30 p.m. Closed December 25. Admission free.

## NATIONAL MUSEUM OF AMERICAN HISTORY

*14th St. and Constitution Ave. N.W., Washington D.C., 202-633-1000; www.americanhistory.si.edu*

More than 17 million artifacts cover aspects of American cultural heritage. Check out Julia Child's cheerfully comfortable kitchen from the famous chef's longtime home in Cambridge, Mass., reassembled here in 2001. Or watch textile conservators take painstaking steps to restore the fragile "Star-Spangled Banner," the actual flag that inspired Francis Scott Key in 1814 to write the poem that became America's national anthem. The museum's collections include the lap desk at which Thomas Jefferson drafted the Declaration of Independence, Henry Ford's 1913 Model-T, first ladies' inaugural gowns and Dorothy's ruby slippers from *The Wizard of Oz*. Children will especially enjoy the Hands-On History Room, where they can harness a life-size model of a mule or tap out a telegraph message in Morse code. This museum is closed for renovations and is due to reopen by November 20, 2009.

## NATIONAL MUSEUM OF HEALTH AND MEDICINE

*Walter Reed Army Medical Center, Building No. 54, 6900 Georgia Avenue and Elder Street, Washington D.C., 202-782-2200; www.nmhm.washingtondc.museum*

One of the most important medical collections in America. Interprets the link between history and technology; AIDS education exhibit; an interactive exhibit on human anatomy and lifestyle choices; and a collection of microscopes, medical teaching aids, tools and instruments (dating from 1862-1965) and famous historical icons exhibits. Daily 10 a.m.-5:30 p.m.; Closed December 25.

## NATIONAL MUSEUM OF NATURAL HISTORY

*Constitution Avenue and 10th Street N.W., Washington D.C., 202-633-1000; www.mnh.si.edu*

Before you enter this museum, stop on the Ninth Street-side of the building to see the mesmerizing Butterfly Garden. The National Museum of Natural History holds more than 124 million artifacts and specimens dating back to the Ice Age. Museum exhibits include an insect zoo with thousands of live specimens, a section on gems (including the 45.52-carat, billion-year-old Hope Diamond), dinosaur skeletons, a live coral reef, and botanical, zoological and geological materials. Daily 10 a.m.-5:30 p.m. Closed December 25. Admission free.

## NATIONAL MUSEUM OF WOMEN IN THE ARTS

*1250 New York Ave. N.W., Washington D.C., 202-783-5000, 800-222-7270; www.nmwa.org*

More than 1,200 works by female artists from the Renaissance to the present. Paintings, drawings, sculpture, pottery, prints. Library, research center by appointment. Performances. Guided tours (by appointment). Monday-Saturday 10 a.m.-5 p.m., Sunday noon-5 p.m.

★
★
★
★
★

### NATIONAL PRESBYTERIAN CHURCH AND CENTER

*4101 Nebraska Ave. N.W., Washington D.C., 202-537-0800; www.natpresch.org*

Chapel of the President contains memorabilia of past U.S. presidents; faceted glass windows depict the history of man and church. Self-guided tours (daily). Guided tours (Sunday following service).

### NATIONAL THEATRE

*1321 Pennsylvania Ave. N.W., Washington D.C., 202-628-6161, 800-447-7400; www.nationaltheatre.org*

Theatrical luminaries such as Sarah Bernhardt, Laurence Olivier and the Barrymores have performed at this historic playhouse, which is said to be haunted by the ghost of a murdered actor. These days, you'll see touring productions of shows such as *West Side Story* or *42nd Street*. On Mondays, there are films in summer and performances drawing on local talent the rest of the year. Saturday mornings feature children's shows. Tours Monday-Friday 11 a.m.-3 p.m. Fees vary by performance.

### NATIONAL ZOO

*3001 Connecticut Ave. N.W., Washington D.C., 202-633-4800; www.nationalzoo.si.edu*

A branch of the Smithsonian Institution, the National Zoo features 5,000 animals of 500 species. Come when the zoo first opens or after 2 p.m. if you want to see giant pandas Tian Tian and Mei Xiang without waiting in long lines. The zoo is set amid the urban greenery of Rock Creek Park. April-October, 10 a.m.-6 p.m.; November-March 10 a.m.-4:30 p.m.

### NAVY MUSEUM

*805 Kidder Breese S.E., Washington D.C., 202-433-6897; www.history.navy.mil*

History of the US Navy from the Revolutionary War to the space age. Dioramas depict achievements of early naval heroes; displays development of naval weapons; fully rigged foremast fighting top and gun deck from frigate *Constitution* on display; World War II guns that can be trained and elevated; submarine room has operating periscopes. Approximately 5,000 objects on display including paintings, ship models, flags, uniforms, naval decorations and the bathyscaphe *Trieste*. Two-acre outdoor park displays 19th- and 20th-century guns, cannon, other naval artifacts; US Navy destroyer *Barry* located on the waterfront. Monday-Friday 9 a.m.-5 p.m., weekends and holidays 10 a.m.-5 p.m. Closed: Thanksgiving, December 24, Christmas and New Years' Day.

### NAVY YARD

*901 M St. S.E., Washington D.C., 202-433-4882*

Founded in 1799 along the Anacostia River at a location chosen by George Washington, the yard was nearly destroyed during the War of 1812. Outside the yard at 636 G St. S.E. is the John Philip Sousa house, where the "March King" wrote many of his famous compositions. The house is private.

### NEW YORK AVENUE PRESBYTERIAN CHURCH

*1313 New York Ave. N.W., Washington D.C., 202-393-3700; www.nyapc.org*

The church where Lincoln worshipped. It was rebuilt in 1950-1951, with Lincoln's pew. Dr. Peter Marshall was pastor from 1937 to 1949. Mementos on display include

**WASHINGTON, D.C.**

★
★
★
★
★

the first draft of the Emancipation Proclamation. Tuesday-Friday, services Sunday morning.

### THE OCTAGON MUSEUM

*1799 New York Ave. N.W., Washington D.C., 202-638-3221;*
*www.archfoundation.org/octagon*
Federal townhouse built for Colonel John Taylor III based on designs by Dr. William Thornton. It served as temporary quarters for President and Mrs. James Madison after the White House burned in the War of 1812; it also was the site of the ratification of the Treaty of Ghent. Restored with period furnishings (1800-1828). Changing exhibits on architecture and allied arts. By appointment only.

### OLD SENATE CHAMBER

*First and Constitution avenues N.E., Washington D.C., 202-225-6827;*
*www.aoc.gov/cc/capitol/old_sen_ch.cfm*
Original Senate chamber has been restored to its 1850s appearance.

### OLD STONE HOUSE

*3051 M St. N.W., Washington D.C., 202-426-6851;*
*www.nps.gov/archive/rocr/oldstonehouse*
Believed to be the oldest pre-Revolutionary building in Washington, dating to 1765. Constructed on parcel No. 3 of the original tract of land that was then Georgetown, the house was used as both a residence and a place of business; five rooms are furnished with household items that reflect a middle-class residence of the late 18th century. The grounds are lush with fruit trees and seasonal blooms. Wednesday-Sunday noon-5 p.m. Open all year by reservation.

### ORGANIZATION OF AMERICAN STATES (OAS)

*17th Street N.W. and Constitution Avenue, Washington D.C., 202-458-3000;*
*www.oas.org*
Headquarters of OAS, set up to maintain international peace and security and to promote integral development in the Americas. Monday-Friday 9 a.m.-5:30 p.m.

### PAVILION AT THE OLD POST OFFICE

*1100 Pennsylvania Ave. N.W., Washington D.C., 202-289-4224;*
*www.oldpostofficedc.com*
Romanesque structure from 1899, which for years was headquarters of the U.S. Postal Service. The building has been remodeled into a marketplace with 100 shops and restaurants and daily entertainment. In the 315-foot tower are replicas of the bells of Westminster Abbey, a bicentennial gift from Great Britain. The tower is the second-highest point in D.C. and offers spectacular views from an open-air observation deck. Above the Pavilion shops are headquarters for the National Endowment for the Arts.

### PETERSEN HOUSE

*511 10th St. N.W., Washington D.C.*
The house where President Lincoln was taken after the shooting at Ford's Theatre; he died here the following morning. The house has been restored to its appearance at that time. Daily 9 a.m.-5 p.m.

## PHILLIPS COLLECTION

*1600 21st St. N.W., Washington D.C., 202-387-2151; www.phillipscollection.org*

First museum of modern art in the nation. Founded in 1918, the museum continues to emphasize the work of emerging as well as established international artists. Permanent collection of 19th- and 20th-century Impressionist, Post-Impressionist and modern painting and sculpture. Tuesday-Saturday 10 a.m.-5 p.m., Thursday 10 a.m.-8:30 p.m., Sunday 11 a.m.-6 p.m.; Concerts October-May, Sunday.

## POTOMAC PARK (EAST AND WEST)

*1100 Ohio St. S.W., Washington D.C., 202-619-7222; www.nps.gov/ncro*

Features 720 riverfront acres divided by Washington's famous Tidal Basin into East and West Potomac parks. East Potomac Park has three golf courses, a large swimming pool, picnic grounds, tennis courts and biking and hiking paths. Pedal boats can be rented at the Tidal Basin. At West Potomac Park, you'll find the Vietnam, Korean, Lincoln, Jefferson and FDR memorials; Constitution gardens; and the Reflecting Pool. Also the site of the famous D.C. cherry trees; enjoy the two-week burst of pink and white cherry blossoms from more than 3,000 trees, a 1912 gift of friendship from Japan, in late March/early April. The Cherry Blossom Festival begins each year with the lighting of the 300-year-old Japanese Stone Lantern, presented by the governor of Tokyo in 1954.

## PRESIDENT KENNEDY'S GRAVESITE

*South Gate, Arlington National Cemetery, Washington D.C.*

## RENWICK GALLERY AT THE AMERICAN ART MUSEUM

*1661 Pennsylvania Ave. at 17th St. N.W., Washington D.C., 202-633-2850;*
*www.americanart.si.edu/renwick*

The American Art Museum's Renwick Gallery, housed in an elegant Second Empire-style building, displays American crafts and decorative arts. The permanent collection features superb, one-of-a-kind pieces in clay, fiber, glass, metal and wood. Make sure to see the sculptural furniture by Sam Maloof and the playful Game Fish by Larry Fuente. Daily 10 a.m.-5:30 p.m. Closed December 25.

## ROCK CREEK PARK

*3545 Williamsburg Lane N.W., Washington D.C., 202-895-6070; www.nps.gov/rocr*

Just five miles from the White House are dozens of miles of clearly marked, well-maintained, easy and moderately hard hiking trails through the park's 1,754 acres of meadows and woodlands. There's also a gentle walk along Beach Drive that takes you through dramatic Rock Creek Gorge; on weekends and holidays, cars are prohibited, making it even more peaceful. Nature Center and Planetarium, Old Stone House. Wednesday-Sunday 9 a.m-5 p.m. Weekend: noon-5 p.m.

## SENATE OFFICE BUILDINGS

*114 Constitution Ave. N.E., Washington D.C.*

Linked by private subway to the Capitol.

**WASHINGTON, D.C.**

★
★
★
★
★

### SEWALL-BELMONT HOUSE

*144 Constitution Ave. N.E., Washington D.C., 202-546-1210;*
*www.sewallbelmont.org*

The Sewall-Belmont House is a monument to Alice Paul, the author of the Equal Rights Amendment. From this house, she spearheaded the fight for the passage of the amendment. Now a national landmark, the house contains portraits and sculptures of women from the beginning of the suffrage movement; extensive collection of artifacts of the suffrage and equal rights movements; historic headquarters of the National Woman's Party. Tuesday-Friday 11 a.m.-3 p.m., Saturday noon-4 p.m.

### SHAKESPEARE THEATRE AT THE LANSBURGH

*450 Seventh St. N.W., Washington D.C., 202-547-1122, 877-487-8849;*
*www.shakespearedc.org*

This company was founded in 1985 and features the Bard's classics.

### SHOPS AT GEORGETOWN PARK

*3222 M St. N.W., Washington D.C., 202-342-8190; www.shopsatgeorgetownpark.com*

This stylish urban mall has four levels of upscale shops and restaurants to explore and is especially strong in apparel. Concierge Center. Monday-Saturday 10 a.m.-9 p.m., Sunday noon-6 p.m.

### SHOPS AT NATIONAL PLACE

*1331 Pennsylvania Ave. N.W., Washington D.C., 202-662-1250;*
*www.downtowndc.org/visit/go/shops-at-national-place-the*

Trilevel marketplace featuring more than 100 specialty shops and restaurants. Monday-Friday 11 a.m.-7 p.m., Saturday noon-6 p.m.

### SMITHSONIAN INSTITUTION

*1000 Jefferson Drive S.W., Washington D.C., 202-633-1000; www.si.edu*

The majority of Smithsonian museums are located on the National Mall. All buildings open daily 10 a.m.-5:30 p.m., except December 25. Anacostia Museum and National Zoo hours may vary.

### ST. JOHN'S CHURCH GEORGETOWN PARISH

*3240 O St. N.W., Washington D.C., 202-338-1796; www.stjohnsgeorgetown.org*

Oldest Episcopal congregation in Georgetown, established 1796; original design of church by William Thornton, architect of the Capitol. Many presidents since Madison have worshiped here. Francis Scott Key was a founding member. Tours (by appointment).

### SUPREME COURT OF THE UNITED STATES

*First Street N.E. and Maryland Avenue, Washington D.C., 202-479-3211;*
*www.supremecourtus.gov*

Designed by Cass Gilbert in Neoclassical style. Court is in session October-April (Monday-Wednesday, at two-week intervals from the first Monday in October) and on the first workday of each week in May and June; court sessions are open to the

★
★★
★★
★★
☆

public (10 a.m. and 1 p.m.), on a first-come, first-served basis; lectures are offered in the courtroom (Monday-Friday except when court is in session; 20-minute lectures hourly on half hour); on the ground floor are exhibits and a film (24 minutes), cafeteria, snack bar and gift shop. Monday-Friday 9 a.m.-4:30 p.m.

## TEXTILE MUSEUM

*2320 S. St. N.W., Washington D.C., 202-667-0441; www.textilemuseum.org*
Founded in 1925 with the collection of George Hewitt Myers, the museum features changing exhibits of non-Western textiles, Oriental rugs and other handmade textile art. Guided tours daily. Monday-Saturday 10 a.m.-5 p.m., Sunday 1-5 p.m.

## THOMAS JEFFERSON MEMORIAL

*East Basin Drive S.W., Washington D.C., 202-426-6841; www.nps.gov/thje*
This memorial, dedicated in 1943, honors the third president and author of both the Declaration of Independence and the Bill of Rights. The white-marble dome surrounded by columns, representing the classic style that Jefferson introduced to the U.S., is quite beautiful when lit up at night. In the basement, you'll find a museum and the plaster statue from which the 19-foot bronze one in the center of the monument was created. Open daily. Rangers: 9:30 a.m.-11:30 p.m. Admission free.

## TOURMOBILE SIGHTSEEING

*1000 Ohio Drive S.W., Washington D.C., 202-554-5100; www.tourmobile.com*
Narrated shuttle tours to 18 historic sites on the National Mall and in Arlington National Cemetery. Unlimited reboarding throughout day (daily). Additional tours separately or in combinations: Arlington National Cemetery; Mount Vernon (seasonal) and Frederick Douglass Home (seasonal).

## TUDOR PLACE

*1644 31st St. N.W., Washington D.C., 202-965-0400; www.tudorplace.org*
This 12-room Federal-style mansion was designed by Dr. William Thornton, architect of the Capitol, for Martha Custis Peter, granddaughter of Martha Washington. The Peter family lived in the house for 180 years. (It was built in 1805.) All furnishings and objects d'art are original. More than five acres of gardens (Monday-Saturday). Guided tours Tuesday-Sunday.

## UNION STATION

*50 Massachusetts Ave. N.E., Washington D.C., 202-289-1908;*
*www.unionstationdc.com*
Architect Daniel Burnham designed Union Station in 1907, and it was restored to its former glory and reopened in 1988. The white granite Beaux Arts masterpiece is still a functioning train station and is now home to more than 130 upscale restaurants and shops, many of them catering to the special needs of travelers. But many locals patronize the shops, too (including former President Bill Clinton, who regularly bought holiday presents here). Also located within the station are the Amtrak depot and Gray Line and Tourmobile Sightseeing operators. Monday-Saturday 10 a.m.-9 p.m., Sunday noon-6 p.m.

WASHINGTON, D.C.

## U.S. BOTANIC GARDEN

*100 Maryland Ave. S.W., Washington D.C., 202-225-8333; www.usbg.gov*

The Botanic Garden, one of the oldest in the country, was established by Congress in 1820 for public education and exhibition. It features plants collected by the famous Wilkes Expedition of the South Seas. Conservatory has tropical, subtropical and desert plants; seasonal displays. Exterior gardens are planted for seasonal blooming; also here is Bartholdi Fountain, designed by the sculptor of the Statue of Liberty. Daily 10 a.m.-5 p.m.

## U.S. HOLOCAUST MEMORIAL MUSEUM

*100 Raoul Wallenberg Plaza S.W., Washington D.C., 202-488-0400; www.ushmm.org*

Opened in 1993, this privately funded museum hosts temporary exhibits that cover everything from the diary of Anne Frank to the role of Oskar Schindler in saving the lives of hundreds of Jews. At the heart of the museum is its self-guided Permanent Exhibition, which includes powerful photos, film footage, eyewitness testimonies, clothing, children's drawings and other victims' belongings, as well as reconstructions of concentration camp buildings. Daily 10 a.m.-5:30 p.m. April-mid-June, 10 a.m.-6:30 p.m.; closed Yom Kippur. Timed daily-use passes are necessary for visiting the museum's permanent exhibition and can be obtained each day at the museum starting at 10 a.m. or in advance by calling 800-400-9373.

## U.S. NATIONAL ARBORETUM

*3501 New York Ave. N.E., Washington D.C., 202-245-2726; www.usna.usda.gov*

Floral displays in spring, summer, fall and winter on 446 acres; Japanese garden, National Bonsai and Penjing Museum (daily); National Herb Garden, major collections of azaleas, wildflowers, ferns, magnolias, crabapples, cherries and dogwoods; aquatic plantings; dwarf conifers (the world's largest evergreen collection). Daily 8 a.m.-5 p.m. Under 16 years admitted only with adult.

## U.S. NAVY MEMORIAL

*701 Pennsylvania Ave. N.W., Washington D.C., 202-737-2300; www.lonesailor.org*

Dedicated to those who have served in the Navy in war and in peacetime. A 100-foot-diameter granite world map dominates the Plaza, where the Lone Sailor, a seven-foot bronze sculpture, stands and the US Navy Band stages performances (Memorial Day-Labor Day, Tuesday evenings). Visitor Center features electronic kiosks with interactive video displays on naval history; also Navy Memorial Log Room and U.S. Presidents' Room. Daily 9:30 a.m.-5 p.m. Closed: Thanksgiving, December 25 and January 1.

## VERIZON CENTER

*601 F St. N.W., Washington D.C., 202-628-3200; www.verizoncenter.com*

This 20,000-seat, state-of-the-art arena, home to the NBA's Washington Wizards, the WNBA's Washington Mystics, the NHL's Washington Capitals and Georgetown Hoyas basketball, is also a popular venue for concerts and other events, from Liza Minnelli to the Harlem Globetrotters. Even when nothing is scheduled, you can check out Nick and Stef's Steakhouse (open for dinner every day, lunch Monday-Friday), the F Street Sports Bar, or Modell's Sporting Goods for team-themed athletic wear. Monday-Saturday; days and fees for events vary.

### VIETNAM VETERANS MEMORIAL

*900 Ohio Drive S.W., Washington D.C., 202-426-6841; www.nps.gov/vive*

Designed by Maya Ying Lin and funded by private citizens' contributions, this memorial's polished black granite walls are inscribed with the names of the 58,175 U.S. servicemen who died in or remain missing from the Vietnam War (a large directory helps visitors locate specific names). Deliberately apolitical, the memorial aims to foster reconciliation and healing given the divisiveness the war caused in American society. Also onsite are the Three Servicemen Statue and Flagpole and the Vietnam Women's Memorial. Daily. Rangers: 9:30 a.m.-11:30 p.m.

### WARNER THEATRE

*13th and E. St. N.W., Washington D.C., 202-783-4000; www.warnertheatre.com*

This theater with more than 1,800 seats has been restored to its 1924 glory, with a sparkling chandelier, stained-glass lamps and Portuguese draperies. The Warner is host to many performances, including comedies, musicals, an annual *Nutcracker* performance and movie premieres from time to time.

### WASHINGTON CAPITALS (NHL)

*Verizon Center, 601 F St. N.W., Washington D.C., 202-661-5065;*
*www.washingtoncapitals.com*

Professional hockey team.

### WASHINGTON CONVENTION CENTER

*801 Mount Vernon Place N.W., Washington D.C., 202-249-3000, 800-368-9000;*
*www.dcconvention.com*

Washington's biggest building is also one of its newest. Opened in 2003, the Washington Convention Center occupies six city blocks, housing 700,000 square feet of exhibit space and 125,000 square feet of meeting space. The roof of the structure alone covers 17 acres. The Washington Convention Center is located immediately north of Mount Vernon Square, offering convenient access to some of the city's finest hotels and restaurants. Many other attractions can be found nearby, including Chinatown, the National Portrait Gallery, Ford's Theatre and the Verizon Center.

### WASHINGTON HARBOUR

*3000 K St. N.W., Washington D.C.*

Dining and shopping complex that features lavish fountains, life-size statuary and a boardwalk with a view of the Potomac River.

### WASHINGTON MONUMENT

*15th St. S.W., Washington D.C., 202-426-6841; www.nps.gov/wamo*

This obelisk, the tallest masonry structure in the world, at 555 feet, was dedicated in 1885 to the memory of the first U.S. president. Before its dedication, it had been under construction for almost 40 years, as a lack of funds and the Civil War interrupted its progress. You can see where construction resumed after a 28-year delay about a quarter of the way up the monument, where two different shades of marble meet. Views of the majestic structure can be enjoyed anytime, but to enter, you must have a ticket. You can try your luck getting one of the free tickets distributed at the kiosk at 15th and Madison starting at 8 a.m. for same-day tours, or you can reserve

WASHINGTON, D.C.

tickets by calling 800-967-2283. There is an elevator to the observation room at the 500-foot level. To take the 898 steps up or down, arrangements must be made in advance. Daily 9 a.m.-5 p.m. Closed: July 4, December 25.

### WASHINGTON MYSTICS (WNBA)

*Verizon Center, 601 F St. N.W., Washington D.C., 202-661-5050;*
*www.wnba.com/mystics*
Professional women's basketball team.

### WASHINGTON NATIONAL CATHEDRAL

*3101 Wisconsin Ave. N.W., Washington D.C., 202-537-6207;*
*www.cathedral.org/cathedral*
This edifice, 83 years in the making, was completed in 1990, its $65 million cost covered by private donations. Graced with intricate carvings inside and out, it has a 30-story central tower and 215 stained-glass windows, including one that contains a piece of lunar rock presented by the astronauts of Apollo 11. Bring binoculars if you want to see close-up the more than 100 gargoyles, which depict not just dragons but also a child with his hand in a cookie jar and *Star Wars* villain Darth Vader. Worshippers of all faiths are welcome at services held daily. There are also frequent musical events, including recitals given on the magnificent pipe organ most Sundays at 5 p.m. Famous Americans interred at the cathedral include President Woodrow Wilson and Helen Keller. Monday-Friday 10 a.m.-5:30 p.m., Saturday 10 a.m.-4:30 p.m., Sunday 8 a.m.-6:30 p.m.

**WASHINGTON, D.C.**

★
★★
★★
★

### WASHINGTON WALKS

*819 G St. S.W., Washington D.C., 202-484-1565; www.washingtonwalks.com*
Guided tours sponsored by Washington Walks are a great way to see the city. The group (along with Children's Concierge) runs two tours that kids will especially enjoy: for "Goodnight Mr. Lincoln," children can show up in pajamas at the Lincoln Memorial for stories, games and music about Honest Abe. The White House Un-Tour offers role-playing (you might be asked to impersonate the president who loved bowling) and fun facts about the executive mansion. April-October, days vary; rest of year by appointment.

### WASHINGTON WIZARDS (NBA)

*Verizon Center, 601 F St. N.W., Washington D.C., 202-661-5050;*
*www.nba.com/wizards*
Professional men's basketball team.

### WEST FRONT

*Capitol Hill, Washington D.C., 202-225-6827;*
*www.aoc.gov/cc/capitol/models/model_l2.cfm*
Along the Capitol's west front are terraces, gardens and lawns designed by Frederick Law Olmsted. Halfway down the hill are the Peace Monument (on the north) and the Garfield Monument (on the south). At the foot of Capitol Hill is Union Square with a Reflecting Pool and the Grant Monument.

## THE WHITE HOUSE

*1600 Pennsylvania Ave. N.W., Washington D.C., 202-456-7041;*
*www.whitehouse.gov*

Constructed in 1800 under George Washington's supervision, the house has hosted every U.S. president since John Adams. The British burned it during the War of 1812, and it was reconstructed under the guidance of James Monroe (from 1817-1825). The West Wing, which includes the Oval Office, was built during Theodore Roosevelt's administration (during 1901-1909); before its construction, executive offices shared the second floor with the president's private quarters. The interior of the White House was gutted and rebuilt using modern construction techniques during the Truman administration. The Library and the Vermeil Room (on the Ground Floor); the East, Green, Blue and Red Rooms, and the State Dining Room (on the State Floor) are accessible to groups of 10 for tours. In this era of heightened security, you'll find Secret Service agents in every room, doubling as tour guides. Obtain tickets through your congressperson or senator. Tuesday-Saturday 7:30 a.m.-12:30 p.m.; closed for presidential functions.

## WOODROW WILSON HOUSE

*2340 S. St. N.W., Washington D.C., 202-387-4062; www.woodrowwilsonhouse.org*
Red brick Georgian Revival townhouse built in 1915 to which President Wilson retired after leaving office; family furnishings and gifts-of-state. Tuesday-Sunday 10 a.m.-4 p.m. Closed Mondays and major holidays.

## WORLD WAR II MEMORIAL

*National Mall, 17th St., Washington D.C., 202-426-6841; www.nps.gov/nwwm*

The World War II Memorial honors America's Greatest Generation, the men and women who emerged from the Depression to serve in a hard-fought war that took the lives of 50 million people worldwide. Situated on the National Mall between the Lincoln Memorial and the Washington Monument, this memorial opened to visitors in spring 2004. Twin Atlantic and Pacific pavilions are divided by an oval-shaped pool, symbolizing a war fought across two oceans. Fifty-six wreath-adorned stone pillars—each representing a U.S. state or territory—form semicircles on the memorial's north and south sides. To the west, the Reflecting Pool cascades over twin waterfalls that bookend the Freedom Wall, which glitters with 4,000 gold stars (one-tenth the number of Americans who lost their lives in the war). National park rangers staff an information station south of the memorial, answering questions and providing brochures. Open daily.

## YELLOW HOUSE

*1430 33rd St. N.W., Washington D.C.*
One of Georgetown's oldest homes (a private residence dating to 1733), typical of the area's mansions.

## SPECIAL EVENTS

### CHERRY BLOSSOM FESTIVAL

*Tidal Basin and Ohio Drive N.W., Washington D.C., 202-789-7000;*
*www.nationalcherryblossomfestival.org*

About 150 trees remain from the original 1912 gift of 3,000 from the city of Tokyo, but thousands of others have been planted in parks along the Tidal Basin, and for two weeks each year their lush pink and white blooms transform the cityscape. The festival

★
★
★
★
★

celebrates this annual event with activities that appeal to visitors of all ages such as the Smithsonian's Kite Festival on the National Mall and the rousing parade or Sakura Matsuri, a day-long Japanese street festival. Visitors can enjoy drummers, traditional dancers and musical performances; demonstrations of flower arranging, calligraphy and martial arts; a Taste of Japan food fair; and the bustling Ginza Arcade, with shops selling everything from origami paper to antique kimonos. Late March-early April.

### CONCERTS

*Independence and 15th St. N.W., Washington D.C., 202-619-7222; www.nps.gov/ncro*
Sylvan Theater, Washington Monument grounds, June-August, days vary, 202-619-7222. U.S. Capitol, west terrace, June-late August, Monday-Wednesday, Friday-Sunday, 202-619-7222. National Gallery of Art, west garden court, October-June, Sunday evenings; first-come basis, 202-842-6941. Phillips Collection, at Dupont-Kalorama Museum, September-May, Sunday, 202-387-2151.

### EASTER EGG ROLL

*White House Lawn, 1600 Pennsylvania Ave. N.W., Washington D.C., 202-456-2200; www.whitehouse.gov/easter*
First introduced to Washington by Dolley Madison. Monday after Easter.

### EVENING PARADE

*Eighth and First streets S.E., Washington D.C., 202-433-6060; www.mbw.usmc.mil/parade_eveningdefault.asp*
Spectacular parade with Marine Band, U.S. Marine Drum and Bugle Corps, Color Guard, Silent Drill Team and marching companies. Submitting a written request for reservations at least three weeks in advance is recommended. Friday evenings, early May-late August.

### FESTIVAL OF AMERICAN FOLKLIFE

*National Mall, Constitution Ave., Washington D.C., 202-357-2700; www.folklife.si.edu/center/festival.html*
Festival of folklife traditions from America and abroad. Sponsored by the Smithsonian Institution and National Park Service. Late June-early July.

### FORT DUPONT SUMMER THEATRE

*Fort Dupont Park, Minnesota Avenue and Randle Circle, Washington D.C.*
Musicals, concerts, plays and dancing. Early July-late August, Saturday evenings.

### GEORGETOWN HOUSE TOUR

*3240 O St. N.W., Washington D.C., 202-338-2287; www.georgetownhousetour.com*
Held since 1927, participants view 8-10 houses in Georgetown. St. John's Episcopal Church members serve as hosts and guides, and serve tea in the Parish Hall in the afternoon. Late April.

### JULY 4TH FIREWORKS ON THE MALL

*National Mall, Washington D.C., 202-426-6841; www.nps.gov/nama/events/july4/july4.htm*
Fireworks over the monuments on the National Mall. One of the best viewing spots is the Capitol, where the National Symphony Orchestra gives a rousing concert before

the fireworks begin. Arrive early (the crowds get quite large) and picnic while you wait. July 4.

### MUSICAL PROGRAMS

*Carter Barron Amphitheater, Rock Creek Park, 16th & Colorado Ave. N.W., Washington D.C., 202-426-0486; www.nps.gov/rocr/planyourvisit/cbarron.htm*
Mid-June-August.

### PAGEANT OF PEACE

*Ellipse, South of White House,15th and E. streets N.W., Washington D.C., 202-619-7222; www.nps.gov/ncro*
Seasonal music, caroling; the president lights a giant Christmas tree near the White House. December.

## HOTELS

### ★★★THE FAIRFAX AT EMBASSY ROW

*2100 Massachusetts Ave. N.W., Washington D.C., 8202-293-2100, 800-434-9990; www.westin.com*
Since 1927, this Embassy Row property has welcomed guests with turn-of-the-century style. All rooms and suites are decorated with Federal and Empire furnishings, including rich fabrics and antique reproductions, and boast beautiful views of Washington National Cathedral and historic Georgetown. Join the distinguished political and social crowd at the Jockey Club for innovative American cuisine. 206 rooms. High-speed Internet access. Restaurant, bar. Fitness center. Business center. $$$

### ★★★THE FAIRMONT WASHINGTON D.C.

*2401 M St. N.W., Washington D.C., 202-429-2400, 800-257-7544; www.fairmont.com*
Located in the West End, this hotel is an ideal base for corporate travelers or vacationers. The well-appointed rooms and suites are comfortable and spacious, and guests on the Gold Floor level are treated to additional perks, such as private check-in and dedicated concierge service. Hotel guests and local denizens celebrate the weekend at the Colonnade's special brunch, while the Juniper is an informal spot for contemporary American fare. 415 rooms. High-speed Internet access. Restaurant. Business center. Pets accepted. $$$

### ★★★★★FOUR SEASONS HOTEL, WASHINGTON D.C.

*2800 Pennsylvania Ave. N.W., Washington D.C., 202-342-0444, 800-332-3442; www.fourseasons.com*
This Four Seasons, located in Washington's historic Georgetown neighborhood, delivers a refined, residential experience that extends from your first step in the modern, sophisticated lobby to lights out in one of the luxuriously appointed guest rooms. Yoga classes, a lap pool and cutting-edge equipment are found in the well-equipped fitness center, while the seven spa treatment rooms are a quiet spot for indulging in signature services like the cherry blossom Champagne body wrap. The hotel's restaurant, Seasons, offers a menu with a focus on fresh, regional ingredients, while the Garden Terrace lounge is the capital's top spot for afternoon tea. 211 rooms. Pets accepted, some restrictions. Wireless Internet access. Restaurant, bar. Fitness room, spa. Indoor pool, whirlpool. Airport transportation available. $$$$

### ★★★GEORGETOWN INN

*1310 Wisconsin Ave. N.W., Washington D.C., 202-333-8900, 800-368-5922;*
*www.georgetowncollection.com*

This hotel, located in the heart of historic Georgetown, puts travelers close to the eclectic and charming shops and restaurants for which this neighborhood is known. Rooms come equipped with marble bathrooms, fluffy terry-cloth robes and complimentary turn-down service. The inn's restaurant, the Daily Grill, serves classic American fare. 96 rooms. $$

### ★★★GRAND HYATT WASHINGTON

*1000 H St. N.W., Washington D.C., 202-582-1234, 800-633-7313;*
*www.grandwashington.hyatt.com*

The Grand Hyatt Washington, D.C., is situated in Penn Quarter, a newly revitalized shopping and dining district, and is close to attractions such as the Verizon Center, the Spy Museum, Ford's Theater and the U.S. Capitol. 888 rooms. High-speed Internet access. Restaurant, bar. Fitness center. Indoor pool, whirlpool. Business center. $$$$

### ★★THE HAMILTON CROWNE PLAZA

*14th and K streets N.W., Washington D.C., 202-682-0111, 800-263-9802;*
*www.hamiltonhoteldc.com*

318 rooms. High-speed Internet access. Restaurant, bar. Fitness center. Business center. $$

### ★★★★THE HAY-ADAMS

*1800 16th St. N.W., Washington D.C., 202-638-6600, 800-424-5054;*
*www.hayadams.com*

Set on Lafayette Square across from the White House, this hotel has welcomed notables since the 1920s. The guest rooms are a happy marriage of historic preservation and 21st-century conveniences—intricately carved plaster ceilings and ornamental fireplaces reside alongside high-speed Internet access and CD players. Windows frame views of the White House, St. John's Church and Lafayette Square. All-day dining is available at Lafayette, while the Off the Record bar is a popular watering hole for politicians and hotel guests. 145 rooms. High-speed Internet access. Restaurant, bar. Airport transportation available. Business center. $$$$

### ★★★HILTON WASHINGTON EMBASSY ROW

*2015 Massachusetts Ave. N.W., Washington D.C., 202-265-1600, 800-445-8661;*
*www.hilton.com*

This elegant hotel is in the heart of D.C.'s international business community and is conveniently located half a block from the Metro transit system. In the evening, you can relax with drinks and hors d'oeuvres in the lobby lounge or take in the fabulous view of D.C. from the seasonal rooftop pool. As its name suggests, the International Marketplace restaurant features cuisine from around the world. 193 rooms. Pool. Restaurant, bar. Children's activity center. $$

### ★★HOLIDAY INN GEORGETOWN

*2101 Wisconsin Ave. N.W., Washington D.C., 202-338-2120, 800-465-4329;*
*www.higeorgetown.com*
296 rooms. Restaurant, bar. Fitness center. Pool. **$**

### ★★HOLIDAY INN ON THE HILL

*415 New Jersey Ave. N.W., Washington D.C., 202-638-1616, 800-282-0244;*
*www.holidayinn.com*
343 rooms. **$**

### ★★★THE HOTEL GEORGE

*15 E. St. N.W., Washington D.C., 202-347-4200, 800-576-8331; www.hotelgeorge.com*
Travelers book this boutique hotel for its dynamic interiors and central Capitol Hill location. The rooms offer bold artwork, monochromatic tones, clean lines and high-tech amenities. The hotel's restaurant, Bistro Bis, is often considered one of the top tables in town and its French bistro fare is a favorite of politicos and celebrities. Those traveling with pets will appreciate the hotel's "Pet Amenity Program," which includes water and food dish, dog mat and special treats. Lonely guests who left their pet at home can take part in the "Guppy Love" program, where the hotel lends a goldfish for guests to keep in their room throughout their stay. 142 rooms. Pets accepted; fee. High-speed Internet access. Restaurant, bar. Fitness center. Business center. **$$$**

### ★★★HOTEL MONACO

*700 F St. N.W., Washington D.C., 202-628-7177; www.monaco-dc.com*
Conveniently located near the Washington Convention Center and Verizon Center, Monaco is a funky alternative to the traditional hotel experience. Housed within the D.C.'s former General Post Office (which was built in 1839 by Robert Mills, who designed the Washington Monument), the all-marble building is fronted by soaring columns—a example of quintessential Washington architecture. Inside, however, a bright palate of colors from the walls to floors to furnishings is a delight for the senses for travelers looking for something out-of-the-ordinary. Uniqueness follows through to things like in-room extras (check out the Nintendos) and services (you can get a temporary pet goldfish delivered to your room, if you start feeling lonely). 184 rooms. Pets accepted. High-speed Internet access. Airport transportation available. Business center. **$$$**

### ★★★HOTEL PALOMAR

*2121 P St. N.W., Washington D.C., 202-448-1800; www.hotelpalomar-dc.com*
The rather bland beige brick exterior belies the trendy style within this art-centric boutique hotel. The marble-floored lobby is filled with striking sculptures and bold, colorful artwork. Art receptions are hosted regularly in a partnership with the Smithsonian and Phillips Collection. And to create a perception of art in motion, the staff has been trained by the Washington, D.C. ballet. The 520-square-foot rooms highlight contemporary design concepts, with zebrawood furnishings and Italian marble floors in the bathrooms. 335 rooms. Pets accepted. Wireless Internet access. Restaurant, bar. Fitness room. Outdoor pool. Airport transportation available. Business center. **$$$**

WASHINGTON, D.C.

★
★
★
★
★

### ★★HOTEL WASHINGTON

*515 15th St. N.W., Washington D.C., 202-638-5900, 800-424-9540;*
*www.hotelwashington.com*

374 rooms. Wireless Internet access. Restaurant, bar. Fitness center. Business center.
**$$$**

### ★★★J. W. MARRIOTT HOTEL ON PENNSYLVANIA AVENUE

*1331 Pennsylvania Ave. N.W., Washington D.C., 202-393-2000;*
*www.marriotthotels.com/wasjw*

Just two blocks from the White House, the J.W. Marriott Hotel offers well-appointed guest rooms with flatscreen TVs and unique black-and-white art. 738 rooms. High-speed Internet access. Restaurant, bar. Fitness center. Spa. Pool. Business center. **$$$**

### ★★★THE JEFFERSON

*1200 16th St. N.W., Washington D.C., 202-347-2200;*
*www.thejeffersonwashingtondc.com*

Built in 1923 just four blocks from the White House, this Beaux Arts hotel is a stylish and centrally located retreat, with antique-filled public rooms and a museum-quality collection of artwork and original documents signed by Thomas Jefferson. A fitness center is available, as are privileges at the University Club, with its Olympic-size pool. The restaurant feels like Old Washington with faux tortoiseshell walls and leather chairs, yet it serves New American cuisine. It is closed for a full renovation and will re-open in mid-2009. 132 rooms. Restaurant, bar. Fitness center. Pool. **$$**

### ★★★L'ENFANT PLAZA HOTEL

*480 L' Enfant Plaza, S.W., Washington D.C., 202-484-1000, 800-636-5065;*
*www.lenfantplazahotel.com*

While The L'Enfant Plaza Hotel offers special packages for kids and pets, in fact it caters to all guests. Rooms are stocked with feather-top mattresses, and the roof comes equipped with a pool and Sunday deck. The hotel is only steps away from the Air and Space museum and Holocaust museum. 370 rooms. Pets accepted; fee. Wireless Internet access. Restaurant, bar. Fitness room. Pool. Business center. **$$**

### ★★★LATHAM HOTEL

*3000 M St. N.W., Washington D.C., 202-339-6318, 888-587-2377;*
*www.georgetowncollection.com*

This European-style boutique hotel is located in the heart of Georgetown, where shopping and dining options abound. But when your stomach growls, you might not want to leave the Latham. Michele Richard, a high-profile local chef with an international reputation, owns and operates the onsite Michele Richard Citronelle, where diners savor award-winning French and American cuisine. Well-appointed guest rooms offer marble showers and high-speed Internet access. In summer, cool off in the rooftop swimming pool. 146 rooms. Wireless Internet access. Restaurant, bar. Fitness center. Pool. Business center. Airport transportation available. **$$**

★
★
★
★
★

### ★★★THE MADISON

*1177 15th St. N.W., Washington D.C., 202-862-1600, 800-424-8577;*
*www.loewshotels.com*

The beautiful Georgian architecture and clock tower cupola distinguish this hotel, as does the hospitable staff. The elegant atmosphere is enhanced by contemporary amenities such as a fitness center and pool. 353 rooms. Airport transportation available. High-speed Internet access. Fitness center. Pool. Restaurant, bar. Airport transportation available. $$$

### ★★★★MANDARIN ORIENTAL, WASHINGTON DC

*1330 Maryland Ave. S.W., Washington D.C., 202-554-8588, 888-888-1778;*
*www.mandarinoriental.com*

Overlooking the Tidal Basin with views of the Jefferson Memorial, this Washington outpost of the Asian hotel brand delivers a scenic and central location on the Potomac River. Guest rooms mix an Eastern sensibility with East Coast style (think preppy plaids and toiles alongside clean-lined furniture and fresh-clipped orchids). Contemporary Asian-influenced cuisine pleases palates in the two restaurants, while the Lounge offers a casual alternative with cocktails and small plates like the lobster salad BLT. A more than 10,000-square-foot spa, fitness center and indoor pool offer water front views, a full spa menu and on-call personal trainers. 400 rooms. Pets accepted, some restrictions; fee. Wireless Internet access. Two restaurants, two bars. Fitness room, fitness classes available, spa. Indoor pool, whirlpool. Airport transportation available. $$$$

### ★★★MARRIOTT WARDMAN PARK HOTEL

*2660 Woodley Road, N.W., Washington D.C., 202-328-2000, 888-733-3222;*
*www.marriotthotels.com/wasdt*

This hotel gracefully combines historic charm, beauty and convenience. Its Wardman Tower, built in 1928, is listed on the National Register of Historic Places. The award-winning gardens have been featured on the *NBC Nightly News* and boast nearly 100,000 seasonal flowers. With an in-house gourmet market, full-service Starbucks and jewelry store, you can easily make this your home away from home. 1,334 rooms. Pets accepted; fee. High-speed Internet access. Restaurant, bar. Fitness center. Pool. Business center. $$

### ★★★OMNI SHOREHAM HOTEL

*2500 Calvert St. N.W., Washington D.C., 202-234-0700, 800-444-6664;*
*www.omnihotels.com*

The Omni Shoreham Hotel is an urban resort. Its full-service spa and fitness center are state-of-the-art. If you prefer the outdoors, hike, bike, jog or horseback ride through the scenic trails of nearby Rock Creek Park, or just relax in a hammock on the hotel's beautiful grounds. The hotel's Woodley Park location puts you close to attractions and restaurants, and the eclectic Adams Morgan neighborhood is only minutes away. 832 rooms. Pets accepted; some restrictions. Wireless Internet access. Restaurant, bar. Fitness center. Spa. Pool. Business center. $$$

**WASHINGTON, D.C.**

★
★
★
★
☆

## ★★ONE WASHINGTON CIRCLE HOTEL

*1 Washington Circle N.W., Washington D.C., 202-872-1680, 800-424-9671;*
*www.onewashcirclehotel.com*
151 rooms. Restaurant, bar. Fitness center. Pool. $$

## ★★★RENAISSANCE MAYFLOWER HOTEL

*1127 Connecticut Ave. N.W., Washington D.C., 202-347-3000;*
*www.renaissancehotels.com*
Built in 1925 for Calvin Coolidge's inauguration, this hotel has played host to the likes of Franklin Delano Roosevelt and J. Edgar Hoover. The block-long lobby features gilded trim, crystal chandeliers and Oriental rugs, but the guest rooms are quite homey. For groups, the Mayflower offers state-of-the-art meeting facilities. 657 rooms. High-speed Internet access. Pets accepted; fee. Fitness center. Business center. $

## ★★★★THE RITZ-CARLTON, GEORGETOWN

*3100 South St. N.W., Washington D.C., 202-912-4100, 800-241-3333;*
*www.ritzcarlton.com*
Embassy delegations often stay at the Ritz-Carlton, Georgetown, with its contemporary décor and historic setting. Many of the hotel's guest rooms offer views of the Potomac River, along with feather duvets, goose-down pillows and marble baths. Sip one of the fire-red martinis in the Degrees Bar and Lounge, then dine on American/ Italian cuisine in Fahrenheit. 86 rooms. High-speed Internet access. Restaurant, bar. Fitness center. Spa. Business center. Pets accepted, some restrictions, fee. Airport transportation available. $$$$

## ★★★★THE RITZ-CARLTON, WASHINGTON D.C.

*1150 22nd St. N.W., Washington D.C., 202-835-0500, 800-241-3333;*
*www.ritzcarlton.com*
The Ritz-Carlton offers noteworthy attention to detail along with innovative amenities. On-call technology butlers can assist with computer woes, while the Luggageless Travel program allows frequent visitors to leave items behind for their next stay. Guests staying in the Club Level rooms are treated to five food and beverage presentations each day. And all guests are granted access to the Sports Club/LA fitness complex next door. 300 rooms. High-speed Internet access. Restaurant, bar. Business center. Pets accepted, some restrictions; fee. Airport transportation available. $$$$

★
★
★
★
⋆

## ★★RIVER INN

*924 25th St. N.W., Washington D.C., 202-337-7600, 888-874-0100;*
*www.theriverinn.com*
126 rooms, all suites. Restaurant, bar. Fitness room. Pets accepted; fee. $$

## ★★★SOFITEL LAFAYETTE SQUARE, WASHINGTON D.C.

*806 15th St. N.W., Washington D.C., 202-730-8800; www.sofitelwashingtondc.com*
Just a short walk from the White House, the National Mall and the Metro, this historic hotel is located in a downtown business area. Its décor is 1930s Art Deco with a contemporary edge. With gold-leaf crown molding, marble and velvet furniture, the Sofitel Lafayette Square has earned a spot on the National Register of Historic Places. Pets receive a welcome bag, silver bowls and a small version of Sofitel's guest bed

with goose-down bedding. 237 rooms. High-speed Internet access. Restaurant, bar. Fitness center. Business center. **$$$**

### ★★★★THE ST. REGIS WASHINGTON, D.C.

*923 16th St. N.W., Washington D.C., 202-638-2626; www.stregis.com/washingtondc*
Built in 1926, the grand hotel has hosted world leaders for more than 80 years—after all, it *is* only two blocks from the White House. Renovated in 2008, rooms and suites include wireless Internet, iPod docking stations on the Bose clock radios, 32-inch LCD televisions and electric mirrors in the bathrooms, with television screens imbedded within the reflective surface of the mirror. Elegant and tasteful furnishings and decor provide a seamless feeling of classic luxury throughout the common areas and the beautiful rooms. 150 rooms, 25 suites, wireless Internet access. Restaurant, bar. Fitness room. Airport transportation available. Business center. **$$$$**

### ★★TOPAZ HOTEL

*1733 North St. N.W., Washington D.C., 202-393-3000, 800-775-1202; www.topazhotel.com*
99 rooms. Complimentary continental breakfast. Restaurant, bar. Pets accepted. **$$**

### ★★★THE WESTIN GRAND

*2350 M St. N.W., Washington D.C., 202-429-0100, 888-627-8406; www.westin.com*
Not as glitzy as many of the other top D.C. hotels, the Westin offers attentive service and a more low-key environment. The stylish rooms offer ultra-comfortable beds, sizable bathrooms, leather furniture and CD players. Westin Doggie Beds offer the same plush sleep experience to four-legged friends. The hotel's location is within walking distance of Georgetown and many waterfront restaurants along the Potomac. 263 rooms. High-speed Internet access. Restaurant, bar. Fitness center. Pool. Business center. Airport transportation available. **$$$**

### ★★★THE WESTIN WASHINGTON, D.C. CITY CENTER

*1400 M St. N.W., Washington D.C., 202-429-1700; www.starwoodhotels.com/westin*
Conveniently located near both Georgetown and Dupont Circle, this hotel offers comfortable rooms that feature Herman Miller Aeron ergonomic desk chairs and flat-screen TVs. Enjoy a meal at the hotel's restaurant, 1400 North, overlooking the main lobby. 352 rooms. Restaurant, bar. Fitness center. Business center. **$$**

### ★★★WILLARD INTERCONTINENTAL, WASHINGTON D.C.

*1401 Pennsylvania Ave. N.W., Washington D.C., 202-628-9100, 877-424-4225; www.washington.interconti.com*
Only two blocks from the White House, this legendary Beaux Arts hotel has been at the center of Washington's political scene since 1850. In the Willard's lobby, Lincoln held fireside staff meetings, Grant escaped the rigors of the White House to enjoy brandy and cigars, and the term "lobbyist" was coined. The guest rooms and suites are a traditional blend of Edwardian and Victorian styles furnished in deep jewel tones. The Jenny Lind suite is perfect for honeymooners, with its mansard roof and canopy bed, while the Oval suite, inspired by the Oval Office, makes guests feel quite presidential indeed. 332 rooms. High-speed Internet access. Restaurant, bar. Fitness center. Spa. Business center. Airport transportation available. **$$$$**

★
★
★
★

### ★WINDSOR PARK HOTEL

*2116 Kalorama Road, N.W., Washington D.C., 202-483-7700, 800-247-3064;*
*www.windsorparkhotel.com*
43 rooms. Complimentary continental breakfast. **$**

## SPECIALTY LODGING
### THE DUPONT AT THE CIRCLE

*1604-06 19th St. N.W., Washington D.C., 202-332-5251, 888-412-0100;*
*www.dupontatthecircle.com*
Built in 1885, this property consists of two connected Victorian townhouses located on a residential street in DuPont Circle. Authentic Victorian décor is mixed with eclectic art, and many rooms come with working fireplaces and whirlpool tubs. Nine rooms. Children over 13 years only. Complimentary continental breakfast. Airport transportation available.

## SPA
### ★★★★THE SPA AT THE MANDARIN ORIENTAL, WASHINGTON, D.C.

*1330 Maryland Ave. S.W., Washington D.C., 202-787-6100; www.mandarinoriental.com*
The staff at the Spa promotes the Time Ritual concept, a customized two- or three-hour experience during which clients receive a one-on-one consultation with a therapist to determine which treatments are best suited to the clients' needs. Clients can also book specific treatments such as facials, massages and body therapies, each enhanced with Eastern philosophies and techniques. In the Spa's signature Cherry Blossom Scrub, the staff uses cherry tea leaves, sugar and nourishing oils to strengthen the immune system and remove dead skin cells.

★
★★
★★
★

## RESTAURANTS
### ★★★701 RESTAURANT

*701 Pennsylvania Ave. N.W., Washington D.C., 202-393-0701;*
*www.701restaurant.com*
Overlooking the Navy Memorial fountains and just steps from the Washington National Mall, this fine-dining restaurant features a diverse menu and a caviar bar. The roomy tables, comfortable chairs and live piano music provide a nice atmosphere. And the lounge, which features a sunken bar, is the perfect place to meet friends for a drink. The Navy Band performs on Tuesday evenings, so try to grab a table on the exterior patio for a great view. American menu. Lunch, dinner. Bar. Business casual attire. Reservations recommended. Valet parking. Outdoor seating. **$$$**

### ★★★1789 RESTAURANT

*1226 36th St. N.W., Washington D.C., 202-965-1789; www.1789restaurant.com*
Located in a restored Federal mansion just on the edge of Georgetown University's campus, this restaurant is a top destination for students with visiting relatives or diners celebrating a special occasion. The restaurant features Victorian decor with fine china, Civil War pictures and artifacts, antiques and a gas fireplace. The menu changes seasonally, but the popular rack of lamb is always available. A chef's tasting menu is offered, as well as a pre/post-theater menu. American menu. Dinner. Bar. Children's menu. Jacket required. Reservations recommended. Valet parking. **$$$**

### ★★ADITI

*3299 M St. N.W., Washington D.C., 202-625-6825; www.image-in-asian.com*

Indian menu. Lunch, dinner. Bar. $

### ★★★★ADOUR

*923 16th St. N.W., Washington D.C., 202-509-8000;*
*www.adour-washingtondc.com*

Adour's Executive Chef Julien Jouhannaud takes the best of local ingredients, such as Maryland blue crab, Amish chicken breast and quail eggs from Virginia, and infuses them with the charm of southwestern French cooking. The ultra-contemporary setting features black walls, white seating and chrome galore. A backdrop of a floor-to-ceiling, temperature-controlled wine vaults serves as a reminder that French fare always goes down better with wine. French, American menu. Breakfast, lunch, dinner. $$$$

### ★AFTERWORDS

*1517 Connecticut Ave. N.W., Washington D.C., 202-387-1462; www.kramers.com*

American menu. Breakfast, lunch, dinner, Saturday-Sunday brunch. Bar. Outdoor seating. $

### ★★ANNA MARIA'S

*1737 Connecticut Ave. N.W., Washington D.C., 202-667-1444;*
*www.annamariasdunmore.com*

Italian menu. Lunch, dinner, late-night. Bar. Casual attire. $$

### ★AUSTIN GRILL

*750 E. St. N.W., Washington D.C., 202-393-3776; www.austingrill.com*

Southwestern menu. Lunch, dinner, Sunday brunch. Bar. $$

### ★BILLY MARTIN'S TAVERN

*1264 Wisconsin Ave. N.W., Washington D.C., 202-333-7370;*
*www.billymartinstavern.com*

American menu. Breakfast, lunch, dinner, late-night, Saturday-Sunday brunch. Bar. Casual attire. $$

### ★★★BISTRO BIS

*15 E. St. N.W., Washington D.C., 202-661-2700; www.bistrobis.com*

This popular French restaurant is located in the contemporary Hotel George on Capitol Hill. Its sleek, modern interior features a zinc bar, cherry wood accents, an open kitchen, leather banquettes, pendant lamps and high ceilings. The menu offers extensive wine pairings. French menu. Breakfast, lunch, dinner, brunch. Bar. Business casual attire. Reservations recommended. Outdoor seating. $$$

### ★★BISTRO FRANCAIS

*3128 M St. N.W., Washington D.C., 202-338-3830; www.bistrofrancaisdc.com*

French menu. Lunch, Saturday-Sunday brunch. $$

### ★★BISTROT LEPIC & WINE BAR

*1736 Wisconsin Ave. N.W., Washington D.C., 202-333-0111; www.bistrotlepic.com*

French menu. Lunch, dinner. Bar. Casual attire. Reservations recommended. $$

### ★★BOMBAY CLUB

*815 Connecticut Ave. N.W., Washington D.C., 202-659-3727;*
*www.bombayclubdc.com*

One of the most respected Indian restaurants in the area, the Bombay Club has an extensive menu that is divided into sections including house, vegetarian, Goan, Mughlai and Northwest Frontier specialties. Indian menu. Lunch, dinner, Sunday brunch. Bar. Outdoor seating. $$

### ★★BOMBAY PALACE

*2020 K St. N.W., Washington D.C., 202-331-4200; www.bombay-palace.com*
Indian menu. Lunch, dinner. Bar. $$

### ★★★BRASSERIE BECK

*1101 K St. N.W., Washington D.C., 202-408-1717; www.beckdc.com*

Belgium comes to the U.S. capital with a bold stroke at this ultra-modern bistro that still manages to feel down-to-earth. The French-Belgian dishes are heavy and filling, and best complemented by a crisp glass of beer. The bistro serves nine draught beers and over 100 varieties by bottle—Belgian, of course. The Chef's Table dinner features five courses with optional wine or beer pairings. And it would be a sin to leave without with a Belgian waffle for dessert. Contemporary Belgian menu. Lunch, dinner, Sunday brunch. $$

### ★THE BREAD LINE

*1751 Pennsylvania Ave. N.W., Washington D.C., 202-822-8900;*
*www.thebreadlinedc.blogspot.com*

Breakfast, lunch. Closed Saturday-Sunday. Outdoor seating. $

### ★BURMA

*740 Sixth St. N.W., Washington D.C., 202-638-1280*
Southeast Asian menu. Lunch, dinner. $

### ★★BUSARA

*2340 Wisconsin Ave. N.W., Washington D.C., 202-337-2340; www.busara.com*
Thai menu. Lunch, dinner. Bar. Casual attire. Outdoor seating. $$

### ★C.F. FOLKS

*1225 19th St. N.W., Washington D.C., 202-293-0162; www.cffolksrestaurant.com*
American menu. Lunch. Closed Saturday-Sunday. Outdoor seating. $

### ★★★CAFE ATLANTICO

*405 Eighth St. N.W., Washington D.C., 202-393-0812; www.cafeatlantico.com*

One of celebrity chef Jose Andres' restaurants, Cafe Atlantico is known for having one of the best cocktail lists in D.C. The caipirinhas and mojitos are delicious, as are the aguas frescas. The menu offers a mix of everything, from strip loin with a plantain puree to a daily fish served Veracruz-style and guacamole made tableside. For brunch, the restaurant offers Latino Dim Sum. Latin American menu. Lunch, dinner, brunch. Bar. Casual attire. Reservations recommended. Valet parking. Outdoor seating. $$$

★
★
★
★

## ★★CAFE MILANO

*3251 Prospect St. N.W., Washington D.C., 202-333-6183; www.cafemilano.net*
Italian menu. Lunch, dinner, late-night. Bar. Casual attire. Reservations recommended. Outdoor seating. $$$

## ★CAFE MOZART

*1331 H St. N.W., Washington D.C., 202-347-5732; www.cafemozartgermandeli.com*
Continental, German menu. Breakfast, lunch, dinner. Bar. Children's menu. German deli on premises. $$

## ★★★THE CAPITAL GRILLE

*601 Pennsylvania Ave. N.W., Washington D.C., 202-737-6200;*
*www.thecapitalgrille.com*
Dark, polished wood accents and dark leather chairs and booths may be reminiscent of a "boys' club" steakhouse, but everyone flocks here for the fresh seafood and signature dry-aged steaks. The restaurant offers an impressive wine list with more than 400 labels. Steak menu. Lunch, dinner. Bar. Business casual attire. Reservations recommended. Valet parking. $$$

## ★★CASHION'S EAT PLACE

*1819 Columbia Road, N.W., Washington D.C., 202-797-1819;*
*www.cashionseatplace.com*
International menu. Dinner, Sunday brunch. Closed Monday. Bar. Casual attire. Reservations recommended. Valet parking. Outdoor seating. $$$

## ★★★CENTRAL MICHEL RICHARD

*1001 Pennsylvania Ave. N.W., Washington D.C., 202-626-0015;*
*www.centralmichelrichard.com*
This restaurant won a 2008 James Beard Award for Best New Restaurant, and we can see why. In a warm atmosphere of earth tones and modern décor, Central is devoted to good, old-fashioned American selections, including macaroni and cheese, burgers, fried chicken with mashed potatoes and gastropub fare such as fish and chips, bangers and mash, and onion soup. Richard's French background, of course, sneaks into dishes like the country pate and ratatouille. Everything is prepared with a focus on the basics. Sometimes, keeping it simple is just the way to go. Classic American menu. Lunch, dinner. Bar. $$$

## ★★★★CITYZEN

*1330 Maryland Ave. S.W., Washington D.C., 202-787-6006;*
*www.mandarinoriental.com*
Under chef Eric Ziebold, CityZcafeen serves modern American-French cuisine. Ziebold offers new three-course prix-fixe menu monthly, including appetizers such as purée of Savoy cabbage soup with a lobster custard, globe artichoke ravioli, sashimi of Japanese hamachi and broiled Boston mackerel. Desserts include crispy brioche bread pudding, a CityZen peanut butter cup or a chocolate mint julep. Ziebold also offers a multi-course tasting menu, available as a vegetarian option. The restaurant and the lounge, designed by the acclaimed Tony Chi, feel intimate despite the large space and vaulted ceilings. American, French menu. Dinner. Closed Sunday-Monday. Bar. Business casual attire. Reservations recommended. Valet parking. $$$$

WASHINGTON, D.C.

★
★
★
★
★

### ★★CLYDE'S OF GEORGETOWN

*3236 M St. N.W., Washington D.C., 202-333-9180; www.clydes.com*

American. Lunch, dinner, Saturday-Sunday brunch. Bar. Children's menu. Atrium dining. $$

### ★★★DC COAST

*1401 K St. N.W., Washington D.C., 202-216-5988; www.dccoast.com*

This restaurant, housed in a Beaux Arts-style building popular in the city, offers a menu heavy on fish dishes. Chef Jeff Tunks shines with dishes such as seared Atlantic salmon, iced Blue point oysters and Tahitian-style tuna tartare. Seafood menu. Lunch, dinner. Closed-Sunday. Bar. Casual attire. $$$

### ★★DISTRICT CHOPHOUSE & BREWERY

*509 Seventh St. N.W., Washington D.C., 202-347-3434; www.districtchophouse.com*

American menu. Lunch, dinner, late-night. Bar. Children's menu. Casual attire. $$$

### ★FELIX RESTAURANT & SPY LOUNGE

*2406 18th St. N.W., Washington D.C., 202-483-3549*

Mediterranean menu. Dinner. Bar. Casual attire. $$

### ★★★GALILEO

*1110 21st St. N.W., Washington D.C., 202-293-7191;*
*www.robertodonna.com/restaurants*

This is the flagship enterprise of Roberto Donna, the celebrity chef behind Il Radicchio, I Matti and many others. In keeping with the cutting-edge trends, there's a much-sought-after kitchen table. The European country décor features terra-cotta floors, small alcoves in the dining room and a mural of Galileo. Italian menu. Lunch, dinner. Bar. Reservations recommended. Valet parking. Outdoor seating. $$$

### ★★★GEORGIA BROWN'S

*950 15th St. N.W., Washington D.C., 202-393-4499; www.gbrowns.com*

At this popular McPherson Square spot, diners have trouble choosing from among the many creative, modern dishes, such as fried green tomatoes stuffed with herbed cream cheese and served on a bed of green tomato relish with lemon-cayenne mayonnaise and watercress. The dining room features blonde wood and a bronzed ceiling scroll. American menu. Lunch, dinner, Sunday brunch. Bar. Casual attire. Reservations recommended. $$

### ★★★GERARD'S PLACE

*915 15th St. N.W., Washington D.C., 202-737-4445; www.gerardsplacedc.net*

Gerard's Place is an intimate hideaway near the White House with high-back chairs, sheaths draped overhead, vibrant colors and a large glass chandelier with amber-colored tones. Two menus are offered nightly: a five-course chef's tasting menu as well as a three-course prix fixe menu. Expect classic French dishes with refined twists, such as sautéed scallops with garlic flan and parsley mousse, braised short ribs with potato galette, and coconut dacquoise with roasted pineapple and lime sorbet. French menu. Lunch, dinner. Closed Sunday. Business casual attire. Outdoor seating. $$$

## ★★GRILL FROM IPANEMA

*1858 Columbia Road, N.W., Washington D.C., 202-986-0757;*
*www.thegrillfromipanema.com*
Brazilian menu. Lunch, dinner. Bar. Casual attire. Outdoor seating. **$$**

## ★GUAPO'S

*4515 Wisconsin Ave. N.W., Washington D.C., 202-686-3588;*
*www.guaposrestaurant.com*
Latin American, Mexican menu. Lunch, dinner. Bar. Outdoor seating. **$$**

## ★GUARDS

*2915 M St. N.W., Washington D.C., 202-965-2350; www.theguardsrestaurant-dc.com*
Seafood, Steak menu. Lunch, dinner, Sunday brunch. Bar. **$$**

## ★HAAD THAI

*1100 New York Ave. N.W., Washington D.C., 202-682-1111;*
*www.haadthairestaurant.co*
Thai menu. Lunch, dinner. Bar.

## ★★★ICI URBAN BISTRO

*Sofitel Lafayette Square Hotel, 806 15th St. N.W., Washington D.C., 202-730-8700;*
*www.iciurbanbistro.com*
Nobody does pastry better than the French. And this is certainly true of the creations of pastry chef Jerome Colin, who grew up in Roanne, France, and began his career in pastries at age 14. If you really want to go all out for maximum decadence, skip dinner altogether and get the sweet Dessert Sampler. But if you must exercise restraint (this *is* a French restaurant, after all), the international-inflected French cuisine and the trendy, modern setting here don't disappoint. Be sure to start with the Cajun pommes frites with Louisiana rémoulade. French menu. Breakfast, lunch, dinner. **$$$**

## ★★JALEO

*480 Seventh St. N.W., Washington D.C., 202-628-7949; www.jaleo.com*
Spanish menu. Lunch, dinner. Bar. Casual attire. Valet parking. Outdoor seating. **$$**

## ★J. PAUL'S

*3218 M St. N.W., Washington D.C., 202-333-3450; www.j-pauls.com*
American menu. Lunch, dinner, Saturday-Sunday brunch. Bar. Children's menu. **$$**

## ★★★THE JEFFERSON

*1200 16th St. N.W., Washington D.C., 202-833-6206;*
*www.thejeffersonwashingtondc.com*
Located inside the Jefferson hotel, this 60-seat restaurant has served politicians, celebrities and dignitaries for years. Nineteenth-century historical prints and portraits from the White House and Blair House are displayed throughout the restaurant. It is closed for a full renovation and will re-open in mid-2009. American menu. Breakfast, lunch, dinner, Sunday brunch. Bar. Children's menu. Casual attire. Valet parking. **$$$**

**47**

**WASHINGTON, D.C.**

★
★
★
★
★

### ★★★KINKEAD'S
*2000 Pennsylvania Ave. N.W., Washington D.C., 202-296-7700; www.kinkead.com*

Senators, journalists, models, financiers and media moguls rub elbows at chef/owner Bob Kinkead's spot for distinctive global fare. The deep, cherry wood-paneled dining room has an intimate, clubby feel to it, with low lighting, vintage wrought-iron staircases and elegant table settings. The menu, which changes daily and draws-influences from Spain, France, Italy, Morocco and Asia, offers a terrific selection of appetizers, soups, salads, chops and seafood. To complement the menu, the user-friendly wine list is color-coded from light to dark according to nose, weight, body and flavor. Kinkead's hosts live jazz in the evenings. Seafood menu. Lunch, dinner. Bar. Business casual attire. Reservations recommended. Valet parking. Outdoor seating. $$$

### ★KRUPIN'S
*4620 Wisconsin Ave. N.W., Washington D.C., 202-686-1989; www.mortysdc.com*

American menu. Breakfast, lunch, dinner. Children's menu. Casual attire. $$

### ★★LA CHAUMIERE
*2813 M St. N.W., Washington D.C., 202-338-1784; www.lachaumieredc.com*

French menu. Lunch, dinner. Closed Sunday. $$

### ★★LAURIOL PLAZA
*1835 18th St. N.W., Washington D.C., 202-387-0035; www.lauriolplaza.com*

Latin American, Mexican menu. Lunch, dinner, Sunday brunch. Bar. Casual attire. Outdoor seating. $$

### ★★LAVANDOU
*3321 Connecticut Ave. N.W., Washington D.C., 202-966-3002; www.lavandoudc.com*

French menu. Lunch, dinner. Closed August. Bar. Casual attire. $$

### ★LES HALLES
*1201 Pennsylvania Ave. N.W., Washington D.C., 202-347-6848; www.leshalles.net*

American, French menu. Lunch, dinner, Saturday-Sunday brunch. Bar. Children's menu. Outdoor seating. $$$

### ★★LUIGINO
*1100 New York Ave. N.W., Washington D.C., 202-371-0595; www.luigino.com*

Italian menu. Lunch, dinner. Closed Labor Day. Bar. Casual attire. Reservations recommended. Outdoor seating. $$

### ★MARKET INN
*200 E. St. S.W., Washington D.C., 202-554-2100; www.marketinndc.com*

American menu. Lunch, dinner, Sunday brunch. Bar. Children's menu. Outdoor seating. $$

### ★★★MENDOCINO GRILL AND WINE BAR
*2917 M St. N.W., Washington D.C., 202-333-2912; www.mendocinodc.com*

The most impressive feature of this restaurant is of course its excellent, all-American wine list. The food is designed to complement the wine. Wood and slate dominate the décor, accented with wall mirrors. American menu. Lunch, dinner. Bar. Business casual attire. Reservations recommended. **$$$**

### ★★★★MICHEL RICHARD CITRONELLE

*3000 M St. N.W., Washington D.C., 202-625-2150; www.citronelledc.com*
Like chef Michel Richard's food, the restaurant is stylish and elegant. Filled with fresh flowers and lit in a creamy, golden glow, the room has a chic vibe and a glass-enclosed open kitchen for a bird's-eye view of the cooks. Ingredients are the stars here; the chef manages to wow diners by highlighting the simple flavors of each dish's main component. Nabbing a seat at one of Richard's coveted tables is like winning the lottery. French menu. Dinner. Bar. Business casual attire. Reservations recommended. Valet parking. Outdoor seating. **$$$$**

### ★★★MIO

*1110 Vermont Ave. N.W., Washington D.C., 202-955-0075; www.miorestaurant.com*
Enjoy sounds of live music from the grand piano in a crisp atmosphere in this two-story bistro. An open kitchen allows diners to take in the action as the chef's staff creates American-style offerings, such as roasted lamb and pan-seared Alaska salmon. Chef Nicholas Stefanelli follows through on his belief of a sustainable approach to cuisine by using local produce and meats, including whole fish and whole animals. For a change of pace, ask for beer pairings with each course. American menu. Lunch, dinner. Closed Sunday. **$$$**

### ★★MONOCLE

*107 D St. N.E., Washington D.C., 202-546-4488; www.themonocle.com*
American menu. Lunch, dinner. Closed-Saturday-Sunday. Bar. Children's menu. Valet parking. **$$**

### ★★MORRISON-CLARK

*1015 L St. N.W., Washington D.C., 202-898-1200; www.morrisonclark.com*
American menu. Dinner. Closed Monday. Bar. Outdoor seating. **$$$**

### ★MR. SMITH'S

*3104 M St. N.W., Washington D.C., 202-333-3104; www.mrsmiths.com*
American menu. Lunch, dinner, Saturday-Sunday brunch. Bar. Outdoor seating. **$$**

### ★MURPHY'S OF DC

*2609 24th St. N.W., Washington D.C., 202-462-7171*
American, Irish menu. Lunch, dinner. Children's menu. Outdoor seating. **$$**

### ★★★NAGE

*Courtyard Marriott Hotel, 1600 Rhode Island Ave. N.W., Washington D.C.,*
*202-448-8005; www.nage.bz*
Tucked off to one side of the Courtyard Marriott Hotel, American and French cuisines find a home in a setting that resembles the Far East, with hanging lamps and hues of red. The D.C. location is the second Nage in the mid-Atlantic, the first being just to the east, in the seashore town of Rehoboth Beach, Delaware. Like its beachside counterpart, the menu features numerous seafood options, such as crab cakes and baked

**WASHINGTON, D.C.**

★
★
★
★
★

oysters. Be sure to check the chalkboard for the chef's specials of the day. American, French menu. Breakfast, lunch, dinner, Sunday brunch. **$$**

### ★NATHAN'S

*3150 M St. N.W., Washington D.C., 202-338-2000; www.nathanslunch.com*

American menu. Lunch, dinner, brunch. Bar. Casual attire. **$$**

### ★★NEW HEIGHTS

*2317 Calvert St. N.W., Washington D.C., 202-234-4110;*
*www.newheightsrestaurant.com*

American menu. Dinner. Closed-Sunday. Bar. Business casual attire. Reservations recommended. Outdoor seating. **$$$**

### ★★★OBELISK

*2029 P St. N.W., Washington D.C., 202-872-1180*

This intimate restaurant in DuPont Circle serves simple and authentic Italian food made from scratch. Homemade breads, pastas, butter and desserts are offered along with artisanal cheeses in an unpretentious—and somewhat romantic—setting. Italian menu. Dinner. Closed Sunday-Monday. Bar. Business casual attire. Reservations recommended. **$$$**

### ★★OCCIDENTAL GRILL

*1475 Pennsylvania Ave. N.W., Washington D.C., 202-783-1475;*
*www.occidentaldc.com*

American menu. Lunch, dinner. Bar. **$$$**

### ★★OLD EBBITT GRILL

*675 15th St. N.W., Washington D.C., 202-347-4800; www.ebbitt.com*

American menu. Breakfast, lunch, dinner, late-night, Saturday-Sunday brunch. Bar. Children's menu. Casual attire. **$$**

### ★★OLD EUROPE

*2434 Wisconsin Ave. N.W., Washington D.C., 202-333-7600; www.old-europe.com*

German menu. Lunch, dinner. Closed-Monday. Bar. Children's menu. Casual attire. **$$**

### ★★OVAL ROOM

*800 Connecticut Ave. N.W., Washington D.C., 202-463-8700; www.ovalroom.com*

American, Mediterranean menu. Lunch, dinner. Closed Sunday. Bar. Outdoor seating. **$$$**

### ★★★★PALENA

*3529 Connecticut Ave. N.W., Washington D.C., 202-537-9250;*
*www.palenarestaurant.com*

Executive chef Frank Ruta and pastry chef Ann Amernick met while working in the White House kitchen in the 1980s and decided to open a restaurant together in 2000. They now offer a seasonal menu of French- and Italian-influenced fare—such as sea scallops with chestnut purée or gnocchi with roasted endive, turnips, black truffle and shaved pecorino—complemented by comforting desserts including a chocolate-toffee

★
★ ★
★ ★
☆
☆

torte and a lime tartlet. American menu. Dinner. Closed Sunday. Bar. Business casual attire. Reservations recommended. $$$

### ★★THE PALM

*1225 19th St. N.W., Washington D.C., 202-293-9091; www.thepalm.com*

Steak menu. Lunch, dinner. Bar. Casual attire. Valet parking. $$$

### ★★PAOLO'S

*1303 Wisconsin Ave. N.W., Washington D.C., 202-333-7353;*
*www.capitalrestaurants.com*

Italian menu. Lunch, dinner, late-night, Saturday-Sunday brunch. Bar. Children's menu. Casual attire. Outdoor seating. $$

### ★★PESCE

*2016 P St. N.W., Washington D.C., 202-466-3474; www.pescebistro.com*

Seafood menu. Lunch, dinner. Casual attire. Valet parking. $$

### ★PIZZERIA PARADISO

*2029 P St. N.W., Washington D.C., 202-223-1245; www.eatyourpizza.com*

Pizza, sandwich menu. Lunch, dinner. Casual attire. $$

### ★★★PRIME RIB

*2020 K St. N.W., Washington D.C., 202-466-8811; www.theprimerib.com*

This K Street business spot features the décor of a 1930s New York supper club. It remains one of the best steakhouses inside the Beltway. Steak menu. Lunch, dinner. Closed-Sunday. Bar. Jacket required. Reservations recommended. Valet parking. $$$

### ★★★PROOF

*775 G St. N.W., Washington, D.C., 202-737-7663; www.proofdc.com*

Wine lovers, rejoice. The 65-page wine menu includes nearly 1,200 bottle selections and 40 choices by glass—the largest wine list in the D.C. area. Sommeliers help match vino to a dynamic assortment of more than 20 artisanal cheeses and a diverse menu that ranges from Mediterranean- to Asian-inspired dishes. An eclectic style mixes old and new with antiques, walnut floors, a French pewter bar and four flat-screen televisions displaying images from the collection at the Smithsonian American Art Museum. Contemporary American menu. Lunch, dinner, late night. $$$

### ★RAKU-AN

*1900 Q St. N.W., Washington D.C., 202-265-7258*

Pan-Asian menu. Lunch, dinner. Bar. Casual attire. Outdoor seating. $$

### ★★★RESTAURANT NORA

*2132 Florida Ave. N.W., Washington D.C., 202-462-5143; www.noras.com*

In this 19th-century grocery store-turned-organic American eatery, seasonal ingredients are the stars. Chef/owner Nora Pouillon is a pioneer in the organic movement; Restaurant Nora was the first certified organic restaurant in the country (95 percent of the products used are organic). Pouillon integrates flavors from the American South to Spain and from Latin America to Asia and India, and the menu changes

**51**

**WASHINGTON, D.C.**

★
★
★
★
★

daily. The rustic dining room is decorated with dried flowers and museum-quality antique Mennonite and Amish quilts. American, Mediterranean menu. Dinner. Closed Sunday; also late August-early-September. Bar. Business casual attire. Reservations recommended. Valet parking. $$$

### ★★★SAM AND HARRY'S
*1200 19th St. N.W., Washington D.C., 202-296-4333; www.samandharrys.com*
This upscale steak house in downtown D.C. is decorated with jazz-themed artwork, green leather booths and dark wood accents. Along with prime aged center New York strip steak, center cut filet mignon and rack of lamb, a number of fresh seafood options are available, from whole Maine lobster to jumbo lump crab cakes. A full bar features a wide selection of liquors and spirits, and the extensive wine list features 25 selections available by the glass. Steak menu. Lunch, dinner. Closed Sunday. Bar. Casual attire. Reservations recommended. Valet parking. $$$

### ★★SEA CATCH
*1054 31st St. N.W., Washington D.C., 202-337-8855; www.seacatchrestaurant.com*
Seafood menu. Lunch, dinner. Closed-Sunday. Bar. Valet parking. Outdoor seating. $$$

### ★★★SEASONS
*2800 Pennsylvania Ave. N.W., Washington D.C., 202-944-2026; www.fourseasons.com*
With deep upholstered armchairs, dark wood and fresh flowers, Seasons is the flagship restaurant of the Four Seasons Hotel. The sophisticated American-French menu offers simple, elegant fare and an extensive wine list. For an afternoon delight, stop by the Garden Terrace for tea service with all the trimmings—scones with clotted cream, cucumber and watercress sandwiches with the crusts cut off, petits fours, chocolate-dipped strawberries and assorted butter cookies. The Sunday brunch should not be missed. American, French menu. Breakfast, lunch, dinner, Sunday brunch. Bar. Children's menu. Business casual attire. Reservations recommended. Valet parking. Outdoor seating. $$$

### ★★SEQUOIA
*3000 K St. N.W., Washington D.C., 202-944-4200; www.arkrestaurants.com*
American menu. Lunch, dinner, Saturday-Sunday brunch. Bar. Casual attire. Outdoor seating. $$

### ★SESTO SENSO
*1214 18th St., Washington D.C., 202-785-9525; www.sesto.com*
Italian menu. Lunch, dinner. Closed Sunday. Bar. Casual attire. $$

### ★SUSHI-KO
*2309 Wisconsin Ave. N.W., Washington D.C., 202-333-4187; www.sushiko.us*
Japanese menu. Lunch, dinner. Casual attire. $$$

### ★★★TABERNA DEL ALABARDERO
*1776 First St. N.W., Washington D.C., 202-429-2200; www.alabardero.com*
For 16 years, Taberna del Alabardero has served classic Spanish cuisine such as chorizo paella with chicken or gazpacho Andaluz to D.C. diners. Executive chef Santi Zabaleta

★
★
★
★

also uses locally grown produce to enhance seasonal menu selections. Spanish. Lunch, dinner. Closed Sunday. Bar. Casual attire. Outdoor seating. **$$$**

### ★★★TEATRO GOLDONI

*1909 K St. N.W., Washington D.C., 202-955-9494; www.teatrogoldoni.com*
Named after a famous Venetian playwright from the 1800s, this downtown restaurant is decorated like a Venetian theater during the carnival, with a wall of masks, velvet curtains, blown-glass pendant lights and harlequin and striped patterns. Innovative but simple Venetian dishes are served, and a pianist performs on weekends. The restaurant also serves a prix fixe theater menu and offers wine dinners and cooking classes. Italian menu. Lunch, dinner. Closed Sunday. Bar. Business casual attire. Reservations recommended. Valet parking. **$$$**

### ★THAI KINGDOM

*2021 K St. N.W., Washington D.C., 202-835-1700; www.thaikingdom.org*
Thai menu. Lunch, dinner. Bar. **$$**

### ★THE TOMBS

*1226 36th St. N.W., Washington D.C., 202-337-6668; www.clydes.com*
American menu. Lunch, dinner, Sunday brunch. Bar. **$$**

### ★TONY AND JOE'S SEAFOOD PLACE

*3000 K St. N.W., Washington D.C., 202-944-4545; www.tonyandjoes.com*
Seafood menu. Lunch, dinner, late-night, Sunday brunch. Bar. Casual attire. Outdoor seating. **$$$**

### ★★TWO QUAIL

*320 Massachusetts Ave. N.E., Washington D.C., 202-543-8030, 800-543-8030; www.twoquail.com*
American, French menu. Lunch, dinner. Casual attire. Reservations recommended. Outdoor seating. **$$**

### ★★★VIDALIA

*1990 M St. N.W., Washington D.C., 202-659-1990; www.vidaliadc.com*
Taking his lead from the South and the Chesapeake Bay area, chef/owner Jeffrey Buben serves up inventive appetizers such as warm crayfish and sweet corn ragout with crispy plantain, piquillo pepper purée, catfish boudin blanc and rich crayfish consommé. Entrées include wild gulf shrimp and creamy anson mill grits with kale, sweet onion ragout and tasso ham ravigote. American menu. Lunch, dinner. Bar. Children's menu. Casual attire. **$$$**

### ★★★WESTEND BISTRO BY ERIC LIPERT

*1150 22nd St. N.W., Washington D.C., 202-974-4900; www.westendbistrodc.com*
Founded by French chef Eric Lipert, one of New York City's top culinary masters, this airy and fun bistro in The Ritz-Carlton, Washington D.C. is yet another example of his tasteful marriage of French and American cuisines. Lipert's vision is carried out by hand-picked protégés and the menu leans toward seafood and beef. For a quirky touch

★
★
★
★
★

not found at most gourmet eateries, try the fries and fish burger topped with roasted tomato and fennel. French, American menu. Lunch, dinner. **$$$**

### ★★★WILLARD ROOM

*1401 Pennsylvania Ave. N.W., Washington D.C., 202-637-7440;*
*www.washington.intercontinental.com*
Located in the Willard Inter Continental Washington hotel, this Victorian-style dining room serves a seasonal, eclectic American-French menu, which includes innovative takes on fish, shellfish, game, lamb, beef and poultry. The also restaurant offers desserts such as the tableside bananas Foster and cherries jubilee, an extensive wine list and a classic cocktail list. American, French menu. Breakfast, lunch, dinner. Closed Columbus Day. Bar. Business casual attire. Reservations recommended. Valet parking. **$$$**

### ★ZED'S ETHIOPIAN CUISINE

*1201 28th St. N.W., Washington D.C., 202-333-4710; www.zeds.net*
Middle Eastern menu. Lunch, dinner. **$$**

**WASHINGTON, D.C.**

★
★
★
★

# DELAWARE

DELAWARE "IS LIKE A DIAMOND, DIMINUTIVE, BUT HAVING WITHIN IT INHERENT VALUE," wrote John Lofland, the eccentric "Bard of Milford," in 1847. Only 96 miles long and from nine to 35 miles wide, the state is a corporate and agricultural superpower. Soybeans, corn, tomatoes, strawberries, asparagus, fruit and other crops bring in about $170 million each year. And favorable state policies have persuaded more than 183,000 corporations to base their headquarters in the "corporate capital of the world."

Within just 2,489 square miles, Delaware boasts rolling, forested hills in the north, stretches of bare sand dunes in the south and miles of marshland along the coast. Visitors can tour a modern agricultural or chemical research center in the morning and search for buried pirate treasures in the afternoon. In fact, Coin Beach in Rehoboth gets its name from the mysterious coins that frequently wash ashore, most likely from the *Faithful Steward,* a passenger vessel lost in 1785. The *deBraak,* another doomed ship that foundered off Lewes in 1798, was raised in 1986 because of the belief that it may have had a fortune in captured Spanish coins or bullion aboard. No such luck, but the artifacts themselves are a treasure.

Despite Delaware's current riches, the state's history started on a grim note. The first 28 colonists landed in the spring of 1631, and after an argument with a Lenni-Lenape chief, their bones were found mingled with those of cattle and strewn over their burned fields. In 1638, a group of Swedes established the first permanent settlement in the state—and the first permanent settlement of Swedes in North America—at Fort Christina, in what is now Wilmington.

Henry Hudson, in Dutch service, first discovered Delaware Bay in 1609. A year later, Thomas Argall reported it to English navigators and named it for his superior, Lord de la Warr, governor of Virginia. Ownership changed rapidly from Swedish to Dutch to English hands. The Maryland-Delaware boundary was set by a British court order in 1750 and surveyed as part of the Mason-Dixon Line in 1763-1767. The boundary with New Jersey, also long disputed, was confirmed by the Supreme Court in 1935.

The "First State" (first to adopt the Constitution, on December 7, 1787) is proud of its history of sturdy independence, both military and political. During the Revolution, the "Delaware line" was a crack regiment of the Continental Army. The men would "fight all day and dance all night," according to a dispatch by General Greene. How well they danced is open to question, but they fought with such gallantry that they received regular praise in the general's dispatches.

Delaware statesman John Dickinson, "penman of the Revolution" and one of the state's five delegates to the Constitutional Convention, was instrumental in the decision to write a new federal constitution rather than to simply patch up the Articles of Confederation.

**FUN FACTS**

Horseshoe crabs may be viewed in large numbers up and down the Delaware shore in May. The crabs, which have remained basically the same since the days of the dinosaur, can endure extreme temperature and salinity and can go for a year without eating.

Along with Lofland and Dickinson, Delaware has produced many literary figures, including the 19th-century playwright and novelist Robert Montgomery Bird, writer and illustrator Howard Pyle, Henry Seidel Canby, founder of the *Saturday Review* and novelist John P. Marquand.

*Information: www.state.de.us*

# BETHANY BEACH

Originally a site for revival camp meetings, Bethany Beach is a quiet beach town on the Atlantic Ocean that offers excellent surf fishing and swimming.

*Information: Bethany-Fenwick Area Chamber of Commerce, 36913 Coastal Highway, Fenwick Island, 302-539-2100, 800-962-7873; www.bethany-fenwick.org*

## WHAT TO SEE AND DO

### HOLTS LANDING STATE PARK

*Bethany Beach, 302-539-9060 (season), 302-227-2800 (off-season); www.beach-net.com/Parkholts.html*

A 203-acre park located along the Indian River Bay offering fishing, crabbing, clamming, sailing, boating (launch ramp providing access to bay) and picnicking, as well as playground and ball fields.

## SPECIAL EVENT

### BOARDWALK ARTS FESTIVAL

*The Boardwalk, Garfield Parkway, Bethany Beach, 800-962-7873; www.bethanybeachartsfestival*

Juried, original handmade works. Woodcarving. Photography. Jewelry. Batik, watercolor paintings. Early September.

## HOTEL

### ★HOLIDAY INN EXPRESS BETHANY BEACH

*39642 Jefferson Bridge Road, Bethany Beach, 302-541-9200, 888-465-4329; www.holidayinn.com*

100 rooms. $

## RESTAURANT

### ★MANGO'S

*97 Garfield Parkway, Bethany Beach, 302-537-6621; www.mangomikes.com*

Caribbean menu. Lunch, dinner. Closed December-February, except December 31; also Monday-Thursday, late March-May and late September-November. Bar. Children's menu. Casual attire. Outdoor seating. $$

# DOVER

Dover, Delaware's capital since 1777, was designed around the city's lovely green by William Penn. Fine 18th- and 19th-century houses still line State Street.

Because of Delaware's favorable corporation laws, more than 60,000 U.S. firms pay taxes in Dover. At Dover Air Force Base, the Military Airlift Command operates one of the biggest air cargo terminals in the world. The city is also home to Delaware

★
★
★
★

State College, Wesley College and the Terry campus of Delaware Technical and Community College.

*Information: Central Delaware Chamber of Commerce, 435 North DuPont Highway, Dover, 302-978-0892; www.cdcc.net*

## WHAT TO SEE AND DO

### AIR MOBILITY COMMAND MUSEUM

*1301 Heritage Road, Dover, 302-677-5938; www.amcmuseum.org*

Located in a historic hangar on Dover Air Force Base, the museum houses a collection of more than two dozen aircraft and historical artifacts dating back to World War II. Tuesday-Saturday 9 a.m.-4 p.m.

### DELAWARE AGRICULTURAL MUSEUM AND VILLAGE

*8866 N. DuPont Highway (Route 13), Dover, 302-734-1618; www.agriculturalmuseum.org*

Museum of farm life from early settlement to 1960. Main exhibition hall and historic structures representing a late-19th-century farming community; includes gristmill, blacksmith-wheelwright shop, farmhouse, outbuildings, one-room schoolhouse, store and train station. Gift shop. Tuesday-Saturday 10 a.m.-4 p.m., Sunday 1-4 p.m.; closed Sunday in winter.

### DELAWARE ARCHEOLOGY MUSEUM

*316 S. Governors Ave., Dover, 302-739-4266; www.delawarearchaeology.org*

Housed in an circa-1790 church, exhibits here are devoted to archaeology. Monday-Saturday 9 a.m.-4:30 p.m., Sunday 1:30-4:30 p.m.

### DELAWARE PUBLIC ARCHIVES

*121 Duke of York St., Dover, 302-744-5000; www.archives.delaware.gov*

Delaware's historical public records. Monday-Tuesday, Friday-Saturday 8 a.m.-4:30 p.m., Wednesday-Thursday 8 a.m.-8 p.m.; closed Sunday.

### DELAWARE STATE VISITOR CENTER

*The Green, 406 Federal St., Dover, 302-739-4266; www.destatemuseums.org/museums/vc/visitors.shtml*

Administered by the Delaware State Museums, the center offers information on attractions throughout the state. Exhibit galleries. Monday-Saturday 9 a.m.-4:30 p.m., Sunday 1:30-4:30 p.m.

### DOVER HERITAGE PARK

*152 S. State St., Dover, 302-739-9194; www.destateparks.com/heritagepark/index.asp*

Guided walking tour of historic areas, buildings and other attractions. Monday-Saturday 9 a.m.-3 p.m., Sunday 1:30-3 p.m.

### JOHN DICKINSON PLANTATION

*340 Kitts Hummrock Road, Dover, 302-739-3277; www.history.delaware.gov/museums/jdp/jdp_main.shtml*

Restored 1740 boyhood residence of Dickinson, the "penman of the Revolution." Reconstructed farm complex. Tuesday-Saturday 10 a.m.-3:30 p.m., Sunday 1:30-4:30 p.m.; closed Sundays in January and February.

### JOHNSON VICTROLA MUSEUM

*Museum Square, 375 S. New St., Dover, 302-739-4266;*
*www.dovermuseums.org/museums/victrola.htm*

Tribute to Eldridge Reeves Johnson, founder of the Victor Talking Machine Company. Collection of talking machines, Victrolas, early recordings and equipment. Monday-Saturday 9 a.m.-4:30 p.m., Sunday 1:30-4:30 p.m.

### MUSEUM OF SMALL TOWN LIFE

*316 S. Governors Ave., Dover, 302-739-4266;*
*www.dovermuseums.org/museums/smalltown.htm*

Turn-of-the-century drugstore. Printing press. Pharmacy. Carpenter shop, general store, post office, shoemaker's shop and printer's shop. Johnson building. Tuesday-Saturday 9 a.m.-4:30 p.m., Sunday 1:30-4:30 p.m.

### THE OLD STATE HOUSE

*The Green, 406 Federal St., Dover, 302-739-4266; www.history.delaware.gov*

Delaware's seat of government since 1787, the State House, restored in 1976, contains a courtroom, ceremonial governor's office, legislative chambers and county offices. A portrait of George Washington in the Senate Chamber was commissioned in 1802 by the legislature as a memorial to the nation's first president. Although Delaware's General Assembly moved to nearby Legislative Hall in 1933, the 1792 State House remains the state's symbolic capital. Tuesday-Saturday 9 a.m.-4:30 p.m., Sunday 1:30-4:30 p.m.

## SPECIAL EVENTS

### DOVER DOWNS HOTEL, CASINO, & INTERNATIONAL SPEEDWAY

*1131 N. DuPont Highway, Dover, 302-674-4600, 800-711-5882;*
*www.doverdowns.com*

Racing events include NASCAR Winston Cup auto racing (June, September); harness racing (mid-November-April). Call for fees and schedule.

### OLD DOVER DAYS

*Dover, 800-233-5368; www.visitdover.com*

Tours of historic houses and gardens are not usually open to the public. Craft exhibits, other activities. Contact Kent County Tourism. First weekend in May.

## HOTELS

### ★COMFORT INN

*222 S. DuPont Highway, Dover, 302-674-3300, 877-424-6423; www.choicehotels.com*

94 rooms. Complimentary continental breakfast. Exercise room. Free continental breakfast. Free wireless Internet access. Pets accepted. $

### ★★★SHERATON DOVER HOTEL

*1570 N. DuPont Highway, Dover, 302-678-8500, 888-625-5144;*
*www.sheratondover.com*

This hotel is conveniently located just a few minutes from shopping and local attractions in historic Dover. 152 rooms. High-speed Internet access. Fitness facility. Heated indoor pool and Jacuzzi. Free shuttle service. Business center. $$

# FENWICK ISLAND

Fenwick Island, at the southeast corner of Delaware, was named after Thomas Fenwick, a wealthy Virginia landowner who purchased the land in 1686. Once known for its "salt making"—after residents James and Jacob Brasure began extracting salt from the ocean in 1775—the island has become a popular summer resort.

*Information: Bethany-Fenwick Area Chamber of Commerce, 36913 Coastal Highway, Fenwick Island, 302-539-2100, 800-962-7873; www.bethany-fenwick.org*

## WHAT TO SEE AND DO

### DISCOVERSEA SHIPWRECK MUSEUM

*708 Ocean Highway, Fenwick Island, 302-539-9366, 888-743-5524; www.discoversea.com*

Contains changing exhibits of shipwreck artifacts recovered on the Delmarva Peninsula. June-August, daily 11 a.m.-8 p.m.; September-May, Saturday-Sunday 11 a.m.-3:30 p.m.

### FENWICK ISLAND LIGHTHOUSE

*146th Street and Lighthouse Lane, Fenwick Island, 302-539-4115*

Built in 1858, this popular attraction is 89 feet tall and houses a mini-museum in its base. A gift shop is nearby. Open most summer days, weather permitting.

### FENWICK ISLAND STATE PARK

*Fenwick Island, 302-539-9060; www.destateparks.com/fenwick/fisp.asp*

This 208-acre seashore park is located between the Atlantic Ocean and Little Assawoman Bay. Surfing, bathhouse, surf fishing and sailing (rentals). Standard hours, fees.

## SPECIAL EVENT

### DELAWARE SEASHORE FALL SURF FISHING CLASSIC

*Highway 1 N., Fenwick Island, 302-539-6243; www.brtackles.com/tournaments/fallclassic.html*

Fishing areas for this competition are located within Delaware Seashore State Park and Fenwick Island State Park. Late September.

## HOTEL

### ★ATLANTIC COAST INN

*37558 Lighthouse Road, Fenwick Island, 302-539-7673, 800-432-8038; www.atlanticcoastinn.com*

48 rooms. Closed October-mid-April. $

# FORT DELAWARE STATE PARK

This grim, gray fort was built as a coastal defense in 1860. The fort was used as a prisoner-of-war depot for three years, housing up to 12,500 Confederate prisoners at a time. Its damp, low-lying terrain and poor conditions encouraged epidemics that led to some 2,400 deaths. The fort was modernized in 1896 and remained in commission until 1943. The site's restoration continues. Available are overlooks of heronry, picnicking

DELAWARE

★
★
★
★
★

and living-history programs. The museum has a scale model of the fort, model Civil War relics and an orientation video. There are special events throughout the summer and a boat trip to the island from Delaware City (mid-June-Labor Day, Wednesday-Sunday; last weekend April-mid-June and September, Saturday, Sunday and holidays).

*Information: Park Superintendent, 45 Clinton St., Delaware City, 302-834-7941; www.destateparks.com/fdsp/index.asp*

# LEWES

Lewes has been home base to Delaware Bay pilots for 300 years. Weather-beaten, cypress-shingled houses still line the streets where pirates plundered and Captain Kidd bargained away his loot. The treacherous sandbars outside the harbor have claimed their share of ships, and stories of sunken treasures have circulated for centuries. Some buildings show scars from cannonballs that hit their mark when the British bombarded Lewes in the War of 1812. Traces of the original stockade were discovered in 1964.

*Information: Chamber of Commerce, Fisher-Martin House, 120 Kings Highway, Lewes, 302-645-8073; www.leweschamber.com*

## WHAT TO SEE AND DO

### BURTON-INGRAM HOUSE

*Second St., Lewes, 302-564-7670; www.historiclewes.org/museums/bih.html*

Circa-1800 log homes made from hand-hewn timbers with cypress shingles. It is home to beautiful antiques.

### CANNONBALL HOUSE & MARINE MUSEUM

*118 Front St., Lewes, 302-645-7670; www.beach-net.com/lewestour/ltour8.html*

Built in late 18th century. Originally called the David Rowland Home, it was hit by a cannonball during the War of 1812 and renamed.

### CAPE HENLOPEN STATE PARK

*42 Cape Henlopen Drive, Lewes, 302-645-8983; www.destateparks.com/chsp/chsp.htm*

More than 3,000 acres at the confluence of Delaware Bay and the Atlantic Ocean; site of decommissioned Fort Miles, part of the U.S. coastal defense system during World War II. Supervised swimming, fishing. Nature center, programs, trails, picnicking. Concession. Camping. Skiing: Standard hours, fees.

### EARLY PLANK HOUSE

*110 Shipcarpenter St., Lewes, 302-564-7670; www.historiclewes.org/museums/eph.html*

Swedish log cabin restored to reflect the home of an early settler.

### HIRAM R. BURTON HOUSE

*Second and Shipcarpenter streets, Lewes, 302-564-7670; www.historiclewes.org/museums/hrbh.html*

Circa-1740 house that features antique furnishings and an 18th-century kitchen. Also includes a reading room with materials dedicated to Delaware history.

★
★
★
★
★

## ATLANTIC BEACHES

Graced with a beautiful 25-mile stretch of Atlantic beach, Delaware has done more than many eastern states to save much of the land from excessive development. From north to south, three state parks maintain the coast's natural look and several small resort towns retain an old-fashioned, early 20th-century flavor.

This one-day drive is rewarding at any time of the year. Begin in Lewes, originally a Dutch whaling colony founded in 1631. Stroll along tree-shaded Second Street, the main street, to browse the town's shops and view its rich architectural heritage, then drive east about a mile on Savannah Road, following the signs to 3,785-acre Cape Henlopen State Park. The park juts between the bay and the ocean, offering hiking and bicycling trails in pine forests, salt marshes and grass-topped dunes. Just inside the park, the Seaside Nature Center features a small aquarium displaying examples of local sea life, including the region's famed blue crabs. In mid-May, the park is a resting stop for shorebirds migrating north from South America to their summer breeding grounds in the Arctic.

From Lewes, take Highway 9 West briefly to State Route 1 South, which runs parallel to the coast for the length of this drive, to Rehoboth Beach. One of mid-Atlantic's most popular beach resorts, Rehoboth hasn't lost its small-town appeal. At sunset, many people stroll along the boardwalk that links one end of the community to the other. In recent years, Rehoboth has grown into a sophisticated destination, with numerous bed and breakfasts, upscale restaurants and quality shops that sell designer beach attire, expensive antiques and contemporary home furnishings. But the town remains true to its roots: Vendors sell burgers and hot dogs on the boardwalk and children enjoy a small amusement arcade called Funland.

South of Rehoboth on Route 1 is Dewey Beach, a much smaller resort town with a cluster of lively pubs that attract a crowd of young singles. To the south is 2,656-acre Delaware Seashore State Park, another natural preserve offering swimming, surfing, fishing, picnicking, hiking and boating on Indian River Bay. Farther south is the little resort town of Bethany Beach, favored by families renting vacation homes or condominiums, and beyond that is 442-acre Fenwick Island State Park, another natural area. End the tour just across the state line in sprawling Ocean City, Maryland, a bustling beach town that stands in sharp contrast to Delaware's quieter beach experience. *Approximately 25 miles.*

DELAWARE

★
★
★
★

---

**LEWES-CAPE MAY, NJ, FERRY**

*43 Henlopen Drive, Lewes, 302-644-6030, 800-643-3779;*
*www.capemaylewesferry.com*

Sole connection between Highway 13 (Ocean Highway) on the Delmarva Peninsula and southern terminus of the Garden State Parkway (NJ). Trip across the Delaware Bay (16 miles) is 70 minutes. Daily; 22 crossings in summer, 10 in winter, 14-18 in spring and fall.

# DUTCH HERITAGE IN LEWES

As an Atlantic beach destination, historic Lewes is an offbeat choice. Lewes is Delaware's oldest community, which began as a Dutch attempt at establishing a whaling station in 1631. The neighborhood adjacent to the pleasure-boat harbor on the Lewes & Rehoboth Canal is dotted with beautifully restored 18th- and 19th-century cottages and mansions that once housed ship pilots working Delaware Bay.

For a one-mile stroll through the Historic District, begin at the Zwaanendael Museum. Built in 1931, it was adapted from the 17th-century town hall of Hoorn in the Netherlands, where Lewes's first colonists came from. The museum details the town's history and explains that all 28 (some sources say 32) original colonists were killed in a dispute with the local Native Americans. Behind the museum, the gambrel-roofed Fisher-Martin House (1730) houses the Visitor Information Center.

From the museum, head up Second Street in the shade of a canopy of giant, old trees. At 218 Second Street, Lewes's oldest home, the little red- and yellow-shingled Ryves Holt House, is believed to have been built around 1665. Once a colonial inn, it also housed the Officer of the Port. A few steps to the right at 118 Front Street, which parallels the canal, a cannonball fired by a British vessel in the War of 1812 still juts from the brick foundation of the Cannonball House Marine Museum. Inside are nautical exhibits. Many of the town's Victorian homes are richly adorned with gingerbread trim, and several are brightly painted. Just off Secondnd Street, the Ann Eliza Baker House is a dazzler in yellow, gold, purple and orange. Head north up Third Street to Shipcarpenter Street, where the Lewes Historical Society maintains an outdoor museum of early Delaware architecture. Several are scooter houses—homes relocated following local custom. Conclude this tour just up Shipcarpenter to the west at Shipcarpenter Square, an attractive development of restored 18th- and 19th-century scooter homes, all private residences, set around a nicely landscaped mall.

**DELAWARE**

★
★
★
★
★

### LEWES HISTORICAL SOCIETY COMPLEX

*110 Shipcarpenter St., Lewes, 302-564-7670; www.historiclewes.org*

The restored buildings were moved here to create a feel for Lewes' early days. June-Labor Day, Tuesday-Saturday. Tickets at Rabbit's Ferry House. Walking tours and events take place during the summer season. Buildings include: Old Doctor's Office, Rabbit's Ferry House, Thompson Country Store and Zwaanendael Museum.

### OLD DOCTOR'S OFFICE

*Third St., Lewes, 302-564-7670; www.historiclewes.org/museums/odo.html*

Circa-1836 medical and dental museum.

### RABBIT'S FERRY HOUSE

*Third St., Lewes, 302-564-7670; www.historiclewes.org/museums/rfh.html*

Circa-1789 farmhouse with original paneling and period pieces.

### THOMPSON COUNTRY STORE

*Third St., Lewes, 302-564-7670; www.historiclewes.org/about/history.html*

Moved from original location in Thompsonville. The Thompson family ran it as a store until 1962.

### ZWAANENDAEL MUSEUM

*102 Kings Highway, Lewes, 302-645-1148;*
*www.history.delaware.gov/museums/zm/zm_main.shtml*

This adaptation of the Hoorn town hall, Holland, was built in 1931 as a memorial to the original 1631 Dutch founders of Lewes. It highlights the town's maritime heritage with colonial, Native American and Dutch exhibits. Tuesday-Saturday 10 a.m.-4:30 p.m., Sunday 1:30-4:30 p.m.; closed Monday.

## SPECIAL EVENTS

### COAST DAY

*University of Delaware Marine Studies Complex, 700 Pilottown Road,*
*Lewes, 302-831-8083; www.ocean.udel.edu/coastday*

Facilities and research vessel open to the public; marine exhibits, research demonstrations, nautical films. First Sunday in October.

### GREAT DELAWARE KITE FESTIVAL

*Cape Henlopen State Park, 42 Henlopen Drive, Lewes,*
*302-645-8983; www.destateparks.com/chsp/chsp.htm*

Festival heralds the beginning of spring on the Friday before Easter.

### LEWES GARDEN TOUR

*Zwaanendael Park, 120 Kings Highway, Lewes,*
*302-645-8073; www.leweschamber.com*

Visit the hidden gardens of Lewes. Vendors. Third Saturday in June.

## HOTELS

### ★★★HOTEL RODNEY

*142 Second St., Lewes, 302-645-6466, 800-824-8754;*
*www.hotelrodneydelaware.com*

Built in 1926, this stylish boutique hotel is located in historic downtown Lewes, minutes from the beach as well as shopping and dining. 18 rooms, five suites. **$$**

### ★★★INN AT CANAL SQUARE

*122 Market St., Lewes, 302-644-3377, 888-644-1911;*
*www.theinnatcanalsquare.com*

Adjacent to the beautiful historic district, this charming "Nantucket-style" bed and breakfast offers private waterfront porches. 24 rooms. Complimentary continental breakfast. Fitness center. High-speed Internet access. **$$**

**DELAWARE**

★
★
★
★

## RESTAURANTS

### ★★★THE BUTTERY

*102 Second St., Lewes, 302-645-7755; www.butteryrestaurant.com*

This charming restaurant located in the restored Trader Mansion offers a variety of entrées, from Maryland crab cakes to Asian pad thai. Try the English bangers at Sunday brunch. French menu. Lunch, dinner, brunch. **$$$**

### ★LIGHTHOUSE

*Savannah and Anglers roads, Lewes, 302-645-6271; www.lighthouselewes.com*

Seafood menu. Breakfast, lunch, dinner. Bar. Children's menu. Outdoor seating. **$$**

# MONTCHANIN

## HOTEL

### ★★★INN AT MONTCHANIN VILLAGE

*Route 100 and Kirk Road, Montchanin, 302-888-2133, 800-269-2473;*
*www.montchanin.com*

Once part of the Winterthur Estate and listed on the National Register of Historic Places, this inn's white picket fence, winding walkways and country sensibilities create a relaxing retreat. Guests can stay in one of several carefully restored houses provided with four-poster beds and modern marble bathrooms. Nearby pastimes include antique stores, scenic country drives and the Longwood Gardens. 28 rooms. **$$**

## RESTAURANT

### ★★★KRAZY KAT'S

*Route 100 and Kirk Road, Montchanin, 302-888-2133, 800-269-2473;*
*www.montchanin.com*

Krazy Kat's is set in a 19th-century blacksmith's shop neighboring the charming and historic Inn at Montchanin Village. Seats covered in plush zebra and leopard prints and the animal portraits adorning the walls set the stage for a menu of signatures like grilled wild boar tenderloin satay with ginger jus, sesame-roasted fingerling potatoes and red cabbage daikon slaw. The wine list is extensive and international. French menu. Breakfast, lunch, dinner. Business casual attire. Reservations recommended. Outdoor seating. **$$$**

# NEW CASTLE

One of Delaware's first settlements, New Castle once served as a meeting place for the Colonial assemblies, as the first capital of the state, and as an early center of culture and communication. Its harbor made it a busy port in the 18th century until Wilmington, a closer neighbor to Philadelphia, took over its commerce. Today, New Castle attracts historians and architects alike. It lies at the foot of the Delaware Memorial Bridge, which connects with the southern end of the New Jersey Turnpike.

*Information: Mayor and Council of New Castle, 220 Delaware St., New Castle,*
*302-322-9801; www.newcastlecity.net*

## WHAT TO SEE AND DO
### AMSTEL HOUSE MUSEUM
*2 E. Fourth St., New Castle, 302-322-2794; www.newcastlehistory.org*
A 1730 restored brick mansion of the seventh governor of Delaware; an earlier structure was incorporated into the service wing. Houses colonial furnishings, arts and a complete colonial kitchen. Tuesday-Saturday 11 a.m.-4 p.m., Sunday 1-4 p.m.

### GEORGE READ II HOUSE
*42 The Strand, New Castle, 302-322-8411; www.hsd.org/read.htm*
A Federal-style house with elegant interior details: gilded fanlights, silver door-hardware, carved woodwork and relief plasterwork. It's furnished with period antiques and the garden design dates back to 1847. March-December, Tuesday-Saturday 10 a.m.-4 p.m., Sunday noon-4 p.m.; January-February, Saturday 10 a.m.-4 p.m., Sunday noon-4 p.m.; weekdays by appointment.

### THE GREEN
*Delaware and Third streets, New Castle*
Laid out under the direction of Peter Stuyvesant, this public square is surrounded by dozens of historically important buildings.

### OLD DUTCH HOUSE
*32 E. Third St., New Castle, 302-322-2794; www.newcastlehistory.org*
Thought to be Delaware's oldest dwelling in its original late 17th-century form. Dutch colonial furnishings. Decorative arts. March-December, Tuesday-Saturday 11 a.m.-4 p.m., Sunday 1-4 p.m.; rest of the year by appointment.

### OLD LIBRARY MUSEUM
*40 E. Third St., New Castle, 302-322-2794; www.newcastlehistory.org*
Unusual semioctagonal Victorian building from 1892 houses temporary exhibits relating to the area. March-December, Saturday-Sunday 1-4 p.m.

### OLD NEW CASTLE COURT HOUSE MUSEUM
*211 Delaware St., New Castle, 302-323-4453;*
*www.history.delaware.gov/museums/ncch/ncch_main.shtml*
Original 1732 colonial capital and oldest surviving courthouse in the state. Furnishings and exhibits on display. Cupola is the center of a 12-mile circle that delineates the Delaware-Pennsylvania border. Tuesday-Saturday 10 a.m.-3:30 p.m., Sunday 1:30-4:30 p.m.; closed Monday.

## SPECIAL EVENTS
### BAND CONCERTS
*Battery Park, Third and Delaware streets, New Castle, 302-328-4188*
Wednesday evenings, June-early August.

### SEPARATION DAY
*220 Delaware St., New Castle, 302-322-9802*
Observance of Delaware's declaration of independence from Great Britain. Regatta, shows, bands, concerts, fireworks. June.

**DELAWARE**

★
★
★
★
★

## HOTEL

### ★BRIDGEVIEW INN - NEW CASTLE

*1612 N. DuPont Highway, New Castle, 302-658-8511; www.choicehotels.com*

120 rooms. Complimentary continental breakfast. **$**

## RESTAURANT

### ★★THE ARSENAL AT OLD NEW CASTLE

*30 Market St., New Castle, 302-323-1812; www.arsenal1812.com*

American menu. Lunch, dinner. Closed Monday. **$$$**

# NEWARK

Newark was established at the crossroads of two well-traveled Native American trails. Nearby, Cooch's bridge was the site of the only Revolutionary War battle on Delaware soil. And according to tradition, Betsy Ross's flag was first raised in battle at the bridge on September 3, 1777.

*Information: Greater Wilmington Convention & Visitors Bureau, 100 W. 10th St., Wilmington, 302-737-4059; www.wilmcvb.org, www.cityofnewarkde.us*

## WHAT TO SEE AND DO

### UNIVERSITY OF DELAWARE

*196 S. College Ave., Newark, 302-831-2792; www.udel.edu*

Student population of 18,000. Founded as a small private academy in 1743 the central campus sits amidst stately elm trees, fine lawns and Georgian-style brick buildings. Tours from Visitors center (Monday-Saturday).

### UNIVERSITY OF DELAWARE MINERAL COLLECTION

*Mineralogical Museum in Penny Hall, Academy Street, Newark, 302-831-8242; www.udel.edu*

Includes fossil exhibit. Tuesday-Thursday noon-4 p.m.

### WHITE CLAY CREEK STATE PARK

*425 Wedgewood Road, Newark, 302-368-6900; www.destateparks.com/wccsp*

A 1,483-acre day park with farmlands, forest and streams. Fishing. Nature and fitness trails, picnicking.

## HOTELS

### ★★DELAWARE INN & CONFERENCE CENTER

*240 Chapman Road, Newark, 302-738-3400, 800-633-3203; www.ramada.com*

99 rooms. Complimentary continental breakfast. Restaurant, bar. **$**

### ★★★HILTON WILMINGTON/CHRISTIANA

*100 Continental Drive, Newark, 302-454-1500, 800-445-8667; www.hilton.com*

This family- and business-friendly hotel is situated on a sprawling country estate. For an afternoon respite, take advantage of the hotel's high tea. Enjoy a meal in one of two restaurants—one casual and one more upscale—or explore shopping and dining in the surrounding area. 266 rooms. High-speed Internet access. Concierge. Fitness center. Restaurant. Business center. Pool. **$$**

## RESTAURANT

### ★KLONDIKE KATE'S

*158 E. Main St., Newark, 302-737-6100; www.klondikekates.com*

American, Southwestern menus. Lunch, dinner. Bar. Children's menu. Outdoor seating. $$

# REHOBOTH BEACH

The "nation's summer capital" got its nickname because it was a favorite of Washington diplomats and legislators. A 2½-hour drive from Washington, D.C., the largest summer resort in Delaware began as a spot for camp meetings amid sweet-smelling pine groves. In the 1920s real estate boomed, triggering Rehoboth Beach's rebirth as a resort town with a variety of accommodations, shopping areas and eateries. The town's deep sea and freshwater fishing, sailing, swimming, biking and strolling along cherry tree-lined Rehoboth Avenue make it a preferred retreat from Washington's summer heat.

*Information: Rehoboth Beach-Dewey Beach Chamber of Commerce,*

*501 Rehoboth Ave., Rehoboth Beach, 302-227-2233, 800-441-1329;*

*www.beach-fun.com*

## WHAT TO SEE AND DO

### DELAWARE SEASHORE STATE PARK

*850 Inlet Road, Rehoboth Beach, 302-227-2800;*

*www.destateparks.com/dssp/dssp.asp*

This 7-mile strip of land separates the Rehoboth and Indian River bays from the Atlantic. Bay and ocean swimming, fishing, surfing, boating (marina, launch, rentals). Picnicking. Concession. Primitive and improved campsites.

### JUNGLE JIM'S

*8 Country Club Road, Rehoboth Beach, 302-227-8444; www.funatjunglejims.com*

Fifteen acres of family fun, including go-karts, batting cages, two miniature golf courses, bumper boats, rock climbing and a water park. Mid-June-Labor Day, daily; late May, early June, late September, limited hours.

### MIDWAY SPEEDWAY

*Midway Shopping Center, Highway 1 N., Rehoboth Beach, 302-644-2042;*

*www.midwayspeedwaypark.com*

This recreational racing park features four tracks, including a Super 8 Track and Family Track, eight different styles of go-karts, a kiddie raceway and bumper boats. Daily.

## SPECIAL EVENTS

### BANDSTAND CONCERTS

*501 Rehoboth Ave., Rehoboth Beach, 302-227-6181; www.rehobothbandstand.com*

Open-air concerts. Memorial Day-Labor Day, Saturday and Sunday evenings.

### SEA WITCH HALLOWEEN AND FIDDLERS' FESTIVAL

*501 Rehoboth Ave., Rehoboth Beach, 302-227-2233, 800-441-1329;*

*www.beach-net.com/events/seawitch.html*

This annual festival features contests, a parade, music and food. Late October.

**DELAWARE**

## HOTELS

### ★★★BOARDWALK PLAZA HOTEL

*Olive Avenue and the Boardwalk, Rehoboth Beach, 302-227-7169, 800-332-3224;*
*www.boardwalkplaza.com*

This Victorian-style hotel on Rehoboth Beach offers state-of-the-art comfort with high-speed Internet access and whirlpool tubs. Enjoy the scenic ocean views at Victoria's restaurant. 84 rooms. High-speed Internet access. Pool. Bar. **$$$**

### ★BRIGHTON SUITES HOTEL

*34 Wilmington Ave., Rehoboth Beach, 302-227-5780, 800-227-5788;*
*www.brightonsuites.com*

66 rooms, all suites. **$**

### ★COMFORT INN

*19210 Coastal Highway, Rehoboth Beach, 302-226-1515, 877-424-6423;*
*www.comfortinn.com*

96 rooms. Complimentary continental breakfast. Business center. Exercise room. Free wireless Internet access. **$**

## SPECIALTY LODGING

### THE BELLMOOR INN

*6 Christian St., Rehoboth Beach, 302-227-5800, 800-425-2355;*
*www.thebellmoor.com*

The Bellmoor Inn is an elegant seaside retreat with Brazilian cherry floors, libraries, game rooms, gardens and a full-service day spa. 78 rooms. Complimentary full breakfast. **$$$**

★
★
★
☆
☆

## RESTAURANTS

### ★★BLUE MOON

*35 Baltimore Ave., Rehoboth Beach, 302-227-6515; www.bluemoonrehoboth.com*

American menu. Dinner, Sunday brunch. Closed January. Bar. **$$$**

### ★★★CHEZ LA MER

*210 Second St., Rehoboth Beach, 302-227-6494; www.chezlamer.com*

With an enticing gourmet menu featuring entrées such as crab imperial and country-style homemade pâté, Chez La Mer is a continual winner of the Award of Excellence from *Wine Spectator* magazine. French menu. Dinner. Closed November-March. Bar. Outdoor seating. Sun porch. **$$$**

### ★IGUANA GRILL

*52 Baltimore Ave., Rehoboth Beach, 302-227-0948; www.iguanagrill.com*

American, Southwestern menu. Lunch, dinner. Closed November-first weekend of March. Bar. Casual attire. Outdoor seating. **$**

### ★★LA LA LAND

*22 Wilmington Ave., Rehoboth Beach, 302-227-3887; www.lalalandrestaurant.com*

American menu. Dinner. Closed December 31-Easter; also Monday-Wednesday from Easter-Memorial Day and October-December 31. Bar. Casual attire. Reservations recommended. Outdoor seating. **$$**

### ★★SYDNEY'S BLUES AND JAZZ RESTAURANT

*25 Christian St., Rehoboth Beach, 302-227-1339, 800-808-1924;*
*www.rehoboth.com/sydneys*

Creole menu. Dinner. Bar. Reservations recommended. Outdoor seating. **$$**

# SMYRNA

In the 1850s, Smyrna—named for the chief seaport of Turkish Asia Minor—was an active shipping center for the produces grown in central Delaware. Today, migratory birds, more than the produce, pass through this small port town.

*Information: Smyrna Visitors Center, 5500 DuPont Highway, Smyrna, 302-653-8910;*
*www.smyrnadelaware.com*

## WHAT TO SEE AND DO

### BOMBAY HOOK NATIONAL WILDLIFE REFUGE

*2591 Whitehall Neck Road, Smyrna, 302-653-6872; www.bombayhook.fws.gov*

This annual fall and spring resting and feeding spot for migratory waterfowl, including a variety of ducks and tens of thousands of snow geese and Canada geese, is also home to bald eagles, shorebirds, deer, fox and muskrat. It includes an auto tour route (12 miles), wildlife foot trails, observation towers and visitor centers offering interpretive and environmental education programs. Visitor center (spring and fall, daily; summer and winter, Monday-Friday). Golden Eagle, Golden Age and Golden Access passports accepted. Daily.

### SMYRNA MUSEUM

*11 S. Main St., Smyrna, 302-653-1320; www.smyrnahistory.org*

Furnishings and memorabilia from early Federal to late Victorian periods; changing exhibits. Tuesday, Thursday and Saturday 10 a.m.-1 p.m., Saturday 1-4 p.m.

## RESTAURANT

### ★WAYSIDE INN

*103 N. DuPont Highway, Smyrna, 302-653-8047; www.thewaysideinn.org*

Seafood, steak menu. Lunch, dinner. Children's menu. **$$**

# WILMINGTON

Wilmington, the "chemical capital of the world" and an international hub of industry and shipping, is the largest city in Delaware. The Swedish, Dutch and British have left their marks on the city. The Swedes settled first, seeking their fortunes and founding the colony of New Sweden. In 1655, Dutch soldiers under Peter Stuyvesant, governor of New Amsterdam, captured the little colony without bloodshed. Nine years later the English arrived, and the town grew into a market and shipping center aided by wealthy Quakers. Wilmington has flourished as an industrial port because of its abundant water power and proximity to other eastern ports. From here come vulcanized fiber, glazed leathers, dyed cotton, rubber hose, autos and many other products.

*Information: Greater Wilmington Convention & Visitors Bureau, 100 W. 10th St.,*
*Wilmington, 302-652-4088, 800-489-6664; www.wilmcvb.org*

**DELAWARE**

★
★
★
★
★

## WHAT TO SEE AND DO

### AMTRAK STATION

*Martin Luther King Boulevard and French Street, Wilmington, 302-429-6530;*
*www.amtrak.com*

Restored Victorian railroad station, still in use, designed by master architect Frank
Furness. Daily.

### BANNING PARK

*22 S. Heald St., Wilmington, 302-323-6422*

Fishing. Tennis. Playing fields. Picnicking. Pavilions. Daily.

### BELLEVUE STATE PARK

*800 Carr Road, Wilmington, 302-761-6963; www.destateparks.com/bvsp/bvsp.htm*

Fishing. Nature, fitness and horseback-riding trails. Bicycling, tennis, game courts.
Picnicking (pavilions).

### BRANDYWINE CREEK STATE PARK

*Routes 92 and 100, Wilmington, 302-577-3534;*
*www.destateparks.com/bcsp/bcsp.asp*

A 1,000-acre day-use park. Fishing. Nature and fitness trails. Cross-country skiing.
Picnicking. Nature center.

### BRANDYWINE SPRINGS PARK

*800 N. French St., Wilmington, 302-395-5652; www.nccde.org*

Site of a once-famous resort hotel for Southern planters and politicos from 1827 to
1845. Here, Lafayette met Washington under the Council Oak before the Battle of
Brandywine in 1777. Picnicking. Fireplaces. Pavilions, baseball fields. On-leash pets
only. Daily.

### BRANDYWINE ZOO AND PARK

*1001 N. Park Drive, Wilmington, 302-571-7788; www.destateparks.com/wilmsp/zoo*

Designed by Frederick Law Olmsted, the park includes the Josephine Garden with a
fountain and roses; stands of Japanese cherry trees. The zoo, along North Park Drive,
features animals from North and South America. Picnicking. Playgrounds. Daily
10 a.m.-4 p.m.

### DELAWARE ART MUSEUM

*2301 Kentmere Parkway, Wilmington, 302-571-9590; www.delart.org*

This museum features the Howard Pyle Collection of American Illustrations, with
works by Pyle, N. C. Wyeth and Maxfield Parrish; American painting collection,
with works by West, Homer, Church, Glackens and Hopper; Bancroft Collection
of English Pre-Raphaelite art, with works by Rossetti and Burne-Jones; and Phelps
Collection of Andrew Wyeth works; also changing exhibits, children's participatory
gallery. Store. Guided tours by appointment. Closed Monday, Tuesday-Saturday
10 a.m.-4 p.m., Sunday noon-4 p.m.

★
★
★
★
☆

## BRANDYWINE VALLEY

The Brandywine Valley, just north of Wilmington, is a serene canvas of rolling hills, broad fields of corn and yellow sunflowers, rambling split-rail fences, horse pastures, ancient stone barns and narrow country roads lined by towering old trees. Tucked into this landscape is a diverse collection of fine arts, history and house museums, most of which were bequeathed by the du Pont family, the wealthy industrialists whose forebear, Pierre Samuel du Pont, arrived from France in 1800. Pierre's son, Eleuthere Irenee (E.I.) du Pont, established a black-powder factory, harnessing Brandywine Creek for power and creating the du Pont fortune.

Nicknamed "Chateau Country," the valley contains many grand homes, typically set far back from the road. For more than 30 years, an environmental organization called the Brandywine Conservancy has worked to protect the valley's open pastoral look from threatening suburban sprawl.

Begin this one-day 50-mile tour into the scenic and artistic riches of the region in Wilmington. Your first stop is the Delaware Art Museum at 2301 Kentmere Parkway, which features a strong collection of American sculpture and painting, including works by the Brandywine resident Andrew Wyeth.

From the museum, return to Route 52 North. Turn right at Route 141 to the Hagley Museum, which is located on the site of the first du Pont powder works, amid 230 acres of gardens and exhibits. The museum recalls industrial life in mid-19th-century-America. A bit farther upstream along Brandywine Creek is the Eleutherian Mills, the lovely Georgian-style house E.I. du Pont built in 1803. Double back on Route 141 to Route 100 North (Montchanin Road) to the village of Montchanin. Here, 11 varied structures that served as homes for workers at the du Pont mills have been converted into a luxury retreat, the 37-room Inn at Montchanin Village. Stroll the block-long cobblestone main street, which is named Privy Lane for the row of gray concrete privies standing behind the dwellings in military precision. (Today the sheds store garden equipment.) Consider lunch at the inn's restaurant, Krazy Kats, one of Brandywine's best.

Continue north on Route 100 to Brandywine State Park for a chance to hike along Brandywine Creek. Stay on Route 100 North to Smith's Bridge Road, then make a left. Continue west via Centerville Road to Route 52, and turn south (left). At the sign, turn left into Winterthur, a nine-story museum of American decorative arts surrounded by 985 acres of gardens. This was the estate of Henry Francis du Pont, who collected antique furniture, porcelain, silver, rugs and draperies crafted from 1640 to 1860. These items are organized in period rooms, including a 17th-century Lancaster, Pa. bedroom and an 18th-century Tidewater, Va., plantation sitting room. The gardens reflect du Pont's goal of creating a masterpiece of 20th-century American naturalism. Return to Wilmington on Route 52 South. *Approximately 50 miles.*

**DELAWARE**

★
★
★
★

## WILMINGTON'S PUBLIC ART

While the Brandywine Valley is known for its museums and gardens, Wilmington itself is no artistic slouch. The historic heart of the old city boasts a wealth of outdoor statuary in public squares and office courtyards. Much of it is representational, but there are also abstract and whimsical pieces. For the past several years, a picture book describing the collection has been published.

A one-mile walk through the city's commercial center is like a stroll through an urban sculpture garden. Begin at Rodney Square outside the elegant Hotel du Pont at 11th and Market streets. Dominating the view is the famous 1923 statue of Caesar Rodney astride his horse, galloping toward Philadelphia to cast the deciding vote for the Declaration of Independence in 1776. A city hallmark, the Rodney statue is a rare example of an equestrian sculpture in which the horse is in full gallop, its two front legs in the air and the weight of the statue resting on the two rear hooves.

Head north on Market Street to 13th Street and two blocks west (left) to Orange Street to the Brandywine Gateway, where you'll see the kinetic fountain at the foot of the Hercules Building (facing 13th Street) in Hercules Plaza. Three solid granite balls rest on three marble pillars in the middle of a large pool. The spheres are arranged so that water flowing over them suggests that they are rotating.

Retrace your path to Eighth and Market streets and then turn east (left) to Spencer and Freedom plazas between French and Market streets. In Spencer Plaza stands "Father and Son," a larger-than-life bronze statue of a man with a child in his arms by Charles Park, a local artist. A plaque notes that this was the one-time site of the Mother African Union Methodist Protestant Church, the first black church in America, wholly controlled by descendants of Africans.

Just across French Street in Freedom Plaza, in the shadow of a cluster of modern municipal buildings, is "The Holocaust." Both abstract and realistic, it shows the victims pressed against three unyielding pillars. End your tour at the plaque honoring abolitionists Harriet Tubman and Thomas Garrett and the Underground Railroad.

### DELAWARE HISTORY MUSEUM

*504 Market St., Wilmington, 302-656-0637; www.hsd.org/dhm.htm*

Changing exhibits on history and decorative arts. Closed Sunday and Monday, Tuesday-Friday 11 a.m.-4 p.m., Saturday 10 a.m.-4 p.m.

### DELAWARE MUSEUM OF NATURAL HISTORY

*4840 Kennett Pike, Wilmington, 302-658-9111; www.delmnh.org*

Exhibits of shells, birds, mammals; also the largest bird egg and a 500-pound clam. Monday-Saturday 9:30 a.m.-4:30 p.m., Sunday noon-4:30 p.m.

## GRAND OPERA HOUSE

*818 Market St., Mall, Wilmington, 302-658-7898; www.grandopera.org*

Historic 1871 landmark built by Masons, this restored Victorian theater now serves as Delaware's Center for the Performing Arts, home of Opera Delaware (November-May) and the Delaware Symphony (September-May). Façade is a fine example of Second Empire style interpreted in cast iron.

## HAGLEY MUSEUM AND LIBRARY

*298 Buck Road, Wilmington, 302-658-2400; www.hagley.lib.de.us*

Old riverside stone mill buildings, a one-room schoolhouse and a millwright shop highlight 19th-century explosive manufacturing and community life; 240-acre historic site of E.I. du Pont's original black-powder mills includes an exhibit building, an operating waterwheel, a stationary steam engine and a fully operable 1875 machine shop. Admission includes a bus ride along the river for a tour of 1803 Eleutherian Mills, a residence with antiques reflecting five generations of du Ponts, a 19th-century garden and a barn with a collection of antique wagons. Museum store. January-mid-March, weekdays one tour 1:30 p.m., weekends 9:30 a.m.-4:30 p.m.; mid-March-January, daily 9:30 a.m.-4:30 p.m.

## HOLY TRINITY (OLD SWEDES) CHURCH AND HENDRICKSON HOUSE

*606 Church St., Wilmington, 302-652-5629; www.oldswedes.org*

Founded by Swedish settlers in 1698, the church stands as originally built and still holds regular services. The house, a Swedish farmhouse built in 1690, is now a museum containing 17th- and 18th-century artifacts. Monday-Saturday.

## NEMOURS MANSION AND GARDENS

*1600 Rockland Road, Wilmington, 302-651-6912, 800-651-6912; www.nemours.org/mansion.html*

Country estate (300 acres) of Alfred I. du Pont. Mansion (1910) is in modified Louis XVI style by Carre and Hastings, with 102 rooms of rare antique furniture, Asian rugs, tapestries and paintings dating from the 12th century. Formal French gardens with terraces, statuary and pools. Tours. May-October, Tuesday-Saturday 9 a.m., 11 a.m., 1 p.m., 3 p.m., Sunday 11 a.m., 1 p.m., 3 p.m.; November-December limited basis; reservations required. Over 12 years only.

## ROCKWOOD MUSEUM

*610 Shipley Road, Wilmington, 302-761-4340; www.rockwood.org*

A 19th-century Gothic Revival estate with gardens in English Romantic style. On grounds are manor house, conservatory, porter's lodge and other outbuildings. Museum furnished with English, European and American decorative arts of the 17th to 19th centuries. Guided tours. Tuesday-Sunday 10 a.m.-3 p.m.

## WILLINGTOWN SQUARE

*505 N. Market St., Mall, Wilmington, 302-655-7161; www.hsd.org/willsq.htm*

Historic square surrounded by four 18th-century houses moved to this location between 1973 and 1976. Serves as office and conference space.

DELAWARE

## WILMINGTON & WESTERN RAILROAD

*Greenbank Station, 2201 Newport Gap Pike, Wilmington,*
*302-998-1930; www.wwrr.com*

Round-trip steam-train ride (nine miles) to and from Mount Cuba picnic grove. May-October, Sunday; for rest of year, schedule varies.

## SPECIAL EVENTS

### HORSE RACING, DELAWARE PARK

*777 Delaware Park Blvd., Wilmington, 302-994-2521, 800-417-5687; www.delpark.com*

Thoroughbred racing. Slot facility. Restaurants. Late April-mid-November.

### VICTORIAN ICE CREAM FESTIVAL

*Rockwood Museum, 610 Shipley Road, Wilmington, 302-761-4340;*
*www.coatesville.org/events/icecream.asp*

Victorian festival featuring high-wheeled bicycles, hot-air balloons, marionettes, old-fashioned medicine show, baby parade and crafts; homemade ice cream. Mid-July.

### WILMINGTON GARDEN DAY

*Wilmington, 302-428-6172; www.gardenday.org*

Tour famous gardens and houses. First Saturday in May.

### WINTERTHUR POINT-TO-POINT RACES

*Highway 52, Wilmington, 302-888-4600, 888-448-3883;*
*www.winterthur.org/calendar/point_to_point.asp*

An old-fashioned country horse race that features five races. May.

## HOTELS

### ★BEST WESTERN BRANDYWINE VALLEY INN

*1807 Concord Pike, Wilmington, 302-656-9436, 800-537-7772;*
*www.brandywineinn.com*

95 rooms. Complimentary continental breakfast. $

### ★★CLARION COLLECTION BRANDYWINE SUITES

*707 N. King St., Wilmington, 302-656-9300, 800-756-0070;*
*www.brandywinesuites.com*

49 rooms, all suites. Complimentary continental breakfast. Airport transportation available. Free wireless Internet access. $

### ★★COURTYARD BY MARRIOTT

*1102 West St., Wilmington, 302-429-7600, 800-321-2211; www.courtyard.com*

123 rooms. Airport transportation available. Pets not accepted. $$

### ★★DOUBLETREE HOTEL WILMINGTON

*4727 Concord Pike, Wilmington, 302-478-6000, 800-222-8733;*
*www.wilmington.doubletree.com*

244 rooms. Pets not accepted. Fitness room. Pool. High-speed Internet access. Restaurant. Business center. $$

### ★★★HOTEL DU PONT

*11th and Market streets, Wilmington, 302-594-3100, 800-441-9019;*
*www.hoteldupont.com*

The Hotel du Pont has been a Delaware institution since 1913. Constructed to rival the grand hotels of Europe with ornate plasterwork and gleaming brass, this palatial hotel enjoys proximity to the city's attractions while remaining in the heart of the scenic Brandywine Valley with its championship golf and estate tours. The guest rooms are classically decorated with mahogany furnishings, cream tones and imported linens. Patrons dine on French cuisine while listening to the gentle strains of a harp at the Green Room. 217 rooms. High-speed Internet access. **$$$**

### ★★★SHERATON SUITES WILMINGTON

*422 Delaware Ave., Wilmington, 302-654-8300, 800-325-3535; www.sheraton.com*

Located in the heart of downtown Wilmington, this all-suite hotel offers spacious rooms and conference facilities just a short drive from a number of museums, within walking distance from headquarters of several Fortune-500 companies and a few miles from major shopping malls. The contemporary guest rooms are decorated in navy and taupe and feature Sweet Sleeper mattresses. 223 rooms, all suites. Wireless Internet access; charge. **$$**

## RESTAURANTS

### ★★821 MARKET STREET BISTRO

*821 N. Market St., Wilmington, 302-652-8821; www.restaurant821.com*

American menu. Lunch, dinner. Closed Sunday; also one week in early January. Bar. Business casual attire. Reservations recommended. Valet parking. **$$$**

### ★★COLUMBUS INN

*2216 Pennsylvania Ave., Wilmington, 302-571-1492; www.columbusinn.com*

American menu. Lunch, dinner, brunch. Bar. Children's menu. Business casual attire. Reservations recommended. Valet parking. Outdoor seating. **$$**

### ★★COSTAS

*1000 N. West St., Wilmington, 302-777-2268; www.costasgrillandwinebar.com*

Greek, Mediterranean menu. Lunch, dinner. Closed last week in August. Bar. Children's menu. Business casual attire. Reservations recommended. **$$$**

### ★★★THE GREEN ROOM

*11th and Market streets, Wilmington, 302-594-3155, 800-441-9019;*
*www.dupont.com/hotel/dining_green.htm*

Located inside the historic Hotel DuPont, this restaurant's sophisticated décor of carved oak paneling and a coffered ceiling is perfect for romantic or special-occasion celebrations. Live music enhances the dining experience Tuesday-Saturday evenings and during Sunday brunch. French menu. Breakfast, lunch, dinner, Sunday brunch. Bar. Children's menu. Jacket required (dinner). Valet parking. **$$$**

**DELAWARE**

★
★
★
★

### ★★★HARRY'S SAVOY GRILL

*2020 Naaman's Road, Wilmington, 302-475-3000; www.harrys-savoy.com*

A Brandywine Valley staple since 1988, Harry's Savoy Grill serves up the classics in an upscale English pub atmosphere. The bar and grill is known for its prime rib, its wine list and its "famous eight-shake martinis." American, seafood, steak menu. Lunch, dinner, late night, Sunday brunch. Bar. Children's menu. Outdoor seating. $$$

### ★KID SHELLEENS CHARCOAL HOUSE & SALOON

*1801 W. 14th St., Wilmington, 302-658-4600; www.kidshelleens.com*

American menu. Lunch, dinner, late night, Sunday brunch. Bar. Children's menu. Casual attire. Outdoor seating. $$

### ★★TOSCANA KITCHEN + BAR

*1412 N. DuPont St., Wilmington, 302-654-8001; www.toscanakitchen.com*

Northern Italian menu. Lunch, dinner. Bar. Business casual attire. Reservations recommended. Outdoor seating. $$

**DELAWARE**

★
★
★
★

# MARYLAND

IN MARYLAND, THE BALTIMORE ORIOLE IS MORE THAN JUST THE STATE BIRD, TURTLES ARE sports heroes and crabs are regular fixtures at the dinner table. The seventh state owns a celebrated sports history, producing superstars such as Babe Ruth and Cal Ripken, Jr., and building the Orioles' Camden Yards, lauded for its classic design. Several noteworthy colleges and universities call Maryland home, including Johns Hopkins University and the University of Maryland, home of the Terrapins. And Maryland's Chesapeake Bay keeps restaurants across the nation well stocked, with crabs, producing more than 50 percent of the United States' harvest of hard-shell crabs.

Maryland prides itself on its varied terrain and diverse economy. Metropolitan areas around Baltimore and Washington, D.C. contrast with life in the rural areas in central and southern Maryland and on the Eastern Shore, across the Chesapeake Bay. Green mountains in the western counties offset the east's white Atlantic beaches. The state's prosperity stems from a flourishing travel industry, central Maryland's agricultural and dairy wealth, the seafood industry, manufacturing and commerce, and federal government and defense contracts.

Named in honor of Henrietta Maria, wife of Charles I, King of England, Maryland was established in 1634 by Leonard Calvert, Lord Baltimore's brother. Calvert and 222 passengers aboard his ships purchased a Native American village and named it "Saint Maries Citty" (now St. Mary's City). The land was cleared, tobacco was planted, and over the years profits built elegant mansions, many of which still stand.

Maryland has played a pivotal role in every war waged on U.S. soil. In 1755, British General Edward Braddock, assisted by Lieutenant Colonel George Washington, trained his army at Cumberland for the fight against the French and Indians. In the War of 1812, Baltimore's Fort McHenry withstood attacks by land and sea. The action was later immortalized in the national anthem by Francis Scott Key, a Frederick lawyer. And in the Civil War, Maryland was a major battleground at Antietam.

*Information: www.mdisfun.org*

★
★
★
★
★

## ABERDEEN

Aberdeen is home to the 75,000-acre Aberdeen Proving Grounds, a federal reservation along Chesapeake Bay, where army materials, ranging from gun sights to tanks, are tested under simulated combat conditions.

*Information: Aberdeen Chamber of Commerce, 115 N. Parke St., Aberdeen, 410-272-2580; www.aberdeencc.com*

### WHAT TO SEE AND DO
#### RECREATION AREA
*Aberdeen, 410-457-5011; www.udel.edu/cecilbirds/sites/funkspond.html*
Fourteen-mile-long man-made lake; swimming pool (fee), boating (ramps, marinas), fishing; fishermen's gallery (over 12 years only); picnicking, hiking.

# DEEP CREEK LAKE, MARYLAND'S WESTERN PLAYGROUND

In western Maryland's Garrett County, Deep Creek Lake is known as the state's hidden secret. But the secret is getting out. The massive lake now hosts waterskiing, whitewater rafting, hiking, back-road bicycling, kayaking, fly-fishing, canoeing, sailing and swimming. On a drive around the lake, you can partake in as many activities as you choose—outfitters are on hand to rent all the necessary equipment—or simply enjoy the sublime mountain views.

Deep Creek, Maryland's largest freshwater lake, is 12 miles long, but so etched with fingerlike coves that the shoreline stretches for 65 miles. Surrounded by the forested ridges and splashing streams of mountain wilderness, the lake, at an altitude of 2,300 feet, treats summer visitors to a cool respite from the city. Begin this two-day, 400-mile drive in Baltimore and head west on Interstate 70 (I-70) and I-68 to exit 14 at Keysers Ridge. Take Highway 219 south to the visitor center just outside the village of McHenry. Plan to spend the night in one of McHenry's inns, hotels or motels.

The trip from Baltimore to McHenry is about 180 miles, a scenic ride that carries you across a series of green mountain ridges. To break up the trip, pull off I-68 at Cumberland. George Washington is said to have assumed his first military command at Fort Cumberland, and his one-room log cabin and remnants of the fort can still be seen here. Cumberland is the terminus of the Chesapeake and Ohio Canal, which originates in Washington, D.C. You can rent a bicycle and ride along the towpath for miles.

At Deep Creek Lake, follow the signs to Deep Creek Lake State Park, which maintains a 700-foot-long sandy swimming beach. The Discovery Center, an attractive structure of stone, wood and soaring windows, features displays about the region's natural history and mining heritage. Ranger talks, walks and canoe trips are offered.

On the second day of your trip, take Highway 219 south from McHenry to the turn-off to Swallow Falls State Park. For an easy hike, follow the 1½-mile path that scrambles in a loop past four waterfalls. At the trail head, the park has preserved a 37-acre stand of virgin hemlock and white pine estimated to be 300 years old. After ¼ mile, Muddy Creek Falls—the state's highest at 52 feet—cascades down a staircase of rocks into a large pool. Next, follow signs south to the town of Oakland and begin your scenic return to Baltimore via Route 135 northeast to Highway 220 north to I-68 east about 10 miles east of Cumberland. Take a break at Rocky Gap State Park, two minutes off the interstate, which tempts with a couple of fine sandy beaches in a forested mountain setting. Approximately 400 miles.

Obtain a day pass at the Maryland Boulevard gate. Daily 9 a.m.-4:45 p.m.

MARYLAND

★
★ ★
★ ★
★

### U.S. ARMY ORDNANCE MUSEUM

*2601 Maryland Blvd., Aberdeen, 410-278-3602;*
*www.goordnance.apg.army.mil/sitefiles/ordnancemuseum.htm*

## HOTEL

### ★★HOLIDAY INN

*1007 Beards Hill Road, Aberdeen, 410-272-8100, 800-315-2621;*
*www.holiday-inn.com/aberdeenmd*

122 rooms. Fitness center. High-speed Internet access. Pool. Wireless Internet access. **$**

# ANNAPOLIS

The capital of Maryland, Annapolis was the first peacetime capital of the United States. Congress met here from November 26, 1783 to August 13, 1784. In 1845, the U.S. Naval Academy was established here at the Army's Fort Severn. Every May at commencement time, thousands of visitors throng the narrow, brick streets.

*Information: Annapolis and Anne Arundel County Conference and Visitors Bureau,*
*26 W. St., Annapolis, 888-302-2852; www.visit-annapolis.org*

## WHAT TO SEE AND DO

### BOAT TRIPS

*980 Awald Road, No. 202, at the City Dock Annapolis, 410-268-7600;*
*www.watermarkcruises.com*

Forty-minute narrated tours of city harbor, USNA and Severn River aboard *Harbor Queen* (Memorial Day-Labor Day: daily); 90-minute cruises to locations aboard *Annapolitan* and *Rebecca,* cruises to St. Michael's aboard the *Annapolitan II* (Memorial Day-Labor Day); 40-minute cruises up Spa Creek, residential areas, city harbor and USNA aboard the *Miss Anne* and *Miss Anne II* (Memorial Day-Labor Day). Some cruises sail early spring and late fall, weather permitting. Fees vary.

### CHESAPEAKE BAY BRIDGE

*357 Pier 1 Road, Annapolis*

The 7¼-mile link of Highway 50 across the Bay. Toll (charged eastbound only).

### CHESAPEAKE SAILING SCHOOL

*7080 Bembe Beach Road, Annapolis, 410-295-0555, 800-966-0032;*
*www.sailingclasses.com*

This school offers everything from weekend sailing classes for beginners (no experience necessary) to live-aboard, five-day cruises on gorgeous Chesapeake Bay, with basic and advanced instruction for individuals, families and corporate groups. You can also rent sailboats and go out on your own. April-October.

### ELIZABETH MYERS MITCHELL ART GALLERY

*Mellon Hall, 60 College Ave., Annapolis, 410-626-2556; www.stjohnscollege.edu*

Displays museum-quality traveling exhibitions. Academic year: Tuesday-Sunday noon-5 p.m., Friday 7-8 p.m.

★
★
★
★

# EASTERN SHORE OF THE CHESAPEAKE BAY

The Chesapeake Bay, North America's largest estuary, commands more than 4,500 miles of shoreline, much of it in Maryland. It is one of the Mid-Atlantic's most popular destinations, known for its rich history and savory shellfish.

A two-day driving tour covering about 250 miles makes a fine introduction to the bay. Begin your drive in Annapolis, Maryland's beautiful old capital, which doubles as the bay's sailing headquarters. In summer, catch the regular Wednesday evening races, when as many as 100 boats may compete. The finish is easily visible from City Dock at the foot of the city's colonial-era streets.

From Annapolis, take Highway 50 east across the soaring Chesapeake Bay Bridge. Just before you reach the bridge, a five-minute detour leads to Sandy Point State Park, the only stop on this drive where you can take a dip in the bay. At the eastern end of the bridge, turn north onto Highway 301 to Route 213 north to Chestertown. Founded in 1706, Chestertown is a pretty village with a collection of 18th- and 19th-century homes, several of them situated along the scenic Chester River.

After browsing the shops of High and Cross streets, take Route 213 south to Highway 50 south. In Easton, take Route 33 west to the historic sailing port of St. Michaels, an inviting place to spend the night. St. Michaels is one of the Mid-Atlantic's prettiest little towns, with lovely inns, fine restaurants, offbeat shops, expansive bay views and charming back streets lined with homes dating to the 18th and 19th centuries. Your first stop should be the Chesapeake Bay Maritime Museum. The museum's 18-acre harbor site features more than a dozen historic structures, including a fully restored 1879 lighthouse. Stop by Waterman's Wharf, where you can try your skill at crab fishing. Boat builders are often at work restoring historic bay work boats for the museum's large collection. The *Patriot*, a cruise ship departing from the museum's dock, takes visitors on a 60-minute tour up the Miles River, a bay tributary.

From St. Michaels, follow Route 33 to its end at Tilghman Island, a charter fishing port. Plan on having lunch at one of its waterside seafood houses. On the return trip to St. Michaels, stop about three miles east of the city and take the road south (right) to Bellevue. There you can catch the little Bellevue-Oxford Ferry for a 10-minute ride across the Tred Avon River to Oxford, a sleepy pleasure-boat port dating back to 1694. To stretch your legs, walk along the Strand, a lovely river promenade, or rent a bicycle and ride along the quiet streets. From Oxford, return to Annapolis via Route 333 and Highway 50, stopping briefly in Easton to admire its attractive town center and to investigate its shops and galleries. Approximately 250 miles.

MARYLAND

★
★★
★★
★

### GOVERNMENT HOUSE
*State Circle, Annapolis, 410-260-3930;*
*www.mdarchives.state.md.us/msa/homepage/html/govhouse.html*
This 1868 Victorian structure was remodeled in 1935 into a Georgian country house; furnishings reflect Maryland's history and culture. Tours by appointment. Monday, Wednesday, Friday 10:30 a.m.-2:30 p.m.

# HISTORY AND GOVERNMENT IN ANNAPOLIS

In the years just prior to the American Revolution, the colonial elite flocked to Annapolis, Maryland's capital on the Chesapeake Bay. This was the city's golden age, and many visitors were drawn by its spirited social life and elegant mansions built by wealthy tobacco planters. You can see some of the same sights on a one-mile stroll through the city's well-preserved historic district.

Begin at the visitor center, 26 W. St., where tourist parking is available. From the center, head east (left) on West Street; detour around St. Anne's Church (1859), noting its Tiffany windows. Pause on School Street to view Government House, the Georgian-style Maryland Governor's residence (remodeled in 1936); and then climb the stairs to the Maryland State House on State Circle (1772), the oldest state capitol in continuous legislative use. Perched atop the city's highest hill, the State House provides a panoramic view of the bay. Inside, the Old Senate Chamber appears as it did on December 23, 1783, when George Washington resigned his commission as the victorious commander of the Continental Army.

Continue east from State Circle on shop-lined Maryland Avenue to the Hammond-Harwood Home (1774) at No. 19. A house museum, this Georgian structure features what is considered by many to be the "prettiest doorway in America." Double back one block on Maryland Avenue, pausing briefly at the Chase-Lloyd House (1769), another elegant Georgian mansion where Francis Scott Key, author of "The Star-Spangled Banner," was married in 1802. Turn toward the harbor (left) onto Prince George Street. The William Paca House (1765) at No. 186 and its two-acre colonial garden, carefully restored for authenticity, are national treasures. Now a house museum, the Paca house was the home of Maryland's Revolutionary War governor and a signer of the Declaration of Independence. Built in a symmetrical five-part format, it is considered one of the best examples of a Georgian home in America. Neighboring Brice House (1767) at 42 E. Street is another magnificent Georgian mansion built by a wealthy merchant. To conclude this tour, continue downhill on Prince George Street, and turn west (right) one block onto Randall Street to City Dark for refreshments at Middleton Tavern. Once an "Inn for Seafaring Men," it has been serving Annapolis visitors since 1754.

**MARYLAND**

★
★
★
★
★

### HAMMOND-HARWOOD HOUSE

*19 Maryland Ave., Annapolis, 410-263-4683; www.hammondharwoodhouse.org*

A 1774 Georgian house designed by William Buckland; antique furnishings; garden. Matthias Hammond, a Revolutionary patriot, was its first owner. Guided tours. Tuesday-Sunday, April-October.

### HISTORIC ANNAPOLIS FOUNDATION

*18 Pinkney St., Annapolis, 410-267-7619, 800-603-4020; www.annapolis.org*

Self-guided digital access audio walking tours. Includes Historic District, State House, Old Treasury, U.S. Naval Academy and William Paca House. Friday-Saturday; also November 7-8.

### HISTORIC ANNAPOLIS FOUNDATION WELCOME CENTER AND MUSEUM STORE

*77 Main St., Annapolis, 410-268-5576, 800-639-9153; www.annapolis.org*

This 1815 building stands on the site of a storehouse for Revolutionary War troops that burned in 1790. Self-guided digital access audio walking tours. Products reflecting Annapolis history. Monday-Thursday 10 a.m.-6 p.m., Friday-Saturday 10 a.m.-8 p.m., Sunday 11 a.m.-6 p.m.

### SAILING TOURS

*80 Compromise St., Annapolis, 410-263-7837; www.schooner-woodwind.com*

Two-hour narrated trips through Chesapeake Bay aboard the 74-foot sailing yacht *Woodwind*. Departs from Pusser's Landing Restaurant at the Annapolis Marriott Waterfront Hotel. May-September: Tuesday-Sunday four trips daily, Monday sunset sail only; April, October, November: schedule varies.

### SANDY POINT STATE PARK

*1100 E. College Parkway, Annapolis, 410-974-2149, 888-432-2267;*
*www.dnr.state.md.us/publiclands/southern/sandypoint.html*

The park's location on the Atlantic Flyway makes it a fine area for bird-watching; view of Bay Bridge and oceangoing vessels. Swimming in the bay at two guarded beaches, two bathhouses, surf fishing, crabbing, boating (rentals, launches); concession. Daily, hours vary; call for schedule.

### ST. JOHN'S COLLEGE

*60 College Ave., Annapolis, 410-263-2371, 800-727-9238; www.sjca.edu/main.html*

475 students. Nonsectarian liberal arts college. This 36-acre campus, one of the oldest in the country, is a National Historic Landmark. The college succeeded King William's School, founded in 1696. George Washington's two nephews and step-grandson studied here; Francis Scott Key was an alumnus.

### STATE HOUSE

*350 Rowe Blvd., State Circle, Annapolis, 410-974-3400, 800-235-4045;*
*www.msa.md.gov*

As the oldest state house in continuous legislative use in United States, this was the first peacetime capitol of the nation. Here in 1784, a few weeks after receiving George Washington's resignation as commander-in-chief, Congress ratified the Treaty of Paris, which officially ended the Revolutionary War. Visitors Information Center. Guide service. Daily.

### WATERMARK TOURS

*26 West St., Annapolis, 410-268-7601, 800-569-9622; www.annapolis-tours.com*

Walking tours of U.S. Naval Academy and Historic District conducted by guides in colonial attire. Tour includes historic Maryland State House, St. John's College, Naval Academy Chapel, crypt of John Paul Jones, Bancroft Hall dormitory and Armel-Leftwich Visitor Center. April-October, daily.

## WILLIAM PACA GARDEN

*186 Prince George St., Annapolis, 410-990-4538, 800-603-4020; www.annapolis.org*

Restored two-acre pleasure garden originally developed in 1765 by William Paca, a signer of the Declaration of Independence and governor of Maryland during the Revolutionary War. Includes waterways, formal parterres and a garden wilderness. Monday-Saturday, Sunday afternoon.

## WILLIAM PACA HOUSE

*186 Prince George St., Annapolis, 410-990-4538, 800-603-4020; www.annapolis.org*

Paca built this five-part Georgian mansion in 1765. Monday-Saturday, Sunday afternoon.

## UNITED STATES NAVAL ACADEMY

*121 Blake Road, Annapolis, 410-263-6933; www.usna.edu*

Opened in 1845, the Naval Academy sits at the edge of the Chesapeake Bay and Severn River, occupying 338 acres. Tours of the campus are available through the academy's Armel-Leftwich Visitor Center. You will see the tomb of John Paul Jones, the chapel, the midshipmen's living quarters and the naval museum. The center also exhibits the original wooden figurehead of the Tecumseh from the *USS Delaware* and displays the *Freedom 7* space capsule. If you time your visit right, you can witness the Noon Formation, during which all present midshipmen line up and march in for the noon meal with military precision. Note: Access to the Academy grounds is limited. Please check the current security restrictions before planning a visit. All visitors over the age of 16 must have a valid picture ID.

## SPECIAL EVENTS

### ANNAPOLIS BY CANDLELIGHT

*18 Pinkney St., Annapolis, 410-267-7619, 800-603-4020; www.annapolis.org*

This self-guided, candlelight walking tour leads visitors through private homes in the historic district. Curator-led tours are also available. For information and reservations contact Historic Annapolis Foundation. Early November.

### CHESAPEAKE APPRECIATION DAYS

*Sandy Point State Park, 1100 E. College Parkway, Annapolis, 410-974-2149; www.dnr.state.md.us*

Skipjack sailing festival honors state's oystermen. Last weekend in October.

### CHRISTMAS IN ANNAPOLIS

*Annapolis, 410-268-8687; www.usna.edu*

Features decorated 18th-century mansions, parade of yachts, private home tours, pub crawls, concerts, holiday meals, First Night celebration, caroling by candlelight at the State House and other events. Call Visitors Bureau for free events calendar. Thanksgiving-January 1.

### MARYLAND RENAISSANCE FESTIVAL

*1821 Crownsville Road, Annapolis, 410-266-7304, 800-296-7304; www.rennfest.com*

Food, crafters, minstrels, dramatic productions. Usually August-October, Saturday-Sunday.

**MARYLAND**

### MARYLAND SEAFOOD FESTIVAL

*Sandy Point State Park, 1100 E. College Parkway, Annapolis, 410-266-3113;*
*www.mda.state.md.us*

This family-friendly event offers up hearty portions of Maryland's favorite seafood dishes, including crab cakes, flounder, oysters, clams, trout and shrimp salad. Visitors will enjoy the beauty of the Chesapeake Bay, more than 50 quality arts and crafts exhibitors, and live musical entertainment. Weekend after Labor Day.

### U.S. POWERBOAT SHOW

*980 Awald Road, Annapolis, 410-268-8828; www.usboat.com*

Extensive in-water display of powerboats; exhibits of related marine products. Mid-October.

### U.S. SAILBOAT SHOW

*980 Awald Road, Annapolis, 410-268-8828; www.usboat.com*

Features world's largest in-water display of sailboats; exhibits of related marine products. Early-mid-October.

## HOTELS

### ★BEST WESTERN ANNAPOLIS

*2520 Riva Road, Annapolis, 410-224-2800, 800-780-7234;*
*www.bestwesternannapolis.com*

151 rooms. Fitness center. High-speed Internet access. Pool. Continental breakfast. $

### ★GIBSON'S LODGINGS

*110 Prince George St., Annapolis, 410-268-5555, 877-330-0057;*
*www.gibsonslodgings.com*

21 rooms. Children over 5 years only. Complimentary continental breakfast. $$

### ★★★LOEWS ANNAPOLIS HOTEL

*126 W. St., Annapolis, 410-263-7777, 800-235-6397; www.loewshotels.com*

The Loews Annapolis Hotel offers 217 newly renovated rooms—18 of which are suites—within walking distance of the city's historic sites, with onsite laundry service, a beauty salon and a spa. 217 rooms. Airport transportation available. $$

### ★★★MARRIOTT ANNAPOLIS WATERFRONT

*80 Compromise St., Annapolis, 410-268-7555, 888-773-0786;*
*www.annapolismarriott.com*

Many of the rooms in the Marriott Annapolis Waterfront offer views of the Chesapeake Bay or Annapolis Harbor. Guest rooms are also decorated in a nautical theme with sea blue tones and comfortable furnishings. 150 rooms. Wireless Internet access. $$$

### ★★★O'CALLAGHAN ANNAPOLIS HOTEL

*174 W. St., Annapolis, 410-263-7700, 800-569-9983; www.ocallaghanhotels.com*

This small, intimate hotel welcomes guests with Irish hospitality and comfortable elegance. Black leather sofas, pale yellow walls and large brass chandeliers give the space a cozy, European touch, making it perfect for couples looking for a weekend getaway. 120 rooms. $$

### ★★★SHERATON BARCELO ANNAPOLIS

*173 Jennifer Road, Annapolis, 410-266-3131, 800-325-3535;*
*www.sheraton.com/annapolis*

This warm, contemporary and newly renovated Sheraton hotel is located just outside the downtown area of Annapolis. Guests can take advantage of the hotel's transportation to get to downtown shops and restaurants. 196 rooms. High-speed Internet access. **$**

## SPECIALTY LODGINGS

### GOVERNOR CALVERT HOUSE

*58 State Circle, Annapolis, 410-263-2641, 800-847-8882; www.annapolisinns.com*

Formerly inhabited by two Maryland governors, the Calverts, this tastefully restored colonial and Victorian residence also has a contemporary conference center. 51 rooms. **$$**

### ROBERT JOHNSON HOUSE

*58 State Circle, Annapolis, 410-263-2641, 800-847-8882; www.annapolisinns.com*

25 rooms. Consists of 18th-century mansion plus two connecting townhouses of the same period. **$$**

### WILLIAM PAGE INN

*8 Martin St., Annapolis, 410-626-1506, 800-364-4160; www.williampageinn.com*

Located in the Annapolis historic district, the William Page Inn puts guests within walking distance of shops, restaurants, the U.S. Naval Academy Visitors Center and the waterfront area. Built in 1908, the inn once served as the Democratic Club. It was carefully renovated in 1987. Five rooms. Closed January. Children over 12 years only. Complimentary full breakfast. Wireless Internet access. **$$**

## RESTAURANTS

### ★★BREEZE

*126 W. St., Annapolis, 410-295-3232; www.loewsannapolis.com*

Seafood, steak menu. Breakfast, lunch, dinner, Sunday brunch. Bar. Children's menu. Valet parking. **$$$**

### ★★CAFÉ NORMANDIE

*185 Main St., Annapolis, 410-263-3382; www.restaurant.com/cafenormandie*

French menu. Breakfast, lunch, dinner. Bar. Children's menu. Outdoor seating. **$$$**

### ★CHICK & RUTH'S DELLY

*165 Main St., Annapolis, 410-269-6737; www.chickandruths.com*

American menu. Breakfast, lunch, dinner. Children's menu. Casual attire. **$**

### ★★FEDERAL HOUSE BAR AND GRILLE

*22 Market Space, Annapolis, 410-268-2576; www.federalhouserestaurant.com*

Seafood, steak menu. Lunch, dinner, Sunday brunch. Bar. Children's menu. **$$**

### ★★HARRY BROWNE'S

*66 State Circle, Annapolis, 410-263-4332; www.harrybrownes.com*

American menu. Lunch, dinner, Sunday brunch. Bar. Business casual attire. Valet parking. Outdoor seating. **$$$**

**MARYLAND**

★
★
★
★
★

### ★JIMMY CANTLER'S RIVERSIDE INN

*458 Forest Beach Road, Annapolis, 410-757-1311; www.cantlers.com*

Seafood menu. Lunch, dinner. Bar. Children's menu. Casual attire. Outdoor seating. **$$**

### ★★LEWNES' STEAKHOUSE

*401 Fourth St., Annapolis, 410-263-1617; www.lewessteakhouse.com*

Seafood, steak menu. Dinner. Bar. Casual attire. Reservations recommended. **$$$**

### ★★MIDDLETON TAVERN

*Second, Market Space, Annapolis, 410-263-3323; www.middletontavern.com*

Seafood menu. Lunch, dinner. Bar. Outdoor seating. **$$$**

### ★★★NORTHWOODS

*609 Melvin Ave., Annapolis, 410-268-2609; www.northwoodsrestaurant.com*

Since 1985, Northwoods has served Italian, Mediterranean and American fare, including beef Wellington, shrimp sorrentina and zuppa de pesce angelico. Continental menu. Dinner. Closed Monday. Bar. Business casual attire. Outdoor seating. **$$$**

### ★★O'LEARY'S SEAFOOD

*310 Third St., Annapolis, 410-263-0884; www.olearysseafood.com*

Seafood menu. Dinner. Bar. Children's menu. **$$$**

### ★★TREATY OF PARIS

*58 State Circle, Annapolis, 410-263-2641; www.historicinnsofannapolis.com*

French, American menu. Lunch, dinner, Sunday brunch. Bar. Reservations recommended. Valet parking. **$$**

## ANTIETAM NATIONAL BATTLEFIELD

On September 17, 1862, the bloodiest day in Civil War annals, more than 23,000 men were killed or wounded as Union forces blocked the first Confederate invasion of the North. The Union gained an advantage beforehand, when a soldier accidentally found Lee's orders wrapped around some cigars. Although he knew Lee's tactical game plan, General McClellan moved cautiously. The battle—critical because British aid to the Confederacy depended on the outcome—was a tactical draw but a strategic victory for the North. This victory allowed Lincoln to issue the Emancipation Proclamation, which expanded the war from simply reuniting the country to a crusade to end slavery. The rebels withdrew across the Potomac on the night of September 18, but for some reason McClellan, with twice the manpower, delayed his pursuit. Lincoln relieved him of command of the Army of the Potomac seven weeks later. Clara Barton, who founded the Red Cross 19 years later, tended the wounded at a field hospital on the battlefield.

Approximately 350 iron tablets, monuments and battlefield maps located on eight miles of paved avenues describe the events of the battle. The visitor center houses a museum and offers information, literature and a 26-minute orientation movie (shown on the hour). Visitor Center (daily); battlefield (daily); ranger-conducted walks, talks and demonstrations (Memorial Day-Labor Day, daily). For information, 301-432-5124.

# BALTIMORE

Baltimore, a city of neighborhoods built on strong ethnic foundations, has achieved an incredible downtown renaissance in the past 20 years. New and renovated sports and entertainment venues have reinvigorated the city. Baseball fans flock to red brick Camden Yards, while football fans come out in force to support the Baltimore Ravens at M&T Bank Stadium. And residents and visitors alike crowd Baltimore's historic Inner Harbor to enjoy its museums, restaurants and nightlife.

Lying midway between the North and South—and enjoying a rich cultural mixture of both—Baltimore is one of the nation's oldest cities. When British troops threatened Philadelphia during the Revolutionary War, the Continental Congress fled to Baltimore, which served as the nation's capital for a little more than two months.

In October 1814, a British fleet attacked the city by land and sea. The defenders of Fort McHenry withstood the naval bombardment for 25 hours until the British gave up. Francis Scott Key saw the huge American flag still flying above the fort and was inspired to pen "The Star-Spangled Banner."

Politics was a preoccupation in the early 19th century, and the city hosted many national party conventions. At least seven presidents and three losing candidates were nominated here. Edgar Allan Poe's mysterious death in the city is rumored to have been at the hands of shady electioneers.

A disastrous fire in 1904 destroyed 140 acres of the business district, but the city recovered rapidly and during the two World Wars it was a major shipbuilding and naval repair center.

In the 1950s and early 1960s, Baltimore was a victim of the apathy and general urban decay that struck the industrial Northeast. But the city fought back, replacing hundreds of acres of slums, rotting wharves and warehouses with gleaming new office plazas, parks and public buildings. The Inner Harbor was transformed into a huge public area with shops, museums, restaurants and frequent concerts and festivals. Millions of tourists and proud Baltimoreans flock downtown to enjoy the sights and activities.

Famous residents and native sons and daughters include Babe Ruth, Edgar Allan Poe, H. L. Mencken, St. Elizabeth Ann Seton, Ogden Nash, Thurgood Marshall, and sports legends Brooks Robinson, Johnny Unitas, Jim Palmer and Cal Ripken, Jr.

*Information: Baltimore Area Convention & Visitors Association, 100 Light St., 12th floor, Baltimore, 410-659-7300, 877-225-8466; www.baltimore.org*

**MARYLAND**

★
★
★
★

## WHAT TO SEE AND DO

### AMERICAN VISIONARY ART MUSEUM

*800 Key Highway, Baltimore, 410-244-1900; www.avam.org*

This museum defines visionary art as works produced by untrained individuals whose art stems from an inner vision. Opened in 1995, the museum displays more than 4,000 pieces. The main building holds seven indoor galleries. There's also a wildflower garden, a wedding chapel and altar built out of tree limbs and flowers, and a tall sculpture barn, which once showcased psychic Uri Geller's art, including a car he covered with 5,000 forks and spoon that was allegedly bent psychically. The museum also plans to add a Thou Art Creative Center, an interactive area for visitors. Tuesday-Sunday 10 a.m.-6 p.m.

## ANTIQUE ROW

*North Howard and West Read streets, Baltimore*

Antique Row, a Baltimore fixture for more than a century, hosts more than 20 dealers and shops, along with restoration services. Shops specialize in items such as European furniture, Tiffany lamps, china and rare books.

## THE AVENUE IN HAMPDEN

*36th St., Baltimore; www.hampdenmainstreet.org*

Novelty shops, vintage clothing stores, casual restaurants and art galleries line Hampden's main drag, with treasures both kitschy and sublime.

## BABE RUTH BIRTHPLACE AND MUSEUM

*301 W. Camden St., Baltimore, 410-727-1539; www.baberuthmuseum.com*

Although Babe Ruth played for the New York Yankees, Baltimore calls him one of its native sons. The house where this legend was born has been transformed into a museum that showcases his life and career. Visitors can see rare family photographs as well as a complete record of his home runs. The museum also features exhibits about the Baltimore Colts and Orioles. Every February 6, the museum commemorates Babe Ruth's birthday by offering free admission to all visitors. April-September, daily 10 a.m.-6 p.m., 10 a.m.-7 p.m. on baseball game days; October-March, daily 10 a.m.-5 p.m.

## BALTIMORE & OHIO RAILROAD MUSEUM

*901 W. Pratt St., Baltimore, 410-752-2490; www.borail.org*

This museum, affiliated with the Smithsonian, celebrates the birthplace of railroading in America and depicts the industry's economic and cultural influences. Encompassing 40 acres, the museum's collection of locomotives is the oldest and most comprehensive in the country. In the Roundhouse, visitors can board and explore more than a dozen of the iron horses, which include a rail post office car and the Tom Thumb train. The second floor of the Annex building has an impressive display of working miniature-scale trains. The Mount Clair Station, exhibiting the story of the B & O Railroad, was built in 1851 to replace the 1829 original, which was the first rail depot in the country. Outside, the museum features more trains, such as the "Chessie," the largest steam locomotive. On certain weekends, visitors can take a train ride. Visitor access by appointment only due to renovations. Daily.

## BALTIMORE MARITIME MUSEUM

*301 E. Pratt St., Baltimore, 410-396-3453; www.baltomaritimemuseum.org*

This museum's featured ships include the *USS Torsk,* a World War II submarine; the Coast Guard cutter *Taney* and the lightship *Chesapeake.* All the ships have been designated National Historic Landmarks. Daily.

## BALTIMORE MUSEUM OF ART

*10 Art Museum Drive, Baltimore, 410-573-1700; www.artbma.org*

Located near Johns Hopkins University, this museum opened in 1923 and was designed by John Russell Pope, the architect of the National Gallery in Washington, D.C. The museum has eight permanent exhibits featuring works from the periods of Impressionism to modern art. It boasts the second largest collection of works by

Andy Warhol. However, its jewel is the Cone collection, which includes more than 3,000 pieces by artists such as Picasso, Van Gogh, Renoir, Cezanne and Matisse. The Matisse collection is the largest in the Western Hemisphere. Visitors will also want to see the three-acre sculpture garden, which contains art by Alexander Calder and Henry Moore. Wednesday-Friday 11 a.m.-5 p.m., Saturday-Sunday 11 a.m.-6 p.m. Free admission the first Thursday of each month.

### BALTIMORE MUSEUM OF INDUSTRY

*Inner Harbor South, 1415 Key Highway, Baltimore, 410-727-4808; www.thebmi.org*

This museum educates visitors about the vital role that industry and manufacturing played in Baltimore's economic and cultural development. Located in a renovated oyster cannery on the west side of the Inner Harbor, the museum opened in 1977. Its exhibits showcase trades such as printing, garment making, canning and metalworking. Guests will learn about the invention of Noxema, the disposable bottle cap and even the first umbrella. Tuesday-Saturday 10 a.m.-4 p.m., Sunday 11 a.m.-4 p.m.; Memorial Day-Labor Day, Monday-Saturday 10 a.m.-4 p.m. Closed holidays.

### BALTIMORE ORIOLES (MLB)

*Oriole Park at Camden Yards, 333 W. Camden St., Baltimore, 410-685-9800, 888-848-2479; www.orioles.mlb.com*

Professional baseball team.

### BALTIMORE RAVENS (NFL)

*M&T Bank Stadium, 1101 Russell St., Baltimore, 410-261-7283; www.baltimoreravens.com*

Professional football team.

### BALTIMORE STREETCAR MUSEUM

*1901 Falls Road, Baltimore, 410-547-0264; www.baltimoremd.com/streetcar*

Eleven electric streetcars and two horse cars used in the city between 1859 and 1963; 1¼-mile rides (fee). Sunday noon-5 p.m.; June-October, Saturday noon-5 p.m.

### BATTLE MONUMENT

*Calvert and Fayette streets, Baltimore*

This an 1815 Memorial is dedicated to those who fell defending the city in the War of 1812. Climb the 228 steps to the top of the monument for a breathtaking view of the city. Wednesday-Sunday 10 a.m.-4 p.m., first Thursday of every month until 8 p.m.

### BUFANO SCULPTURE GARDEN

*3400 N. Charles St., Baltimore; www.jhu.edu*

A wooded retreat with animals sculpted by artist Beniamino Bufano.

### CHARLES CENTER

*36 S. Charles St., Baltimore*

Bounded by Charles, Liberty, Saratoga and Lombard streets, downtown, this business area is packed with European-style plazas, shops, restaurants and outdoor activities. A prize-winning office building by Mies van der Rohe borders center plaza.

## CHURCH HOME AND HOSPITAL

*Broadway and Fairmount avenues, East Baltimore*

Edgar Allan Poe died here in 1849.

## CITY COURT HOUSE

*100 N. Calvert St., Baltimore*

On the steps is a statue of Cecil Calvert, brother of Leonard and founder of Maryland as the second Lord Baltimore.

## CITY HALL

*100 N. Holiday St., Baltimore, 410-396-3100; www.baltimorecity.gov*

Post-Civil War architecture, restored to original detail. Tours by appointment.

## CITY OF BALTIMORE CONSERVATORY

*Druid Hill Park, 2600 Madison Ave., Baltimore, 410-396-0180; www.baltimorecity.gov*

This graceful building (circa 1885) houses a variety of tropical plants. Special shows during Easter, November and the holidays. Thursday-Sunday 10 a.m.-3 p.m.

## CLYBURN ARBORETUM

*4915 Greenspring Ave., Baltimore, 410-367-2217; www.cylburnassociation.org*

Marked nature trails. Nature museum, ornithological room, horticultural library in a restored mansion; shade and formal gardens, All-American Selection Garden, Garden of the Senses. Grounds are open from dawn to dusk; Mansion: Monday-Friday 7:30 a.m.-3:30 p.m.; Museums: Tuesday, Thursday 1-3 p.m.

## DUCKPIN BOWLING

No ducks on the lanes, just smaller pins and balls in this game designed in Baltimore back in 1900. Alleys are open throughout Baltimore, including at Taylor's Stoneleigh Duckpin Bowling Center, 6703 York Road, 410-377-8115.

## EDGAR ALLAN POE GRAVE

*Westminster Hall and Burial Grounds, 519 W. Fayette St., Baltimore, 410-706-2072; www.ci.baltimore.md.us*

Baltimore's oldest cemeteries also contain the graves of many prominent early Marylanders. Westminster Burying Ground and Catacomb tours by appointment. April-November, first and third Friday and Saturday.

## EDGAR ALLAN POE HOUSE AND MUSEUM

*203 N. Amity St., Baltimore, 410-396-7932; www.ci.baltimore.md.us/government/historic/poehouse.html*

The famed author and father of the macabre lived in this house from 1832 to 1835. Haunted or not, the house and museum have scared up many Poe artifacts such as period furniture, a desk and telescope owned by Poe, and Gustave Dore's illustrations of "The Raven." Around January 19, the museum hosts a birthday celebration that includes readings and theatrical performances of Poe's work. April-early December, Wednesday-Saturday noon-3:45 p.m.

## ENOCH PRATT FREE LIBRARY

*400 Cathedral St., Baltimore, 410-396-5430; www.pratt.lib.md.us*

Includes H.L. Mencken and Edgar Allan Poe collections. Monday-Wednesday 10 a.m.-8 p.m., Thursday 10 a.m.-5:30 p.m., Friday-Saturday till 5 p.m., also Sunday 1-5 p.m. from October-May.

## EVERGREEN HOUSE

*4545 N. Charles St., Baltimore, 410-516-0341; www.jhu.edu*

On 26 wooded acres; features Classical Revival architecture and a formal garden. Library. Post-Impressionist paintings, Japanese and Chinese collections and Tiffany glass. Tours (Tuesday-Sunday).

## FEDERAL HILL

*Charles and Cross streets, Baltimore*

Bordered by Hughes Street, Key Highway, Hanover Street and Cross Street Inner Harbor area. View of the city harbor and skyline. Named after a celebration that occurred here in 1788 to mark Maryland's ratification of the Constitution.

## FELL'S POINT

*Visitors Center, 812 S. Ann St., Baltimore, 410-675-6750; www.fellspoint.us*

Shipbuilding and maritime center, this neighborhood dates back to 1730; approximately 350 original residential structures. Working tugboats and tankers can be observed from the docks.

## FIRST UNITARIAN CHURCH

*Charles and Franklin streets, Baltimore, 410-685-2330; www.firstunitarian.net*

William Ellery Channing preached a sermon here that hastened the establishment of the Unitarian denomination. The church is also an example of Classic Revival architecture.

## FLAG HOUSE & STAR-SPANGLED BANNER MUSEUM

*844 E. Pratt St., Baltimore, 410-837-1793; www.flaghouse.org*

Open to the public for more than 75 years, this museum was the home of Mary Pickersgill, who sewed the flag that Francis Scott Key eternalized in America's national anthem. Although the flag now hangs in the Smithsonian's National Museum of American History, visitors can tour the house to learn about its origins and Pickersgill's life. The house has an adjoining War of 1812 museum, which exhibits military and domestic artifacts and presents an award-winning video. Tuesday-Saturday 10 a.m.-4 p.m.

## FORT MCHENRY NATIONAL MONUMENT AND HISTORIC SHRINE

*End of East Fort Avenue, Baltimore, 410-962-4290; www.nps.gov/fomc*

Fort McHenry boasts a stunning view of the harbor, authentic re-created structures and a wealth of living history. Not only was it the site of the battle that inspired Francis Scott Key to pen the national anthem in 1814, but the fort was also a defensive position during the Revolutionary War, a P.O.W. camp for Confederate prisoners during the Civil War and an army hospital during World War I. Summer weekends feature precision drills and music performed by volunteers in Revolutionary War uniforms. Labor Day-Memorial Day, daily 8 a.m.-4:45 p.m.; Memorial Day-Labor Day, daily 8 a.m.-7:45 p.m.

MARYLAND

★
★
★
★
★

## HARBOR CRUISES
*561 Light St., Baltimore, 410-347-5560; www.harborcruises.com*
Depart from Inner Harbor.

## HARBORPLACE
*200 E. Pratt St., Baltimore, 410-332-4191; www.harborplace.com*
This shopping mecca boasts more than 130 stores and restaurants. Visitors who want to take a break can go outside and walk on the brick-paved promenade that runs along the water's edge. Harborplace also has a small outdoor amphitheater, where in good weather, guests are treated to free performances by jugglers, musicians, singers and military and concert bands. Daily.

## HOLOCAUST MEMORIAL
*Water, Gay and Lombard streets, Baltimore*
A simple marble slab memorial to the victims of the Holocaust.

## HOMEWOOD HOUSE MUSEUM
*3400 N. Charles St., Baltimore, 410-516-5589; www.jhu.edu*
Former country home of Charles Carroll, Jr., whose father was a signer of the Declaration of Independence; period furnishings. Guided tours every half hour. Tuesday-Friday 11 a.m.-4 p.m., Saturday-Sunday noon-4 p.m.

## JEWISH MUSEUM OF MARYLAND
*15 Lloyd St., Baltimore, 410-732-6400; www.jhsm.org*
Buildings include Lloyd St. Synagogue, the oldest in Maryland; B'nai Israel Synagogue and the Jewish Museum of Maryland. Tuesday-Thursday, Sunday noon-4 p.m. or by appointment; closed Jewish holidays. Research archives. Monday-Friday, by appointment.

## JOHNS HOPKINS MEDICAL INSTITUTIONS
*600 N. Wolf St., Baltimore, 410-955-5000; www.hopkinsmedicine.org*
Widely known as a leading medical school, research center and teaching hospital. Victorian buildings from 1889.

## JOHNS HOPKINS UNIVERSITY
*3400 N. Charles St., Baltimore, 410-516-8000; www.jhu.edu*
Founded in 1876 and located in northern Baltimore, Johns Hopkins enrolls 18,000 students and is renowned for the Bloomberg School of Public Health, the Peabody Institute (a music conservatory) and its Applied Physics Laboratory located 30 minutes outside of Baltimore. *US News & World Report* continuously ranks its affiliated hospital, which has its own separate campus in eastern Baltimore, as one of the top medical facilities in the country.

## JOSEPH MEYERHOFF SYMPHONY HALL
*1212 Cathedral St., Baltimore, 410-783-8000, 877-276-1444;*
*www.baltimoresymphony.org*
Permanent residence of the Baltimore Symphony Orchestra.

## LACROSSE HALL OF FAME MUSEUM

*113 W. University Parkway, Baltimore, 410-235-6882; www.lacrosse.org/museum*

Team trophies, lacrosse artifacts and memorabilia, including rare photographs and art, vintage equipment and uniforms. Also historical video documentary. February-May, Tuesday-Saturday 10 a.m.-3 p.m.; June-January, Monday-Friday 10 a.m.-3 p.m.

## LEXINGTON MARKET

*400 W. Lexington St., Baltimore, 410-685-6169; www.lexingtonmarket.com*

This under-roof market is more than two centuries old. Covering two blocks, it has more than 130 stalls offering fresh vegetables, seafood, meats, baked goods and pre-pared foods. Vendors outside the market sell clothing, jewelry, T-shirts and other items. Throughout the year, the market hosts several events, such as the Chocolate Festival in October, which boasts free samples and a chocolate-eating contest. But the most anticipated event at the market is Lunch with the Elephants. Every March, Ringling Bros. and Barnum & Bailey Circus elephants parade up Eutaw Street accompanied by fanfare, live music and clowns. When they finally reach the market, they are served lunch, consisting of 1,100 oranges, 1,000 apples, 500 heads of lettuce, 700 bananas, 400 pears and 500 carrots. Monday-Saturday 8:30 a.m.-6 p.m.

## LOVELY LANE MUSEUM

*The Lovely Lane United Methodist Church, 2200 St. Paul St., Baltimore, 410-889-4458; www.lovelylanemuseum.com*

Permanent and changing exhibits of items of Methodist church history since 1760. Guided tours. Thursday-Friday.

## MARYLAND HISTORICAL SOCIETY

*201 W. Monument St., Baltimore, 410-685-3750; www.mdhs.org*

The state's oldest cultural institution includes a library, a museum and even a small press that promotes scholarship about Maryland's history and material culture. The library has more than 5.4 million works and is a valuable resource for genealogists. The society's collection of historical artifacts includes the original draft of "The Star Spangled Banner." Museum: Wednesday-Sunday 10 a.m.-5 p.m.; until 8 p.m. the first Thursday of every month. History and Genealogy Reading Room: Wednesday-Saturday 10 a.m.-4:30 p.m. Special Collections Reading Room: Wednesday-Friday 10 a.m.-4:30 p.m.; also open to the public the third Saturday of every month.

## MARYLAND INSTITUTE, COLLEGE OF ART

*1300 Mount Royal Ave., Baltimore, 410-669-9200; www.mica.edu*

Institute hosts frequent contemporary art exhibitions. Campus distinguished by recy-cled buildings and white marble Italianate main building. Daily.

## MARYLAND SCIENCE CENTER & DAVIS PLANETARIUM

*601 Light St., Baltimore, 410-685-5225; www.mdsci.org*

Located in the Inner Harbor, the three-story building contains hundreds of exhibits guaranteed to spark young (and old) minds. In the Chesapeake Bay exhibit, you can learn about the bay's delicate ecosystem. Or you can explore the mysteries of the human body in BodyLink. The Kids Room, for guests eight and younger, gives children the

**93**

**MARYLAND**

★
★
★
★

chance to operate a fish camera or dress up like turtles. Don't miss the Hubble Space Telescope National Visitor Center, a 4,000-square-foot interactive space gallery with 120 high-resolution images that allow guests to see space through the Hubble's eye. Labor Day-Memorial Day, Tuesday-Friday 10 a.m.-5 p.m., Saturday 10 a.m.-6 p.m., Sunday noon-5 p.m.; Memorial Day-Labor Day, Sunday-Wednesday 10 a.m.-6 p.m., Thursday-Saturday until 8 p.m. IMAX theater is open later.

### MARYLAND ZOO

*Druid Hill Park Lake Drive, Baltimore, 410-366-5466; www.marylandzoo.org*

Located in Druid Hill Park, the third-oldest zoo in the United States covers 180 acres and features more than 2,250 animals. Children can visit the giraffes and elephants in the African Safari exhibit, as well as ride the carousel or try out the climbing wall. The zoo also hosts special events during Halloween and Christmas. March-December, daily 10 a.m.-4 p.m.

### MINNIE V HARBOR TOURS

*Baltimore, 410-685-9062*

Docks near Pier 1, Pratt St., Inner Harbor area. A 45-foot Chesapeake Bay skipjack sloop built in 1906. Ninety-minute harbor tours give 24 passengers the opportunity to help crew the boat (open summer weekends).

### MORGAN STATE UNIVERSITY

*1700 E. Cold Spring Lane, Baltimore, 443-885-3333; www.morgan.edu*

The James E. Lewis Museum of Art has changing exhibits. Monday-Friday; weekends by appointment.

★
★
★
★

### MOTHER SETON HOUSE

*600 N. Paca St., Baltimore, 410-523-3443;*
*www.nps.gov/history/nr/travel/baltimore/b13.htm*

Home of St. Elizabeth Ann Bayley Seton from 1808 to 1809. Here she established the forerunner of the parochial school system, as well as an order of nuns that eventually became the Daughters & Sisters of Charity in the U.S. and Canada. Saturday-Sunday 1-3 p.m., also by appointment.

### MOUNT CLARE MUSEUM HOUSE

*1500 Washington Blvd., Baltimore, 410-837-3262;*
*www.cr.nps.gov/nr/travel/baltimore/b2.htm*

Oldest mansion in Baltimore, dating back to 1760, it is the former home of barrister Charles Carroll. Eighteenth- and 19th-century furnishings. Guided tours on the hour. Tuesday-Saturday 10 a.m.-4 p.m.; closed January.

### MOUNT VERNON PLACE UNITED METHODIST CHURCH

*10 E. Mount Vernon Place, Baltimore, 410-685-5290;*
*www.gbgm-umc.org/mtvernonplumc*

Circa-1850 brownstone with balcony and grillwork extending the entire width of the house; spiral staircase suspended from three floors; library with century-old painting on the ceiling; drawing room. Daily; closed the Monday after Easter.

## MV LADY BALTIMORE

*561 Light St., Baltimore, 410-727-3113, 800-695-5239; www.harborcruises.com*

West Bulkhead. Round-trip cruises to Annapolis (June-August, Wednesday); also cruises to the Chesapeake & Delaware Canal (three selected Sundays in October). *Bay Lady* has lunch and dinner cruises. April-October, daily; limited schedule rest of the year.

## NATIONAL AQUARIUM

*501 E. Pratt St., Baltimore, 410-576-3800; www.aqua.org*

The National Aquarium introduces guests to stingrays, sharks, puffins, seals and a giant Pacific octopus. Visitors can explore the danger and mystery of a living South American tropical rainforest complete with poisonous frogs, exotic birds, piranha and swinging tamarin monkeys, or delight in the underwater beauty of the replicated Atlantic coral reef. The Children's Cove, a touch pool, provides an interactive experience for kids. Feeding schedules are posted in the lobby. Daily.

## MARINE MAMMAL PAVILION

*501 E. Pratt St., Baltimore, 410-576-3800; www.aqua.org*

This unique structure features a 1,300-seat amphitheater surrounding a 1.2-million-gallon pool that houses Atlantic bottlenose dolphins underwater viewing areas enable visitors to observe the mammals from below the surface. The Discovery Room houses a collection of marine artifacts, the Resource Center is an aquatic learning center for school visitors and the library boasts an extensive collection of marine science material. Daily.

## OLD OTTERBEIN UNITED METHODIST CHURCH

*112 W. Conway St., Baltimore, 410-685-4703; www.oldotterbein.com*

Fine Georgian architecture; mother church of United Brethren. Tours of historic building run Saturday-Sunday.

## OLD TOWN MALL

*414 N. Gay St., Baltimore*

This 150-year-old, brick-lined commercial area has been beautifully refurbished; it's closed to vehicular traffic.

## STIRLING STREET

*1000 block of Monument St.*

First community urban "homesteading" venture in the U.S. Renovated homes date back to the 1830s. Original facades have been maintained; interior rehabilitation ranges in style from the antique to the avant-garde.

## OTTERBEIN "HOMESTEADING"

*Area around South Sharp Street, Inner Harbor area*

The original neighborhood dates back to 1785. Houses have been restored.

**MARYLAND**

★
★
★
★
☆

## PATTERSON PARK

*200 S. Linwood Ave., Baltimore, 410-396-3932; www.pattersonpark.com*

Defenses here helped stop the British attack in 1814. Breastworks and artillery pieces are displayed.

## PEABODY INSTITUTE OF THE JOHNS HOPKINS UNIVERSITY

*1 E. Mount Vernon Place, Baltimore, 410-659-8100; www.peabody.jhu.edu*

Music conservatory founded by philanthropist George Peabody; now affiliated with Johns Hopkins. Research and reference collection in library accessible to the public (Monday-Friday). The Miriam A. Friedberg Concert Hall seats 800. Orchestral, recital and opera performances.

## PORT DISCOVERY

*35 Market Place, Baltimore, 410-727-8120; www.portdiscovery.org*

Opened in 1998 in collaboration with Walt Disney Imagineering, Port Discovery has been ranked the fourth best children's museum in the country by *Child* magazine. Kids will have a blast exploring the three-story urban tree house. In MPT Studioworks, they can become producers of their own television broadcasts. The museum also operates the HiFlyer, a giant helium balloon anchored 450 feet above the Inner Harbor. The enclosed gondola holds 20 to 25 passengers and offers a spectacular view of the city. October-May, Tuesday-Friday 9:30 a.m.-4:30 p.m., Saturday 10 a.m.-5 p.m., Sunday noon-5 p.m.; Memorial Day-Labor Day, Monday-Saturday 10 a.m.-5 p.m., Sunday noon-5 p.m.

★
★
★
★

## POWER PLANT

*601 E. Pratt St., Baltimore, 410-752-5444; www.powerplantlive.com*

This commercial complex was once a power plant owned by Baltimore Gas & Electric. The renovated plant now houses a two-story Barnes & Noble bookstore, a Hard Rock Café and the original ESPN Zone, a 35,000-square-foot sports-themed restaurant and arcade.

## PUBLIC WORKS MUSEUM & STREETSCAPE

*Pier 7, 751 Eastern Ave., Baltimore, 410-396-5565;*
*baltimorepublicworksmuseum.org/portfolio*

Museum exhibits the history and artifacts of public works. Located in a historic sewage pumping station. Streetscape sculpture outside depicts the various utility lines and ducts under a typical city street, in a walk-through model. Tuesday-Sunday 10 a.m.-4 p.m.

## SAIL BALTIMORE

*1809 Thames St., Baltimore, 410-522-7300; www.sailbaltimore.org*

Sail Baltimore, a nonprofit organization, informs the public about a variety of citywide boating events that take place throughout the year. Its Web site provides an updated schedule of the different boats and ships that will be visiting the Inner Harbor. It also hosts the Great Chesapeake Bay Schooner Race in October, among other seasonal events.

## SENATOR THEATRE

*5904 York Road, North Baltimore, 410-435-8338; www.senator.com*

Movie buffs will appreciate the charm and history of the Senator, which *USA Today* rated as one of the top theaters in the country. Showing first-run, independent and classic films, the theater seats 900 and has a 40-foot-wide screen. Listed on the National Register of Historic Places, its architecture is elegant Art Deco. The theater recently added its own mini Walk of Fame outside its entrance.

## SHERWOOD GARDENS

*Stratford Road, and Greenway, Baltimore, 410-785-0444*

More than 6 acres in size, the gardens reach their peak of splendor in late April and early May, when thousands of tulips, azaleas and flowering shrubs bloom. Daily dawn-dusk.

## TOP OF THE WORLD

*World Trade Center, 401 E. Pratt St., Baltimore, 410-837-8439; www.baltimore.to*

Observation deck and museum on the 27th floor of the World Trade Center, which was designed by I. M. Pei. Exhibits describe the city's history, famous residents and the activities of the port. September-Memorial Day, Wednesday-Sunday; Memorial Day-Labor Day, daily.

## UNIVERSITY OF MARYLAND AT BALTIMORE

*520 W. Lombard St., Baltimore, 410-706-3100; www.umaryland.edu*

The 32-acre downtown campus includes six professional schools; the University of Maryland Medical System and the Graduate School. Davidge Hall is the oldest medical teaching building in continuous use in the western hemisphere dating back to 1812.

## USS CONSTELLATION

*301 E. Pratt St., Pier 1, Baltimore, 410-539-1797; www.constellation.org*

This retired sloop, anchored at Pier 1 in the Inner Harbor, has a proud naval history that spans from the Civil War to World War II. Visitors can board the ship for a self-guided audio tour. Kids can participate in the Powder Monkey program, in which they learn what it was like to serve in President Lincoln's navy. June-mid-August, daily 10 a.m.-6 p.m.; mid-September-April, daily 10 a.m.-4:30 p.m. Extended hours may be available June-August.

## VAGABOND PLAYERS

*806 S. Broadway, Baltimore, 410-563-9135; www.vagabondplayers.com*

Oldest continuously operating "little theater" in the United States. Recent Broadway shows, revivals and original scripts are performed. Early June-early July, Friday-Sunday.

## WALTERS ART MUSEUM

*600 N. Charles St., Baltimore, 410-547-9000; www.thewalters.org*

This museum's collection traces the history of the world from ancient times to the present day. Father and son William and Henry Walters gave the museum and its

MARYLAND

numerous holdings to Baltimore, though the New York Metropolitan Museum of Art also coveted it. With more than 30,000 pieces of art, the collection is renowned for its French paintings and Renaissance and Asian art. The museum also exhibits Imperial Fabergé eggs, paintings by Raphael and El Greco, and an impressive assortment of ivories and Art Deco jewelry. Visitors will also want to check out the unique Roman sarcophagus. Wednesday-Sunday 10 a.m.-5 p.m.

### WASHINGTON MONUMENT
*600 Charles St., Baltimore, 410-396-1049; www.museumsusa.org*
The first major monument to honor George Washington. There's a museum in the base; view the city from the top. Other monuments nearby honor Lafayette, Chief Justice Roger Brooke Taney, philanthropist George Peabody, lawyer Severn Teackle Wallis and Revolutionary War hero John Eager Howard.

## SPECIAL EVENTS
### AMERICAN CRAFT COUNCIL BALTIMORE-WINTER SHOW
*Convention Center, 1 W. Pratt St., Baltimore, 410-649-7000, 800-836-3470; www.craftcouncil.org*
Craft festival features the works of nearly 800 artisans, with crafts ranging from clay and glass to furniture and toys. Three-day weekend in late February.

### ARTSCAPE
*1200 block of Mount Royal Ave., Baltimore, 877-225-8466; www.baltimore.org*
This festival celebrates the area's abundance of visual, literary and performing arts. The three-day event takes place in the cultural corridor of the city's Bolton Hill neighborhood. It features live music performances, poetry and fiction readings by regional writers and even a one-act opera. The Artists' Market exhibits and sells the work of more than 140 artists. The festival includes a wide variety of activities for children, which in the past have included a youth Shakespearean performance and an interactive art tent. Mid-July, Friday-Saturday noon-10 p.m., Sunday noon-8 p.m.

### COCKPIT IN COURT SUMMER THEATRE
*Essex Community College, 7201 Rossville Blvd., Baltimore, 410-780-6369; www.ccbcmd.edu/cockpit/boxoffice.html*
Theater in residence at Essex Community College. Four separate theaters offer a diverse collection of plays, including Broadway productions, contemporary drama, revues and Shakespeare. Mid-June-mid-August.

### MARYLAND FILM FESTIVAL
*107 E. Read St., Baltimore, 410-752-8083; www.mdfilmfest.com*
Since 1999, this four-day festival has become a premier cinema event for Baltimore, presenting more than 120 foreign, domestic and short films throughout the city's movie houses, including the famous Senator Theatre. Most screenings are followed by a discussion with the film's director or producer. The festival has also hosted films for children, such as a silent version of *Peter Pan* accompanied by an orchestra. Late April or early May.

MARYLAND

★
★
★
★
★

### PIER 6 CONCERT PAVILION

*731 Eastern Ave., Pier 6, Baltimore; www.piersixpavilion.com*

Summertime outdoor concerts and plays at the water's edge. Some covered seating. June-September. Evenings.

### PIMLICO RACE COURSE

*5201 Park Heights Ave., Baltimore, 410-542-9400; www.pimlico.com*

Home to the world-famous Preakness Stakes, this track features a 70-foot-wide and one-mile-long track, more than 750 betting windows, and a clubhouse and two grandstands that can accommodate more than 13,000 people. August.

### PREAKNESS STAKES AND CELEBRATION WEEK

*Pimlico Race Course, 5201 Park Heights Ave., Baltimore,*
*410-542-9400, 877-206-8042; www.preaknesscelebration.org*

The Preakness Stakes, the second jewel in horse racing's Triple Crown, is a time-honored tradition in Baltimore. On the third Saturday in May, nearly 100,000 people from Maryland and around the world gather at the Pimlico Race Course. Celebration festivities begin one week before the race, with activities that include a parade, a hot-air balloon festival, outdoor concerts, boat races and 5K and 10K runs. On race day, the Preakness is the second-to-last race and begins at around 5:30 p.m. Visitors looking for a good value and an eye-level view of the horses should reserve seats in the infield. Those willing to spend more money—and dress more formally—should choose seats in the clubhouse or grandstand.

### SHOWCASE OF NATIONS ETHNIC FESTIVALS

*7 E. Redwood St., Baltimore, 877-225-8466; www.baltimore.org*

Presenting the food, music and crafts of a different culture each weekend. June-October.

### TASTE OF BALTIMORE

*Camden Yards, 333 W. Camden St., Baltimore, 888-848-2473;*
*www.tasteofbaltimore.com*

Dozens of restaurants set up shop in the ballpark to offer hungry attendees samples of their finest dishes, from Polish sausage and cheesesteak to pizza and Italian ice. Part of the proceeds from the event go to the Children's Cancer Foundation. Live music and family activities provide entertainment between bites. Mid-September.

## HOTELS

### ★★ADMIRAL FELL INN

*888 S. Broadway, Baltimore, 410-522-7380, 866-583-4162; www.harbormagic.com*

80 rooms. $$

### ★CELIE'S WATERFRONT INN

*1714 Thames St., Baltimore, 410-522-2323, 800-432-0184; www.celieswaterfront.com*

Nine rooms. Complimentary continental breakfast. Wireless Internet access. $$

**MARYLAND**

★
★
★
★
☆

### ★★CLARION HOTEL PEABODY COURT

*612 Cathedral St., Baltimore, 410-727-7101, 800-292-5500;*
*www.peabodycourthotel.com*
104 rooms. Fitness center. Business center. Parking. **$$**

### ★★DAYS INN INNER HARBOR HOTEL

*100 Hopkins Place, Baltimore, 410-576-1000, 800-329-7466;*
*www.daysinnerharbor.com*
250 rooms. Complimentary wireless Internet access. Business center. **$$**

### ★★★HYATT REGENCY BALTIMORE ON THE INNER HARBOR

*300 Light St., Baltimore, 410-528-1234, 800-233-1234; www.baltimore.hyatt.com*
Conveniently located across the street from Baltimore's Inner Harbor, this hotel is
linked by a skywalk to the convention center and shopping at Harbor place. It is
also situated within minutes of the National Aquarium, Maryland Science Center and
Oriole Park. Guest rooms are decorated with off-white wall coverings resembling
white leather, white bedding with gold accents and marble bathrooms. In addition to
a rooftop pool and a huge fitness center, amenities include a basketball half-court,
putting green and jogging track, along with 29,000 square feet of meeting space. 488
rooms. **$$$**

### ★INN AT HENDERSON'S WHARF

*1000 Fell St., Baltimore, 410-522-7777, 800-522-2088; www.hendersonswharf.com*
38 rooms. Complimentary full breakfast. Fitness center. High-speed Internet access.
Parking. **$$**

★
★
★
★
☆

### ★★INN AT THE COLONNADE

*4 W. University Parkway, Baltimore, 410-235-5400, 800-222-8733;*
*www.colonnadebaltimore.com*
125 rooms. **$$**

### ★★★INTERCONTINENTAL HARBOR COURT HOTEL

*550 Light St., Baltimore, 410-234-0550, 800-496-7621;*
*www.intercontinental.com/baltimore*
The InterContinental Harbor Court Hotel, located across the street from the Inner
Harbor and Harborplace, re-creates the spirit of a grand English manor home. Guest
rooms offer views of the harbor or the garden on the courtside. The professional staff
attends to every need, even offering hot, buttery popcorn for guests enjoying in-room
movies. The hotel has a fitness center and yoga studio for athletic-minded guests.
195 rooms. **$$**

### ★★★MARRIOTT BALTIMORE WATERFRONT

*700 Aliceanna St., Baltimore, 410-385-3000, 800-228-9290; www.marriott.com*
From its large rooms offering stunning views of the harbor to its amenities, this hotel
puts you in the center of Baltimore's Inner Harbor. Walk (or take a water taxi) to
some of the city's premier tourist destinations: Little Italy, Pier 6 Concert Pavilion or
Harborplace. 751 rooms. **$$$**

### ★★★RENAISSANCE HARBORPLACE HOTEL

*202 E. Pratt St., Baltimore, 410-547-1200, 800-535-1201;*
*www.renaissancehotels.com/bwish*

This hotel adjoins the upscale Gallery mall, with four floors of shopping and dining. Nearby attractions include the National Aquarium, the Baltimore Convention Center and Ride the Ducks of Baltimore. Many guest rooms offer views of the harbor. 622 rooms. $$$

### ★★TREMONT PARK HOTEL

*8 E. Pleasant St., Baltimore, 410-576-1200, 800-873-6668; www.1800tremont.com*

58 rooms, all suites. Complimentary continental breakfast. $$

## RESTAURANTS
### ★THE BAYOU CAFÉ

*8133-A Honeygo Blvd., Baltimore, 410-931-2583; www.thebayoucafe.com*

American, Cajun menu. Lunch, dinner, Sunday brunch. Bar. Children's menu. Casual attire. Outdoor seating. $$

### ★BERTHA'S

*734 S. Broadway, Baltimore, 410-327-5795; www.berthas.com*

Seafood menu. Lunch, dinner. Bar. Children's menu. Casual attire. $$

### ★★★BLACK OLIVE

*814 S. Bond St., Baltimore, 410-276-7141; www.theblackolive.com*

This Mediterranean restaurant, formerly Fells Point's General Store, has retained the building's original hardwood floors and brick archways. The restaurant also offers outdoor dining under a grape arbor. The food here is organic, and fresh fish is displayed in front of the open kitchen. Each fish entrée is filleted tableside. The carrot cake is a perfect finale. Mediterranean, seafood menu. Lunch, dinner. Bar. Children's menu. Business casual attire. Reservations recommended. Valet parking. Outdoor seating. $$$

### ★★★BOCCACCIO

*925 Eastern Ave., Baltimore, 410-234-1322; www.boccaccio-restaurant.com*

This Little Italy restaurant's specialty is classic Northern Italian fare. Specials change on a seasonal basis to reflect the chef's fresh, locally obtained ingredients. Italian menu. Lunch, dinner. Bar. Business casual attire. Reservations recommended. Valet parking. $$$

### ★★BRASSERIE TATIN

*105 W. 39th St., Baltimore, 443-278-9110; www.brasserietatin.com*

French menu. Lunch, dinner. Bar. Business casual attire. Reservations recommended. Outdoor seating. $$

### ★CAFÉ HON

*1002 W. 36th St., Baltimore, 410-243-1230; www.cafehon.com*

American menu. Breakfast, lunch, dinner, brunch. Bar. Children's menu. Casual attire. $$

**MARYLAND**

★
★
★
★

### ★★★★CHARLESTON

*1000 Lancaster St., Baltimore, 410-332-7373; www.charlestonrestaurant.com*

Chef/owner Cindy Wolf's regional American/French restaurant serves up dishes such as sautéed heads-on Gulf shrimp with andouille sausage and Tasso ham with creamy stone-milled grits. The restaurant also has an impressive wine program that includes several dozen sparkling wines and a selection of about 600 well-chosen whites and reds from the New World (Australia, South Africa, New Zealand and Chile) and the Old (France, Italy and Spain). Charleston also offers more than a dozen microbrews and imported beers. American, French menu. Dinner. Closed Sunday. Bar. Business casual attire. Reservations recommended. Valet parking. Outdoor seating. $$$

### ★★★DELLA NOTTE

*801 Eastern Ave., Baltimore, 410-837-5500; www.dellanotte.com*

A popular spot, Della Notte's interior is replete with faux-white brick walls covered with murals and busts of Roman emperors. The menu offers a selection of antipasti, fish, meats and daily specials, along with a vast wine list of more than 1,400 selections. After dinner, settle into the Emperor's Lounge with an after-dinner drink and enjoy the live entertainment offered daily. Italian menu. Lunch, dinner. Bar. Business casual attire. Reservations recommended. Valet parking. $$$

### ★★GERMANO'S TRATTORIA

*300 S. High St., Baltimore, 410-752-4515; www.germanostrattoria.com*

Italian menu. Lunch, dinner. Bar. Casual attire. Reservations recommended. Valet parking. $$

★
★
★
★

### ★★THE HELMAND

*806 N. Charles St., Baltimore, 410-752-0311; www.helmand.com*

Middle Eastern menu. Dinner. Lunch, Bar. Business casual attire. Reservations recommended. $$

### ★★★IXIA

*518 N. Charles St., Baltimore, 410-727-1800; www.ixia-online.com*

This eclectic, international restaurant serves entrées such as rockfish and lump crab cake or French "moulard" confit. The lounge offers jazz on Friday nights. International menu. Dinner. Closed Sunday-Monday. Bar. Business casual attire. Reservations recommended. $$$

### ★★JOHN STEVEN, LTD.

*1800 Thames St., Baltimore, 410-327-0489; www.johnstevenltd.com*

Seafood menu. Lunch, dinner. Bar. Children's menu. Casual attire. Reservations recommended. Outdoor seating. $$$

### ★★LA SCALA

*1012 Eastern Ave., Baltimore, 410-783-9209; www.lascaladining.com*

Italian menu. Dinner. Bar. Business casual attire. Reservations recommended. Valet parking. $$

## ★★MT. WASHINGTON TAVERN

*5700 Newbury St., Baltimore, 410-367-6903; www.mtwashingtontavern.com*

American menu. Lunch, dinner, Sunday brunch. Bar. **$$$**

## ★★OBRYCKI'S CRAB HOUSE

*1727 E. Pratt St., Baltimore, 410-732-6399; www.obryckis.com*

Seafood menu. Lunch, dinner. Closed mid-November-mid-March Bar. Children's menu. Casual attire. Reservations recommended. **$$**

## ★★★THE OCEANAIRE SEAFOOD ROOM

*801 Aliceanna St., Baltimore, 443-872-0000; www.theoceanaire.com*

The restaurant's upscale décor features hardwood floors, rich cherry wood accents, wood blinds and leather. The menu changes daily, since seafood is the specialty and the restaurant has it flown and trucked in every morning. Diners can choose how they would like their fish prepared—grilled, broiled, sautéed, steamed or fried. Seafood menu. Dinner. Bar. Business casual attire. Reservations recommended. Valet parking. **$$$**

## ★★★PAZO

*1425 Aliceanna, Baltimore, 410-534-7296; www.pazorestaurant.com*

Group dining is popular, with diners ordering multiple tapas entrées to share. The restaurant's soft lighting, wood tables, soaring high ceilings and wrought-iron accents make it a romantic spot. Mediterranean, Tapas menu. Dinner. Bar. Casual attire. Valet parking. **$$$**

## ★★PIERPOINT

*1822 Aliceanna St., Baltimore, 410-675-2080; www.pierpointrestaurant.com*

American menu. Lunch, dinner, brunch. Closed Monday. Bar. Business casual attire. Reservations recommended. Breakfast. **$$**

## ★★★THE PRIME RIB

*1101 N. Calvert St., Baltimore, 410-539-1804; www.theprimerib.com*

The Prime Rib has been serving consistently good steaks, chops and seafood since 1965. With black walls, candlelit tables and tuxedoed waitstaff, it's known as "the civilized steakhouse." America, steak menu. Dinner. Bar. Jacket required. Reservations recommended. Valet parking. **$$$**

## ★★★RUTH'S CHRIS STEAK HOUSE

*600 Water St., Baltimore, 410-783-0033; www.ruthschris.com*

Born from a single New Orleans restaurant that Ruth Fertel bought in 1965 for $22,000, the Ruth's Chris Steak House chain has made it to the top of every steak-lover's list. Aged prime Midwestern beef is broiled to your liking and served on a heated plate, sizzling in butter. Sides such as creamed spinach and fresh asparagus with hollandaise are not to be missed. Choose from seven different potato preparations, from a one-pound baked potato with everything to au gratin potatoes with cream sauce and topped with cheese. Steak menu. Dinner. Bar. Business casual attire. Reservations recommended. Valet parking. **$$$**

**MARYLAND**

★
★
★
★

### ★★SOTTO SOPRA

*405 N. Charles St., Baltimore, 410-625-0534; www.sottosoprainc.com*
Italian menu. Lunch, dinner. Bar. Business casual attire. Reservations recommended.
Valet parking. Outdoor seating. $$

### ★★TAPAS TEATRO

*1711 N. Charles St., Baltimore, 410-332-0110; www.tapasteatro.net*
Mediterranean, Spanish, Tapas menu. Dinner. Closed Monday. Bar. Casual attire.
Outdoor seating. $$

# BALTIMORE/WASHINGTON INTERNATIONAL (BWI) AIRPORT AREA

## HOTELS

### ★★EMBASSY SUITES

*1300 Concourse Drive, Linthicum, 410-850-0747, 800-362-2779;*
*www.embassy-suites.com*
251 rooms, all suites. Complimentary full breakfast. Airport transportation available. $$

### ★★★FOUR POINTS BY SHERATON BWI AIRPORT

*7032 Elm Road, Baltimore, 410-859-3300, 800-368-7764; www.fourpoints.com*
Whether you are homeward bound or heading out for business or pleasure, this hotel
at Baltimore's major airport can be a stepping stone to your final destination. City
attractions, such as the Inner Harbor, Camden Yards and Laurel Racecourse, are less
than 20 minutes away. 201 rooms. Airport transportation available. $$

### ★HAMPTON INN

*829 Elkridge Landing Road, Linthicum, 410-850-0600, 800-426-7866;*
*www.hamptoninnbwiairport.com*
182 rooms. Complimentary continental breakfast. Airport transportation available. $

### ★★★MARRIOTT BALTIMORE WASHINGTON INTERNATIONAL AIRPORT

*1743 W. Nursery Road, Linthicum, 410-859-8300, 800-228-9290; www.marriott.com*
310 rooms. Airport transportation available. High-speed Internet access. Unlimited
local phone calls. $$

# BERLIN

## WHAT TO SEE AND DO

### ASSATEAGUE ISLAND NATIONAL SEASHORE

*7206 National Seashore Lane, Berlin, 410-641-1441, 800-365-2267; www.nps.gov/asis*
Visitors interested in sandy beaches and wildlife should visit Assateague Island,
which is about a four-hour drive from Baltimore. Straddling Maryland and Virginia,
it contains a state park and a wildlife refuge with swimming, hiking, canoeing, sea
kayaking, biking and camping on the beach, and some of the best surf-fishing on the
Atlantic Coast. Guests also come to see the wild horses. According to legend, the

horses, which are only the size of ponies, swam to the island from a shipwrecked Spanish galleon. On every last Wednesday and Thursday in July, the world-famous Pony Penning event occurs. During this event, the horses swim from the Maryland side of the island to the Virginia side with a crowd of spectators cheering them on. The visitor center offers more information about the horses as well as the seashore's many activities. Daily.

### ASSATEAGUE STATE PARK

*7307 Stephen Decatur Highway, Berlin, 410-641-2120, 888-432-2267;*
*www.dnr.state.md.us*
Has 755 acres with two miles of ocean frontage and gentle, sloping beaches. Swimming, fishing, boat launch; picnicking, concession (summer), bicycle and hiking trails, camping. April-October.

## SPECIAL EVENT
### HARNESS RACING

*Ocean Downs, 10218 Racetrack Road, Berlin, 410-641-0600;*
*www.oceandowns.com*
Nightly Tuesday-Sunday. Children with an adult only. Late July-Labor Day.

## HOTEL
### ★★★ATLANTIC HOTEL

*2 N. Main St., Berlin, 410-641-3589, 800-814-7672; www.atlantichotel.com*
The Atlantic Hotel offers Victorian-decorated rooms centrally located in Berlin's historic district. Complimentary morning Starbucks coffee service and wireless Internet access are just a few of the perks you'll find here. 17 rooms. Complimentary full breakfast. Restaurant, bar. $

## SPECIALTY LODGING
### MERRY SHERWOOD PLANTATION

*8909 Worcester Highway, Berlin, 410-641-2112, 800-660-0358;*
*www.merrysherwood.com*
Eight rooms. Children over 8 years only. Complimentary full breakfast. Built in 1859, on grounds of a former plantation. $$

# BETHESDA

A suburb of Washington, D.C., Bethesda is home to both the National Institutes of Health and Bethesda Naval Hospital.
*Information: The Greater Bethesda-Chevy Chase Chamber of Commerce,*
*Landow Building, 7910 Woodmont Ave., 301-652-4900; www.bcchamber.org*

## WHAT TO SEE AND DO
### NATIONAL LIBRARY OF MEDICINE

*8600 Rockville Pike, Bethesda, 301-594-5983, 888-346-3656; www.nlm.nih.gov*
World's largest biomedical library; rare books, manuscripts, prints; medical art displays. Monday-Saturday; closed Saturday before Monday holidays. Visitors center and guided tour. Monday-Friday, one departure each day.

★
★
★
★
★

## HOTELS

### ★★★HYATT REGENCY BETHESDA

*1 Bethesda Metro Center, Bethesda, 301-657-1234; www.bethesda.hyatt.com*

Located at Metro Center and within steps to restaurants, theaters and shopping, this hotel is perfect for both the business and leisure traveler. The rooms offer Hyatt Grand beds, iPod docking stations and deluxe bathrooms with Portico products. 390 rooms. Children's activity center. **$$**

### ★★MARRIOTT SUITES BETHESDA

*6711 Democracy Blvd., Bethesda, 301-897-5600, 800-228-9290;*
*www.marriotthotels.com*

274 rooms, all suites. **$$**

## RESTAURANTS

### ★★AUSTIN GRILL

*7278 Woodmont Ave., Bethesda, 301-656-1366; www.austingrill.com*

Tex-Mex menu. Lunch, dinner, late-night, brunch. Bar. Children's menu. Casual attire. Outdoor seating. **$$**

### ★★BACCHUS BETHESDA

*7945 Norfolk Ave., Bethesda, 301-657-1722; www.bacchusoflebanon.com*

Middle Eastern menu. Lunch, dinner. Casual attire. Valet parking. Outdoor seating. **$$**

### ★BETHESDA CRAB HOUSE

*4958 Bethesda Ave., Bethesda, 301-652-3382; www.bethesda.org/arts/arts.htm*

Seafood menu. Lunch, dinner, late-night. Casual attire. Outdoor seating. **$$**

### ★★★CESCO TRATTORIA

*4871 Cordell Ave., Bethesda, 301-654-8333*

This cute Italian restaurant features breads that are baked fresh daily in a wood-burning oven, which is visible to diners. You can't go wrong with any of the pasta dishes. Italian menu. Lunch, dinner. Bar. Casual attire. Valet parking (dinner). Outdoor seating. **$$$**

### ★★FOONG LIN

*7710 Norfolk Ave., Bethesda, 301-656-3427; www.foonglin.com*

Chinese menu. Lunch, dinner. Bar. Casual attire. **$$**

### ★★FRASCATI

*4806 Rugby Ave., Bethesda, 301-652-9514*

Italian menu. Lunch, dinner. Closed Monday. Reservations recommended. Outdoor seating. **$$**

### ★★JEAN-MICHEL

*10223 Old Georgetown Road, Bethesda, 301-564-4910;*
*www.jeanmichelrestaurant.com*

French menu. Lunch, dinner. Closed Sunday in July-August. Casual attire. **$$$**

### ★★★LE VIEUX LOGIS

*7925 Old Georgetown Road, 301-652-6816*

Mixing American and Scandinavian techniques with the classic French menu creates dishes that are innovative and delicious. The ambience is romantic with dim lighting and warm color tones. French menu. Dinner. Closed Sunday. Casual attire. Free valet parking. Outdoor seating. **$$$**

### ★RAKU

*7240 Woodmont Ave., Bethesda, 301-718-8680*

Pan-Asian menu. Lunch, dinner. Children's menu. Outdoor seating. **$$**

### ★★★RUTH'S CHRIS STEAK HOUSE

*7315 Wisconsin Ave., Bethesda, 301-652-7877; www.ruthschris.com*

This chain started as a single New Orleans restaurant Ruth Fertel bought in 1965 by mortgaging her house. Thick, juicy USDA Prime steaks slathered with butter as well as market-fresh seafood are the hallmarks of Ruth's Chris. On the ground floor of the Air Rights building, the dining room features a relaxed, informal atmosphere with dark wood accents, a large lobster tank and a cigar lounge. Steak menu. Dinner. Bar. Business casual attire. Valet parking. **$$$**

### ★★THYME SQUARE

*4735 Bethesda Ave., Bethesda, 301-657-9077*

Seafood, American menu. Lunch, dinner. Bar. Children's menu. Casual attire. Outdoor seating. **$$**

### ★★★TRAGARA

*4935 Cordell Ave., Bethesda, 301-951-4935; www.tragara.com*

Bathed in soft light with fresh roses on every linen-topped table, Tragara offers satisfying Italian cuisine and impeccable service. Tables fill up quickly during lunch and dinner. The impressive Italian kitchen offers a tempting menu of pastas, fish, meat and antipasti, but be sure to save room for the house-made gelato. Italian menu. Lunch, dinner. Casual attire. Valet parking. Bar. **$$$**

# BOONSBORO

*Information: Hagerstown/Washington County Chamber of Commerce,*
*28 W. Washington St., Hagerstown, 301-739-2015; www.hagerstown.org*

## WHAT TO SEE AND DO

### CRYSTAL GROTTOES CAVERNS

*19821 Shepherdstown Pike, Boonsboro, 301-432-6336;*
*www.goodearthgraphics.com/showcave/md/crystal.html*

Limestone caverns may be viewed from walkways. Picnicking. Guided tours. April-October, daily 9 a.m.-6 p.m.; November-March, Saturday-Sunday 11 a.m.-4 p.m.

**MARYLAND**

★
★
★
★
☆

### GATHLAND STATE PARK

*21843 National Pike, Boonsboro, 301-791-4767, 888-432-2267;*
*www.dnr.state.md.us/publiclands/western/gathland.html*

A site once owned by George Townsend, Civil War reporter. A monument was built in 1896 to honor Civil War correspondents. The visitor center contains original papers. Picnicking, walking tour, winter sports.

### GREENBRIER STATE PARK

*21843 National Pike, Boonsboro, 301-791-4767, 888-432-2267;*
*www.dnr.state.md.us/publiclands/western/greenbrier.html*

The Appalachian Trail passes near this 1,275-acre park and its 42-acre man-made lake. Swimming (Memorial Day-Labor Day, daily), fishing, boating (rentals; no gas motors); nature and hiking trails, picnicking.

### WASHINGTON MONUMENT STATE PARK

*21843 National Pike Road, Boonsboro, 301-791-4767, 888-432-2267;*
*www.dnr.state.md.us/publiclands/western/washington.html*

A 34-foot tower of native stone was the first completed monument to honor George Washington. Views of nearby battlefields, two states (Pennsylvania and West Virginia). History Center displays firearms and Civil War mementos (by appointment). The Appalachian Trail leads through the park; hiking and picnicking.

# BOWIE

*Information: Greater Bowie Chamber of Commerce, 6911 Laurel Bowie Road, Bowie, 301-262-0920; www.bowiechamber.org*
*Information is also available from Prince George's Conference & Visitors Bureau, 9475 Lottsford Road No.130, Landover, 301-925-8300*

## WHAT TO SEE AND DO

### BELAIR MANSION

*12207 Tulip Grove Drive, Bowie, 301-809-3089;*
*www.cityofbowie.org/Museums/museums.asp*

Georgian-style house was the home of Governor Samuel Ogle in the 1700s; later owned by the Woodward family, prominent racehorse breeders in the first half of the 20th century. Tours. Wednesday-Sunday noon-4 p.m., groups by appointment.

### BELAIR STABLE MUSEUM

*2835 Belair Drive, Bowie, 301-809-3089; www.cityofbowie.org/Museums/museums.asp*

Part of famed Belair Stud, one of the premier thoroughbred racing stables of the '30s, '40s and '50s. Was home to two Triple Crown winners—Gallant Fox and Omaha—and the 1955 Horse of the Year, Nashua. Wednesday-Sunday noon-4 p.m., groups by appointment.

## SPECIAL EVENT

### HERITAGE DAY

*Belair Mansion and Stable, 2835 Belair Drive, Bowie, 301-809-3089*

Belair Mansion and Stable. Performance by Congress' Own Regiment; tour of stables and grounds; battle reenactments; demonstrations of colonial crafts. Third Sunday in May.

## HOTEL

### ★HAMPTON INN BOWIE

*15202 Major Lansdale Blvd., Bowie, 301-809-1800; www.hamptoninn.com*
301 rooms. **$**

# BUCKEYSTOWN

## SPECIALTY LODGINGS

### CATOCTIN INN

*3619 Buckeystown Pike, Buckeystown, 301-874-5555, 800-730-5550*
20 rooms. Complimentary full breakfast. **$**

### INN AT BUCKEYSTOWN

*3521 Buckeystown Pike, Buckeystown, 301-874-5755, 800-272-1190;*
*www.innatbuckeystown.com*
This stately and elegant mansion opened its doors in 1981, and today continues to enchant guests with touches of luxury and the charm of another era. Located in a National Registered Historic Village, this mansion delights with its warm hospitality, Victorian-style décor and wonderful appointment of collectibles and period pieces. Nine rooms. **$$**

# CAMBRIDGE

On the Eastern Shore, Cambridge is Maryland's second-largest deep-water port. Boating and fishing opportunities are found in the Choptank and Honga rivers and Chesapeake, Tar and Fishing bays.

*Information: Dorchester County Visitors Center, 2 Rose Hill Place,*
*410-228-1000, 800-522-8687; www.tourdorchester.org*

★
★
★
☆

## WHAT TO SEE AND DO

### BLACKWATER NATIONAL WILDLIFE REFUGE

*2145 Key Wallace Drive, Cambridge, 410-228-2677; www.fws.gov/blackwater*
Over 20,000 acres of rich tidal marsh, freshwater ponds and woodlands. One of the chief wintering areas for Canada geese and ducks using the Atlantic Flyway; in fall, as many as 33,000 geese and 17,000 ducks swell the bird population. Also a haven for the bald eagle, the Delmarva fox squirrel and the peregrine falcon. Scenic drive, woodland trails, photo blind. Visitor center, daily.

## SPECIAL EVENT

### NATIONAL OUTDOOR SHOW

*Cambridge, 800-522-8687; www.nationaloutdoorshow.com*
Goose and duck calling, log sawing, crab picking, trap setting contests; entertainment. Last weekend in February.

## CHESAPEAKE AND OHIO CANAL NATIONAL HISTORICAL PARK

As early as 1754, the enterprising George Washington (who was only in his twenties) proposed a system of navigation along the Potomac River valley. His Patowmack Canal Company, organized in 1785, cleared obstructions and built skirting canals to facilitate the transportation of goods from settlements beyond the Allegheny Mountains to the lower Potomac River towns.

These improvements eventually were rendered inadequate, and with Erie Canal's renown, the Chesapeake and Ohio Canal Company was formed in 1828 to connect Georgetown with the Ohio Valley by river and canal. On July 4, 1828, President John Quincy Adams led the ground-breaking ceremony, declaring, "To subdue the earth is preeminently the purpose of this undertaking." Unfortunately, the earth was not easily subdued. President Adams bent his shovel with several attempts before breaking into an energetic frenzy and successfully getting a shovelful of dirt.

The groundbreaking ceremony's difficulty foreshadowed the canal's short-lived future as a major transportation artery. Completed in 1850 as far as Cumberland, Maryland, (184½ miles from Georgetown), the waterway was used extensively for the transportation of coal, flour, grain and lumber. Financial and legal difficulties, the decline of commerce after the Civil War, the Baltimore & Ohio Railroad and the advent of improved roads cut deeply into the commerce of the waterway, and it gradually faded into obsolescence. The canal still had limited commercial use as late as 1924, when a flood destroyed many of the canal locks and nothing was restored.

The C & O Canal's unfortunate demise is now a blessing for hikers, canoeists and bikers, who can find access to the towpath along the banks of the waterway. One of the least altered of old American canals, the Chesapeake and Ohio is flanked by ample foliage throughout most of its 20,239 acres.

Many points of interest include exhibits in Cumberland, Georgetown, Hancock and Williamsport, and at a museum near the Great Falls of the Potomac. Mule-drawn canal boat rides are offered from April to October at Georgetown and Great Falls. Camping for hikers and bikers is available throughout the park.

For information about the canal, contact the C & O Canal National Historical Park, Sharpsburg, 301-739-4200. Visitor centers are located in Cumberland, Georgetown, Great Falls, Hancock and Williamsport.

# CHESAPEAKE BAY BRIDGE AREA

The majestic twin spans of the Chesapeake Bay Bridge carry visitors to the Eastern Shore, a patchwork of small picturesque towns, lighthouses and fishing villages tucked away from the city. Scenic rivers and bays, wildlife, gardens and wildflowers fill the countryside. The main attractions of any visit, however, are the many fine inns and the restaurants specializing in local seafood.

## WHAT TO SEE AND DO
### WYE OAK STATE PARK
*Highway 662, Wye Mills, 410-820-1668;*
*www.dnr.state.md.us/publiclands/eastern/wyeoak.html*

On the Eastern Shore in Talbot County, approximately one mile from the junction of Routes 50 and 404. The official state tree of Maryland is in this 29-acre park; it is the largest white oak in the United States (108 feet high, 28 feet around) and is believed to be more than 460 years old; a new tree has been started from one of its acorns. A restored 18th-century one-room schoolhouse and the Old Wye Mill (late 1600s) are nearby.

## HOTELS
### ★COMFORT SUITES
*160 Scheeler Road, Chestertown, 410-810-0555, 877-424-6423; www.comfortinn.com*
53 rooms. Complimentary continental breakfast. $

### ★★★KENT MANOR INN
*500 Kent Manor Drive, Stevensville, 410-643-7716, 800-820-4511;*
*www.kentmanor.com*
This historic 1820 inn sits among 220 wooded acres on picturesque Thompson Creek, a tributary to the Chesapeake Bay. Just 12 miles from Annapolis, the hotel is a convenient spot for both business and leisure travelers. The guest rooms feature poster beds, Italian marble fireplaces and stunning views of the grounds. Several rooms also have window seats and porches—perfect spots to curl up with a good book. There are many outdoor activities for guests to enjoy, including bike and paddleboat rentals. 24 rooms. Complimentary continental breakfast. $$

## SPECIALTY LODGINGS
### HUNTINGFIELD MANOR
*4928 Eastern Neck Road, Rock Hall, 410-639-7779, 800-720-8788;*
*www.huntingfield.com*
Six rooms. Complimentary continental breakfast. Telescope-type house on a working farm that dates to the middle 1600s. $

### INN AT MITCHELL HOUSE
*8796 Maryland Parkway, Chestertown, 410-778-6500; www.innatmitchellhouse.com*
Built in 1743, this historic manor house welcomes guests with friendly service, set amid lush woods and 10 beautiful acres. Five rooms. Complimentary full breakfast. $$

### WHITE SWAN TAVERN
*231 High St., Chestertown, 410-778-2300; www.whiteswantavern.com*
Six rooms. Complimentary continental breakfast. Former house and tavern built in 1733 and 1793, respectively; restored with antique furnishings; museum. $

**MARYLAND**

★
★
★
★

## RESTAURANTS

### ★★FISHERMAN'S INN AND CRAB DECK

*3116 Main St., Kent Narrows, 410-827-8807; www.fishermansinn.com*

Seafood, steak menu. Lunch, dinner. Bar. Children's menu. Casual attire. **$$**

### ★HARRIS CRAB HOUSE

*433 Kent Narrows Way North, Grasonville, 410-827-9500; www.harriscrabhouse.com*

American, seafood menu. Lunch, dinner. Bar. Children's menu. Casual attire. Outdoor seating. **$$**

### ★★★NARROWS

*3023 Kent Narrows Way South, Grasonville, 410-827-8113;*
*www.thenarrowsrestaurant.com*

This restaurant offers waterfront dining with a spectacular view of the narrows. The crab cakes are a must here. In fact, they have become so popular that the restaurant now ships them anywhere in the country. Fried oysters are another signature dish. Regional eastern shore menu. Lunch, dinner, brunch. Bar. Children's menu. **$$**

### ★WATERMAN'S CRAB HOUSE

*21055 Sharp St., Rick Hall, 410-639-2261; www.watermanscrabhouse.com*

Seafood menu. Breakfast, lunch, dinner. Bar. Children's menu. Casual attire. Reservations recommended. Outdoor seating. **$$**

# CHEVY CHASE

## RESTAURANT

### ★★★LA FERME

*7101 Brookville Road, Chevy Chase, 301-986-5255; www.lafermerestaurant.com*

In a French country-house setting, La Ferme serves entrées such as a hickory-smoked and grilled double-cut pork chops with potato gratin, grilled vegetables and Meaux mustard sauce. In warmer weather, the outdoor terrace is on the perfect spot to grab a quick lunch or romantic dinner. French menu. Lunch, dinner. Bar. Closed Monday. Reservations recommended. Outdoor seating. **$$**

## HOTEL

### ★★HOLIDAY INN

*5520 Wisconsin Ave., Chevy Chase, 301-656-1500, 800-315-2621;*
*www.holiday-inn.com*

215 rooms. **$**

# COCKEYSVILLE

*Information: Baltimore County Chamber of Commerce, 102 W. Pennsylvania Ave.,*
*Towson, 410-825-6200; www.baltcountycc.com*

## SPECIAL EVENT

### POINT-TO-POINT STEEPLECHASE

*Cockeysville, 410-825-6200*

Three well-known meets on consecutive weekends: My Lady's Manor in Monkton, Mid-April. Grand National in Butler, Mid-April. Maryland Hunt Cup in Glyndon, Late April.

# COLLEGE PARK

*Information: Prince George's County Conference & Visitors Bureau, 9200 Basil Court, Largo, 301-925-8300, 888-925-8300; www.visitprincegeorges.com*

## WHAT TO SEE AND DO

### COLLEGE PARK AVIATION MUSEUM

*1985 Corporal Frank Scott Drive, College Park, 301-864-6029; www.collegeparkaviationmuseum.com*

World's oldest operating airport, started by Wilbur Wright in 1909 to train two military officers in the operation of aircraft. First airplane machine gun and radio navigational aids were tested here; first air mail and controlled helicopter flights. Museum (daily 10 a.m.-5 p.m.).

### GREENBELT PARK

*6565 Greenbelt Road, College Park, 301-344-3948; www.hikercentral.com/parks/gree*

A 1,100-acre wooded park operated by the National Park Service that includes 174 sites. Nature trails, picnicking, camping, skiing. Self-registration; first-come, first-served. Standard fees.

### UNIVERSITY OF MARYLAND

*Highway 1, College Park, 301-405-1000; www.umd.edu*

This university is attended by 35,000 students. Tawes Fine Arts Theater has plays, musicals, concerts, dance, opera and music festivals. Tours.

## HOTEL

### ★★HOLIDAY INN

*10000 Baltimore Ave., College Park, 301-345-6700, 800-315-2621; www.holidayinncollegepark.com*

222 rooms. $

# COLUMBIA

A planned city built on a tract of land larger than Manhattan Island, Columbia comprises 11 villages surrounding a central downtown service area. Construction of the city began in 1966.

*Information: Howard County Tourism Council, 8267 Main St., Ellicott City, 410-313-1900, 800-288-8747; www.howardcountymd.gov*

## WHAT TO SEE AND DO

### AFRICAN ART MUSEUM OF MARYLAND

*5430 Vantage Point Road, Columbia, 410-730-7106; www.africanartmuseum.org*

Masks, sculptured figures, textiles, basketry, household items and musical instruments displayed in a 19th-century manor. Tuesday-Friday 10 a.m.-4 p.m., Sunday noon-4 p.m.

### HOWARD COUNTY CENTER OF AFRICAN-AMERICAN CULTURE

*5434 Vantage Point Road, Columbia, 410-715-1921; www.hccaacres.org*

Contains artifacts and memorabilia depicting images of African-Americans over the last 200 years. Extensive collection of spiritual, jazz and rap music; more than 2,000 books and periodicals; hands-on exhibit for children. Tuesday-Friday noon-5 p.m., Saturday noon-4 p.m., Sunday by appointment.

## SPECIAL EVENTS

### COLUMBIA FESTIVAL OF THE ARTS

*5575 Sterrett Place, Columbia, 410-715-3044; www.columbiafestival.com*
Music, dance, theater, lakeside entertainment. Ten days in mid-June.

### SYMPHONY OF LIGHTS

*8267 Main St., Columbia, 410-313-1900; www.visithowardcounty.com*
Animated lighting displays along a 1½-mile park route. Late November-early January.

### WINE IN THE WOODS

*Symphony Woods, 7120 Oakland Mills Road, Columbia, 410-313-4700;*
*www.wineinthewoods.com*
Symphony Woods at Merriweather Post Pavilion. Two-day celebration featuring Maryland wines, gourmet food, entertainment, arts and crafts. Third weekend in May.

## HOTELS

### ★★★HILTON COLUMBIA

*5485 Twin Knolls Road, Columbia, 410-997-1060, 800-445-8667;*
*www.columbia.hilton.com*
Located in the heart of Columbia in a parklike setting, this hotel offers a very relaxing stay, with a glassed atrium and well-appointed guest rooms. A state-of-the-art fitness center and indoor pool make this a good choice for the active set. 152 rooms. Wireless Internet access. Restaurant, bar. $$

### ★★★SHERATON COLUMBIA HOTEL

*10207 Wincopin Circle, Columbia, 410-730-3900, 800-638-2817;*
*www.sheratoncolumbia.com*
Recognized for its gracious accommodations, superb service and well-appointed guest rooms, this hotel is a welcome retreat for both business and leisure travelers. Guest rooms have been updated to include flat-screen TVs and ibahn high-speed Internet access. 290 rooms. Suites. High-speed Internet access. Pets accepted. $$

## RESTAURANT

### ★★★KING'S CONTRIVANCE

*10150 Shaker Drive, Columbia, 410-995-0500; www.thekingscontrivance.com*
Guests can enjoy fine country dining in this 1900 mansion with Early American décor. The menu offers selections such as crab cakes, venison and rack of lamb, as well as an extensive wine list. American menu. Lunch, dinner. Bar. Children's menu. Reservations recommended. Valet parking (weekends). $$$

# CRISFIELD

*Information: Crisfield Area Chamber of Commerce, 906 W. Main St., Crisfield,*
*410-968-2500, 800-782-3913; www.crisfieldchamber.org*

## WHAT TO SEE AND DO
### JANES ISLAND STATE PARK
*26280 Alfred J. Lawson Drive, Crisfield, 410-968-1565, 800-521-9189;*
*www.dnr.state.md.us/publiclands/eastern/janesisland.html*
These 3,147 acres are nearly surrounded by Chesapeake Bay and its inlets. Swimming, fishing, boat ramp (rentals); cabins, camping. Standard fees.

### SMITH ISLAND CRUISES
*Somers Cove Marina, Seventh Street, Crisfield, 410-425-2771;*
*www.smithislandcruises.com*
The *Chelsea's Lane Tyler* and the *Captain Tyler* make approximately one-hour cruises to Smith Island. There are also bus tours of the two villages on the island, with spare time to visit the rest of the island. Memorial Day-mid-October.

### TANGIER ISLAND CRUISES
*1001 W. Main St., Crisfield, 410-968-2338; www.tangierislandcruises.com*
Trips to the fishing village of Tangier Island, VA. Mid-May-October.

## SPECIAL EVENT
### NATIONAL HARD CRAB DERBY & FAIR
*Somers Cove Marina, Seventh Street, Crisfield, 410-968-2500, 800-782-3913;*
*www.crisfieldchamber.com/crabderby.htm*
Cooking, crab picking, boat docking contests; crab racing; fireworks and parade. Friday-Sunday, Labor Day weekend.

## HOTEL
### ★PINES MOTEL
*127 N. Somerset Ave., Crisfield, 410-968-0900; www.crisfield.com/pines*
40 rooms. $

# CUMBERLAND

Cumberland is nestled between Pennsylvania and West Virginia in western Maryland. George Washington, who once defended the town, thought the nation's primary east-west route would eventually pass through Cumberland. In 1833, the National Road (Highway 40 Alternate) made the town a supply terminus for overland commerce. Today's economy includes services and recreational facilities.

*Information: Allegany County Convention & Visitors Bureau, 13 Canal St., Cumberland, 301-777-5132, 800-425-2067; www.mdmountainside.com*

## WHAT TO SEE AND DO
### FORT CUMBERLAND TRAIL
*Cumberland*
Walking trail covers several city blocks downtown around the site of Fort Cumberland. Includes boundary markers, narrative plaques.

115

**MARYLAND**

★
★
★
★
☆

### GORDON-ROBERTS HOUSE

*218 Washington St., Cumberland, 301-777-8678; www.historyhouse.allconet.org/house*

Restored 18-room Victorian house Circa 1867, with nine period rooms; research room. Tuesday-Saturday 10 a.m.-5 p.m.

### THE NARROWS

*Route 40, Cumberland*

Picturesque 1,000-foot gap through Alleghenies (Highway 40A) used by pioneers on their way West.

### ROCKY GAP STATE PARK

*12500 Pleasant Valley Road N.E., Cumberland, 301-722-1480, 888-432-2267;*
*www.dnr.state.md.us/publiclands/western/rockygap.html*

Mountain scenery around 243-acre lake with three swimming beaches. Swimming, fishing, boating (electric motors only; rentals); nature and hiking trails, picnicking, cafe, improved camping (reservations accepted one year in advance), winter activities. Resort; 18-hole golf course. Standard fees.

### WESTERN MARYLAND STATION CENTER

*13 Canal St., Cumberland, 301-724-3655;*
*www.nps.gov/history/nr/travel/cumberland/WMD.HTM*

This 1913 railroad station houses Canal Place Authority, Industrial and Transportation Museum; C & O Canal National—Historical Park Visitors Center and Allegany County Visitors Center. Daily.

★
★★
★★
★
★

### WESTERN MARYLAND SCENIC RAILROAD

*13 Canal St., Cumberland, 301-759-4400, 800-872-4650; www.wmsr.com*

Excursion train makes scenic trip 17 miles to Frostburg and back. May-October: Tuesday-Sunday; November-mid-December, weekends.

## SPECIAL EVENTS
### AGRICULTURAL EXPO AND FAIR

*Allegany County Fairgrounds, 11490 Moss Ave., 301-729-1200;*
*www.alleganycofair.org*

Poultry, livestock, carnival, entertainment. Late July.

### DRUMFEST

*Greenway Avenue Stadium, 500 Greenway Ave., Cumberland, 301-777-8325*

Drum and bugle corps championship. Last Saturday in July.

### STREET ROD ROUNDUP

*Cumberland Fairgrounds, 301-729-5555*

Hundreds of pre-1950 hot rods on display and in competitions. Labor Day weekend.

## HOTEL
### ★★HOLIDAY INN

*100 S. George St., Cumberland, 301-724-8800, 800-315-2621;*
*www.hicumberland.com*

130 rooms. Airport transportation available. **$**

## SPECIALTY LODGING
### INN AT WALNUT BOTTOM

*120 Greene St., Cumberland, 301-777-0003, 800-286-9718; www.iwbinfo.com*

At this elegant retreat, guests are offered their choice of two accommodations. The Georgian-style architecture of the Cowden House welcomes guests with a formal doorway and chimneys at each end, while the Queen Anne-style Dent House features a round turret on the corner. 12 rooms. Complimentary full breakfast. **$**

# EASTON

*Information: Talbot County Chamber of Commerce, 11 S. Harrison St., Easton, 410-770-8000; www.talbotchamber.org*

## WHAT TO SEE AND DO
### ACADEMY ART MUSEUM

*106 South St., Easton, 410-822-2787; www.art-academy.org*

Housed in a renovated 1820s schoolhouse, the Academy exhibits works of local and national artists in its permanent collection. Also hosts more than 250 visual and performing arts programs annually. Monday-Saturday 10 a.m.-4 p.m., Wednesday 10 a.m.-9 p.m.

### HISTORICAL SOCIETY OF TALBOT COUNTY

*25 S. Washington St., Easton, 410-822-0773; www.hstc.org*

A three-gallery museum in a renovated early commercial building; changing exhibits, museum shop. Historic houses: 1810 Federal town house, 1700s Quaker cabinetmaker's cottage, period gardens; tours. Monday-Saturday 10 a.m.-4 p.m., by advance appointment.

### THIRD HAVEN FRIENDS MEETING HOUSE

*405 S. Washington St., Easton, 410-822-0293; www.thirdhaven.org*

One of the oldest frame-construction houses of worship in the U.S. Daily.

## SPECIAL EVENTS
### EASTERN SHORE CHAMBER MUSIC FESTIVAL

*21 S. Harrison St., Easton, 410-819-0380; www.chesapeakechambermusic.org*

World-class chamber music. Two weeks in June.

### TUCKAHOE STEAM AND GAS SHOW AND REUNION

*11472 Ocean Gateway, Easton, 410-643-6123; www.tuckahoesteam.org*

Old steam and gas engines; antique tractors and cars. Demonstrations in soap and broom making; flour milling. Gas and steam wheat threshing, sawmill working, flea market, crafts, parade, entertainment. Usually the weekend after July 4.

### WATERFOWL FESTIVAL

*40 S. Harrison St., Easton, 410-822-4567; www.waterfowlfestival.org*

Downtown and various locations in and around town. Exhibits on waterfowl, pictures, carvings, food. First or second weekend in November.

**MARYLAND**

★
★
★
★
☆

## HOTELS

### ★★BISHOP'S HOUSE

*214 Goldsborough St., Easton, 410-820-7290, 800-223-7290; www.bishopshouse.com*
Five rooms. Closed January-February. Children over 12 years only. Complimentary full breakfast. **$**

### ★HOLIDAY INN EXPRESS

*8561 Ocean Gateway, Easton, 410-819-6500, 877-327-8661; www.hotel-easex.com*
73 rooms. Complimentary continental breakfast. **$**

### ★★★ROBERT MORRIS INN

*314 N. Morris St., Oxford, 410-226-5111, 888-823-4012; www.robertmorrisinn.com*
Rooms at the Robert Morris Inn include private porches with views of the Chesapeake Bay. Relax in an Adirondack chair on the inn's property, which rolls down to the water's edge. Or visit the marine museum, go for a bike ride or scout for antiques in nearby Oxford. 35 rooms. Closed December-March. Children over 10 years only. Restaurant. **$$**

## RESTAURANTS

### ★★★★THE INN AT EASTON

*28 S. Harrison St., Easton, 410-822-4910; www.theinnateaston.com*
Housed in a Federal-style mansion, the dining room at the Inn at Easton delivers the unexpected. The room is fresh and contemporary, not stuffy, and the food is modern Australian, not classic American. Chef Andrew Evans puts his knowledge of clean, unfussy, fresh Down Under cuisine (he spent a year cooking in Brisbane and married an Aussie) to work in recipes like barramundi en papillote with red Thai curry and jasmine rice, or coffee-crusted rack of lamb with potato purée and wilted spinach. The wine list draws heavily from Australian produces, whose bold shirazes and chardonnays pair well with Andrews' inventive food. Australian menu. Dinner. Closed Monday-Tuesday. Business casual attire. Reservations recommended. Outdoor seating. **$$**

### ★★★RESTAURANT LOCAL

*101 E. Dover St., Easton, 410-822-1300; www.tidewaterinn.com*
Opened in 2006 as part of the Historic Tidewater Inn's renovations, Restaurant Local serves contemporary American cuisine in a modern but casual setting. Entrées include a local rockfish filet with shrimp and basil risotto, mushrooms and saffron butter, and filet mignon with roasted garlic potatoes, grilled asparagus and wild mushroom bordelaise. American menu. Breakfast, lunch, dinner, Sunday brunch. Bar. Valet parking. Outdoor seating. **$$**

# ELLICOTT CITY

Originally named Ellicott Mills, this town was founded by three Quaker brothers as the site of their gristmill. Charles Carroll of Carrollton, whose Doughoregan Manor can still be seen nearby, lent financial help to the Ellicotts, and the town eventually became the site of ironworks, rolling mills and the first railroad terminus in the United States. The famous Tom Thumb locomotive race with a horse took place near here.

Many of the town's original stone houses and log cabins, on hills above the Patapsco River, have been preserved.

*Information: Howard County Tourism Council, 8267 Main St., Ellicott City, 410-313-1900, 800-288-8747; www.howardcountymd.gov*

## WHAT TO SEE AND DO

### ELLICOTT CITY B & O RAILROAD STATION MUSEUM

*2711 Maryland Ave., Ellicott City, 410-461-1945; www.ecborail.org*

Completed by the Baltimore and Ohio Railroad in 1830, the Ellicott City Station is the oldest surviving railroad station in America and the site of the original terminus of the first 13 miles of commercial track constructed in the United States. In the 1970s the station was restored as a museum, and a second restoration in 1999 returned the building to its 1857 appearance. Today, the site interprets the story of transportation and travel in early America through seasonal exhibits, education programs and living history programs. Wednesday-Sunday 11 a.m.-4 p.m.; last admission is one half-hour before closing.

### PATAPSCO VALLEY STATE PARK

*8020 Baltimore National Pike, Ellicott City, 410-461-5005, 888-432-2267; www.dnr.state.md.us/publiclands/central/patapscovalley.html*

Spread across three counties, this great nature and recreational area runs along a 32-mile stretch of the scenic Patapsco River, spans 14,000 acres and contains five sites. Guests can hike, bike, ride horses, fish, camp, canoe, tube or picnic. The park also includes the world's largest multiple-arched stone railroad bridge, a 300-foot suspension bridge and a paved hiking trail for the disabled. Park: daily dawn-dusk. Information desk: daily 8 a.m.-4:30 p.m.

## HOTEL

### ★★★TURF VALLEY RESORT AND CONFERENCE CENTER

*2700 Turf Valley Road, Ellicott City, 410-465-1500, 888-833-8873; www.turfvalley.com*

This full-service resort (formerly a thoroughbred farm and country club) is convenient to Baltimore and offers well-appointed guest rooms. The resort also features a full-service European spa, two golf courses, tennis courts and a nightly hors d'oeuvres and cocktail reception. 234 rooms. Free parking. High-speed Internet access. Spa. **$$**

## RESTAURANTS

### ★★CRAB SHANTY

*3410 Plumtree Drive, Ellicott City, 410-465-9660; www.crabshanty.com*

Seafood menu. Lunch, dinner, brunch. Bar. Children's menu. Business casual attire. **$$**

### ★★★TERSIGUEL'S

*8293 Main St., Ellicott City, 410-465-4004; www.tersiguels.com*

Tersiguel's offers fine dining in a 19th-century home with six individual dining rooms. Chefs prepare seasonal cuisine with fresh vegetables and herbs from their garden, and chèvre cheese is made daily. French menu. Lunch, dinner. Bar. Business casual attire. Reservations recommended. **$$$**

**MARYLAND**

★
★
★
★

# FLINTSTONE

## WHAT TO SEE AND DO

### GREEN RIDGE STATE FOREST

*28700 Headquarters Drive Northeast, Flintstone, 301-478-3124;*
*www.dnr.state.md.us/publiclands/western/greenridge.html*

These 44,000 acres of forest land stretch across mountains of western Maryland and occupy portions of Town Hill, Polish Mountain and Green Ridge Mountain. Abundant wildlife. Fishing, boat launch, canoeing; hiking trails, camping, winter sports. C & O Canal runs through here into 3,118-foot Paw-Paw Tunnel.

## HOTEL

### ★★ROCKY GAP LODGE & GOLF RESORT

*16701 Lakeview Road Northeast, Flintstone, 301-784-8400, 800-724-0828;*
*www.rockygapresort.com*

217 rooms. Children's activity center. Beach. Airport transportation available. $$

# FREDERICK

Home of fearless Barbara Frietschie, who reportedly spoke her mind to Stonewall Jackson and his "rebel hordes," Frederick is a town filled with history. Named for Frederick Calvert, sixth Lord Baltimore, it is the seat of one of America's richest agricultural counties. Francis Scott Key and Chief Justice Roger Brooke Taney made their homes here. Court House Square was the scene of several important events during the Revolutionary War, including the famed protest against the Stamp Act, in which an effigy of the stamp distributor was burned.

During the Civil War, Frederick was a focal point for strategic operations by both sides. In the campaign of 1862, the Confederacy's first invasions of the North were made at nearby South Mountain and Sharpsburg, at Antietam Creek. Thousands of wounded men were cared for here. In July 1864, the town was forced to pay a $200,000 ransom to Confederate General Jubal Early before he fought the Battle of Monocacy a few miles south. Frederick today is an educational center, tourist attraction, the location of Fort Detrick army installation, and home to diversified small industry. A 33-block area has been designated a Historic District.

*Information: Tourism Council of Frederick County, 19 E. Church St., Frederick,*
*301-663-3687, 800-999-3613; www.visitfrederick.org*

## WHAT TO SEE AND DO

### BARBARA FRIETSCHIE HOUSE AND MUSEUM

*154 W. Patrick St., Frederick, 301-698-0630*

Exhibits include quilts, clothing made by Frietschie, her rocker and Bible, the bed in which she died, and other items; 10-minute film; garden. April-September, Monday, Thursday-Sunday; October-November, Saturday-Sunday.

★
★
★
★
★

# CIVIL WAR SITES OF FREDERICK

A well-preserved city of elegant 18th- and 19th-century structures, Frederick is a necessary stop on any tour of Civil War landmarks. It is an especially appropriate sequel to visit after nearby Antietam National Battlefield, the site of the single bloodiest day of the Civil War—September 17, 1862. At the end of the battle, thousands of Union wounded were transported to Frederick, where 29 buildings were turned into makeshift hospitals. President Lincoln later praised townsfolk for their humanity. This heritage led to Frederick's selection as the site of the National Museum of Civil War Medicine.

Begin an hour-long, one-mile walking tour of the city's historic district at the museum at 48 East Patrick St. The museum tells the story of radical improvements in medical treatment during the four-years war, as the divided nation coped with the flood of ill or wounded soldiers on both sides of the Mason-Dixon line. From the museum, walk three blocks west (left) to the reconstructed Barbara Frietschie House & Museum at 154 West Patrick. Frietschie was immortalized in John Greenleaf Whittier's Civil War poem, "Shoot if you must, this old gray head, but spare your country's flag." According to legend, she waved a Union flag defiantly at Stonewall Jackson, who was leading a Confederate army through the city. In truth, she may have waved a flag, but to honor Union troops passing by later.

Double back on Patrick Street to Court Street and walk north (left) one block to tour Courthouse Square. On Court Street, opposite City Hall, is the small office where Francis Scott Key, author of "The Star-Spangled Banner," practiced law. Revolutionary War General Lafayette was a guest at 103 Council St. during his ceremonial U.S. tour in 1824. At 119 Record St. Lincoln visited a wounded general and addressed a crowd from its steps after the Antietam battle. Head east (left) on West Church Street. Conclude your tour two blocks east at the Historical Society of Fredericksburg at 24 East Church. A large 1820 home, it is maintained as a house museum furnished with local antiques—appropriately so, because nearby East Patrick Street has been dubbed "Antique Row" for its many antique shops.

★
★
★
★
★

### CHILDREN'S MUSEUM OF ROSE HILL MANOR

*1611 N. Market St., Frederick, 301-694-1646, 800-999-3613;*
*www.rosehillmuseum.com*

Hands-on exhibits of 19th-century family life; carriage museum, colonial herb and fragrant gardens, farm museum, blacksmith shop, log cabin. April-October, daily; November, Saturday-Sunday.

### EVANGELICAL REFORMED CHURCH

*15 W. Church St., Frederick, 301-662-2762; www.erucc.org*

A Grecian-style building modeled after the Erechtheum, with two towers resembling Lanterns of Demosthenes. Here Andrew "Stonewall" Jackson slept through a pro-Union sermon before the Battle of Antietam; Barbara Frietschie was a member.

## GAMBRILL STATE PARK

*8602 Gambrill Park Road, Frederick, 301-271-7574, 888-432-2267;*
*www.dnr.state.md.us/publiclands/western/gambrill.html*
Park has 1,136 acres with two developed areas. Fishing; nature and hiking trails, picnicking, tent and trailer sites (fees). Tea room. Two overlooks.

## HISTORICAL SOCIETY OF FREDERICK COUNTY MUSEUM

*24 E. Church St., Frederick, 301-663-1188; www.hsfcinfo.org*
House built in early 1800s shows both Georgian and Federal-style details. Portraits of early Frederick residents. Genealogy library (Tuesday-Saturday). Monday-Saturday; also Sunday afternoons.

## MONOCACY NATIONAL BATTLEFIELD

*4801 Urbana Pike, Frederick, 301-662-3515; www.nps.gov/mono/home.htm*
On July 9, 1864, Union General Lew Wallace and 5,000 men delayed General Jubal Early and his 23,000 Confederate soldiers for 24 hours, during which Grant was able to reinforce and save Washington, D.C., New Jersey, Vermont and Pennsylvania. Confederate monuments mark the area. Labor Day-Memorial Day 8 a.m.-4:30 p.m., Memorial Day-Labor Day 8:30 a.m.-5 p.m.

## MOUNT OLIVET CEMETERY

*515 S. Market St., Frederick, 301-662-1164, 888-662-1164;*
*www.mountolivetcemeteryinc.com*
Monuments mark graves of Francis Scott Key and Barbara Frietschie. A flag flies over Key's grave.

**122**

★
★
★
★
★

## ROGER BROOKE TANEY HOME

*121 S. Bentz St., Frederick, 301-663-8687*
Chief Justice of the United States from 1835 to 1864, Taney was chosen by Andrew Jackson to succeed John Marshall. He swore in seven presidents, including Abraham Lincoln, and issued the famous Dred Scott Decision. He is buried in the cemetery of St. John's Catholic Church at East Third and East streets. April-October, weekends.

## SCHIFFERSTADT ARCHITECTURAL MUSEUM

*1110 Rosemont Ave., Frederick, 301-663-3885;*
*www.smallmuseum.org/schifferstadt.htm*
Fine example of German Colonial farmhouse architecture. Tours of architectural museum. Gift shop. April-mid-December, Wednesday-Friday 10 a.m.-4 p.m.; Saturday-Sunday noon-4 p.m.

## TRINITY CHAPEL

*West Church Street, Frederick, 301-694-2489*
Graceful colonial church; Francis Scott Key was baptized here. Steeple houses town clock and 10-bell chimes; chimes play every Saturday evening.

## SPECIAL EVENTS

### BEYOND THE GARDEN GATES TOUR

*19 E. Church St., Frederick, 301-394-2489; www.celebratefrederick.com*

Downtown. Tour historic and contemporary gardens. Early May.

### FALL FESTIVAL

*Rose Hill Manor, 1611 N. Market St., Frederick, 301-600-1650;*
*www.co.frederick.md.us/Parks/rosehill.html*

Apple butter making, music, crafts demonstrations, tractor pull, hay rides, country cooking. Early October.

### GREAT FREDERICK FAIR

*797 E. Patrick St., Frederick, 301-663-5895; www.thegreatfrederickfair.com*

Frederick county fair. Mid-late September.

### LOTUS BLOSSOM FESTIVAL

*Lilypons Water Garden, 6800 Lilypons Road, Buckeystown,*
*301-874-5133, 800-723-7667; www.lilypons.com*

Endless blooms of water lilies and lotus, water garden; arts and crafts, food, entertainment, lectures. First double-digit weekend in July.

## HOTELS

### ★FAIRFIELD INN

*5220 Westview Drive, Frederick, 301-631-2000, 800-228-2800; www.marriott.com*

**123**

105 rooms. Complimentary continental breakfast. Free high-speed Internet access. $

### ★★HAMPTON INN

*5311 Buckeystown Pike, Frederick, 301-698-2500, 800-426-7866;*
*www.hamptoninnfrederick.com*

161 rooms. Complimentary continental breakfast. Business center. High-speed Internet access. $

## RESTAURANT

### ★★RED HORSE STEAK HOUSE

*996 W. Patrick St., Frederick, 301-663-3030; www.redhorseusa.com*

Steak menu. Dinner. Bar. Children's menu. Casual attire. Reservations recommended. $$

# FROSTBURG

## RESTAURANT

### ★★★AU PETIT PARIS

*86 E. Main St., Frostburg, 301-689-8946; www.aupetitparis.com*

The atmosphere at this cozy French bistro is intimate and relaxed. The à la carte menu will satisfy even the most discriminating gourmet with dishes like duck a l'orange and le coq au vin. The wine cellar boasts the most extensive collection in western Maryland. French menu. Dinner. Closed Sunday-Monday. Bar. Children's menu. $$$

# GAITHERSBURG

*Information: Chamber of Commerce, 9 Park Ave., Gaithersburg, 301-840-1400;*
*www.ggchamber.org*

## WHAT TO SEE AND DO
### SENECA CREEK STATE PARK
*11950 Clopper Road, Gaithersburg, 301-924-2127, 888-432-2267;*
*www.dnr.state.md.us/publiclands/central/seneca.html*
This park comprises 6,109 acres with a 90-acre lake. Historic sites with old mills, an old schoolhouse, stone quarries. Fishing, boating (rentals); picnicking, disc golf, hiking, bicycle and bridle trails, winter sports. Standard fees.

## SPECIAL EVENT
### MONTGOMERY COUNTY AGRICULTURAL FAIR
*16 Chestnut St., Gaithersburg, 301-926-3100; www.mcagfair.com*
One of the East Coast's leading county fairs. Mid-late August.

## HOTELS
### ★COMFORT INN
*16216 Frederick Road, Gaithersburg, 301-330-0023, 877-424-6423;*
*www.choicehotels.com*
127 rooms. Complimentary full breakfast. Free wireless Internet access. Free local calls. **$**

★
★ ★
★ ★
★

### ★★COURTYARD BY MARRIOTT
*805 Russell Ave., Gaithersburg, 301-670-0008, 800-336-6880; www.marriott.com*
203 rooms. **$**

### ★★★HILTON GAITHERSBURG
*620 Perry Parkway, Gaithersburg, 301-977-8900, 800-445-8667; www.hilton.com*
Enjoy newly renovated guest rooms with pillow-top beds, wireless Internet access, dual-line telephone and updated furnishings. The staff is friendly and accommodating and the location just outside the Nation's Capital means sightseeing opportunities abound. 301 rooms. High-speed Internet access. Business center. Fitness room. Pets accepted. **$$**

### ★★HOLIDAY INN
*2 Montgomery Village Ave., Gaithersburg, 301-948-8900, 800-465-4329;*
*www.higaithersburg.com*
301 rooms. Wireless Internet access. Business center. **$**

### ★★★RESIDENCE INN BY MARRIOTT GAITHERSBURG WASHINGTONIAN CENTER
*9751 Washingtonian Blvd., Gaithersburg, 301-590-0044;*
*www.residenceinngaithersburg.com*
This hotel offers suites with full kitchens and a social hour Monday-Thursday. It is also conveniently located near happening restaurants, shops and a multiplex theater. 284 rooms. Wireless Internet access. Restaurant, bar. Business center. **$$**

## RESTAURANTS

### ★★GOLDEN BULL GRAND CAFÉ

*7 Dalamar St., Gaithersburg, 301-948-3666; www.golden-bull.com*

American menu. Lunch, dinner. Bar. Children's menu. Casual attire. Reservations recommended. $$

### ★★OLD SIAM

*108 E. Diamond Ave., Gaithersburg, 301-926-9199*

Thai menu. Lunch, dinner. Casual attire. $

### ★★PEKING CHEERS

*519 Quince Orchard Road, Gaithersburg, 301-216-2090*

Chinese menu. Lunch, dinner. Casual attire. Reservations recommended. $

### ★ROY'S PLACE

*2 E. Diamond Ave., Gaithersburg, 301-948-5548; www.roysplacerestaurant.com*

American menu. Lunch, dinner. Bar. Casual attire. Outdoor seating. $$

# GRANTSVILLE

*Information: Garrett County Chamber of Commerce, 15 Visitors Center Drive, McHenry, 301-387-4386; www.garrettchamber.com*

## WHAT TO SEE AND DO

### CASSELMAN RIVER BRIDGE STATE PARK

*349 Headquarters Lane, Grantsville, 301-895-5453; www.dnr.state.md.us/publiclands/western/casselman.html*

This single-span stone arch bridge over the Casselman River was built in 1813.

### NEW GERMANY STATE PARK

*349 Headquarters Lane, Grantsville, 301-895-5453, 888-432-2267; www.dnr.state.md.us/publiclands/western/newgermany.html*

A 13-acre lake built on the site of a once-prosperous milling center. Swimming, fishing, boating; nature, hiking trails, winter sports, picnicking, playground, concession, improved campsites, cabins (fee).

### SAVAGE RIVER STATE FOREST

*127 Headquarters Lane, Grantsville, 301-895-5759; www.dnr.state.md.us/publiclands/western/savageriver.html*

Largest of Maryland's state forests comprises about 52,800 acres of near wilderness. A strategic watershed area, the northern hardwood forest surrounds the Savage River Dam. Fishing, hunting, hiking trails, winter sports, primitive camping (permit required).

### SPRUCE FOREST ARTISAN VILLAGE

*177 Casselman Road, Grantsville, 301-895-3332; www.spruceforest.org*

Original log cabins and other historic buildings serve as studios for a potter, internationally recognized bird carver, weaver, spinner stained-glass maker and other artisans. Village. Monday-Saturday 10 a.m.-5 p.m. Special events (summer; fee). Restaurant.

**MARYLAND**

★
★
★
★
☆

## SPECIAL EVENT
### SPRUCE FOREST SUMMERFEST AND QUILT SHOW

*Spruce Forest Artisan Village, 177 Casselman Road, Grantsville, 301-895-3332;*
*www.spruceforest.org*

More than 200 quilts on display. Second full Thursday, Friday and Saturday weekend in July.

## RESTAURANT
### ★★PENN ALPS

*125 Casselman Road, Grantsville, 301-895-5985; www.pennalps.com*
Dutch menu. Breakfast, lunch, dinner, Sunday brunch. Children's menu. **$$**

# GREENBELT

## WHAT TO SEE AND DO
### NASA/GODDARD VISITOR CENTER

*Greenbelt, 301-286-3978; www.gsfc.nasa.gov/vc*
Satellites, rockets, capsules and exhibits in all phases of space research. Monday-Friday 9 a.m.-4 p.m.

## HOTELS
### ★★COURTYARD BY MARRIOTT

*6301 Golden Triangle Drive, Greenbelt, 301-441-3311, 800-321-2211;*
*www.marriott.com*
152 rooms. Pets not accepted. High-speed Internet access. **$**

### ★★★MARRIOTT GREENBELT

*6400 Ivy Lane, Greenbelt, 301-441-3700, 800-228-9290; www.marriott.com*
The close proximity to BWI airport and downtown Washington, D.C., along with laptop plug-in connections to flat-screen HDTVs, makes this a hotel ideal for business travelers. And the pillow-top beds guarantee that you'll be well rested for your morning meeting. 288 rooms. Children's activity center. High-speed Internet access. Unlimited local phone calls. **$$**

## RESTAURANT
### ★★SIRI'S CHEF'S SECRET

*5810 Greenbelt Road, Greenbelt, 301-345-6101; www.sirichef.com*
Thai menu. Lunch, dinner. Business casual attire. **$$**

# HAGERSTOWN

Visitors to Hagerstown might appear lost in thought, alternately staring at their shoes and turning their gaze to the heavens as they walk. But they're actually soaking in some history on the town's walking tour—points of interest are marked on downtown sidewalks and walking paths in city parks. South Prospect Street is one of the city's oldest neighborhoods, listed on the National Register of Historic Places. The tree-lined street is graced by homes dating back to the early 1800s.

*Information: Hagerstown/Washington County Tourism Office, 16 Public Square,*
*Hagerstown, 301-791-3246, 888-257-2600; www.marylandmemories.org*

## WHAT TO SEE AND DO

### HAGERSTOWN ROUNDHOUSE MUSEUM

*300 S. Burhans Blvd., Hagerstown, 301-739-4665; www.roundhouse.org*

Museum houses photographic exhibits of the seven railroads of Hagerstown; historic railroad memorabilia, tools and equipment; archives of maps, books, papers and related items. Gift shop. Friday-Sunday 1-5 p.m.

### JONATHAN HAGER HOUSE AND MUSEUM

*110 Key St., Hagerstown, 301-739-8393; www.fortedwards.org/cwffa/hager.htm*

Stone house in park setting; authentic 18th-century furnishings. April-December, Tuesday-Saturday 10 a.m.-4 p.m., Sunday 2-5 p.m.

### MILLER HOUSE

*135 W. Washington St., Hagerstown, 301-797-8782*

Washington County Historical Society Headquarters. Federal townhouse circa 1820; three-story spiral staircase, period furnishings, garden, clock, doll and Bell pottery collections; Chesapeake and Ohio Canal and Civil War exhibits; 19th-century country store display. April-December, Wednesday-Saturday 1-4 p.m., Sunday afternoons; closed first two weeks in December.

### WASHINGTON COUNTY MUSEUM OF FINE ARTS

*91 Key St., Hagerstown, 301-739-5727; www.wcmfa.org*

Paintings, sculpture, changing exhibits; concerts, lectures. Tuesday-Friday 9 a.m.-5 p.m., Saturday 9 a.m.-4 p.m., Sunday 1-5 p.m.; closed Monday.

## SPECIAL EVENTS

### ALSATIA MUMMERS HALLOWEEN PARADE FESTIVAL

*Hagerstown, 301-739-2044*

Ten thousand participants enter this downtown Hagerstown parade, which includes floats, bands, organizations and mummers. Saturday of weekend closest to Halloween.

### HAGERSTOWN RAILROAD HERITAGE DAYS

*Hagerstown Roundhouse Museum, 300 S. Burhans Blvd., Hagerstown, 301-739-4665; www.roundhouse.org*

Special events centered on the Roundhouse Museum. Mid-June.

### JONATHAN HAGER FRONTIER CRAFT DAY

*Jonathan Hager House and Museum, 110 Key St., Hagerstown, 301-739-8393; www.fortedwards.org/cwffa/hager.htm*

Colonial crafts, Bluegrass music, food. First weekend in August.

### LEITERSBURG PEACH FESTIVAL

*21378 Leiters Mill Road, Hagerstown*

Peach-related edibles, farmers market, bluegrass music. Second weekend in August.

**MARYLAND**

★
★
★
★

### WILLIAMSPORT C & O CANAL DAYS

*30 W. Potomac St., Hagerstown, 301-767-3714; www.candocanal.org*

Arts and crafts, Indian Village, National Park Service activities; food. Late August.

## HOTELS
### ★★CLARION HOTEL

*901 Dual Highway, Hagerstown, 301-733-5100, 877-424-6423; www.clarionhotels.com*

144 rooms. Airport transportation available. Free wireless Internet access. $

### ★★PLAZA HOTEL

*1718 Underpass Way, Hagerstown, 301-797-2500, 800-732-0906;*
*www.plazahotelhagerstown.com*

159 rooms. Airport transportation available. Fitness center. Wireless Internet access. $

# HAVRE DE GRACE

*Information: Chamber of Commerce, 450 Pennington Ave., Havre de Grace,*
*410-939-3303, 800-851-7756; www.hdgchamber.com*

## WHAT TO SEE AND DO
### CONCORD POINT LIGHTHOUSE

*At foot of Lafayette Street, Havre de Grace;*
*www.nps.gov/history/maritime/light/concord.htm*

Built of granite, considered the oldest continuously used lighthouse on the East Coast. It was automated in 1928. May-October, weekends and holidays only.

### DECOY MUSEUM

*215 Giles St., Havre de Grace, 410-939-3739; www.decoymuseum.com*

Adjacent to the blue waters of Chesapeake Bay is a museum dedicated to a sport the locals call waterfowling. The museum houses a large collection of working and decorative decoys used in the Chesapeake Bay area. It also offers workshops on creating effective decoys, honors some of the great decoy makers and hunters of the area and even hosts talks from those currently in the practice of decoy making. Daily 11 a.m.-4 p.m.

### SUSQUEHANNA STATE PARK

*4122 Wilkinson Road, Havre de Grace, 410-734-9035, 888-432-2267;*
*www.dnr.state.md.us/publiclands/central/susquehanna.html*

A 2,639-acre park. Fishing, boat launch; nature, riding and hiking trails; cross-country skiing, picnicking, camping. May-September; fee.

### STEPPINGSTONE MUSEUM

*461 Quaker Bottom Road, Havre de Grace, 410-939-2299, 888-419-1762;*
*www.steppingstonemuseum.org*

Self-guided tour of museum grounds includes sites of a once working Harford County farm; farmhouse is furnished as a turn-of-the-century country home; nearby shops and barn hold many displays and exhibits of the 1880-1920 period; demonstrations of rural arts and crafts of the period. Also here are blacksmith, woodworking, cooper and dairy shops. May-September, Saturday-Sunday 1-5 p.m. Special events held throughout the year.

## SPECIAL EVENTS

### DECOY & WILDLIFE ART FESTIVAL

*Decoy Museum, 215 Giles St., Havre de Grace, 410-939-3739;*
*www.decoymuseum.com*

Decoys on display, auction. Carving, gunning and calling contests. Refreshments.
Early May.

### FALL HARVEST FESTIVAL AND CRAFT SHOW

*Steppingstone Museum, 461 Quaker Bottom Road, Havre de Grace,*
*410-939-2299, 888-419-1762; www.steppingstonemuseum.org*

Features activities related to the harvest and preparation for winter: apple pressing,
scarecrow stuffing and other events. Entertainment. Last full weekend in September.

## SPECIALTY LODGING

### VANDIVER INN

*301 S. Union Ave., Havre de Grace, 410-939-5200, 800-245-1655;*
*www.vandiverinn.com*

This elegant Victorian mansion was built in 1886 and is listed on the National Historic
Register. Located just blocks from the Chesapeake Bay, charming antique stores and
numerous water activities, this inn offers a relaxing veranda and elegantly appointed
guest rooms. 17 rooms. Complimentary full breakfast. $

## RESTAURANT

### ★★BAYOU

*927 Pulaski Highway (Route 40), Havre de Grace, 410-939-3565;*
*www.bayourestaurant.net*

Seafood menu. Lunch, dinner. Closed Monday; also week of July 4. Children's menu.
Casual attire. $$

# HUNT VALLEY

## HOTEL

### ★★★MARRIOTT HUNT VALLEY INN

*245 Shawan Road, Hunt Valley, 410-785-7000; www.marriott.com*

Located on 18 acres of land 20 minutes north of Baltimore's Inner Harbor, this hotel
offers comfortable guest rooms with the amenities that business and leisure travelers
expect. Play a round of golf at one of the six nearby golf courses. For your business
needs, take advantage of Marriott's Wired for Business program that offers high-
speed Internet access and unlimited local and long distance calls for a low daily fee.
390 rooms. High-speed Internet access. Business center. Unlimited local phone calls.
Pets accepted. $$

## RESTAURANT

### ★★★THE OREGON GRILLE

*1201 Shawan Road, Hunt Valley, 410-771-0505; www.theoregongrille.com*

The Oregon Grille succeeds in differentiating itself from the fray by offering not only
a terrific selection of impeccably prepared steaks (all beef is dry-aged USDA Prime),

★
★
★
★

but also a creative selection of classic American cuisine, including free-range poultry, fresh seafood and vibrant first courses with regional ingredients. The restaurant, set in a renovated 19th-century stone farmhouse, has four fireplaces and is filled with deep, luxurious banquettes. American menu. Lunch, dinner, Sunday brunch. Bar. Jacket required. Reservations recommended. Outdoor seating. **$$$**

# LA PLATA

*Information: Charles County Chamber of Commerce, 6360 Crain Highway, La Plata, 301-932-6500 or the Department of Tourism, 301-645-0558; www.charlescountychamber.org*

## HOTEL

### ★BEST WESTERN LA PLATA INN

*6900 Crain Highway, Route 301, La Plata, 301-934-4900, 877-356-4900; www.bestwestern.com*

73 rooms. Complimentary continental breakfast. Fitness center. High-speed Internet access. Free parking. **$**

# LAUREL

*Information: Baltimore/Washington Corridor Chamber of Commerce, 312 Marshall Ave., Laurel, 301-725-4000; www.laurel.md.us*

## WHAT TO SEE AND DO

### MONTPELIER MANSION

*9650 Muirkirk Drive, Laurel, 301-377-7817; www.pgparks.com/places/eleganthistoric/montpelier_visitor.html*

Circa-1780 mansion built and owned for generations by Maryland's Snowden family; Georgian architecture. George Washington and Abigail Adams were among its early visitors. On the grounds are boxwood gardens, an 18th-century herb garden and a small summer house. Tours; purchase ticket in gift shop. March-November, Sunday-Thursday noon-3 p.m.; December-February, Sunday 1, 2 p.m.; weekday groups by appointment. Candlelight tours held in early December.

### NATIONAL WILDLIFE VISITOR CENTER

*10901 Scarlet Tanager Loop, Laurel, 301-497-5760; www.pwrc.usgs.gov*

A 12,750-acre national wildlife refuge and research area. Interactive exhibits focus on global environmental issues, migratory birds, wildlife habitats and endangered species. Tram tours available of surrounding forests and lakes (weather permitting; fee). Trails. Gift shop. Daily 9 a.m.-4:30 p.m.

## SPECIAL EVENT

### THOROUGHBRED RACING

*Laurel Race Course, Racetrack Road and Route 198, Laurel, 301-725-0400, 800-638-1859; www.laurelpark.com*

## HOTEL

### ★★RAMADA INN LAUREL

*3400 Fort Meade Road, Laurel, 301-498-0900; www.ramadalaurel.com*

166 rooms. Free newspaper. Free parking. Free airport shuttle. **$**

# LA VALE

## WHAT TO SEE AND DO

### TOLL GATE HOUSE

*Highway 40, La Vale, 301-777-5132; www.mdmountainside.com*

Built to collect tolls from users of Cumberland Road (National Road); only remaining toll house in the state; restored. Late May-late October, Saturday-Sunday 1:30-4:30 p.m.

## HOTELS

### ★★BEST WESTERN BRADDOCK MOTOR INN

*1268 National Highway, La Vale, 301-729-3300, 800-296-6006;*
*www.bestwesternbraddock.com*

100 rooms. Complimentary continental breakfast. Airport transportation available. High-speed Internet access. **$**

### ★SUPER 8

*1301 National Highway, La Vale, 301-729-6265, 800-800-8000; www.super8.com*

63 rooms. Complimentary continental breakfast. Free high-speed Internet access. Pets accepted. **$**

# LEONARDTOWN

*Information: St. Mary's County Division of Tourism, 23115 Leonard Hall Drive,*
*Leonardtown, 301-475-4411, 800-327-9023; www.co.saint-marys.md.us*

## WHAT TO SEE AND DO

### CALVERT MARINE MUSEUM

*14150 Solomons Island Road, Leonardtown, 410-326-2042;*
*www.calvertmarinemuseum.com*

Museum complex with exhibits relating to the culture and marine environment of Chesapeake Bay and Patuxent River estuary; fossils of marine life; estuarine biology displays, aquariums, touch-tank; maritime history exhibits, includes boat-building gallery. Also here is the restored Drum Point Lighthouse, built in 1883. Daily 10 a.m.-5 p.m.

### OLD JAIL MUSEUM

*11 Court House Drive, Leonardtown, 301-475-2467*

Local historical exhibits housed in an old jail; also a genealogy library for researchers. A cannon from Leonard Calvert's ship, the *Ark*, is mounted in front. Tuesday-Saturday 10 a.m.-4 p.m.; closed last week in December.

## SPECIAL EVENTS

### ST. MARY'S COUNTY FAIR

*County Fairgrounds, Route 5, Leonardtown, 301-475-2256*

Midway, seafood, horse shows. Late September.

### ST. MARY'S COUNTY OYSTER FESTIVAL

*County Fairgrounds, Route 5, Leonardtown, 301-863-5015; www.usoysterfest.com*

National oyster-shucking contest; oyster cook-off, seafood and crafts. Third weekend in October.

# MCHENRY

## SPECIAL EVENTS

### GARRETT COUNTY AGRICUTURAL FAIR

*Garrett County Fairgrounds, Route 219, McHenry, 301-533-1010;*
*www.garrettcountyfair.org*

Agricultural exhibits, animals, a 4-H sale and carnival are among the attractions at this county fair. Early August.

### MCHENRY HIGHLAND FESTIVAL

*Route 219, McHenry, 301-387-4200; www.highlandfest.info*

Deep Creek Lake in McHenry. Traditional Scottish and Celtic festival. First Saturday in June.

## RESTAURANT

### ★★POINT VIEW INN

*609 Deep Creek Drive, McHenry, 301-387-5555; www.pointviewinn.com*

American menu. Breakfast, lunch, dinner. Closed November-April. Bar. Casual attire. Outdoor seating. $$

# OAKLAND

*Information: Garrett County Chamber of Commerce, 200 S. Third St., Oakland,*
*301-387-4386; www.garrettchamber.com*

## WHAT TO SEE AND DO

### BACKBONE MOUNTAIN

Highest point in the state (3,360 feet).

★
★
★
★
★

### GARRETT STATE FOREST

*1431 Potomac Camp Road, Oakland, 301-334-2038;*
*www.dnr.state.md.us/publiclands/western/garrett.html*

Approximately 6,800 acres. The forest contains much wildlife. Fishing; hunting, hiking and riding trails, winter activities, primitive camping. Forestry demonstration area.

### HERRINGTON MANOR STATE PARK

*222 Herrington Manor Road, Oakland, 301-334-9180, 888-432-2267;*
*www.dnr.state.md.us/publiclands/western/herringtonmanor.html*

Well-developed 365-acre park with housekeeping cabins, 53-acre lake. Swimming, fishing, boating (launch, rentals); hiking trails, concession, picnicking, cross-country skiing (rentals). Interpretive programs (summer). Standard fees.

### SWALLOW FALLS STATE PARK

*222 Herrington Lane, Oakland, 301-387-6938, 888-432-2267;*
*www.dnr.state.md.us/publiclands/western/swallowfalls.html*

Surrounding 257 acres, the Youghiogheny River tumbles along the park's boundaries, passing through shaded rocky gorges and over sunny rapids. Muddy Creek produces a 52-foot waterfall. The last remaining stand of virgin hemlock dwarfs visitors. Fishing; nature trails, hiking, picnicking, improved campsites. Pets at registered campsites only. Standard fees.

### POTOMAC STATE FOREST

*1431 Potomac Camp Road, Oakland, 301-334-2038;*
*www.dnr.state.md.us/publiclands/western/potomacforest.html*

More than 10,685 acres for hiking, riding and hunting. Primitive camping. Timber is harvested regularly here. The area is important in the management of watershed and wildlife programs.

## SPECIAL EVENTS
### AUTUMN GLORY FESTIVAL

*Countywide, Oakland, 301-387-4386; www.garrettchamber.com*

Celebrates fall foliage. Features arts and crafts, five-string banjo contest, state fiddle contest, western Maryland tournament of bands, parades, antique show. Mid-October.

### WINTERFEST

*15 Visitors Center Drive, Oakland*

Deep Creek Lake in McHenry. Ski races, parade, fireworks. Late February or early March.

## SPECIALTY LODGING
### HALEY FARM BED AND BREAKFAST SPA & RETREAT CENTER

*16766 Garrett Highway, Oakland, 301-387-9050, 888-231-3276; www.haleyfarm.com*

Built in 1923; formerly a working farm; near Deep Creek Lake, Swallow Falls and five state parks. 10 rooms. Children over 12 years only. Complimentary full breakfast. $

# OCEAN CITY

Deep-sea fishing is highly regarded in Maryland's only Atlantic Ocean resort town. The white-sand beach, three-mile boardwalk, amusements, golf courses and boating draw thousands of visitors every summer.

*Information: Chamber of Commerce, 12320 Ocean Gateway, Ocean City,*
*410-213-0552; www.oceancity.org*

## SPECIAL EVENT
### FISHING CONTESTS AND TOURNAMENTS

*Ocean City, 410-213-0552*

Many held throughout the year. For exact dates contact the Chamber of Commerce.

**MARYLAND**

★
★
★
★
☆

## HOTELS

### ★BEST WESTERN OCEAN CITY HOTEL & SUITES

*5501 Coastal Highway, Ocean City, 443-664-4001; www.bestwestern.com*

72 rooms. Complimentary breakfast. High-speed Internet access. Free parking. **$$**

### ★★CLARION RESORT FOUNTAINEBLEAU HOTEL

*10100 Coastal Highway, Ocean City, 410-524-3535, 877-424-6423;*
*www.clarioninn.com*

250 rooms. Airport transportation available. Free wireless Internet access. Free weekday newspaper. **$$**

### ★COMFORT INN

*507 Atlantic Ave., Ocean City, 410-289-5155, 800-228-5150;*
*www.comfortinnboardwalk.com*

84 rooms. Closed December-February. Complimentary continental breakfast. Free deluxe continental breakfast. Free wireless Internet access. **$$**

### ★★HOLIDAY INN

*6600 Coastal Highway, Ocean City, 410-524-1600, 800-315-2621;*
*www.holiday-inn.com*

216 rooms. Children's activity center. Beach. **$$**

### ★★PRINCESS ROYALE OCEAN FRONT RESORT

*9100 Coastal Highway, Ocean City, 410-524-7777, 800-476-9253;*
*www.princessroyale.com*

310 rooms. Swimming beach, ocean deck, private boardwalk. Free parking. **$**

### ★★QUALITY INN

*5400 Coastal Highway, Ocean City, 410-524-7200, 877-424-6423;*
*www.choicehotels.com*

130 rooms. Swimming beach. Free local calls. **$**

## SPECIALTY LODGING

### THE LIGHTHOUSE CLUB HOTEL

*56th St. in the Bay, Ocean City, 410-524-5400, 888-371-5400; www.fagers.com*

Located on the Isle of Wight Bay at Fager's Island, this three-story octagonal hotel offers elegant, beachy accommodations with spectacular views of waterfowl in flight and sunsets over the natural wetlands. 23 rooms. Complimentary continental breakfast. **$$**

## RESTAURANTS

### ★★BONFIRE

*71st St., Ocean City, 410-524-7171; www.thebonfirerestaurant.com*

American menu. Dinner. Closed Monday-Thursday in winter. Bar. Children's menu. **$$**

### ★★EMBERS

*2305 Philadelphia Ave., Ocean City, 410-289-3322; www.embers.com*

American menu. Dinner. Closed December-February. Bar. Children's menu. **$$**

### ★★★FAGER'S ISLAND
*201 60th St., Ocean City, 410-524-5500; www.fagers.com*
The outdoor deck overlooking the bay is the perfect spot to take in a glorious summer sunset. The menu does well with standard and creative seafood preparations as well as classics like prime rib. Choose from a wine list that features over 500 bottles to accompany your meal. Pacific-Rim/Pan-Asian, seafood menu. Lunch, dinner, brunch. Bar. $$

### ★★HARRISON'S HARBOR WATCH
*806 S. Boardwalk, Ocean City, 410-289-5121; www.ocmdhotels.com*
Seafood menu. Dinner. Closed Monday-Thursday December-March. Bar. Children's menu. $$

### ★★★HOBBIT
*101 81st St., Ocean City, 410-524-8100*
This restaurant serves many of your old favorites, as well as creative new items. The crab cakes are outstanding. After dinner, browse through the unique gift shop for Hobbit memorabilia. American, seafood menu. Lunch, dinner. Bar. Children's menu. $$

### ★MARINA DECK RESTAURANT
*306 Dorchester St., Ocean City, 410-289-4411; www.marinadeckrestaurant.com*
Seafood, steak menu. Breakfast, lunch, dinner. Closed mid-November-mid-March. Bar. Children's menu. Casual attire. Outdoor seating. $

### ★★OCEAN CLUB
*49th St., Ocean City, 410-524-7500*
Seafood menu. Breakfast, lunch, dinner. Closed Monday-Tuesday off-season; mid January-February. Bar. Children's menu. $$

### ★★PHILLIPS CRAB HOUSE
*2004 Philadelphia Ave., Ocean City, 410-289-6821; www.phillipsoc.com*
Seafood menu. Lunch, dinner. Closed November-March. Bar. Children's menu. $$

### ★★PHILLIPS SEAFOOD HOUSE
*14101 Coastal Highway, Ocean City, 410-250-1200, 800-799-2788;*
*www.phillipscrabhouse.com*
Seafood menu. Lunch, dinner. Closed late November-late February. Bar. Children's menu. $$

# OWINGS MILLS

## WHAT TO SEE AND DO
### MPT (MARYLAND PUBLIC TELEVISION)
*11767 Owings Mills Blvd., Owings Mills, 410-356-5600, 800-223-3678; www.mpt.org*
Tours of the state's television network studios. By appointment.

### SOLDIERS DELIGHT NATURAL ENVIRONMENT AREA

*5100 Deer Park Road, Owings Mills, 410-461-5005;*
*www.dnr.state.md.us/publiclands/central/soldiers.html*

This 1,725-acre park has 19th-century chrome mines; restored log cabin, scenic overlook, hiking and nature trails, picnicking (at visitor center only). It is the only undisturbed Barren Serpentine in the state. Pets must be on leash. Visitor center: Wednesday-Sunday 9 a.m.-4 p.m.

### RESTAURANT

#### ★★★LINWOOD'S

*25 Crossroads Drive, Owings Mills, 410-356-3030; www.linwoods.com*

This sophisticated, clubbish restaurant is one of Baltimore's most popular and for good reason. The dining room is formal but not stuffy and the menu is inventive and enticing. Dishes have included honey-lavender grouper with porcini and leek risotto and grilled asparagus; grilled black Angus steak with truffle-infused pommes frites, jumbo asparagus and black pepper steak sauce; and grilled veal chop with caramelized peaches, buttered spinach and potato Ann. American menu. Lunch, dinner. Bar. Business casual attire. Reservations recommended. Outdoor seating. **$$$**

# POTOMAC

### RESTAURANTS

#### ★★★NORMANDIE FARM

*10710 Falls Road, Potomac, 301-983-8838; www.popovers.com*

Normandie Farm is reminiscent of a country home, serving entrées such as fresh soft-shell crab with bacon, scallions, pine nuts and citrus beurre blanc or tenderloin tips with mushrooms, sun-dried tomatoes and cabernet sauce. The atmosphere is relaxed and welcoming. French, seafood menu. Lunch, dinner, brunch. Closed Monday. Bar. **$$**

#### ★★★OLD ANGLER'S INN

*10801 MacArthur Blvd., Potomac, 301-299-9097; www.oldanglersinn.com*

Located in a Tudor-style house built in 1860, the rustic dining room is a perfect spot for a cozy evening. In winter get a table near the fireplace. In summer the terrace provides a lovely setting. New Point oysters are always on the menu and the wild Chesapeake rockfish with corn salad is delicious. Seafood menu. Lunch, dinner. Closed Monday. Bar. Outdoor seating. **$$**

# ROCKVILLE

Located at the northern edge of D.C., Rockville is the second-largest city in Maryland. The Great Falls of the Potomac are nine miles south off Highway 189. Stone locks and levels are still visible from the Chesapeake & Ohio Canal, which was built to circumvent the falls. St. Mary's Cemetery holds the graves of F. Scott and Zelda Fitzgerald.

*Information: Chamber of Commerce, 250 Hungerford Drive, Rockville,*
*301-424-9300; www.rockvillechamber.org*

## WHAT TO SEE AND DO

### BEALL-DAWSON HOUSE

*103 W. Montgomery Ave., Rockville, 301-762-1492; www.rockvillemd.gov*
Federal architecture; period furnishings, library; museum shop, 19th-century doctor's office. Tours guided by docents. Tuesday-Saturday noon-4 p.m.

### CABIN JOHN REGIONAL PARK

*7700 Tuckerman Lane, Rockville, 301-299-0024; www.mcparkandplanning.org*
This 551-acre park has playgrounds, miniature train ride, nature center; concerts (summer evenings; free); tennis courts, game fields, ice rink, nature trails and picnicking. Fee for some activities. Daily.

## SPECIAL EVENT

### HOMETOWN HOLIDAYS

*Rockville, 301-424-9300; www.rockvillechamber.org*
Family entertainment; carnival rides and games, arts and crafts, music, food, skate park. Memorial Day weekend.

## HOTELS

### ★★COURTYARD BY MARRIOTT

*2500 Research Blvd., Rockville, 301-670-6700; www.courtyard.com*
147 rooms. High-speed Internet access. $

### ★CROWNE PLAZA

*3 Research Court, Rockville, 301-840-0200, 800-496-7621; www.crowneplaza.com*
124 rooms. Complimentary full breakfast. High-speed Internet access. Fitness center. $

### ★★HILTON EXECUTIVE MEETING CENTER

*1750 Rockville Pike, Rockville, 301-468-1100, 800-445-8661; www.hilton.com*
315 rooms. High-speed Internet access. Business center. $$

## RESTAURANTS

### ★A AND J

*1319-C Rockville Pike, Rockville, 301-251-7878*
Chinese menu. Lunch, dinner. Casual attire. $

### ★★ADDIE'S

*11120 Rockville Pike, Rockville, 301-881-0081; www.addiesrestaurant.com*
American menu. Lunch, dinner, brunch. Closed Sunday. Bar. Children's menu. Outdoor seating. $$

### ★★BOMBAY BISTRO

*98 W. Montgomery Ave., Rockville, 301-762-8798; www.bombaybistro.com*
Indian, vegetarian menu. Lunch, dinner. Closed Labor Day. $$

MARYLAND

★
★
★
★
★

### ★★COPELAND'S OF NEW ORLEANS

*10200 Wincopin Circle, Columbia, 301-230-0968; www.copelandsofneworleans.com*
Cajun/Creole, seafood menu. Lunch, dinner. Bar. Children's menu. $

### ★HARD TIMES CAFÉ

*1117 Nelson St., Rockville, 301-294-9720; www.hardtimes.com*
American menu. Lunch, dinner. Bar. Children's menu. $

### ★★IL PIZZICO

*15209 Frederick Road, Rockville, 301-309-0610; www.ilpizzico.com*
Italian menu. Lunch, dinner. Closed Sunday. Bar. $

### ★RED HOT & BLUE

*16811 Crabbs Branch Way, Rockville, 301-948-7333; www.redhotandblue.com*
American menu. Lunch, dinner. Bar. Children's menu. Outdoor seating. $$

### ★SEVEN SEAS

*1776 E. Jefferson St., Rockville, 301-770-5020; www.sevenseasrestaurant.com*
Chinese, Japanese menu. Lunch, dinner. Bar. $$

### ★SILVER DINER

*11806 Rockville Pike, Rockville, 301-770-0333; www.silverdiner.com*
American menu. Breakfast, lunch, dinner. Children's menu. $

### ★★TARA ASIA

*199D E. Montgomery Ave., Rockville, 301-315-8008*
Pan-Asian menu. Lunch, dinner. Bar. Casual attire. Outdoor seating. $$

### ★★TASTE OF SAIGON

*20 A Maryland Ave., Rockville, 301-424-7222*
Vietnamese menu. Lunch, dinner. Bar. Outdoor seating. $$

### ★★THAT'S AMORE

*15201 Shady Grove Road, Rockville, 240-268-0681; www.thatsamore.com*
Italian menu. Lunch, dinner. Bar. $$

# SALISBURY

"Central City of the Eastern Shore" and of the Delmarva Peninsula, Salisbury has a marina on the Wicomico River providing access to Chesapeake Bay. It lies within 30 miles of duck hunting and deep-sea fishing.
*Information: Wicomico County Convention & Visitors Bureau, 8480 Ocean Highway, Delmar, 410-548-4914, 800-332-8687.*
*Information is also available from the Chamber of Commerce, 144 E. Main St., 410-749-0144; www.salisburyarea.com*

MARYLAND

## WHAT TO SEE AND DO

### POPLAR HILL MANSION

*117 Elizabeth St., Salisbury, 410-749-1776; www.poplarhillmansion.org*

Example of Georgian- and Federal-style architecture; Palladian and bull's-eye windows, large brass box locks on doors, woodwork, mantels and fireplaces. Period furniture; country garden. First and third Sunday of the month 1-4 p.m.; Tuesday-Saturday by appointment. Admission is free on Sunday.

### SALISBURY ZOOLOGICAL PARK

*755 S. Park Drive, Salisbury, 410-548-3188; www.salisburyzoo.org*

Natural habitats for almost 400 mammals, birds and reptiles. Major exhibits include bears, monkeys, jaguars, bison, waterfowl. Also exotic plants. Memorial Day-Labor Day, daily 8 a.m.-7:30 p.m.; rest of year, daily 8 a.m.-4:30 p.m.

### WARD MUSEUM OF WILDFOWL ART

*909 S. Schumaker Drive, Salisbury, 410-742-4988; www.wardmuseum.org*

Displays include the history of decoy and wildfowl carving in North America; wildfowl habitats; contemporary wildfowl art. Changing exhibits. Gift shop. Monday-Saturday 10 a.m.-5 p.m., Sunday noon-5 p.m.

## HOTELS

### ★COMFORT INN

*2701 N. Salisbury Blvd., Salisbury, 410-543-4666, 800-638-7949; www.choicehotels.com*

96 rooms. Complimentary continental breakfast. Free wireless Internet access. **$**

### ★★RAMADA INN

*300 S. Salisbury Blvd., Salisbury, 410-546-4400; www.ramada.com*

156 rooms. Airport transportation available. Business center. High-speed Internet access. Pets accepted. **$**

# SEVERNA PARK

## RESTAURANT

### ★★★CAFÉ BRETTON

*849 Baltimore-Annapolis Blvd., Severna Park, 410-647-8222*

Whether or not you like French cooking, the amicable waitstaff, appealing atmosphere and classically prepared dishes will win you over. If the Chilean sea bass is on the menu, order it. Also be sure to try a glass of wine from the extensive (though affordable) wine list. French menu. Dinner. Closed Sunday-Monday. Bar. Reservations recommended. **$$$**

# SILVER SPRING

*Information: Chamber of Commerce, 8601 Georgia Ave., Silver Spring, 301-565-3777; www.gsscc.org*

★
★
★
★
★

## RESTAURANTS
### ★★BLAIR MANSION INN
*7711 Eastern Ave., Silver Spring, 301-588-1688; www.blairmansion.com*
American menu. Lunch, dinner. Closed Monday. Bar. 1890s Victorian mansion; gaslight chandelier, seven fireplaces. Murder mystery dinners. Thursday-Sunday. **$$**

### ★★MRS. K'S TOLL HOUSE
*9201 Colesville Road, Silver Spring, 301-589-3500; www.mrsks.com*
American menu. Lunch, dinner, Sunday brunch. Closed Monday. Children's menu. Business casual attire. Reservations recommended. Outdoor seating. **$$**

### ★VICINO`
*959 Sligo Ave., Silver Spring, 301-588-3372; www.mealstoyou.com*
Italian menu. Lunch, dinner. Children's menu. Outdoor seating. **$$**

# SNOW HILL

## WHAT TO SEE AND DO
### NASSAWANGO IRON FURNACE
*Pocomoke Forest, Old Furnace Road, Snow Hill, 410-632-2032*
One of the oldest industrial sites in Maryland and one of the earliest hot blast mechanisms still intact. The stack was restored in 1966; archaeological excavations were made and a canal, dike and a portion of the old waterwheel used in the manufacturing process were found. The remains of the area are undergoing restoration. April-October, daily 11 a.m.-5 p.m.

### FURNACE TOWN
*Pocomoke Forest, 3816 Old Furnace Road, Snow Hill, 410-632-3732;*
*www.dnr.state.md.us/publiclands/eastern/pocomokeforest.html*
This 1840s industrial village occupies 22 acres and includes six historic structures, a working 19th-century blacksmith shop, a museum and company store and archaeological excavations. Nature trail and picnic area. Special events take place throughout the season. Same hours and fees as Nassawango Iron Furnace.

## SPECIALTY LODGING
### RIVER HOUSE INN
*201 E. Market St., Snow Hill, 410-632-2722; www.riverhouseinn.com*
Eight rooms. This inn was built in 1860. **$**

# SPARKS

## RESTAURANT
### ★★★THE MILTON INN
*14833 York Road, Sparks, 410-771-4366; www.miltoninn.com*
This old stone house has been restored for use as a country inn that serves exceptional food in an authentic colonial atmosphere. Candle-lit to up the romantic ambience, this cozy spot serves tasty dishes including roast Hudson Valley duck and cinnamon-crusted

Atlantic salmon. American menu. Lunch, dinner. Closed Saturday. Bar. Children's menu. Business casual attire. Reservations recommended. Outdoor seating. $$$

# ST. MARY'S CITY

Under the leadership of Leonard Calvert, Maryland's first colonists bought a Native American village on this site upon their arrival in the New World. The settlement was the capital and hub of the area until 1694, when the colonial capital was moved to Annapolis, and the town gradually disappeared. The city and county are still rich in historical attractions.

*Information: St. Mary's County Division of Tourism, 23115 Leonard Hall Drive,*
*Leonardtown, 301-475-4411, 800-327-9023; www.co.saint-marys.md.us*

## WHAT TO SEE AND DO
### HISTORIC ST. MARY'S CITY
*Route 5 and Rosecroft Road, St. Mary's City, 240-895-4990, 800-762-1634;*
*www.stmaryscity.org*
Outdoor museum at site of Maryland's first capital includes reconstructed State House replica of the original capitol building; other exhibits include the "Maryland Dove," replica of a 17th-century ship and archaeological exhibits. Also a 17th-century tobacco plantation, reconstructed 17th-century inn; visitor center, outdoor café. Call or visit the Web site for hours.

### MARGARET BRENT MEMORIAL
*Trinity Churchyard, 18751 Hogaboom Lane, St. Mary's City*
Gazebo overlooking the river; memorial to the woman who, being a wealthy landowner, requested the right to vote in the Maryland Assembly in 1648 to settle Leonard Calvert's affairs after his death.

### LEONARD CALVERT MONUMENT
*Trinity Churchyard, 18751 Hogaboom Lane, St. Mary's City*
Monument to Maryland's first colonial governor.

### POINT LOOKOUT STATE PARK
*St. Mary's City, 301-872-5688, 888-432-2267;*
*www.dnr.state.md.us/publiclands/southern/pointlookout.html*
Site of Confederate Monument, the only memorial erected by U.S. government to honor P.O.W.s who died in Point Lookout Prison Camp during Civil War (3,384 died here). Swimming, fishing, boating; hiking, picnicking, improved camping. April-October; self-contained camping units year-round. Nature center. Civil War museum. Standard fees. May-September, weekends.

## SPECIAL EVENTS
### CRAB FESTIVAL
*41348 Medley's Neck Road, St. Mary's City; www.crabfestival.org*
Steamed crabs, and other dishes. Arts and crafts, antique and classic car show. First Sunday in June.

**MARYLAND**

★
★
★
★
☆

**MARYLAND DAYS**

*38370 Point Breeze Road, St. Mary's City*

Boat rides, seafood, 17th-century militia musters. Third weekend in March.

# ST. MICHAELS

Chartered in 1804, Saint Michaels now offers visitors an abundance of shops, marinas, restaurants, bed and breakfasts and country inns, as well as many Federal- and Victorian-period buildings.

*Information: Talbot County Chamber of Commerce, Easton Plaza Suite 53, Easton, 410-822-4653; www.talbotchamber.org*

## WHAT TO SEE AND DO

### CHESAPEAKE BAY MARITIME MUSEUM

*Mill Street and Navy Point, St. Michaels, 410-745-2916; www.cbmm.org*

This waterside museum consists of nine buildings and includes a historic lighthouse, floating exhibits, boat-building shop with working exhibit, ship models, small boats and more. Daily 9 a.m.-5 p.m.

### THE FOOTBRIDGE

*109 S. Talbot St., St. Michaels*

Joins Navy Point to Cherry St. Only remaining bridge of three that once connected the town with areas across the harbor.

### THE PATRIOT

*Chesapeake Bay Museum Dock, St. Michaels, 410-745-3100; www.patriotcruises.com*

A one-hour narrated cruise on Miles River. Four trips daily at 11 a.m., 12:30 p.m., 2:30 p.m., 4 p.m. April-October.

### ST. MARY'S SQUARE

This public square was laid out in 1770 by Englishman James Braddock. Several buildings date to the early 1800s, including the Cannonball House and Dr. Miller's Farmhouse. The Ship's Carpenter Bell was cast in 1842; across from the bell stand two cannons, one dating from the Revolution, the other from the War of 1812.

### ST. MARY'S SQUARE MUSEUM

*409 St. Mary's Square, St. Michaels, 410-745-9561*

Mid-19th-century home of "half-timber" construction; one of the earliest buildings in St. Michaels. Exhibits of historical and local interest. Early May-late October, Saturday-Sunday 10 a.m.-4 p.m.; also by appointment. Inquire about the town walk-ing tour brochures.

## SPECIAL EVENT

### MID-ATLANTIC MARITIME FESTIVAL

*Chesapeake Bay Maritime Museum, Mill Street at Navy Point, St. Michaels, 410-745-2916; www.cbmm.org*

Nautical celebration with fly-fishing demonstration, skipjack races, boat building contest, boat parade, seafood festival cooking contest. Three days in mid-May.

## HOTELS
### ★★HARBOURTOWNE GOLF RESORT & CONFERENCE CENTER
*Route 33 and Martingham Drive, St. Michaels, 410-745-9066, 800-446-9066; www.harbourtowne.com*
111 rooms. Complimentary full breakfast. Golf. **$$**

### ★★★INN AT PERRY CABIN
*308 Watkins Lane, St. Michaels, 410-745-2200, 866-278-9601; www.perrycabin.com*
Built just after the War of 1812, the Inn at Perry Cabin looks and feels like a gracious manor house, with mahogany sleigh beds, antiques and views of the Miles River. Cycling, golfing and sailing are popular pastimes. The inn offers high tea and scones with Devonshire cream and shortbread served at evening turndown. 81 rooms. Children over 10 only. Spa. **$$$**

### ★★★ST. MICHAELS HARBOUR INN, MARINA & SPA
*101 N. Harbor Road, St. Michaels, 410-745-9001, 800-955-9001; www.harbourinn.com*
From this waterfront resort, visitors can take a short stroll down the main road to shops, museums and historical sites. Rooms are spacious and many have Jacuzzi tubs and panoramic views of the harbor. The onsite spa offers relaxing treatments after a day of activity around the bay. 46 rooms. Restaurant. Spa. **$$$**

## SPECIALTY LODGINGS
### PARSONAGE INN
*210 N. Talbot, St. Michaels, 410-745-5519, 800-394-5519; www.parsonage-inn.com*
Restored in 1985, this inn is located just steps from the Maritime Museum, restaurants and shops. Guests are welcome to borrow the inn's bicycles to explore the historic area. 8 rooms. Complimentary full breakfast. **$$**

### WADE'S POINT INN
*Wades Point Road, St. Michaels, 410-745-2500, 888-923-3466; www.wadespoint.com*
This bed and breakfast is located just outside historic St. Michaels. It is situated on 120 acres of fields, woodlands and a half mile of coastline overlooking Chesapeake Bay. 24 rooms. Closed mid-December-mid-March. Complimentary continental breakfast. **$$**

## RESTAURANTS
### ★★★208 TALBOT
*208 N. Talbot St., St. Michaels, 410-745-3838; www.208talbot.com*
Chef Brendan Keegan puts a sophisticated, soulful twist on local ingredients, serving entrées including cornflake-crusted fried mahi mahi with basil potato salad, sweet corn cream and grape tomato relish; and braised pork shoulder with peach chutney, a corn tamale and salsa roja. The atmosphere is as upscale and sophisticated at the cuisine, with rich décor accents and a knowledgeable waitstaff. **$$$**

### ★★BISTRO ST. MICHAELS
*403 S. Talbot St., St. Michaels, 410-745-9111; www.bistrostmichaels.com*
French bistro menu. Dinner. Closed Tuesday-Wednesday; February. Bar. Casual attire. Outdoor seating. **$$$**

### ★★CHESAPEAKE LANDING SEAFOOD

*23713 St. Michael's Road, St. Michaels, 410-745-9600*
Seafood menu. Lunch, dinner. Children's menu. Casual attire. **$$**

### ★★★SHERWOOD'S LANDING

*308 Watkin Lane, St. Michaels, 410-745-2200, 866-278-9601; www.perrycabin.com*
Located in the Inn at Perry Cabin, Sherwood Landing serves continental selections made with regional ingredients such as crab spring rolls with pink grapefruit, avocado and toasted almonds; and honey- and tarragon-glazed lamb shank with sun-dried tomato sauce. American menu. Breakfast, lunch, dinner. Bar. Children's menu. Valet parking. Outdoor seating. **$$$**

### ★★SHORE RESTAURANT & LOUNGE

*101 N. Harbor Road, St. Michaels, 410-924-4769; www.shorerestaurant.net*
American, International menu. Breakfast, lunch, dinner, Sunday brunch. Bar. Business casual attire. Outdoor seating. **$$$**

### ★ST. MICHAELS CRAB HOUSE

*305 Mulberry St., St. Michaels, 410-745-3737; www.stmichaelscrabhouse.com*
Seafood menu. Lunch, dinner. Closed Wednesday; mid-December-March. Bar. Children's menu. Casual attire. Outdoor seating. **$$**

# SWANTON

## WHAT TO SEE AND DO
### DEEP CREEK LAKE STATE PARK

*898 State Park Road, Swanton, 301-387-4111, 888-432-2267;*
*www.dnr.state.md.gov/publiclands/western/deepcreeklake.html*
Approximately 1,800 acres with 3,900-acre man-made lake. Swimming, bathhouse, fishing, hiking trails, picnicking, playground, concession, improved campsites.

## SPECIALTY LODGING
### CARMEL COVE BED AND BREAKFAST

*105 Monastery Way, Oakland, 301-387-0067; www.carmelcoveinn.com*
This bed and breakfast was once a monastery and now offers fine accommodations surrounded by beautiful mountains and the clear lake. 10 rooms. Children over 12 only. Complimentary full breakfast. Whirlpool. Built in 1945. **$$**

# TANEYTOWN

## SPECIALTY LODGING
### ANTRIM 1844

*30 Trevanion Road, Taneytown, 410-756-6812, 800-858-1844; www.antrim1844.com*
This country inn is located on 23 acres in the Catoctin Mountains. Guest rooms and suites are decorated with antiques. 27 rooms. Complimentary full breakfast. Spa. **$$**

## RESTAURANT
### ★★★ANTRIM 1844
*30 Trevanion Road, Taneytown, 410-756-6812, 800-858-1844; www.antrim1844.com*

The Paris-trained chef at Antrim 1844 serves a unique menu each night, with entrées such as filet mignon with bacon and walnut, braised lamb volcano or porcupine shrimp. On a nice night, there isn't a better seat than on the spacious verandah overlooking the formal gardens. American, French menu. Breakfast, dinner. Bar. Business casual attire. Reservations recommended. Outdoor seating. $$$$

# THURMONT
*Information: Tourism Council of Frederick County, 19 E. Church St., Frederick, 301-228-2888, 800-999-3613; www.visitfrrederick.org*

## WHAT TO SEE AND DO
### CATOCTIN MOUNTAIN NATIONAL PARK
*Park Central Road, Thurmont, 301-663-9388; www.nps.gov/cato*

Located one hour outside Baltimore, this 5,810-acre forest is an easily accessible nature retreat. The park is adjacent to two state parks and Camp David, the weekend mountain home of the U.S. president. The park offers camping, picnicking areas, fishing and playgrounds. Park: Open year-round during daylight hours. Visitor center: Monday-Thursday 10 a.m.-4:30 p.m., Friday 10 a.m.-5 p.m., Saturday-Sunday 8:30 a.m.-5 p.m.

### CUNNINGHAM FALLS STATE PARK
*14039 Catoctin Hollow Road, Thurmont, 301-271-7574, 888-432-2267;*
*www.dnr.state.md.us/publiclands/western/CunninghamFalls.html*

This state park encompasses 4,950 acres in the Catoctin Mountains. Two recreation areas: Houck, five miles west of town, has swimming, fishing, boating (rentals); picnicking, camping, hiking trails that lead to 78-foot falls and scenic overlooks. Manor Area, three miles south of town on Route 15, has picnicking, camping, playground. Trout fishing in Big Hunting Creek. Ruins of Iron Masters Mansion and the industrial village that surrounded it are also here.

## SPECIAL EVENTS
### CATOCTIN COLORFEST
*6602 Foxville Road, Thurmont, 301-271-4432; www.colorfest.org*

Fall foliage; arts and crafts show. Second weekend in October.

### MAPLE SYRUP DEMONSTRATION
*Cunningham Falls State Park, 14039 Catoctin Hollow Road, Thurmont,301-271-7574;*
*www.dnr.state.md.us/publiclands/western/cunninghamfalls.html*

Tree tapping, sap boiling; carriage rides; food; children's storytelling corner. Usually second and third weekends in March.

## HOTEL
### ★★COZY COUNTRY INN THURMONT
*103 Frederick Road, Thurmont, 301-271-4301; www.cozyvillage.com*

21 rooms. Complimentary continental breakfast. Restaurant, bar. Children's activity center. $

**MARYLAND**

★
★
★
★
★

# TILGHMAN ISLAND

## SPECIALTY LODGINGS

### CHESAPEAKE WOOD DUCK INN

*21490 Gibsontown Road at Dogwood Harbor, Tilghman Island,*
*410-886-2070, 800-956-2070; www.woodduckinn.com*

This waterfront, Victorian-style bed and breakfast was first used as a boarding house but has since been remodeled to provide comfortable and intimate lodging for guests. Seven rooms. Children over 14 years permitted. Complimentary full breakfast. **$$**

### LAZYJACK INN

*5907 Tilghman Island Road, Tilghman Island, 410-886-2215, 800-690-5080;*
*www.lazyjackinn.com*

Four rooms. Children over 12 years only. Complimentary full breakfast. **$$**

## RESTAURANTS

### ★★BAY HUNDRED RESTAURANT

*6178 Tilghman Island Road, Tilghman, 410-886-2126; www.bayhundredrestaurant.net*

Seafood menu. Lunch, dinner, brunch. Children's menu. Outdoor seating. **$$**

### ★★THE BRIDGE

*6136 Tilghman Island Road, Tilghman Island, 410-886-2330;*
*www.bridge-restaurant.com*

American menu. Lunch, dinner. Bar. Children's menu. Casual attire. Reservations recommended. Outdoor seating. **$$**

# TIMONIUM

## SPECIAL EVENT

### MARYLAND STATE FAIR

*Maryland Fairgrounds, 2100 York Road, Timonium, 410-252-0200;*
*www.marylandstatefair.com*

Ten-day festival of home arts; entertainment, midway; agricultural demonstrations, Thoroughbred horse racing, livestock presentations. Late August-early September.

## RESTAURANT

### ★★LIBERATORE'S

*9515 Derreco Road, Timonium, 410-561-3300; www.liberatores.com*

Italian menu. Dinner. Bar. Business casual attire. Reservations recommended. Outdoor seating. **$$**

# TOWSON

*Information: Baltimore County Chamber of Commerce, 102 W. Pennsylvania Ave.,*
*Towson, 410-825-6200*

## WHAT TO SEE AND DO
### HAMPTON NATIONAL HISTORIC SITE
*535 Hampton Lane, Towson, 410-823-1309; www.nps.gov/hamp*
Includes tours of ornate Georgian mansion circa 1790, formal gardens and plantation outbuildings. Gift shop. Grounds: daily 9 a.m.-5 p.m. Mansion tours: daily on the hour, 9 a.m.-4 p.m. Tea room open for lunch. Daily; closed six weeks mid-January-early March.

### TOWSON STATE UNIVERSITY
*8000 York Road, Towson, 410-704-2000; www.towson.edu*
On campus are three art galleries, including Holtzman Art Gallery, with an extensive collection of art media. September-May, Tuesday-Saturday. Concerts and sporting events are held in the Towson Center.

## SPECIAL EVENT
### MARYLAND HOUSE AND GARDEN PILGRIMAGE
*1105-A Providence Road, Towson, 410-821-6933; www.mhgp.org*
More than 100 homes and gardens throughout the state are open. Late April-early May.

## HOTEL
### ★★★SHERATON BALTIMORE NORTH
*903 Dulaney Valley Road, Towson, 410-321-7400, 800-423-7619;*
*www.sheratonbaltimore.com*
It doesn't get much more convenient than this. Locatd near the Towson business district, Baltimore's Inner Harbor, Camden Yard and the Timonium Fairgrounds, the hotel has endless entertainment options. The guest rooms are roomy and the heated indoor pool provides a built-in playground for the family. 282 rooms. $$

## RESTAURANT
### ★★CAFÉ TROIA
*28 W. Allegheny Ave., Towson, 410-337-0133; www.cafetroia.com*
Italian menu. Lunch, dinner. Closed Sunday. Bar. Casual attire. Reservations recommended. Outdoor seating. $$

# UPPER MARLBORO

## WHAT TO SEE AND DO
### MARLTON GOLF CLUB
*9413 Midland Turn, Upper Marlboro, 301-856-7566; www.marltongolf.com*
Marlton is a very narrow course that like many others in the area requires the ability to play a number of different types of shots. Some holes require arrow-straight drives, some fly over large expanses of water to medium-sized greens and some make approaching the green impossible from one side of the fairway. However, for the challenge, the price is cheap: $24 for 18 holes on weekdays.

MARYLAND

★
★
★
★
★

# WALDORF

*Information: Tourism Director, La Plata, 301-645-0558, 800-766-3386;*
*www.explorecharlescomd.com*

## WHAT TO SEE AND DO

### DR. SAMUEL A. MUDD HOUSE MUSEUM

*3725 Drive Samuel Mudd Road, Waldorf, 301-645-6870*

Where Dr. Mudd set John Wilkes Booth's broken leg, unaware that Booth had just shot the president. Mudd was convicted and imprisoned for life, but pardoned four years later by President Andrew Johnson. Tours conducted by costumed docents, some of whom are Dr. Mudd's descendants. April-November, Saturday-Sunday, Wednesday 11 a.m.-4 p.m.; last tour at 3:30 p.m.

### FARMERS MARKET AND AUCTION

*29890 Three Notch Road, Waldorf, 301-884-3108*

Nearby Amish farms offer fresh baked goods and produce (auction Wednesday) for sale; more than 90 shops. Antique dealers. Wednesday and Saturday.

## SPECIAL EVENT

### JOHN WILKES BOOTH ESCAPE ROUTE TOUR

*Surrat House and Tavern, 9118 Brandywine Road, Waldorf, 301-868-1121;*
*www.surratt.org/su_bert.html*

Daylong bus tour of Booth's route from Ford's Theatre, Washington, through southern Maryland to site of Garrett's farm, Virginia, with expert commentary. Select dates in April, May, September and October.

## HOTEL

### ★★HOLIDAY INN

*45 St. Patrick's Drive, Waldorf, 301-645-8200, 800-645-8277;*
*waldorfmd.holiday-inn.com*

191 rooms. High-speed Internet access. **$**

# WESTMINSTER

Westminster, a Union supply depot at the Battle of Gettysburg, saw scattered action before the battle. It was the first town in the United States to offer complete rural free delivery mail service (started in 1899 with four two-horse wagons).

## HOTEL

### ★BEST WESTERN WESTMINSTER CATERING & CONFERENCE CENTER

*451 WMC Drive, Westminster, 410-857-1900, 800-780-7234;*
*www.bestwesternwestminster.com*

102 rooms. Complimentary continental breakfast. High-speed Internet access. **$**

## RESTAURANT

### ★★JOHANSSON'S DINING HOUSE

*4 W. Main St., Westminster, 410-876-0101; www.johanssonsdininghouse.com*

American menu. Lunch, dinner. Bar. Children's menu. Business casual attire. **$$**

★
★
★
★
★

# NEW JERSEY

FROM INDUSTRIAL CITIES TO LUSH TREE-SHADED, 18TH-CENTURY TOWNS TO SMALL SEASIDE communities, New Jersey is a state of contrasts. Hard-working areas such as Newark and Elizabeth might lead the unacquainted visitor to believe that the Garden State is a misnomer, but traveling deeper into New Jersey—out of the cities and off the highways—will reveal the flourishing greenery that earned the state its nickname.

The swampy meadows west of the New Jersey Turnpike have been reclaimed and transformed into commercial and industrial areas. The Meadowlands, a multimillion-dollar sports complex, offers horse racing, the New York Giants and the New York Jets NFL football teams, the New Jersey Devils NHL hockey team and the New Jersey Nets NBA basketball team. But commercial and industrial interests have reached only so far into the state's natural resources. More than 800 lakes and ponds, 100 rivers and streams and 1,400 miles of freshly stocked trout streams are scattered throughout the state's wooded, scenic northwest corner. The coastline, stretching 127 miles from Sandy Hook to Cape May, offers excellent swimming and ocean fishing.

New Jersey is also rich in history. George Washington spent a quarter of his time as commander-in-chief of the Revolutionary Army here. On Christmas night in 1776, he crossed the Delaware and surprised the Hessians at Trenton. A few days later, he marched to Princeton and defeated three British regiments. He then spent the winter in Morristown, where the memories of his campaign are preserved in a national historical park.

*Information: www.state.nj.us/travel*

## ALLAIRE STATE PARK

Allaire State Park has more than 3,000 acres and offers a fishing pond for children under 14; multiuse trails, picnic facilities, playground, camping (summer) and the opportunity to visit a historic 19th-century village. Park (daily).

*Information: 732-938-2371; www.state.nj.us/dep/parksandforests/parks/allaire.html*

### WHAT TO SEE AND DO
#### HISTORIC ALLAIRE VILLAGE
*524 Allaire Road, Farmingdale, 732-915-3500; www.allairevillage.org*

In 1822, James Allaire bought this site as a source of bog ore for his ironworks. The furnace also produced items such as hollowware pots and kettles, stoves, sadirons and pipes for New York City's waterworks. Today, visitors can explore the bakery, general store, blacksmith and carpentry shops, worker's houses, the community church and other buildings still much as they were in 1836. Village grounds and center (daily 10 a.m.-4 p.m.); village buildings (Memorial Day-Labor Day, 10 a.m.-5 p.m.; Labor Day-November, Saturday-Sunday 8 a.m.-8 p.m.); special events (February-December).

### TRAIN RIDES

*Historic Allaire Village, Allaire State Road, Farmingdale, 732-915-3500*
Narrow-gauge steam and diesel locomotive rides. April-mid-October, daily.

# ASBURY PARK

This popular shore resort was bought in 1871 by New York brush manufacturer James
A. Bradley and named for Francis Asbury, first American Bishop of the Methodist
Episcopal Church. Bradley established a town for temperance advocates and good
neighbors. The beach and the three lakes proved so attractive that by 1874, Asbury
Park had grown into a borough, and by 1897, a city. It is the home of the famous
boardwalk, Convention Hall and the Paramount Theatre. In September 1934, the *SS
Morro Castle* was grounded off this beach and burned with a loss of 122 lives. Asbury
Park became the birthplace of a favorite sweet when a local confectioner introduced
saltwater taffy. Today, this is a popular resort area for swimming and fishing.
*Information: Greater Asbury Park Chamber of Commerce, 1420 Asbury Ave.,*
*Asbury Park, 732-897-0010; www.asburyparkchamber.com*

## WHAT TO SEE AND DO
### STEPHEN CRANE HOUSE

*508 Fourth Ave., Asbury Park, 732-775-5682*
Early home of the author of *The Red Badge of Courage* contains photos, drawings and
other artifacts. Tours by appointment.

### THE STONE PONY

*913 Ocean Ave., Asbury Park, 732-502-0600; www.stoneponyonline.com*
This legendary nightclub is known for unexpected visits from Bruce Springsteen and
others. Includes the Asbury Park Gallery, with a collection of photographs and other
memorabilia. Daily.

## SPECIAL EVENTS
### HORSE RACING

*Monmouth Park, 175 Oceanport Ave., Oceanport, 732-222-5100;*
*www.monmouthpark.com*
Thoroughbred racing. Memorial Day-Labor Day, Daily.

### JAZZ FEST

*1 Municipal Plaza, Asbury Park, 732-775-7676*
Late June.

### METRO LYRIC OPERA SERIES

*Paramount Theatre, Asbury Park, 732-720-9200; www.mlonj.com*
At the Paramount Theatre on the Boardwalk. Saturday evenings, July-August.

### OCEAN GROVE HOUSE TOUR

*54 Pitman Ave., Ocean Grove, 732-775-0035; www.oceangrove.org*
Tour of Victorian cottages. July.

★
★
★
★
★

## RESTAURANT

### ★★MOONSTRUCK

*517 Lake Ave., Asbury Park, 732-988-0123; www.moonstrucknj.com*

Italian, Mediterranean menu. Dinner. Closed Monday-Tuesday, also January-mid-February. Outdoor seating. $$

# ATLANTIC CITY

Honeymooners, conventioneers, Miss America and some 37 million annual visitors have made Atlantic City the best-known New Jersey beach resort. Built on Absecon Island, the curve of the coast shields it from battering northeastern storms while the nearby Gulf Stream warms its waters, helping to make it a year-round resort. A 60-foot-wide boardwalk extends along five miles of beaches. Hand-pushed wicker rolling chairs take visitors up and down the Boardwalk. Absecon Lighthouse ("Old Ab"), a well-known landmark, was first lit in 1857 and now stands in an uptown city park.

*Information: Atlantic City Convention & Visitors Authority, 2314 Pacific Ave.,*
*Atlantic City, 609-348-7100, 888-262-7892, 800-228-4748; www.atlanticcitynj.com*

## WHAT TO SEE AND DO

### ABSECON LIGHTHOUSE

*31 S. Rhode Island Ave., Atlantic City, 609-449-1360; www.abseconlighthouse.org*

Climb the 228 steps to the top of this 1857 lighthouse, designed by Civil War general George Gordon Meade. Tallest lighthouse in New Jersey, third-tallest in the

## THE AMUSEMENTS OF THE JERSEY SHORE

Pennsylvania Route 40 leads to the Jersey Shore, Atlantic City, Ocean City and historic Cape May. Atlantic City offers fun activities for everyone. Children love Lucy the Margate Elephant, a six-story, elephant-shaped building with an observation deck on her back, and Storybook Land, with its rides, animals, playground and more than 50 storybook buildings. Older children will enjoy the *Ripley's Believe It or Not* Museum. And adults will have a great time exploring the Renault Winery, Noyes Museum and Smithville's specialty shops and restaurants. Travelers can also visit one of the many recreation areas or amusement piers along the coast, as well as the Marine Mammal Stranding Center and Museum, the Edwin B. Forsythe National Wildlife Refuge and the casinos.

Head south from Atlantic City to Ocean City, a popular family resort with eight miles of beaches. Walk along the boardwalk. Take a ride to the top of the 140-foot Ferris wheel, or take a turn at the video arcades, roller coasters and water slides. Stop for a snack at one of the outdoor cafes or fill up on ice cream and cotton candy.

Cape May, the nation's oldest seaside resort, is at New Jersey's southernmost tip. Explore historic Cold Spring Village, a restored 1870 farm village with craft shops and demonstrations. Take the ferry across Delaware Bay, or take a guided walking tour of the historic district or a one-hour Ocean Walk tour of the area's beaches and marine life. Approximately 125 miles.

United States. July-August, daily 10 a.m.-5 p.m.; September-June, Thursday-Monday 11 a.m.-4 p.m.

### ATLANTIC CITY BOARDWALK HALL

*2301 Boardwalk, Atlantic City, 609-348-7000, 800-736-1420; www.boardwalkhall.com*
Seats 13,800; special events, concerts, boxing, ice shows, sports events; site of the annual Miss America Pageant.

### EDWIN B. FORSYTHE NATIONAL WILDLIFE REFUGE, BRIGANTINE DIVISION

*Box 72, Great Creek Road, Oceanville, 609-652-1665; www.forsythe.fws.gov*
Wildlife drive; interpretive nature trails (daily). Over the years, more than 200 species of birds have been observed at this 45,000-acre refuge. Public-use area has an eight-mile wildlife drive through diversified wetlands and uplands habitat; most popular in the spring and fall, during the course of the waterbird migration and at sunset, when the birds roost for the evening. Refuge headquarters. Weekdays 10 a.m.-3 p.m.

### FISHING

Surf and deep-sea fishing. License may be required, check locally. Charter boats (March-November). Many tournaments are scheduled.

### GARDEN PIER

*Boardwalk and New Jersey Avenue, Atlantic City, 609-347-5837; www.acmuseum.org*
The Atlantic City Art Center and Atlantic City Historical Museum are located here. Daily 10 a.m.-4 p.m.

### HISTORIC GARDNER'S BASIN

*800 New Hampshire Ave., Atlantic City, 609-348-2880; www.gardnersbasin.com*
An eight-acre, sea-oriented park featuring working lobstermen; Ocean Life Center, eight tanks totaling 29,800 gallons of aquariums, exhibiting more than 100 varieties of fish and marine animals, 10 exhibits featuring themes on the marine and maritime environment. Picnicking. Daily 10 a.m.-5 p.m.

★
★
★
★
★

## SPECIAL EVENTS

### ATLANTIC CITY MARATHON

*2181, Ventnor City, New Jersey, 609-822-6911; www.atlanticcitymarathon.org*
Mid-October.

### MISS AMERICA PAGEANT

*Atlantic City Boardwalk Hall, 2301 Boardwalk, Atlantic City, 609-449-2064;*
*www.missamerica.com*
Usually first or second weekend after Labor Day.

### SHOPRITE LPGA ATLANTIC CITY CLASSIC

*Seaview Marriott Resort & Spa, 401 S. New York Road, Galloway Township,*
*609-652-1800; www.seaviewmarriott.com*
Late June.

## HOTELS

### ★★★BALLY'S PARK PLACE CASINO RESORT

*Park Place and Boardwalk, Atlantic City, 609-340-2000, 800-225-5977;*
*www.ballysac.com*

A geometric glass chandelier twinkles overhead at the entrance to this large, classic Boardwalk casino. There are several dining options to choose from, including some that fit into the Wild West theme of the hotel's annex casino. 1,246 rooms. Spa. Casino. Whirlpools. Outdoor deck. Daily. $$

### ★★★BORGATA CASINO HOTEL AND SPA

*1 Borgata Way, Atlantic City, 609-317-1000, 866-638-6748; www.theborgata.com*

The Borgata Hotel Casino and Spa is a stylish resort, where the rooms and suites are luxurious havens from the traditional casino style, with cool earth tones, contemporary furnishings and advanced in-room technology. The hotel's five restaurants include Wolfgang Puck's American Grille and Bobby Flay Steak. Those who may not succeed at the blackjack tables find themselves lucky to be ensconced in the confines of Spa Toccare, where a wide variety of relaxing treatments melt tension away, or in the hotel's several high-end boutiques. 2,000 rooms. Spa. Casino. $$$

### ★★★CAESARS ATLANTIC CITY HOTEL CASINO

*2100 Pacific Ave., Atlantic City, 609-348-4411, 800-223-7277; www.caesarsac.com*

This oceanfront hotel, dubbed "Rome on the Jersey shore," houses 26,000 square feet of meeting space and a nicely appointed business center. Enjoy an international dish at the hotel's Chinese, Japanese and American restaurants, Roman-themed eateries, casual restaurants and lounges. 1,144 rooms. Spa. Beach. Casino. Reservations recommended. $$

### ★HAMPTON INN

*7079 Black Horse Pike, West Atlantic City, 609-484-1900, 800-426-7866;*
*www.hamptoninn.com*

144 rooms. Complimentary continental breakfast. Pets not accepted. $

### ★★★HILTON CASINO RESORT

*Boston and the Boardwalk, Atlantic City, 609-340-7235, 800-257-8677;*
*www.hiltonac.com*

The Hilton Casino Resort offers convenient access to everything in the area, though the luxurious hotel might lure guests inside. Onsite offerings include a 9,000-square-foot pool, full-service health spa, 60,000-square-foot casino with poker room and Asian gaming room, an assortment of fine dining restaurants and an entertainment venue. 804 rooms. Spa. Beach. Casino. Reservations recommended. $$

### ★★★RESORTS ATLANTIC CITY

*1133 Boardwalk, Atlantic City, 609-344-6000, 800-336-6378; www.resortsac.com*

Opened in 1978, Resorts Atlantic City offered the first casino in the area. The hotel's charmingly beachy 480-room Ocean Tower offers views of and convenient access to the boardwalk, and the newly renovated Rendezvous Tower boasts the largest guest rooms in Atlantic City. 412 rooms. Whirlpool. Airport transportation available. Casino. High-speed Internet access. Pool. $$

★
★
★
★
☆

### ★★★SHERATON ATLANTIC CITY CONVENTION CENTER HOTEL

*2 Miss America Way, Atlantic City, 609-344-3535, 800-325-3535; www.sheraton.com*

This tower hotel with Art Deco accents is near Atlantic City's boardwalk as well as designer outlet shops. Guests will appreciate the Sheraton's signature "Sweet Sleeper Bed" (also available for man's best friend) and in-room movies and games, while business travelers will be able to work in comfort with oversized desks, ergonomic chairs and an in-room fax/copier/printer. During the summer, in-room massages and poolside massages are available. Dogs up to 80 pounds are welcome and receive treats and bowls. 502 rooms. $$

### ★★★TRUMP PLAZA HOTEL & CASINO

*The Boardwalk and Mississippi Avenue, Atlantic City, 609-441-6000, 800-677-7378; www.trumpplaza.com*

When you've had enough casino excitement and want to unwind, head to the hotel's health spa, where you can relax in the sauna or Jacuzzi, indulge in a massage, body scrub or wrap, or take in a workout in the well-equipped fitness center. 904 rooms. Spa. Casino. Reservations recommended. $$

### ★★★TRUMP TAJ MAHAL CASINO RESORT

*1000 Boardwalk, Atlantic City, 609-449-1000, 800-825-8888; www.trumptaj.com*

This opulent property boasts a 4,500-square-foot suite named for Alexander the Great that features its own steam room, sauna, weight room, lounge and pantry. And rooms for the guests who aren't rolling in riches are impressive enough to make them feel like millionaires. 1,250 rooms. Spa. Casino. Reservations recommended. $$

## RESTAURANTS

### ★★★BRIGHTON STEAKHOUSE

*Indiana Avenue at Brighton Park, Atlantic City, 609-441-4259*

This classic steak house in the Sands Casino Hotel offers thick cuts of steak, veal and lamb as well as fresh seafood and poultry dishes. Escape into the warm, rose-colored décor to unwind from the casino's hectic pace. Steak menu. Dinner. Closed Tuesday-Wednesday. Bar. Business casual attire. Reservations recommended. Valet parking. $$$

### ★★CHEF VOLA'S

*111 S. Albion Place, Atlantic City, 609-345-2022; www.chefvolas.com*

Italian, American menu. Dinner. Closed Monday. Casual attire. Reservations recommended. $$$

### ★★DOCK'S OYSTER HOUSE

*2405 Atlantic Ave., Atlantic City, 609-345-0092; www.docksoysterhouse.com*

Seafood menu. Dinner. Bar. Business casual attire. Reservations recommended. $$$

### ★IRISH PUB AND INN

*164 St. James Place and Boardwalk, Atlantic City, 609-344-9063; www.theirishpub.com*

American, Irish menu. Lunch, dinner, late-night. Bar. Casual attire. Outdoor seating. $

### ★★OLD WATERWAY INN

*1660 W. Riverside Drive, Atlantic City, 609-347-1793*

Seafood menu. Dinner. Closed Monday-Tuesday; open only on weekends January-February. Bar. Children's menu. Casual attire. Reservations recommended. Outdoor seating. **$$**

### ★SCANNICCHIO'S

*119 S. California Ave., Atlantic City, 609-348-6378; www.epictrip.com*

American, Italian menu. Dinner. Bar. Casual attire. Reservations recommended. **$$**

### ★★★SEABLUE BY MICHAEL MINA

*1 Borgata Way, Atlantic City, 609-317-1000, 866-692-6742; www.theborgata.com*

Fresh fish options are grilled over mesquite wood in a tandoor oven. The eight-page menu includes a page for guests to design their own salads—crayons are placed on the table for filling in the blanks—and dessert consists of three different items, always with one ice cream or sherbet. Seafood menu. Dinner. Bar. Business casual attire. Reservations recommended. Valet parking. Casino. **$$$**

### ★★★SPECCHIO

*1 Borgata Way, Atlantic City, 609-317-1000, 866-692-6742; www.theborgata.com*

Specchio, at the Borgata Casino Hotel and Spa, features contemporary design with an eye-catching Dale Chihuly glass sculpture suspended from the ceiling. The menu offers Italian cooking with a modern twist. Fish and meat figure largely in the offerings, while pasta and risotto dishes are always crowd-pleasers. Many antipasti and entrée selections have a suggested wine pairing. Italian menu. Dinner, late-night. Closed Wednesday in July-September, Sunday-Monday in October-June. Business casual attire. Reservations recommended. Valet parking. Casino. **$$$**

## SPA

### ★★★SPA TOCCARE

*1 Borgata Way, Atlantic City, 609-317-7555, 866-692-6742; www.theborgata.com*

Facials use bilberry for sensitive skin and rainforest propolis for hydration. A special treatment menu for men offers unique baths, massages therapies and facials created for their needs. Casino. Indoor pool.

# AVALON

## HOTELS

### ★★AVALON GOLDEN INN HOTEL & CONFERENCE CENTER

*78th Street and the oceanfront, Avalon, 609-368-5155; www.goldeninn.com*

154 rooms. Children's activity center. Beach. **$**

### ★★DESERT SAND RESORT COMPLEX

*7888 Dune Drive, Avalon, 609-368-5133, 800-458-6008; www.desertsand.com*

90 rooms. Closed November-mid-April. Wireless Internet access. Indoor and outdoor Pools. **$**

**NEW JERSEY**

★
★
★
★
★

## RESTAURANTS

### ★ANTONIO'S PIZZERIA & THE CATALINA CABARET

*230 Crescent Ave., Avalon, 310-510-0008; www.catalinahotspots.com*

Italian menu. Breakfast, lunch, dinner. Bar. Casual attire. Outdoor seating. $$

### ★★MIRAGE

*7888 Dune Drive, Avalon, 609-368-1919; www.desertsand.com*

Continental menu. Breakfast, dinner. Closed November-March. Bar. Children's menu. Casual attire. Reservations recommended. Friday-Monday from 8 a.m. $$

# BATSTO

The Batsto Iron Works, established in 1766, made munitions for the Revolutionary Army from the bog iron ore found nearby. Its furnaces shut down for the last time in 1848. Eighteen years later, Joseph Wharton, whose immense estate totaled nearly 100,000 acres, bought the land. In 1954, the state of New Jersey bought nearly 150 square miles of land in this area, including the entire Wharton tract, for a state forest.

## WHAT TO SEE AND DO

### ATSION RECREATION AREA

*744 Highway 206, Batsto, 609-268-0444*

Swimming, canoeing; picnicking, camping.

### WHARTON STATE FOREST

*31 Batsto Road, Hammonton, 609-561-0024;*
*www.state.nj.us/dep/parksandforests/parks/wharton.html*

Streams wind through 110,000 acres of wilderness. Swimming, fishing, canoeing; limited picnicking, tent and trailer sites, cabins. Standard fees. Also here is hunting, boating.

# BEACH HAVEN

## SPECIAL EVENT

### SURFLIGHT THEATRE

*Beach and Engleside avenues, Beach Haven, 609-492-9477; www.surflight.org*

Broadway musicals nightly. Children's theater, Wednesday-Saturday 6 p.m. May-mid-October.

## HOTEL

### ★★THE ENGLESIDE INN

*30 E. Engleside Ave., Beach Haven, 609-492-1251, 800-762-2214; www.engleside.com*

72 rooms. Beach. Pets accepted. $$

## RESTAURANT

### ★ROBERTO'S DOLCE VITA

*12907 Long Beach Blvd., Beach Haven Terrace, 609-492-1001*

Italian menu. Dinner. Casual attire. Reservations recommended. $$

★
★
★
★
★

# BEAR MOUNTAIN

## WHAT TO SEE AND DO
### PALISADES INTERSTATE PARKS
*Bear Mountain, 914-786-2701; www.gorp.away.com*

This 81,008-acre system of conservation and recreation areas extends along the west side of the Hudson River from the George Washington Bridge at Fort Lee, N.J., to Saugerties, N.Y. The main unit is the 51,680-acre tract of Bear Mountain and Harriman state parks. Included in the system are 17 parks and six historic sites. Bear Mountain (5,067 acres) extends westward from the Hudson River opposite Peekskill. Only 45 miles from New York City via the Palisades Interstate Parkway, this is a popular recreation area, with all-year facilities mainly for one-day visits. Bear Mountain has picnic areas, hiking trails, a swimming pool with bathhouse, boating on Hessian Lake, fishing and an artificial ice rink. Perkins Memorial Drive goes to the top of Bear Mountain, where there is a picnic area and a sightseeing tower. Near the site of Fort Clinton, just west of Bear Mountain Bridge, is Trailside Museums and Wildlife Center, with native animals and exhibit buildings (daily; 845-786-2701). Harriman (46,613 acres), southwest of Bear Mountain, consists of wilder country. Fishing, boating, scenic drives, lakes, bathing beaches at Lakes Tiorati, Welch and Sebago; tent camping at Lake Welch, and cabins (primarily for family groups) at Lake Sebago. The Silver Mine Area, four miles west of Bear Mountain, has fishing, boating and picnicking. Charges for parking and for most activities vary.

# BERNARDSVILLE

## HOTEL
### ★★★BERNARDS INN
*27 Mine Brook Road, Bernardsville, 908-766-0002, 888-766-0002; www.bernardsinn.com*

This historic property is a favored retreat for locals looking for a night out. Guest rooms are individually decorated with antiques and reproductions. The restaurant serves sophisticated American food in an upscale, clubby setting. 20 rooms. Complimentary full breakfast. Reservations recommended. $$

## RESTAURANT
### ★★★THE BERNARDS INN
*27 Mine Brook Road, Bernardsville, 908-766-0002, 888-766-0002; www.bernardsinn.com*

This traditional dining room features chef Edward Stone's creative contemporary American menu—along with an 8,000-bottle wine cellar—in a rustic, intimate setting that's just a short drive from New York City. American menu. Lunch, dinner. Closed Sunday. Bar. Business casual attire. Reservations recommended. Valet parking. Outdoor seating. Complimentary wireless Internet access. $$$

# BORDENTOWN

Bordentown was once a busy shipping center and a key stop on the Delaware and Raritan Canal. In January 1778, Bordentown citizens filled numerous kegs with gunpowder and sent them down the Delaware River to Philadelphia hoping to blow

**NEW JERSEY**

★
★
★
★

up the British fleet stationed there. But the plan was discovered, and British troops intercepted the kegs and discharged them. In 1816, Joseph Bonaparte, exiled king of Spain and brother of Napoleon, bought 1,500 acres and settled here.

*Information: Historical Society Visitors Center, 302 Farnsworth Ave., Bordentown, 609-298-1740; www.bordentownhistory.org*

## WHAT TO SEE AND DO
### CLARA BARTON SCHOOLHOUSE
*100 Crosswicks St., Bordentown, 609-298-0676; www.bordentown.k12.nj.us*
This building was in use as a school in Revolutionary days. In 1851, Clara Barton, founder of the American Red Cross, established one of the first free public schools in the country here. By appointment.

# BRIDGETON
Bridgeton has been recognized as New Jersey's largest historic district, with more than 2,200 registered historical landmarks. There are many styles of architecture here, some of which date back nearly 300 years.

*Information: Bridgeton-Cumberland Tourist Association, 50 E. Broad St., Bridgeton, 856-451-4802, 800-319-3379*

## WHAT TO SEE AND DO
### CITY PARK
*Mayor Aitken Drive, Bridgeton, 856-455-3230*
A 1,100-acre wooded area with swimming (protected beaches, Memorial Day-Labor Day), fishing, boating (floating dock), canoeing. Picnic grounds, recreation center; zoo. Daily.

### GEORGE J. WOODRUFF MUSEUM OF INDIAN ARTIFACTS
*Bridgeton Public Library, 150 E. Commerce St., Bridgeton, 856-451-2620; www.bridgetonlibrary.org*
Approximately 20,000 local Native American artifacts, some up to 10,000 years old; clay pots, pipes, implements. September-May, Monday-Saturday 1-4 p.m.; June-August, Saturday 11 a.m.-2 p.m.; rest of year, by appointment.

### NEW SWEDEN FARMSTEAD MUSEUM
*City Park, Mayor Aitken Drive, Bridgeton, 856-455-9785; www.cityofbridgeton.com*
Reconstruction of the first permanent European settlement in Delaware Valley. Seven log buildings including smokehouse/sauna, horse barn, cow and goat barn, threshing barn; blacksmith shop; family residence with period furnishings. Costumed guides. May-Labor Day, Saturday 11 a.m.-5 p.m., Sunday noon-5 p.m.; rest of year, by appointment.

### OLD BROAD STREET CHURCH
*West Broad Street and West Avenue, Bridgeton*
(1792) Outstanding example of Georgian architecture, with Palladian window, high-backed wooden pews, wine glass pulpit, brick-paved aisles and brass lamps that once held whale oil.

# BURLINGTON

In 1774, like New York, Philadelphia and Boston, Burlington was a thriving port. A Quaker settlement, it was one of the first to provide public education. A 1682 Act of Assembly gave Matinicunk (now Burlington) Island in the Delaware River to the town with the stipulation that the revenue it generated would be used for public schools; that act is still upheld. Burlington was the capital of West Jersey; the legislature met here and in the East Jersey capital of Perth Amboy from 1681 until after the Revolution. In 1776, the Provincial Congress adopted the state constitution here.

*Information: Burlington County Chamber of Commerce,100 Technology Way,*
*Mount Laurel, 856-439-2520; www.bccoc.com*

## WHAT TO SEE AND DO

### BURLINGTON COUNTY HISTORICAL SOCIETY

*451 High St., Burlington, 609-386-4773; www.tourburlington.org*
The society maintains D. B. Pugh Library. Also includes Revolutionary War exhibit; James Fenimore Cooper House (circa 1780), birthplace of the famous author; Bard-How House (circa 1740) with period furnishings; Captain James Lawrence House, birthplace of the commander of the *Chesapeake* during the War of 1812 and speaker of the immortal words "Don't give up the ship." Tours: Tuesday-Saturday 1-5 p.m.; tours leave every 50 minutes.

### FRIENDS MEETING HOUSE

*340 High St., Burlington, 609-387-3875; www.pym.org*
The 1784 house is now a regional conference center for Southeastern Pennsylvania/ New Jersey Quakers operated by the Philadelphia Yearly Meeting. By appointment.

### HISTORIC TOURS

*Foot of High Street, Burlington, 609-386-3993; www.tourburlington.org*
Guided walking tours of 33 historic sites (1685-1829), eight of which are open to the public. Daily.

### OLD ST. MARY'S CHURCH

*145 W. Broad St., Burlington, 609-386-0902; www.stmarysburlington.org*
The oldest Episcopal Church building (1703) in the state. By appointment.

### THOMAS REVELL HOUSE

*213 Wood St., Burlington, 609-386-3993; www.tourburlington.org*
The oldest building (1685) in Burlington County. Included in Burlington County Historical Society home tour. By appointment and during Wood Street Fair.

## SPECIAL EVENT

### WOOD STREET FAIR

*609-386-0200; www.woodstreetfair.com*
Recreation of colonial fair; crafts, antique exhibits; food, entertainment. First Saturday after Labor Day 9 a.m.-4 p.m. Pets not accepted.

**NEW JERSEY**

★
★
★
★
★

## PHILADELPHIA AND WESTERN NEW JERSEY

This drive meanders up New Jersey's western border, following the scenic Delaware River from the greater Philadelphia area through the timberlands of Delaware Water Gap National Recreation Area.

From Philadelphia, follow Route 130 to Route 73 N. Turn left and then right onto County Route 543. The drive becomes leisurely, following local roads through the small towns of Palmyra, Riverton and Riverside. It merges with Route 130, a major thoroughfare just south of Burlington. In Burlington, go south onto High Street and into the historic district, which dates back to 1677. (Ben Franklin learned the printing trade here.) The Burlington Center offers walking tours (609-298-1740), and the Burlington County Historical Society is at 457 High Street. Tours are also offered of the James Fenimore Cooper House. The town offers several fine restaurants.

Leave Burlington northbound on County Route 656, bringing you back to Route 130. Take 130 N. into Trenton, the state capital and home of the Old Barracks Museum, the State House, the Contemporary Victorian Museum, the War Memorial Theater and the New Jersey State Museum and Planetarium. Leave Trenton on NJ 29 N. Near the junction of Interstate 95 (I-95) stands the New Jersey State Police Museum, and soon after Titusville, Washington Crossing State Park. Washington's crossing of the Delaware is reenacted here every Christmas Day. The park also offers walking paths, river views, picnic areas and historical information. Also in Titusville is the Howell Living History Farm at 101 Hunter Road, a circa-1900 horse-powered farm where visitors join in field, barn and craft programs on weekends.

Continue on NJ 29 northbound into Lambertville, a well-maintained town with many Federal-style and Victorian buildings, antiques shops, bed and breakfasts and access to the Delaware & Raritan Canal State Park. NJ 29 continues north along the river. The Stockton Inn on Main Street in Stockton offers nice accommodations. The Prallsville Mills at Delaware & Raritan Canal State Park consists of nine structures from 1796. The Bull's Island Recreation Area offers 30 miles of hiking trails and great bird-watching. In Frenchtown, Hunterdon House and the Guesthouse at Frenchtown Brown's Old Homestead are two fine bed and breakfasts, and Poor Richard's Winery offers tours and tastings.

In Frenchtown, go left on Ridge Street, then right on Harrison Street, which becomes Millford-Frenchtown Road and eventually Frenchtown Road, leading into Milford, home to the Ship Inn, New Jersey's first brewpub. Follow County Route 627 out of Milford. In Holland Township, the Vollendam Windmill Museum shows its operational gristmill and replica windmills on summer weekends. In Mount Joy, Route 627 veers inland. Follow it to the merge with Route 173, bearing right, then to the junction of I-78 (exit 6). Take I-78 westbound to exit 4, and follow County Route 687 towards Lower Harmony, switching to County Route 519 northbound in Harmony. Follow Route 519 to Belvidere and visit Four Sisters Winery at Matarazzo Farms, which not only produces nice wines, but also has an excellent bakery and stages special events. The Pequest River Book Company, which stocks local historical books and has an art gallery and café, is also in town.

★
★
★
★
★

Continue on Route 519 N. until it meets US 46/I-80 at Columbia. Follow I-80 westbound to exit 1 and stop to visit the Delaware Water Gap National Recreation Area, with its swimming, fishing, camping, cross-country skiing and other outdoor activities. The Kittatinny Ranger Station offers an audio-visual program and displays, and rangers present impromptu "Terrace Talks" on weekends. Make the trip to Millbrook Village, located about 12 miles north of I-80 along Old Mine Road, a 19th-century settlement in an ongoing process of restoration. Approximately 115 miles.

## RESTAURANT

### ★★★CAFÉ GALLERY

*219 High St., Burlington, 609-386-6150; www.cafegalleryburlington.com*

Local artwork adorns the walls and large windows offer views of the Delaware River and the brick terrace. The well-landscaped outdoor terrace is set with umbrella-topped tables and a large fountain. The creative menu includes options such as roast Long Island duckling with orange and cognac sauce, braised pork loin in champagne with baked apples and pineapple, and sautéed rainbow trout on crust with almond butter sauce. Continental, French menu. Lunch, dinner, Sunday brunch. Bar. Children's menu. Business casual attire. Reservations recommended. Outdoor seating. $$

# CALDWELL

## WHAT TO SEE AND DO

### GROVER CLEVELAND BIRTHPLACE STATE HISTORIC SITE

*207 Bloomfield Ave., Caldwell, 973-226-0001; www.gcbirthpalce.org*

Built in 1832, this building served as the parsonage of the First Presbyterian Church. It is the birthplace of Grover Cleveland, the only president born in New Jersey. He lived here from 1837 to 1841. The house is listed on the New Jersey and National Registers of Historic Places. Self-guided and guided tours are available, and reservations are recommended. Wednesday-Sunday afternoons, call for hours.

# CAMDEN

Camden's growth as the leading industrial, marketing and transportation center of southern New Jersey dates from post-Civil War days. Its location across the Delaware River from Philadelphia prompted large companies such as Campbell's Soup (national headquarters) to establish plants here. Walt Whitman spent the last 20 years of his life in Camden.

## WHAT TO SEE AND DO

### CAMDEN COUNTY HISTORICAL SOCIETY-POMONA HALL

*1900 Park Blvd., Camden, 856-964-3333; www.cchsnj.com*

Brick Georgian house that belonged to descendants of William Cooper, an early Camden settler; period furnishings. Museum exhibits focus on regional history and include antique glass, lamps, toys and early hand tools; fire-fighting equipment;

**NEW JERSEY**

★
★
★
★
★

Victor Talking Machines. Library (fee) has more than 20,000 books, as well as maps (17th century-present), newspapers (18th-20th century), oral history tapes, photographs and genealogical material. Tuesday-Thursday, Sunday; closed August.

### NEW JERSEY STATE AQUARIUM

*1 Riverside Drive, Camden, 856-365-0352; www.njaquarium.org*

This home to more than 4,000 total fish of some 500 species is just minutes across the Ben Franklin Bridge in Camden, on the Delaware River waterfront. Curious kids can find out how fish sleep and which fish can change from male to female and back again. You will also find exhibits of seals, penguins, sharks, turtles and tropical fish, as well as elaborate rain forest, water filtration and conservation awareness displays. January-February, 10 a.m.-3 p.m.; March-April and September-December, 9:30 a.m.-3 p.m.; May-August, 9:30 a.m.-5 p.m.

### TOMB OF WALT WHITMAN

*Harleigh Cemetery, 1640 Haddon Ave., Camden, 856-963-0122;*
*www.harlighcemetery.org*

The vault of the "good gray poet," designed by the poet himself, is of rough-cut stone with a grillwork door.

### USS *NEW JERSEY*

*62 Battleship Place, Camden, 856-966-1652, 866-877-6262;*
*www.battleshipnewjersey.org*

The United States Navy permanently berthed the USS *New Jersey* (or "Big J"), one of the nation's largest and most decorated battleships, at the Camden Waterfront in 2000 and has transformed it into a floating museum. First launched in 1942, the ship was commissioned for operations during World War II at Iwo Jima and Okinawa. The ship conducted its last mission, providing fire support to Marines in embattled Beirut, Lebanon, in 1983. Military history buffs will be awed by the guided two-hour tour through this 887-foot, 11-story, 212,000-horsepower, Iowa-class ship. Big J is available for special events, retreats and overnight encampments. April-September, daily 9 a.m.-5 p.m.; October-March, daily 9 a.m.-3 p.m.

### WALT WHITMAN ARTS CENTER

*Second and Cooper streets, Camden, 856-964-8300; www.waltwhitmancenter.org*

Poetry readings, concerts and gallery exhibits (October-May). Children's theater (late June-August, Friday). Art gallery Saturday. Center (Monday-Friday).

### WALT WHITMAN HOUSE STATE HISTORIC SITE

*328 Mickle Blvd., Camden, 856-964-5383; www.waltwhitman.org*

The last residence of the poet and the only house he ever owned; he lived here from 1884 until his death on March 26, 1892. Contains original furnishings, books and mementos. Wednesday-Saturday, also Sunday afternoons.

# CAPE MAY

Cape May, the nation's oldest seashore resort, is located on the southernmost tip of the state. Popular with Philadelphia and New York society since 1766, Cape May has been host to presidents Lincoln, Grant, Pierce, Buchanan and Harrison, as well as notables such as John Wanamaker and Horace Greeley. The entire town has been proclaimed a National Historic Landmark because it has more than 600 Victorian homes and buildings, many of which have been restored. The downtown Washington Street Victorian Mall features three blocks of shops and restaurants. Four miles of beaches and a 1¼-mile paved promenade offer vacationers varied entertainment. "Cape May diamonds," often found on the shores of Delaware Bay by visitors, are actually pieces of pure quartz, rounded by the waves.

*Information: Chamber of Commerce, 609-884-5508 or Welcome Center,*
*405 Lafayette St., Cape May, 609-884-9562; www.capemaychamber.com*

## CAPE MAY: AN ARCHITECTURAL BOUNTY

The Center for the Arts, located at the historic Emlen Physick Estate at 1048 Washington Street (609-884-5404), is a good place to begin a walking tour that explores some of more than 600 Victorian-era buildings in Cape May. Take the 45-minute house tour. Leaving the estate, turn left, go right onto Madison, and having arrived at the corner of Virginia Street, turn left and walk the grid created by Madison, Philadelphia and Reading streets as they intersect Virginia, Ohio, Cape May, Idaho, Maryland, New York and New Jersey streets. The entire neighborhood is rich in antique homes.

Return to Madison. Turn left onto Sewell, then right onto Franklin. At the corner of Columbia Avenue, note the Clivedon Inn (709 Columbia) on the right. Turn left on Columbia. Here stand the Henry Sawyer Inn (722 Columbia) with its magnificent garden; the Dormer House (800 Columbia), a Colonial Revivalist home; the Inn at Journeys End (710 Columbia) and the Mainstay Inn (635 Columbia), once a gentlemen's gambling house.

Walk toward the ocean on Howard Street. At Beach Drive is the Hotel Macomber (727 Beach Drive), built in the Shingle style. Turn right, walk three blocks to Ocean Street, turn right and look for the Queen Anne-style Columbia House (26 Ocean St.) and Twin Gables (731 Ocean St.). Go left on Hughes to Decatur, turn right and in three short blocks enter the downtown shopping district. Here, along the Washington Street Mall, Lyle Lane, Jackson Street and Perry Street are dozens of shops, restaurants and inns. Stop at the corner of the Washington Street Mall and Perry to look at Congress Hall, a gargantuan hotel. At 9 Perry, near Beach Drive, stands the Kings Cottage, built in the Mansard style with Stick-style detailing. Another excellent Queen Anne-style building, the Inn at 22 Jackson, is found on Jackson Street parallel to Perry. Nearby, the Virginia Hotel (25 Jackson) serves elegant meals in its upscale dining room. You could also enjoy a meal at the Mad Batter (19 Jackson), a Victorian bed and breakfast inn, where breakfast on the veranda is a long-standing Cape May tradition.

For a classic Jersey Shore finish, return to the beach (at Jackson and Beach Drive) and stroll along the water's edge, or shop and snack along the Promenade. On a summer's eve, another option is to take in a play performed by the professional Cape May Stage. To reach them, stroll back up Jackson (away from the ocean), past the Washington Street Mall to Lafayette Street. Turn right—the theater is in the Visitor Center.

163

NEW JERSEY

★
★
★
★
★

## WHAT TO SEE AND DO

### CAPE MAY INNTERIORS TOUR & TEA

*202 Ocean St., Cape May, 809-884-5404; www.capemaymac.org*

Features a different group of houses each week, visiting five or more bed and breakfast inns and guesthouses. Innkeepers greet guests and describe experiences. Summer, Monday; rest of year, Saturday; no tours December-January.

### CAPE MAY-LEWES (DEL.) FERRY

*Sandman Boulevard and Lincoln Drive, North Cape May, 609-889-7200,*
*800-643-3779; www.capemaylewesferry.com*

Sole connection between southern terminus of Garden State Parkway and Highway 13 (Ocean Highway) on the Delmarva Peninsula. 17-mile, 80-minute trip across Delaware Bay. Daily.

### COMBINATION TOURS

*Cape May, 609-884-5404; www.capemaymac.org*

Begin at Emlen Physick Estate.

### EMLEN PHYSICK ESTATE

*1048 Washington St., Cape May, 609-884-5404; www.capemaymac.org*

Authentically restored 18-room Victorian mansion (1879) designed by Frank Furness. Mansion is also headquarters for the Mid-Atlantic Center for the Arts. Daily.

### HISTORIC COLD SPRING VILLAGE

*720 Route 9, Cape May, 609-898-2300; www.hcsv.org*

Restored early 1800s South Jersey farm village; 25 restored historic buildings on 22 acres. Craft shops, spinning, blacksmithing, weaving, pottery, broom making, ship modeling demonstrations, folk art; bakery and food shops, restaurant. Memorial Day-June and Labor Day-mid-September, weekends 10 a.m.-4:30 p.m.; May 31st-late July, July-Labor Day, Saturday-Tuesday 10 a.m.-4:30 p.m.

### TOURS

*1048 Washington St., Cape May, 609-884-5404, 800-275-4278; www.capemaymac.org*

The Mid-Atlantic Center for the Arts offers the following tours:

### MANSIONS BY GASLIGHT

*Cape May, 609-884-5404; www.capemaymac.org*

Three-hour tour begins at Emlen Physick Estate. Visits four Victorian landmarks: Emlen Physick House, the Abbey (1869), Mainstay Inn (1872) and Humphrey Hughes House (1903); shuttle bus between houses. Mid-June-September, Wednesday evenings; rest of year, holiday and special tours.

### OCEAN WALK TOURS

*Promenade and Beach drives, Cape May, 609-884-5404; www.capemaymac.org*

A 1½-hour guided tour of Cape May's beaches. Guide discusses marine life and history of the beaches, including legends of buried treasure. May-September, Tuesday-Saturday.

## TROLLEYS

*Cape May, 609-884-5404; www.capemaymac.org*

Half-hour tours on enclosed trolley bus or open-air carriage; three routes beginning at Ocean Street opposite the Washington Street Mall. June-October, daily; reduced schedule rest of year.

## WALKING TOURS OF THE HISTORIC DISTRICT

*Washington Street Mall and Ocean Street, Cape May, 609-884-5404;*
*www.capemaymac.org*

Begin at Information Booth on Washington Street Mall at Ocean Street Three 90-minute guided tours give historical insight into the customs and traditions of the Victorians and their ornate architecture. June-September: daily; reduced schedule rest of year.

## SPECIAL EVENTS
### TULIP FESTIVAL

*513 Washington, Cape May, 609-884-5508*

Celebrate Dutch heritage with ethnic foods and dancing, craft show, street fair, garden and house tours. April.

### VICTORIAN WEEK

Tours, antiques, crafts, period fashion shows. Mid-October.

## HOTELS
### ★AVONDALE BY THE SEA

*Beach and Gurney avenues, Cape May, 609-884-2332, 800-676-7030;*
*www.avondalebythesea.com*

46 rooms. Complimentary continental breakfast. Swimming pool. Pets not accepted. **$$**

### ★★CARROLL VILLA HOTEL

*19 Jackson St., Cape May, 609-884-5970, 877-275-8452; www.carrollvilla.com*

22 rooms. Complimentary continental breakfast. Reservations recommended. **$$**

### ★★★CONGRESS HALL

*251 Beach Ave., Cape May, 609-884-8421, 888-944-1816; www.congresshall.com*

Guests feel like royalty when they step beneath the 32-foot tall colonnade and into Congress Hall's beautiful lobby, complete with the hotel's original black-and-white marble floor, 12-foot tall doors and black wicker furniture. The guest rooms feature views of the Atlantic, antiques, custom furnishings and large bathrooms with 1920s-style tubs and pedestal sinks. The Blue Pig Tavern is a great place to stop for a bite to eat or meet up with new friends, and the Grand Ballroom is not to be missed. 108 rooms. Closed mid-week January and February. Children's activity center. Beach. Complimentary wireless Internet access. Valet parking. Fitness room. Pool. **$$$**

### ★★★MAINSTAY INN

*635 Columbia Ave., Cape May, 609-884-8690; www.mainstayinn.com*

This Victorian-style inn near the water offers breakfast by the fireplace or on the private porch. 16 rooms. Children over 12 years only. Complimentary full breakfast. Wireless Internet access. Parking. **$$$**

### ★★MONTREAL INN

*Beach at Madison Ave., Cape May, 609-884-7011, 800-525-7011;*
*www.montreal-inn.com*

70 rooms. Closed December-mid-March. Children's activity center. Airport transportation available. Reservations recommended. $

### ★★★THE SOUTHERN MANSION

*720 Washington St., Cape May, 609-884-7171, 800-381-3888;*
*www.southernmansion.com*

Originally built as a country estate in 1863 by Philadelphia industrialist George Allen, the Victorian décor of this painstakingly restored home has graced the covers of several magazines. Each room is meticulously decorated with antiques and vibrant colors, and features private bathrooms. The hotel's location puts guest within walking distance of beaches, shops and restaurants. 24 rooms. Children over 10 years only. Complimentary full breakfast. Parking. Pets not accepted. $$$

### ★★★VIRGINIA HOTEL

*25 Jackson St., Cape May, 609-884-5700, 800-732-4236; www.virginiahotel.com*

This hotel, built in 1879, has been remodeled and no detail was overlooked. Bright and airy rooms feature flatscreen televisions, Italian duvet covers, Belgian linens and Bulgari bath products. 24 rooms. Closed January-February. Complimentary continental breakfast. Valet parking. Complimentary wireless Internet access. $$$

## SPECIALTY LODGINGS

### ANGEL OF THE SEA

*5 Trenton Ave., Cape May, 609-884-3369, 800-848-3369; www.angelofthesea.com*

Just steps from the beach, this Victorian inn offers wraparound porches and balconies from which to take in the ocean view. 27 rooms. Children over eight years only. Complimentary full breakfast. Reservations recommended. $$

### QUEEN'S HOTEL

*601 Ocean St., Columbia Ave., Cape May, 609-884-1613; www.capemaytimes.com*

11 rooms. Complimentary continental breakfast. Complimentary bicycles. Beach. Whirlpool. $$

### THE QUEEN VICTORIA BED & BREAKFAST INN

*102 Ocean St., Cape May, 609-884-8702; www.queenvictoria.com*

Guests at this historic inn can enjoy British high tea just steps from the ocean. 32 rooms. Complimentary full breakfast. Whirlpool. Wireless Internet access. Reservations recommended. $$

### VICTORIAN LACE INN

*901 Stockton Ave., Cape May, 609-884-1772; www.victorianlaceinn.com*

Spacious suites feature kitchenettes as well as fireplaces to curl up to on cool nights, while a barbecue grill and picnic table are found outside on the well-manicured lawns. Eight rooms, all suites. Closed January-mid-February. Children over 5 years only. Complimentary full breakfast. Built in 1869. Reservations recommended. $$

## RESTAURANTS

### ★★410 BANK STREET

*410 Bank St., Cape May, 609-884-2127; www.410bankstreet.com*

Cajun, Caribbean menu, Seafood dinner. Closed October-May. Outdoor seating. Restored 1840 Cape May residence. Casual attire. Reservations recommended. **$$$**

### ★★ALEATHEA'S

*7 Ocean St., Cape May, 609-884-5555, 800-582-5933; www.aleatheas.com*

American menu. Breakfast, lunch, dinner, brunch. Closed various days in October-March. Bar. Children's menu. Casual attire. Reservations recommended. **$$**

### ★★ALEXANDER'S INN

*653 Washington St., Cape May, 609-884-2555, 877-484-2555; www.alexandersinn.com*

French menu. Dinner, Sunday brunch. Closed early January-mid-February. Casual attire. Reservations recommended. Outdoor seating. Complimentary full breakfast. **$$$**

### ★★BLUE PIG TAVERN

*251 Beach Ave., Cape May, 609-884-8421, 888-944-1816; www.congresshall.com*

American menu. Breakfast, lunch, dinner. Closed mid-week January and mid-week February. Bar. Children's menu. Casual attire. Reservations recommended. Valet parking. Outdoor seating. **$$**

### ★★★EBBITT ROOM

*25 Jackson St., Cape May, 609-884-5700, 800-732-4236; www.virginiahotel.com*

Nestled in an 1870s Victorian in the charming Virginia Hotel, the equally charming Ebbitt Room reflects the quaint Cape May atmosphere while serving plates of contemporary American fare. American menu. Dinner. Closed mid-January-February. Bar. Valet Parking. Casual attire. Reservations recommended. Outdoor seating. Intimate Victorian dining room. **$$$**

### ★★MAD BATTER

*19 Jackson St., Cape May, 609-884-5970; www.madbatter.com*

American menu. Breakfast, lunch, dinner. Bar. Children's menu. Outdoor seating. Casual attire. Reservations recommended. Outdoor dining. **$$**

### ★★MERION INN

*106 Decatur St., Cape May, 609-884-8363; www.merioninn.com*

Seafood, steak menu. Dinner, late-night. Closed weekdays in January-February; also Memorial Day. Bar. Children's menu. Outdoor seating. Casual attire. Reservations recommended. Valet parking. **$$$**

### ★★★WASHINGTON INN

*801 Washington St., Cape May, 609-884-5697; www.washingtoninn.com*

The Washington Inn is located in a former plantation house in the heart of the Cape May Historic District. An impressive wine list beautifully complements the seasonal American menu, which may include appetizers like a warm goat cheese tart and

**NEW JERSEY**

★
★
★
★
★

entrées such as pan-seared filet mignon and fig- and hazelnut-crusted rack of lamb. American menu. Dinner. Closed January-mid-February. Bar. Business casual attire. Reservations recommended. Valet parking. Fireside seating. $$$

# CAPE MAY COURT HOUSE

To be accurately named, this county seat would have to be called Cape May Court Houses because there are two of them; the white 19th-century building is now used as a meeting hall.

*Information: Cape May County Chamber of Commerce, Cape May Court House, 609-465-7181; www.cmccofc.com*

## WHAT TO SEE AND DO
### CAPE MAY COUNTY HISTORICAL MUSEUM

*504 N. Highway 9, Cape May Court House, 609-465-3535; www.cmcmuseum.org*

Period dining room (predating 1820), 18th-century kitchen, doctor's room, military room with Merrimac flag, Cape May diamonds. Barn exhibits, whaling implements, Indian artifacts, pioneer tools, lens from Cape May Point Lighthouse. Genealogical library. October-May, Saturday 10 a.m.-2 p.m.; September, Friday-Saturday 10 a.m.-2 p.m.; admission free.

### CAPE MAY COUNTY PARK

*4 Moore Road, Cape May Court House, 609-465-5271*

Zoo has more than 100 types of animals. Jogging path, bike trail, tennis courts, picnicking, playground. Daily 10 a.m.-3:45 p.m.

### VICTORIAN HOUSES

Over 600 fine examples of 19th-century architecture located in the area. Information can be obtained at the Chamber of Commerce Information Center, Crest Haven Road and Garden State Parkway, milepost 11. Easter-mid-October, daily; rest of year, Monday-Friday.

# CHATHAM

*Information: Township of Chatham, 58 Meyersville Road, Chatham, 973-635-4600; www.chathamtownship.org*

## RESTAURANT
### ★★★RESTAURANT SERENADE

*6 Roosevelt Ave., Chatham, 973-701-0303; www.restaurantserenade.com*

Owned by husband-and-wife team James and Nancy Sheridan Laird, Restaurant Serenade opened in 1996. The kitchen uses seasonal local ingredients to create innovative, contemporary French cuisine with Asian flair, such as seared sea bass with cantaloupe risotto, opal basil, purslane and Romano beans, or roasted rack of lamb with grilled corn, escarole, feta cheese and spicy tomato coulis. Lunch, dinner. Closed Sunday. Bar. Jacket required. Reservations recommended. $$$

★
★
★
★

# CHERRY HILL

*Information: Chamber of Commerce, 1060 Kings Highway North, Cherry Hill,*
*856-667-1600; www.cherryhillregional.com*

## WHAT TO SEE AND DO

### BARCLAY FARMSTEAD

*209 Barclay Lane, Cherry Hill, 856-795-6225; www.barclayfarmstead.org*

One of the earliest properties settled in what is now Cherry Hill; origins traced to
1684. The township-owned site consists of 32 acres of open space; restored Federal-
style farmhouse; Victorian spring house. Grounds (all year); house tours. Tuesday-
Friday noon-4 p.m., first Sunday each month 1-4 p.m.; and by appointment.

## HOTELS

### ★★CLARION HOTEL

*1450 Route 70 E., Cherry Hill, 856-428-2300, 877-424-6423; www.choicehotels.com*

197 rooms. Airport transportation available. Free parking. Pets accepted. **$**

### ★★★CROWNE PLAZA HOTEL

*2349 W. Marlton Pike, Cherry Hill, 856-665-6666, 800-496-7621;*
*www.crowneplaza.com*

This suburban hotel is located only 10 minutes from Philadelphia's historic and business districts, and just a few miles from the Aquarium and the Cherry Hill Mall. 408
rooms. Outdoor pool. High-speed Internet access. Fitness center. Airport transportation available. Pets not accepted. **$**

### ★★HOLIDAY INN

*2175 Marlton Pike, Cherry Hill, 856-663-5300, 800-315-2621; www.holiday-inn.com*

186 rooms. Indoor and outdoor pool. High-speed Internet access. **$**

## RESTAURANTS

### ★★★LA CAMPAGNE

*312 Kresson Road, Cherry Hill, 856-429-7647; www.lacampagne.com*

This 150-year-old restaurant and farmhouse serves country French cuisine with an
emphasis on the Provençal region of southeast France. French menu. Dinner Sunday
brunch. Closed Monday; also one week in July. Children's menu. Business casual
attire. Reservations recommended. Outdoor seating. **$$$**

### ★★MELANGE CAFÉ

*1601 Chapel Ave., Cherry Hill, 856-663-7339; www.melangecafe.com*

Cajun/Creole, Italian menu. Lunch, dinner. Closed Monday. Children's menu. Busi-
ness casual attire. Reservations recommended. Outdoor seating. **$$**

### ★RED HOT & BLUE

*2175 Route 70, Cherry Hill, 856-665-7427; www.redhotandblue.com*

American menu. Breakfast, lunch, dinner, late-night. Bar. Children's menu. Casual
attire. Outdoor seating. Blues Friday-Saturday. **$**

**NEW JERSEY**

★
★
★
★

### ★★SIRI'S THAI FRENCH CUISINE
*2117 Route 70 W., Cherry Hill, 856-663-6781; www.siris-nj.com*
Thai, French menu. Lunch Monday-Saturday, dinner daily. Casual attire. Reservations recommended. **$$**

# CLIFTON
*Information: North Jersey Regional Chamber of Commerce, 1033 Route 46 E., Clifton, 973-470-9300; www.njrcc.org*

## WHAT TO SEE AND DO
### HAMILTON HOUSE MUSEUM
*971 Valley Road, Clifton, 973-744-5707; www.cliftonnj.org*
Early 19th-century sandstone farmhouse with period furniture; country store, exhibits. Open-hearth cooking demonstrations by costumed guides. March-December, Sundays from 2-4 p.m.; closed holiday weekends.

## HOTEL
### ★WELLESLEY INN
*265 Route 3 E., Clifton, 973-778-6500, 800-444-8888; www.wellesleyonline.com*
231 rooms. Complimentary continental breakfast. Free wireless Internet access. Pets accepted. Free parking. Fitness center. Pool. **$**

# CLINTON

## WHAT TO SEE AND DO
### RED MILL MUSEUM VILLAGE
*56 Main St., Clinton, 908-735-4101; www.theredmill.org*
Four-story gristmill (circa 1810). Ten-acre park houses education center, quarry and lime kilns, blacksmith shop, general store, one-room schoolhouse, log cabin, machinery sheds, herb garden. Also home of Clinton's landmark red mill. April-October, Tuesday-Saturday 10 a.m.-4 p.m., Sunday noon-5 p.m.; closed on Easter Sunday, Memorial Day, Labor Day. Outdoor concerts some Saturday evenings in summer (fee).

### ROUND VALLEY STATE PARK
*1220 Lebanon Stanton Road, Clinton, 908-236-6355;*
*www.state.nj.us/dep/parksandforests/parks/round.html*
A 4,003-acre park. Swimming, fishing, boating; picnicking, concession (Memorial Day-Labor Day), wilderness camping (access to campsites via hiking or boating only). Standard fees.

### SPRUCE RUN STATE RECREATION AREA
*Van Syckles Road, Clinton, 908-638-8572;*
*www.state.nj.us/dep/parksandforests/parks/spruce.html*
Swimming, fishing, boating (launch, rentals); picnicking, concession, camping. April-October. Standard fees.

## HOTEL

### ★★HOLIDAY INN

*111 Route 173, Clinton, 908-735-5111, 800-315-2621; www.holiday-inn.com*

142 rooms. **$**

## RESTAURANT

### ★★CLINTON HOUSE

*2 W. Main St., Clinton, 908-730-9300; www.theclintonhouse.com*

American menu. Lunch, dinner. Bar. Business casual attire. Reservations recommended. **$$**

# EDISON

Although Thomas A. Edison's house has been destroyed, Menlo Park and the Edison Memorial Tower stand in tribute to the great American inventor. It was here, on December 6, 1877, that Edison invented the phonograph. Two years later, he perfected the first practical incandescent light, designing and constructing electrical equipment we now take for granted. (His workshop has been moved to the Ford Museum in Dearborn, Mich.) Edison also built the first electric railway locomotive here in 1880; it ran 1½ miles over the fields of Pumptown.

*Information: Chamber of Commerce, 336 Raritan Center Parkway, Campus Plaza 6, Edison, 732-738-9482; www.edisonchamber.com*

## WHAT TO SEE AND DO

### EDISON MEMORIAL TOWER AND MENLO PARK MUSEUM

*37 Christie St., Edison, 732-248-7298; www.menloparkmuseum.com*

A 131-foot tower topped by a 13½-foot-high electric light bulb stands at the birthplace of recorded sound. Museum contains some of Edison's inventions. Thursday-Saturday 10 a.m.-4 p.m.

## HOTELS

### ★★CLARION HOTEL

*2055 Lincoln Highway, Edison, 732-287-3500, 877-424-6423; www.choicehotels.com*

169 rooms. Complimentary full breakfast. Airport transportation available. **$**

### ★★★SHERATON EDISON HOTEL RARITAN CENTER

*125 Raritan Center Parkway, Edison, 732-225-8300, 800-325-3535; www.sheraton.com/edison*

The Sheraton Edison Hotel Raritan Center is just half an hour from New York City. A large indoor pool, well-equipped fitness facility and sauna offer onsite recreation, while Lily's Restaurant is the hotel's casual bistro. 276 rooms. **$$**

## RESTAURANTS

### ★★CHARLIE BROWN'S

*222 Plainfield Road, Edison, 732-494-6135; www.menuism.com*

American menu. Lunch, dinner, late-night. Bar. Children's menu. Casual attire. Outdoor seating. **$$**

★
★
★
★
★

### ★★MOGHUL
*1665-195 Oaktree Center, Edison, 732-549-5050; www.moghul.com*
Indian menu. Lunch, dinner, brunch. Closed Monday. Business casual attire. Reservations recommended. **$$$**

# EGG HARBOR CITY

## WHAT TO SEE AND DO
### RENAULT WINERY
*72 N. Bremen Ave., Egg Harbor City, 609-965-2111; www.renaultwinery.com*
Guided tour (approximately 45 minutes) includes wine-aging cellars; free wine tasting. Restaurants. Guided tours and wine tasting: Monday-Friday 11 a.m.-3 p.m., Saturday 11 a.m.-8 p.m., Sunday noon-4 p.m. Free tour with dinner on Saturday night.

### STORYBOOK LAND
*6415 Black Horse Pike, Egg Harbor Township, 609-641-7847; www.storybookland.com*
More than 50 storybook buildings and displays depicting children's stories; live animals, rides, picnic area, concession. Christmas Fantasy with Lights and visiting with Mr. and Mrs. Santa (Thanksgiving-December 30, nightly). Admission includes attractions and unlimited rides. Schedule varies, call for hours.

## HOTEL
### ★DAYS INN
*6708 Tilton Road, Egg Harbor City, 609-641-4500, 800-329-7466; www.daysinn.com*
117 rooms. Complimentary continental breakfast. **$**

## RESTAURANT
### ★★★RENAULT WINERY
*72 N. Bremen Ave., Egg Harbor City, 609-965-2111; www.renaultwinery.com*
This gourmet restaurant offers three different dining experiences: Guests may enjoy a six-course dinner with two wine samplings (reservations are required), relax at the garden café for an afternoon meal or try the Sunday country brunch. Dinner, Sunday brunch. Closed Monday-Thursday. Reservations recommended. **$$$**

# ELIZABETH
More than 1,200 manufacturing industries are located in Elizabeth and Union County. Long before the Revolution, Elizabeth was not only the capital of New Jersey but also a thriving industrial town. The first Colonial Assembly met here from 1669 to 1692. Princeton University began in Elizabeth in 1746 as the College of New Jersey. More than 20 pre-Revolutionary buildings still stand. Noteworthy citizens include: William Livingston, first governor of New Jersey; Elias Boudinot, first president of the Continental Congress; Alexander Hamilton; Aaron Burr; General Winfield Scott; John Philip Holland, builder of the first successful submarine and Admiral William J. Halsey. The Elizabeth-Port Authority Marine Terminal is the largest container port in the United States.
*Information: Union County Chamber of Commerce, 135 Jefferson Ave., Elizabeth, 908-352-0900; www.gatewaychamber.com*

★
★
★
★
★

## WHAT TO SEE AND DO

### BOXWOOD HALL STATE HISTORIC SITE

*1073 E. Jersey St., Elizabeth, 973-648-4540*

Home of Elias Boudinot, president of the Continental Congress (1783) and director of the U.S. Mint. Boudinot entertained George Washington here on April 23, 1789, when Washington was on his way to his inauguration. Monday-Saturday.

### FIRST PRESBYTERIAN CHURCH AND GRAVEYARD

*42 Broad St., Elizabeth, 908-353-1518*

The first General Assembly of New Jersey convened in an earlier building in 1668. The burned-out church was rebuilt in 1785-1787 and again in 1949. The Reverend James Caldwell was an early pastor. Alexander Hamilton and Aaron Burr attended an academy where the parish house now stands.

### TRAILSIDE NATURE AND SCIENCE CENTER

*452 New Providence Road, Mountainside, 908-789-3670; www.museumsusa.org*

Nature exhibits, special programs, planetarium shows (Sunday; fee). Museum (late March-mid-November, daily; rest of year, weekends only). Visitor Center with live reptile exhibit (daily, afternoons).

### WARINANCO PARK

*Elizabethtown Town Plaza, Elizabeth, 908-527-4900;*
*www.elizabethnj.org/parks_recreation.html*

One of the largest Union County parks. Fishing, boating (rentals June-September, daily); running track, parcourse fitness circuit, tennis (late April-early October), handball, horseshoes, indoor ice-skating (early October-early April, daily). Henry S. Chatfield Memorial Garden features tulip blooms each spring; azaleas and Japanese cherry trees; summer and fall flower displays. Some fees.

### WATCHUNG RESERVATION

*Between Routes 22 and 78, Elizabeth, 908-527-4900; www.ucnj.org/home.cfm*

A 2,000-wooded-acre reservation in the Watchung Mountains includes the 25-acre Surprise Lake. Nature and bridle trails, ice-skating, picnic areas, playground. Ten-acre nursery and rhododendron display garden.

## HOTEL

### ★★★HILTON NEWARK AIRPORT

*1170 Spring St., Elizabeth, 908-351-3900, 800-445-8667; www.hilton.com*

With the airport at its doorstep and a fully equipped business center, the Hilton Newark Airport is an ideal choice for business travelers. But with kids' movies and games available in rooms and dining menus just for the little ones, the hotel is also great for families. 374 rooms. Airport transportation available. **$$**

173

NEW JERSEY

★
★
★
★
★

# FLEMINGTON

Originally a farming community, Flemington became a center for the production of pottery and cut glass at the turn of the century.

*Information: Hunterdon County Chamber of Commerce, 2200 Route 31, Lebanon, 908-735-5955; www.hunterdon-chamber.org*

## WHAT TO SEE AND DO

### BLACK RIVER & WESTERN RAILROAD

*Route 12, Flemington, 908-782-9600; www.brwrr.com*

Excursion ride on old steam train, 11-mile round trip to the town of Ringoes; museum; Picnic area. July-August, Thursday-Sunday; April-June and September-December, Saturday-Sunday and holidays.

### COUNTY COURTHOUSE

*Main Street, Flemington*

(1828) For 46 days in 1935, world attention was focused on this Greek Revival building where Bruno Hauptmann was tried for the kidnapping and murder of the Lindbergh baby.

### FLEMING CASTLE

*5 Bonnell St., Flemington, 908-782-4607; www.flemingcastle.com*

(1756) Typical two-story colonial house built as a residence and inn by Samuel Fleming, for whom the town is named. By appointment.

## RESTAURANT

### ★★UNION HOTEL

*76 Main St., Flemington, 908-788-7474; www.unionhotelrestaurant.com*

American menu. Lunch, dinner. Bar. Casual attire. Reservations recommended. Outdoor seating. $$

# FORKED RIVER

## RESTAURANT

### ★★CAPTAIN'S INN

*304 E. Lacey Road, Forked River, 609-693-3351; www.captainsinnnj.com*

American menu. Breakfast, lunch, dinner. Bar. Children's menu. Docking. $$

# FORT LEE

North and south of the George Washington Bridge, Fort Lee is named for Gen. Charles Lee, who served in the Revolutionary Army under George Washington. Its rocky bluff achieved fame as the cliff from which Pearl White hung in the early movie serial *The Adventures of Pearl White*. From 1907 to 1916, 21 companies and seven studios produced motion pictures in Fort Lee. Stars such as Mary Pickford, Mabel Normand, Theda Bara and Clara Kimball Young made movies here.

*Information: Greater Fort Lee Chamber of Commerce, 2357 Lemoine Ave., Fort Lee, 201-944-7575; www.greaterfortleechamber.com*

## WHAT TO SEE AND DO
### ★★★FORT LEE HISTORIC PARK
*Hudson Terrace and Palisades Interstate, Fort Lee, 201-461-3956;*
*www.njpalisades.org/flhp.htm*
33-acre Historic Park.

## HOTELS
### ★★CROWNE PLAZA HOTEL ENGLEWOOD
*401 S. Van Brunt St., Englewood, 201-871-2020, 800-496-7621;*
*www.crowneplaza.com*
194 rooms. $$

### ★★★DOUBLE TREE HOTEL
*2117 Route 4, Fort Lee, 201-461-9000, 800-445-8667; www.doubletree.com*
This hotel sits near the George Washington Bridge. Along with its convenient location, this Hilton offers its guests two restaurants, a lounge, a karaoke night club, an indoor pool and a modern fitness center. 236 rooms. $$

### ★★HOLIDAY INN
*2339 Route 4 E., Fort Lee, 201-944-5000, 800-315-2621; www.holiday-inn.com*
184 rooms. $

# FREEHOLD

George Washington and the Revolutionary Army defeated the British under General Sir Henry Clinton at the Battle of Monmouth near here on June 28, 1778. Molly Hays carried water to artillerymen in a pitcher, and from that day on she has been known as "Molly Pitcher." Formerly known as Monmouth Courthouse, Freehold is the seat of Monmouth County.
*Information: Western Monmouth Chamber of Commerce, 17 Broad St., Freehold,*
*732-462-3030; www.wmchamber.com*

**NEW JERSEY**

★
★
★
★
★

## WHAT TO SEE AND DO
### COVENHOVEN HOUSE
*150 W. Main St., Freehold, 732-462-1466; www.monmouthhistory.org*
1756 House with period furnishings; once occupied by General Sir Henry Clinton prior to the Battle of Monmouth in 1778. May-September, Tuesday, Thursday, Saturday and Sunday afternoons.

### MONMOUTH COUNTY HISTORICAL MUSEUM AND LIBRARY
*70 Court St., Freehold, 732-462-1466; www.monmouthhistory.org*
Headquarters of the Monmouth County Historical Association. Changing exhibits center on aspects of life in Monmouth county and include collections of silver, ceramics and paintings, exhibits on the Battle of Monmouth. Museum (Tuesday-Saturday 10 a.m.-4 p.m.); library (Wednesday-Saturday).

### TURKEY SWAMP PARK

*200 Georgia Road, Freehold, 732-462-7286;*
*www.monmouthcountyparks.com/parks/turket.asp*

An 1,004-acre park with fishing, boating (rentals); hiking trails, ice-skating, picnicking (shelter), playfields, camping. (March-November; fee). Special events.

### SPECIAL EVENT
#### HARNESS RACING

*Freehold Raceway, Routes 9 and 33, Freehold, 732-462-3800;*
*www.freeholdraceway.com*

The nation's oldest and fastest daytime half-mile harness racing track features Standard-bred harness races for trotters and pacers. Mid-August-May, Tuesday-Saturday.

### RESTAURANT
#### ★GOLDEN BELL DINER

*3320 Route 9, Freehold, 908-462-7259; www.goldenbelldinerbanquet.com*
Italian, American menu. Lunch, dinner. Children's menu. Greenhouse atrium. **$$**

# GALLOWAY

### HOTEL
#### ★★★MARRIOTT SEAVIEW RESORT AND SPA

*401 S. New York Road, Galloway, 609-652-1800, 800-205-6518; www.seaviewgolf.com*
A golfer's dream, this hotel is located on 670 secluded acres near Reeds Bay and offers two 18-hole championship golf courses. It is also only 15 minutes from the bright lights of Atlantic City. The hotel's lobby has a traditional 1912 elegance and features black-and-white antique golf pictures, mahogany furniture and bar, overstuffed brown leather chairs and large windows with views of the grounds. Guests can enjoy a well-equipped recreation room with pool tables and PlayStations, volleyball and basketball courts, a kids' playground, the Faldo Golf School and the Elizabeth Arden Red Door Spa. 297 rooms. **$$$**

### RESTAURANT
#### ★★★RAM'S HEAD INN

*9 W. White Horse Pike, Galloway City, 609-652-1700; www.ramsheadinn.com*
This continental restaurant is also a busy banquet facility that can accommodate up to 350 people. Dine in a glass-enclosed veranda, ballroom or brick courtyard. Continental menu. Lunch, dinner. Closed Monday. Bar. Children's menu. Jacket required. Reservations recommended. Valet parking. Outdoor seating. **$$$**

# GATEWAY NATIONAL RECREATION AREA (SANDY HOOK UNIT)

Sandy Hook is a barrier peninsula that was first sighted by the crew of Henry Hudson's *Half Moon* (1609). It once was owned (1692) by Richard Hartshorne, an English Quaker, but has been government property since the 18th century. Fort Hancock (1895) was an important harbor defense from the Spanish-American War through the Cold War era. Among Sandy Hook's most significant features are the Sandy Hook Lighthouse

(1764), the oldest operating lighthouse in the United States, and the U.S. Army Proving Ground (1874-1919), the army's first new-weapons testing site.

The park offers swimming (lifeguards in summer), fishing; guided and self-guided walks, picnicking and a concession. Visitors are advised to obtain literature at the Visitor Center (daily). There is no charge for entrance and activities scheduled by the National Park Service. Parking fee, Memorial Day weekend-Labor Day. Daily, sunrise-sunset; some facilities closed in winter.

*Information: 732-354-4606; www.nps.gov/gate*

## WHAT TO SEE AND DO
### TWIN LIGHTS STATE HISTORIC SITE
*Route 36 and Light House Road, Highlands, 732-872-1814; www.twin-lights.org*
(1862) A lighthouse built to guide ships into New York harbor; now a marine museum operated by the State Park Service. May-October, daily 10 a.m.-4:30 p.m.; rest of year, Wednesday-Sunday 10 a.m.-4:30 p.m. Free admission.

## RESTAURANTS
### ★★BAHR'S RESTAURANT & MARINA
*2 Bay Ave., Highlands, 732-872-1245; www.bahrs.com*
Seafood menu. Lunch, dinner. Bar. Children's menu. **$$**

### ★★DORIS & ED'S
*348 Shore Drive, Highlands, 732-872-1565; www.doris-and-eds.com*
Dinner. Closed Monday-Tuesday, also January-February. Children's menu. **$$$**

# HACKENSACK

Hackensack was officially known as New Barbados until 1921 when it received its charter under its present name, thought to be derived from the Native American word "Hacquinsacq." The influence of the original Dutch settlers who established a trading post here remained strong even after British conquest. A strategic place during the Revolutionary War, the city contains a number of historical sites from that era. Hackensack is the hub for industry, business and government in Bergen County. Edward Williams College is located here.

*Information: Chamber of Commerce, 190 Main St., Hackensack, 201-489-3700; www.hackensackchamber.org*

## WHAT TO SEE AND DO
### CHURCH ON THE GREEN
*42 Court St., Hackensack, 201-342-7050*
Organized in 1686, the original building was built in 1696 (13 monogrammed stones preserved in the east wall) and rebuilt in 1791 in Stone Dutch architectural style. It is the oldest church building in Bergen County. Museum contains pictures, books and colonial items. Enoch Poor, a Revolutionary War general, is buried in the cemetery. Tours. Weekdays on request.

### USS LING SUBMARINE
*Court and River streets, Hackensack, 201-342-3268; www.njnm.com*
Restored World War II fleet submarine; New Jersey Naval Museum. Saturday-Sunday afternoons.

## RESTAURANT

### ★★★STONY HILL INN

*231 Polifly Road, Hackensack, 201-342-4085; www.stonyhillinn.com*

Housed in a historic Dutch colonial house (1818), this restaurant offers seven dining rooms, all decorated in 18th-century style. Some rooms are themed, such as the Pipe Room or Herb Room, while others, such as the Green Room and Apricot Room, are more sophisticated. Menu specialties include chateaubriand bouquetiere for two and grilled double-cut loin veal chop. The cigar-friendly bar is decorated in deep, rich tones and mahogany woodwork. On Friday and Saturday evenings, guests can enjoy live entertainment performed in the Garden Room. American menu. Lunch, dinner. Bar. Business casual attire. Reservations recommended. Valet parking. $$$

# HACKETTSTOWN

First called Helm's Mills and then Musconetcong, citizens renamed this town in honor of Samuel Hackett, the largest local landowner. His popularity increased when he treated the town to unlimited free drinks at the christening of a new hotel. Hackettstown is located in the Musconetcong Valley between the Schooleys and Upper Pohatcong mountains.

*Information: Town Hall, 215 Stiger St., Hackettstown, 908-852-3130;*
*www.hackettstown.net*

## WHAT TO SEE AND DO

### ALLAMUCHY MOUNTAIN STATE PARK, STEPHENS SECTION

*800 Willow Grove St., Hackettstown, 908-852-3790;*
*www.state.nj.us/dep/parksandforests/parks/allamuch.html*

Allamuchy Mountain State Park (7,263 acres) is divided into sections. The Stephens Section (482 acres) is developed and the rest (Allamuchy) is natural. Fishing in Musconetcong River; hunting, hiking, picnicking, playground, camping.

# HADDONFIELD

Haddonfield is named for Elizabeth Haddon, a 20-year-old Quaker girl whose father sent her here from England in 1701 to develop 400 acres of land. This assertive young woman built a house, started a colony and proposed to a Quaker missionary who promptly married her. The *Theologian's Tale* in Longfellow's *Tales of a Wayside Inn* celebrates Elizabeth Haddon's romance with the missionary.

*Information: Visitor/Information Center, 114 Kings Highway East, Haddonfield,*
*856-216-7253; www.haddonfieldnj.org*

## WHAT TO SEE AND DO

### GREENFIELD HALL

*343 Kings Highway E. (Route 41), Haddonfield, 856-429-7375;*
*www.historicalsocietyofhaddonfield.org*

Haddonfield's Historical Society headquarters in old Gill House (1747-1841) contains personal items of Elizabeth Haddon; furniture, costumes, doll collection. Boxwood garden; library on local history. On grounds is a house (circa 1735) once owned by Elizabeth Haddon. Library: Tuesday, Thursday mornings. Museum: Wednesday-Friday afternoons, other days by appointment; closed August.

### INDIAN KING TAVERN MUSEUM STATE HISTORIC SITE

*233 Kings Highway E., Haddonfield, 856-429-6792; www.waymarking.com*

Built as an inn; state legislatures met here frequently, passing a bill (1777) substituting "State" for "Colony" in all state papers. Colonial furnishings. Guided tours. Wednesday-Sunday; closed Wednesday if following a Monday or Tuesday holiday.

### THE SITE OF THE ELIZABETH HADDON HOUSE

*Wood Lane and Merion Avenue, Haddonfield*

Isaac Wood built this house in 1842, on the foundation of Elizabeth Haddon's 1713 brick mansion, immediately after it was destroyed by fire. The original brew house Elizabeth built and the English yew trees she brought over from England in 1712 are in the yard. Private residence; not open to the public.

## HOTEL

### ★★★HADDONFIELD INN

*44 West End Ave., Haddonfield, 856-428-2195, 800-269-0014;*
*www.haddonfieldinn.com*

Located in a Victorian home, the Haddonfield Inn offers well-appointed rooms and suites with varying styles and themes, including the Dolley Madison Room, with an antique desk, Franklin stove and pewter light fixtures, and the Dublynn Room, with antiques and a lace-canopied, four-poster King bed. All rooms feature fireplaces and high-speed Internet access. Each morning, a gourmet breakfast is served in the dining room or on the wraparound porch and complimentary beverages, coffee, tea and snacks are available throughout the day. Nine rooms. Complimentary full breakfast. Airport transportation available. $$

# HASBROUCK HEIGHTS

## HOTEL

### ★★★HILTON HASBROUCK HEIGHTS

*650 Terrace Ave., Hasbrouck Heights, 201-288-6100, 800-445-8667; www.hilton.com*

The Hilton Hasbrouck Heights is conveniently located near New York City and the Meadowlands. The onsite restaurant, Bistro 650, offers casual American fare for breakfast, lunch and dinner. 355 rooms. Airport transportation available. $$

# HIGH POINT STATE PARK

High Point's elevation (1,803 feet), the highest point in New Jersey, gave this 15,000-acre park its name. Marked by a 220-foot stone war memorial, the spot offers a magnificent view overlooking Tri-State—the point where New Jersey, New York and Pennsylvania meet—with the Catskill Mountains to the north, the Pocono Mountains to the west and hills, valleys and lakes all around. Elsewhere in the forests of this Kittatinny Mountain park are facilities for swimming, fishing, boating; nature center, picnicking, tent camping. Standard fees.

*Information: 973-875-4800; www.state.nj.us/dep/parksandforests/parks/highpoint.html*

**NEW JERSEY**

★
★
★
★
★

# HO-HO-KUS

In colonial times, Ho-Ho-Kus was known as Hoppertown. Its present name is derived from the Chihohokies, who also had a settlement on this spot.

*Information: Borough of Ho-Ho-Kus, 333 Warren Ave., 201-652-4400; www.ho-ho-kusboro.com*

## WHAT TO SEE AND DO

### THE HERMITAGE

*335 N. Franklin Turnpike, Ho-Ho-Kus, 201-445-8311; www.thehermitage.org*

Stone Victorian house of Gothic Revival architecture superimposed on original 18th-century house. Grounds consist of five wooded acres, including a second stone Victorian house. Docents conduct tours of site and the Hermitage. Changing exhibits. Special events held throughout the year. Tours.

# HOBOKEN

In the early 19th century, beer gardens and other amusement centers dotted the Hoboken shore, enticing New Yorkers across the Hudson. John Jacob Astor, Washington Irving, William Cullen Bryant and Martin Van Buren were among the fashionable visitors. By the second half of the century, industries and shipping began to encroach on the fun. Today, Hoboken is returning to its roots, as bars, restaurants and shops do steady business there, and young commuters flock to the birthplace of Frank Sinatra for more affordable housing than New York can provide. Hoboken is connected to Manhattan by the PATH rapid-transit system and New Jersey Transit buses.

*Information: Hoboken Community Development, 94 Washington St., Hoboken, 201-420-2013; www.hobokennj.org*

## WHAT TO SEE AND DO

### DAVIDSON LABORATORY

*Hudson and Seventh streets, Hoboken, 201-216-5290; www.stevens.edu/press/cgi-bin/wordpress/?p=28*

One of the largest privately owned hydrodynamic labs of its kind in the world. Testing site for models of ships, hydrofoils, America's Cup participants and the Apollo command capsule. Limited public access.

### SAMUEL C. WILLIAMS LIBRARY

*Stevens University, Hoboken, 201-216-5421; www.stevens.edu*

(1969) Special collections include a set of facsimiles of every drawing by Leonardo da Vinci; library of 3,000 volumes by and about da Vinci; Alexander Calder mobile; the Frederick Winslow Taylor Collection of Scientific Management. Academic year.

### STEVENS CENTER

(1962) The 14-story hub of campus. Excellent view of Manhattan from George Washington Bridge to the Verrazano-Narrows Bridge.

### STEVENS INSTITUTE OF TECHNOLOGY

*Hudson and Eighth streets, Hoboken, 201-216-5105; www.stevens.edu*

(1870) A leading college of engineering, science, computer science management and the humanities (3,600 students); also a center for research. Campus tours.

## RESTAURANTS

### ★★BAJA MEXICAN CUISINE
*104 14th St., Hoboken, 201-653-0610; www.bajamexicancuisine.com*
Mexican menu. Lunch, dinner, brunch. Bar. Casual attire. Reservations recommended. **$$**

### ★CAFÉ MICHELINA
*423 Bloomfield St., Hoboken, 201-659-3663; www.cafemichelina.com*
Italian menu. Dinner. Closed Monday. Casual attire. Reservations recommended. Outdoor seating. Daily. **$**

### ★GRIMALDI'S
*133 Clinton St., Hoboken, 201-792-0800; www.grimaldis.com*
Italian menu. Lunch, dinner. Closed Monday. Outdoor seating. **$$**

### ★ODD FELLOWS
*80 River St., Hoboken, 201-656-9009; www.oddfellowsrest.com*
Creole/Cajun menu. Lunch, dinner. Bar. Casual attire. Outdoor seating. Blues Thursday, Sunday. **$$**

# HOPE

## WHAT TO SEE AND DO
### LAND OF MAKE BELIEVE
*354 Great Meadows Road, Hope, 908-459-9000; www.thelandofmakebelieve.com*
Amusement park at foot of Jenny Jump Mountain includes the Old McDonald's Farm, the Red Baron airplane, Santa Claus at the North Pole, a Civil War train, a maze, water park, hayrides, picnic grove, fudge factory. Mid-June-Labor Day, daily; Memorial Day weekend-mid-June, weekends; September, weekend after Labor Day.

## HOTEL
### ★★★THE INN AT MILLRACE POND
*313 Johnsonberg Road, Route 519 N., Hope, 908-459-4884, 800-746-6467;*
*www.innatmillracepond.com*
This colonial-style bed and breakfast features guest rooms in three historic buildings: the Grist Mill, built in 1769 by Moravian settlers; the Miracle House, built in the early 19th century and the Stone Cottage, the home of the mill's caretaker. Some accommodations feature fireplaces, televisions and whirlpool tubs. The onsite restaurant offers a freshly prepared, contemporary American menu for dinner, while the Colonial Tavern features casual pub fare in 18th-century surroundings. 17 rooms. Complimentary full breakfast. Restaurant. Airport transportation available. **$**

# JERSEY CITY

Located on the Hudson River, due west of the southern end of Manhattan Island, Jersey City is now the second-largest city in New Jersey. New Yorkers across the bay tell time by the Colgate-Palmolive Clock at 105 Hudson Street; the dial is 50 feet across, and the minute hand, weighing 2,200 pounds, moves 23 inches each minute. Linking Jersey City with New York are the 8,557-foot Holland Tunnel, which is

★
★
★
★
★

72 feet below water level; the Port Authority Trans-Hudson (PATH) rapid-transit system; and New York Waterways Ferries, which run between Exchange Place, the city's Financial District and the World Financial Center in lower Manhattan.

*Information: Jersey City Cultural Affairs, 1 Chapel Ave., Jersey City, 201-547-5522*

## WHAT TO SEE AND DO
### LIBERTY STATE PARK
*Morris Pesin Drive, Jersey City, 201-915-3400; www.libertystatepark.org*

Off NJ Turnpike, exit 14B; on the New York Harbor, less than 2,000 feet from the Statue of Liberty. Offers breathtaking view of New York City skyline; flag display includes state, historic and U.S. flags; boat launch; fitness course, picnic area. Historic railroad terminal has been partially restored. The Interpretive Center houses an exhibit area; adjacent to the Center is a 60-acre natural area consisting mostly of salt marsh. Nature trails and observation points complement this wildlife habitat. Boat tours and ferry service to Ellis Island and Statue of Liberty are available. Daily.

### LIBERTY SCIENCE CENTER
*251 Phillip St., Jersey City, 201-200-1000; www.lsc.org*

Four-story structure encompasses Environment, Health and Invention areas that feature more than 250 hands-on exhibits. Geodesic dome houses IMAX Theater with a six-story screen. Daily.

# LAKE HOPATCONG

★
★
★
★
☆

## WHAT TO SEE AND DO
### HOPATCONG STATE PARK
*Lakeside Boulevard, Landing, 973-398-7010;*
*www.state.nj.us/dep/parksandforests/parks/hopatcong.html*

Southwest shore of lake Hopatcong. A 113-acre park with swimming, bathhouse, fishing; picnicking, playground, concession. Historic museum (Sunday afternoons). Standard fees.

### LAKE HOPATCONG
*NJ 15, Rockaway*

The largest lake in New Jersey, Hopatcong's popularity as a resort is second only to the seacoast spots. It covers 2,443 acres and has a hilly shoreline of approximately 40 miles. The area offers swimming, stocked fishing and boating.

## HOTEL
### ★★COURTYARD BY MARRIOTT
*15 Howard Blvd., Mount Arlington, 973-770-2000, 800-321-3211;*
*www.marriot.com/ewrma*

125 rooms. **$**

# LAKEWOOD

A well-known winter resort in the 1890s, many socially prominent New Yorkers such as the Astors, Goulds, Rhinelanders, Rockefellers and Vanderbilts maintained large homes on the shores of Lake Carasaljo.

*Information: Chamber of Commerce, 395 Route 70 W. Lakewood, 732-363-0012;*
*www.mylakewoodchamber.com*

## WHAT TO SEE AND DO
### OCEAN COUNTY PARK NO.1

*659 Ocean Ave., Lakewood, 732-506-9090; www.ocean.nj.us*

The 325-acre former Rockefeller estate. Lake swimming, children's fishing lake; tennis, platform tennis, picnicking (grills), playground, athletic fields. Daily. Entrance fee. July-August, weekends.

## HOTEL
### ★★BEST WESTERN LEISURE INN

*1600 Route 70, Lakewood, 732-367-0900; www.bestwestern.com*

105 rooms. Restaurant, bar. **$**

# LAMBERTVILLE

*Information: Lambertville Area Chamber of Commerce, 60 Wilson St., Lambertville,*
*609-397-0055; www.lambertville.org*

## WHAT TO SEE AND DO
### JOHN HOLCOMBE HOUSE

*260 N. Main St., Lambertville, 609-397-2752*

Washington stayed here just before crossing the Delaware. Privately owned residence.

### MARSHALL HOUSE

*62 Bridge St., Lambertville, 609-397-0770; www.lambertvillehistoricalsociety.org*

(1816) James Marshall, who first discovered gold at Sutter's Mill in California in 1848, lived here until 1834. Period furnishings; memorabilia of Lambertville; small museum collection. May-mid-October, weekends or by appointment.

## HOTELS
### CHIMNEY HILL FARM ESTATE

*207 Goat Hill Road, Lambertville, 609-397-1516, 800-211-4667;*
*www.chimneyhillinn.com*

12 rooms. Children over 12 years only. Complimentary full breakfast. Elegant stone and frame manor house built in 1820; furnishings are antiques and period reproductions. **$$**

### ★★★INN AT LAMBERTVILLE STATION

*11 Bridge St., Lambertville, 609-397-4400, 800-524-1091; www.lambertvillestation.com*

On the banks of the Delaware River, the Inn at Lambertville Station offers beautiful views and accommodations inspired by different time periods and international locations. A complimentary continental breakfast is served each morning, and the Lambertville Station restaurant serves a menu of creative American cuisine for brunch, lunch and dinner. 45 rooms. Complimentary continental breakfast. Restaurant. **$**

NEW JERSEY

★
★
★
★
★

## LAMBERTVILLE'S UNIQUE SHOPPING

Once the country's hairpin-making capital, Lambertville is now a fine antiques and art center, rich in history, antique shops, fine restaurants and historic Federalist and Victorian homes. The town's streets are set out in a grid, with Union and Main streets running north and south, parallel to the river and a series of short cross-streets passing between them. Lambertville has long been the state's shad-fishing center and still celebrates the annual Shad Festival.

This tour can cover anywhere from 1.5 to many miles, depending on your chosen route. Start at the historic Marshall House at 62 Bridge Street. A classic Federal-style building, this is the home of the Lambertville Historical Society, which leads one-hour guided walking tours from late June through September, presents a 30-minute film on Lambertville's history and can supply you with a guide to the town's historic buildings. After visiting the Marshall House, proceed west to Union Street and head north into the heart of the shopping district, where you'll find: **Phoenix Books** (*49 N. Union*), a treasure trove of rare and out-of-print volumes; the **Five and Dime** (*40 N. Union*), which houses an equally fascinating collection of antique toys; and all along the street, a number of high-quality antique shops and galleries.

At the north end of **Union** (*10 blocks north*), turn right onto Cherry Street. Follow Cherry to North Main, turn right and begin weaving among the cross streets between North Union and North Main back to Bridge Street. Along North Main, A Mano Gallery specializes in American crafts, jewelry and glass, while Almirah focuses on colonial-era Native American antique furniture and gifts. Shopping, window-shopping and gallery hopping are best done on Perry, York, Coryell, Church Bridge and Ferry streets. More shops can be found on **Kline's Court** (*one block on the left from Bridge St.*) and **Lambert Lane** (*just across the canal on the right*). From Lambert Lane, cross the footbridge onto Lewis Island, home of Fred Lewis, the state's only commercially licensed freshwater shad fisherman.

Back on Bridge Street, take a break at Lambertville Station, which serves New American cuisine, or return to town for other dining options, including the **Fish House** (*2 Canal St.*) for local catches of the day, Anton's at the **Swan** (*43 South Main St.*) for upscale dining in an historical building, or the **Church Street Bistro** (*11 Church St.*) for intimate dining.

For those with stamina, add one of the two extended walk options. Follow the walking/biking path along the Delaware & Raritan Canal, which travels south for many miles, presenting a bucolic view of the canal and the Delaware River. Another option is to cross the Delaware on the Bridge Street bridge and enter New Hope, Pennsylvania, a treasure trove of antique shops and restaurants.

**184**

**NEW JERSEY**

★
★
★
★
★

## RESTAURANTS

### ★★ANTON'S AT THE SWAN

*43 S. Main St., Lambertville, 609-397-1960; www.antons-at-the-swan.com*

American menu. Dinner. Closed Monday. Bar. **$$$**

### ★★LAMBERTVILLE STATION

*11 Bridge St., Lambertville, 609-397-8300, 800-524-1091; www.lambertvillestation.com*

American menu. Lunch, dinner, Sunday brunch. Bar. Children's menu. Casual attire. Reservations recommended. **$$**

# LIVINGSTON

This suburban community in southwestern Essex County is named for William Livingston, the first governor of New Jersey.

*Information:*

## HOTEL

### ★★★HOTEL WESTMINSTER

*550 W. Mount Pleasant Ave., Livingston, 973-533-0600; www.westminsterhotel.net*

The Hotel Westminster provides classic, sophisticated accommodations in the heart of Livingston. Guest rooms feature Egyptian cotton sheets and marble baths. The hotel also offers a well-equipped business center, state-of-the-art fitness facility and spa. 187 rooms. Complimentary continental breakfast. **$$**

# LONG BEACH ISLAND

Six miles out to sea, this island is separated from the New Jersey mainland by Barnegat and Little Egg Harbor bays. Route 72, going east from Manahawkin on the mainland, enters the island at Ship Bottom. The island is no more than three blocks wide in some places and extends 18 miles from historic Barnegat Lighthouse to the north. It includes towns such as Loveladies, Harvey Cedars, Surf City, Ship Bottom, Brant Beach and the Beach Havens at the southern tip. A popular family resort, the island offers fishing, boating, swimming in the bay and in the ocean's surf.

Tales are told of pirate coins buried on the island and over the years, silver and gold pieces have occasionally turned up. Whether they are part of pirate treasure or the refuse of shipwrecks remains a mystery.

*Information: www.longbeachisland.com*

## WHAT TO SEE AND DO

### BARNEGAT LIGHTHOUSE STATE PARK

*Long Beach Island, 609-494-2016;*
*www.state.nj.us/dep/parksandforests/parks/barnlig.html*

Barnegat Lighthouse, a 167-foot red and white tower, was engineered by General George G. Meade and completed in 1858; its 217-step spiral staircase leading to the lookout offers a spectacular view. Fishing; picnicking. Park (daily); lighthouse (Memorial Day-Labor Day, daily; May and Labor Day-October, weekends only).

### FANTASY ISLAND AMUSEMENT PARK

*320 W. Seventh St., Beach Haven, 609-492-4000; www.fantasyislandpark.com*

Family-oriented amusement park featuring rides and games; family casino arcade. June-August, daily; May and September, weekends; schedule varies.

**NEW JERSEY**

★
★
★
★
★

## SPECIAL EVENT
### SURFLIGHT THEATRE
*Beach and Engleside avenues, Beach Haven, 609-492-9477; www.surflight.org*
Broadway musicals nightly. Children's theater, Wednesday-Saturday. May-mid-October.

## HOTELS
### ★★THE ENGLESIDE INN
*30 E. Engleside Ave., Beach Haven, 609-492-1251, 800-762-2214; www.engleside.com*
72 rooms. $$

### ★★★SAND CASTLE BED AND BREAKFAST
*710 Bayview Ave., Barnegat Light, 609-494-6555, 800-253-0353;*
*www.sandcastlelbi.com*
This intimate bayfront bed and breakfast features five uniquely appointed guest rooms and two spacious, luxurious suites. Each morning, guests awaken to find a full breakfast served in the dining room, while complimentary tea, coffee and soft drinks are available throughout the day. The outdoor pool is a popular spot. Seven rooms. Closed December-January. No children accepted. Complimentary full breakfast. $$

## SPECIALTY LODGING
### AMBER STREET INN BED & BREAKFAST
*118 Amber St., Beach Haven, 609-492-1611*
This 1885 building has been lovingly restored. Each guest room is unique, with king or queen-sized beds, ceiling fans, private verandas and sitting rooms. Six rooms. Closed November-January. Children over 14 years only. Complimentary full breakfast. Built in 1885; antiques. $$

## RESTAURANTS
### ★★BUCKALEW'S
*101 N. Bay Ave., Beach Haven, 609-492-1065; www.buckalews.com*
American menu. Breakfast, lunch, dinner. Bar. Children's menu. Casual attire. Reservations recommended. $$

### ★★LEEWARD ROOM
*30 E. Engleside Ave., Beach Haven, 609-492-5116, 800-762-2214; www.engleside.com*
American, sushi menu. Lunch, dinner. Children's menu. Casual attire. Outdoor seating. $$

### ★★TUCKER'S
*Engleside Avenue and West Street, Beach Haven, 609-492-2300;*
*www.weloveourlife.com*
American, seafood menu. Lunch, dinner. Bar. Children's menu. Casual attire. Outdoor seating. $$

★
★
★
★
★

# MADISON
For many years, the quiet suburban town of Madison was called the "Rose City" because of the thousands of bouquets produced in its many greenhouses.
*Information: Chamber of Commerce, 155 Main St., Madison, 973-377-7830;*
*www.madisonnjchamber.org*

## WHAT TO SEE AND DO

### DREW UNIVERSITY

*36 Madison Ave., Madison, 973-408-3000; www.drew.edu*

(1867) A 186-acre wooded campus (2,100 students) west of town. College of Liberal Arts, Theological School and Graduate School. On campus are a Neoclassical administration building (1833), the United Methodist Archives and History Center, and the Rose Memorial Library containing Nestorian Cross collection, government and UN documents, and manuscripts and memorabilia of early Methodism. Tours.

### FAIRLEIGH DICKINSON UNIVERSITY-FLORHAM-MADISON CAMPUS

*285 Madison Ave., Madison, 973-443-8661; www.fdu.edu*

(1958) (3,889 students) (One of three campuses.) On site of Twombly Estate (1895); many original buildings still in use. Friendship Library houses numerous special collections including Harry A. Chesler collection of comic art and collections devoted to printing and the graphic arts. Academic year, Monday-Friday; closed school holidays. Tours of campus by appointment.

### MUSEUM OF EARLY TRADES AND CRAFTS

*9 Main St., Madison, 973-377-2982; www.metc.org*

Hands-on look at 18th- and 19th-century artisans. Special events include Bottle Hill Craft Festival (October). Tours. Tuesday-Saturday, also Sunday afternoons.

## SPECIAL EVENT

### NEW JERSEY SHAKESPEARE FESTIVAL

*36 Madison Ave., Madison, 973-408-5600; www.njshakespeare.org*

In residence at Drew University. Professional theater company. Includes Shakespearean, classic and modern plays; special guest attractions and classic films. Mid-May-December.

# MAHWAH

## WHAT TO SEE AND DO

### CAMPGAW MOUNTAIN SKI AREA

*200 Campgaw Road, Mahwah, 201-327-7800; www.skicampgaw.com*

Two double chairlifts, T-bar, two rope tows; patrol, school, rentals, snowmaking; cafeteria. Eight runs, longest run 600 feet; vertical drop 275 feet. Early December-mid-March, daily. Lighted cross-country trails; half-pipe, cross-country and snowboard rentals, night skiing (Monday-Saturday), snow tubing.

## HOTEL

### ★★★SHERATON CROSSROADS HOTEL

*1 International Blvd., Mahwah, 201-529-1660, 800-325-3535;*
*www.sheraton.com/crossroads*

This hotel offers rooms with a garden or a fountain view as well as an indoor heated pool, tennis courts, two restaurants and two lounges. Golfers will enjoy the nearby courses. 225 rooms. **$$**

# MARGATE

## WHAT TO SEE AND DO
### LUCY, THE MARGATE ELEPHANT
*9200 Atlantic Ave., Margate City, 609-823-6473; www.lucytheelephant.org*
Guided tour and exhibit inside this six-story elephant-shaped building. Built in 1881; spiral stairs in Lucy's legs lead to main hall and observation area on her back. Gift shop. Mid-June-Labor Day, daily; September-December, Saturday-Sunday 10 a.m.-5 p.m.

## RESTAURANT
### ★★STEVE AND COOKIE'S BY THE BAY
*9700 Amherst Ave., Margate, 609-823-1163; www.steveandcookies.com*
American menu. Dinner, brunch. Bar. Children's menu. Casual attire. $$

# MATAWAN
*Information: Matawan-Aberdeen Chamber of Commerce, Matawan, 732-290-1125; www.matabchamber.org*

## WHAT TO SEE AND DO
### CHEESEQUAKE STATE PARK
*300 Gordon Road, Matawan, 732-566-2161; www.state.nj.us/dep/parksandforests/parks/cheesequake.html*
This 1,300-acre park offers swimming, bathhouse, fishing; nature tours, picnicking, playground, concession, camping (fee; dump station).

## SPECIAL EVENT
### CONCERTS
*PNC Bank Arts Center, 3215 Route 35, Matawan, 732-442-9200; www.gsafoundation.org*
A 5,302-seat amphitheater; lawn area seats 4,500-5,500. Contemporary, classical, pop and rock concerts. Mid-June-September.

## RESTAURANT
### ★★BUTTONWOOD MANOR
*845 Route 34, Matawan, 732-566-6220; www.buttonwoodmanor.com*
Seafood, steak menu. Lunch, dinner. Bar. Children's menu. Lakeside dining. $$

# MEDFORD

## RESTAURANTS
### ★★★BEAU RIVAGE
*128 Taunton Blvd., Medford, 856-983-1999; www.beaurivage-restaurant.com*
Beau Rivage offers a casual but classic dining atmosphere. Menu selections include jumbo lump crab cakes with plum tomato salsa, and roast half duck with blueberry and lemon compote. French menu. Lunch, dinner. Closed Monday. Bar. Business casual attire. Reservations recommended. Two dining areas, one upstairs. $$$

### ★★★BRADDOCK'S TAVERN
*39 S. Main St., Medford Village, 609-654-1604; www.braddocks.com*
This casual restaurant features traditional American cuisine with European influences. Don't miss the cooking classes held throughout the year. American menu. Lunch, dinner, Sunday brunch. Bar. Business casual attire. Reservations recommended. **$$**

# MILLVILLE
*Information: Chamber of Commerce, 4 City Park Drive, Millville, 856-825-2600;*
*www.millville-nj.com*

## WHAT TO SEE AND DO
### WHEATON VILLAGE
*1501 Glasstown Road, Millville, 856-825-6800, 800-998-4552; www.wheatonvillage.org*
Buildings include the Museum of American Glass, which houses an extensive glass collection; working factory where demonstrations of glassmaking are given; general store; restored train station; 1876 one-room schoolhouse. Crafts demonstrations, arcade, shops. Restaurant, hotel. Self-guided tours. January-February, Friday-Sunday; March, Wednesday-Sunday; April-December, daily.

## HOTEL
### ★★COUNTRY INNS & SUITES
*1125 Village Drive at Wade Blvd., Millville, 856-825-3100, 888-201-1746;*
*www.countryinns.com*
100 rooms. **$**

# MONTCLAIR
Originally a part of Newark, the area that includes Montclair was purchased from Native Americans in 1678 for "two guns, three coats and 13 cans of rum." The first settlers were English farmers from Connecticut who came here to form a Puritan church of their own. Shortly after, Dutch from Hackensack arrived and two communities were created: Cranetown and Speertown. The two communities later were absorbed into West Bloomfield.

In the early 1800s, manufacturing began, new roads opened and the area grew. In 1856-57, a rail controversy arose: West Bloomfield citizens wanted a rail connection with New York City; Bloomfield residents saw no need for it. In 1868, the two towns separated and West Bloomfield became Montclair. One of the town's schools is named for painter George Inness, who once lived here.
*Information: North Essex Chamber of Commerce, 3 Fairfield Ave., West Caldwell,*
*973-226-5500; www.northessexchamber.com*

## WHAT TO SEE AND DO
### ISRAEL CRANE HOUSE
*108 Orange Road, Montclair, 973-744-1796; montclairhistorical.org*
(1796) Federal mansion with period rooms; working 18th-century kitchen, school room; special exhibits during the year. Country Store and Post Office have authentic items; old-time crafts demonstrations. Research library. June-August, Thursday-Saturday; September-May, Sunday afternoons; other times by appointment.

**NEW JERSEY**

★
★
★
★
☆

### THE MONTCLAIR ART MUSEUM

*3 S. Mountain Ave., Montclair, 973-746-5555; www.montclairartmuseum.org*

American art, Native American gallery, changing exhibits. (Tuesday-Sunday.) Gallery lectures (Sunday). Concerts; film series.

### PRESBY IRIS GARDENS

*Mountainside Park, 474 Upper Mountain Ave., Montclair, 973-783-5974;*
*www.presbyirisgardens.org*

Height of bloom in mid-May or early June.

# MORRISTOWN

Today, Morristown is primarily residential, but the town and its surrounding area were developed thanks to the iron industry, so desperately needed during the Revolutionary War. George Washington and his army spent two winters here, operating throughout the area until the fall of 1781. Morristown was the site of the first successful experiments with the telegraph by Samuel F.B. Morse and Stephen Vail. Cartoonist Thomas Nast, writers Bret Harte and Frank Stockton, and millionaire Otto Kahn all lived here.

*Information: Historic Morris Visitors Center, 6 Court St., Morristown, 973-631-5151;*
*www.morristourism.org*

## WHAT TO SEE AND DO

### ACORN HALL

*68 Morris Ave., Morristown, 973-267-3465; www.acornhall.org*

(1853) Victorian Italianate house; original furnishings, reference library, restored garden. Monday, Thursday, Sunday; group tours by appointment.

### FOSTERFIELDS LIVING HISTORICAL FARM

*73 Kahdena Road, Morristown, 973-326-7645; www.njskylands.com*

Turn-of-the-century living history farm (200 acres). Self-guided trail; displays, audiovisual presentations, workshops, farming demonstrations; restored Gothic Revival house. Visitor Center. April-October, Wednesday-Sunday.

### FRELINGHUYSEN ARBORETUM

*53 E. Hanover Ave., Morristown, 973-326-7600; www.arboretumfriends.org*

Features 127 acres of forest and open fields, natural and formal gardens, spring and fall bulb displays, labeled collections of trees and shrubs, Braille trail. Gift shop. Grounds Daily.

### HISTORIC SPEEDWELL

*333 Speedwell Ave., Morristown, 973-540-0211; www.morrisparks.net*

Home and factory of Stephen Vail, iron master, who in 1818 manufactured the engine for the *S.S. Savannah,* the first steamship to cross the Atlantic. In 1838, Alfred Vail (Stephen's son) and Samuel F.B. Morse perfected the telegraph and first publicly demonstrated it here in the factory. Displays include period furnishings in the mansion, exhibit on Speedwell Iron Works, exhibits on history of the telegraph; water wheel, carriage house and granary. Gift shop. Picnic area. May-September, Sunday, Thursday.

### MACCULLOCH HALL HISTORICAL MUSEUM

*45 Macculloch Ave., Morristown, 973-538-2404; www.maccullochhall.org*

Restored 1810 house and garden; home of George P. Macculloch, initiator of the Morris Canal, and his descendants for more than 140 years. American, European decorative arts from the 18th and 19th centuries. Illustrations by Thomas Nast. Garden. Wednesday, Thursday and Sunday afternoons.

### MORRIS MUSEUM

*6 Normandy Heights Road, Morristown, 973-971-3700; www.morrismuseum.org*

Art, science and history exhibits. Musical, theatrical events; lectures and films. (Tuesday-Sunday.) Free admission Thursday afternoons.

### SCHUYLER-HAMILTON HOUSE

*5 Olyphant Place, Morristown, 973-267-4039*

(1760) Former home of Dr. Jabez Campfield. Alexander Hamilton courted Betsy Schuyler here. Period furniture; colonial garden. Sunday afternoons; other times by appointment.

## HOTELS

### ★★★THE MADISON HOTEL

*1 Convent Road, Morristown, 973-285-1800, 800-526-0729;*
*www.themadisonhotel.com*

Family-owned since 1951, this Georgian-style hotel offers individually appointed guest rooms that combine Victorian style with modern comforts, including high-speed Internet access. Rod's Steak and Seafood Grille serves diners in two turn-of-the-century Pullman cars. New York City is just an hour-long train ride away via the nearby Convent Station stop of the Midtown Direct Train. 200 rooms. Complimentary continental breakfast. $$

### ★★★THE WESTIN GOVERNOR MORRIS

*2 Whippany Road, Morristown, 973-539-7300, 800-937-8461;*
*www.westin.com/morristown*

Accommodations at the Westin Governor Morris are comfortable and contemporary, with high-speed Internet access, spacious work desks with ergonomic chairs, luxurious bath amenities and Westin's signature Heavenly Beds and Heavenly Showers. 224 rooms. $$$

## RESTAURANT

### ★★ROD'S STEAK AND SEAFOOD GRILLE

*Highway 124, Convent Station, 973-539-6666; www.rodssteak-seafoodgrill.com*

Seafood, steak menu. Breakfast, lunch, dinner, Sunday brunch. Bar. Children's menu. Business casual attire. Reservations recommended. Valet parking. $$$

# MORRISTOWN NATIONAL HISTORICAL PARK

Morristown National Historic Park was created by an Act of Congress in 1933, the first national historical park to be established and maintained by the federal government. Its three units cover more than 1,600 acres, and all but Jockey Hollow and the

New Jersey Brigade Area are within Morristown's limits. The Continental Army's main body stayed here in the winter of 1779-1780.

Headquarters and museum (daily 9 a.m.-5 p.m.); Jockey Hollow buildings (summer: daily; rest of year schedule varies, phone ahead).

*Information: Chief of Interpretation, 30 Washington Place, Morristown, 973-539-2016*

## WHAT TO SEE AND DO
### FORD MANSION

*10 Washington Place, Morristown National Historical Park, Morristown, 973-539-2085; www.nps.gov/archive/morr/morr1.htm*

One of the finest early houses in Morristown was built in 1772-1774 by Colonel Jacob Ford, Jr., who produced gunpowder for American troops during the Revolutionary War. His widow rented the house to the army for General and Mrs. Washington when the Continental Army spent the winter of 1779-1780 here. The Ford Mansion is open daily, Ranger Guided tours only. Tours are given hourly at 10 a.m., 11 a.m., 1 p.m., 2 p.m., 3 p.m. and 4 p.m.

### FORT NONSENSE

*Ann Street, Morristown, 908-766-8215; www.nps.gov/morr/historyculture/fortnonsense.htm*

Its name came long after residents had forgotten the real reason for earthworks constructed here in 1777. Overlook commemorates fortifications which were built at Washington's order to defend military supplies stored in the village.

### JOCKEY HOLLOW

*30 Washington Place, Morristown National Historical Park, 973-543-4030; www.nps.gov/mor*

The site of the Continental Army's winter quarters in 1779-1780 and the 1781 mutiny of the Pennsylvania Line. Signs indicate locations of various brigades. There are typical log huts and an officer's hut, among other landmarks. Demonstrations of military and colonial farm life (summer). Visitor center has exhibits and audiovisual programs.

### WICK HOUSE

*30 Washington Place., Morristown National Historical Park, Morristown, 973-543-4030; www.nps.gov/morr*

Farmer Henry Wick lived here with his wife and daughter. Used as quarters by Major General Arthur St. Clair in 1779-1780. Restored with period furnishings.

## MOUNT HOLLY

The rock formation after which this old Quaker town was named is more a mound than a mountain: It stands only 183 feet high. For two months in 1779, Mount Holly was the capital of the state. Today, it is the seat of Burlington County.

*Information: www.mountholly.com*

## WHAT TO SEE AND DO

### JOHN WOOLMAN MEMORIAL

*99 Branch St., Mount Holly, 609-267-3226; www.woolmancentral.com*

(1783) John Woolman, the noted Quaker abolitionist whose "Journal" is still appreciated today, owned the property on which this small, three-story red brick house was built; garden. Picnicking. Wednesday-Friday; also by appointment.

### MANSION AT SMITHVILLE

*801 Smithville Road, Mount Holly, 609-265-5068; www.co.burlington.nj.us*

(1840) Victorian mansion and village of inventor/entrepreneur Hezekiah B. Smith; home of the "Star" hi-wheel bicycle. Guided tours. May-October, Wednesday and Sunday. Victorian Christmas tours December; fee.

### MOUNT HOLLY LIBRARY

*307 High St., Mount Holly, 609-267-7111; www.mtholly.lib.nj.us*

Chartered in 1765 by King George III, the library is currently housed in a Georgian mansion built in 1830. Historic Lyceum contains original crystal chandeliers, blue marble fireplaces, boxwood gardens; archives date to original 1765 collection. July-August, Tuesday-Thursday; rest of year, Monday-Saturday, limited hours.

## RESTAURANT

### ★★CHARLEY'S OTHER BROTHER

*1383 Monmouth Road, Eastampton Township, 609-261-1555;*
*www.charleysotherbrother.com*

American menu. Lunch, dinner. Bar. Children's menu. Casual attire. Reservations recommended. $$

# NEW BRUNSWICK

On the south bank of the Raritan River, New Brunswick is both a college town and a diversified commercial and retail city. Rutgers University, the eighth-oldest institution of higher learning in the country and the only state university with a colonial charter, was founded in 1766 as Queens College and opened in 1771 with a faculty of one—aged 18. Livingston College, Cook College and Douglass College (for women), all part of the university, are also located here. The headquarters for Johnson & Johnson is located downtown. The poet Joyce Kilmer was born in New Brunswick; his house, at 17 Joyce Kilmer Avenue, is open to visitors.

*Information: Middlesex County Regional Chamber of Commerce, One Distribution Way, Monmouth Junction, 732-821-1700; www.mcrcc.org*

## WHAT TO SEE AND DO

### BUCCLEUCH MANSION

*George Street and Easton Avenue, New Brunswick, 732-745-5094*

Built in 1739 by Anthony White, son-in-law of Lewis Morris, a colonial governor of New Jersey. Period rooms. June-October, Sunday afternoons. Under 10 only with adult.

### CROSSROADS THEATRE

*7 Livingston Ave., New Brunswick, 732-545-8100; www.crossroadstheatrecompany.org*
Professional African-American theater company offering plays, musicals, touring programs and workshops. October-May, Wednesday-Sunday.

### GEOLOGY MUSEUM

*George and Somerset streets, New Brunswick, 732-932-7243*
Displays of New Jersey minerals, mammals, including a mastodon; Egyptian exhibit with mummy. Monday-Friday; call for weekend/summer hours.

### GEORGE STREET PLAYHOUSE

*9 Livingston Ave., New Brunswick, 732-246-7717; www.georgestplayhouse.org*
Regional theater; six-show season of plays and musicals; touring Outreach program for students. Café. Cabaret. Tuesday-Sunday.

### HUNGARIAN HERITAGE CENTER

*300 Somerset St., New Brunswick, 732-846-5777; www.ahfoundation.org*
Museum of changing exhibits that focus on Hungarian folk life, fine and folk art; library, archives. Tuesday-Sunday.

### JANE VOORHEES ZIMMERLI ART MUSEUM

*George and Hamilton streets, New Brunswick, 732-932-7237;*
*www.zimmerlimuseum.rutgers.edu*
Paintings from early 16th century through the present; changing exhibits. Tuesday-Friday, also Saturday and Sunday afternoons.

### NEW JERSEY MUSEUM OF AGRICULTURE

*103 College Farm Road, New Brunswick, 732-249-2077; www.agriculturemuseum.org*
Large collection of farm implements covers three centuries of farming history. Interactive science and history exhibits. Tuesday-Sunday.

### RUTGERS-THE STATE UNIVERSITY OF NEW JERSEY

*126 College Ave., New Brunswick, 732-932-1766; www.rutgers.edu*
(1766) Multiple campuses include 30 colleges serving 50,000 students at all levels through postdoctoral studies; main campus on College Avenue.

### THE RUTGERS GARDENS

*112 Ryder's Lane (Route 1), New Brunswick, 732-932-8451;*
*www.rutgersgardens.rutgers.edu*
Features extensive display of American holly. Daily.

## SPECIAL EVENT
### MIDDLESEX COUNTY FAIR

*Cranbury-South River Road, East Brunswick, 732-257-8858; middlesexcountyfair.org*
August.

## HOTELS

### ★★★HILTON EAST BRUNSWICK

*3 Tower Center Blvd., East Brunswick, 732-828-2000, 800-445-8667; www.hilton.com*

The Hilton East Brunswick offers spacious guest rooms with high-speed Internet access and the Hilton's Serenity Collection bedding that features pillow-top mattresses and luxurious bed linens. Nearby attractions include Princeton University, Six Flags Great Adventure Theme Park and outlet shopping. 405 rooms. Airport transportation available. **$$**

### ★★★HYATT REGENCY NEW BRUNSWICK

*2 Albany St., New Brunswick, 732-873-1234, 800-233-1234; www.hyatt.com*

This property is located downtown on a six-acre lot, midway between New York and Philadelphia. 288 rooms. Tennis. **$$**

## RESTAURANTS

### ★★DELTA'S

*19 Dennis St., New Brunswick, 732-249-1551; www.deltasrestaurant.com*

American menu. Lunch, dinner. Bar. **$$**

### ★★★THE FROG AND THE PEACH

*29 Dennis St., New Brunswick, 732-846-3216; www.frogandpeach.com*

Housed in a converted factory, this restaurant has been in business since 1983 and features painted brick walls and exposed ductwork. Entrées include summer mushroom and local chard strudel with goat cheese and Jersey tomato emulsion; and Moroccan-spiced lamb sirloin with corn and garlic flan, popcorn shoots and pine nut yogurt sauce. American menu. Lunch, dinner. Bar. Children's menu. Casual attire. Reservations recommended. Outdoor seating. **$$$**

### ★★MAKEDA ETHIOPIAN RESTAURANT

*338 George St., New Brunswick, 732-545-5115; www.makedas.com*

Ethiopian menu. Lunch, dinner. Bar. Casual attire. Reservations recommended. **$$**

### ★★THE OLD BAY

*61-63 Church St., New Brunswick, 732-246-3111; www.oldbayrest.com*

French Creole menu. Lunch, dinner. Closed Sunday. Bar. Outdoor seating. **$$**

### ★★★STAGE LEFT: AN AMERICAN CAFÉ

*5 Livingston Ave., New Brunswick, 732-828-4444; www.stageleft.com*

Since 1992, Stage Left has been serving up creative American cuisine in a warm setting. Selections from an extensive wine list can be paired with menu options such as pistachio-studded organic free-range chicken breast, pan-roasted cod and apple cider-braised pork belly. Wine-tasting dinners with guest speakers and festive brunches are among the special events offered. American menu. Lunch, dinner. Bar. Business casual attire. Reservations recommended. Valet parking. Outdoor seating. **$$$**

# NEWARK

Once a strict Puritan settlement, Newark has grown to become the largest city in the state and one of the country's leading manufacturing cities. Major insurance firms and banks have large offices in Newark, dominating the city's financial life. Newark was the birthplace of Stephen Crane (1871-1900), author of *The Red Badge of Courage,* and Mary Mapes Dodge (1838-1905), author of the children's book *Hans Brinker, or the Silver Skates.* Newark is also an educational center with Newark College of Rutgers University, College of Medicine and Dentistry of New Jersey, New Jersey Institute of Technology, Seton Hall Law School and Essex County College.
*Information: www.state.nj.us/travel*

## WHAT TO SEE AND DO

### BRIDGE MEMORIAL
*Broad Street and Washington Place, Newark*
This sculpture of a Native American and a Puritan stands on the site of a colonial marketplace.

### MINOR BASILICA OF THE SACRED HEART
*89 Ridge St., Newark, 973-484-4600; www.cathedralbasilica.org*
French Gothic in design, it resembles the cathedral at Rheims. Hand-carved reredos. Daily.

### NEW JERSEY HISTORICAL SOCIETY
*52 Park Place, Newark, 973-596-8500; www.jerseyhistory.org*
Museum with collections of paintings, prints, furniture, decorative arts. Reference and research library of state and local history; manuscripts, documents, maps. Tuesday-Saturday 10 a.m.-5 p.m.

### NEW JERSEY PERFORMING ARTS CENTER
*1 Center St., Newark, 973-297-5857, 888-466-5722, 973-642-8989; www.njpac.org*
Home of the New Jersey Symphony Orchestra and host to many other performances.

### NEWARK MUSEUM
*49 Washington St., Newark, 973-596-6550; www.newarkmuseum.org*
Museum of art and science, with changing exhibitions. American paintings and sculpture; American and European decorative arts; classical art; and more. Also here are the Junior Museum, Mini Zoo, Dreyfuss Planetarium and the Newark Fire Museum. Special programs, lectures, concerts, café (lunch). Wednesday-Sunday noon-5 p.m.

### OLD PLUME HOUSE
*407 Broad St., Newark, 973-483-8202*
The current rectory of the adjoining House of Prayer Episcopal Church is thought to have been standing as early as 1710, which would make it the oldest building in Newark.

### STATUE OF ABRAHAM LINCOLN
*Springfield Avenue and Market Street, Newark*
Essex County Courthouse.

★
★
★
★
★

## IRONBOUND NEWARK

Once moribund, Newark is experiencing a renaissance. The city now offers fascinating history, modern facilities and some of the finest Spanish/Portugese dining around. This walk first covers the historic Ironbound section. Named for the surrounding railroads, this area has been the settling site for immigrants since the 1830s and is now home to about 40 ethnic groups. The walk then continues into the resurgent Four Corners/Military Park section.

Start at Pennsylvania Station, built in 1933 and beautifully decorated with Art Deco wall reliefs and ceiling sculptures. Walk east on Market Street, passing diminutive Mother Cabrini Park, site of a bust of Jose Marti, liberator of Cuba. Turn right onto Union Street. In one block, at Ferry Street, Our Lady of Mount Carmel Roman Catholic Church stands opposite at McWhorter Street. Originally opened in 1848, this building is now home to the Ironbound Educational and Cultural Center. Turn left onto Ferry Street. This is the commercial heart of the Ironbound, and is filled with shops and restaurants.

Turn right onto Prospect Street. Number 76 is the Gothic Revival-style Christ Episcopal Church, completed in 1850. Destroyed by vandalism and fire, it was restored in 1978 and now serves as the Chancery Professional Center. At the corner of Lafayette Street stands St. Joseph's Roman Catholic Church, circa 1858, now called Immaculate Heart of Mary. Its basement holds hidden catacombs that are replicas of those found in Rome, complete with crypts featuring wax likenesses of Spanish saints. Turn left on Lafayette and walk six blocks to Van Duren. Turn right two blocks to Independence Park. Covering 12½ acres, this was one of the city's first neighborhood parks (1896). Turn left on New York Avenue, go one block and turn right on Pulaski Street. Pass East Side High School, and come to St. Casimir's Roman Catholic Church, built in 1919 in the Italian Renaissance style. Continue to Chestnut Street and turn right. Five blocks down the road stand the remains of the Murphy Varnish Company, once comprising six major structures; note the carving of a Roman chariot carrying a can of Murphy Varnish on the west side of the building.

Follow Chestnut under the railroad and across McCarter Highway to Broad Street. Turn right and walk through the business district to the Prudential Building at the heart of the Four Corners Historic District. Among the many historic buildings are the National Newark Building (744 Broad St.), a 34-story neoclassical structure completed in 1930, and at 1180 Raymond Blvd. another Depression-era skyscraper. In two more blocks, Military Park appears. Walk on the left side of the park to the New Jersey Historical Society (52 Park Place), which has an onsite museum and is next door to the historic Robert Treat Hotel. At the end of the park on Center Street stands the architecturally stunning New Jersey Performing Arts Center. Opened in 1997, it has become a world-renowned performance space. Return on Center Street towards Military Park, turn left on Central Street and go two blocks to the Newark Museum (49 Washington St.), site of the largest collection of Tibetan art outside Tibet, the Dreyfus Planetarium and the historic 1885 Ballantine House.

NEW JERSEY

★
★
★
★
★

### SYMPHONY HALL

*1020 Broad St., Newark, 973-643-4550; www.newarksymphonyhall.org*

(1925) A 2,811-seat auditorium; home of New Jersey State Opera and the New Jersey Symphony Orchestra; also here is the famous Terrace Ballroom.

### THE WARS OF AMERICA

*Broad Street and Park Place, Newark, www.hmdb.org*

Military Park, bounded by Broad Street, Park Place, Rector Street, Raymond Boulevard. Sculptured bronze group by Gutzon Borglum features 42 human figures representing soldiers in the major conflicts in U.S. history.

## HOTEL

### ★★★MARRIOTT NEWARK AIRPORT

*Newark International Airport, Newark, 973-623-0006, 800-882-1037; www.marriott.com*

Located on the premises of Newark Airport, this Marriott features a connecting indoor/outdoor pool, complimentary coffee in the lobby, laundry and dry cleaning and babysitting services. The hotel's three restaurants—Mangiare di Casa, JW Prime Steakhouse and Chatfields English Pub—cater to all tastes. Area attractions include Ellis Island and the Statue of Liberty, the Jersey Gardens Outlet Mall and Six Flags Great Adventure. 591 rooms. Airport transportation available. $$

# OCEAN CITY

Families from all over the country come to this popular resort year after year, as do conventions and religious conferences. In accordance with its founder's instructions, liquor cannot be sold here. Ocean City is an island that lies between the Atlantic Ocean and Great Egg Harbor. It has eight miles of beaches, more than two miles of boardwalk, an enclosed entertainment auditorium on the boardwalk and excellent swimming, fishing, boating, golf and tennis.

*Information: Public Relations Department, City of Ocean City, Ninth and Asbury Ave., Ocean City, 609-525-9300*

## WHAT TO SEE AND DO

### OCEAN CITY HISTORICAL MUSEUM

*1735 Simpson Ave., Ocean City, 609-399-1801; www.ocnjmuseum.org*

Victorian furnishings and fashions; doll exhibit, local shipwreck, historical tours, research library. Gift shop. Monday-Saturday. Winter, Tuesday-Friday 10 a.m.-4 p.m. and in Saturdays 11 a.m.-2 p.m. Closed Sundays, Mondays and most major holidays.

## SPECIAL EVENTS

### BOARDWALK ART SHOW

*Arts Center, 1735 Simpson Ave., Ocean City, 609-399-7628;*
*www.oceancityartscenter.org*

International and regional artists. August.

### CONCERTS

*Music Pier, Highways 152 and 40, Ocean City, 732-316-1095*

Pops orchestra and dance band. Monday-Wednesday, Sunday. Late June-September.

★
★
★
★
☆

**FLOWER SHOW**

*Music Pier, Ocean City*
June.

**HERMIT CRAB RACE, MISS CRUSTACEAN CONTEST**

*Sixth St. Beach, Ocean City, 609-525-9300, 800-232-2465*
Crab beauty pageant, races. Early August.

**NIGHT IN VENICE**

*Ocean City, 609-525-9300*
Decorated boat parade. Mid-July.

## HOTELS
### ★★BEACH CLUB HOTEL

*1280 Boardwalk, Ocean City, 609-399-8555; www.ochotels.com*
82 rooms. Closed December-April. Restaurant. Children's pool. Beach. **$$**

### ★★PORT-O-CALL HOTEL

*1510 Boardwalk, Ocean City, 609-399-8812, 800-334-4546; www.portocallhotel.com*
99 rooms. **$**

### ★★SERENDIPITY BED & BREAKFAST

*712 E. Ninth St., Ocean City, 609-399-1554, 800-842-8544; www.serendipitynj.com*
5 rooms. Children over 12 years only. Complimentary full breakfast. **$**

# PARAMUS

Now a well-known shopping area with a handful of sizeable malls, Paramus was once a Dutch farm community. Beginning in the Revolutionary War, the city was an important hub of transportation and western Paramus was headquarters for the Continental Army. Paramus has grown as a residential community from 4,000 inhabitants in 1946 to more than 25,000 today.
*Information: Chamber of Commerce, 58 E. Midland Ave., Paramus, 201-261-3344;*
*www.paramuschamber.com*
*Office hours: 9 a.m.-5 p.m. Monday-Friday*

## WHAT TO SEE AND DO
### NEW JERSEY CHILDREN'S MUSEUM

*599 Valley Health Plaza, Paramus, 201-262-5151; www.njcm.com*
Interactive displays on aviation, firefighting; TV studio, hospital. Gift shop. Daily. Hours Weekdays, Monday-Friday 10 a.m.-6 p.m., Weekends, October 1-April 30, 10 a.m.-6 p.m., May 1-September 30, 10 a.m.-5 p.m.

### VAN SAUN COUNTY PARK

*216 Forest Ave., Paramus, 201-336-7275; www.co.bergen.nj.us/parks/Parks*
Fishing lake; bike trail, tennis (fee), horseshoes, shuffleboard, ice-skating, sledding, picnicking, concession, playgrounds, ball fields (permit). Zoo, train, pony rides (fees). Garden surrounding historic Washington Spring. Park. Daily.

**NEW JERSEY**

★
★
★
★
★

## HOTEL

### ★★CROWNE PLAZA HOTEL AT PARAMUS PARK

*601 From Road, Paramus, 201-262-6900, 800-496-7621; www.crowneplaza.com*
120 rooms. High-speed Internet access. $$

# PARK RIDGE

## RESTAURANT

### ★★★THE PARK STEAKHOUSE

*151 Kinderkamack Road, Park Ridge, 201-930-1300; www.theparksteakhouse.com*
This classic American steakhouse is a local favorite, specializing in 21-day dry-aged sirloins (done on premises) and a variety of fish entrées. The chef uses the freshest ingredients in the creative cuisine, and the wine list includes nearly 200 selections. Steak menu. Lunch, dinner. Bar. Children's menu. Business casual attire. Reservations recommended. Valet parking. $$$

# PARSIPPANY

## WHAT TO SEE AND DO

### SIX FLAGS GREAT ADVENTURE THEME PARK/SIX FLAGS WILD SAFARI ANIMAL PARK

*1 Six Flags Blvd., Jackson, 732-928-1821; www.sixflags.com/national*
This family entertainment center includes a 350-acre drive-through safari park with more than 1,200 free-roaming animals from six continents and a 125-acre theme park featuring more than 100 rides, shows and attractions. Late March-late October; schedule varies.

## HOTELS

### ★★BEST WESTERN FAIRFIELD EXECUTIVE INN

*216-234 Route 46 E., Fairfield, 973-575-7700, 800-937-8376; www.bwfei.com*
170 rooms. Complimentary full breakfast. Complimentary high-speed Internet access. Indoor heated pool with whirlpool and outdoor patio area. Fitness room. $

### ★HAMPTON INN

*1 Hilton Court, Parsippany, 973-267-7373, 800-445-8667; www.hampton-inn.com*
Pool, wireless Internet. $

### ★★★HILTON PARSIPPANY

*1 Hilton Court, Parsippany, 973-267-7373, 800-445-8667; www.parsippany.hilton.com*
The Hilton Parsippany is located 25 minutes from the Newark International Airport and 27 miles from New York. 509 rooms. High-speed Internet service. $$

### ★★PRIME HOTEL & SUITES FAIRFIELD

*690 Route 46 E., Fairfield, 973-227-9200, 800-496-7621; www.crowneplaza.com*
204 rooms. $$

★
★
★
★

# PATERSON

Named after Governor William Paterson, this city owes its present and historic emi-
nence as an industrial city to Alexander Hamilton. He was the first to realize the
possibility of harnessing the Great Falls of the Passaic River for industrial purposes.
As Secretary of the Treasury, he helped to form the Society for Establishment of Use-
ful Manufactures in 1791, and a year later he was instrumental in choosing Paterson
as the site of its initial ventures. Paterson was the country's major silk-producing town
in the late 1800s. Today, it is a diversified industrial center. The area surrounding the
Great Falls is now being restored and preserved as a historic district.

*Information: Great Falls Visitor Center, 65 McBride Ave. across from the Great Falls,
Paterson, 973-279-9587 or Special Events Office, 72 McBride Ave., Paterson,
973-523-9201; www.patersonnj.gov*

## WHAT TO SEE AND DO

### AMERICAN LABOR MUSEUM-BOTTO HOUSE NATIONAL LANDMARK

*83 Norwood St., Haledon, 973-595-7953; www.museumsusa.org*

The history of the working class is presented through restored period rooms, changing
exhibits and ethnic gardens. Tours, seminars and workshops are offered. Wednesday-
Saturday afternoons. Museum Hours: Other times by appointment.; Museum:
Wednesday-Saturday 1-5 p.m.; Office: Monday-Friday 9 a.m.-5 p.m.

### GARRET MOUNTAIN RESERVATION

*Rifle Camp Road and Mountain Avenue, Paterson, 973-881-4832*

A 575-acre woodland park on a 502-foot-high plateau. Fishing pond (stocked with
trout), boat dock, rowboats, paddleboats; trails, stables, picnic groves.

**201**

### GREAT FALLS HISTORIC DISTRICT CULTURAL CENTER

*65 McBride Ave., Paterson, Location: City Hall Room 155 Market St., Paterson, NJ,
973-321-9587; www.patcity.com*

Includes 77-foot-high falls, park and picnic area, renovated raceway system, restored
19th-century buildings. Office hours: Monday-Friday 9 a.m.-4.30 p.m.

### LAMBERT CASTLE

*3 Valley Road, Paterson, 973-247-0085; www.lambertcastle.com*

Built by an English immigrant who rose to wealth as a silk manufacturer. The 1893
castle of brownstone and granite houses a local history museum; restored period
rooms, art-history gallery, library. Wednesday, Friday, Sunday.

### RIFLE CAMP PARK

*Rifle Camp Road, West Paterson, 973-881-4832*

This 158-acre park is 584 feet above sea level. Includes nature and geology trails, nature
center with astronomical observatory, walking paths, fitness course. Picnic areas.

**NEW JERSEY**

# PENNSVILLE

## WHAT TO SEE AND DO
### FORT MOTT STATE PARK
*454 Fort Mott Road, Pennsville, 856-935-3218;*
*www.state.nj.us/dep/parksandforests/parks/fortmott.html*
*Directions: Take I-295 or NJ Turnpike to exit 1 at Pennsville, Route 49 E to Fort Mott*
*Road. Turn right onto Fort Mott Road and travel three miles. Park is located on right.*
A 104-acre park at Finns Point; established in 1837 as a defense of the port of
Philadelphia. North of the park is Finns Point National Cemetery, where more than
2,500 Union and Confederate soldiers are buried. Fishing, ferry ride, picnicking,
playground, overlook.

## RESTAURANT
### ★★J. G. COOK'S RIVERVIEW INN
*60 Main St., Pennsville, 856-678-3700; www.riverviewinn.nets*
Lunch, dinner. Closed Monday. Bar. Children's menu. Outdoor seating. Hours:
Monday and Tuesday Closed; Wednesday and Thursday, Lunch 11:30 a.m.-4 p.m.
Dinner 4-10 p.m., Friday and Saturday, Lunch 11:30 a.m.-4 p.m. Dinner 4-11 p.m.,
Sunday, Dinner Only 2-9 p.m. **$$$**

# POINT PLEASANT BEACH

## RESTAURANT

### ★★MARLINS CAFÉ
*1901 Ocean Ave., Point Pleasant Beach, 732-714-8035*
American menu. Lunch, dinner. Bar. Children's menu. Casual attire. **$$**

# PRINCETON
In 1776, the first State Legislature of New Jersey met in Princeton University's Nassau Hall. Washington and his troops surprised and defeated a superior British Army
in the 1777 Battle of Princeton. From June to November 1783, Princeton was the
new nation's capital. Around the same time, Washington was staying at Rockingham
in nearby Rocky Hill, where he wrote and delivered his famous "Farewell Orders to
the Armies."

Princeton's life is greatly influenced by the university, which opened here in
1756; at that time it was known as the College of New Jersey. In 1896, on the 150th
anniversary of its charter, the institution became Princeton University. Woodrow
Wilson, the first president of the university who was not a clergyman, held the office
from 1902 to 1910. Princeton is also the home of the Institute for Advanced Study,
where Albert Einstein spent the last years of his life.
*Information: Chamber of Commerce, 9 Vandeventer Ave., Princeton, 609-520-1776;*
*www.princetonchamber.org*

## WHAT TO SEE AND DO
### BAINBRIDGE HOUSE
*158 Nassau St., Princeton, 609-921-6748; www.princetonhistory.org*
Circa-1766 birthplace of commander of the *USS Constitution* during the War of 1812.
Changing exhibits on Princeton history; research library (Tuesday, Saturday; fee).
Museum shops. Also offers walking tours of historic district (Sunday; fee).

## KUSER FARM MANSION AND PARK

*Newkirk Ave., Princeton, 609-890-3630; www.state.nj.us*

Farm and 1890s summer mansion of Fred Kuser; more than 20 rooms open, which include many original furnishings. Grounds consist of 22 acres with original buildings including coachman's house, chicken house, tennis pavilion. Park with picnic areas, quoit courts, lawn bowling, walking trails; formal garden, gazebo. Tours May-November, Thursday-Sunday; February-April, Saturday and Sunday; limited hours, call for schedule and holiday closings. Self-guided tour maps of grounds. Special programs, lectures and video evenings throughout the year.

## MCCARTER THEATRE

*91 University Place, Princeton, 608-258-2787, 888-278-7932; www.mccarter.org*

Professional repertory company performs classical and modern drama; concerts, ballet; other special programs year-round.

## MORVEN

*55 Stockton St., Princeton, 609-924-8144; www.historicmorven.org*

Circa-1750 house of Richard Stockton, signer of the Declaration of Independence. April-October, Wednesday-Friday, Sunday.

## NASSAU HALL

*Princeton University, Princeton, 609-258-3000; www.princeton.edu*

(1756) Provided all college facilities, classrooms, dormitories, library and prayer hall for about 50 years. New Jersey's first legislature met here in 1776, and the Continental Congress met here in 1783, when Princeton was the capital. During the Revolution, it served as a barracks and hospital for Continental and British troops.

## PRINCETON BATTLE MONUMENT

*Monument Drive and Stockton streets, Princeton*

The work of Frederick W. MacMonnies, this 50-foot block of Indiana limestone commemorates the famous 1777 battle when George Washington's troops defeated the British.

## PRINCETON CEMETERY

*Witherspoon and Wiggens streets, Princeton, 609-924-1369;*
*www.princetonol.com/groups/cemetery*

Buried in the Presidents' Plot are 11 university Presidents, including Aaron Burr, Sr., Jonathan Edwards and John Witherspoon. Monument to Grover Cleveland and grave of Paul Tulane, in whose honor Tulane University was named.

## PRINCETON UNIVERSITY

*1 Nassau Hall, Princeton, 609-258-3603; www.princeton.edu*

(1746) An Ivy League college (4,500 undergraduate students, 1,650 graduate students) that has been coeducational since 1969. A campus guide service shows the visitor points of interest on the main campus. Daily.

**NEW JERSEY**

★
★
★
★
☆

### THE PUTNAM SCULPTURES

One of the largest modern outdoor sculpture showcases in the country, with 19 sculptures on display throughout the campus, including pieces by Picasso, Moore, Noguchi, Calder and Lipchitz.

### WOODROW WILSON SCHOOL OF PUBLIC AND INTERNATIONAL AFFAIRS

*Princeton University, Robertson Hall Princeton, 609-258-4831; wws.princeton.edu*
Designed by Minoru Yamasaki; reflecting pool and "Fountain of Freedom" by James Fitzgerald.

## HOTELS

### ★★★HYATT REGENCY PRINCETON

*102 Carnegie Center, Princeton, 609-987-1234, 800-233-1234; www.hyatt.com*
This hotel is nestled on 16 acres of landscaped property just one mile from the city's business center and near the Princeton Junction Train Station. Guests receive a complimentary shuttle to anywhere within a five-mile radius of the property. 347 newly renovated stylish guestrooms. Airport transportation available. **$$**

### ★★NASSAU INN

*10 Palmer Square, Princeton, 609-921-7500, 800-862-7728; www.nassauinn.com*
203 rooms. Complimentary continental breakfast. 24-hour fitness center. High-speed Internet access **$$**

### ★★★PEACOCK INN

*20 Bayard Lane, Princeton, 609-924-1707; www.peacockinn.com*
This colonial structure was built in the 1700s and was once the home to a number of prominent members of the Princeton community, including John Deare, a member of the 1783 Continental Congress. Each guest room is named after a previous owner. Rooms like Swain and Lindsay feature four-poster queen beds, down quilts, fireplaces and full baths with tubs, whereas the Deare includes an antique French double bed. The inn's restaurant, Le Plumet Royal, features a delectable menu that includes maple-seared duck breast and roasted rack of lamb. Princeton University is just two blocks away. 17 rooms. Complimentary continental breakfast. **$$**

### ★★★PRINCETON MARRIOTT HOTEL & CONFERENCE CENTER AT FORRESTAL

*100 College Road, East, Princeton, 609-452-7800, 800-943-6709; www.marriott.com*
Located on 25 wooded acres, this newly renovated hotel offers a full-service spa, health club, pool and jogging and recreational facilities. 290 rooms. Airport transportation available. High-speed Internet access. Business center. Express check-in/check-out. Concierge. Complimentary on-site parking. **$**

### ★★THE PRINCETON PREMIER HOTEL

*4355 Route 1 S, Princeton, 609-452-2400; www.princetonpremier.com*
241 rooms. Pets allowed. Onsite swimming pool. High-speed Internet access. Onsite Whirlpool. Wireless Internet access. **$$**

## RESTAURANTS
### ★★ALCHEMIST AND BARRISTER

*28 Witherspoon, Princeton, 609-924-5555; www.alchemistandbarrister.com*
Lunch, dinner, Sunday brunch 11 a.m.-3 p.m. Bar. Outdoor seating. $$$

### ★★★TRE PIANI

*120 Rockingham Row, Princeton, 609-452-1515; www.trepiani.com*
In its dining room, bistro and banquet space, Tre Piani (meaning three floors in Italian) serves entrées such as grilled filet mignon with wild mushroom ragu and a crispy potato and cheese galette; prosciutto-wrapped tuna loin with white bean stew and cherry tomatoes; and breast of Muscovy duck with duck confit and walnut risotto. Italian, Mediterranean menu. Lunch, dinner. Bar. Casual attire. Outdoor seating. $$$

# RED BANK

Formed in 1870, Red Bank is a historic community on the shores of the Navesink River in New Jersey's Monmouth County.

## HOTEL
### ★★COURTYARD BY MARRIOTT

*245 Half Mile Road, Red Bank, 732-530-5552, 800-321-2211; www.courtyard.com*
146 rooms. High-speed Internet access. Bar. Pool (indoor pool, outdoor pool). $$

## RESTAURANTS
### ★★2 SENZA RISTORANTE

*2 Bridge Ave., Building 5, Red Bank, 732-758-0999; www.2senza.com*
Italian, Mediterranean menu. Lunch, dinner. Closed Monday. Children's menu. Casual attire. Outdoor seating. $$

### ★★★FROMAGERIE

*26 Ridge Road, Rumson, 732-842-8088; www.fromagerierestaurant.com*
This romantic French restaurant first opened in 1972. Classical French cuisine is paired with an award-winning selection of wines, some of which may be sampled during special gourmet wine dinners. French menu. Lunch, dinner. Bar. Jacket required. Valet parking. Dinner: Tuesday-Thursday 5 p.m.-10 p.m., Friday and Saturday 5-11 p.m., Lunch: Friday 11.30 a.m.-2.30 p.m., Sunday Brunch: 10.30 a.m.-3 p.m., Sunday Dinner: 4-9 p.m. $$$

### ★GAETANO'S

*10 Wallace St., Red Bank, 732-741-1321; www.gaetanosrebank.com*
Italian menu. Lunch, dinner. Casual attire. Outdoor seating. $$

### ★OAK BRIDGE TAVERN

*115 Oakland St., Red Bank, 732-842-4830; www.oakbridgetavern.com*
German menu. Dinner. Closed Monday. Bar. Children's menu. Casual attire. Outdoor seating. $$

NEW JERSEY

★
★
★
★
★

### ★★★MOLLY PITCHER INN

*88 Riverside Ave., Red Bank, 732-747-2500, 800-221-1372;*
*www.mollypitcher-oysterpoint.com*

Located in a waterfront hotel on the banks of the Navensink river, this sophisticated restaurant serves up dishes like country duck with smoked bacon, roasted pearl onions and cous cous or salmon with California avocado mashed potatoes and overnight tomatoes. Breakfast, lunch, dinner, Sunday brunch. Bar. Children's menu. Jacket required. Wireless Internet connectivity. Fitness room. Pool. **$$**

### ★★★THE RAVEN & THE PEACH

*740 River Road, Fair Haven, 732-747-4666; www.ravenandthepeach.net*
Guests will enjoy dining at this popular, casual restaurant. French menu. Lunch, dinner. Bar. Children's menu. Valet parking. Outdoor seating. **$$$**

# RUTHERFORD

## WHAT TO SEE AND DO

### FAIRLEIGH DICKINSON UNIVERSITY-RUTHERFORD CAMPUS

*West Passaic and Montross Avenues, Rutherford, 201-692-7032;*
*www.view.fdu.edu/default.aspx?id=2050*

(1942) On campus (2,300 students) is the Kingsland House (1670), in which George Washington stayed in August 1783; and the Castle, an 1888 copy of Chateau d'Amboise in France.

### MEADOWLANDS RACETRACK

*50 Highway 120, East Rutherford, 201-935-8500; www.meadowlands.com*
The suburban leafy Meadowlands complex offers fine thoroughbred racing from September-mid-December and harness racing for the remainder of the year. Wednesday-Sunday.

### NEW JERSEY DEVILS (NHL)

*Continental Airlines Arena, 50 Highway 120 N., East Rutherford, 800-653-3845;*
*www.nhl.com/devils*
Professional hockey team.

### NEW JERSEY NETS (NBA)

*Continental Airlines Arena, 50 Highway 120, East Rutherford, 201-935-8888;*
*www.nba.com/nets*
Professional basketball team.

### NEW YORK GIANTS (NFL)

*Giants Stadium, 50 Highway 120, East Rutherford, 201-935-8111; www.giants.com*
Professional football team.

### NEW YORK JETS (NFL)

*The Meadowlands, 50 Highway 120, East Rutherford, 201-583-7000;*
*www.newyorkjets.com*
Professional football team.

**NEW YORK RED BULLS (MLS)**

*One Harmon Plaza Eighth Floor, Secaucus, 201-583-7000; www.web.mlsnet.com/t107*
Professional soccer team.

## HOTELS

### ★FAIRFIELD INN

*850 Paterson Plank Road, East Rutherford, 201-507-5222, 800-228-2800;*
*www.fairfieldinn.com*
141 rooms. Complimentary continental breakfast. Pets not accepted. **$**

# SKYLANDS AT RINGWOOD STATE PARK

Skylands, the official state garden of New Jersey, covers 96 acres, with Skylands Manor House at its center. The Tudor-style manor house, circa 1922, holds an outstanding collection of antique stained-glass medallions set in leaded windows. Guided house tours are offered one Sunday each month from March through December (973-962-9534).

The walking here is largely on marked dirt paths, with some paved drives and paths. Start at the Visitors Center/Carriage House and pick up a self-guided tour brochure. Walk first to the right (in the general direction of Parking Lot A), skirting the manor house counter-clockwise. The Winter Garden contains New Jersey's largest Jeffery pine, a century-old upright beech and an elegant weeping beech. The Japanese umbrella pine is distinctive for its dark green needles. Also on display here are Atlas cedars and an Algerian fir, a tree that produces seven-inch-tall, purple standing cones.

Walk around the house along the lawn to the Terrace Garden. This garden comprises five terraces, each with its own particular ambience. Continue past a pair of Sweet Bay Magnolias to the third level. Here the centerpiece is a rectangular reflecting pool that in summer displays water lilies and tropical fish. Surrounding it is a large collection of azaleas and rhododendrons that bloom in many colors. Next comes the Summer Garden, home to annuals and day lilies, followed by the final terrace level, the Peony Garden.

Walk to the left into the Lilac Garden, which peaks in mid-May. Step onto Maple Avenue, the paved lane, and walk back toward the house. On the right, you'll see the Perennial Garden. A constant flow of color is maintained here from March until November. Just beyond that stands the Annual Garden, a frequently changing formal garden centered on a 16th-century Italian marble well. Move from there to the right, turn around and walk along Crab Apple Vista, a 1,600-foot grassy corridor of 166 Carmine crab apple trees that erupts into full bloom in early- to mid-May. At the end of the Vista stands a series of sculptures known as the "Four Continents Statues" and to the left, a collection of horse chestnut trees.

Turn left at the horse chestnut trees, and another world appears, revealing woodland paths that travel past swan ponds and through a bog. The paths also travel through a cactus collection, a wildflower garden and a heather garden and end at a colorful yet formal Rhododendron Display Garden. From here, follow East Cottage Road as it winds its way back to the Carriage House.

NEW JERSEY

★
★
★
★
★

### ★★★SHERATON MEADOWLANDS HOTEL AND CONFERENCE CENTER

*2 Meadowlands Plaza, East Rutherford, 201-896-0500, 800-325-3535;*
*www.sheraton.com*

Located just across the river, this newly renovated hotel is only minutes from Manhattan. Many guest rooms offer views of the city's sparkling skyline. Grab a cup of coffee from the full-service Starbucks on site before heading out to shop at the nearby outlets, or hunker down in the Chairman's Grill for a hearty bite before the Giants game. 443 rooms. Airport transportation available. High-speed Internet access. **$$**

# SALEM

Salem is said to be the oldest English settlement on the Delaware River. The town and its surrounding area have more than 60 18th-century houses and buildings, as well as many points of historical interest. In the Friends Burying Ground on Broadway stands the 600-year-old Salem Oak, under which John Fenwick, the town's founder, signed a treaty with the Lenni-Lenape tribe.

*Information: Salem County Chamber of Commerce, 91A S. Virginia Ave.,*
*Carneys Point, 856-299-6699; www.salemnjchamber.homestead.com*

## WHAT TO SEE AND DO
### ALEXANDER GRANT HOUSE

*79-83 Market St., Salem, 856-935-5004; www.nps.gov*

Headquarters of Salem County Historical Society (1721). Twenty rooms with period furniture; Wistarburg glass, Native American relics, dolls, paintings; genealogy library; stone barn. Tuesday-Friday afternoons; also open the second Saturday afternoon of each month.

★
★
★
★
★

# SCOTCH PLAINS

## RESTAURANT
### ★★★STAGE HOUSE INN

*366 Park Ave., Scotch Plains, 908-322-4224; www.stagehouserestaurant.com*

A local favorite, this establishment offers lightened versions of classic French dishes, beautifully presented and full of flavor. Guests enjoy the simple, refined atmosphere and the casual patio dining. American menu. Lunch, dinner. Bar. Business casual attire. Reservations recommended. Outdoor seating. **$$$**

# SEASIDE PARK

## WHAT TO SEE AND DO
### ISLAND BEACH STATE PARK

*Seaside Park, 732-793-0506; www.state.nj.us/dep/parksandforests/parks/island.html*

This strip of land (3,002 acres) is across the water, north of Long Beach Island and faces Barnegat Lighthouse. There are two natural areas (Northern Area and Southern Area) and a recreational zone in the center. Excellent swimming and fishing in Atlantic Ocean (seasonal). Nature tours. Picnicking. Daily.

## HOTEL

### ★★WINDJAMMER MOTOR INN

*First and Central avenues, Seaside Park, 732-830-2555;*
*www.windjammermotorinn.com*

39 rooms. Happy hour daily: 3-7 p.m. Free hors d'oeuvres. **$**

# SECAUCUS

## HOTEL

### ★★HOLIDAY INN HARMON MEADOW SPORTPLEX

*300 Plaza Drive, Secaucus, 201-348-2000, 888-465-4329;*
*www.holiday-inn.com/secaucusnj*

161 rooms. **$**

# SHORT HILLS

## WHAT TO SEE AND DO

### CORA HARTSHORN ARBORETUM AND BIRD SANCTUARY

*324 Forest Drive S., Short Hills, 973-376-3587; www.hartshornarboretum.org*

A 17-acre sanctuary with nature trails; guided walks. Stone House Museum with nature exhibits (late September-mid-June, Tuesday, Thursday and Saturday). Grounds daily.

### PAPER MILL PLAYHOUSE

*Brookside Drive and Old Shore Hills Road, Millburn, 973-376-4343;*
*www.papermill.org/papermill.html*

State Theater of New Jersey. A variety of plays, musicals and children's theater (Wednesday-Sunday); matinees (Thursday, Saturday and Sunday).

## HOTEL

### ★★★HILTON SHORT HILLS

*41 John F. Kennedy Parkway, Short Hills, 973-379-0100, 800-445-8667;*
*www.hiltonshorthills.com*

Executives visiting the New York metropolitan area appreciate this hotel's proximity to Manhattan, New Jersey's businesses and Newark airport—yet this hotel is not just a destination for corporate travelers. Located across from the fabulous Short Hills Mall, the Hilton Short Hills is also a favorite stomping ground for shopaholics. A beauty salon keeps guests properly primped, whereas a fitness center and pool are a boon for fitness enthusiasts. 308 rooms. Airport transportation available. Children's menu. Fitness room. Pool. **$$**

## RESTAURANT

### ★★★THE DINING ROOM

*41 John F. Kennedy Parkway, Short Hills, 973-379-0100; www.hilton.com*

American, French menu. Dinner. Closed Sunday. Bar. Jacket required. Valet parking. **$$$**

# SHREWSBURY

## WHAT TO SEE AND DO

### ALLEN HOUSE

*400 Sycamore Ave., Shrewsbury, 732-462-1466; www.monmouthhistory.org*

(Circa 1750) Lower floor restored as tavern of the Revolutionary period; traveler's bedrooms upstairs.

## HOTEL

### ★★★SHADOWBROOK

*Route 35, Shrewsbury, 732-747-0200, 800-634-0078; www.shadowbrook.com*

Established in 1942, this restaurant is set in an authentic Georgian mansion. Catering for weddings is its specialty, with bridal suites, attended restrooms and beautiful gardens for cocktail parties or receptions. Dinner. Closed Monday. Bar. Children's menu. Jacket required. Valet parking. $$$

# SOMERS POINT

## RESTAURANTS

### ★★CRAB TRAP

*2 Broadway, Somers Point, 609-927-7377; www.thecrabtrap.com*

Seafood menu. Lunch, dinner. Bar. Children's menu. Casual attire. Outdoor seating. On the bay. Lunch: Every day 11 a.m.-3 p.m., Dinner: Sunday-Thursday 3-10 p.m., Friday-Saturday 3-11 p.m. $$

### ★GREGORY'S

*900 Shore Road, Somers Point, 609-927-6665; www.gregorysbar.com*

Seafood menu. Lunch, dinner, late-night. Bar. Children's menu. Casual attire. Outdoor seating. $$

### ★★MAC'S

*908 Shore Road, Somers Point, 609-927-2759; www.macsrestaurant.com*

Italian, American menu. Dinner. Bar. Children's menu. Casual attire. Reservations recommended. $$$

# SOMERSET

## HOTELS

### ★★DOUBLETREE HOTEL

*200 Atrium Drive, Somerset, 732-469-2600, 800-222-8733;*
*www.somerset.doubletree.com*

361 rooms. High-speed Internet access. $$

### ★★★MARRIOTT SOMERSET

*110 Davidson Ave., Somerset, 732-560-0500, 800-228-9290;*
*www.crowneplaza.com/somersetnj*

Sleep comfortably on the Marriott Somerset's 300 thread-count sheets. And if you can pull the kids away from the hotel's connecting indoor/outdoor pool, you can visit

★
★
★
★
★

nearby attractions, including Six Flags Great Adventure, golf courses and Rutgers University. The Garden State Exhibit Center and Ukrainian Cultural Center are adjacent to the hotel. 440 rooms. Indoor pool. Outdoor pool. Whirlpool. $$

# SOMERVILLE

*Information: Somerset County Chamber of Commerce, 64 W. End Ave., Somerville, 908-725-1552; www.somersetcountychamber.com*

## WHAT TO SEE AND DO

### DUKE GARDENS
*80 Route 206 S., Somerville, 908-722-3700; www.dukefarms.org*
Features 11 gardens under glass, including colonial, desert, Italian, Asian, English and tropical; 45-minute guided tour (October-May, daily). No high heels, no cameras. Reservations required; contact Duke Gardens Foundation (Monday-Friday).

### OLD DUTCH PARSONAGE STATE HISTORIC SITE
*38 Washington Place, Somerville, 908-725-1015; www.state.nj.us*
Moved from its original 1751 location, from 1758 to 1781 this brick building was the home of the Reverend Jacob Hardenbergh, who founded Queens College, now Rutgers University. Some furnishings and memorabilia on display. Wednesday-Sunday; hours may vary.

### WALLACE HOUSE STATE HISTORIC SITE
*38 Washington Place, Somerville, 908-725-1015; www.state.nj.us*
General and Mrs. Washington made their headquarters here immediately after the house was built in 1778, whereas the army was stationed at Camp Middlebrook. Period furnishings. Wednesday-Sunday; hours may vary.

# SPRING LAKE

## HOTELS

### ★★★HEWITT WELLINGTON HOTEL
*200 Monmouth Ave., Spring Lake, 732-974-1212; www.hewittwellington.com*
Situated on Spring Lake in the town of the same name, this Victorian-style hotel offers well-appointed rooms and suites with wireless Internet access, along with a wraparound porch on which guests can relax. Those who wish to explore the area will find golf courses and tennis courts just a short distance away as well as unique shops and restaurants. 29 rooms. Children over 12 years only. $$

### ★★SPRING LAKE INN
*104 Salem Ave., Spring Lake, 732-449-2010; www.springlakeinn.com*
16 rooms. Complimentary full breakfast. $$

## SPECIALTY LODGINGS

### ASHLING COTTAGE
*106 Sussex Ave., Spring Lake, 732-449-3553, 888-274-5464; www.ashlingcottage.com*
A Victorian-style frame house, Ashling Cottage was built in 1877 with materials from the Philadelphia Bicentennial agricultural exhibit by James Hulett, a prominent

Philadelphia architect. 11 rooms. Closed November-March. Children over 14 years only. Complimentary full breakfast. **$$**

### CHATEAU INN AND SUITES

*500 Warren Ave., Spring Lake, 732-974-2000, 877-974-5253; www.chateauinn.com*
The Chateau Inn and Suites offers high-speed Internet access, bathrooms with imported marble and flatscreen televisions, along with wood-burning fireplaces and patios or balconies. 36 rooms. Renovated Victorian hotel (1888). Overlooks parks, lake. **$$**

### NORMANDY INN

*21 Tuttle Ave., Spring Lake, 732-449-7172, 800-449-1888; www.normandyinn.com*
Found on the National Register of Historic Places, the Normandy Inn offers guests a true Victorian experience. All guest rooms include antiques, private baths and high-speed Internet access and some feature four-poster Tester beds, Jacuzzis, fireplaces and private porches. The inn's complimentary bicycles are great for exploring all that the scenic Spring Lake area has to offer. 18 rooms. Complimentary full breakfast. Built as a private residence in 1888; 19th-century antiques. **$$**

### THE SANDPIPER INN

*7 Atlantic Ave., Spring Lake, 732-449-6060, 800-824-2779; www.sandpiperinn.com*
The Sandpiper Inn features a wraparound porch and a glass-enclosed heated pool. 15 rooms. Complimentary full breakfast. Opposite beach. **$$**

### WHITE LILAC INN

*414 Central Ave., Spring Lake, 732-449-0211; www.whitelilac.com*
Set on a tree-lined street just a few blocks from the Atlantic Ocean, the White Lilac Inn features wraparound porches on each level and uniquely themed rooms with in-room fireplaces and period furnishings. Each morning, breakfast is served in the dining area and on the enclosed porch. Nine rooms. Closed January. Children over 14 years only. Complimentary full breakfast. **$$**

## RESTAURANTS

### ★★THE BLACK TRUMPET

*7 Atlantic Ave., Spring Lake, 732-449-4700; www.theblacktrumpet.com*
American menu. Lunch, dinner. Casual attire. Reservations recommended. **$$**

### ★★★MILL INN

*Old Mill Road, Spring Lake, 732-449-1800; www.themillatslh.com*
For more than 60 years, the Mill has been a popular New Jersey dining destination, serving contemporary American cuisine such as fresh seafood and prime aged steaks. On special nights, the Mill features supper club events with comedians and musicians, as well as big band nights. American menu. Lunch, dinner. Closed Monday. Bar. Children's menu. Casual attire. Reservations recommended. Valet parking. Outdoor seating. **$$**

# STANHOPE

## WHAT TO SEE AND DO

### WATERLOO VILLAGE RESTORATION

*525 Waterloo Road, Stanhope, 973-347-0900; www.waterloovillage.org*

Known as the Andover Forge during the Revolutionary War, this was once a busy town on the Morris Canal. The 18th-century buildings include Stagecoach Inn, houses, craft barns, gristmill, apothecary shop, general store. Music festival during summer (fee). Mid-April-mid-November, Wednesday-Sunday.

## RESTAURANT

### ★★THE BLACK FOREST INN

*249 Route 206 N., Stanhope, 973-347-3344; www.blackforestinn.com*

German, Continental menu. Lunch, dinner. Closed Tuesday. Bar. Casual attire. **$$**

# STONE HARBOR

*Information: Stone Harbor Chamber of Commerce, 212 96th St., Stone Harbor, 609-368-6101 or Cape May County Chamber of Commerce, 609-465-7181; www.capemaycountychamber.com*

## WHAT TO SEE AND DO

### WETLANDS INSTITUTE

*1075 Stone Harbor Blvd., Stone Harbor, 609-368-1211; www.wetlandsinstitute.org*

Environmental center focusing on coastal ecology. Also includes observation tower, marsh trail, aquarium, films and guided walks (July and August, daily). Bookstore. Mid-May-mid-October, daily; rest of year, Tuesday-Saturday; two weeks in late December-early January.

## SPECIAL EVENTS

### SAIL INTO SUMMER BOAT SHOW

*212 96th St., Stone Harbor, 609-368-6101; www.stoneharborbeach.com*

Pleasure boating, family entertainment, musicians, food. First weekend in May. 10 a.m.-7 p.m.

### WINGS 'N WATER FESTIVAL

*1075 Stone Harbor Blvd., Stone Harbor, 609-368-1211; www.wetlandsinstitute.org*

Arts and crafts, entertainment, seafood. Third full weekend in September.

# STRATHMERE

## RESTAURANT

### ★★DEAUVILLE INN

*201 Willard Road, Strathmere, 609-263-2080; www.deauvilleinn.com*

Seafood, steak menu. Lunch, dinner, late-night. Closed Tuesday-Wednesday in September 30-April 15. March. Bar. Children's menu. Casual attire. Reservations recommended. Valet parking. Outdoor seating. **$$$**

**213**

**NEW JERSEY**

★
★
★
★
★

# TEANECK

## HOTEL

### ★★★MARRIOTT GLENPOINTE

*100 Frank W. Burr Blvd., Teaneck, 201-836-0600, 800-992-7752;*
*www.teaneckmarriott.com*
Onsite dining options at the Marriott Glenpointe include elegant Tuscan cuisine at the Grille Restaurant and light American fare at Glen Lounge. For a day of total relaxation, guests can head to The Spa at Glenpointe, whereas golf enthusiasts have a choice of seven nearby courses. 347 rooms. **$$**

# TOMS RIVER

*Information: Toms River-Ocean County Chamber of Commerce, 1200 Hooper Ave.,*
*Toms River, 732-349-0220; www.oc-chamber.com*

## WHAT TO SEE AND DO

### COOPER ENVIRONMENTAL CENTER

*1170 Cattus Island Blvd., Toms River, 732-270-6960;*
*www.ocean.nj.us/Parks/cattus.html*
A 530-acre facility with three-mile bay front. Boat tours (summer; free); seven miles of marked trails, picnicking (grills), playground. Nature center. Daily.

## HOTELS

### ★★HOLIDAY INN TOMS RIVER

*290 Route 37 E. and Clifton Ave., Toms River, 732-244-4000, 888-465-4329;*
*www.holidayinn.com*
122 rooms. **$**

### ★★RAMADA INN

*2373 Route 9, Toms River, 732-905-2626; www.ramada.com*
154 rooms. Complimentary continental breakfast. Restaurant, bar. Tennis. **$**

## RESTAURANT

### ★THE OLD TIME TAVERN

*Dover Mall Route 166, Toms River, 732-349-2387*
American menu. Lunch, dinner. Bar. Children's menu. Casual attire. **$$**

# TRENTON

The capital of New Jersey since 1790, Trenton is one of the fastest-growing business and industrial areas in the country and has been a leading rubber manufacturing center since colonial times.
*Information: Mercer County Chamber of Commerce, 214 W. State St., Trenton,*
*609-393-4143; www.mercerchamber.org*

## WHAT TO SEE AND DO

### AUDITORIUM

*205 W. State St., Trenton, 609-292-6464*
Lectures, films, music, children's theater. Some fees.

## COLLEGE ART GALLERY
*Trenton, 609-771-2652*
February-May and September-December, Monday-Friday, Sunday.

## COLLEGE OF NEW JERSEY
*Trenton, 609-771-1855; www.tcnj.edu*
(1855) (6,150 students.) A 250-acre wooded campus with two lakes. Tours of campus.

## FERRY HOUSE STATE HISTORIC SITE
*355 Washington Crossing, Trenton, 609-737-2515;*
*www.state.nj.us/dep/parksandforests/histori*
This building sheltered Washington and some of his men on December 25, 1776 after they had crossed the Delaware from Pennsylvania. It is believed that the strategy for the attack on Trenton was discussed here. Restored as a living history colonial farmhouse; special programs throughout the year. Wednesday-Sunday.

## MAIN BUILDING
Fine art, cultural history, archaeology and natural science exhibits. Tuesday-Sunday.

## NEW JERSEY STATE MUSEUM
*125 W. State St., Trenton, 609-292-6464; www.newjerseystatemuseum.org*
Adjacent to Capitol. Tuesday-Sunday. Saturday 9 a.m.-5 p.m., Sunday noon-5 p.m. Closed Mondays and State Holidays.

## OLD BARRACKS MUSEUM
*Barrack St., Trenton, 609-396-1776; www.oldbarracks.org*
One of the finest examples of colonial barracks in the United States. Built between 1758 and 1759, it housed British, Hessian and Continental troops during the Revolutionary War. Museum contains restored soldiers' squad room, antique furniture, ceramics, firearms, dioramas. Guides in period costumes. Daily.

**215**

## PLANETARIUM
*New Jersey State Museum, 125 W. State St., Trenton, 609-292-6303;*
*www.nj.gov/state/museum/index.htm*
One of few Intermediate Space Transit planetariums that duplicates motions of space vehicles in the world. Programs (weekends; July-August, Tuesday-Sunday). Children over four years only, except during special children's programs. Tickets 30 minutes in advance.

## SESAME PLACE
*100 Sesame Road, Langhorne, 215-752-7070; www.sesameplace.com*
A family play park featuring characters from *Sesame Street*.

## WASHINGTON CROSSING STATE PARK
*355 Washington Crossing-Pennington Road, Titusville, 609-737-0623;*
*www.state.nj.us/dep/parksandforests/parks/washcros.html*
This 996-acre park commemorates the famous crossing on Christmas night, 1776, by the Continental Army under the command of General George Washington. Nature

**NEW JERSEY**

★
★
★
★

trails. Picnicking, playground. Visitor center and nature center (Wednesday-Sunday); open-air summer theater (fee). Admission: $5 per vehicle on weekends, free weekdays. Free for walk-ins or bicycles.

### WILLIAM TRENT HOUSE

*15 Market St., Trenton, 609-989-3027; www.williamtrenthouse.org*

Trenton's oldest house (1719) is an example of Georgian architecture. It was the home of Chief Justice William Trent, for whom the city was named. Colonial garden. Daily, afternoons.

## SPECIAL EVENTS

### REENACTMENT OF CROSSING OF THE DELAWARE

*Washington Crossing State Park, 355 Washington Crossing Road, Trenton, 609-737-9303; www.state.nj.us/dep/parksandforests/historic*

Departs on the afternoon of December 25.

### TRENTON KENNEL CLUB DOG SHOW

*Mercer County Park, Old Trenton and South Post Roads, West Windsor Township, 609-448-6247; www.trentonkennelclub.net/shows.html*

Mercer County Central Park. Early May.

## HOTEL

### ★★★LAFAYETTE YARD MARRIOTT

*1 W. Lafayette St., Trenton, 609-421-4000, 888-796-4662; www.marriott.com/hotels/travel/ttnmc-trenton-marriott-at-lafayette-yard*

Like all Marriott hotels, the Lafayette Yard offers guest rooms with luxurious linens, fluffy comforters and pillows, and a host of amenities including high-speed Internet access. Archives restaurant offers an American menu for breakfast, lunch and dinner, whereas the Archives Bar and Lounge features lighter fare. 197 rooms. Airport transportation available. $$

## RESTAURANT

### ★★MARSILIO'S

*541 Roebling Ave., Trenton, 609-695-1916; www.marsilios.com*

Italian menu. Lunch, dinner. Closed Sunday. Bar. Children's menu. Business casual attire. Reservations recommended. Valet parking. $$

# VERNON

*Information: Vernon Township Municipal Building, 21 Church St., Vernon, 973-764-4055; www.vernontwp.com*

## WHAT TO SEE AND DO

### ACTION PARK

*200 Route 94, Vernon, 973-827-2000, 888-767-0762; www.mountaincreek.com*

Theme park includes 75 self-operative rides, shows and attractions. Action Park has more than 40 water rides, including river rides and Tidal Wave Pool; also Grand Prix racecars, bungee jumping, miniature golf, children's park; food, picnic area. Three daily shows, weekend festival series. Mid-June-Labor Day, daily; late May-mid-June, Thursday-Sunday.

### MOUNTAIN CREEK SKI RESORT

*200 NJ 94, Vernon, 973-827-2000, 888-767-0762; www.mountaincreek.com*

Gondola; four quad, triple, double chairlifts; three surface lifts, rope tow; school, rentals, snowmaking; cafeterias, restaurants, bars, night club; nursery. Forty-three runs; vertical drop 1,040 feet. December-March, daily Night skiing. Spa, country club (daily).

## HOTEL

### ★★★MINERAL HOTEL AND SPA

*2 Chamonix Drive, Vernon, 973-827-5996; www.crystalgolfresort.com*

Located in the Kittaninny Mountains just an hour from New York City, Minerals Hotel and Spa offers 175 guest rooms, all of which include unlimited access to the sports club on site. 201 rooms. Golf, 100 holes. Ski in/ski out. Dial-up Internet access. $$

# WARREN

## HOTEL

### ★★★SOMERSET HILLS HOTEL

*200 Liberty Corner Road, Warren, 908-647-6700, 800-688-0700; www.shh.com*

Visitors will find that this hotel, located in the Watchung Mountains, combines the service of a country inn with the facilities, entertainment and accommodations expected from a full-service hotel. 111 rooms. Complimentary full breakfast. Wireless Internet access. Pets accepted. $$

# WAYNE

Wayne is the home of William Paterson University of New Jersey (1855).

*Information: Tri-County Chamber of Commerce, 2055 Hamburg Turnpike, Wayne, 973-831-7788; www.tricounty.org*

## WHAT TO SEE AND DO

### DEY MANSION

*199 Totowa Road, Wayne, 973-696-1776; www.passaiccountynj.org*

Circa-1740. Restoration of Washington's headquarters was done in 1780; period furnishings. Guided tours. Picnic tables. Wednesday-Sunday.

### MEAD VAN DUYNE HOUSE

*530 Berdan Ave., Wayne, 973-694-7192*

Restored Dutch farmhouse.

### RINGWOOD STATE PARK

*1304 Sloatsburg Road, 973-962-7031;*
*www.state.nj.us/dep/parksandforests/parks/Ringwood*

Ringwood State Park lies in upper Passaic County, near the town of Ringwood, within the heart of the Ramapo Mountains. Consisting of 6,196 acres, the park can be reached by routes 23 and 511 from the west and Route 17 and Sloatsburg Road from the east. Standard fees are charged for each section Memorial Day-Labor Day.

**NEW JERSEY**

★
★
★
★
☆

### RINGWOOD MANOR SECTION

This section features a 51-room mansion containing a collection of Americana; relics of iron-making days (1740); formal gardens. Interpretive tours. Fishing in Ringwood River. Picnic facilities nearby. Tours Wednesday-Sunday.

*Information: Ringwood Manor, Sloatsburg Road, Ringwood, 973-962-2240; www.ringwoodmanor.com*

### SHEPHERD LAKE SECTION

A 541-acre wooded area has trap and skeet shooting all year (fee). The 74-acre Shepherd Lake provides a swimming beach and bathhouse, fishing, boating (ramp). Picnicking.

### SKYLANDS SECTION

Located here is a 44-room mansion modeled after an English baronial house (open to the public on select days). The gardens (90 acres) surrounding the manor house comprise the only botanical garden in the state park system (guided tours upon request; 973-962-7527). This 1,119-acre section also offers fishing, hunting, hiking, mountain biking. Ringwood, www.njbg.org

### TERHUNE MEMORIAL PARK (SUNNYBANK)

*475 Valley Road, Wayne, 973-694-1800; www.waynetownship.com*
Estate of the late Albert Payson Terhune, author of *Lad, a Dog* (1919) and many other books about his collies. Scenic garden; picnic area. Daily.

### VAN RIPER-HOPPER (WAYNE) MUSEUM

*533 Berdan Ave., Wayne, 973-694-7192; www.passaiccountynj.org/ParksHistorical/Historical_Attractions/vanripperhopper*
Circa-1786 Dutch Colonial farmhouse with 18th- and 19th-century furnishings, local historical objects, herb garden, bird sanctuary.

# WEST ORANGE

*Information: West Orange Chamber of Commerce, 973-731-0360; www.westorangechamber.com*

## WHAT TO SEE AND DO

### EAGLE ROCK RESERVATION

*Prospect and Eagle Rock avenues, West Orange, 973-268-3500; www.eaglerockreservation.org*
A 644-foot elevation in the Orange Mountains; visitors see a heavily populated area that stretches from the Passaic River Valley east to New York City. Hiking trails, picnicking, bridle paths. Restaurant. Daily.

### EDISON NATIONAL HISTORIC SITE

*Main Street and Lake Side Avenues, West Orange, 973-324-9973; www.nps.gov/edis*

### EDISON LABORATORY

*Main Street and Lakeside Avenues, West Orange, 973-736-5050; www.nps.gov/edis*
Built by Thomas A. Edison in 1887, this was his laboratory for 44 years. During that time, he was granted more than half of his 1,093 patents (an all-time record).

Here he perfected the phonograph, motion picture camera and electric storage battery. One-hour lab tour (no video cameras, strollers) includes the chemistry lab and library; demonstrations of early phonographs. Visitor center has exhibits; films. Daily.

### SOUTH MOUNTAIN ARENA

*560 Northfield Ave., West Orange, 973-731-3828; www.essexcountynj.org*
Indoor ice rink. Hockey games, special events.

### TURTLE BACK ZOO

*560 Northfield Ave., West Orange, 973-731-5800; www.turtlebackzoo.com*
This 20-acre park features animals in natural surroundings; sea lion pool; miniature train ride (one mile). Picnicking, concessions. Daily Zoo Hours: 10 a.m.-3:30 p.m. Limited schedule December-March.

## RESTAURANTS
### ★★★HIGHLAWN PAVILION

*Eagle Rock Reservation, West Orange, 973-731-3463; www.highlawn.com*
This restaurant offers a picturesque view of the Manhattan skyline. The 1909 building was restored and opened as a restaurant in 1986. A French rotisserie and Italian brick wood-burning oven bring out the flavors of the American cuisine. American menu. Lunch, dinner, late-night. Bar. Jacket required. Reservations recommended. Valet parking. Outdoor seating. $$$

### ★★★THE MANOR

*111 Prospect Ave., West Orange, 973-731-2360; www.themanorrestaurant.com*
One of the most well-known (and most formal) restaurants in New Jersey, the Manor offers dishes such as cilantro sesame seed-coated halibut filet, pan-seared veal tournados and lobster bisque. American menu. Lunch, dinner, Sunday brunch. Closed Monday. Bar. Jacket required. Reservations recommended. Valet parking. $$$

# WHITEHOUSE

## RESTAURANT
### ★★★THE RYLAND INN

*Highway 22 W., Whitehouse, 908-534-4011; www.therylandinn.com*
Using ingredients culled from his seven acres of gardens, chef/owner Craig Shelton creates a simple, seasonal French cuisine at this country-estate restaurant. The decor ranges from homey to hunting lodge, and the wine list is long and varied. French menu. Dinner. Bar. Children's menu. Jacket required. Reservations recommended. Valet parking. $$$$

# WILDWOOD AND WILDWOOD CREST

Wildwood's busy boardwalk extends for approximately two miles along the five miles of protected sandy beach it shares with North Wildwood and Wildwood Crest, two neighboring resorts. The area offers swimming, waterskiing, ocean and bay fishing, boating, sailing, bicycling, golf, tennis and shuffleboard.
*Information: Greater Wildwood Chamber of Commerce, 3306 Pacific Ave., Wildwood, 609-729-4000; www.gwcoc.com*

## HOTELS

### ★ARMADA BY THE SEA

*6503 Ocean Ave., Wildwood Crest, 609-729-3000, 800-399-3001; www.armadamotel.com*
56 rooms. Closed October-mid-April. Free high-speed wireless Internet. **$$**

### ★★EL CORONADO MOTOR INN

*8501 Atlantic Ave., Wildwood Crest, 609-729-1000, 800-227-5302;*
*www.elcoronado.com*
113 rooms. Closed November-April. Restaurant. Children's activity center. Wireless
Internet access in Resort Lobby. Exercise room. **$**

### ★FLEUR DE LIS

*6105 Ocean Ave., Wildwood Crest, 609-522-0123; www.fleurdelismotel.com*
44 rooms. Closed mid-October-mid-April. On beach. Wireless Internet access. Free
parking-one car per unit. **$**

### ★JOLLY ROGER MOTEL

*6805 Atlantic Ave., Wildwood Crest, 609-522-6915, 800-337-5232;*
*www.jollyrogermotel.com*
74 rooms. Closed late September-mid-May. Children's activity center. Free parking.
Swimming pool. **$**

### ★NASSAU INN

*6201 Ocean Ave., Wildwood Crest, 609-729-9077, 800-336-9077;*
*www.nassauinnmotel.com*
56 rooms. Closed mid-October-April. On beach. Wireless network. **$**

### ★★PAN AMERICAN HOTEL

*5901 Ocean Ave., Wildwood Crest, 609-522-6936; www.panamericanhotel.com*
78 rooms. Closed mid-October-mid-May. Children's activity center. Adult swimming
pool. Wireless internet access. **$$**

### ★★PORT ROYAL HOTEL

*6801 Ocean Ave., Wildwood Crest, 609-729-2000; www.portroyalhotel.com*
100 rooms. Closed mid-October-April. Children's activity center. Kiddie pool. **$$**

## SPECIALTY LODGING

### CANDLELIGHT INN

*2310 Central Ave., North Wildwood, 609-522-6200, 800-992-2632;*
*www.candlelight-inn.com*
10 rooms. No children accepted. Complimentary full breakfast. Queen Anne/Victorian-
style house (circa 1905); restored. **$$**

## RESTAURANT

### ★★GARFIELD'S GIARDINO RISTORANTE

*3800 Pacific Ave., Wildwood, 609-729-0120; www.garfieldsnj.net*
Italian, seafood menu. Dinner. Bar. Children's menu. **$$**

# PENNSYLVANIA

FROM ITS EASTERNMOST TIP NEAR BORDENTOWN, NEW JERSEY, TO ITS STRAIGHT WESTERN boundary with Ohio and West Virginia, Pennsylvania's 300-mile stride across the country covers a mountain-and-farm, river-and-stream, mine-and-mill topography. Its cities, people and resources are just as diverse. In the eastern part of the state, Philadelphia is a treasure chest of tradition and historical shrines; in the west, Pittsburgh is a mighty museum of our nation's industrial heritage. Pennsylvania miners dig nearly all the anthracite coal in the United States and still work some of the oldest iron mines in the country. Oil employees work more than 19,000 producing wells, and 55,000 farm families make up 20 percent of the Pennsylvania workforce.

The state is a leader in cigar leaf tobacco, apples, grapes, ice cream, chocolate products, mushrooms and soft drinks, plus factory and farm machinery, electronic equipment, scientific instruments, watches, textile machines, railroad cars, ships, assorted metal products and electrical machinery.

Pennsylvania has also been a keystone of culture. The first serious music in the colonies was heard in Bethlehem; today, both Pittsburgh and Philadelphia have well-known symphonies. Celebrated art galleries, museums and more than 140 institutions of higher learning (including the oldest medical school in the United States at the University of Pennsylvania) are based here.

Swedes made the first settlement on this fertile land in 1643 at Tinicum Island in the Delaware River. The territory became Dutch in 1655 and British in 1664. After Charles II granted William Penn a charter that made him proprietor of "Pennsilvania," the Quaker statesman landed here in 1682 and invested the land with his money and leadership. Commercial, agricultural and industrial growth came quickly.

The Declaration of Independence was signed in Pennsylvania, and the Constitution was drafted here.

*Information: www.state.pa.us*

**★ FUN FACTS** Benjamin Franklin founded the Philadelphia Zoo, the first zoo in the United States.

## ALLENTOWN

Situated in the heart of Pennsylvania Dutch country, Allentown is conveniently accessible via a network of major highways. Allentown was originally incorporated as Northamptontown. The city later took the name of its founder, William Allen, a Chief Justice of Pennsylvania. Allentown was greatly influenced by the Pennsylvania Germans who settled the surrounding countryside and helped the city become the business hub for a rich agricultural community.

*Information: Lehigh Valley Convention & Visitors Bureau, 840 Hamilton St., Allentown, 610-882-9200, 800-747-0561; www.lehighvalleypa.org*

## WHAT TO SEE AND DO
### CEDAR CREST COLLEGE
*100 College Drive, Allentown, 610-437-4471, 800-360-1222; www.cedarcrest.edu*
The women's college, which was founded in 1867 and is now home to 1,700 students, is on an 84-acre campus that includes nationally registered William F. Curtis Arboretum (tours); chapel with stained-glass windows portraying outstanding women in history; art galleries, sculpture gardens, museum and theater. Campus tours.

### DORNEY PARK AND WILDWATER KINGDOM
*3830 Dorney Park Road, Allentown, 610-395-3724*
This amusement and water park is one of the country's oldest. A former fish hatchery, the 200-acre park is home to nearly 100 rides, 11 water slides and four roller coasters. Little ones can discover turtle fountains and squirt guns. Bigger kids can climb and play on a submarine. Older kids may want to torpedo through an enclosed tube or float slowly down a 1,600-foot winding river. Just an hour from Philadelphia, the park also features song and dance revues and 40 food locations, including two air-conditioned, dine-in restaurants. Daily; closed November-April.

### FRANK BUCHMAN HOUSE
*117 N. 11th St., Allentown, 610-435-1074*
Constructed in 1892, this three-story row house, typical of Allentown's inner city, is an example of Victorian architecture; period rooms. Saturday and Sunday afternoons; also by appointment.

### LEHIGH COUNTY MUSEUM
*432 W. Walnut St., Allentown, 610-435-1074; www.lchs.museum*
Exhibits illustrate the economic, social and cultural history of the county. Monday-Saturday 10 a.m.-4 p.m., Sunday 2-4 p.m.

### LIBERTY BELL SHRINE
*622 Hamilton St., Allentown, 610-435-4232;*
*www.libertybellmuseum.org/museum/hours_location.html*
This reconstructed Zion's church has a shrine in basement area where the Liberty Bell was hidden in 1777; contains a full-size replica of the original bell; other historical exhibits, art collection. February-April, Wednesday-Saturday afternoons; May-November, Monday-Saturday afternoons.

★
★
★
★

### LOCK RIDGE FURNACE MUSEUM
*525 N. Franklin St., Allentown, 610-435-4664; www.lchs.museum*
Exhibits on the development of the U.S. iron and steel industry. May-September, Saturday and Sunday afternoons; also by appointment.

### MUHLENBERG COLLEGE
*2400 W. Chew St., Allentown, 484-664-3100; www.muhlenberg.edu*
(1848) (2,000 students.) Founded by the Lutheran Church to honor patriarch of Lutheranism in America. On campus is the Gideon F. Egner Memorial Chapel, an example of Gothic architecture. Also here is the Center for the Arts, a dramatic building designed by renowned architect Philip Johnson, which houses the Muhlenberg Theater Association. Campus tours.

### SAYLOR PARK CEMENT INDUSTRY MUSEUM
*245 N. Second St., Coplay, 610-435-4664; www.nps.gov*
Outdoor historic site featuring remains of cement kilns. Saturday and Sunday 1-4 p.m.

### TREXLER-LEHIGH COUNTY GAME PRESERVE
*5150 Game Preserve Road, Allentown, 610-799-4171; www.lvzoo.org*
A 1,200-acre zoo, petting farm and wilderness tour that is home to more than 350 animals. Scenic overlooks; picnic area. April-October, daily 9:30 a.m.-4 p.m.

### TREXLER MEMORIAL PARK
*Cedar Crest Boulevard and Broadway, Allentown, 610-437-7628*
Spring outdoor bulb display (April-May). Gross Memorial Rose Garden (at peak bloom the second week in June): Trout Nursery and Fish-for-Fun stream. Picnic areas. Band concerts June-August.

### TROUT HALL
*414 W. Walnut St., Allentown, 610-435-4664; www.lchs.museum*
Oldest house in city, Georgian Colonial was built in 1770 and has been restored. Period rooms, museum. Guided tours. April-November, Tuesday-Sunday afternoons; also by appointment.

## SPECIAL EVENTS
### DAS AWKSCHT FESCHT
*Macungie Memorial Park, Allentown, 610-967-2317; www.awkscht.com*
2,500 antique, classic and special-interest autos; entertainment, food, fireworks. First weekend in August.

### DRUM CORPS INTERNATIONAL-EASTERN REGIONAL CHAMPIONSHIP
*J. Birney Crum Stadium, 21st and Linden streets, Allentown, 610-966-5344; www.dci.org*
Drum and bugle corps competition. September.

### GREAT ALLENTOWN FAIR
*Fairgrounds, 17th and Chew streets, Allentown, 610-435-7469; www.allentownfair.com*
Farm and commercial exhibits, rides, games, food, entertainment. Late August-early September.

### MAYFAIR FESTIVAL OF THE ARTS
*Allentown, 610-437-6900; www.mayfairfestival.org*
Allentown parks. Family arts festival with 150 free musical performances; crafts and food. Monday and Thursday-Sunday, Memorial Day weekend.

## HOTELS
### ★COMFORT INN
*3712 Hamilton Blvd., Allentown, 610-437-9100, 877-424-6423; www.Comfortinn.com*
121 rooms. Complimentary continental breakfast. High-speed Internet access. Airport transportation available. **$**

### ★CROWNE PLAZA

*904 Hamilton Mall, Allentown, 610-433-2221, 877-424-4225; www.crowneplaza.com*
224 rooms. Pets accepted; fee. High-speed Internet acces. Fitness center. Indoor pool.
Airport transportation available. **$**

### ★★FOUR POINTS BY SHERATON

*3400 Airport Road, Allentown, 610-266-1000; www.fourpoints.com*
147 rooms. High-speed Internet access. **$**

### ★HAMPTON INN

*7471 Keebler Way, Allentown, 610-391-1500, 800-426-7866; www.hamptoninn.com*
124 rooms. Complimentary continental breakfast. Airport transportation available.
Fitness room. **$**

## RESTAURANTS

### ★★ALADDIN RESTAURANT

*651 Union Blvd., Allentown, 610-437-4023*
Middle Eastern menu. Lunch, dinner. Closed Monday, children's menu. Casual attire. **$$**

### ★★BAY LEAF

*935 W. Hamilton St., Allentown, 610-433-4211; www.allentownbayleaf.com*
Thai menu. Lunch, dinner. Closed Sunday. Bar. Reservations recommended. **$$**

### ★★FEDERAL GRILL

*536 Hamilton St., Allentown, 610-776-7600; www.federalgrill.com*
Seafood menu. Lunch, dinner. Saturday-Sunday brunch. Bar. Reservations recommended. Outdoor seating. **$$**

# ALTOONA

The rough, high Alleghenies ring this city, which was founded by the Pennsylvania
Railroad. Altoona expanded rapidly after 1852, when the difficult task of spanning
the Alleghenies with track to link Philadelphia and Pittsburgh was completed. The
railroad shops still offer substantial employment for residents of the city and Blair
County.

*Information: Allegheny Mountains Convention & Visitors Bureau,*
*One Convention Center Drive, Altoona, 814-943-4183, 800-842-5866;*
*www.alleghenymountains.com*

## WHAT TO SEE AND DO

### BAKER MANSION MUSEUM

*3500 Oak Lane, Altoona, 814-942-3916; www.blairhistory.org*
Stone Greek Revival house of early ironmaster was built from 1844-1848; now occupied
by Blair County Historical Society. Hand-carved Belgian furniture of the period; transportation exhibits, gun collection, clothing, housewares. Memorial Day-Labor Day,
Tuesday-Sunday; mid-April-Memorial Day and Labor Day-October, Saturday-Sunday.

★
★★
★★
★

## CANOE CREEK STATE PARK

*Altoona, 814-695-6807; www.dcnr.state.pa.us*

Approximately 950-acre park features 155-acre lake. Swimming beach, fishing, boating (launches, rentals); hiking, picnicking (reservations for pavilion), cross-country skiing, sledding, ice boating, ice skating, cabins.

## DELGROSSOS PARK

*Altoona, 814-684-3538; www.delgrossos.com*

More than 30 rides and attractions include antique carousel, miniature golf and pony rides. Also here are arcade games, picnic pavilions and restaurant. May-September, Tuesday-Sunday.

## FORT ROBERDEAU

*Altoona, 814-946-0048; www.fortroberdeau.org*

Reconstructed Revolutionary War fort with horizontal logs; contains blacksmith shop, barracks, storehouse, powder magazine. Costumed guides; weekend reenactments. Visitor center. Picnicking, nature trails. May-October, daily; Tuesday-Saturday 11 a.m.-5 p.m., Sunday and Monday 1-5 p.m.

## HORSESHOE CURVE VISITORS CENTER

*Altoona, 814-946-0834; www.railroadcity.com*

World-famous engineering feat, carrying main-line Conrail and Amtrak trains around western grade of 91 feet per mile. Curve is 2,375 feet long and has a central angle of 220 degrees. Funicular railway runs between interpretive center and observation area. Gift shop. April-December, daily.

**225**

## LAKEMONT PARK

*700 Park Ave., Altoona, 800-434-8006; www.lakemontparkfun.com*

An amusement park with more than 30 rides and attractions; home of the nation's oldest wooden roller coaster; water park, miniature golf, entertainment. May-September, closed Monday-Tuesday.

## PRINCE GALLITZIN STATE PARK

*Highway 53 and Beaver Valley Road, Flinton, 814-674-1000;*
*www.dcnr.state.pa.us/stateparks/parks*

Approximately 6,200 acres; 26 miles of shoreline on 1,600-acre lake. Swimming beach, fishing, boating (rentals, mooring, launching, marina); hiking trails, horseback riding, cross-country skiing, snowmobiling, iceskating, ice fishing; picnicking, snack bar, store, laundry facilities, tent and trailer sites, cabins. Standard fees.

## RAILROADER'S MEMORIAL MUSEUM

*1300 Nineth Ave., Altoona, 814-946-0834, 888-428-6662; www.railroadcity.com*

Exhibits feature railroad artifacts, art and theme displays. Railroad rolling stock, steam and electric locomotive collections. Daily.

**PENNSYLVANIA**

★
★
★
★

#### WOPSONONOCK MOUNTAIN
*Altoona*
Lookout provides view of six-county area from height of 2,580 feet; offers one of the best views in the state.

## SPECIAL EVENTS
### BLAIR COUNTY ARTS FESTIVAL
*Penn State Altoona Campus, 3000 Ivyside Park, Altoona, 814-949-2787;*
*www.mishlertheatre.org*
Arts, crafts, hobbies on display. Mid-May.

### KEYSTONE COUNTRY FESTIVAL
*Lakemont Park, 700 Park Ave., Altoona, 814-943-4183, 800-842-5866;*
*www.alleghenymountains.com*
Arts and crafts, music, food. Contact Convention and Visitors Bureau. Weekend after Labor Day.

### RAILFEST
*1300 Ninth Ave., Altoona, 814-946-0834*
A celebration of Altoona's rich rail heritage. October.

## HOTEL
### ★★RAMADA INN
*I-99 Exit 31 Plank Road Route. 220 and Plank Road exit Altoona,*
*814-946-1631, 800-311-5192; www.ramadainnaltoona.com*
215 rooms. Complimentary continental breakfast. High-speed Internet access. Airport transportation available. Business center. Fitness center. Pool. **$**

## RESTAURANT
### ★★ALLEGRO
*3926 Broad Ave., Altoona, 814-946-5216, 800-372-5524; www.allegro-restaurant.com*
American, Italian menu. Dinner. Closed Sunday. Bar. Children's menu. **$$**

# AMBRIDGE
Founded by the American Bridge Company, this city rests on part of the site of Old Economy Village. In 1825, under the leadership of George Rapp, the Harmony Society established a communal pietistic colony that was important in the industrial development of western Pennsylvania for many decades. Despite its spiritual emphasis, Old Economy Village enjoyed a great material prosperity; farms were productive, craft shops were busy and factories made textiles widely acclaimed for their quality. Surplus funds financed railroads and industrial enterprises throughout the upper Ohio Valley. After celibacy was adopted and unwise investments were made, productivity decreased. Officially dissolved in 1905, the remains of the community were taken over by the Commonwealth of Pennsylvania in 1916.
*Information: Beaver County Recreation & Tourism Department, 121 Brady's Run*
*Road, Beaver Falls, 724-891-7030, 800-342-8192; www.visitbeavercounty.com*

## WHAT TO SEE AND DO
### OLD ECONOMY VILLAGE

*270 16th St., Ambridge, 724-266-4500; www.oldeconomyvillage.com*

Seventeen original Harmony Society buildings located on six acres, restored and filled with furnishings of the community. Included are the communal leader's 32-room Great House, the Feast Hall, the Grotto in the Gardens, wine cellars, a five-story granary, shops, dwellings and community kitchens. Cobblestone streets link the buildings. Special festivals and events. Tuesday-Sunday.

## SPECIAL EVENT
### NATIONALITY DAYS

Ethnic cultural displays, foods, native music, dancing. Mid-May.

# BEAVER FALLS

Founded as Brighton, the town changed its name for the falls in the Beaver River. The plates from which U.S. currency is printed are made in Beaver Falls. Geneva College (1848) is located here.

*Information: Beaver County Recreation & Tourism Department, 121 Brady's Run Road, Beaver Falls, 724-891-7030, 800-342-8192; www.visitbeavercounty.com*

## HOTELS
### ★BEAVER VALLEY MOTEL

*7257 Big Beaver Blvd., Beaver Falls, 724-843-0630, 800-400-8312; www.bvmotel.com*
27 rooms. High-speed Internet access. **$**

### ★★CONLEY INN

*7099 Big Beaver Blvd., Beaver Falls, 724-843-9300, 800-345-6819; www.super8.com*
56 rooms. **$**

### ★★HOLIDAY INN

*7195 Eastwood Road, Beaver Falls, 724-846-3700, 800-282-0244;*
*www.holidayinn.com*
156 rooms. Pets accepted. High-speed Internet access. Fitness center. Indoor pool. **$**

## RESTAURANT
### ★★WOODEN ANGEL

*308 Leopard Lane, Beaver, 724-774-7880; www.wooden-angel.com*
Seafood menu. Lunch, dinner. Closed Sunday-Monday. Bar. **$$$**

# BEDFORD

Fort Bedford was a major frontier outpost in pre-Revolutionary War days. After the war, it became an important stopover along the route of western migration. Garrett Pendergrass, the second settler here, built Pendergrass's Tavern, which figures in a number of novels by Hervey Allen.

*Information: Bedford County Conference & Visitors Bureau, 131 S. Juliana St., Bedford, 814-623-1771, 800-765-3331; www.bedfordcounty.net*

**PENNSYLVANIA**

★
★
★
★
★

## WHAT TO SEE AND DO

### BEDFORD COUNTY COURTHOUSE

*230 S. Juliana St., Building 2, Bedford, 814-623-4807*

Federal-style building constructed in 1828 has unique hanging spiral staircase; oldest courthouse still in operation in Pennsylvania. Monday-Friday.

### FORT BEDFORD PARK AND MUSEUM

*Fort Bedford Drive, North end of Juliana St., Bedford,*
*814-623-8891, 800-259-4284; www.motherbedford.com*

Log blockhouse, erected during Bedford's bicentennial. Contains large-scale replica of original fort, displays of colonial antiques and relics, Native American artifacts. Park along Raystown River. May-late October, daily 10 a.m.-5 p.m.

### OLD BEDFORD VILLAGE

*220 Sawblade Road, Bedford, 814-623-1156, 800-238-4347;*
*www.oldbedfordvillage.com*

More than 40 authentic log and frame structures built between 1750-1851 house historical exhibits; crafts demonstrations, operating pioneer farm. Many special events throughout the year. Memorial Day weekend-Labor Day, closed Wednesdays; September-October, Thursday-Sunday.

## SPECIAL EVENTS

### CIVIL WAR REENACTMENT

Old Bedford Village. Early September.

### FALL FOLIAGE FESTIVAL DAYS

*141 S. Juliana St., Bedford; www.bedfordcounty.net/fall*

Entertainment, ethnic foods, antique cars, more than 350 craft booths. First two full weekends in October.

## HOTELS

### ★★BEST WESTERN BEDFORD INN

*4517 Business 220, Bedford, 814-623-9006, 800-752-8592; www.bestwestern.com*

104 rooms. Pets accepted. Complimentary breakfast. High-speed Internet access. Fitness center. Pool. $

### ★★QUALITY INN

*4407 Business 220, Bedford, 814-623-5188, 877-424-6423; www.choicehotels.com*

65 rooms. Pets accepted. Complimentary continental breakfast. High-speed Internet access. Outdoor pool. $

## RESTAURANT

### ★★ED'S STEAK HOUSE

*4476 Business 220, Bedford, 814-623-8894*

Seafood, steak menu. Breakfast, lunch, dinner. Bar. Children's menu. $$

## LAUREL HIGHLANDS

As the name suggests, the Laurel Highlands—spread across the Allegheny Mountains in southwestern Pennsylvania—is a region of lofty, wooded ridges, farm valleys, and streams and lakes, many boasting swimming beaches. Here and there you come upon covered bridges. Early on, the beauty of the setting drew many travelers, and it continues to do so. Today the Highlands serve as a year-round playground where you can raft, kayak, fish, swim, ski and bicycle.

This two-day, 150-mile drive meanders though the Highlands while visiting several important historic sites. This is a one-way trip between Bedford in the east and Uniontown in the west. You can drive in either direction, but we'll begin at Bedford, just off the Pennsylvania Turnpike. Stop in Bedford at the Old Bedford Village, which preserves more than 40 original farm buildings and other structures in a villagelike cluster. One that catches the eye is the eight-sided schoolhouse built nearby in 1851. Called an "Eight Square," the octagon shape had a specific purpose: It gave every student an equal share of window light and proximity to the pot-bellied stove in the center. In summer, craftsmen demonstrate blacksmithing, barrel-making, broom-making and other pioneer skills.

From Bedford, take I-99 North to State Route 56 northwest to Johnstown. Two sites here capture the horror of the Johnstown Flood of 1889, which struck the small, steel-manufacturing city with a sudden ferocity that left 2,200 people dead. Just east of the city, the National Park Service operates the Johnstown Flood National Memorial. It overlooks the dry basin of what was once a man-made lake that emptied when heavy rains collapsed an earthen dam. In town, the Johnstown Flood Museum illustrates the damage wrought by the flood and Johnstown's determination to rebuild.

Ahead on the drive, two reconstructed 18th-century forts, Fort Ligonier in Ligonier and Fort Necessity National Battlefield near Farmington, recount British colonial efforts to wrest the Ohio River Valley west of the Alleghenies from French control. Both forts played a role in the ultimate defeat of the French at Fort Duquesne, which became the site of Pittsburgh. Ligonier is the more imposing of the two forts, but Fort Necessity may be more memorable. To reach it, take Route 271 West from Johnstown to Ligonier, and plan to spend the night there. To reach Fort Necessity, head two miles southeast on US 30 to Route 381 to Farmington, and turn right on US 40. At Fort Necessity, a modest ring of stakes marks the site of George Washington's only military surrender, a lesson that surely must have aided him two decades later as commander of the Continental Army.

The route from Ligonier to Farmington edges past Fallingwater, architect Frank Lloyd Wright's masterpiece on Bear Run. The structure, stair-stepping down a wooded mountainside, combines architecture and nature in a glorious piece of artwork. A stop here is a must, but allow at least three hours to take an escorted tour and to walk the grounds. Exhibits at the Entrance Pavilion explain the construction of the house, built in 1936 as a mountain retreat for a wealthy Pittsburgh department store owner. Inside the house, you'll learn about Wright's daring use of new construction materials and his fascination with the possibilities of

PENNSYLVANIA

★
★
★
★
★

space. Short in stature, Wright designed the house with surprisingly low ceilings.

A couple of miles down the road, the village of Ohiopyle is a center for whitewater rafting. Sign up for thrills, or watch helmet-clad rafters arriving or departing on upper and lower stretches of the Youghiogheny River (also called the "Yock"). From Fort Necessity, continue west on US 40 to Uniontown to conclude this tour. Approximately 150 miles.

# BELLEFONTE

When Talleyrand, the exiled French minister, saw the Big Spring here in 1794, his exclamation—"Beautiful fountain"—gave the town its name. Bellefonte is perched on seven hills at the southeast base of Bald Eagle Mountain.

*Information: Bellefonte Intervalley Area Chamber of Commerce,*
*Train Station, 320 W. High St., Bellefonte, 814-355-2917; www.bellefontechamber.org*

## WHAT TO SEE AND DO
### BLACK MOSHANNON STATE PARK
*814-342-5960; www.stateparks.com/black_moshannon.html*
Approximately 3,450 acres. Swimming beach, fishing, boating (rentals, mooring, launching); hunting, hiking, cross-country skiing, snowmobiling, ice skating, ice fishing, ice boating; picnicking, snack bar, tent and trailer sites, cabins.

### CENTRE COUNTY LIBRARY AND HISTORICAL MUSEUM
*200 N. Allegheny St., Bellefonte, 814-355-1516; www.centrecountylibrary.org*
Local museum includes central Pennsylvania historical and genealogical books, records. Monday-Saturday.

## RESTAURANT
### ★★GAMBLE MILL RESTAURANT
*160 Dunlap St., Bellefonte, 814-355-7764; www.gamblemill.com*
American menu. Lunch, dinner. Closed Sunday. Bar. $$

# BETHLEHEM

Bethlehem Steel products have put this city on the map, but Bethlehem is also known for its Bach Festival, for its historic district, and for Lehigh University (1865) and Moravian College (1807).

Not surprisingly, Bethlehem has earned itself the nickname, "America's Christmas city." Moravians, members of a very old Protestant denomination, assembled here on Christmas Evening 1741 in a log house that was part stable, which was the only building in the area at the time. Singing a hymn that praised Bethlehem, they found a name for their village. Their private musical performance also was the first of many in Bethlehem; string quartets and symphonies were heard here before any other place in the colonies.

The Lehigh Canal's 1829 opening kicked off the area's industrialization, along with the development of the borough of South Bethlehem (1865), which was incorporated into Bethlehem in 1917.

*Information: Bethlehem Tourism Authority, 52 W. Broad St., Bethlehem,*
*610-868-1513, 800-360-8687; www.bethlehem.info*

★
★
★
★
★

## WHAT TO SEE AND DO

### APOTHECARY MUSEUM

*424 Main St., Bethlehem, 610-867-0173; www.historicbethlehem.org*

Features the original 1752 fireplace where prescriptions were compounded; collection of artifacts includes retorts, grinders, mortars and pestles, scales, blown-glass bottles, labels and a set of Delft Tobacco jars from 1743; herb and flower garden. By appointment.

### BRETHREN'S HOUSE

*Church and Main streets, Bethlehem, 610-861-3916*

Built in 1748, this was a residence and shop area for single men of the Moravian community. It now serves Moravian College as its Center for Music and Art.

### CENTRAL MORAVIAN CHURCH

*40 W. Church St., Bethlehem*

Federal-style church built in 1806 features hand-carved detail, considered foremost Moravian church in the U.S. Noted for its music, including a trombone choir in existence since 1754.

### GOD'S ACRE

*Church and Market streets, Bethlehem*

Old Moravian cemetery (1742-1910) following Moravian tradition that all gravestones are laid flat, indicating that all are equal in the sight of God.

### GOUNDIE HOUSE

*501 Main St., Bethlehem*

Restored Federal-style brick house from 1810 has period-furnished rooms and interpretive exhibits.

### HILL-TO-HILL BRIDGE

Joins old and new parts of the city and provides excellent view of historic area, river and Bethlehem Steel plant.

### HISTORIC BETHLEHEM INC'S 18TH-CENTURY INDUSTRIAL QUARTER

*459 Old York Road, Bethlehem, 610-691-0603*

Ohio Road and Main St. (pedestrian entrance); Old York Road and Union Boulevard (parking lot entrance). Guided tours July-August, Saturday; late November-late December, weekends).

### KEMERER MUSEUM OF DECORATIVE ARTS

*459 Old York Road, Bethlehem, 610-691-6055, 800-360-3687;*
*www.historicbethlehem.org*

Exhibits include art, Bohemian glass, toys, prints, china; regional German folk art from 1750-1900; Federal furniture, period room settings. Tuesday-Saturday 10 a.m.-5 p.m., Sunday noon-5 p.m.; closed Monday.

**PENNSYLVANIA**

★
★
★
★
★

## LUCKENBACH MILL

*459 Old York Road, Bethlehem; www.historicbethlehem.org*
Restored gristmill contains contemporary craft gallery and museum shop; also the offices of Bethlehem Area Chamber of Commerce and Historic Bethlehem Inc. Interpretive display here is included in guided tour.

## MORAVIAN MUSEUM (GEMEINHAUS)

*66 W. Church St., Bethlehem, 610-867-0173; www.historicbethlehem.org*
This five-story log building was built in 1741 and is the oldest structure in the city; docents interpret the history and culture of early Bethlehem and the Moravians. 45-minute tour. Tuesday-Sunday; closed January.

## OLD CHAPEL

*Heckewelder Place, adjacent to Moravian Museum, Bethlehem*
Once called the "Indian chapel" because so many Native Americans attended the services, this stone structure, the second church for the Moravian congregation, was built in 1751 and is still used frequently. May be toured only in combination with Moravian Museum community walking tour.

## SPRINGHOUSE

*459 Old York Road, Bethlehem*
Reconstruction on site of original spring that served Moravian community as a water source from the time of settlement in 1741 until 1912.

## TANNERY

*459 Old York Road, Bethlehem*
Exhibits Moravian crafts, trades and industries. Includes a working model of the original oil mill.

## WATERWORKS

*459 Old York Road, Bethlehem*
Reconstructed 18-foot wooden waterwheel and pumping mechanisms.

# SPECIAL EVENTS

## BACH FESTIVAL

*Packer Church, 18 University Drive, Bethlehem, 610-866-4382; www.Bach.org*
Lehigh University campus. One of the country's outstanding musical events. Famous artists and the Bach Choir of Bethlehem participate. Mid-late May.

## LIVE BETHLEHEM CHRISTMAS PAGEANT

*1424 Catasauqua Road, Bethlehem, 610-867-2893*
Scores of volunteers (garbed in biblical costumes) and live animals (including camels, horses, donkey and sheep) join together to re-create the nativity story; narrated. First weekend in December.

## MORAVIAN COLLEGE ALUMNI ASSOCIATION ANTIQUES SHOW

*Johnston Hall, Moravian College Campus, 1200 Main St., Bethlehem, 610-861-1366*
Early June.

## MUSIKFEST

*25 W. Third St., Bethlehem, 610-861-0678; www.musikfest.org*

Nine-day festival celebrating Bethlehem's rich musical and ethnic heritage. More than 600 performances (most free) of all types of music including folk, big-band, jazz, country-western, chamber, classical, gospel, rock, swing. Also children's activities. Late August.

## SHAD FESTIVAL

*459 Old York Road, Bethlehem, 610-691-0603; www.historicbethlehem.org*

Historic Bethlehem's 18th-century Industrial Quarter. Old-fashioned planked shad bake (reservations required for dinner), exhibits, demonstrations. First Sunday in May.

## HOTELS

### ★★BEST WESTERN HOTEL

*300 Gateway Drive, Bethlehem, 610-866-5800; www.bestwestern.com*

192 rooms. Pets accepted. Complimentary continental breakfast. High-speed Internet access. Fitness center. Pool. Airport transportation available. **$**

### ★COMFORT INN

*3191 Highfield Drive, Bethlehem, 610-865-6300, 877-424-6423;*
*www.choicehotels.com*

112 rooms. Pets accepted. Complimentary continental breakfast. High-speed Internet access. Fitness center. **$**

### WYDNOR HALL INN

*3612 Old Philadelphia Pike, Bethlehem, 610-867-6851, 800-839-0020;*
*www.mysite.vrizon.net/wydnorhall*

5 rooms. Complimentary continental breakfast. European-style inn that was built in 1895. **$**

## RESTAURANTS

### ★★CAFÉ

*221 W. Broad St., Bethlehem, 610-866-1686*

International menu. Lunch, dinner. Closed Sunday-Monday. Reservations recommended. **$$**

### ★EASTERN CHINESE

*3926 Linden St., Bethlehem, 610-868-0299*

Chinese menu. Lunch, dinner. Bar. Reservations recommended. **$$**

### ★★INN OF THE FALCON

*1740 Seidersville Road, Bethlehem, 610-868-6505; www.innofthefalcon.com*

American menu. Dinner. Closed Sunday. Bar. Reservations recommended. **$$**

### ★★★MAIN STREET DEPOT

*61 W. Lehigh St., Bethlehem, 610-868-7123; www.mainstreetdepotrestaurant.com*

On the National Registry of Historic Buildings, the location out of which the Main Street Depot now operates was built in 1873 and served as a station for the Jersey Central

**PENNSYLVANIA**

★
★
★
★
★

railroad. Grab a depot burger at the bar, or sit down for dinner and enjoy an entrée like butter rum chicken with cashews, coconut and fresh pineapple over rice or filet mignon wrapped in bacon and served with asparagus and béarnaise sauce. American menu. Lunch, dinner. Closed Sunday. Bar. Reservations recommended. $$$

### ★★MINSI TRAIL INN
*626 Stefko Blvd., Bethlehem, 610-691-5613; www.minsitrailinn.com*
American, Greek menu. Lunch, dinner. Sunday brunch. Bar. Children's menu. Reservations recommended. $$

# BIRD-IN-HAND
This Pennsylvania Dutch farming village got its name from the signboard of an early inn.
*Information: Pennsylvania Dutch Convention and Visitors Bureau, 501 Greenfield Road, Lancaster, 717-299-8901, 800-723-8824; www.padutchcountry.com*

## WHAT TO SEE AND DO
### ABE'S BUGGY RIDES
*2596 Old Philadelphia Pike, Bird-in-Hand, 717-392-1794; www.abesbuggyrides.com*
A tour through Amish country in an authentic family carriage. Monday-Saturday.

### AMISH COUNTRY TOURS
*3121 Old Philadelphia Pike (Highway 340), Bird-In-Hand, 717-768-3600*
Tours of Amish farmlands and Philadelphia.

### BIRD-IN-HAND FARMERS MARKET
*2710 Old Philadelphia Pike, Bird-In-Hand, 717-393-9674;*
*www.birdinhandfarmersmarket.com*
Indoor market with a wide variety of Pennsylvania Dutch foods and gifts. July-October, Wednesday-Saturday; April-June and November, Wednesday, Friday and Saturday; rest of year, Friday and Saturday 8.30 a.m.-5.30 p.m.

### WEAVERTOWN ONE-ROOM SCHOOLHOUSE
*Highway 340 Bird-in-Hand Pennsylvania, 717-768-3976*
Life-size animated re-creation of activities at a one-room schoolhouse. Early April-October, daily; March and November, weekends.

## HOTEL
### ★★★BIRD-IN-HAND FAMILY INN
*2740 Old Philadelphia Pike, Bird-In-Hand, 717-768-8271, 800-665-8780;*
*www.bird-in-hand.com/familyinn*
In the small town of Bird-in-Hand, this quiet inn offers a comfortable escape. Guests are welcome to visit the inn's petting zoo, picnic pavilion and playground, or to take complimentary two-hour tours of Amish farmland. 125 rooms. High-speed Internet access. Restaurant. Outdoor pool. Tennis. $

**PENNSYLVANIA**

★
★★
★★
★★
★☆

## SPECIALTY LODGINGS

### GREYSTONE MANOR BED AND BREAKFAST

*2658 Old Philadelphia Pike, Bird-in-Hand, 717-393-4233; www.greystonemanor.com*

This inn was built in the mid-1880s and is used today as a heritage lodging site. Situated on eight acres of landscaped property, the inn offers guests Victorian charm and style for a relaxing stay. 10 rooms. Closed January. Complimentary full breakfast. Victorian mansion built in 1883. $

### VILLAGE INN

*2695 Old Philadelphia Pike, Bird-in-Hand, 717-293-8369, 800-665-8780;*
*www.bird-in-hand.com/villageinn*

Closed early December-early February. Children over 13 only. Complimentary continental breakfast. Built in 1734 as inn on Old Philadelphia Pike. Victorian interior ambience. 24 Rooms. High-speed Internet access. $

## RESTAURANT

### ★PLAIN AND FANCY FARM

*3121 Old Philadelphia Pike, Bird-in-Hand, 717-768-4400; www.plainandfancyfarm.com*

Pennsylvania Dutch menu. Lunch, dinner. Children's menu. $$

# BLAKESLEE

## WHAT TO SEE AND DO

### FERN RIDGE CAMPGROUNDS

*Highway 115, Blakeslee, 570-646-2267*

More than 200 shaded tent and RV campsites with water, electric hook-ups, picnic tables and fire rings. Heated pool, hot showers, volleyball, basketball, horseshoes, mountain biking, fishing stream and playground available. Convenience store with groceries, propane, ice and firewood. Laundry. Dump station and pump-out service. Rental cabins also available.

### JACK FROST

*Highway 940, Blakeslee, 570-443-8425; www.jfbb.com*

Two triple, five double chairlifts; patrol, school, rentals, snowmaking; cafeteria, restaurant, bar; nursery. Longest run approximately ½ mile; vertical drop 600 feet. December-March, daily; Half-day rate.

### WT FAMILY CAMPING

*Highway 115, Blakeslee, 570-646-9255; www.wtfamily.com*

This clean, friendly campground a couple of miles south of Pocono Raceway has plenty of activities for the entire family. The wooded sites have picnic tables and fire rings. RV, trailer and tent sites; full hook-ups. Propane station, restrooms, convenience store, ice, wood. Outdoor pool, miniature golf. Monday-Thursday noon-5 p.m., Friday noon-10 p.m., Saturday noon-9 p.m., Sunday noon-5 p.m.

# BLOOMSBURG

On the north bank of the Susquehanna River, Bloomsburg was a center for mining, transportation and industry during the 19th and early 20th centuries. While it remains

★
★
★
★
★

a manufacturing town, Bloomsburg retains the relaxed atmosphere of earlier days with its lush scenery and covered bridges. In nearby Orangeville, Fishing Creek offers trout, bass and pickerel.

*Information: Columbia-Montour Visitors Bureau, 121 Papermill Road, Bloomsburg, 570-784-8279, 800-847-4810; www.cmtpa.org*

## WHAT TO SEE AND DO
### BLOOMSBURG UNIVERSITY OF PENNSYLVANIA
*400 Second St., Bloomsburg, 570-389-4316; www.bloomu.edu*
Established in 1839, this campus of 6,000 students features Carver Hall (1867); the Harvey A. Andruss Library (1966); Haas Center for the Arts (1967) with 2,000-seat auditorium and art gallery; McCormick Center for Human Services (1985); Redman Stadium and Nelson Field House. Tours (academic year, Monday-Friday).

### THE CHILDREN'S MUSEUM
*2 W. Seventh St., Bloomsburg, 570-389-9206; www.the-childrens-museum.org*
This museum has more than 50 hands-on activities that aim to make learning about our world and the environment fun. The museum has a new theme each year, and most of the exhibits change as well. Mid-June-mid-December, Tuesday-Saturday 10 a.m.-4 p.m.

### HISTORIC DISTRICT
*Bounded by West, Fifth, First, Lake streets, Bloomsburg, 570-784-7703*
More than 650 structures spanning architectural styles from Georgian to Art Deco. Center of town.

★
★
★
★
★

## SPECIAL EVENTS
### BLOOMSBURG THEATRE ENSEMBLE
*Alvina Krause Theatre, 226 Center St., Bloomsburg, 570-784-8181; www.bte.org*
Three to four weeks of performances for each of six plays. Main stage: October-June (special performances rest of year).

### COVERED BRIDGE & ARTS FESTIVAL
*I-80, exit 35.*
Tours of covered bridges; apple-butter boil; weaving, old-fashioned arts and crafts. Early October.

## HOTELS
### ★BUDGET HOST PATRIOT INN
*6305 Columbia Blvd., Bloomsburg, 570-387-1776, 800-873-1180; www.budgethost.com*
59 rooms. High-speed Internet access. $

### ★★★INN AT TURKEY HILL
*991 Central Road, Bloomsburg, 570-387-1500; www.innatturkeyhill.com*
This inn's 1839 brick farmhouse offers two guest bedrooms with whirlpool tubs. 16 additional rooms are available on the property. Visit the inn's gazebo, duck pond and two resident ducks. 18 rooms. Pets accepted. High-speed Internet access. Complimentary continental breakfast. Airport transportation available. $

# BRADFORD

When oil was discovered in Bradford in the late 1800s, the price of land jumped from about six cents to $1,000 an acre, and wells appeared on front lawns, in backyards and even in a cemetery. An oil exchange was established in 1877, two years after the first producing well was brought in. A Ranger District office of the Allegheny National Forest is located here.

*Information: Bradford Area Chamber of Commerce, 10 Marilyn Horne Way, Bradford, 814-368-7115; www.bradfordpa.com*

## WHAT TO SEE AND DO

### BRADFORD LANDMARK SOCIETY

*45 E. Corydon St., Bradford, 814-362-3906; www.bradfordlandmark.org*
Headquartered in restored bakery; local history exhibits, period rooms. Monday, Wednesday and Friday.

### CROOK FARM

*Seaward Avenue Exit, Bradford, 814-362-3906; Near the Tuna Crossroad*
Original home of Erastus and Betsy Crook was built in 1848 and restored to the 1870s period. May-September, Tuesday-Friday afternoons, also Saturday by appointment.

### CARPENTER SHOP

Reconstruction of original 1870 shop, featuring old hand tools.

### OLD BARN

Identical to the 1870 original; moved to Crook Farm in 1981 and rebuilt on the site of the original barn.

### OLD ONE-ROOM SCHOOLHOUSE #8

Authentic 1880 structure where classes are still held occasionally.

## SPECIAL EVENT

### CROOK FARM COUNTRY FAIR

*Crook Farm, Seaward Avenue, at Tuna Crossroad, Bradford, 914-362-3906*
Arts and crafts, exhibits, entertainment, food. Last weekend in August.

## HOTEL

### ★★BEST WESTERN BRADFORD INN

*100 Davis St., Bradford, 814-362-4501; www.bestwestern.com*
112 rooms. Pets accepted. Complimentary breakfast. High-speed Internet access. Fitness center. Pool. $

### ★★★GLENDORN

*1000 Glendorn Drive, Bradford, 814-362-6511, 800-843-8568; www.glendorn.com*
Set on 1,280 acres, this one-time private estate offers a sophisticated twist on the traditional wooded retreat. A long, private drive welcomes visitors to this hideaway, where guests enjoy walks in the woods, canoe and fishing trips, hiking and biking adventures, and a host of other outdoor pursuits. The accommodations in the Big House reflect a warm, country house spirit, while the cabin suites have a rugged

**PENNSYLVANIA**

★
★
★
★
☆

charm. Fine dining is a hallmark of this country lodge, with hearty country breakfasts, delicious lunches and four-course prix fixe dinners. 17 rooms. Pets accepted. Children over 12 only. **$$$$**

# BRISTOL

Bristol, founded in 1681, was on the main thoroughfare between Philadelphia and New York. It has been frequented by famous visitors including Joseph Bonaparte, brother of Napoleon, and General Lafayette. There are homes dating from the 1700s, most of which have been restored.

*Information: Bucks County Conference and Visitors Bureau, 152 Swamp Road, Doylestown, 215-345-4552, 800-836-2825; www.buckscountycvb.org*

## WHAT TO SEE AND DO
### GRAVE OF CAPTAIN JOHN GREEN
*St. James Protestant Episcopal Church Burial Ground, Cedar and Walnut streets, Bristol*
Grave of U.S. Navy captain who piloted the *Columbia* around the world in 1787-1789 on first such voyage by a vessel flying the American flag.

### PENNSBURY MANOR
*400 Pennsbury Memorial Road, Bristol, 215-946-0400; www.pennsburymanor.org*
Reconstruction of William Penn's 17th-century country manor; formal and kitchen gardens; livestock. Craft demonstrations; hands-on workshops. April-November, Tuesday-Sunday.

# BROOKVILLE

*Information: Brookville Area Chamber of Commerce, 175 Main St., Brookville, 814-849-8448; www.brookvillechamber.com*

## WHAT TO SEE AND DO
### CLEAR CREEK STATE PARK
*Brookville, 814-752-2368;*
*www.dcnr.state.pa.us/stateparks/parks/clearcreek.aspx#contacts*
Approximately 1,600 acres. Swimming beach, fishing, canoeing; hiking trails, cross-country skiing, picnicking, playing field, camping, cabins. Nature center; interpretive activities.

## HOTEL
### ★HOLIDAY INN EXPRESS
*235 Allegheny Blvd., Brookville, 814-849-8381, 800-315-2621; www.holidayinn.com*
68 rooms. Complimentary continental breakfast. High-speed Internet access. Fitness center. **$**

## RESTAURANT
### ★★MEETING PLACE
*209 Main St., Brookville, 814-849-2557*
American menu. Breakfast, lunch, dinner. Closed Sunday. Bar. Children's menu. **$$**

# BRYN MAWR

## WHAT TO SEE AND DO
### HARRITON HOUSE

*500 Harriton Road, Bryn Mawr, 610-525-0201; www.haritonhouse.org*

(1704) Early American domestic architecture of the Philadelphia area. Originally 700-acre estate, now 16½ acres. House of Charles Thomson, Secretary of the Continental Congresses; restored to early 18th-century period. Nature park. Wednesday-Saturday 10 a.m.-4 p.m.; Sunday by appointment.

## RESTAURANT
### ★★WILD ONION

*900 Conestoga Road, Bryn Mawr, 610-527-4826; www.thewildonion.com*

Seafood menu. Lunch, dinner. Bar. Children's menu. **$$**

# BUTLER

Robert Morris of Philadelphia, financier of the Revolutionary War, once owned the hills in which Butler now sits. The city is named for General Richard Butler, who died in the St. Clair Indian Expedition. During the 1930s, the Butler-based American Austin Company—later called American Bantam Company—pioneered the development of small, lightweight cars in America and invented the prototype of the jeep.

*Information: Butler County Chamber of Commerce, 101 E. Diamond St., Butler, 724-283-2222; www.butlercountychamber.com*

## HOTELS
### ★★CONLEY RESORT

*740 Pittsburgh Road, Butler, 724-586-7711, 800-344-7303; www.conleyresort.com*

56 rooms. 150-foot indoor water park. Complimentary breakfast. Pool. Sauna. Golf. **$**

### ★FAIRFIELD INN BY MARRIOTT BUTLER

*200 Fairfield Lane, Butler, 724-283-0009, 800-228-2800; www.fairfieldinn.com*

75 rooms. Fitness center. Indoor Pool. Spa. **$**

# CAMBRIDGE SPRINGS

## HOTEL
### ★★★RIVERSIDE INN

*1 Fountain Ave., Cambridge Springs, 814-398-4645, 800-964-5173; www.theriversideinn.com*

Opened in 1885, this inn continues to provide excellent service to its visitors. It's nestled in a quiet and peaceful area overlooking French Creek. Guests will enjoy golf, swimming, tennis and other activities. 74 rooms. Closed January-mid-April. Complimentary full breakfast. **$**

**PENNSYLVANIA**

★
★
★
★
★

# CANADENSIS

## SPECIALTY LODGING
### BROOKVIEW MANOR INN
*2960 Highway 447, Canadensis, 570-595-2451, 800-585-7974;*
*www.brookviewmanor.com*
Brookview Manor Inn sits on five acres in the Pocono Mountains and is surrounded by 200 acres of privately owned forests. Relax in a rocking chair on the inn's wraparound porch. Or head out to shop at the area's wide selection of outlet stores and antiques shops. 10 rooms. Children over 12 years only. Complimentary full breakfast. **$$**

# CARLISLE
In the historically strategic Cumberland Valley, Carlisle was a vital point for Native American fighting during the Revolutionary and Civil wars.

The Carlisle Barracks is one of the oldest military posts in America. Soldiers mounted guard here as early as 1750 to protect the frontier. In 1794 President Washington reviewed troops assembled here to march against the "Whiskey Rebels," and troops went from the Barracks to the Mexican and Civil wars. The Barracks was reopened in 1920 as the Medical Field Service School. It is now home to the U.S. Army War College. George Ross, James Wilson and James Smith, all signers of the Declaration of Independence, lived in Carlisle, as did Molly Pitcher.
*Information: Greater Area Chamber of Commerce, 212 N. Hanover St., Carlisle,*
*717-243-4515; www.carlislechamber.org*

★
★
★
★
★

## WHAT TO SEE AND DO
### CUMBERLAND COUNTY HISTORICAL SOCIETY AND HAMILTON LIBRARY ASSOCIATION
*21 N. Pitt St., Carlisle, 717-249-7610; www.historicalsociety.com*
Woodcarvings, furniture, silver, tools, redware, ironware, tall-case clocks, coverlets, paintings by local artisans; mementos of the Carlisle Indian School; special exhibits and programs. Library contains books, tax lists, early photographs, genealogical material. Tuesday-Saturday 10 a.m.-4 p.m., Monday 3-9 p.m.

### DICKINSON COLLEGE
*242 W. High St., Carlisle, 717-243-5121; www.dickinson.edu*
Founded in 1773, Dickinson is the tenth college chartered in the United States. President James Buchanan was a graduate. On campus is "Old West" (1804), a building registered as a National Historic Landmark that was designed by Benjamin Henry Latrobe, one of the designers of the Capitol in Washington. Tours of campus.

### GRAVE OF MOLLY PITCHER
*In Old Graveyard, E. South St., Carlisle www.dickinson.edu*
Soldiers in the Battle of Monmouth (June 1778) gave Molly Ludwig Hays McCauley her nickname because of her devotion to her husband and others who were fighting by bringing them pitchers of water. When her husband was wounded, Molly took his place at a cannon and continued fighting for him.

## PINE GROVE FURNACE STATE PARK

*1212 Pine Grove Road, Carlisle, 717-486-7575;*
*www.dcnr.state.pa.us/stateParks/parks/pinegrovefurnace.aspx*
Pre-Revolutionary iron, slate and brick works were in this area. Approximately 696 acres. Swimming beaches, fishing, boating (rentals, mooring, launching); hunting, hiking, bicycling (rentals), cross-country skiing, ice skating, ice fishing; picnicking, snack bar, store, tent and trailer sites. Visitor center. Lodging available.

## THE TROUT GALLERY

*West High St., Carlisle, 717-245-1711; www.dickinson.edu*
Emil R. Weiss Center for the Arts. Permanent and temporary exhibits. September-mid-June, Tuesday-Saturday.

## HOTELS

### ★★ALLENBERRY RESORT INN

*1559 Boiling Springs Road, Boiling Springs, 717-258-3211, 800-430-5468;*
*www.allenberry.com*
69 rooms. Airport transportation available. Outdoor pool. Tennis courts. **$**

### ★★CLARION HOTEL

*1700 Harrisburg Pike, Carlisle, 717-243-1717, 800-692-7315; www.hotelcarlisle.com*
267 rooms. High-speed Internet access. Fitness center. Business center. **$**

### ★DAYS INN

*101 Alexander Spring Road, Carlisle, 717-258-4147, 800-329-7466; www.daysinn.com*
136 rooms. Pets accepted. Complimentary continental breakfast. High-speed Internet access. Fitness center. Pool. Business center. Airport transportation available. **$**

### ★★HOLIDAY INN

*1450 Harrisburg Pike, Carlisle, 717-245-2400, 800-315-2621; www.holidayinn.com*
100 rooms. Pets accepted, fee. Outdoor pool. Fitness center. **$**

### ★QUALITY INN

*1255 Harrisburg Pike, Carlisle, 717-243-6000, 877-424-6423; www.qualityinn.com*
96 rooms. Complimentary continental breakfast. **$**

## RESTAURANTS

### ★★BOILING SPRINGS TAVERN

*Front and First streets, Boiling Springs, 717-258-3614; www.boilingspringstavern.net*
American menu. Lunch, dinner. Closed Sunday-Monday. Bar. Children's menu. An 1832 stone structure, originally an inn. **$$**

### ★★CALIFORNIA CAFÉ

*38 W. Pomfret St., Carlisle, 717-249-2028; www.calcaf.com*
California, French menu. Lunch, dinner. Closed Memorial Day weekend. **$$**

★
★
★
★
★

# CHADDS FORD

## WHAT TO SEE AND DO
### BARNS-BRINTON HOUSE
*1736 North Creek Road, (Old U.S. Route 100) Chadds Ford, 610-388-7376; www.chaddsfordhistor.org*

Authentically restored 1714 tavern, now a house museum furnished in the period. Guides in colonial costume offer interpretive tours; domestic art demonstrations. May-September, weekends.

### BRANDYWINE BATTLEFIELD
*1491 Baltimore Pike, Chadds Ford, 610-459-3342; www.ushistory.org/Brandywine*

The Battle of the Brandywine took place here in 1777 and around Chadds Ford—a decisive battle for Washington—includes Lafayette's quarters and Washington's headquarters. Visitor center with exhibits; tours of historic buildings; museum shop. Picnicking. March, weekends; April-November, Tuesday-Sunday; December-February, Thursday-Sunday.

### BRANDYWINE RIVER MUSEUM
*Highway 1, Chadds Ford, 610-388-2700; www.brandywinerivermuseum.org*

Converted 19th-century gristmill houses largest collection of paintings by Andrew Wyeth and other Wyeth family members; also collections of American illustration, still life and landscape painting. Nature trail, wildflower gardens; restaurant, museum shop, guided tours. Daily 9:30 a.m.-4:30 p.m.

### CHADDSFORD WINERY
*632 Baltimore Pike, Chadds Ford, 610-388-6221; www.chaddsford.com*

Tours of boutique winery, housed in renovated old barn; view of production process; tasting room. Tours; tastings. Schedule varies.

### JOHN CHADDS HOUSE
*1736 Creek Road, Chadds Ford, 610-388-7376; www.chaddsfordhistory.org*

Stone building, built in 1725, is fine example of early 18th-century Pennsylvania architecture; authentically restored and furnished as a house museum. Narrated tours by guides in colonial costume; baking demonstrations in beehive oven. May-September, Saturday-Sunday; also by appointment.

## HOTEL
### ★BRANDYWINE RIVER HOTEL
*Highways 1 and 100, Chadds Ford, 610-388-1200, 800-274-9644; www.brandywineriverhotel.com*

40 rooms. Pets accepted. Complimentary continental breakfast. High-speed Internet access. Airport transportation available. $

# CHAMBERSBURG

Named for Colonel Benjamin Chambers, a Scottish-Irish pioneer, this is an industrial county seat amid peach and apple orchards. John Brown had his headquarters here.

During the Civil War, Confederate cavalry burned down the town, destroying 537 buildings after the citizens refused to pay an indemnity of $100,000.

*Information: Chamber of Commerce, 75 S. Second St., 717-264-7101.*

*Information is also available at the Visitors Station, 1235 Lincoln Way East, Chambersburg, 717-261-1200; www.chambersburg.org*

## WHAT TO SEE AND DO

### CAPITOL THEATRE

*159 S. Main St., Chambersburg, 717-263-0202; www.thecapitoltheatre.org*

This 1927 movie house presents performances ranging from classical concerts to big bands; theatrical presentations. Features a 1928 Moller pipe organ.

### THE OLD JAIL

*175 E. King St., Chambersburg, 717-264-1667; www.pafc.tripod.com*

Jail complex originally built in 1818 was restored and renovated for use as the Kittochtinny Historical Society's Museum and Library. An 1880 cell block houses community cultural activities, art and historical exhibits. Also on grounds are Colonial, Fragrance and Japanese gardens; 19th-century barn; agricultural museum. Cultural programs (May-October). Tours. May-November, Thursday-Saturday.

## SPECIAL EVENTS

### CHAMBERSFEST

*Emil R. Weiss Center for the Performing Arts, 100 Lincoln Way East, Chambersburg, 717-264-7101; www.chambersburg.org*

Civil War festival with crafts, food, reenactments, parade of pets. July.

### FRANKLIN COUNTY FAIR

*Rod and Gun Club Farm, 5995 Warm Springs, Chambersburg, 717-369-4100*

Arts and crafts displays, needlework, home and dairy products, state turkey-calling contest, tractor pull, agricultural and livestock exhibits, entertainment. Third full week in August.

### TOTEM POLE PLAYHOUSE

*Caledonia State Park, 9555 Golf Course Road, Fayetteville, 717-352-2164; www.totempoleplayhouse.org*

Resident professional theater company performs dramas, comedies and musicals in 453-seat proscenium theater. Tuesday-Sunday evenings; matinees Wednesday, Saturday-Sunday. June-August.

## HOTELS

### ★HAMPTON INN

*955 Lesher Road, Chambersburg, 717-261-9185, 800-486-7866; www.hamptoninn.com*

119 rooms. Complimentary continental breakfast. Business center. $

### ★★QUALITY INN

*1095 Wayne Ave., Chambersburg, 717-263-3400; www.qualityinnchambersburg.com*

139 rooms. Complimentary continental breakfast. High-speed Internet access. Fitness center. $

PENNSYLVANIA

★
★
★
★
★

## RESTAURANT

### ★★COPPER KETTLE

*1049 Lincoln Way East (Highway 30), Chambersburg, 717-264-3109*
Seafood, steak menu. Dinner. Closed Sunday. Bar. Children's menu. **$$**

# CHAMPION

## SPECIAL EVENT

### SEVEN SPRINGS WINE AND FOOD FESTIVAL

*777 Waterwheel Drive, Champion, 814-352-7777, 800-452-2223; www.7springs.com*
Sample some of the best local producers have to offer and drink from the complimentary wine glass that comes with the price of admission. With easy access from the Pennsylvania turnpike, you can head to Champion to stomp grapes or simply enjoy the cuisine of the Keystone State. Third weekend in August.

## HOTEL

### ★★SEVEN SPRINGS MOUNTAIN RESORT

*Road 1, County Line Road, Champion, 814-352-7777, 866-437-1300;*
*www.7springs.com*
418 rooms. High-speed Internet access. Children's activity center. Airport transportation available. **$**

## RESTAURANT

### ★★★HELEN'S

*777 Waterwheel Drive, Champion, 814-352-7777; www.7springs.com*
The formal service, complete with tableside carving and preparations, is a surprise considering the rural setting. Though the menu changes with the seasons, it leans towards classics with dishes such as veal osso buco with summer squash risotto and seafood linguine in a garlic cream sauce. American menu. Lunch, dinner. Bar. Reservations recommended. **$$$**

# CHESTER

The oldest settlement in the state, Chester was established by the Swedish Trading-Company as Upland. William Penn came to Upland in 1682 to begin colonization of the land granted to him by King Charles II. He renamed the settlement in honor of Chester, a Quaker center in Cheshire, England. The first Assembly here adopted Penn's framework of government, enacted the first laws and organized the county of Chester—from which Delaware County broke off in 1789. On the Delaware River, 15 miles southwest of Philadelphia, Chester is a busy port and home of shipyards where every type of vessel has been built for the navy and merchant marine.

*Information: Delaware County Convention & Tourist Bureau, 200 E. Estate St., Media,*
*610-565-3679, 800-343-3983; www.brandywinecvb.org*

## WHAT TO SEE AND DO

### PENN MEMORIAL LANDING STONE

*Front and Penn streets, Chester, 610-447-7881*
Marks spot where William Penn first landed October 28, 1682.

### WIDENER UNIVERSITY

*3800 Vartan Road, Chester, 610-499-4000; www.widener.edu*

Founded in 1821, the campus features Old Main, a national historic landmark, and the University Art Museum, with a permanent collection of 19th- and 20th-century American Impressionist and European academic art as well as contemporary exhibits. September-May, Tuesday-Saturday; June and August, Monday-Thursday; closed July. Also here is Wolfgram Memorial Library. Campus tours.

# CLARION

Once the forests were so thick and tall here that, according to tradition, the wind in the treetops sounded like a distant clarion. Today many campers and sports and outdoors enthusiasts enjoy the beauty and recreation that the Clarion area offers.

*Information: Clarion Area Chamber of Business and Industry, 41 S. Fifth Ave., Clarion, 814-226-9161; www.clarionpa.com*

## WHAT TO SEE AND DO
### CLARION COUNTY HISTORICAL SOCIETY

*18 Grant St., Clarion, 814-226-4450*

Museum housed in mid-19th century Sutton-Ditz house. Contains exhibits on county industry and business; Victorian bedroom and parlor; genealogical and historical library (researchers may call ahead for appointment other than regular hours); changing exhibits. April-December, Tuesday, Thursday and Friday afternoons.

## SPECIAL EVENTS
### AUTUMN LEAF FESTIVAL

Parade, carnival, autorama, scholarship pageants, concerts, flea market, craft shows. Late September-early October.

### SPRING FLING

Concerts, food concessions, games, entertainment. Early May.

## HOTELS
### ★★HOLIDAY INN

*45 Holiday Inn Drive, Clarion, 814-226-8850, 800-596-1313; www.holidayinn.com*

121 rooms. High-speed Internet access. Indoor pool. Fitness center. Airport transportation available. $

### ★SUPER 8

*135 Hotel Drive, I-80 and Exit 62 Clarion, 814-226-4550, 800-800-8000; www.super8.com*

99 rooms. Pets accepted. Complimentary continental breakfast. High-speed Internet access. Pool. $

# CLARK

## HOTEL
### ★★★TARA COUNTRY INN

*2844 Lake Road, Clark, 724-962-3535, 800-782-2803; www.tara-inn.com*

Inspired by *Gone With the Wind,* this pillared inn brings Southern charm and hospitality to the northeast. All 27 rooms boast personalized décor and furnishings such as

★
★
★
★
★

floral wallpaper, antique four-poster beds and hand-carved mantels. Ashley's Gourmet Dining Room downstairs continues the upscale vibe. 27 rooms. No children allowed. Golf. Indoor pool. Sauna. Spa. $$$

# CLARKS SUMMIT

## HOTEL
### ★★INN AT NICHOLS VILLAGE
*1101 Northern Blvd., Clarks Summit, 570-587-1135, 800-642-2215;*
*www.nicholsvillage.com*
135 rooms. High-speed Internet access. Fitness center. Sauna. Spa. Airport transportation available. 12 acres include over 1,000 rhododendrons; forestland. $

# CLEARFIELD
The old and important Native American town of Chinklacamoose occupied this site until it was burned in 1757. Coal and clay mining and more than 20 diversified plants producing school supplies, firebrick, fur products, precision instruments, electronic products and sportswear now occupy what used to be cleared fields.
*Information: Clearfield Chamber of Commerce, 125 E. Market St., 814-765-7567;*
*www.clearfieldchamber.com*

## WHAT TO SEE AND DO
### PARKER DAM
*28 Fairview Road, Clearfield, 814-765-0630;*
*www.dcnr.state.pa.us/stateparks/parks/parkerdam.aspx*
Approximately 950 acres in Moshannon State Forest. Swimming beach, fishing, boating (launch, rentals); hiking, cross-country skiing, snowmobiling, sledding, ice skating, ice fishing, snack bar, tent and trailer sites, cabins. Nature center.

### S. B. ELLIOTT STATE PARK
*814-765-7271, www.dcnr.state.pa.us/stateparks/parks/sbelliott.aspx*
Approximately 300 acres in the heart of the Moshannon State Forest; entirely wooded; display of mountain laurel in season. Fishing in small mountain streams surrounding the park. Hiking, snowmobile trails, tent and trailer sites, cabins. Standard fees.

## SPECIAL EVENTS
### CLEARFIELD COUNTY FAIR
*Clearfield County Fairgrounds, Mill Road and Turnpike Avenue, Clearfield,*
*814-765-4629; www.clearfieldcountyfair.com*
Late July-early August.

### HIGH COUNTRY ARTS & CRAFT FAIR
*814-765-9804*
S. B. Elliott State Park. Sunday after July Fourth.

## HOTEL
### ★DAYS INN
*Route 879 and I-80, Clearfield, 814-765-5381, 800-329-7466;*
*www.daysinn.com*

★
★
★
★
★

119 rooms. Pets accepted. Complimentary continental breakfast. High-speed Internet access. Fitness center. Pool. Business center. **$**

# COATESVILLE

## WHAT TO SEE AND DO
### HIBERNIA COUNTY PARK
*1 Park Ave., Coatesville, 610-384-0290*
Once the center of an iron works community, it is now the largest of the county parks, encompassing 800 acres of woodlands and meadows. The west branch of the Brandywine Creek, Birch Run and a pond are stocked with trout; hiking trails, picnicking, tent and trailer camping. Park features Hibernia Mansion; portions of house date from 1798, period furnishings. Tours of mansion. Memorial Day-Labor Day, Sunday.

## SPECIAL EVENTS
### HIBERNIA MANSION CHRISTMAS TOURS
*Hibernia County Park, 1 Park Ave., Coatesville*
First week in December.

### OLD FIDDLERS' PICNIC
*Hibernia County Park, 1 Park Ave., Coatesville*
Second Saturday in August.

# CONNELLSVILLE

George Washington once owned land in the region, and many places are named in his honor. The restored Crawford Cabin near the river was the home of Colonel William Crawford, surveyor of these properties and Washington's surveying pupil.

Northwest of town in Perryopolis, the town square is named for Washington, who some believe planned the design of the town.
*Information: Greater Connellsville Chamber of Commerce, 923 W. Crawford Ave., 724-628-5500; www.greaterconnellsville.org*

## WHAT TO SEE AND DO
### FALLINGWATER (KAUFMANN CONSERVATION ON BEAR RUN)
*Highway 381 S., Mill Run, Connellsville, 724-329-8501;*
*www.wpconline.org/fallingwaterhome.htm*
One of the most famous structures of the 20th century, Fallingwater, designed by Frank Lloyd Wright in 1936, is cantilevered on three levels over a waterfall; interior features Wright-designed furniture, textiles and lighting, as well as sculpture by modern masters; extensive grounds are heavily wooded and planted with rhododendron, which blooms in early July. Visitor center with self-guided orientation program, concession, gift shop. Guided tours. Mid-March-Thanksgiving, Tuesday-Sunday; winter, Saturday-Sunday. No children under age 6; child-care center. Reservations required.

**PENNSYLVANIA**

★
★
★
★
★

### NEWMYER HOUSE

*507 S. Pittsburgh St., Connellsville, 724-626-0141*

Restored Queen Anne-style mansion built in 1892; antiques. 4 rooms. Children over 12 only. Complimentary full breakfast. **$**

# CORNWALL

The Cornwall Ore Banks were a major source of magnetic iron ore for nearly 250 years.

*Information: Pennsylvania Rainbow Region Vacation Bureau,*
*625 Quentin Road, Lebanon, 717-272-8555; www.visitlebanoncounty.com*

## WHAT TO SEE AND DO

### CORNWALL IRON FURNACE

*Rexmont Road and Boyd St., Cornwall, 717-272-9711; www.cornwallironfurnace.org*

In operation 1742-1883. Open pit mine; 19th-century Miners Village still occupied. Furnace building houses "great wheel" and 19th-century steam engine. Visitor center, exhibits, book store. Tuesday-Sunday 9 a.m.-5 p.m., Sunday noon-5 p.m.

### HISTORIC SCHAEFFERSTOWN

*Highway 419 N., Schaefferstown, Cornwall, 717-949-2244; www.hsimuseum.org*

An 18th-century farm established by Swiss-German settlers. Village square with authentic log and stone and half-timber buildings; site of first waterworks in U.S., still in operation. Schaeffer Farm Museum has Swiss Bank House and Barn; early farm tools; colonial farm garden. The museum north of the square has antiques and artifacts of settlers. House and museum (open during festivals; also June-September, by appointment).

## SPECIAL EVENT

### HISTORIC SCHAEFFERSTOWN EVENTS

*www.hsimuseum.org*

Events during the year include Cherry Fair, fourth Saturday in June; Folk Festival, mid-July; Harvest Fair and Horse Plowing Contest, second weekend in September.

# DANVILLE

*Information: Columbia-Montour Visitors Bureau, 316 Mill St., Danville, 570-275-8185*

## WHAT TO SEE AND DO

### PP & L MONTOUR PRESERVE

*700 Preserve Road, Danville, 570-437-3131; www.fish.state.pa.us*

Fishing, boating (no gasoline motors) on 165-acre Lake Chillisquaque. Hiking and nature trails, picnicking. Birds of prey exhibit in visitor center; scheduled programs (daily, fee for some).

## HOTELS

### ★★★PINE BARN INN

*1 Pine Barn Place, Danville, 570-275-2071, 800-627-2276; www.pinebarninn.com*

This quiet inn is only a 20-minute drive from downtown and the lake. Behind its comfortably rustic exterior, it displays a modern touch with amenities such as Jacuzzi tubs. 99 rooms. Restaurant, bar. Wireless Internet access. Fitness center. Pool. **$**

### ★QUALITY INN

*15 Valley West Road, Danville, 570-275-5100, 877-424-6423; www.choicehotels.com*
77 rooms. Pets accepted. High-speed Internet. Fitness center. Pool. Business center. $

## RESTAURANT
### ★★PINE BARN INN

*1 Pine Barn Place, Danville, 570-275-2071; www.pinebarninn.com*
Seafood, steak menu. Breakfast, lunch, dinner. Sunday brunch. Bar. Children's menu. Converted 19th-century barn. Outdoor seating. $$

# DELAWARE WATER GAP NATIONAL RECREATION AREA

It is difficult to believe that the quiet Delaware River could carve a path through the Kittatinny Mountains, which are nearly a quarter of a mile high at this point. Conflicting geological theories account for this natural phenomenon. The prevailing theory is that the mountains were formed after the advent of the river, rising up from the earth so slowly that the course of the Delaware was never altered.

Despite the speculation about its origin, there is no doubt about the area's recreational value. A relatively unspoiled area along the river boundary between Pennsylvania and New Jersey, stretching approximately 35 miles from Matamoras to an area just south of I-80, the site of the Delaware Water Gap is managed by the National Park Service.

Trails and overlooks offer scenic views. Also here are canoeing and boating, and hunting and fishing; camping is nearby at the Dingmans Campground within the recreation area. Swimming and picnicking at Smithfield and Milford beaches. Dingmans Falls and Silver Thread Falls, two of the highest waterfalls in the Poconos, are near here. Several 19th-century buildings are in the area, including Millbrook Village (several buildings open May-October) and Peters Valley. The visitor center is located off I-80 in New Jersey, at Kittatinny Point (April-November, daily; rest of year; Saturday and Sunday only). Park headquarters are in Bushkill.
*Information: 570-426-2452; www.nps.gov/dewa*

# DENVER/ADAMSTOWN

Just off the Pennsylvania Turnpike, Denver and Adamstown are in the center of an active antique marketing area, which preserves its Pennsylvania German heritage.
*Information: Pennsylvania Dutch Convention and Visitors Bureau, 501 Greenfield Road, Lancaster, 717-299-8901, 800-723-8834; www.padutchcountry.com*

## WHAT TO SEE AND DO
### STOUDT'S BLACK ANGUS ANTIQUES MALL

*Route 272, 2800 North Reading Road, Adamstown, 717-484-4386; www.stoudtsbeer.com*
More than 350 dealers display quality antiques for sale. Sunday.

## SPECIAL EVENT

### BAVARIAN SUMMER FEST

*Adamstown, 717-484-4385; www.stoudtbeer.com*

Oompah bands, schuhplattler dance groups; Oktoberfest atmosphere. Includes special events, German folklore, German food, displays, shops. Early August-Labor Day, Friday-Sunday; October, Sunday only.

## HOTELS

### ★★BLACK HORSE LODGE & SUITES

*2180 N. Reading Road, Denver, 717-336-7563, 800-610-3805;*
*www.blackhorselodge.com*

74 rooms. Complimentary full breakfast. High-speed Internet access. Restaurant, bar. $

### ★★HOLIDAY INN

*1 Denver Road, Denver, 717-336-7541, 800-315-2621; www.holidayinn.com*

110 rooms. High-speed Internet access. Fitness center. Pool. Business center. $

## SPECIALTY LODGING

### INNS OF ADAMSTOWN

*62 W. Main St., Adamstown, 717-484-0800, 800-594-4808; www.adamstown.com*

Two inns (Adamstown Inn and Amethyst Inn); built in 1925; Victorian décor; antiques, family heirlooms. Nine rooms. Pets accepted. Children over 12 years only. Complimentary continental breakfast. High-speed Internet access. $

## RESTAURANT

### ★★BLACK HORSE

*2180 N. Reading Road, Denver, 717-336-6555; www.blackhorselodge.com*

Seafood, steak menu. Dinner. Bar. Children's menu. $$$

# DONEGAL

## WHAT TO SEE AND DO

### SEVEN SPRINGS MOUNTAIN RESORT SKI AREA

*Donegal, 800-452-2223; www.7springs.com*

Three quad, five triple chairlifts; two rope tows, six-passenger high-speed chair; patrol, school, rentals, snowmaking; cafeteria, restaurant, bar, lodge. Longest run 1¼ miles; vertical drop 750 feet. Night skiing. (December-March, daily) Alpine slide (May-September, daily). Hotel and conference center; summer activities include 18-hole golf, tennis, rope course, horseback riding and swimming.

## HOTEL

### ★DAYS INN

*Highway 31, Donegal, 724-593-7536, 800-329-7466; www.daysinn.com*

50 rooms. Complimentary continental breakfast. High-speed Internet access. Fitness center. Pool. Business center. $

# DOWNINGTOWN

Settled by emigrants from Birmingham, England, Downingtown honors Thomas Downing, who erected a log cabin here in 1702. The borough was first called Mill-town, after the mill built here by Roger Hunt in 1765. The town, with its many histori-cally interesting homes, retains much of its colonial charm. Jacob Eichholtz, a leading early American portrait artist, was born here.

*Information: Chester County Conference and Visitors Bureau,*
*400 Exton Square Parkway, Exton, 610-280-6145, 800-228-9933;*
*www.brandywinevalley.com*

## HOTEL

### ★★★SHERATON GREAT VALLEY HOTEL

*707 Lancaster Pike, Downingtown, 610-524-5500, 800-325-3535; www.sheraton.com*

Located in Chester County, this full-service hotel is conveniently located near area attractions and corporate offices. Historic Philadelphia is about 30 miles away, and Exton Square and King of Prussia Mall are nearby. Guests can get comfortable in the spacious guest rooms, which feature large work desks and the Sheraton Sweet Sleeper Beds (also available for dogs). The hotel offers a complimentary shuttle service to the surrounding area for guests who would like to see the sites or need a ride to the office. The White Horse Tavern, a historic 18th-century farmhouse, serves traditional American fare. Guests can also find a bite to eat or a drink at the casual Chesterfields Lounge, located just off the main lobby. 198 rooms. High-speed Internet access. Business center. $$

# DOYLESTOWN (BUCKS COUNTY)

*Information: Bucks County Conference and Visitors Bureau, 152 Swamp Road,*
*Doylestown, 215-345-4552, 800-836-2825; www.buckscountycvb.org*

## WHAT TO SEE AND DO

### COVERED BRIDGES

Descriptive list, map of 11 bridges in Bucks County may be obtained at Bucks County Tourist Commission.

### JAMES A. MICHENER ART MUSEUM

*138 S. Pine St., Doylestown, 215-340-9800; www.michenerartmuseum.org*

This museum, a former prison modeled after the Eastern State Penitentiary in Philadelphia, is as large as a football field and was named for Doylestown's most famous son, the Pulitzer Prize-winning writer James Michener. He supported the arts and dreamed of a regional art museum dedicated to preserving, interpreting and exhibiting the art and cultural heritage of the Bucks County region. The museum is now home to more than 2,500 paintings, sculptures, drawings and photographs, as well as stained glass collections and an outdoor gallery paying homage to the local landscape. Tuesday-Sunday.

### MERCER MILE

Three reinforced-concrete structures built between 1910-1916 within a one-mile radius by Dr. Henry Chapman Mercer, archaeologist, historian, a major proponent of the Arts and Crafts movement in America.

**PENNSYLVANIA**

★
★
★
★
☆

### FONTHILL MUSEUM

*525 E. Court St., Doylestown, 215-348-9461; www.mercermuseum.org*

Concrete castle of Henry Chapman Mercer, displays his collection of tiles and prints from around the world. Guided tours (times vary).

### MERCER MUSEUM

*84 S. Pine St., Doylestown, 215-345-0210; www.mercermuseum.org*

In this towering castle built in 1969, visitors will find implements, folk art and furnishings of early America before mechanization. See a Conestoga wagon, a whaling boat, carriages and an antique fire engine. Fifty thousand pieces of more than 60 early American crafts and varying trade tools on display. Monday-Saturday 10 a.m.-5 p.m., Sunday noon-5 p.m.

### THE MORAVIAN POTTERY AND TILE WORKS

*130 Swamp Road, Doylestown, 215-345-6722; www.buckscounty.org*

This historic landmark is a working history museum in which visitors can witness tiles produced by hand. Visitors may purchase tiles made on site in the tile shop. Daily.

## DUBOIS

At the entrance to the lowest pass of the Allegheny Range, DuBois is a transportation center, which was once the apex of huge lumbering operations. Destroyed by fire in 1888, the town was rebuilt on the ashes of the old community and today ranks as one of the 12 major trading centers in the state.

*Information: DuBois Area Chamber of Commerce, 31 N. Brady St., DuBois, 814-371-5010; www.duboispachamber.com*

### HOTELS

#### ★★CLARION HOTEL

*1896 Rich Highway, DuBois, 814-371-5100, 877-424-6423; www.choicehotels.com*

160 rooms. High-speed Internet access. Pool. Spa. Fitness center. Business center. Airport transportation available. $

#### ★HAMPTON INN

*1582 Bee Line Highway, DuBois, 814-375-1000, 800-426-7866; www.hamptoninn.com*

96 rooms. Pets accepted. Complimentary continental breakfast. High-speed Internet access. Pool, whirlpool. Fitness center. Business cetner. $

## EASTON

Easton is part of a larger metropolitan area, the Lehigh Valley, which also includes Allentown and Bethlehem. Lafayette College, with its beautiful campus and the historic Great Square is of interest.

*Information: Two Rivers Area Chamber of Commerce, 1 S. Third St., Easton, 610-253-4211*

## WHAT TO SEE AND DO

### CANAL MUSEUM NATIONAL

*30 Centre Square, Easton, 610-559-6613; www.canals.org*

Exhibits include photographs, models, documents and artifacts from the era of mule-drawn canal boats in the 1800s; electronic map and audiovisual programs. Changing exhibits. Memorial Day-Labor Day, daily; rest of year, Tuesday-Sunday.

### CRAYOLA FACTORY

*Two Rivers Landing, 30 Centre Square, Easton, 610-515-8000, 800-272-9652; www.crayola.com/factory*

This is not the main factory, which is several miles away, but it explains well how crayons and markers are manufactured. There are lots of colorful interactive exhibits and plenty of opportunities to draw and color to your heart's content. Hours vary.

### THE GREAT SQUARE

Center of business district. Now called Center Square. Dominated by Soldiers' and Sailors' Monument. Bronze marker shows replica of Old Courthouse, which stood until 1862 on land rented from the Penns for one red rose a year. From Old Courthouse steps, the Declaration of Independence was read on July 8, 1776, when the Easton Flag, the first Stars and Stripes of the united colonies, was unfurled here.

### LAFAYETTE COLLEGE

*Highways 22 and 78, Easton, 610-330-5000; www.lafayette.edu*

A bronze statue of Lafayette created in 1826 by Daniel Chester French stands in front of college chapel; American historical portrait collection in Kirby Hall of Civil Rights. Tour of campus.

### NORTHAMPTON COUNTY HISTORICAL SOCIETY

*101-107 S. Fourth St., Easton, 610-253-1222; www.northamptonctymuseum.org*

Changing exhibits; library; museum. Monday-Friday 9 a.m.-4 p.m. Closed Saturday-Sunday.

## RESTAURANT

### ★★PEARLY BAKER'S ALE HOUSE

*11 Centre Square, Easton, 610-253-9949; www.pearlybakers.net*

International menu. Lunch, dinner. Closed Monday. Bar. Children's menu. Reservations recommended. Outdoor seating. **$$**

# EDINBORO

## HOTELS

### ★★EDINBORO INN RESORT AND CONFERENCE CENTER

*401 W. Plum St., Edinboro, 814-734-5650; www.edinboroinn.com*

105 rooms. Pets accepted. High-speed Internet access. Pool. Business center. **$**

# EMMAUS

## RESTAURANT
### ★★THE FARMHOUSE
*1449 Chestnut St., Emmaus, 610-967-6225; www.thefarmhouse.com*
American menu. Dinner. Closed Sunday-Monday. Bar. Outdoor seating. Business casual. $$$

# EPHRATA
*Information: Chamber of Commerce, 16 E. Main St., Ephrata, 717-738-9010;*
*www.ephrata-area.org*

## WHAT TO SEE AND DO
### EPHRATA CLOISTER
*632 W. Main St., Ephrata, 717-733-6600; www.ephratacloister.org*
Buildings stand as a monument to an unusual religious experiment. In 1732 Conrad Beissel, a German Seventh-Day Baptist, began to lead a hermit's life here. Within a few years he established a religious community of recluses, with a Brotherhood, a Sisterhood and a group of married "householders." The members of the solitary order dressed in concealing white habits; the buildings were without adornment, the halls were narrow, the doorways were low, and board benches served as beds and wooden blocks as pillows. Their religious zeal and charity, however, proved to be their undoing. After the Battle of Brandywine, the cloistered community nursed the Revolutionary sick and wounded but contracted typhus, which decimated their numbers. Celibacy also contributed to the decline of the community, but the Society was not formally dissolved until 1934. An orientation exhibit and video prepare each visitor for their journey back through time. Craft demonstrations (summer). Daily.

### MUSEUM AND LIBRARY OF THE HISTORICAL SOCIETY OF COCALICO VALLEY
*249 W. Main St., Ephrata, 717-733-1616; www.cocalicovalleyhs.org*
Italianate Victorian mansion contains period displays, historical exhibits, genealogical and historical research library (fee) on Cocalico Valley area and residents. Monday, Wednesday, Thursday, Saturday.

## SPECIAL EVENT
### STREET FAIR
*717-733-4451; www.ephratafair.org*
One of largest in the state. Last full week in September.

## SPECIALTY LODGINGS
### THE INNS AT DONECKERS
*409 N. State St., Ephrata, 717-738-9502, 800-377-2206; www.doneckers.com*
31 rooms. Complimentary continental breakfast. High-speed Internet access. $

### SMITHTON BED AND BREAKFAST COUNTRY INN
*900 W. Main St., Ephrata, 717-733-6094, 877-755-4590; www.historicsmithtoninn.com*
Historic stone inn. 17 rooms. Complimentary full breakfast. Whirlpool. $

★
★
★
★
☆

## RESTAURANT

### ★★★THE RESTAURANT AT DONECKERS

*333 N. State St., Ephrata, 717-738-9501; www.doneckers.com*

Guests can opt for a formal atmosphere amidst antiques and artwork in the main dining room, or a more casual setting in the bistro. Entrées include sautéed trout on black beluga lentils with roast garlic and a saffron-roasted red pepper broth or filet mignon with a crispy truffled risotto cake, celery gremolata and Malmsey Madeira sauce. Check for special events, such as theme dinners and wine tastings. American, French menu. Lunch, dinner. Closed Wednesday, Sunday. Bar. Children's menu. $$$

# ERIE

The third-largest city in Pennsylvania, Erie is the state's only port on the Great Lakes and boasts a wealth of natural beauty and fascinating historical tales. Visitors enjoy Presque Isle State Park, with its seven miles of sandy beaches, hiking and biking trails. Downtown offers cultural and entertainment options including Broadway shows, classical ballet, philharmonic performances and comedy clubs. Explore acres of vineyards at local wineries, take in a play at the Erie Playhouse or the Roadhouse Theater, cheer for the AA Seawolves Baseball or the Otters OHL professional hockey team, splash around at northwest Pennsylvania's only indoor water park, or strap on your skis for downhill or cross-country fun.

The lake and city take their name from the Erie tribe, who were killed by the Seneca about 1654. On the south shore of Presque Isle Bay, Commodore Oliver Hazard Perry built his fleet, floated the ships across the sandbars and fought the British in the Battle of Lake Erie. Fort Presque Isle, built by the French in 1753 and destroyed by them in 1759, was rebuilt by the English, burned by Native Americans, and rebuilt again in 1794 by Americans.

*Information: Erie Area Convention and Visitors Bureau, 208 E. Bayfront Parkway, Erie, 814-454-7191, 800-524-3743; www.visiteriepa.com*

## WHAT TO SEE AND DO

### BICENTENNIAL TOWER

*7 Dobbins Landing, Erie, 814-455-6055*

Commemorating Erie's 200th birthday, this 187-foot tower features two observation decks with an aerial view of the city, bay and Lake Erie. Concessions in tower lobby. April-September, daily; rest of year: call for schedule. Free admission on Tuesday.

### ERIE ART MUSEUM

*411 State St., Erie, 814-459-5477; www.erieartmuseum.org*

Temporary art exhibits in a variety of media; regional artwork and lectures in the restored Greek Revival Old Customs House. Art classes, concerts, lectures and workshops are also offered. Tuesday-Saturday, Sunday afternoons. Free admission on Wednesday.

### ERIE ZOO

*423 W. 38th St., Erie, 814-864-4091; www.eriezoo.org*

Zoo houses more than 300 animals, including gorillas, polar bears and giraffes; children's zoo (May-September); one-mile tour of grounds on Safariland Express Train (fee). Indoor ice rink. September-March, daily 10 a.m.-5 p.m.

**PENNSYLVANIA**

★
★
★
★
★

## FIREFIGHTERS HISTORICAL MUSEUM

*428 Chestnut St., Erie, 814-456-5969; www.museumstuff.com*

More than 1,300 items of firefighting memorabilia are displayed in the old #4 Fire-house. Exhibits include fire apparatus dating from 1823, alarm systems, uniforms, badges, ribbons, helmets, nozzles, fire marks and fire extinguishers; fire safety films are shown in the Hay Loft Theater. May-October, Saturday-Sunday.

## GRIDLEY'S GRAVE

*Lakeside Cemetery, 1718 E. Lake Road, Erie, 814-459-8200*

Final resting place of Captain Charles Vernon Gridley, to whom, at the Battle of Manila Bay in 1898, Admiral Dewey said, "You may fire when ready, Gridley." Gridley died in Japan; his body was returned here for burial. Four old Spanish cannons from Manila Harbor, built in 1777, guard the grave. Offers view of peninsula, Lake Erie and entrance to Erie Harbor from cliff by Gridley Circle.

## LAND LIGHTHOUSE

*2 Lighthouse St., Erie, 814-452-3937; www.nps.gov/maritime/light/erieland.htm*

The first lighthouse on the Great Lakes was constructed on this site in 1813.

## MISERY BAY

*N.E. corner of Presque Isle Bay, Erie*

State monument to Perry; named after Perry defeated British and the fleet suffered cold and privations of a bitter winter.

## PRESQUE ISLE STATE PARK

*1 Peninsula Drive, Erie, 814-833-7424; www.presqueisle.org*

Peninsula stretches seven miles into Lake Erie and curves back toward city. Approximately 3,200 acres of recreation and conservation areas. Swimming, fishing, boating (rentals, mooring, launching, marina); hiking, birding, trails, cross-country skiing, ice skating, ice fishing, ice boating, picnicking, concessions. Visitor center, environmental education and interpretive programs.

## WALDAMEER PARK & WATER WORLD

*220 Peninsula Drive., Erie, 814-838-3591; www.waldameer.com*

At entrance to Presque Isle State Park. Rides, midway, kiddieland, water park, picnic area, food, dance pavilion. Memorial Day-Labor Day, Tuesday-Sunday open. Monday holiday.

## WATSON-CURTZE MANSION

*356 W. Sixth St., Erie, 814-871-5790; www.eriecountyhistory.org*

Housed in 1890s Victorian mansion. Museum features regional history and decorative arts exhibits, restored period rooms, changing exhibits (Wednesday-Sunday afternoons). Also planetarium with shows Saturday afternoons.

## WAYNE MEMORIAL BLOCKHOUSE

*560 E. Third St., Erie, 814-871-4531; www.ushistory.org*

On grounds of State Soldiers' and Sailors' Home. Replica of blockhouse in which General Anthony Wayne died December 15, 1796, after becoming ill on a voyage from Detroit. He was buried at the foot of the flagpole; later, his son had the body disinterred and the remains moved to Radnor. Memorial Day-Labor Day, daily.

## HOTELS

### ★COMFORT INN

*3041 W. 12th St., Erie, 814-835-4200, 877-424-6423; www.choicehotels.com*
100 rooms. Complimentary continental breakfast. Wireless Internet access. Pool. Business center. Airport transportation available. **$**

### ★★DOWNTOWN ERIE HOTEL

*18 W. 18th St., Erie, 814-456-2961, 800-832-9101; www.downtowneriehotel.com*
133 rooms. Complimentary full breakfast. Wireless Internet access. Pool. Fitness center. Business center. Airport transportation available. **$**

### ★GLASS HOUSE INN

*3202 W. 26th St., Erie, 814-833-7751, 800-956-7222; www.glasshouseinn.com*
30 rooms. Complimentary continental breakfast. Wireless Internet access. Pool. **$**

### ★QUALITY INN & SUITES

*8040 Perry Highway, Erie, 814-864-4911, 877-424-6423; www.qualityinn.com*
109 rooms. Complimentary continental breakfast. Wireless Internet access. Pool, whirlpool. Business center. Airport transportation available. **$**

## RESTAURANTS

### ★★PUFFERBELLY

*414 French St., Erie, 814-454-1557; www.thepufferbelly.com*
Restored firehouse. Dinner. Sunday brunch. Bar. Outdoor seating. **$$**

### ★★THE STONEHOUSE INN

*4753 W. Lake Road, Erie, 814-838-9296; www.stonehouse-inn.com*
International/fusion menu. Dinner. Closed Sunday-Monday; also Holy Week. Bar. Business casual attire. Reservations recommended. **$$$**

# ERWINNA

## HOTEL

### ★★★GOLDEN PHEASANT INN

*763 River Road, Erwinna, 610-294-9595, 800-830-4474; www.goldenpheasant.com*
Located an hour and a half from New York City and 20 minutes outside of Philadelphia, this provincial and romantic weekend hideaway sits between the Delaware River and the Pennsylvania Canal. The guest rooms are homey and unique (if a little snug) with canopy beds and plush carpeting. Don't miss dinner at the restaurant, as it turns out spectacular French cuisine. 6 rooms. Complimentary continental breakfast. **$**

## RESTAURANT

### ★★★GOLDEN PHEASANT INN

*763 River Road, Erwinna, 610-294-9595; www.goldenpheasant.com*
Enjoy entrées such as roasted pheasant with apple and calvados sauce or grilled petite lamb chops with a roasted shallot and mint sauce. The interior is decorated in dark

woods and beamed ceilings, and chandeliers hang throughout the dining room. French menu. Dinner, Sunday brunch. Closed Monday. Bar. **$$**

# EXTON

## HOTELS

### ★★★DULING-KURTZ HOUSE & COUNTRY INN

*146 S. Whitford Road, Exton, 610-524-1830; www.duling-kurtz.com*

Rich in history and comfort, this small inn offers a homey, elegant atmosphere for relaxation. The Duling-Kurtz House was built in 1783 and is located within walking distance of shopping, the train station and more. Rooms are small but comfortable and cozy. 20 rooms. Complimentary continental breakfast. **$**

### ★★INN AT CHESTER SPRINGS

*815 N. Pottstown Pike, Exton, 610-363-1100, 888-253-6119;*
*www.innatchestersprings.com*

225 rooms. Restaurant, bar. Wireless Internet access. Fitness center. Business center. Airport transportation available. **$**

## RESTAURANT

### ★★DULING-KURTZ HOUSE

*146 S. Whitford Road, Exton, 610-524-1830; www.duling-kurtz.com*

French menu. Lunch, dinner. Bar. Valet parking Friday, Saturday. Seven dining rooms. **$$$**

# FARMINGTON

★
★
★
★
★

## WHAT TO SEE AND DO

### BRADDOCK'S GRAVE

*200 Caverns Park Road, Farmington*

Granite monument marks burial place of British General Edward Braddock, who was wounded in battle with French and Native American forces on July 9, 1755, and died four days later.

### LAUREL CAVERNS

*200 Caverns Park Road, Farmington, 724-438-2070, 800-515-4150;*
*www.laurelcaverns.com*

Colored lighting, unusual formations. Indoor miniature golf. Repelling (fee). Guided tours. Exploring trips. May-October, daily 9 a.m.-5 p.m.

## HOTELS

### ★★★★FALLING ROCK

*150 Falling Rock Blvd., Farmington, 724-329-8555; www.nemacolin.com/fallingrock*

Inspired by the architecture of Frank Lloyd Wright, Falling Rock extends almost organically from the Pennsylvania countryside with its natural stone exterior, fountains and seasonally open, heated outdoor infinity pool. All rooms include 24-hour butler service and 1,200-thread-count sheets. But perhaps its most indulgent quality, at least for duffers, is its location—at the 18th hole of the Mystic Rock Golf Course, within the Nemacolin Woodlands Resort, and the accompanying 50,000-square-foot clubhouse. 38 rooms, four suites. Wireless Internet access. Restaurant, bar. Fitness room. Outdoor pool. Airport transportation available. Business center. **$$$**

### ★★★★NEMACOLIN WOODLANDS RESORT & SPA

*1001 Lafayette Drive, Farmington, 724-329-8555, 866-344-6957; www.nemacolin.com*

Tucked away in Pennsylvania's scenic Laurel Highlands, this comprehensive resort offers a multitude of recreational opportunities, from the Hummer driving club, equestrian center and shooting academy to the adventure and activities centers, culinary classes and art museums. Two golf courses and a renowned golf academy delight players, while special activities entertain children and teenagers. Grand European style defines the guest accommodations at Chateau LaFayette, while the Lodge maintains a rustic charm. Families enjoy the spacious accommodations in the townhouses, while the luxury homes add a touch of class to group travel. 220 rooms. High-speed Internet access. Pool. Spa. Fitness center. Children's activity center. **$$$**

### ★★★SUMMIT INN RESORT

*101 Skyline Drive, Farmington, 724-438-8594, 800-433-8594;*
*www.summitinnresort.com*

Located at the peak of Mount Summit, the Summit Inn Resort offers sparkling panoramic views of the surrounding counties. The 1907 inn is an architecture lover's dream: It's located near Frank Lloyd Wright's Fallingwater and has its own spot on the National Register of Historic Places. 100 rooms. Closed early November-mid-April. Atop Mount Summit. Pool. Bar. **$**

## SPA

### ★★★★WOODLANDS SPA AT NEMACOLIN RESORT

*1001 Lafayette Drive, Farmington, 724-329-8555, 800-422-2736; www.nemacolin.com*

Famed interior designer Clodagh created the look of this spa using natural materials and the guiding properties of feng shui, the ancient Chinese philosophy of balancing the forces of nature. Achieving inner tranquility is the mission here, and the treatments embrace this guiding principle. An extensive massage menu includes favorites such as Swedish, sports, aromatherapy, shiatsu and deep tissue as well as Eastern methods such as reflexology and reiki. From Japanese citrus and Balinese hibiscus to German chamomile and Greek mint, the body scrubs embody international personalities. Fitness and nutrition consultations help you gain insight into your body and its needs. The onsite spa restaurant makes healthy eating easier. **$$**

## RESTAURANTS

### ★★★AQUEOUS

*Falling Rock Hotel, 150 Falling Rock Blvd., Farmington, 724-329-8555;*
*www.nemacolin.com/aqueous*

Plunge into a true farm-to-table experience with local meats and produce at this upscale American steakhouse overlooking the Mystic Rock Golf Course. Porterhouse, bone-in ribeye, filet mignon and New York strip are available with a choice of delectable sauces, such as classic béarnaise and roasted red pepper. Country-style

**PENNSYLVANIA**

★
★
★
★
★

sides "big enough for two" include creamed spinach, creamed corn, onion rings and plenty of potatoes. Don't forget the surf and turf with king crab, jumbo shrimp and Maine lobster tail. American steakhouse menu. Breakfast, lunch, dinner. **$$$**

### ★★★★★LAUTREC

*Chateau LaFayette, 1001 LaFayette Drive, Farmington, 724-329-8555; www.nemacolin.com/lautrec*

Savor a bit of fine French cuisine—the restaurant wasn't named after French artist Henri de Toulouse-Lautrec for nothing—in Pennsylvania's Laurel Highlands. Self-taught chef Dave Racicot achieved high accolades while in his twenties with his frequently changing menu, driven by the availability of the freshest ingredients. Spend an entire evening focusing on the complexities of a four-course meal plus dessert, or go all out with the Grand Tasting Menu that includes over a dozen selections. Wine pairings are offered as well. French menu. Dinner. Jacket suggested. **$$$**

# FOGELSVILLE

## HOTEL

### ★★★THE GLASBERN INN

*2141 Pack House Road, Fogelsville, 610-285-4723; www.glasbern.com*

Stay in rustic luxury, amidst antique furnishings and all of the contemporary comforts. Built in the late 1800s on 100 acres near Allentown, the inn is housed in an old farm and includes a renovated farmhouse, barn, gate house and carriage house. 38 rooms. Pets accepted. Complimentary full breakfast. High-speed Internet access. Pool. Spa. Fitness center. Business center. **$**

# FORT WASHINGTON

*Information: Valley Forge Convention & Visitors Bureau, 600 W. Germantown Pike, Plymouth Meeting, 610-834-1550; www.valleyforge.org*

## WHAT TO SEE AND DO

### FORT WASHINGTON STATE PARK

*500 Bethlehem Pike, Fort Washington, 215-646-2942; www.dcnr.state.pa.us*

Commemorates the site of Washington's northern defense line against the British in 1777. Fishing, hiking, ball fields, picnicking.

### THE HIGHLANDS

*7001 Sheaff Lane, Fort Washington, 215-641-2687; www.highlandshistorical.org*

Late-Georgian mansion on 43 acres built by Anthony Morris, active in both state and federal government. Formal gardens and crenellated walls built circa 1845. Tours. Monday-Friday 1:30 a.m. and 3 p.m.

### HOPE LODGE

*553 Bethlehem Pike, Fort Washington, 215-646-1595; www.ushistory.org*

Colonial Georgian mansion; headquarters for Surgeon General John Cochran after Battle of Germantown. Historic furnishings, paintings, ceramics. Tuesday-Sunday.

## RESTAURANT
### ★★PALACE OF ASIA
*285 Commerce Drive, Fort Washington, 215-646-2133; www.palaceofasia.net*
Indian menu. Lunch, dinner. Brunch. Bar. Reservations recommended. $$

# FRANKLIN

A series of French and British forts was erected in this area. The last one, Fort Franklin, was razed by local settlers who used the stone and timber in their own buildings. Old Garrison took its place in 1796 and later served as the Venango County Jail. In 1859, James Evans, a blacksmith, made tools to drill an oil well, bringing an oil boom to the area. For years, oil was the area's dominant industry.

*Information: Franklin Area Chamber of Commerce, 1259 Liberty St., Franklin, 814-432-5823, 888-547-2377; www.franklin-pa.org*

## WHAT TO SEE AND DO
### HOGE-OSMER HOUSE
*301 S. Park St., Franklin, 814-437-2275; www.vpa.org*
Museum owned by Venango County Historical Society; displays materials and artifacts relating to Venango County history; period furnishings, research library. House open May-December, Tuesday-Thursday and Saturday; rest of year, Saturday. Inquire for genealogy library hours.

### PIONEER CEMETERY
*Otter and 15th streets, Franklin*
Self-guided walking tour booklets can be purchased at the Chamber of Commerce.

### VENANGO COUNTY COURTHOUSE
*1168 Liberty St., Franklin, 814-432-9500; www.co.venango.pa.us*
Built in 1868, this courthouse features unique Unique styling; contains display of Native American artifacts. Monday-Friday.

## SPECIAL EVENTS
### APPLEFEST
*1259 Liberty St., Franklin, 814-432-5823, 888-547-2377; www.franklinapplefest.com*
Apple pie-baking contest, arts and crafts, entertainment, classic car show, 5K race, horse-drawn buggy rides. First full weekend in October.

### FRANKLIN SILVER CORNET BAND CONCERTS
*City Park*
Thursday, mid-June-August.

### ROCKY GROVE FIREMAN'S FAIR & PARADE
*www.rgvfd.com*
Late June.

## SPECIALTY LODGING
### LAMBERTON HOUSE BED AND BREAKFAST
*1331 Otter St., Franklin, 814-432-7908, 866-632-7908; www.lambertonhouse.com*
5 rooms. Complimentary full breakfast. $

★
★
★
★
★

# GETTYSBURG

Because of the many historical attractions in this town, visitors may want to stop in at the Gettysburg Convention & Visitors Bureau for complete information about bus tours, guide service (including a tape-recorded and self-guided tour) and help in planning their visit here.

*Information: Convention & Visitors Bureau, 102 Carlisle St., Gettysburg, 717-334-6274, 800-337-5015; www.gettysburg.travel*

## WHAT TO SEE AND DO

### A. LINCOLN'S PLACE

*571 Steinwehr Ave., Gettysburg, 717-334-6049*

Live portrayal of the 16th president; 45 minutes. Mid-June-Labor Day: Monday-Friday.

## A TOWN GRIPPED BY WAR

In July 1863, a three-day Civil War battle unfolded about a mile outside Gettysburg, a small rural community. Gettysburg suffered greatly in the battle.

This one-mile walking tour visits several of the well-preserved buildings that withstood the conflict. Begin at Lincoln Square, the commercial heart of Gettysburg. Abraham Lincoln stayed at the David Wills House, now a small museum at No. 12, the night before he delivered the "Gettysburg Address" in the National Cemetery nearby. Just outside the door is an odd, life-size statue of Lincoln, dressed somberly, appearing to help a visitor dressed in a colorful sweater and corduroys—known to the town's residents as the "Perry Como statue" because of the tourist's strange garb.

Head south on Baltimore Street to Nos. 242-246, the Jennie Wade Birthplace. Wade, the only civilian killed in the battle, was supposedly shot by a Confederate soldier while baking bread and biscuits for Union troops in her sister's house nearby. Between the two homes, stop at the Schriver House at 309 Baltimore. Built for George Schriver and his family, the house contains a garret that was occupied by Confederate sharpshooters who poked still-visible holes in the wall for their rifles. Now a museum, the Schriver House details life in the town during and immediately after the battle.

Across the street at No. 304, formerly the Methodist parsonage, note the shell near the second story window in front. The parson's daughter, Laura, was said to have narrowly escaped injury when a shell crashed through the brick wall into her room. Later, the shell was placed in the hole to mark the spot.

Return to Lincoln Square via Washington Street. At the corner of West Middle Street, pause in front of the Michael Jacobs House at No. 101. A meteorologist, Jacobs recorded the weather throughout his life, leaving important details of the battle's weather and cloud conditions to posterity.

PENNSYLVANIA

★
★★
★★★
★★
★

## BOYD'S BEAR COUNTRY

*75 Cunningham Road, Gettysburg, 717-630-2600, 866-367-8338;*
*www.boydsbearcountry.com*

"The World's Most Humongous Teddy Bear Store" features four floors of bears (plus rabbits, moose and other furry friends) in a giant barn. At the Boyd's Teddy Bear Nursery, kids can adopt their very own baby bear; personalize your bear at the Make-N-Take-Craft Center. Live entertainment every weekend adds to the merriment. Restaurant; museum. Daily 10 a.m.-6 p.m.

## EISENHOWER NATIONAL HISTORIC SITE

*Rural Route 9, Gettysburg*

## GENERAL LEE'S HEADQUARTERS

*401 Buford Ave., Gettysburg, 717-334-3141; www.civilwarheadquarters.com*

Robert E. Lee planned Confederate strategy for the Gettysburg battle in this house; contains collection of historical items from the battle. Mid-March-mid-November, daily 9 a.m.-5 p.m.

## GETTYSBURG BATTLE THEATRE

*571 Steinwehr Ave., Gettysburg, 717-334-6100*

Battlefield diorama with 25,000 figures; 30-minute film and electronic maps program showing battle strategy. March-November, daily.

## GETTYSBURG COLLEGE

*300 N. Washington St., Gettysburg, 717-337-6300; www.gettysburg.edu*

Small liberal arts college of 2,000 students. Founded in 1832, this is the oldest Lutheran-affiliated college in the U.S. Liberal arts; Pennsylvania Hall was used as Civil War hospital; Eisenhower House and statue on grounds. Tour of campus.

## GETTYSBURG SCENIC RAIL TOURS

*Washington St., Gettysburg, 717-334-6932; www.gettysburgrail.com*

A 22-mile round trip to Aspers on a steam train. Also charter trips and special runs. June, Thursday-Sunday; July-August, Tuesday-Sunday; September, Saturday-Sunday.

## GHOSTS OF GETTYSBURG CANDLELIGHT WALKING TOURS

*271 Baltimore St., Gettysburg, 717-337-0445; www.ghostsofgettysburg.com*

Armed with tales from Mark Nesbitt's "Ghosts of Gettysburg" books, knowledgeable guides lead 1¼-hour tours through sections of town that were bloody battlefields 130 years ago. March and November, weekends; April-October, daily.

## HALL OF PRESIDENTS AND FIRST LADIES

*789 Baltimore St., Gettysburg, 717-334-5717; www.gettysburgbattle.com*

Costumed life-size wax figures of all the presidents and reproductions of their wives' inaugural gowns. Mid-March-November, daily.

**PENNSYLVANIA**

★
★
★
★
★

## LAND OF LITTLE HORSES

*125 Glenwood Drive, Gettysburg, 717-334-7259; www.landoflittlehorses.com*

A variety of performing horses—all in miniature. Continuous entertainment; indoor arena; exotic animal races. Saddle and wagon rides. Picnic area, snack bar, gift shop. April-August, daily; September-October, Saturday-Sunday.

## LINCOLN TRAIN MUSEUM

*425 Steinwehr Ave., Gettysburg, 717-334-5678;*
*www.gettysburgbattlefieldtours.com/Lincoln.html*

Museum features more than 1,000 model trains and railroad memorabilia; Lincoln Train Ride—simulated trip of 15 minutes. March-November, daily.

## LUTHERAN THEOLOGICAL SEMINARY

*61 Seminary Ridge, Gettysburg, 717-334-6286; www.ltsg.edu*

Oldest Lutheran seminary in the United States, which was founded in 1826; cupola on campus used as Confederate lookout during battle. Old Dorm, now home of Adams County Historical Society, served as hospital for both Union and Confederate soldiers.

## NATIONAL CIVIL WAR WAX MUSEUM

*297 Steinwehr Ave., Gettysburg, 717-334-6245; www.gettysburgmuseum.com*

Highlights Civil War era and Battle of Gettysburg. March-December, daily; rest of year, Saturday-Sunday.

## SCHRIVER HOUSE

*309 Baltimore St., Gettysburg, 717-337-2800; www.schriverhouse.com*

Built prior to the Civil War, this two-story brick house was used by Confederate sharpshooters, who knocked still-visible holes in the garret walls through which to aim their weapons. Private owners have restored and furnished the house as a period museum; the 30-minute guided tour details the Schriver family's experience during the battle, as well as the experience of other townspeople. Monday-Saturday 10 a.m.-5 p.m., Sunday noon-5 p.m.

## SOLDIERS' NATIONAL MUSEUM

*777 Baltimore St., Gettysburg, 717-334-4890;*
*www.gettysburgbattlefieldtours.com/Soldiers.html*

Dioramas of major battles; Civil War collection. March-November, daily.

## SPECIAL EVENTS

### APPLE BLOSSOM FESTIVAL

*South Mountain Fairgrounds, 35 Carlisle St., Gettysburg*

Early May.

### APPLE HARVEST FESTIVAL

*South Mountain Fairgrounds, 218 Mercer St., Gettysburg*

Demonstrations, arts and crafts, guided tours of orchard, mountain areas. First and second weekend in October.

### CIVIL WAR HERITAGE DAYS

Lectures by historians, Civil War collectors' show, entertainment, fireworks. Late June-early July.

## HOTELS

### ★BEST INN

*301 Steinwehr Ave., Gettysburg, 717-334-1188, 800-237-8466;*
*www.gettysburgbestinn.com*

77 rooms. Complimentary continental breakfast. Pool. **$**

### ★★BEST WESTERN GETTYSBURG HOTEL

*1 Lincoln Square, Gettysburg, 717-337-2000, 866-378-1797; www.bestwestern.com*

119 rooms. High-speed Internet access. Pool. Spa. Fitness center. Business center. **$**

### ★★★THE HERR TAVERN AND PUBLICK HOUSE

*900 Chambersburg Road, Gettysburg, 717-334-4332, 800-362-9849;*
*www.herrtavern.com*

Built in 1815, this inn served as the first Confederate hospital during the Battle of Gettysburg. Guest rooms have been modernized with a light touch that has not marred their quaint, historic charm. 16 rooms. Children over 12 only. Complimentary continental breakfast. Restaurant. Spa. Pool. **$$**

### ★HOLIDAY INN EXPRESS

*869 York Road, Gettysburg, 717-337-1400, 800-315-2621; www.hiexpress.com*

162 rooms. Pets accepted. Complimentary continental breakfast. Bar. Wireless Internet access. Pool, whirlpool. Spa. Fitness center. Business center. **$**

### ★QUALITY INN

*401 Buford Ave., Gettysburg, 717-334-3141, 877-424-6423; www.choicehotels.com*

48 rooms. Complimentary continental breakfast. High-speed Internet access. Restaurant. Pool, whirlpool. Fitness center. Business center. **$**

## SPECIALTY LODGINGS

### BALADERRY INN

*40 Hospital Road, Gettysburg, 717-337-1342, 800-220-0025; www.baladerryinn.com*

10 rooms. Children over 12 years only. Complimentary full breakfast. **$**

### BATTLEFIELD BED AND BREAKFAST INN

*2264 Emmitsburg Road, Gettysburg, 717-334-8804, 888-766-3897;*
*www.gettysburgbattlefield.com*

Built in 1809, this Civil War inn is located on the Gettysburg battlefield. Guests can enjoy a carriage ride and a historic demonstration with real muskets, cannons and cavalry. 8 rooms. Pets accepted. Complimentary full breakfast. **$$**

### BRAFFERTON INN

*44 York St., Gettysburg, 717-337-3423, 866-337-3423; www.brafferton.com*

18 rooms. Children over 8 only. Complimentary full breakfast. Wireless Internet access. Business center. **$**

### THE GASLIGHT INN

*33 E. Middle St., Gettysburg, 717-337-9100, 800-914-5698; www.thegaslightinn.com*
This bed and breakfast is located in the center of historic Gettysburg, near shopping, restaurants and local attractions. 9 rooms. Children over 11 years only. Complimentary full breakfast. Restaurant. **$$**

### JAMES GETTYS HOTEL

*27 Chambersburg St., Gettysburg, 717-337-1334, 888-900-5275;*
*www.jamesgettyshotel.com*
112 rooms, all suites. Complimentary continental breakfast. **$$**

## RESTAURANTS
### ★★DOBBIN HOUSE TAVERN

*89 Steinwehr Ave., Gettysburg, 717-334-2100; www.dobbinhouse.com*
American menu. Lunch, dinner. Closed first Monday in January and second Monday in June. Bar. Children's menu. Business casual attire. Reservations recommended. **$$$**

### ★★FARNSWORTH HOUSE INN

*401 Baltimore St., Gettysburg, 717-334-8838; www.farnsworthhouseinn.com*
American menu. Dinner. Children's menu. Outdoor seating. **$$**

### ★GINGERBREAD MAN

*217 Steinwehr Ave., Gettysburg, 717-334-1100; www.thegingerbreadman.net*
American menu. Lunch, dinner. Bar. Children's menu. **$$**

### ★★★HERR TAVERN AND PUBLICK HOUSE

*900 Chambersburg Road, Gettysburg, 717-334-4332, 800-362-9849;*
*www.herrtavern.com*
This restaurant is housed in the historic country inn of the same name, which served as the first Confederate hospital during the Battle of Gettysburg. Guests here are treated to friendly, pleasant service and an appetizing menu of American-inspired fare that includes some Mediterranean influences. Because most ingredients are obtained from local farmers, the menu frequently changes. Past dishes included shrimp and scallops in red pepper fondue with baby spinach and fettuccine; and Black Angus filet mignon with port wine demi-glace and a stuffed potato. American menu. Lunch, dinner. Bar. Children's menu. Business casual attire. Reservations recommended. **$$$**

# GETTYSBURG NATIONAL MILITARY PARK

The hallowed battlefield of Gettysburg, the site of one of the Civil War's most decisive battles and immortalized by Lincoln's Gettysburg Address, is preserved by the National Park Service. The town itself is still a college community, as it was more than a hundred years ago on July 1-3, 1863, when General Robert E. Lee led his Confederate Army in its greatest invasion of the North. The defending Northerners, under Union General George Meade, repulsed the Southern assault after three days of fierce fighting, which left 51,000 men dead, wounded or missing.

The Gettysburg National Military Park has more than 35 miles of roads through 5,900 acres of the battlefield area. There are more than 1,300 monuments, markers and tablets of granite and bronze, as well as 400 cannons.

Visitors may wish to tour the battlefield with a Battlefield Guide who is licensed by the National Park Service (two-hour tour; fee). The guides escort visitors to all points of interest and sketch the movement of troops and details of the battle. Or visitors may wish to first orient themselves at the Electric Map at the Visitor Center; then using the park folder, the battlefield can be toured without a guide. Audio cassettes are also available for self-guided tours.

The late President Dwight D. Eisenhower's retirement farm, a National Historic Site, adjoins the battlefield. It is open to the public on a limited-tour basis. All visitors must obtain tour tickets at the information center, located at the lobby of the Visitor Center-Electric Map building. Transportation to the farm is by shuttle.

*Information: Gettysburg National Military Park, 97 Taneytown Road, Gettysburg, 717-334-1124; www.nps.gov/gett*

## WHAT TO SEE AND DO

### THE ANGLE

Spot where Pickett's Charge was repulsed on July 3, referred to as "high water mark" of the Confederacy.

### CULP'S HILL

Site of longest sustained fighting during battle.

### CYCLORAMA CENTER

*97 Taneytown Road, Gettysburg*

Adjacent to visitor center. Instructive film and exhibits: 356-foot Cyclorama painting of Pickett's Charge. Daily.

### DEVIL'S DEN

Stronghold of Confederate sharpshooters following its capture during action on the second day.

### EAST CEMETERY HILL

Rallying point for Union forces on first day of battle. Scene of fierce fighting on evening of second day.

### EISENHOWER NATIONAL HISTORIC SITE

*(Visitor Center) 97 Taneytown Road, Gettysburg, 717-338-9114; www.nps.gov/eise*

Farm and home of the 34th President of the United States and his wife, Mamie. Tour of grounds and home take 1½-2 hours. Self-guided tours explore the farm and skeet range. Reception Center houses exhibits and bookstore; 11-minute video is shown. Access to site is by shuttle only, from the National Park Service Visitor Center. Daily.

### ETERNAL LIGHT PEACE MEMORIAL

On Oak Ridge. Erected in 1938 and dedicated by President Roosevelt to "peace eternal in a nation united."

**PENNSYLVANIA**

### GETTYSBURG NATIONAL CEMETERY
Site of Lincoln's Gettysburg Address.

### LITTLE ROUND TOP
Key Union position during second and third days of battle.

### MEMORIALS TO STATE UNITS
Includes Pennsylvania State Monument, with names of more than 34,500 Pennsylvanian soldiers who participated in the battle.

### SEMINARY RIDGE
Main Confederate battle line.

### VISITOR CENTER-ELECTRIC MAP-GETTYSBURG MUSEUM OF THE CIVIL WAR
*35 Carlisle St., Gettysburg*
Visits to the park should begin here. Park information, including a self-guided auto tour, and guides may be obtained at the center. Story of battle told on 750-square-foot electric map surrounded by 525 seats (every 45 minutes; fee). Gettysburg Museum of the Civil War has an extensive collection of Civil War relics (free). Daily.

### WHEATFIELD AND PEACH ORCHARD
Scene of heavy Union and Confederate losses on the second day of fighting.

### WHITWORTH GUNS ON OAK HILL
Only breech-loading cannon used here.

# GREENSBURG
Greensburg was named for Revolutionary General Nathanael Greene.
*Information: Laurel Highlands Visitors Bureau, 120 E. Main St., Ligonier, 724-238-5661; www.laurelhighlands.org*

## WHAT TO SEE AND DO
### HISTORIC HANNA'S TOWN
*951 Old Salem Road, Greensburg, 724-836-1800*
Costumed tour guide tells story of Hanna's Town, site of first court west of Alleghenies. Includes reconstructed courthouse, tavern, jail and stockaded fort; picnic area. June-August, Tuesday-Sunday; May, September-October, Saturday-Sunday.

### LINCOLN HIGHWAY HERITAGE CORRIDOR
*114 S. Market St., Greensburg, 724-238-9030; www.lhhc.org*
A 140-mile stretch of Highway 30 extending from Greensburg to Chambersburg. Pass through and explore countless historical and recreational areas. Driving guide available.

### WESTMORELAND COUNTY COURTHOUSE
*Main and Pittsburgh streets, Greensburg, 724-830-3000; www.co.westmoreland.pa.us*
Building in style of Italian Renaissance; restored in 1982. Monday-Friday.

### WESTMORELAND MUSEUM OF AMERICAN ART

*221 N. Main St., Greensburg, 724-837-1500; www.wmuseumaa.org*

18th-, 19th- and early 20th-century American paintings, sculpture, furniture and decorative arts. 19th- and early 20th-century southwestern Pennsylvania paintings. Extensive toy collection. Lectures, guided tours. Wednesday-Sunday 11 a.m.-5 p.m., Thursday, 11 a.m.-9 p.m. Closed Monday-Tuesday.

## HOTEL

### ★★FOUR POINTS BY SHERATON

*100 Sheraton Drive (Route 30 E.), Greensburg, 724-836-6060, 800-325-3535;*
*www.sheraton.com*

146 rooms. Pets accepted. High-speed Internet access. Pool. Fitness center. Business center. **$**

# GWYNEDD

## HOTEL

### ★★★WILLIAM PENN INN

*US 202 & Sumneytown Pike, Gwynedd, 215-699-9272; www.williampenninn.com*

6 rooms. Complimentary continental breakfast. Wireless Internet access. Business center. **$**

## RESTAURANT

### ★★WILLIAM PENN INN

*US 202 and Sumneytown Pike, Gwynedd, 215-699-9272; www.williampenninn.com*

Claiming more than 300 years of service and experience in the kitchen, this picturesque dining spot is a popular choice for weddings and other celebratory events. The menu leans heavily on seafood with such signature dishes as snapper soup and baked Maryland crab imperial. The Sunday brunch is a hit with locals. American menu. Lunch, dinner, Sunday brunch. Bar. Originally built as a tavern. **$$$**

# HANOVER

Hanover was once known as "McAllisterstown" (for founder Colonel Richard McAllister) and "Rogue's Harbor" (for its lack of law enforcement). Here, on June 30, 1863, Confederate General J. E. B. Stuart's cavalry tangled with Union forces under Generals Kilpatrick and Custer. The battle prevented Stuart from reaching Gettysburg in time to function as "the eyes of Lee's army." Among the products of the town's diversified industry are books, wirecloth, yarns, furniture, industrial machinery, textiles and foods, including the famous pretzel maker, Snyder's of Hanover.

*Information: Hanover Area Chamber of Commerce, 146 Carlisle St., Hanover,*
*717-637-6130; www.hanoverchamber.com*

## WHAT TO SEE AND DO

### CODORUS STATE PARK

*1066 Blooming Grove Road, Hanover*

Approximately 3,300 acres. Swimming pool, fishing in 1,275-acre Lake Marburg, boating (rentals, mooring, launching, marina); hunting, hiking, bridle trails, cross-country skiing, snowmobiling, sledding, ice skating, ice boating, ice fishing, picnicking, mountain biking, snack bar, tent and trailer sites.

PENNSYLVANIA

★
★
★
★
★

### CONEWAGO CHAPEL

*30 Basilica Drive, Hanover, 717-637-2721*

Built in 1741, this is the oldest stone Catholic church in the U.S. Designated Sacred Heart Basilica in 1962. Cemetery dates from 1752. Daily.

### NEAS HOUSE MUSEUM

*113 W. Chestnut St., Hanover, 717-632-3207; www.hanoverareahistoricalsociety.org*

Neas House, restored Georgian mansion, serves as local history museum. May-November, Tuesday-Friday. Special events: spring, summer, late December.

### UTZ QUALITY FOODS, INC

*900 High St., Hanover, 717-637-6644; www.utzsnacks.com*

Producers of potato chips and snack foods. Glass-enclosed tour gallery overlooks production area; push-to-talk audio program and closed-circuit TV monitors. Monday-Saturday 8 a.m.-7 p.m., Sunday 11 a.m.-6 p.m.

## SPECIALTY LODGING

### THE BEECHMONT BED AND BREAKFAST INN

*315 Broadway, Hanover, 717-632-3013, 800-553-7009; www.thebeechmont.com*

Built in 1834, this bed and breakfast is located just 14 miles outside of Gettysburg. It offers four large guest rooms and three suites, each furnished with fine antiques. Breakfast can be enjoyed in the dining room, on the porch or in the rooms. 7 rooms. Children over 12 only. Complimentary full breakfast. Wireless Internet access. Business center. $

# HARRISBURG

This mid-state metropolis holds what many consider the finest capitol building in the nation. Other showplaces include the city's riverside park (known as City Island), Italian Lake, unique museum and beautiful Forum.

Harrisburg's location was viewed in 1615 by Etienne Brul on a trip down the Susquehanna, but more than a century passed before John Harris, the first settler, opened his trading post here. His son established the town in 1785. The cornerstone of the first capitol building was laid in 1819.

*Information: Capital Regional Chamber of Commerce, 3211 N. Front St., Harrisburg, 717-232-4099 or the Harrisburg-Hershey-Carlisle Tourism & Convention Bureau, 25 N. Front St., Harrisburg, 717-231-7788; www.harrisburgregionalchamber.org*

## WHAT TO SEE AND DO

### CAPITOL HILL BUILDINGS

*North Third and Walnut streets, Harrisburg, 717-787-6810; www.harrisburgpa.gov*

Clustered in a 45-acre complex, the major buildings are:

### CAPITOL

*Third and state streets, Harrisburg*

Italian Renaissance building was dedicated in 1906 and covers two acres and has 651 rooms; 26,000-ton, 272-foot dome, imitating that of St. Peter's in Rome, dominates city skyline. Includes murals by Abbey and Okley. Tours. Daily.

## DAUPHIN COUNTY COURTHOUSE

*Front and Market streets, Harrisburg, 717-255-2741; www.dauphincounty.org*

Seven imposing courtrooms; outline map on floor of main foyer pictures borough and township boundaries. Monday-Friday.

## FINANCE BUILDING

*Seventh and North streets*

Ceiling murals by Maragliotti, Eugene Savage; mural in south vestibule illustrates "The Collection of Taxes." Monday-Friday.

## FORUM BUILDING

*Walnut Street at Commonwealth Avenue*

Includes auditorium below constellation-bedecked ceiling; walls review man's progress through time. Lobby boasts a Maragliotti ceiling. General and law libraries.

## NORTH OFFICE BUILDING

*North Street at Commonwealth Avenue*

Map inscribed on lobby floor shows state highways, seals of Pennsylvania cities.

## SOUTH OFFICE BUILDING

*Commonwealth Avenue*

Colorful murals by Edward Trumbull depict "Penn's Treaty with the Indians" and "The Industries of Pittsburgh."

## THE STATE MUSEUM OF PENNSYLVANIA

*300 N. St., Harrisburg, 717-787-4980; www.statemuseumpa.org*

A six-story circular building housing four stories of galleries, authentic early country store, Native American life exhibit, technological and industrial exhibits, collection of antique autos and period carriages; planetarium; natural history and geology exhibits and one of the world's largest framed paintings, Rothermel's "The Battle of Gettysburg." Planetarium has public shows on Saturday and Sunday. Tuesday-Sunday.

## FORT HUNTER PARK

*5300 N. Front St., Harrisburg, 717-599-5751; www.forthunter.org*

Historic 37-acre property; site of British-built fort erected in 1754 to combat mounting threats prior to the French and Indian War. In 1787, the land was purchased and became a farm that eventually grew into a self-sufficient village. The Pennsylvania Canal runs through the park; on the grounds are historic buttonwood trees dating from William Penn's time, a 19th-century boxwood garden and picnic area.

## FORT HUNTER MANSION

*5300 N. Front St., Harrisburg, 717-599-5751; www.forthunter.org*

Federal-style stone mansion, built in three sections. Front stone portions were built in 1786 and 1814; rear wooden portion built in 1870. Spacious mansion displays period furnishings, clothing, toys and other artifacts. Guided tours. May-December, Tuesday-Saturday 10:30 a.m.-4:30 p.m., Sunday 12-4:40 p.m. Closed Mondays and holidays.

## ITALIAN LAKE

**PENNSYLVANIA**

★
★
★
★
★

*North Third and Division streets, Harrisburg*
Bordered with flowers, shrubs and shade trees in summer.

### JOHN HARRIS MANSION

*219 S. Front St., Harrisburg, 717-233-3462; www.dauphincountyhistory.org*
Home of city's founder, now Historical Society of Dauphin County headquarters.
Stone house has 19th-century furnishings, library (Monday-Thursday; fee), collection
of county artifacts. Tours April-December, Monday-Thursday.

### RESERVOIR PARK

*Walnut and N. 19th streets, Harrisburg*
View of east end of city, five nearby counties.

### RIVERFRONT PARK

Four miles along Susquehanna River, with park promenade flanking Front Street.

### ROCKVILLE BRIDGE

A 3,810-foot stone-arch bridge built in 1902; 48 spans carry four tracks of Penn
Central Railroad main line.

## SPECIAL EVENTS

### EASTERN SPORTS & OUTDOOR SHOW

*State Farm Show Complex, 2301 N. Cameron, Harrisburg, 717-787-5373;*
*www.agriculture.state.pa.us*
Early-mid-February.

### KIPONA

*www.harrisburgevents.com*
Boating and water-related activites. Labor Day weekend.

### PENNSYLVANIA NATIONAL HORSE SHOW

*1509 Cedar Cliff Drive, Harrisburg, 717-975-3677; www.panational.org*
Ten days in mid-October.

### PENNSYLVANIA STATE FARM SHOW

*State Farm Show Complex, 2300 N. Cameron St., Harrisburg, 717-787-5373*
State fair. Early-mid-January.

★
★
★
★
★

## HOTELS

### ★★BEST WESTERN HARRISBURG/HERSHEY HOTEL & SUITES

*300 N. Mountain Road, Harrisburg, 717-652-7180; www.bestwestern.com*
101 rooms. Pets accepted. Complimentary breakfast. High-speed Internet access.
Pool. Spa. Fitness center. Business center. $

### ★★★CROWNE PLAZA

*23 S. Second St., Harrisburg, 717-234-5021, 800-496-7621; www.crowneplaza.com*

A smart choice for families and budget travelers, this full-service hotel is near all the attractions of Harrisburg but does not leave the wallet empty. Hershey Park is minutes away, as are Chocolate World, the Carlisle Fairgrounds, the National Civil War Museum and the Capitol Complex. Restaurant Row (a collection of more than 30 restaurants, clubs, pubs and shops) is literally outside the front door and should not be missed. After a busy day, a nap in one of the contemporary guest rooms is the answer. 261 rooms. Pets accepted. Wireless Internet acccess. Pool. Fitness center. Business center. Airport transportation available. $

### ★DAYS INN

*3919 N. Front St., Harrisburg, 717-233-3100, 800-329-7466; www.daysinn.com*
116 rooms. Pets accepted. Complimentary continental breakfast. Wireless Internet access. Restaurant. Pool. Fitness center. Business center. Children's activity center. $

### ★★FOUR POINTS BY SHERATON

*800 E. Park Drive, Harrisburg, 717-561-2800, 800-325-3535; www.starwoodhotels.com*
174 rooms. High-speed Internet access. Pool. Fitness center. Business center. $

### ★HAMPTON INN

*4230 Union Deposit Road, Harrisburg, 717-545-9595, 800-426-7866;*
*www.hamptoninn.com*
145 rooms. Complimentary continental breakfast. High-speed Internet access. Pool. Fitness center. Business center. Airport transportation available. $

### ★★★HILTON HARRISBURG AND TOWERS

*1 N. Second St., Harrisburg, 717-233-6000, 800-445-8667; www.harrisburg.hilton.com*
This elegant, family-friendly hotel is located in the heart of historic Harrisburg and is connected to the Whitaker Center by an enclosed walkway. Although the standard guest rooms are well-appointed, guests who choose to upgrade to Tower Level rooms will enjoy upgraded amenities including access to a private lounge that serves complimentary continental breakfast and evening hors d'oeuvres. The hotel also offers three restaurants, as well as a seasonal (summer) restaurant. 341 rooms. High-speed Internet access. Pool. Fitness center. Business center. Airport transportation available. Pets accepted. $$

### ★★RADISSON PENN HARRIS HOTEL & CONVENTION CENTER

*1150 Camp Hill Bypass, Camp Hill, 717-763-7117, 800-333-3333; www.radisson.com*
250 rooms. Pets accepted. Wireless Internet access. Pool. Fitness center. Airport transportation available. $

### ★★★SHERATON HARRISBURG HERSHEY HOTEL

*4650 Lindle Road, Harrisburg, 717-564-5511, 800-325-3535; www.sheraton.com*
Minutes from downtown Harrisburg and the airport, this full-service hotel is also near many attractions such as Hershey Park, Hershey Chocolate World, historic Gettysburg, the Pennsylvania Dutch Country and the State Museum of Pennsylvania. The traditional-style guest rooms are spacious and include large work desks. The Dog and Pony Restaurant serves breakfast, lunch and dinner in a casually elegant setting, and the Dog and Pony Pub is a nice place for a nightcap. 348 rooms. Pets accepted. Wireless Internet access. Pool. Business center. Airport transportation available. $

PENNSYLVANIA

# HAWLEY

A major attraction in this Pocono resort area is man-made Lake Wallenpaupack, offering summer recreation and winter recreation nearby.

*Information: Pocono Mountains Vacation Bureau, 1004 Main St., Stroudsburg, 570-424-6050, 800-762-6667; www.poconos.org*

## WHAT TO SEE AND DO

### GRAVITY COACH

Car used on Pennsylvania Gravity Railroad.

### LAKE WALLENPAUPACK

*Highway 6, Hawley, 570-226-2141*

One of the largest man-made lakes in the state (5,600 acres), formed by the damming of Wallenpaupack Creek. Swimming beach (Memorial Day-Labor Day), fishing, boating, water sports; ice fishing, camping. The information center is ½ mile NW on Highway 6 at Highway 507. Daily.

## HOTELS

### ★GRESHAM'S LAKE VIEW MOTEL

*Highway 6, Hawley, 570-226-4621; www.greshems.net*

21 rooms. Complimentary breakfast. Restaurant. Pool. Fitness center. Business center. $

### ★★★SETTLERS INN AT BINGHAM PARK

*4 Main Ave., Hawley, 570-226-2993, 800-833-8527; www.thesettlersinn.com*

The Settlers Inn, a Craftsmen mountain lodge, was built in 1927. Guests can request in-room massages, or champagne and flowers to greet them upon their arrival. 21 rooms. Complimentary full breakfast. Wireless Internet access. Restaurant. Pool. Fitness room. Business center. Airport transportation available. $

## RESTAURANT

### ★★THE SETTLERS INN

*4 Main Ave., Hawley, 570-226-2993; www.thesettlersinn.com*

Seafood menu. Lunch, dinner, Sunday brunch. Bar. Children's menu. Reservations recommended. $$

# HAZLETON

On top of Spring Mountain, Hazleton calls itself the highest city in Pennsylvania. Rich agricultural land surrounds it, and its early and rapid economic growth was spurred by the rich anthracite coal reserves found in the area. Although coal dominated the town's economy during the 19th century, today there are many diversified industries located here.

*Information: Greater Hazleton Chamber of Commerce, 1 S. Church St., Hazleton, 570-455-1509; www.hazletonchamber.org*

## HOTELS

### ★BEST WESTERN GENETTI LODGE

*1341 N. Church St., Hazleton, 570-454-2494, 800-780-7234; www.bestwestern.com*

PENNSYLVANIA

★
★
★
★

85 rooms. Pets accepted. Complimentary continental breakfast. Outdoor pool. **$**

### ★★RAMADA INN
*Route 309 N., Hazleton, 570-455-2061, 800-272-6232; www.ramada.com*
106 rooms. Pets accepted. High-speed Internet access. Restaurant. Pool. Fitness center. **$**

# HERSHEY
One of America's most fascinating success stories, this planned community takes its name from founder M. S. Hershey, who established his world-famous chocolate factory here in 1903, then built a town around it. The streets have names like Chocolate and Cocoa and streetlights are shaped like chocolate kisses. But there's more than chocolate here. Today, Hershey is known as one of the most diverse entertainment and resort areas in the eastern United States. Hershey is also known as the "golf capital of Pennsylvania" and has a number of well-known golf courses.
*Information: Hersheypark, 100 W. Hersheypark Drive, Hershey, 800-HERSHEY (information) or 800-533-3131 (reservations); www.800hershey.com*

## WHAT TO SEE AND DO
### FOUNDERS HALL
*801 Spartan Lane, Hershey, 717-520-2000; www.mhs-pa.org*
Campus center of Milton Hershey School, noted for its striking rotunda. Daily.

### HERSHEY GARDENS
*170 Hotel Road, Hershey, 717-534-3492; www.hersheygardens.org*
From mid-June to first frost, 8,000 rose plants bloom on 23 acres. Tulip garden (mid-April-mid-May); chrysanthemums and annuals; butterfly house featuring 400-500 butterflies; six theme gardens. Daily.

### HERSHEY MUSEUM
*111 W. Chocolate Ave., Hershey, 717-534-3439; www.hersheymuseum.org*
Pennsylvania German, Native American, Eskimo collections; displays of Stiegel glass; "Apostolic Clock" depicting life of Christ; Milton Hershey history. Daily.

### HERSHEY PARK
*100 W. Hershey Park Drive, Hershey, 800-437-7439; www.800hershey.com*
This 110-acre theme park includes Rhine Land, Tudor Square, Dutch crafts barn; more than 60 rides include six roller coasters; live family shows. Mid-May-Labor Day, daily; May and September, selected weekends.

### HERSHEYPARK STADIUM/STAR PAVILION
*100 W. Hershey Park Drive, Hershey, 717-534-3911, 800-437-7439; www.hersheypark.com*
Sports and entertainment events.

### HERSHEYPARK ARENA
*100 Hershey Park Drive, Hershey, 717-534-3911; www.hersheypark.com*
Capacity 10,000; professional hockey, basketball, ice skating, variety shows, concerts.

★
★
★
★
☆

### HERSHEY'S CHOCOLATE WORLD

*251 Park Blvd., Hershey, 717-534-4900; www.hersheys.com/chocolateworld*

Tour via automated conveyance; simulates steps of chocolate production from cacao bean plantations through chocolate-making in Hershey. Also tropical gardens, shopping village. Daily.

### SELTZER'S LEBANON BOLOGNA COMPANY

*230 N. College St., 717-838-6336; www.seltzerslebanonbologna.com*

Outdoor wooden smokehouses since 1902. Monday-Saturday.

### ZOO AMERICA

*100 W. Hershey Park Drive, Hershey, 717-534-3900; www.zooamerica.com*

An 11-acre environmental zoo featuring five climatic regions of North America; home to more than 200 animals. Daily. Combination admission with Hersheypark available.

## SPECIAL EVENTS

### ANTIQUE AUTOMOBILE CLUB

National fall rally. Second weekend in October.

### CHOCOLATE-COVERED FEBRUARY IN HERSHEY

*Various locations; www.hersheypa.com*

February.

### CHRISTMAS CANDYLANE

*Hersheypark, 100 W. Hershey Park Drive, Hershey; www.hersheypa.com*

Hersheypark is transformed into "Christmas Candylane" to mark the beginning of the Christmas season. Mid-November-December.

### HERSHEYPARK BALLOONFEST

*Hersheypark, 100 W. Hershey Park Drive, Hershey, 717-534-3900; www.hersheypark.com*

October.

## HOTELS

### ★DAYS INN

*350 W. Chocolate Ave., Hershey, 717-534-2162, 800-329-7466; www.daysinn.com/hershey06452*

100 rooms. Pets accepted. Complimentary continental breakfast. High-speed Internet access. Restaurant. Pool. Business center. Airport transportation available. **$**

### ★★★HERSHEY LODGE AND CONVENTION CENTER

*West Chocolate Avenue and University Drive, Hershey, 717-533-3311, 800-437-7439*

The Hershey Lodge stays true to its name, with chocolate-themed décor in every guest room and special Hersheypark privileges including discounted tickets and early access to certain rides. Kids can even check themselves in at their own check-in desk and greet the friendly Hershey's product characters who might make an appearance in the lobby. 665 rooms. Complimentary breakfast. Wireless Internet access. Restaurant, bar. Children's activity center. Pool. Fitness center. Business center. Airport transportation available. **$$**

### ★★★★THE HOTEL HERSHEY

*100 Hotel Road, Hershey, 717-533-2171, 800-437-7439; www.thehotelhershey.com*

Perched atop a hill overlooking town, the Hotel Hershey sits on 300 acres of formal gardens, fountains and reflecting pools. Instead of mints, you'll find chocolate kisses on your pillow at evening turndown. Recreational opportunities abound, from 72 holes of golf, six miles of nature trails, basketball, volleyball and tennis courts to the pools and fitness center. Rest your sweet tooth with a meal at the Fountain Cafe, or grab snacks and light meals at the coffeehouse or fireside lounge. The Spa at Hotel Hershey is a wonderfully sinful place, with whipped cocoa baths and chocolate fondue wraps. 230 rooms. Complimentary breakfast. High-speed Internet access. Children's activity center. Pool. Fitness center. Airport transportation available. **$$$**

### ★SPINNERS INN

*845 E. Chocolate Ave., Hershey, 717-533-9157, 800-800-5845; www.spinnersinn.com*

52 rooms. Complimentary continental breakfast. Wireless Internet access. Pool. Fitness center. **$**

## SPA
### ★★★THE SPA AT THE HOTEL HERSHEY

*100 W. Hersheypark Drive, Hershey, 717-533-2171, 800-437-7439;*
*www.spaathotelhershey.com*

The Spa at Hotel Hershey doesn't skimp on using its signature luscious ingredient. Chocolate reigns at this spa, from the chocolate bean polish and whipped cocoa bath to the chocolate fondue wrap and the chocolate scrub. The facility includes an inhalation room, a quiet room for meditation, soaking tubs, steam rooms, saunas and signature showers for hydrotherapy treatments. **$$**

## RESTAURANTS
### ★★★CIRCULAR DINING ROOM

*1 Hotel Road, Hershey, 717-534-8800, 800-437-7439; www.hersheypa.com*

This elegant dining destination is tucked away in the Hotel Hershey. Its circular design—the idea of founder Milton S. Hershey—affords all guests, no matter where they are seated, unobstructed views of the exquisite formal gardens and reflecting pools from the room's soaring windows. The contemporary-American menu is as refined as the restaurant's surroundings, and changes seasonally to ensure only the freshest and most flavorful ingredients are used. Past menus have included cocoa-braised beef short ribs, pulled pork shoulder with house-made sauerkraut, and grilled beef filet with truffled dauphinoise potatoes. Decadent desserts feature many choices for chocolate lovers, like warm chocolate soufflé, chocolate and blood orange bombe, and the Chocolate Evolution, a tasting of chocolate. American menu. Breakfast, lunch, dinner. brunch. Children's menu. Jacket required (for dinner, Sunday

**PENNSYLVANIA**

★
★
★
★
★

brunch). Reservations recommended. $$$

### ★★DIMITRI'S
*1311 E. Chocolate Ave., Hershey, 717-533-3403*
Greek. Lunch, dinner. Closed Sunday. Bar. Children's menu. $$$

### ★★UNION CANAL HOUSE
*107 S. Hanover St., Hershey, 717-566-0054, 888-566-5867;*
*www.unioncanalhouse.com*
American menu. Dinner. Closed Sunday. Bar. Children's menu. Business casual attire.
Reservations recommended. $$$

# HONESDALE

Named in honor of Philip Hone, a mayor of New York City and first president of
the Delaware & Hudson Canal Company, Honesdale was for many years the world's
largest coal storage center, shipping millions of tons of anthracite. A gravity railroad
brought coal here in winter; in spring it was reshipped by canal boats to tidewater.
The Stourbridge Lion, first steam locomotive to operate in the United States, was
used by the Delaware & Hudson Canal Company, but when the rail bed proved too
weak, mule power replaced the steam engine. Today, Honesdale manufactures textile
products, business forms and furniture, and is surrounded by dairy farms in the beau-
tiful rolling countryside.

*Information: Wayne County Chamber of Commerce, 32 Commercial St., Honesdale,*
*570-253-1960, 800-433-9008; www.waynecountycc.com*

★
★
★
★
☆

## WHAT TO SEE AND DO
### REPLICA OF THE STOURBRIDGE LION
*Main Street, Honesdale*
The original is in Smithsonian Institution, which was the first steam locomotive to
operate in the U.S.

### STOURBRIDGE RAIL EXCURSIONS
*www.waynecountycc.com*
Scenic rail excursions from Honesdale to Lackawaxen, centering on the change of
seasons, with entertainment and activities.

### TRIPLE W RIDING STABLE
*Honesdale, 570-226-2620, 800-540-2620; www.triplewstable.com*
A 181-acre horse ranch in the Northeast range of the Pocono Mountains. Variety of
trail rides for beginners or advanced riders; half- and full-day trips; overnight camp-
ing trips. Hay and sleigh rides (seasonal; by appointment). Daily.

### WAYNE COUNTY HISTORICAL SOCIETY MUSEUM
*810 Main St., Honesdale, 570-253-3240; www.waynehistorypa.org*
Delaware and Hudson-Canal exhibit, Native American exhibit. April-December,
Wednesday-Saturday.

# HOPEWELL FURNACE NATIONAL HISTORIC SITE

Hopewell, an early industrial community, was built around a charcoal-burning cold-blast furnace, which made pig iron and many other iron products from 1771-1883. Nearby mines and forests supplied ore and charcoal for the furnace. The National Park Service has restored the buildings, and interpretive programs emphasize the community's role in the history of American industry. Hopewell is surrounded by French Creek State Park.

The Visitor Center has a museum and audiovisual program on iron-making and community life. A self-guided tour includes charcoal house, blacksmith shop, office store and more. Stove molding and casting demonstrations (late June-Labor Day). Captioned slide program for the hearing impaired; Braille map and large-print pamphlets for the visually impaired; wheelchair access. Daily. Closed winter holidays.
*2 Mark Bird Lane, Elverson, 610-582-8773; www.berksweb.com*

# HOPWOOD

## RESTAURANTS

### ★★★CHEZ GERARD AUTHENTIC FRENCH RESTAURANT
*1187 National Pike, Highway 40 E., Hopwood, 724-437-9001; www.chezgerard.net*
Chez Gerard is located in the historic Hopwood House, which dates to 1790. The all-French staff prides itself on providing the most authentic French experience, serving entrees such as magret de canard aux deux facons (grilled and smoked duck breasts with a plum and ginger reduction, grilled marinated zucchini and potato au gratin). French menu. Lunch, dinner, Sunday brunch. Closed Tuesday. Bar. Children's menu. Outdoor seating. Reservations recommended. $$$

### ★★SUNDAY PORCH
*Highway 40 E., Hopwood, 724-439-5734*
Lunch, dinner. Closed Monday. Children's menu. $$

# HUNTINGDON

Founded on the site of an Oneida village in the Juniata Valley, Huntingdon was first called Standing Stone for a 14-foot-etched stone pillar venerated by Native Americans.
*Information: Huntingdon County Visitors Bureau, Seven Points Road, Hesston, 814-658-0060, 800-729-7869; www.raystown.org*

## WHAT TO SEE AND DO

### GREENWOOD FURNACE STATE PARK
*15795 Greenwood Road, Huntingdon, 814-667-1800; www.dcnr.state.pa.us*
Remains of Greenwood Works, last iron furnace to operate in area (circa 1833-1904); restored stack. Approximately 400 acres. Swimming beach, fishing; hiking, snowmobiling, ice skating, ice fishing, picnicking, playground, snack bar, store, tent and trailer sites. Visitor center, interpretive program.

### LINCOLN CAVERNS
*7703 William Penn Highway, U.S. Route 22, Huntingdon, 814-643-0268;*

★
★
★
★
☆

The one-hour tour of two caves includes Frozen Niagara, Diamond Cascade; visitor center and gift shop. April-November, daily; March and December, weekends only.

# INDIANA

Named after the area's Native American population, this borough was established on 250 acres donated for a county seat by George Clymer of Philadelphia, a signer of the Declaration of Independence. Indiana University of Pennsylvania is located here. This is also the birthplace of actor Jimmy Stewart.

*Information: Indiana County Tourist Bureau, 2334 Oakland Ave., Indiana,*
*724-463-7505; www.visitindianacountypa.org*

## WHAT TO SEE AND DO
### COUNTY PARKS

*1128 Blue Spruce Road, Indiana, 724-463-8636; www.indianacountyparks.org*

Blue Spruce park covers 420 acres. Fishing for bass, perch, catfish and crappie; boating (rowboat, canoe rentals); winter sports area, picnicking, grills, playground. Daily. Pine Ridge covers 630 acres. Trout fishing; hiking, picnicking. Nature study. Daily. Hemlock Lake park covers 200 acres. Fishing; small game hunting, hiking, ice skating. Nature study, photography. Daily.

### JIMMY STEWART MUSEUM

*Indiana Public Library Building, 835 Philadelphia St., Indiana, 724-349-6112,*
*800-835-4669; www.jimmy.org*

Highlights the namesake's accomplishments on film, radio and TV. His roles as a military hero, civic leader, family man and world citizen are woven into displays, film presentations and gallery talks. Fifty-seat vintage theater. Monday-Saturday 10 a.m.-5 p.m., Sunday noon-5 p.m.

## HOTELS
### ★★BEST WESTERN UNIVERSITY INN

*1545 Wayne Ave., Indiana, 724-349-9620, 888-299-9620; www.bestwestern.com*

100 rooms. Complimentary breakfast. Restaurant. Pool. Business center. $

### ★★HOLIDAY INN

*1395 Wayne Ave., Indiana, 724-463-3561, 800-315-2621; www.holidayinn.com*

159 rooms. Complimentary breakfast. High-speed Internet access. Indoor pool. Business center. $

# JIM THORPE

The twin towns, Mauch Chunk (Bear Mountain) and East Mauch Chunk, built on the sides of a narrow gorge of the Lehigh River, merged in 1954 and adopted the name of Jim Thorpe, the great Native American athlete. This, together with a "nickel-a-week" plan whereby each man, woman and child paid five cents to promote the community and attract industry, gave the area (formerly dependent on coal mining) a new lease on economic life. Little has changed in appearance after more than a century; a walking tour will reveal 19th-century architecture.

*Information: Carbon County Tourist Promotion Agency Information Center,*

## WHAT TO SEE AND DO

### ASA PACKER MANSION MUSEUM

*Packer Hill, Jim Thorpe, 570-325-3673; www.asapackermansionmuseum.homestead.com*

Former showplace home of founder of Lehigh Valley Railroad and Lehigh University, one of state's wealthiest men. Packer's house, treasures and money were left to the borough. June-November, daily; April-May, weekends; closed first two weeks in December.

### BLUE MOUNTAIN SPORTS

*34 Susquehanna St., Jim Thorpe, 570-325-4421, 800-599-4421;*
*www.bikejimthorpe.com*

Blue Mountain Sports offers whitewater rafting, kayaking and mountain biking.

### JIM THORPE MEMORIAL

A 20-ton granite mausoleum built in memory of the 1912 Olympic champion.

### JIM THORPE RIVER ADVENTURES, INC

*One Adventure Lane, Jim Thorpe, 570-325-2570; www.jtraft.com*

National Geographic Adventure. March-November, daily.

### OLD JAIL MUSEUM

*128 W. Broadway, Jim Thorpe, 570-325-5259; www.theoldjailmuseum.com*

Built in 1871, the Old Jail, which was an active prison until January 1995, contains 28 original cells, warden's living quarters and 16 dungeon cells. Famous for hangings of the Molly Maguires, a group of rebel union organizers. Late May-early November.

### POCONO WHITEWATER ADVENTURES

*1519 State Route 903, Jim Thorpe, 570-325-3655; www.poconowhitewater.com*

Also bike tours. March-November, daily.

### STONE ROW

*Race Street, Jim Thorpe*

Sixteen town houses built by Asa Packer for the engineers on his railroad; reminiscent of Philadelphia's Elfreth's Alley. Some are stores open to the public.

### ST. MARK'S CHURCH

*21 Race St., Jim Thorpe, 570-325-2241; www.stmarkandjohn.org*

Has Tiffany windows and copy of reredos from Windsor Castle. June-October, Wednesday-Saturday afternoons.

### WHITEWATER RAFTING

On upper and lower gorges of Lehigh River.

## SPECIAL EVENTS

### FALL FOLIAGE FESTIVAL

Arts and crafts, food, entertainment. Scenic three-hour train rides. Second weekend

**281**

**PENNSYLVANIA**

★
★
★
★
★

in October.

## LAUREL BLOSSOM FESTIVAL
Arts and crafts, entertainment, food, steam train rides. Second weekend in June.

## SPECIALTY LODGING
### HARRY PACKER MANSION
*One Packer Hill Road, Jim Thorpe, 570-325-8566; www.murdermansion.com*
This mansion's ornate, brick facade served as a model for the haunted mansion at Disney World, but its regal, lived in quality is elegant and inviting. The interior features 15-foot ceilings, marble fireplaces and gilded mirrors. The mansion hosts special events and murder mystery weekends. 13 rooms. Children over 12 years only. Complimentary full breakfast. Internet access. Pool. Business center. **$**

# JOHNSTOWN
On May 31, 1889, a break in the South Fork Dam that impounded an old reservoir 10 miles to the east poured a wall of water onto the city, causing the disastrous "Johnstown Flood." The death toll rose to 2,209 and property damage totaled $17 million. The city has been flooded 22 times since 1850, most recently in 1977.

Founded by a Swiss Mennonite, Joseph Johns, the city is now the center of Cambria County's iron and steel industry, producing iron and steel bars, railroad cars, parts and railroad supplies.

*Information: Greater Johnstown/Cambria County Convention & Visitors Bureau,*
*416 Main St., Johnstown, 814-536-7993, 800-237-8590; www.visitjohnstownpa.com*

## WHAT TO SEE AND DO
### CONEMAUGH GAP
Located at the West end of the city. Gorge, seven miles long and 1,700 feet deep, cuts between Laurel Hill Ridge and Chestnut Ridge.

### INCLINED PLANE RAILWAY
*711 Edgehill Drive, Johnstown, 814-536-1816; www.inclinedplane.com*
Joins Johnstown and Westmont. Ride is on steep (72 percent grade) passenger incline with 500-foot ascent. Counterbalanced cable cars take 50 passengers and two automobiles each. Daily.

### JOHNSTOWN FLOOD MUSEUM
*304 Washington St., Johnstown, 814-539-1889; www.jaha.org*
Museum depicts history of Johnstown, with permanent exhibits on 1889 Johnstown Flood; Academy Award-winning film, photographs, artifacts, memorabilia. Daily.

### JOHNSTOWN FLOOD NATIONAL MEMORIAL
*733 Lake Road, Johnstown, 814-495-4643; www.nps.gov/jofl*
Commemorates 1889 Johnstown Flood; preserved remnants of the South Fork Dam. Visitor center with exhibits, 30-minute movie. Daily.

## HOTELS

### ★COMFORT INN

*455 Theatre Drive, Johnstown, 814-266-3678; www.choicehotels.com*

115 rooms. Pets accepted. Complimentary continental breakfast. High-speed Internet access. Restaurant. Pool. Airport transportation available. **$**

### ★★HOLIDAY INN

*250 Market St., Johnstown, 814-535-7777, 800-443-5663; www.holidayinn.com*

159 rooms. High-speed Internet access. Pool. Business center. Airport transportation available. **$**

### ★SLEEP INN

*453 Theatre Drive, Johnstown, 814-262-9292, 877-424-6423; www.sleepinn.com*

62 rooms. Pets accepted. Complimentary continental breakfast. High-speed Internet access. Pool. Business center. Airport transportation available. **$**

## RESTAURANT

### ★★SURF N' TURF

*100 Valley Pike, Johnstown, 814-536-9250*

Seafood, steak menu. Dinner. Bar. Children's menu. **$$**

# KANE

Situated on a lofty plateau, Kane offers hunting, fishing and abundant winter sports. Summers are cool and winters are bracing. Allegheny National Forest is to the north, west and south; there are scenic drives through 4,000 acres of virgin timber. General Thomas L. Kane of "Mormon War" fame settled here and laid out the community, which prospered as a lumber and railroad town. General Ulysses Grant was once arrested here for fishing without a license.

*Information: Seneca Highlands Tourist Association, junction Highways 770 West and 219, Custer City, 814-368-9370; www.visitanf.com*

## WHAT TO SEE AND DO

### THOMAS L. KANE MEMORIAL CHAPEL

*30 Chestnut St., Kane, 814-837-9729*

Built as a chapel for the new town under the direction of General Kane, a Civil War hero and humanitarian who championed the persecuted Mormons. Visitor center includes film of General Kane's life; small museum. Tuesday-Saturday.

### TWIN LAKES

*Route 321, Kane, 814-723-5150*

Swimming, fishing, hiking, picnicking, camping.

# KEMPTON

## WHAT TO SEE AND DO

### HAWK MOUNTAIN SANCTUARY

**PENNSYLVANIA**

★
★
★
★
★

*1700 Hawk Mountain Road, Kempton, 610-756-6961; www.hawkmountain.org*
Hawk and eagle flights visible with binoculars from lookouts mid-August-mid-December; museum, bookstore.

### WANAMAKER, KEMPTON & SOUTHERN, INC
*42 Community Center Drive, Kempton, 610-756-6469; www.kemptontrain.com*
A six-mile, 40-minute round trip on steam or diesel train along the Ontelaunee Creek at the foot of Hawk Mountain. Model railroad, antique shop. Snack bar, picnic area. Steam train (July-August and October, Saturday and Sunday afternoons; May and June, Sunday afternoons). Diesel train (June and September, first and third Saturday afternoons only). Also special events throughout the year.

# KENNETT SQUARE
*Information: Chester County Conference and Visitors Bureau,*
*400 Exton Square Parkway, Exton, 610-280-6145, 800-228-9933 or*
*the Southeastern Chester County Chamber of Commerce, 206 E. State St.,*
*Kennett Square, 610-444-0774; www.scccc.com*

## WHAT TO SEE AND DO
### LONGWOOD GARDENS
*Route 1, Kennett Square, 610-388-1000; www.longwoodgardens.org*
Longwood Gardens is a stately horticultural display garden created by Pierre S. du Pont, offering more than 1,000 acres of indoor and outdoor gardens, woodlands and meadows. Lovers of living things are treated to greenhouses heated year-round, more than 10,000 different types of plants, spectacular fountains, flower shows and gardening demonstrations. Children's programs are available as well. The Orangery and Exhibition Hall are centerpieces, with a sunken marble floor flooded with reflective water. Daily.

## SPECIALTY LODGING
### KENNETT HOUSE BED AND BREAKFAST
*503 W. State St., Kennett Square, 610-444-9592, 800-820-9592;*
*www.kennetthouse.com*
4 rooms. Complimentary full breakfast. Wireless Internet access. Pool. Business center. $

## RESTAURANTS
### ★★KENNETT SQUARE INN
*201 E. State St., Kennett Square, 610-444-5687; www.kennettinn.com*
American menu. Lunch, dinner. Bar. Reservations recommended. $$$

### ★★TERRACE
*Longwood Gardens, Kennett Square, 610-388-6771; www.longwoodgardens.org*
Lunch, dinner. Closed January-March. Bar. Children's menu. Outdoor seating. Admis-

★
★
★
★
★

sion to Longwood Gardens required. **$$**

# KING OF PRUSSIA

Originally named Reeseville for the Welsh family that owned the land, the town renamed itself after the local inn, which is still standing.

*Information: Valley Forge Convention & Visitors Bureau, 600 W. Germantown Pike, Plymouth Meeting, 610-834-1550; www.valleyforge.org*

## WHAT TO SEE AND DO

### KING OF PRUSSIA MALL

*160 N. Gulph Road, King of Prussia, 610-265-5727; www.kingofprussiamall.com*

The king of malls on the eastern seaboard is located just 18 miles west of central Philadelphia. Bloomingdales, Neiman Marcus, Nordstrom, Macy's, Lord & Taylor, JCPenney, Sears and Strawbridge's anchor this mall, and its 365 specialty shops and 40 restaurants will keep you from staying in one place too long.

## HOTELS

### ★BEST WESTERN THE INN AT KING OF PRUSSIA

*127 S. Gulph Road, King of Prussia, 610-265-4500, 800-780-7234; www.bestwestern.com*

166 rooms. Complimentary continental breakfast. High-speed Internet access. Pool. Fitness center. Airport transportation available. **$**

### ★★CROWNE PLAZA

*260 Mall Blvd., King of Prussia, 610-265-7500, 800-496-7621; www.crowneplaza.com*

225 rooms. High-speed Internet access. Pool. Fitness center. Business center. **$**

### ★★DOUBLETREE HOTEL

*640 W. Germantown Pike, Plymouth Meeting, 610-834-8300, 800-222-8733; www.doubletree.com*

253 rooms, all suites. Wirless Internet access. Pool. Business center. Airport transportation available. **$**

### ★HOLIDAY INN EXPRESS HOTEL & SUITES KING OF PRUSSIA

*260 N. Gulph Road, King of Prussia, 610-768-9500, 800-315-2621*

205 rooms. Complimentary continental breakfast. High-speed Internet access. Fitness center. Business center. **$**

### ★★★THE RADNOR HOTEL

*591 E. Lancaster Ave., Saint Davids, 610-688-5800, 800-537-3000; www.radnorhotel.com*

This beautiful hotel has formal gardens often used for weddings, and charming accomodations fit for any traveler. Take a dip in the expansive outdoor swimming pool in the summer. 171 rooms. Complimentary breakfast. High-speed Internet access. Business center. Airport transportation available. **$$**

### ★SPRINGHILL SUITES

*430 Plymouth Road, Plymouth Meeting, 610-940-0400; www.marriott.com*

199 rooms. Complimentary continental breakfast. High-speed Internet access. Pool.

★
★
★
★
★

Business center. $

## RESTAURANTS
### ★★CREED'S
*499 N. Gulph Road, King of Prussia, 610-265-2550; www.creedskop.com*
Seafood, steak menu. Lunch, dinner. Closed Sunday; also first week in July. Bar. $$

### ★★LOTUS INN
*402 W. Swedesford Road, Berwyn, 610-725-8888*
Chinese, Japanese menu. Lunch, dinner. Closed Sunday (except Mother's Day) Bar. Children's menu. Reservations recommended. $$

# KULPSVILLE
*Information: Valley Forge Country Convention & Visitors Bureau,*
*600 W. Germantown Pike, Plymouth Meeting, 610-834-1550; www.valleyforge.org*

## WHAT TO SEE AND DO
### MORGAN LOG HOUSE
*850 Weikel Road, Kulpsville, 215-368-2480; www.morganloghouse.org*
Built by the grandfather of General Daniel Morgan and Daniel Boone, this is the oldest and finest surviving medieval-style log house in the country. Partially restored; authentic early 18th-century furnishings. It exhibits fine, early antiques, including 18th-century Pennsylvania furniture. Guided tours. April-December, weekends; other times by appointment.

## RESTAURANT
### ★★MAINLAND INN
*17 Main St., Kulpsville, 215-256-8500; www.themainlandinn.com*
Seafood menu. Lunch, dinner, Sunday brunch. Bar. Reservations recommended. $$$

# KUTZTOWN
Home of a popular folk festival, Kutztown is named for its founder, George Kutz. The town's population includes many descendants of the Pennsylvania Germans.

## WHAT TO SEE AND DO
### CRYSTAL CAVE PARK
*963 Crystal Cave Road, Kutztown, 610-683-6765; www.crystalcavepa.com*
Discovered in 1871; crystal formations, stalactites, stalagmites, natural bridges all enhanced by indirect lighting. Also museum (July-September); nature trail; miniature golf (July-September); theater. Cafe, rock shop, gift shop. Tours. March-November, Daily.

## SPECIAL EVENT
### FOLK FESTIVAL
*Festival Grounds, Kutztown, 215-679-9610; www.kutztownfestival.com*

PENNSYLVANIA

★
★
★
★
★

Celebration of Pennsylvania Dutch folk culture; quilts, music, dancing and food of Plain and Fancy Dutch. Craftspeople make baskets, brooms, rugs, toleware and other handcrafts. Late June-early July.

## RESTAURANT
### ★★NEW SMITHVILLE COUNTRY INN
*10425 Old Route 22, Kutztown, 610-285-2987*
Breakfast, lunch, dinner. Closed Memorial Day, Labor Day. Bar. Children's menu. **$$**

# LAHASKA

## WHAT TO SEE AND DO
### PEDDLER'S VILLAGE
*Highways 202 and 263, Lahaska, 215-794-4000; www.peddlersvillage.com*
This 18th-century-style country village with 42 acres of landscaped gardens and winding brick paths makes a great day trip from Philadelphia. Browse through a selection of more than 70 specialty shops for handicrafts, toys, accessories, leather goods, collectibles and gourmet foods. Take the kids for a ride on an antique carousel, or take advantage of the many free family events and seasonal festivals. Daily.

## SPECIAL EVENTS
### SCARECROW FESTIVAL
*Peddler's Village, between Highways 202 and 263, Lahaska, 215-794-4000; www.peddlersvillage.com*
Scarecrow making, pumpkin painting. Jack-o-lantern and gourd art contest. Square dancing, entertainment. September.

### TEDDY BEAR'S PICNIC
*Peddler's Village, between Highways 202 and 263, Lahaska, 215-794-4000; www.peddlersvillage.com*
Teddy bear vendors, parades, competitions. "Bear clinic" for "hurt" bears. Appraisals. Music. July.

## HOTEL
### ★★★GOLDEN PLOUGH INN
*41 Peddlersvillage, Lahaska, 215-794-4004; www.peddlersvillage.com*
Scattered throughout Peddler's Village on 42 acres, this inn is charming no matter the season. Many of the beautifully appointed rooms have gas-lit fireplaces and whirlpools. In case you're hungry, guests are greeted with a snack basket upon arrival. 71 rooms. Complimentary continental breakfast. High-speed Internet access. Pool. Business center. **$**

## RESTAURANT
### ★★COCK N' BULL
*Highways 202 and 263, Lahaska, 215-794-4000; www.peddlersvillage.com*
Steak menu. Lunch, dinner, Sunday brunch. Bar. Reservations recommended. **$$**

# LAKE HARMONY

PENNSYLVANIA

★
★
★
★
★

## WHAT TO SEE AND DO
### BIG BOULDER
*Highway 940 and Moseywood Road, Lake Harmony, 570-722-0100; www.jfbb.com*
Five double, two triple chairlifts; patrol, school, rentals, snowmaking; cafeteria, bar, nursery, lodge. Night skiing. Longest run approximately ¾ mile; vertical drop 475 feet. December-March, daily.

## HOTEL
### ★★RAMADA
*1-476 Exit 95 & I-80 Exit 277, Lake Harmony, 570-443-8471, 800-251-2610; www.ramada.com*
138 rooms. Pets accepted. High-speed Internet access. Pool. Business center. Airport transportation available. $

# LAKEVILLE

## WHAT TO SEE AND DO
### CLAWS 'N PAWS WILD ANIMAL PARK
*1475 Ledgedale Road, Lakeville, 570-698-6154; www.clawsnpaws.com*
A zoo in the woods with more than 100 species of exotic animals. Petting zoo with tame deer, lambs and goats. Farmyard area. Parrot, reptile shows; zookeeper talks (schedule varies). Picnicking, snack bar. May-October, daily.

## HOTEL

### ★★CAESARS COVE HAVEN
*Highway 590, Lakeville, 570-226-2101; www.caesarspoconoresorts.com*
276 rooms. Complimentary continental breakfast. Airport transportation available. $$

# LANCASTER
Lancaster blends the industrial modern, the colonial past and the Pennsylvania Dutch present. It is in the heart of the Pennsylvania Dutch Area, one of the East's most colorful tourist attractions. To fully appreciate the area, visitors should leave the main highways and travel on country roads, which Amish buggies share with automobiles. Lancaster was an important provisioning area for the armies of the French and Indian and Revolutionary wars. Its crafters turned out fine guns, which brought the city fame as the "arsenal of the Colonies." When Congress, fleeing Philadelphia, paused here on September 27, 1777, the city was the national capital for one day. It was the state capital from 1799 to 1812.
*Information: Pennsylvania Dutch Convention & Visitors Bureau, 501 Greenfield Road, Lancaster, 717-299-0470, 800-723-8824; www.padutchcountry.com*

## WHAT TO SEE AND DO
### AMISH FARM AND HOUSE
*2395 Lincoln Highway, East Lancaster, 717-394-6185; www.amishfarmandhouse.com*
Typical Amish farm in operation. Lecture on the Amish and tour through early 19th-century stone buildings furnished and decorated as old-order Amish household; waterwheels, windmill, hand-dug well, carriages, spring wagon, sleighs. Daily.

### BRUNSWICK TOURS
*2102 Lincoln Highway, East Lancaster, 717-397-7541; www.brunswicktours.com*

## PENNSYLVANIA DUTCH AREA

In the 18th century, great waves of immigrants from Germany's Rhineland and Palatinate settled in Pennsylvania, first near Philadelphia and then farther west. Because they retained their customs and speech, and developed bountiful farms, the Pennsylvania Dutch (corruption of the German "Deutsch") and their communities are one of the state's greatest tourist attractions.

Descendants of Pennsylvania's original German immigrants all share tremendous vigor, family devotion, love of the Bible and belief in thrift and hard work. Many of the plain people—Amish, Old Order Mennonites and Bretren (Dunkards)—still live much as they did a century ago. Married men wear beards, black coats and low-crowned hats. Women wear bonnets and long, simple dresses. They drive horses and buggies rather than cars, work long hours in the field and shun the use of modern farm machinery, and turn to the Bible for guidance. Despite their dated methods, they are master farmers, among the first to rotate crops and practice modern fertilization methods. Their harvests are among the best in the country.

Many Amish regard photographs as "graven images." Visitors should not take pictures of individuals without their permission.
*Information: www.padutch.com*

Private guide and auto tape tours. America Music Theater. Daily.

★
★
★
★
☆

### DUTCH WONDERLAND
*2249 Lincoln Highway, East Lancaster, 866-386-2839; www.dutchwonderland.com*
Family fun park with rides, botanical gardens, diving shows, shops. Monorail. Memorial Day-Labor Day, daily; Mid-May-Memorial Day and after Labor Day-October, Saturday and Sunday.

### FRANKLIN AND MARSHALL COLLEGE
*Race and College avenues, Lancaster, 717-291-3981; www.fandm.edu*
A liberal arts college with 1,810 students. Rothman Gallery showcases Pennsylvania-German artifacts: quilts, Fraktur and stoneware. More than 200 varieties of trees, plants and shrubs on grounds. Tours of campus, daily.

### FULTON OPERA HOUSE
*12 N. Prince St., Lancaster, 717-394-7133; www.thefulton.org*
First opened in 1852, this is one of the oldest American theaters and many legendary people have performed here. It is believed that more than one ghost haunts the theater's Victorian interior. Professional regional theater; home of community theater, opera and symphony organizations.

### HANS HERR HOUSE
*1849 Hans Herr Drive, Lancaster, 717-464-4438; www.hansherr.org*

Built in 1719, this is a fine example of medieval Germanic architecture. The house served as an early Mennonite meetinghouse and colonial residence of the Herr family. Mennonite rural life exhibit; blacksmith shop. House tours. April-November, Monday-Saturday; rest of year by appointment.

### HEBREW TABERNACLE REPRODUCTION

*2209 Millstream Road, Lancaster, 717-299-0954; www.mennoniteinfoctr.com*
Tours Monday-Saturday.

### HERITAGE CENTER MUSEUM OF LANCASTER COUNTY

*13 W. King St., Lancaster, 717-299-6440; www.lancasterheritage.com*
Houses examples of early Lancaster County arts and crafts. Furniture, tall clocks, quilts, needlework, silver, pewter, rifles. Mid-April-early January, Tuesday-Saturday.

### HISTORIC LANCASTER WALKING TOUR

*100 S. Queen St., Lancaster, 717-392-1776; www.padutchcountry.com*
A 90-minute tour of historic downtown area. Costumed guide narrates 50 points of architectural or historic interest covering six square blocks. April-October: two tours daily Friday-Saturday, one tour daily, Monday-Thursday and Sunday; rest of year, by appointment.

### HISTORIC ROCK FORD

*881 Rockford Road, Lancaster, 717-392-7223; www.rockfordplantation.org*
The preserved 1794 home of General Edward Hand, Revolutionary War commander, member of Continental Congress. April-October, Monday-Saturday.

★
★
★
★
★

### JAMES BUCHANAN'S WHEATLAND

*1120 Marietta Ave., Lancaster, 717-392-8721; www.wheatland.org*
Built in 1828, this building served as residence of President James Buchanan from 1848 to 1868; restored Federal mansion with period rooms containing American Empire and Victorian furniture and decorative arts. Guided tours. April-October, daily; November, Friday-Monday. Christmas candlelight tours early December.

### JOSEPH R. GRUNDY OBSERVATORY

*Lancaster, 717-291-4136*
Holds 11-inch refractor and 16-inch-reflecting telescope demonstrations.

### LANDIS VALLEY MUSEUM

*2451 Kissel Hill Road, Lancaster, 717-569-0401; www.landisvalleymuseum.org*
Interprets Pennsylvania German rural life. Largest collection of Pennsylvania-German objects in U.S.; craft and living history demonstrations (May-October); farmsteads, tavern, country store among other exhibit buildings. March-December, Monday-Saturday. Closed New Year's Day.

### MENNONITE INFORMATION CENTER

*2209 Millstream Road, Lancaster, 717-299-0954; www.mennoniteinfoctr.com*

Tourist information; interpretation of Mennonite and Amish origins beliefs. Free video. Monday-Saturday.

## MUDDY RUN LLC

*Lancaster, 717-284-4325*

Covers 700 acres with 100-acre lake for boating (rentals; no power boats), fishing; picnicking, playgrounds, snack bar, concession, camping, Park. April-early November.

## NATIONAL WAX MUSEUM OF LANCASTER COUNTY

*2251 Lincoln Highway, East Lancaster, 717-393-3679*

Figures re-create Lancaster County's history from the 1700s to present. Daily.

## NORTH MUSEUM OF NATURAL HISTORY AND SCIENCE

*400 College Ave., Lancaster, 717-291-3941; www.northmuseum.org*

General science and natural history; planetarium shows (Saturday and Sunday); Children's Discovery Room; film series; monthly art exhibits. Tuesday-Sunday.

## ROBERT FULTON BIRTHPLACE

*1932 Fulton Highway, Lancaster, 717-548-2679; www.lyhr.org*

Robert Fulton, a great inventor and accomplished artist, is best known for having built the steamboat Clermont, which in 1807 successfully made a trip up the Hudson River against winds and strong current. This little stone house, where Fulton was born, was nearly destroyed by fire about 1822; now refurbished. Memorial Day-Labor Day, Saturday-Sunday.

## THE WATCH AND CLOCK MUSEUM

*514 Poplar St., Lancaster, 717-684-8261; www.nawcc.org/museum/museum.htm*

National Association of Watch and Clock Collectors living museum of timepieces and related tools and memorabilia. More than 8,000 items representing the 1600s to the present. Extensive research library. Special exhibitions. April-November, Tuesday-Sunday; December-March, Tuesday-Saturday.

## SPECIAL EVENTS

### HARVEST DAYS

*Landis Valley Museum, 2451 Kissel Hill Road, Lancaster, 717-569-0401*

Demonstrations of more than 80 traditional craft and harvest-time activities. Columbus Day weekend.

### OLD-FASHIONED SUNDAY

*1120 Marietta Ave., Lancaster, 717-392-8721; www.wheatland.org*

On grounds of Wheatland. Festivities include entertainment, magic show and 19th-century activities. Mid-May.

### SHEEP SHEARING

*Animal Farm and House, 2395 Lincoln Highway, East Lancaster, 717-394-6185; www.amishfarmandhouse.com*

Last Thursday and Friday in April, first Friday in October.

### VICTORIAN CHRISTMAS WEEK

★
★
★
★
★

*Wheatland, 1120 Marietta Ave., Lancaster, 717-392-8721; www.wheatland.org*
Early December.

## HOTELS

### ★★BEST WESTERN EDEN RESORT INN & SUITES

*222 Eden Road, Lancaster, 717-569-6444; www.bestwestern.com*
276 rooms. Pets accepted. Complimentary breakfast. High-speed Internet access. Restaurant. Pool. Fitness center. Airport transportation available. $

### ★★DAYS INN

*30 Keller Ave., Lancaster, 717-299-5700, 800-329-7466; www.daysinn.com*
193 rooms. Complimentary breakfast. High-speed Internet access. Restaurant. Pool. Fitness center. $$

### ★GARDEN SPOT MOTEL

*2291 Lincoln Highway, East Lancaster, 717-394-4736; www.gardenspotmotel.com*
19 rooms. Closed December-March. Complimentary breakfast. High-speed Internet access. Pool. $

### ★HERSHEY FARM MOTOR INN

*240 Hartman Bridge Road, Ronks, 717-687-8635, 800-827-8635;*
*www.hersheyfarm.com*
59 rooms. Complimentary full breakfast. High-speed Internet access. Pool. Business center. $

### ★★HILTON GARDEN INN LANCASTER

*101 Granite Run Drive, Lancaster, 717-560-0880, 877-782-9444*
156 rooms. High-speed Internet access. Pool. Fitness center. Business center. $

### ★★HOLIDAY INN

*24 S. Willowdale Drive, Lancaster, 717-293-9500, 800-524-3817; www.holidayinn.com*
112 rooms. Complimentary breakfast. High-speed Internet access. Outdoor pool. Business center. $

### ★★HOLIDAY INN

*521 Greenfield Road, Lancaster, 717-299-2551; www.holidayinn.com*
189 rooms. Complimentary breakfast. High-speed Internet access. Pool. Business center. $

### ★★HOTEL BRUNSWICK

*151 Queen St., Lancaster, 717-397-4800, 800-821-9258; www.hotelbrunswick.com*
221 rooms. Complimentary breakfast. High-speed Internet acces. Pool. Fitness center. Business center. $

### ★★WILLOW VALLEY RESORT

*2416 Willow St., Pike, Lancaster, 717-464-2711, 800-444-1714; www.willowvalley.com*
342 rooms. High-speed Internet access. Restaurant. Indoor/outdoor pool. Fitness center. Business center. Airport transportation available. $

## SPECIALTY LODGINGS

### AUSTRALIAN WALKABOUT INN BED AND BREAKFAST

*837 Village Road, Lancaster, 717-464-0707; www.walkaboutinn.com*

8 rooms. Children over 10 years only. Complimentary full breakfast. High-speed Internet access. Pool. Fitness center. **$$**

### COUNTRY LIVING INN

*2406 Old Philadelphia Pike, Lancaster, 717-295-7295; www.countrylivinginn.com*

34 rooms. Complimentary breakfast. High-speed Internet access. Pool. Business center. **$**

### KING'S COTTAGE

*1049 E. King St., Lancaster, 717-397-1017, 800-747-8717; www.kingscottagebb.com*

This bed and breakfast is nestled in the center of scenic Lancaster County. It provides a perfect location for travelers looking to explore Pennsylvania Dutch Country. The inn is a Spanish-style mansion providing a comfortable stay for travelers. 8 rooms. Children over 12 years only. Complimentary full breakfast. Wireless Internet access. Business center. **$$**

### O'FLAHERTY'S DINGELDEIN HOUSE

*1105 E. King St., Lancaster, 717-293-1723, 800-779-7765; www.dingeldeinhouse.com*

7 rooms. Complimentary full breakfast. High-speed Internet access. Pool. Business center. Airport transportation available. **$**

## RESTAURANTS

### ★★D & S BRASSERIE

*1679 Lincoln Highway East, Lancaster, 717-299-1694; www.dandsbrasserie.com*

American menu. Lunch, dinner. Bar. House built in 1925; original woodwork, fireplaces. Outdoor seating. Reservations recommended. **$$$**

### ★★★HAYDN ZUG'S

*1987 State St., East Petersburg, 717-569-5746; www.haydnzugs.com*

Owner and Chef Terry Lee hails from Petersburg. With its award-winning wine list and exceptional cuisine, Lee's restaurant makes a day journey worthwhile. Winner of the Wine Spectator Award of Excellence. American menu. Lunch, dinner. Closed Sunday-Monday. Bar. Casual attire. Reservations recommended. **$$**

### ★★OLDE GREENFIELD INN

*595 Greenfield Road, Lancaster, 717-393-0668; www.theoldegreenfieldinn.com*

American menu. Lunch, dinner. Bar. Children's menu. Casual attire. Outdoor seating. Reservations recommended. **$$$**

# LEBANON

This industrial city, steeped in German traditions, is the marketplace for colorful Lebanon County. Many Hessians were confined here after the Battle of Trenton. Today, Lebanon bologna factories and food processing are important to the city's economy.

*Information: Pennsylvania Rainbow Region Vacation Bureau, 625 Quentin Road, Lebanon, 717-272-8555; www.visitlebanoncounty.com*

★
★
★
★
★

## WHAT TO SEE AND DO
### COLEMAN MEMORIAL PARK

*1408 W. Maple St., Lebanon, 717-272-7271; www.colemanmemorialpark.org*

This 100-acre former estate has a swimming pool (Memorial Day-Labor Day, daily; fee); tennis courts, athletic fields, picnic facilities. Fee for some activities. Park. Daily.

### DANIEL WEAVER COMPANY

*15th Avenue and 1415 Weavertown Road, Lebanon, 717-274-6100, 800-932-8377; www.godshall.com*

A manufacturer, since 1885, of Weaver's Famous Lebanon Bologna and other wood-smoked gourmet meats; smoked in 100-year-old outdoor smokehouses. Samples. Tours. Monday-Saturday.

### STOEVERS DAM RECREATIONAL AREA

*943 Miller St., Lebanon, 717-228-4470; www.lebanonpa.org*

A 153-acre park with a 52-acre lake for fishing, boating (electric motors only), canoeing; 1½-mile trail for jogging, hiking and bicycling; primitive camping (permit only; fee). Nature trails; nature barn (April-October, Tuesday-Sunday; winter, by appointment). Community park. Daily.

### STOY MUSEUM OF THE LEBANON COUNTY HISTORICAL SOCIETY

*924 Cumberland St., Lebanon, 717-272-1473; www.lebanonhistory.org*

Local historical museum containing 30 permanent room and shop displays on three floors of house built in 1773 and used as first county courthouse; research library. Tours. Monday-Friday, Sunday; closed Monday and Sunday of holiday weekends.

## HOTEL
### ★★QUALITY INN

*625 Quentin Road, Lebanon, 717-273-6771, 800-626-8242; www.choicehotels.com*

130 rooms. Pets accepted. Wireless Internet access. Restaurant. Outdoor pool. Business center. $

# LEWISBERRY

## WHAT TO SEE AND DO
### GIFFORD PINCHOT STATE PARK

*2200 Rosstown Road, Lewisberry, 717-432-5011; www.dcnr.state.pa.us*

Approximately 2,300 acres; 340-acre lake. Fishing, boating (rentals, mooring, launching). Hunting; hiking cross-country skiing, ice skating, ice fishing, ice boating. Picnicking, store. Tent and trailer sites, cabins. Nature center, interpretive center. Monday-Saturday.

### SKI ROUNDTOP

*925 Roundtop Road, Lewisberry, 717-432-9631, 800-767-4766; www.skiroundtop.com*

Two quad, triple, two double chairlifts; two J-bars, one magic carpet, two tubing lifts; patrol, school, rentals, snowmaking; cafeteria, nursery. Longest run 4,100 feet; vertical drop 600 feet. Mid-November-mid-March, daily.

# LEWISBURG

Home of Bucknell University, this college community also has light industry. The Native American village of Old Muncy Town was located nearby before the region was opened by Ludwig (Lewis) Doerr.

*Information: Susquehanna Valley Visitors Bureau, Rural Route 3, 81 Hafer Road, Lewisburg, 570-524-7234, 800-525-7320; www.svvb.com*

## WHAT TO SEE AND DO

### PACKWOOD HOUSE MUSEUM

*15 N. Water St., Lewisburg, 570-524-0323; www.packwoodhousemuseum.com*

A three-story, 27-room log-and-frame building begun in the late 18th century. Former hostelry houses a wide ranging collection of Americana, period furnishings, textiles and decorative arts. Changing exhibits; museum shop. Tours. Tuesday-Saturday 10 a.m.-5 p.m.

### SLIFER HOUSE MUSEUM

*80 Magnolia Drive, Lewisburg, 570-524-2245; www.albrightcare.org*

Elaborate three-story, 20 room Victorian mansion. First and second floors have been restored, complete with Victorian parlor, dining room, library and five bedrooms. April-late-December, Tuesday-Sunday; rest of year, Tuesday-Friday afternoons, also by appointment.

## HOTEL

### ★BEST WESTERN COUNTRY CUPBOARD INN

*Route 15 North, Lewisburg, 570-524-5500, 800-780-7234; www.bestwestern.com*

141 rooms. Complimentary continental breakfast. High-speed Internet access. Restaurant. Pool. Fitness center. $

## RESTAURANT

### ★COUNTRY CUPBOARD

*101 Hafer Road, Lewisburg, 570-523-3211*

American menu. Breakfast, lunch, dinner. Children's menu. $$

**PENNSYLVANIA**

★
★
★
★

# LEWISTOWN

Surrounded by rich farmland and beautiful forested mountain ranges, Lewistown lies in the scenic Juniata River Valley in the heart of central Pennsylvania. Lewistown retains the charm of its rustic surroundings, which yearly attract thousands of sportsmen and outdoor enthusiasts to the area's fine hunting, fishing and camping facilities. A large Amish population that thrives on the farmland of the Kishacoquillas Valley has contributed greatly to the area's culture and heritage.

*Information: Juniata Valley Area Chamber of Commerce, 1 W. Market St., Lewistown, 717-248-6713, 877-568-9739; www.juniatarivervalley.org*

## WHAT TO SEE AND DO

### REEDS GAP STATE PARK

*1405 New Lancaster Valley Road, Lewistown, 717-667-3622; www.dcnr.state.pa.us*

Approximately 200 acres. Swimming pool, fishing; hiking, picnicking, snack bar. Tent sites only.

## HOTEL

### ★★CLARION HOTEL

*13015 Furguson Valley Road, Burnham, 717-248-4961, 877-424-6423;*
*www.choicehotels.com*

111 rooms. Pets accepted. Complimentary continental breakfast. High-speed Internet access. Restaurant. Business center. **$**

# LIGONIER

Fort Ligonier, built in 1758 by the British, was the scene of one of the key battles of the French and Indian War. It also served as a supply base during Pontiac's War in 1763.

*Information: Ligonier Valley Chamber of Commerce, Town Hall, 120 E. Main St.,*
*Ligonier, 724-238-4200; www.ligonier.com*

## WHAT TO SEE AND DO

### FORT LIGONIER

*200 S. Market St., Ligonier, 724-238-9701; www.fortligonier.org*

Reconstructed 18th-century British fort; includes buildings with period furnishings. Museum houses outstanding French and Indian War collection, 18th-century artifacts; introductory film. May-October, daily.

### IDLEWILD PARK

*Highway 30 E., Ligonier, 724-238-3666; www.idlewild.com*

Amusement rides, entertainment, picnicking, children's play area, water park. Memorial Day-late August, Daily.

### STORY BOOK FOREST

*US 30 E., Ligonier, 724-238-3666; www.idlewild.com*

Admission included with Idlewild Park. Children's park with animals, people and buildings portraying nursery rhymes. Memorial Day-late August, Tuesday-Sunday.

## SPECIAL EVENTS

### FORT LIGONIER DAYS

*120 E. Main St., Ligonier, 724-238-4200; www.ligonier.com*

Living history program of the French and Indian War. Parade, 150 juried crafters, food and special events. Usually second weekend in October.

### LIGONIER HIGHLAND GAMES AND GATHERING OF THE CLANS
### OF SCOTLAND

*Route 30 East, Ligonier, 724-238-3666; www.idlewild.com*

Sports, massed pipe bands, Highland dancing competitions, Scottish fiddling; sheep dog, wool spinning and weaving demonstrations; genealogy booth. Scottish fair. First Saturday after Labor Day.

### LIGONIER ICE FEST

*Ligonier, 724-238-4200; www.ligonier250.com*

Professional ice sculptures on the Diamond and in front of businesses; collegiate ice-carving competition. Super Bowl weekend.

## HOTEL

### ★★RAMADA

*216 W. Loyalhanna St., Ligonier, 724-238-9545, 800-272-6232; www.ramada.com*
66 rooms. High-speed Internet access. Restaurant. Pool. Fitness center. **$**

# LIMERICK

*Information: Valley Forge Convention & Visitors Bureau, 600 W. Germantown Pike,*
*Plymouth Meeting, 610-834-1550; www.valleyforge.org*

## WHAT TO SEE AND DO

### SPRING MOUNTAIN SKI AREA

*757 Spring Mount Road, Spring Mount Limerick, 610-287-7900;*
*www.springmountain-fun.com*
One triple, three double chairlifts; two rope tows; patrol, school, rentals, snowmaking; cafeteria, lodge. Longest run ½ mile; vertical drop 420 feet. Also camping available, (fee; hookups). Mid-December-mid-March, daily.

# LOCK HAVEN

Founded on the site of pre-Revolutionary Fort Reed, the community takes its name from two sources. The lock of the Pennsylvania Canal once crossed the West Branch of the Susquehanna River here and the town was once a "haven" for the rafts and lumberjacks of nearby logging camps. Near the geographic center of the state, the town today is a center of commerce and small industry.

*Information: Clinton County Tourist Promotion Agency, Court House Annex,*
*151 Susquehanna Ave., Lock Haven, 570-893-4037; www.clintoncountyinfo.com*

## WHAT TO SEE AND DO

### BUCKTAIL NATURAL AREA

Scenic area extends from mountain rim to mountain rim for 75 miles from Lock Haven north to Renovo and west to Emporium. Connecting the three towns and weaving through the park is Highway 120, an outstanding drive through mountain scenery. Historic site west of Renovo commemorates Bucktail Trail, which served pioneers and Civil War volunteers. Fishing.

### HEISEY MUSEUM

*362 E. Water St., Lock Haven, 570-748-7254; www.clintoncountyhistory.com*
Victorian house museum; early 1800s kitchen; ice house containing logging, farming and canal artifacts. Monday-Friday; also by appointment.

### HYNER VIEW

At 2,000 feet, "Laurel Drive to the top of the world" provides panoramic view of valley, river, highway and forest. Site of state and national hang gliding competitions.

## SPECIALTY LODGING

### VICTORIAN INN BED AND BREAKFAST

*402 E. Water St., Lock Haven, 570-748-8688, 888-653-8688; www.victorianinnbnb.com*
12 rooms. No children allowed. Complimentary full breakfast. High-speed Internet access. Built in 1859; garden atrium. **$**

**PENNSYLVANIA**

★
★
★
★
☆

# LUMBERVILLE

## SPECIALTY LODGING
### 1740 HOUSE
*1740 River Road, Route 32, Lumberville, 215-297-5661; www.1740house.com*

23 rooms. Complimentary full breakfast. High-speed Internet access. Bar. Pool. Business center. $$

## RESTAURANT
### ★★CUTTALOSSA INN
*3478 River Road, Route 32, Lumberville, 215-297-5082; www.cuttalossainn.com*

American menu. Lunch, dinner. Closed Sunday; three weeks in January. Bar. Outdoor seating. $$$

# MANHEIM

Baron Henry William Stiegel founded Manheim and started manufacturing the flint glassware that bore his name. In 1770 he owned the town; by 1774 he was in debtor's prison, the victim of his own generosity and his poor choice of business associates. After his imprisonment, he made a meager living teaching here.

*Information: Manheim Area Chamber of Commerce, 13 E. High St., Manheim, 717-665-6330; www.manheimchamber.com*

## WHAT TO SEE AND DO
### MOUNT HOPE ESTATE & WINERY
*2775 Lebanon Road, Manheim, 717-665-7021; www.parenfaire.com*

This restored sandstone mansion was originally built in the Federal style, then increased its size to 32 rooms with an extension built in 1895, which changed the house's style to Victorian. Turrets, winding walnut staircase, hand-painted 18-foot ceilings, Egyptian marble fireplaces, grand ballroom, crystal chandeliers; greenhouse, solarium, gardens. Wine tasting in billiards room. Daily.

### ZION LUTHERAN CHURCH
*2 S. Hazel St., Manheim, 717-665-5880; www.zionmanheim.com*

Victorian-Gothic structure built on site of original church; Stiegel donated the ground in exchange for one red rose from the congregation every year. Monday-Friday. Sunday church school.

## SPECIAL EVENTS
### PENNSYLVANIA RENAISSANCE FAIRE
*83 Mansion House Road, Manheim*

Mt. Hope Estate and Winery. A 16th-century village is created in the acres of gardens surrounding the mansion. Eleven stages include a jousting arena with capacity of 6,000. Highlights includes a medieval jousting tournament, trial and dunking, human chess match, knighthood ceremonies. August-mid-October, weekends.

### ROSE FESTIVAL
Celebration during which a Stiegel descendant accepts annual rent of one red rose for church grounds. Second Sunday in June.

# MEADVILLE

David Mead—Revolutionary War ensign, tavern-keeper and major general in the War of 1812—and his brothers established Mead's Settlement in 1788. Colonel Lewis Walker started the manufacture of "hookless slide fasteners" here; since 1923 these fasteners (now known as zippers) have been the leading local industry. The city is also a major producer of yarn and thread, and is home to many tool-and-die manufacturers.

*Information: Crawford County Convention & Visitors Bureau,*
*16709 Conneaut Lake Road, Meadville, 814-333-1258, 800-332-2338;*
*www.visitcrawford.org*

## WHAT TO SEE AND DO
### ALLEGHENY COLLEGE
*520 N. Main St., Meadville, 814-332-3100; www.allegheny.edu*
This college of 1,850 students was established in 1815 and features Bentley Hall, which is a fine example of Federalist architecture. Also on campus are Bowman, Penelec and Megahan Art Galleries. Library has colonial, Ida Tarbell and Lincoln collections. Tours of campus.

### BALDWIN-REYNOLDS HOUSE MUSEUM
*411 Chestnut St., Meadville, 814-333-9882; www.baldwinreynolds.org*
Restored mansion of Henry Baldwin, congressman and U.S. Supreme Court justice. First and second floors refurbished in period; basement exhibits 19th-century kitchen and Land Office. Also on grounds is 1890 doctor's office. Elaborate landscaping on three-acre grounds feature pond and icehouse. Tours. Late May-Labor Day, Wednesday-Sunday.

### COLONEL CRAWFORD PARK
*Woodcock Creek Lake, Meadville, 814-724-6879; www.visitcrawford.org/index.html*
Within park is Woodcock Creek Lake. Swimming (fee), fishing, boating; hunting, nature trail, picnicking, camping (fee). Park. Memorial Day-Labor Day, daily.

## SPECIAL EVENT
### CRAWFORD COUNTY FAIR
*Dickson Road, Meadville, 814-337-2154*
Third week in August.

## HOTEL
### ★DAYS INN
*18360 Conneaut Lake Road, Meadville, 814-337-4264, 800-329-7466;*
*www.daysinn.com*
163 rooms. Pets accepted. High-speed Internet access. Restaurant. Pool. Fitness center. **$**

★
★
★
★
★

# MEDIA

*Information: Delaware County Convention & Visitors Bureau, 200 E. State St., Media, 610-565-3679, 800-343-3983; www.brandywinecvb.org*

## WHAT TO SEE AND DO
### RIDLEY CREEK STATE PARK
*1023 Sycamore Mills Road, Media, 610-892-3900; www.dcnr.state.pa.us*
Approximately 2,600 acres of woodlands and meadows. Fishing, hiking, bicycling, sledding, picnicking, playground.

### COLONIAL PENNSYLVANIA PLANTATION
*Media, 610-566-1725; www.colonialplantation.org*
A 200-year-old farm is a living history museum that re-creates the life of a typical farm family of the late 1700s. Period tools and methods are used to perform seasonal and daily chores. Tours. Tuesday-Friday, by appointment. Visitors may participate in some activities. Mid-April-November, Saturday and Sunday.

### TYLER ARBORETUM
*515 Painter Road, Media, 610-566-9134; www.tylerarboretum.org*
Approximately 650 acres of ornamental and native plants. Outdoor "living museum" with a 20-mile system of trails; special fragrant garden and bird garden; notable trees planted in the 1800s; bookstore. Guided walks and educational programs each week.

## RESTAURANT
### ★★D'IGNAZIO'S TOWNE HOUSE
*117 Veterans Square, Media, 610-566-6141; www.townehouse.com*
Italian, seafood menu. Lunch, dinner. Bar. Children's menu. Singing maitre'd. Reservation recommended. **$$**

# MENDENHALL

## HOTEL
### ★★MENDENHALL HOTEL
*323 Kennett Pike, Mendenhall, 610-388-2100; www.mendenhallinn.com*
70 rooms. Complimentary continental breakfast. High-speed Internet access. Pool. Fitness room. Business center. Airport transportation available. **$**

## SPECIALTY LODGING
### FAIRVILLE INN
*506 Kennett Pike, Mendenhall, 610-388-5900, 877-285-7772; www.fairvilleinn.com*
15 rooms. No children allowed. Complimentary continental breakfast. High-speed Internet access. Pool. Fitness center. Built in 1826; antiques, period décor. View of surrounding countryside. **$$**

## RESTAURANT
### ★★MENDENHALL INN
*Highway 52, Mendenhall, 610-388-1184; www.mendenhallinn.com*
American, French menu. Dinner, Sunday brunch. Bar. Children's menu. Business casual attire. Reservations recommended. Valet parking. **$$$**

# MERCER

*Information: Mercer Area Chamber of Commerce, 143 N. Diamond St., Mercer, 724-662-4185; www.mercerareachamber.com*

## WHAT TO SEE AND DO
### MAGOFFIN HOUSE MUSEUM

*119 S. Pitt St., Mercer, 724-662-3490; www.mchspa.org*

The museum, which was built in 1821, houses collection of Native-American artifacts, pioneer tools, furniture, children's toys, clothing and military items. Some original furnishings, memorabilia. Special collection of artifacts from John Goodsell's trip to the North Pole with Peary in 1908-1909, as well as early maps, historic records. Restored print shop. Tuesday-Saturday.

## SPECIAL EVENT
### WAYNE COUNTY FAIR

*545 W. Butler St., Mercer*

Exhibits, livestock, horse racing. First full week in August.

## HOTEL
### ★★HOWARD JOHNSON

*835 Perry Highway, Mercer, 724-748-3030, 800-542-7674; www.hojo.com*

102 rooms. Amish craft shop in lobby. $

# MERCERSBURG

## HOTEL
### ★★★MERCERSBURG INN

*405 S. Main St., Mercersburg, 717-328-5231; www.mercersburginn.com*

Located between the civil war battlefield and other historic sites, the Mercersburg Inn is a 15-room turn-of-the-century Georgian mansion. Golf courses, tennis facilities, skiing, fly fishing, mountain biking and hiking trails are all located within a short distance. 15 rooms. Complimentary full breakfast. $

## RESTAURANT
### ★★★MERCERSBURG INN

*405 S. Main St., Mercersburg, 717-328-5231; www.mercersburginn.com*

Built in 1909, this Georgian-style mansion resides in a charming, 230-year-old village. With both a prix fixe and an à la carte menu, the inn's restaurant serves entrées such as sautéed skate a la meuniere with capers, preserved lemon and caramelized onion risotto or rosemary lemon Cornish hen with roasted fingerling potatoes. French menu. Dinner. Closed Monday-Wednesday. Bar. Reservations recommended. $$$

# MIDDLETOWN

## RESTAURANT
### ★★★ALFRED'S VICTORIAN RESTAURANT

*38 N. Union St., Middletown, 717-944-5373; www.alfredsvictorian.com*

Housed in a picturesque, 1888-Victorian brownstone, this 30-year-old restaurant offers five intimate dining rooms, each with authentically restored design elements

**PENNSYLVANIA**

★
★
★
★
★

and period décor. The menu shows a Northern Italian influence and offers 30 different entrées, including lobster tail and filet mignon. American, Italian menu. Lunch, dinner. Closed Monday; also early January. Bar. Reservations recommended. Outdoor seating. $$$

# MILFORD

The borough of Milford was settled by Thomas Quick, a Hollander. Noted forester and conservationist Governor Gifford Pinchot lived here. His house, Grey Towers, is near the town.

*Information: Pocono Mountains Vacation Bureau, 1004 Main St., Stroudsburg, 570-424-6050, 800-762-6667; www.poconos.org*

## WHAT TO SEE AND DO
### CANOEING, RAFTING, KAYAKING AND TUBING
*Kittatinny Canoes, Milford, 570-828-2338, 800-356-2852; www.kittatinny.com*
Trips travel down the Delaware River. Camping. Mid-April-October, Daily.

### GREY TOWERS
*151 Grey Tower Drive, Milford, 570-296-6401; www.fs.fed.us/gt*
A 100-acre estate originally built in 1886 as summer house for philanthropist James W. Pinchot; became residence of his son, Gifford Pinchot, "father of American conservation," governor of Pennsylvania and first chief of USDA Forest Service. Now, site of Pinchot Institute for Conservation Studies. Tours. Memorial Day weekend-Labor Day weekend, daily; after Labor Day-Veterans Day, Monday afternoons and Friday-Sunday; rest of year, by appointment. Occasionally closed for conferences.

## HOTELS
### ★★★CLIFF PARK INN
*155 Cliff Park Road, Milford, 570-296-6491, 800-225-6535; www.cliffparkinn.com*
The Cliff Park Inn (originally a farmhouse, built in 1820) is located on 500 acres overlooking the Delaware River. With 14 guest rooms, three restaurants, seven miles of hiking trails, a nine-hole golf course and free wireless Internet access, this inn might encourage you to extend your stay. Nearby activities include cross-country skiing, hiking trails, swimming and more. 14 rooms. Golf. Reservations recommended. $

### ★MYER MOTEL
*600 Routes 6 and 209, Milford, 570-296-7223, 800-764-6937;*
*www.myermotel.com*
20 rooms. Wireless Internet access. $

# MONTGOMERYVILLE

## HOTELS
### ★COMFORT INN
*Route 309, 678 Bethlehem Pike, Montgomeryville, 215-361-3600, 877-424-6423;*
*www.choicehotels.com*
84 rooms. Complimentary continental breakfast. Wireless Internet access. $

## RESTAURANT
### ★★★JOSEPH AMBLER INN

*1005 Horsham Road, Montgomeryville, 215-362-7500; www.josephamblerinn.com*

Complex combinations of local fare and European cuisine make up the innovative menu at this rustic country inn. Executive Chef Meg Votta and her team offer entrées such as grilled day boat scallops with sweet corn, potato, bacon chowder and tarragon butter; and Lancaster County roasted half-chicken with citrus, a rosemary and garlic rub, creamed potatoes and summer beans. Lunch, dinner. Bar. In 1820s-era stone barn. Outdoor seating. $$$

# MOUNT JOY

## WHAT TO SEE AND DO
### BUBE'S BREWERY

*102 N. Market St., Mount Joy, 717-653-2056; www.bubesbrewery.com*

Historic brewery built before the Civil War is the only one in the country that has remained intact since the mid-1800s; it now operates as a restaurant. Guided tours take visitors 43 feet below the street into the brewery's aging vaults and passages, which were built from a cave and later became part of the Underground Railroad. A narrator tells the history of the brewery and explains methods of producing beer in the Victorian-age. Tours. Memorial Day-Labor Day, daily. Restaurant open all year. Free tour included with reservations for Catacombs restaurant.

### DONEGAL MILLS PLANTATION & INN

*Mount Joy, 717-653-2168*

Historic 1736 village and resort. Mansion, bake house, gardens. Restaurant and lodging (year-round). Plantation tours March-December, Saturday and Sunday afternoons.

## RESTAURANTS
### ★★CATACOMBS AT BUBE'S BREWERY

*102 N. Market St., Mount Joy, 717-653-2056; www.bubesbrewery.com*

American menu. Dinner. Bar. Outdoor seating. Guided tours. Reservations recommended. $$$

### ★★GROFF'S FARM RESTAURANT

*650 Pinkerton Road, Mount Joy, 717-653-2048; www.groffsfarmgolfclub.com*

Dinner. Closed weekdays January-mid-February. Children's menu. Reservations recommended. $$

# MOUNT POCONO

One of the many thriving resort communities in the heart of the Pocono Mountains, Mount Pocono offers recreation year-round in nearby parks, lakes and ski areas.

*Information: Pocono Mountains Vacation Bureau, 1004 Main St., Stroudsburg, 570-424-6050, 800-762-6667; www.800poconos.com*

**PENNSYLVANIA**

★
★
★
★
★

## WHAT TO SEE AND DO

### MEMORYTOWN, USA

*Grange Road, Mount Pocono, 570-839-1680*

Old-time village includes hex shop, country store, store with artifacts, ice-cream parlor. Paddle boats, entertainment. Lodging, restaurant and tavern. Summer festivals. Fee for some activities. Daily.

### MOUNT POCONO CAMPGROUND

*30 Edgewood Road, Mount Pocono, 570-839-8950; www.mtpoconocampground.com*

Enjoy 185 seasonal campsites for every need on 42 wooded acres in sunny or shaded locations. RV, trailer and tent sites; full hook-ups (with cable), water and electrical hook-ups, electrical hook-ups, or no hook-ups. Convenience store. Outdoor pool, children's pool. Hiking, playground, volleyball court, picnic areas, game room.

### POCONO KNOB

*Southeast edge of town of Mount Pocono*

Excellent view of surrounding countryside.

### SUMMIT LANES

*Three Park Drive E., Pocono Summit, 570-839-9635; www.summitlanespa.com*

Summit Lanes is a terrific bowling center with 36 new state-of-the-art synthetic lanes and automatic scorers with color monitors. It also has a billiards area, food court, pro shop, lounge and video-game room. Daily. Glow bowling Saturday 9:30 p.m.-2 a.m. Children's playroom.

## HOTELS

### ★★★CAESARS PARADISE STREAM

*Highway 940, Mount Pocono, 570-226-2101, 800-432-9932;*
*www.caesarsparadisestream.com*

For that honeymoon experience the Poconos are so well known for, Caesars is the place to stay. These are all-inclusive resorts, with heart-shaped tubs, round beds and champagne glass-shaped whirlpools that offer a romantic contrast to a day at the races. Big-name entertainers often appear at Caesars. 164 rooms. No children accepted. High-speed Internet access. Restaurant, bar. Tennis. $$$

### ★★★CRESCENT LODGE

*191 Paradise Valley, Mount Pocono, 570-595-7486, 800-392-9400;*
*www.crescentlodge.com*

Nestled in the heart of the Pocono Mountains, the Cresecnt Lodge is elegant and welcoming. Guests enjoy uniquely furnished guest rooms, with some rooms boasting sunken Jacuzzis, private patios and sundecks overlooking the well-maintained grounds. 31 rooms. Complimentary continental breakfast. Pool. Fitness center. $

### ★★★POCONO MANOR INN AND GOLF CLUB

*Highway 314, Pocono Manor, 570-839-7111, 800-233-8150; www.poconomanor.com*

Less than two hours from New York, this "Grand Lady of the Mountains" has been in business since 1902. Its rooms are well appointed and tasteful, in keeping with its spot on the National Register of Historic Places. Golf, horseback riding, swimming and tennis are all available on the 3,100-acre estate, as are fishing, clay shooting and more. 255 rooms. Wireless Internet access. Spa. Children's activity center. $$

### ★★★SKYTOP LODGE
*One Skytop, Mount Pocono, 570-595-7401, 800-345-7759; www.skytop.com*

Skytop Lodge is the ultimate mountain getaway for outdoor enthusiasts, with an 18-hole golf course, seven tennis courts, a clay shooting range, indoor and outdoor pools and fly fishing in the natural streams found throughout the property. This retreat in the heart of the Poconos is easily accessed from New York or Philadelphia. Accommodations are offered within the historic hotel, four-bedroom cottages or the intimate golf-course inn. The continental menu at the Windsor Dining Room (jacket required) draws a crowd, while more-casual dining is available at the Lake View Dining Room and the Tap Room. 185 rooms. Children's activity center. Beach. Spa. $$$$

## RESTAURANT
### ★TOKYO TEAHOUSE
*Highway 940, Pocono Summit, 570-839-8880; www.tokyoteahouse.us*

Japanese menu. Lunch, dinner. Closed Tuesday. Reservations recommended. $$

# NEW CASTLE

At the junction of the Shenango, Mahoning and Beaver rivers, New Castle was long an important Native American trading center. Today, the fireworks and plastics industries have become an integral part of the community.

*Information: Lawrence County Tourist Promotion Agency, Celli Central Station,*
*229 S. Jefferson, New Castle, 724-654-8408, 888-284-7599; www.newcastlepa.org*

## WHAT TO SEE AND DO

### GREER HOUSE
*408 N. Jefferson, New Castle, 724-658-4022; www.lawrencechs.org*

Turn-of-the-century restored mansion houses the Lawrence County Historical Society. Museum has extensive Shenango and Castleton china collections, Sports "Hall of Fame," fireworks room. Archives, workshops and speakers. Tuesday-Saturday; also by appointment.

### HOYT INSTITUTE OF FINE ARTS
*124 E. Leasure Ave., New Castle, 724-652-2882; www.hoytartcenter.org*

Cultural arts center housed in two early 20th-century mansions on four acres of landscaped grounds; permanent art collection, changing exhibits, period rooms, performing arts programs, classes. Tours: Tuesday-Saturday.

### LIVING TREASURES ANIMAL PARK
*Highway 422, New Castle, 724-924-9571; www.ltanimalpark.com*

Visitors can pet and feed over 100 species from around the world. Memorial Day-Labor Day, daily; May, September, October, weekends.

### MCCONNELL'S MILL STATE PARK
*New Castle, 724-368-8091; www.dcnr.state.pa.us*

Approximately 2,500 acres. Century-old mill surrounded by beautiful landscape and scenery. Fishing, hunting, whitewater boating. Hiking. Picnicking. Store. Historical center. Interpretive program.

**PENNSYLVANIA**

★
★
★
★
☆

### SCOTTISH RITE CATHEDRAL
*110 E. Lincoln Ave., New Castle, 724-654-6683; www.cathedralnewcastle.com*
On hillside; six 32-foot columns dominate city's skyline. Large auditorium, ballroom. Local Masonic headquarters. Tours by appointment.

## HOTEL
### ★COMFORT INN
*1740 New Butler Road, New Castle, 724-658-7700, 877-424-6423; www.choicehotels.com*
79 rooms. Pets accepted. Complimentary continental breakfast. Business center. **$**

## RESTAURANT
### ★★THE TAVERN
*108 N. Market St., New Wilmington, 724-946-2020*
Bar menu. Lunch, dinner. Outdoor Dining. **$$**

# NEW HOPE
The river village of New Hope was originally the largest part of a 1,000-acre land grant from William Penn to Thomas Woolrich of Shalford, England. In the 20th century, the area gained fame as the home of artists and literary and theatrical personalities.
*Information: Information Center, One W. Mechanic St., New Hope, 215-862-5030 or Bucks County Conference and Visitors Bureau, 152 Swamp Road, Doylestown, 215-345-4552, 800-836-2825; www.newhopevisitorscenter.org*

## WHAT TO SEE AND DO
### CORYELL'S FERRY
*22 S. Main St., New Hope, 215-862-2050*
Passenger and chartered rides aboard the Major William C. Barnett, a 65-foot Mississippi-style stern-wheel riverboat, on the Delaware River. Memorial Day-Labor Day, daily; call for extended season.

### NEW HOPE & IVYLAND RAILROAD
*32 W. Bridge St., New Hope, 215-862-2332; www.newhoperailroad.com*
A nine-mile, 50-minute narrated train ride through Bucks County. Reading Railroad passenger coaches from the 1920s depart from restored 1890 New Hope Station. Early April-November, daily; December, special Santa Train Friday-Sunday; rest of year, weekends.

### PARRY BARN
*South Main Street, New Hope*
Owned by New Hope Historical Society, this building (1784) operated as commercial art gallery. Opposite the Parry mansion museum.

### PARRY MANSION MUSEUM
*South Main and Ferry streets, New Hope, 215-862-5652; www.newhopehistoricalsociety.org*
Restored stone house built in 1784 by Benjamin Parry, a prosperous merchant and mill owner. Eleven rooms on view, restored and furnished to depict period styles from late 18th to early 20th centuries. May-December, Friday-Sunday; also by appointment.

**PENNSYLVANIA**

★
★
★
★
☆

# BUCKS COUNTY

Over the years, literary references to Bucks County, just north of Philadelphia, have been plentiful—and with good reason. Manhattan literati, including Broadway's Moss Hart and George S. Kaufman, and the acerbic writer Dorothy Parker, have favored this woodland retreat along the Delaware River for decades. Though estate-sized homes are popping up in the privileged realm, the rumpled landscape retains the look of a Currier and Ives print. Stately, old fieldstone houses stand beneath towering trees, and stalks of ripening corn march across the fields. Nearby, the wide and peaceful Delaware flows quietly past.

A one-day, 75-mile loop out of New Hope provides a rewarding glimpse of Bucks County's scenic and cultural appeal. Begin in New Hope. A colonial-era ferry crossing on the main road between Philadelphia and New York, the town is dotted with old stone structures sandwiched between the river and the Delaware Canal. Shops here are worth visiting; several feature exquisite handmade crafts of local and national artisans. Many visitors come simply to stroll along the old streets and enjoy the cafés, pubs and ice cream parlors. You can hike or bicycle on the canal tow path. If you're in town on Saturday or Tuesday morning, drop by Rice's Market on Greenhill Road, a 10-minute drive northwest of New Hope. Set in a 30-acre field, the market is the next best thing to an old-fashioned county fair. More than 200 vendors set up booths selling merchandise such as produce, plants and flowers, crafts, furniture pieces and clothing, often at bargain prices.

To see more of the county, return to New Hope and take River Road (SR 32) north. The road winds alongside the Delaware River for about 25 miles to Kintnersville. Quaint river towns, mostly a cluster of old homes, dot the route. The stretch of road between New Hope and Lumberville passes a river setting that, in the early years of the century, drew a number of landscape artists who formed a colony of Pennsylvania Impressionists in the hamlet of Phillips Mill. You can't miss it; River Road makes a sharp turn here. Today, their work can be seen in a permanent exhibit called Visual Heritage of Bucks County at the James A. Michener Art Museum in Doylestown, ahead on this drive.

In Kintnersville take Route 611, the Lackawanna Trail, south to Doylestown. Visit the Michener Museum, which also features an exhibit detailing the Broadway and Hollywood legends who have lived in the county. Save time for the three castlelike structures that archeologist and historian Henry Chapman Mercer bequeathed his hometown. Turrets, towers and parapets adorn the buildings, all built between 1908 and 1916 in a free-form style of reinforced concrete. The Moravian Pottery and Tile Works, which resembles a Spanish-colonial mission, houses Mercer's innovative tile factory. On the same 70-acre grounds stands Fonthill, Mercer's 44-room mansion, a fairy-tale creation of strange nooks and crannies adorned with decorative titles from his factory and around the world. A mile away, the seven-story Mercer Museum houses an important collection of furnishings, folk art and implements of early America. Conclude this drive by returning to New Hope via Routes 202 and 179. Approximately 75 miles. www.buckscounty.org

PENNSYLVANIA

★
★ ★
★ ★
★ ★
★

## SPECIAL EVENT

### NEW HOPE ARTS AND CRAFTS FESTIVAL

*One W. Mechanic St., New Hope, 215-862-5880; www.newhopevisitorscenter.org*

Contemporary and traditional crafts. Painting, photography, sculpture. October.

## HOTELS

### ★★★HOTEL DU VILLAGE

*2535 N. River Road, New Hope, 215-862-9911; www.hotelduvillage.com*

Simple and intimate, Hotel du Village offers 20 cozy guest rooms, two tennis courts, a pool and a restaurant that specializes in French country cuisine. Situated just north of New Hope, the inn is only a short distance to shops, art galleries and entertainment options. 20 rooms. Complimentary full breakfast. Tennis. Reservations recommended. $

### ★★★THE INN AT BOWMAN'S HILL

*518 Lurgan Road, New Hope, 215-862-8090; www.theinnatbowmanshill.com*

The Inn at Bowman's Hill consists of stone and stucco buildings sitting on five acres of well-manicured grounds. An 80-foot stream runs out front, and the property adjoins the Bowman's Hill Wildflower Preserve. The décor and furnishings are rustic but very upscale, with lots of natural wood. Guest rooms are intimate, with gas fireplaces and large whirlpool tubs. Guests can enjoy a three-course gourmet breakfast in the breakfast room or in their own rooms, and afternoon snacks are offered from 3-7 p.m. 6 rooms. No children accepted. Complimentary full breakfast. Pool. $$$

### ★★★THE MANSION INN

*Nine S. Main St., New Hope, 215-862-1231; www.themansioninn.com*

This grand 1865 Baroque Victorian mansion is located along a tranquil canal in the center of downtown New Hope, within walking distance to numerous shops and restaurants, as well as the Michener Art Museum. The stately building welcomes guests with its garden, gazebo, refreshing outdoor pool and beautifully decorated Empire/French Victorian rooms. 7 rooms. Children over 14 years only. Complimentary full breakfast. Wireless Internet access. Restaurant, bar. Pool. $$

## SPECIALTY LODGINGS

### 1870 WEDGWOOD INN OF NEW HOPE

*111 W. Bridge St., New Hope, 215-862-3936; www.1870wedgwoodinn.com*

Built in 1870, this inn features antiques and a large Wedgwood collection. Carriage rides are available. 12 rooms. Complimentary full breakfast. Wireless Internet access. Pool. $

### AARON BURR HOUSE

*80 W. Bridge St., New Hope, 215-862-2343; www.aaronburrhouse.com*

5 rooms. Complimentary full breakfast. Built in 1873. $

### FOX AND HOUND BED AND BREAKFAST OF NEW HOPE

*246 W. Bridge St., New Hope, 215-862-5082, 800-862-5082; www.foxhoundinn.com*

8 rooms. Children over 12 only. Complimentary continental breakfast. Stone manor house built in 1850. Golf. Museum. Spa. $

### PINEAPPLE HILL BED AND BREAKFAST

*1324 River Road, New Hope, 215-862-1790, 888-866-8404; www.pineapplehill.com*

8 rooms. Complimentary full breakfast. Wireless Internet access. Built in 1790. **$**

## RESTAURANTS

### ★★CENTRE BRIDGE INN

*2998 N. River Road, New Hope, 215-862-9139; www.centrebridgeinn.com*

International/Fusion menu. Dinner. Closed Monday-Tuesday. Bar. Business casual attire. Reservations recommended. Valet parking. Outdoor seating. **$$$**

### ★★★THE CHAMPAGNE ROOM

*Nine S. Main St., New Hope, 215-862-1231; www.themansioninn.com*

Situated in the Mansion Inn, this casual yet stately restaurant offers continental cuisine in candlelit dining rooms. Along with a signature champagne cocktail, the restaurant serves entrées including pan-seared sea scallops with lobster ravioli, porcini mushrooms, cream sauce and sautéed organic spinach or a pan-seared rack of lamb chops with coriander and cumin served over yellow beet Yukon gold mash and topped with goat cheese, crispy shoestring sweet potatoes and port wine demi glaze. Continental menu. Lunch, dinner. Bar. Business casual attire. Reservations recommended. Outdoor seating. **$$$**

### ★★THE INN AT PHILLIPS MILL

*2590 N. River Road, New Hope, 215-862-9919; www.theinnatphillipsmill.com*

French menu. Dinner. Closed four weeks in January/early February. Casual attire. Reservations recommended. Outdoor seating. No credit cards accepted. **$$$**

### ★SPOTTED HOG

*Highways 202 and 263, New Hope, 215-794-4000; www.peddlersvillage.com*

American menu. Breakfast, lunch, dinner. Bar. Children's menu. **$$**

# NEW STANTON

*Information: Laurel Highlands Visitors Bureau, Town Hall, 120 E. Main St., Ligonier, 724-238-5661; www.laurelhighlands.org*

## WHAT TO SEE AND DO

### L. E. SMITH GLASS CO

*1900 Liberty St., New Stanton, 724-547-3544; www.lesmithglass.com*

Reproductions of several styles of antique handcrafted glass. Tours. Children under 6 not admitted on tour. Monday-Friday; closed first two weeks in July.

## HOTEL

### ★★DAYS INN

*127 W. Byers Ave., New Stanton, 724-925-3591, 800-329-7466; www.daysinn.com*

135 rooms. Pets accepted. Complimentary breakfast. Wireless Internet access. Pool. Fitness center. **$**

# NORRISTOWN

★
★
★
★

William Penn, Jr., owner of the 7,600-acre tract around Norristown, sold it to Isaac Norris and William Trent for 50 cents an acre in 1704. It became a crossroads for colonial merchants and soldiers; Washington's army camped nearby. Dutch, German, Swedish, Welsh and English immigrants all left their mark on the city. Today, Norristown is still a transportation hub.

*Information: Valley Forge Convention and Visitors Bureau, 600 W. Germantown Pike, Plymouth Meeting, 610-834-1550; www.valleyforge.org*

## WHAT TO SEE AND DO
### ELMWOOD PARK ZOO

*1661 Harding Blvd., Norristown, 610-277-3825; www.elmwoodparkzoo.org*
Features extensive North American waterfowl area. Cougars, bobcats, bison, elk. Outdoor aviary. Children's zoo barn. Museum with exhibit on animal senses. Daily.

## HOTEL
### ★★★SHERATON BUCKS COUNTY HOTEL

*400 Oxford Valley Road, Norristown, 215-547-4100, 800-325-3535; www.sheraton.com*
Only 25 miles from Philadelphia in the foothills of Bucks County, this full-service hotel features well-appointed rooms, as well as complimentary aerobics classes and certified personal trainers in its fitness center. 186 rooms. Restaurant, bar. Pets accepted. Fitness center. business center. Pool. **$$**

## RESTAURANT
### ★★★THE JEFFERSON HOUSE

*2519 DeKalb Pike, Norristown, 610-275-3407; www.jefferson-house.com*
Since 1926, this casual lakefront dining spot has been pleasing locals with a hankering for fresh seafood and friendly service. Try the shrimp scampi or the handmade cheeseburger with a side of perfectly browned fries. American menu. Lunch, dinner, Sunday brunch. Bar. Children's menu. **$$$**

# NORTH EAST
When Pennsylvania bought the tract containing North East from the federal government in 1778, the state gained 46 miles of Lake Erie frontage, a fine harbor and some of the best Concord grape terrain in the nation.

*Information: Chamber of Commerce, 21 S. Lake St., North East, 814-725-4262; www.nechamber.org*

## WHAT TO SEE AND DO
### HERITAGE WINE CELLARS

*12160 E. Main Road, North East, 814-725-8015, 800-747-0083; www.heritagewine.biz*
Guided tours. Wine tastings. Daily.

### MAZZA VINEYARDS

*11815 E. Lake Road, North East, 814-725-8695; www.mazzawines.com*
Guided tours. Wine tastings. Daily.

### PENN-SHORE VINEYARDS AND WINERY

*10225 E. Lake Road, North East, 814-725-8688; www.pennshore.com*
Guided tours. Wine tastings. Daily. Largest and longest established winery in the state.

**CHERRY FESTIVAL**

*Northeast*

Concessions. Rides, games, parade. Mid-July.

**WINE COUNTRY HARVEST FESTIVAL**

*21 S. Lake St., North East, 814-725-4262; www.nechamber.org*

Gravel Pit Park and Gibson Park. Arts and crafts. Bands. Buses to wineries. Food. Last full weekend in September.

# OIL CITY

Spreading on both sides of Oil Creek and the Allegheny River, Oil City was born of the oil boom. Oil refining and the manufacture of oil machinery are still its major occupations today. Nearby are natural gas fields.

Seven miles northwest stood the famous oil-boom town of Pithole, now a ghost town. In 1865, Pithole expanded from a single farmhouse to a population of more than 10,000 in five months as its first oil well brought in 250 barrels a day. When the oil began to run out, the town fell to pieces.

## HOTEL

### ★★ARLINGTON HOTEL

*First Seneca St., Oil City, 814-677-1221, 877-677-1222; www.oilcityhotel.com*

106 rooms. Pool. Reservations recommended. $

# PHILADELPHIA

311

**PENNSYLVANIA**

★
★
★
★
★

In the mid-18th century, it was the second largest city in the English-speaking world. Today, Philadelphia is the second largest city on the East Coast and the fifth largest in the country. Here, in William Penn's City of Brotherly Love, the Declaration of Independence was written and adopted, the Constitution was molded and signed, the Liberty Bell was rung, Betsy Ross was said to have sewn her flag and Washington served most of his years as president.

This is the city of "firsts," including the first American hospital, medical college, women's medical college, bank, paper mill, steamboat, zoo, sugar refinery, daily newspaper, U.S. mint and public school for black children.

The first Quakers, who came here in 1681, lived in caves dug into the banks of the Delaware River. During the first year, 80 houses were raised; by the following year, William Penn's "greene countrie towne" was a city of 600 buildings. The Quakers prospered in trade and commerce, and Philadelphia became the leading port in the colonies. Its leading citizen for many years was Benjamin Franklin.

The fires of colonial indignation burned hot and early in Philadelphia. Soon after the Boston Tea Party, a protest rally of 8,000 Philadelphians frightened off a British tea ship. In May 1774, when Paul Revere rode from Boston to Philadelphia to report Boston's harbor had been closed, all of Philadelphia went into mourning. The first and second Continental Congresses convened here, and Philadelphia became the headquarters of the Revolution. After the Declaration of Independence was composed and accepted by Congress, the city gave its men, factories and shipyards to the cause. But, British General Howe and 18,000 soldiers poured in on September 26, 1777, to spend a comfortable and social winter here while Washington's troops endured the bitter winter at Valley Forge. When the British evacuated the city, Congress returned.

Philadelphia continued as the seat of government until 1800, except for a short period when New York City held the honor. Since those historic days, Philadelphia has figured prominently in the country's politics, economy and culture.

More than 1,400 churches and synagogues grace the city. There are more than 25 colleges, universities and professional schools in Philadelphia as well. Fine restaurants are in abundance, along with exciting nightlife to top off an evening. Entertainment is offered by the world-renowned Philadelphia Orchestra, theaters, college and professional sports, outstanding parks, recreation centers and playgrounds. Shoppers may browse major department stores and hundreds of specialty and antique shops.

*Information: Convention & Visitors Bureau, 1700 Market St., Philadelphia, 215-636-3300; www.pcvb.org*

## WHAT TO SEE AND DO
### ACADEMY OF MUSIC
*Broad and Locust streets, Philadelphia, 215-893-1999; www.academyofmusic.org*
The city's opera house and concert hall, this academy was built in 1857 and is home of the Philadelphia Orchestra, Philly Pops, Opera Company of Philadelphia and Pennsylvania Ballet.

### ACADEMY OF NATURAL SCIENCES MUSEUM
*1900 Ben Franklin Parkway, Philadelphia, 215-299-1000; www.acnatsci.org*
Dinosaurs, Egyptian mummies, animal displays in natural habitats, live animal programs. Hands-on children's museum. Daily.

### AFRICAN-AMERICAN MUSEUM OF PHILADELPHIA
*701 Arch St., Philadelphia, 215-574-0380; www.aampmuseum.org*
Built to house and interpret African-American culture. Changing exhibits. Public events include lectures, workshops, films and concerts. Tuesday-Sunday.

### AMERICAN SWEDISH HISTORICAL MUSEUM
*1900 Pattison Ave., Philadelphia, 215-389-1776; www.americanswedish.org*
From tapestries to technology, the museum celebrates Swedish influence on American life. Special exhibits on the New Sweden Colony. Research library, collections. Tuesday-Sunday.

### ANTIQUE ROW
*From Ninth to 17th streets along Pine Street, Philadelphia*
Dozens of antique, craft and curio shops.

### ARCH STREET MEETINGHOUSE
*Fourth and Arch streets, Philadelphia, 215-627-2667; www.archstreetfriends.org*
Built in 1804, this is perhaps the largest friends meetinghouse in the world. Exhibits, slide show, tours. Daily except Sunday.

### ATHENAEUM OF PHILADELPHIA
*219 S. Sixth St., Philadelphia, 215-925-2688; www.athenaonline.org*
Landmark example of Italian Renaissance architecture (1845-1847). This restored building has American neoclassical-style decorative arts, paintings, sculpture;

**PENNSYLVANIA**

★
★
★
★
★

research library; furniture and art from the collection of Joseph Bonaparte, King of Spain and older brother of Napoleon; changing exhibits of architectural drawings, photos and rare books. Tours by appointment. Monday-Friday.

## ATWATER KENT MUSEUM OF PHILADELPHIA

*15 S. Seventh St., Philadelphia, 215-685-4830; www.philadelphiahistory.org*

Hundreds of fascinating artifacts, toys and miniatures, maps, prints, paintings and photographs reflect the city's social and cultural history. Wednesday-Sunday 1-5 p.m.

## BETSY ROSS HOUSE

*239 Arch St., Philadelphia, 215-686-1252; www.betsyrosshouse.org*

Where the famous seamstress is said to have made the first American flag. Upholsterer's shop, memorabilia. Flag Day ceremonies, June 14. April-September, daily; October-March, closed Monday.

## BISHOP WHITE HOUSE

*309 Walnut St., Philadelphia*

House of Bishop William White, first Episcopal Bishop of Pennsylvania. This house was built from from 1786-1787 and have been restored and furnished. Free tickets at park's Visitor center. Admission by tour only.

## BLUE CROSS RIVER RINK

*Festival Pier at Penn's Landing, Columbus Boulevard and Spring Garden Street, Philadelphia, 215-925-7465; www.riverrink.com*

Few outdoor ice-skating rinks are as well-located as this one along the Delaware River. Visitors have a great vantage point from which to view the Benjamin Franklin Bridge and the Philadelphia skyline. This Olympic-size rink, at 200 feet x 85 feet, can accommodate 500 skaters. After a hearty skate, warm yourself in the heated pavilion, which features a video game area and concessions. November-February, daily.

## THE BOURSE

*South Fifth St., 111 S. Independence Mall E., Philadelphia, 215-625-0300; www.bourse-pa.com*

Restored Victorian building (1893-1895) houses shops and restaurants. Daily.

## BURIAL GROUND OF CONGREGATION MIKVEH ISRAEL

*Spruce and Eighth streets, Philadelphia*

Graves of Haym Salomon, Revolutionary War financier and Rebecca Gratz, probable model for Rebecca of Sir Walter Scott's "Ivanhoe."

## CARPENTERS' HALL

*320 Chestnut St., Philadelphia*

Constructed as guild hall; meeting site of First Continental Congress (1774). Historical museum since 1857; still operated by Carpenters Co. Contains original chairs; exhibits of early tools. Tuesday-Sunday, daily.

**PENNSYLVANIA**

★
★
★
★
★

## CENTIPEDE TOURS

*1315 Walnut St., Philadelphia, 215-735-3123; www.centipedeinc.com*

Candlelight strolls (1½ hours) through historic Philadelphia and Society Hill areas led by guides in 18th-century dress; begins and ends at City Tavern. Mid-May-Mid-October, Saturday. Reservations preferred.

## CHRIST CHURCH AND BURIAL GROUND

*Second and Market streets, Philadelphia, 215-922-1695; www.oldchristchurch.org*

Patriots, loyalists and heroes have worshiped at this Episcopal church since 1695. Sit in pews once occupied by Washington, Franklin and Betsy Ross. Burial ground resting place of Benjamin Franklin, his wife, Deborah, and six other signers of the Declaration of Independence. Monday-Saturday 9 a.m.-5 p.m., Sunday 9 a.m.-5 p.m.; Closed Mondays and Tuesdays in January and February. Closed holidays.

## CITY HALL

*Broad and Market streets, Philadelphia, 215-686-2840; www.phila.gov*

A granite statue of William Penn stands 510 feet high above the heart of the city on top of this municipal building, which is larger than the Capitol. It's known as Penn Square and was designated by Penn as the location for a building of public concerns. It also functions as Philadelphia's City Hall and is one of the finest examples of French Second-Empire architectural style. Boasting the tallest statue (37,000 feet) in the world on its top, this building took 30 years to construct. Penn's famous hat is more than seven feet in diameter, and the brim creates a two-foot-wide track. There are more than 250 sculptures around this marble, granite and limestone structure, 20 elevators, and a four-faced, 50-ton clock. Monday-Friday.

## CIVIL WAR AND UNDERGROUND RAILROAD MUSEUM OF PHILADELPHIA

*1805 Pine St., Philadelphia, 215-405-8719; www.cwurmuseum.org*

Four-story, 19th-century brick townhouse filled with 18,000 books and periodicals dealing with Civil War. Unique collection of arms, uniforms, flags of the period, memorabilia and artifacts. Begun in 1888 by former officers of the Union Army. Exhibits on Lincoln, Grant and Meade. Thursday-Saturday 11 a.m.-4:30 p.m.; also by appointment.

★
★
★
★
☆

## CLIVEDEN

*6401 Germantown Ave., Philadelphia, 215-848-1777; www.cliveden.org*

A 2½-story stone Georgian house built in 1767 as a summer home by Benjamin Chew, Chief Justice of colonial Pennsylvania. On October 4, 1777, British soldiers used the house as a fortress to repulse Washington's attempt to recapture Philadelphia. Used as the Chew family residence for 200 years; many original furnishings. A National Trust for Historic Preservation property. April-December, Thursday-Sunday afternoons.

## COLONIAL MANSIONS

*4231 N. Concourse Drive, Philadelphia, 215-683-0200; www.fairmountpark.org*

Handsome 18th-century dwellings in varying architectural styles, authentically preserved and furnished, include Mount Pleasant (Tuesday-Sunday); Cedar Grove (Tuesday-Sunday); Strawberry Mansion (Tuesday-Sunday); Sweetbriar (Monday, Wednesday-Sunday); Lemon Hill (Wednesday-Sunday); Woodford (Tuesday-Sunday);

Laurel Hill (Wednesday-Sunday). Further details and guided tours from Park House office at Philadelphia Museum of Art.

## CONGRESS HALL

*Sixth and Chestnut streets, Philadelphia, 215-965-2305; www.nps.gov/inde*

Congress met here during the last decade of the 18th century. House of Representatives and Senate chambers are restored.

## DECLARATION HOUSE

*701 Market St., Philadelphia, 215-965-2305; www.ushistory.org*

Reconstructed house on the site of the writing of the Declaration of Independence by Thomas Jefferson. Two rooms that Jefferson rented have been reproduced. Short orientation and movie about Jefferson, his philosophy on the common man, and the history of the house.

## DESHLER-MORRIS HOUSE

*5442 Germantown Ave., Philadelphia, 215-596-1748; www.nps.gov/demo*

Residence of President Washington in the summers of 1793 and 1794. Period furnishings, garden. Friday-Sunday afternoons, or by appointment.

## EDGAR ALLAN POE NATIONAL HISTORIC SITE

*532 N. Seventh St., Philadelphia, 215-597-8780; www.nps.gov/edal*

Where Poe lived before his move to New York in 1844. The site is the nation's memorial to the literary genius of Edgar Allan Poe. Exhibits, slide show, tours and special programs. September-November, Wednesday-Sunday 9 a.m.-5 p.m.

**315**

## ELECTRIC FACTORY

*421 N. Seventh St., Philadelphia, 215-627-1332; www.electricfactory.com*

This all ages live-music venue offers accessibility to lesser-known bands, though Tori Amos, Garbage, Brian Setzer and other well-known artists have played here. Arrive early to set a bar table in the upstairs balcony overlooking the stage. Daily.

## ELFRETH'S ALLEY

*126 Elfreth's Alley, Philadelphia, 215-574-0560; www.elfrethsalley.org*

Philadelphians still live in these Georgian- and Federal-style homes along cobblestoned Elfreth's Alley, the nation's oldest continued-use residential street. A few homes have been converted into museums, offering guided tours, a quaint gift shop and handcrafted memorabilia. Culture and architecture fans will pick up all sorts of historical facts through photos and the collections. March-October, Monday-Sunday; November-February, Thursday-Saturday.

## FAIRMOUNT PARK

*4231 N. Concourse Drive, Philadelphia, 215-683-0200; www.phila.gov/fairpark*

At 8,900 acres, Fairmount Park is the largest city park in America. It is home to 100 miles of beautifully landscaped paths for walking and horseback riding. Cyclists love to bike along the Pennypack and Wissahickon trails. Walkers stroll or power-hike in Valley Green alongside the ducks. In-line skaters and rowing and sculling enthusiasts at Boathouse Row enjoy the sights along the Schuykill River on Kelly Drive. Within

**PENNSYLVANIA**

★
★
★
★
★

the park are the Philadelphia Zoo, the Shofuso Japanese House, the Philadelphia Museum of Art, the outdoor festival center Robin Hood Dell and the Philadelphia Orchestra's summer amphitheater (Mann Music Center), as well as 127 tennis courts and numerous picnic spots. The park contains America's largest collection of authentic colonial homes, features majestic outdoor sculptures, and includes Memorial Hall, the only building remaining from the 1876 Centennial Exhibition. Daily.

### FIREMAN'S HALL MUSEUM

*147 N. Second St., Philadelphia, 215-923-1438; www.firemanshall.org*
Collection of antique firefighting equipment; displays and exhibits of fire department history since its beginning in 1736. Library. Tuesday-Saturday daily and the first Friday of every month until 9 p.m.

### FIRST BANK OF THE UNITED STATES

*Third and Walnut streets, Philadelphia*
Organized by Alexander Hamilton. Country's oldest bank building. Restored exterior. Closed to the public.

### FIRST PRESBYTERIAN CHURCH

*201 S. 21st St., Philadelphia, 215-567-0532; www.fpcphila.org*
This more than 300-year-old church was designed in the Victorian-Gothic style, combining French and English medieval Gothic cathedral motifs with massive details, flamboyant decoration and mixed materials, including granite, sand-toned brick, six types of marble, terra-cotta and stone. No plaster was used anywhere within the original building, a matter of some architectural significance toward the end of the 19th century. Call ahead to arrange visit.

### THE FIVE SPOT

*5 S. Bank St., Philadelphia, 215-574-0070; www.phillytown.com/fivespot.htm*
Originally opened as a swing club during the late 1990s swing trend, The Five Spot is now a live music and dance club that features everything from rock music and live DJs to salsa and swing. Daily.

### FORT MIFFLIN

*Fort Mifflin Road and Enterprise Avenue, Philadelphia, 215-685-4167; www.fortmifflin.us*
Fort Mifflin, a Revolutionary War fort strategically located in the Delaware River at the mouth of the Schuylkill, is a complex of 11 restored buildings. Here, you can climb into a bombproof enclosure used to shelter troops; witness the uniform and weapons demonstrations that take place throughout the year; explore the four-foot-thick walls of the Arsenal, soldiers' barracks, officers' quarters and blacksmith's shop; or simply enjoy the spectacular view of Philadelphia and the Delaware from the Northeast Bastion. Self-guided and one-hour guided tours are available. April-November, Wednesday-Sunday.

### FRANKLIN COURT

*316-322 Market St., Philadelphia, 215-965-2305; www.ushistory.org/franklin*
The site of Benjamin Franklin's house has been developed as a tribute to him. Area includes working printing office and bindery, underground museum with multimedia exhibits, an archaeological exhibit and the B. Franklin. Post office.

★
★
★
★
★

## FRANKLIN INSTITUTE SCIENCE MUSEUM

*222 N. 20th St., Philadelphia, 215-448-1200; www2.fi.edu*

This 300,000-square-foot science museum complex and memorial hall brings biology, earth science, physics, mechanics, aviation, astronomy, communications and technology to life with a variety of highly interactive exhibits honoring Philadelphia's mechanical inventor Ben Franklin. (A 30-foot marble statue of Franklin sits in a Roman Pantheon-inspired chamber known as the Benjamin Franklin National Memorial.) The kids can play tic-tac-toe with a strategically adept computer, climb into the cockpit of an Air Force jet trainer, or test water quality in the Mandell Center, located in a 38,000-square-foot garden. Stargazers can witness the birth of the universe, see galaxies form, or discover wondrous nebulae under the Fels Planetarium dome. Budding physicists and bike fanatics will appreciate the 28-foot-high bicycle perched on a one-inch cable demonstrating gyroscopic stability in the Sky Bike exhibit. Daily.

## FRANKLIN MILLS MALL

*1455 Franklin Mills Circle, Philadelphia, 215-632-1500; www.simon.com*

Bargain hunters will feel like they've hit the jackpot in the more than 200 discount stores in this mega shopping complex, just 15 miles outside the city center, which touts itself as Pennsylvania's most visited attraction. Shoppers will find outlets of retailers like Kenneth Cole, Tommy Hilfiger, Neiman Marcus, Saks Fifth Avenue and Marshalls. There is no sales tax on apparel in Pennsylvania, which makes slashed prices even more appealing. If you don't want to fight for a parking spot, take advantage of the daily shuttle services from area hotels, airport and train stations. Monday-Saturday 10 a.m.-9:30 p.m., Sunday 11 a.m.-7 p.m.

## FREE LIBRARY

*Logan Square, 1901 Vine St., Philadelphia, 215-686-5322; www.library.phila.gov*

Large central library with more than 9 million indexed items in all fields. Rare books, maps, theater scripts and orchestral scores. Automobile reference collections. Changing exhibits. Daily.

## THE GALLERY

*Ninth and Market streets, Philadelphia, 215-625-4962; www.galleryatmarketeast.com*

Concentration of 250 shops and restaurants in a four-level mall with glass elevators, trees, fountains and benches. Daily.

**PENNSYLVANIA**

★
★
★
★

## GLORIA DEI CHURCH NATIONAL HISTORIC SITE

*143 S. Third St., Philadelphia, 215-389-1513; www.nps.gov/glde*

The state's oldest church was built in 1700. Memorial to John Hansen, president of the Continental Congress under the Articles of Confederation. Daily.

## HISTORIC BARTRAM'S GARDEN

*54th Street and Lindbergh Boulevard, Philadelphia, 215-729-5281;*
*www.bartramsgarden.org*

Pre-Revolutionary home of John Bartram, the royal botanist to the colonies under George III, naturalist and plant explorer. The 18th-century stone farmhouse, barn, stable and cider mill overlook the Schuylkill River. Museum shop. Closed Monday.

### HISTORICAL SOCIETY OF PENNSYLVANIA

*1300 Locust St., Philadelphia, 215-732-6200; www.hsp.org*

Museum exhibit features a first draft of the U.S. Constitution, 500 artifacts and manuscripts, plus video tours of turn-of-the-century urban and suburban neighborhoods. Research library and archives house historical and genealogical collections. Tuesday-Friday daily and Wednesday evening.

### INDEPENDENCE HALL

*Fifth and Chestnut streets, Philadelphia, 215-965-2305; www.nps.gov/inde*

Built in the mid-1700s, Independence Hall is the site of the first public reading of the Declaration of Independence. It also played host to large political rallies during the country's founding years. It is considered a fine example of Georgian architecture. Visitors often find the Hall a good first stop for their tour of Independence National Historic Park, which includes the Liberty Bell, Congress Hall, Old City Hall and Carpenters' Hall. The building is open for tours only. Admission by tour only. Daily.

### INDEPENDENCE NATIONAL HISTORICAL PARK

*Third and Chestnut streets, Philadelphia, 215-965-2305; www.nps.gov/inde*

The park has been called "America's most historic square mile." The Independence Visitor Center at Sixth and Market streets has a tour map, information on all park activities and attractions, and a 30-minute film entitled "Independence." Unless otherwise indicated, all historic sites and museums in the park are free and open daily.

### INDEPENDENCE SEAPORT MUSEUM

*211 S. Columbus Blvd., Philadelphia, 215-413-8655; www.phillyseaport.org*

Maritime enthusiasts of all ages will appreciate the creative interactive exhibits about the science, history and art of boat building along the region's waterways at the Independence Seaport Museum. Oral histories of the men and women who have lived and worked here take visitors through immigration, commerce, defense, industry and the recreational aspects of boats. You can watch how builders assemble a boat, walk (or crawl) through a full-size replica of a Delaware River Shad Skiff, or pull shapes through a 10-foot tank of water to examine drag affecting speed. Daily.

### INDEPENDENCE SQUARE

Known as State House Yard in colonial times. Contains Independence Hall, Congress Hall, Old City Hall and Philosophical Hall.

### INDEPENDENCE VISITOR CENTER

*First N. Independence Mall W., Philadelphia, 215-965-2307;*
*www.independencevisitorcenter.com*

Reconstruction of Quaker merchant's house. Now shop with items relating to historic sites.

### JAPANESE EXHIBITION HOUSE

*Fairmount Park Horticulture Center, Philadelphia, 215-878-5097; www.shofuso.com*

Recreates a bit of Japan, complete with garden, pond, bridge. September-October, Tuesday-Sunday; May-August, daily.

## JEWELER'S ROW

*Seventh and Sansom streets, Philadelphia*

Largest jewelry district in the country other than New York City. More than 300 shops, including wholesalers and diamond cutters.

## JOHN HEINZ NATIONAL WILDLIFE REFUGE AT TINICUM

*8601 Lindbergh Blvd., Philadelphia, 215-365-3118; www.fws.gov/northeast/heinz*

Largest remaining freshwater tidal wetland in the state, protecting more than 1,000 acres of wildlife habitat. Area was first diked by Swedish farmers in 1643; Dutch farmers and the colonial government added dikes during the Revolutionary War. More than 280 species of birds and 13 resident mammal species. Hiking, bicycling, nature observation, canoeing on Darby Creek. Fishing. Daily 8:30 a.m.-4 p.m.

## LIBERTY BELL

*Liberty Bell Center, Market and Sixth streets, Philadelphia, 215-597-8974*

An international icon and one of the most venerated stops in Independence Park, this mostly copper symbol of religious freedom, justice and independence is believed to hang from its original yoke. Daily.

## LIBRARY HALL

*105 S. Fifth St., Philadelphia, 215-440-3400; www.amphilsoc.org*

## MANAYUNK

*111 Grape St., Philadelphia, 215-482-9565; www.manayunk.com*

This historic district, just seven miles from Center City, makes a great destination point or place to hang out. Old rail lines, canal locks and textile mills dot this quaint town. Joggers, walkers, hikers and off-road cyclists will enjoy traveling the towpath that edges the town while their shopaholic counterparts check out the more than 70 boutiques and galleries.

## MASONIC TEMPLE

*One N. Broad St., Philadelphia, 215-988-1900; www.pagrandlodge.org*

Philadelphia's Masonic Temple was designed for the Fraternal Order of Freemasons, of which Benjamin Franklin and George Washington were members. The interior houses seven different halls, including the Gothic Hall, Oriental Hall and the better-known Egyptian Hall. It showcases treasures of freemasonry, including a book written by Franklin and Washington's Masonic apron. Open for tours only. Tuesday-Friday.

## MERCHANT'S EXCHANGE

*Third and Walnut streets, Philadelphia*

Designed by William Strickland, this building is one of the East's finest examples of Greek Revival architecture. Exterior restored; now houses regional offices of the National Park Service. Closed to the public.

## MORRIS ARBORETUM OF THE UNIVERSITY OF PENNSYLVANIA

*100 E. Northwestern Ave., Philadelphia, 215-247-5777; www.upenn.edu/arboretum*

Established in 1887, this public garden features more than 14,000 accessioned plants on 166 acres; special garden areas such as Swan Pond, Rose Garden and Japanese gardens. Tours. Daily.

**PENNSYLVANIA**

★
★
★
★
★

## MUMMER'S MUSEUM

*1100 S. Second St., Philadelphia, 215-336-3050; www.riverfrontmummers.com*

Participatory exhibits and displays highlighting the history and tradition of the Mummer's Parade. Costumes and videotapes of past parades. Free outdoor string band concerts (May-September, Tuesday evenings, weather permitting). 20 string bands, different every week. Tuesday-Saturday; closed Monday and Sunday.

## MUTTER MUSEUM

*19 S. 22nd St., Philadelphia, 215-563-3737; www.collphyphil.org*

This collection of one-of-a-kind, hair-raising medical curiosities includes President Cleveland's jawbone; the thorax of John Wilkes Booth; a plaster cast of Siamese twins; human bones shattered by bullets; a liver in a jar; and a drawer full of buttons, coins and teeth removed from human stomachs without surgery. Located at the esteemed College of Physicians of Philadelphia, the gallery holds an internationally revered collection of creepy anatomical and pathological specimens, medical instruments and illustrations. Daily 10 a.m.-5 p.m. and Friday evenings.

## NATIONAL MUSEUM OF AMERICAN JEWISH HISTORY

*Independence Mall East, 55 N. Fifth St., Philadelphia, 215-923-3811; www.nmajh.org*

The museum presents experiences and educational programs that preserve, explore, and celebrate the history of Jews in America. Sunday-Friday: daily.

## NEW HALL MILITARY MUSEUM

*Fourth and Chestnut streets, Philadelphia, 215-965-2305; www.ushistory.org*

This reconstruction houses the U.S. Marine Corps Memorial Museum, featuring exhibits on the early history of the Marines, and the Army-Navy Museum. Wednesday-Sunday 3-5 p.m.

## NINTH STREET ITALIAN MARKET

*Ninth Sreet, between Wharton and Fitzwater, Philadelphia, 215-923-5637;*
*www.phillyitalianmarket.com*

Sip on Italian gourmet coffee, inhale imported cheeses or treat yourself to a cannoli. With more than 100 merchants selling their wares, this is the largest working outdoor market in the United States. Pining choices range from fine Italian dining to lunch counters to an outdoor snack tent. Tuesday-Sunday.

## OLD CITY HALL

*Fifth and Chestnut streets, Philadelphia; www.ushistory.org*

Built as City Hall in 1789, this was also home of first U.S. Supreme Court from 1791-1800. Restored exterior. Interior depicts the judicial phase of the building.

## OLD PINE STREET PRESBYTERIAN CHURCH

*412 Pine St., Philadelphia, 215-925-8051; www.oldpine.org*

Colonial church and graveyard built in 1768 and renovated in 1850s in Greek Revival style. Daily.

★
★
★
★
★

### OLD ST. GEORGE'S UNITED METHODIST CHURCH

*235 N. Fourth St., Philadelphia, 215-925-7788; www.historicstgeorges.org*

Oldest Methodist Church in continuous service in the United States. Colonial architecture; collection of Methodist memorabilia; has only Bishop Asbury bible and John Wesley chalice cup in America. Daily.

### OLD ST. MARY'S CHURCH

*252 S. Fourth St., Philadelphia, 215-923-7930; www.ushistory.org*

Commodore John Barry, "father of the US Navy," is interred in graveyard behind the city's first Catholic cathedral. Daily.

### PENN'S LANDING

*Columbus Boulevard and Spruce Street, Philadelphia*

### PENNSYLVANIA ACADEMY OF FINE ARTS

*118 N. Broad St., Philadelphia, 215-972-7600; www.pafa.org*

This is the nation's oldest art museum and school of fine arts. Within the Gothic-Victorian structure are paintings, works on paper and sculptures by American artists ranging from colonial masters to contemporary artists. Many of the nation's finest artists, including Charles Willson Peale, Mary Cassatt, William Merritt Chase and Maxfield Parrish, were founders, teachers or students here. Sunday 11 a.m.-5 p.m., Tuesday-Saturday 10 a.m.-5 p.m.

### PENNSYLVANIA BALLET

*1819 JFK Blvd., Philadelphia, 215-551-7000; www.paballet.org*

This company with a George Balanchine influence includes a varied repertoire of ballets ranging from classics like "The Nutcracker" to original works. Performances are held at the Academy of Music and the Merriam Theatre.

### PENNSYLVANIA HOSPITAL

*Eighth and Spruce streets, Philadelphia*

First hospital in the country, was founded in 1751 by Benjamin Franklin.

### PENTIMENTI GALLERY

*145 N. Second St., Philadelphia, 215-625-9990; www.pentimenti.com*

Exhibiting works of art in all modes ranging from figurative to abstract by local, regional and international artists. Wednesday-Saturday.

### PHILADELPHIA 76ERS (NBA)

*Wachovia Complex, 3601 S. Broad St., Philadelphia; www.nba.com/sixers*

Professional basketball team.

### PHILADELPHIA CARRIAGE COMPANY

*500 N. 13th St., Philadelphia, 215-922-6840; www.philacarriage.com*

Guided tours via horse-drawn carriage covering Society Hill and other historic areas. Begin and end on Fifth Street at Chestnut. Daily, weather permitting.

**PENNSYLVANIA**

★
★
★
★
☆

## PHILADELPHIA EAGLES (NFL)

*Lincoln Financial Field, 11th Street and Pattison Avenue, Philadelphia, 215-463-2500;*
*www.philadelphiaeagles.com*
Professional football team.

## PHILADELPHIA FLYERS (NHL)

*Wachovia Complex, 3601 S. Broad St., Philadelphia, 215-336-2000;*
*www.flyers.nhl.com*
Professional hockey team.

## PHILADELPHIA PHILLIES (MLB)

*Citizens Bank Park, One Citizens Bank Way, Philadelphia, 215-463-5000;*
*www.philadelphiaphillies.com*
Professional baseball team.

## PHILADELPHIA MUSEUM OF ART

*26th Street and the Benjamin Franklin Parkway, Philadelphia, 215-763-8100;*
*www.philamuseum.org*
Modeled after a Greco-Roman temple, this massive museum amplifies the beauty of more than 300,000 works of art, and offers spectacular natural views. From the top of the steps outside (made famous by Sylvester Stallone in "Rocky"), visitors discover a breathtaking view of the Ben Franklin Parkway toward City Hall. Inside, the collections span 2,000 years and many more miles. There's a lavish collection of period rooms, a Japanese teahouse and a Chinese palace hall. Art lovers will also find Indian and Himalayan pieces, European decorative arts, medieval sculptures, Impressionist and Post-Impressionist paintings, and modern and contemporary works in many media. Tuesday-Sunday 10 a.m-5 p.m., Friday until 8:45 p.m.

## PHILADELPHIA ORCHESTRA

*260 S. Broad St. No. 1600, Philadelphia, 215-893-1900*
The internationally renowned Philadelphia Orchestra has distinguished itself through a century of acclaimed performances, historic international tours and best-selling recordings. Performances are held at the Kimmel Center for the Performing Arts at Broad and Spruce streets; the Mann Center for the Performing Arts, 52nd Street and Parkside Avenue; Saratoga Performing Arts Center in upstate New York; and annually at New York's Carnegie Hall. Working Monday-Friday.

## PHILADELPHIA SOFT PRETZEL

The famous Philadelphia soft pretzel is a hand-rolled, freshly baked, coarsely salted, buttery, golden-brown comfort food in a paper bag. A Philadelphia pretzel's texture is as vital as its taste: not too dry and certainly not too moist. Aficionados claim that Amish girls in hairnets sell the best ones, at Fisher's in Reading Terminal Market. But serious pretzel hunters can also find these chewy twists of dough, considered to be the country's oldest snack food, in food carts at city intersections, family-owned restaurants and the airport. Try one with a dollop or two of yellow mustard.

PENNSYLVANIA

★
★
★
★

## PHILADELPHIA ZOO

*3400 W. Girard Ave., Philadelphia, 215-243-1100; www.philadelphiazoo.org*

The Philadelphia Zoo may have been America's first zoo (it was home to the nation's first white lions and witnessed its first successful chimpanzee birth), but you'll see no signs of old age here. Over the last century, the zoo has transformed itself into a preservation spot for rare and endangered animals and as a garden and wildlife destination point. The zoo is home to 1,600 live animals, from red pandas to Rodrigues fruit bats. Take a pony, camel or elephant ride; feed nectar to a parrot in a walk-through aviary; or engage with a playful wallaby. Pedal a boat around Bird Lake. Or take a soaring balloon 400 feet up on the country's first passenger-carrying Zooballoon. March-November, daily 9:30 a.m.-5 p.m.; December-February, daily 9:30 a.m.-4 p.m.

## PHILOSOPHICAL HALL

*104 S. Fifth St., Philadelphia; www.amphilsoc.org*

Home of the American Philosophical Society, oldest learned society in America, founded by Benjamin Franklin. Not open to the public.

## PHYSICK HOUSE

*321 S. Fourth St., Philadelphia, 215-925-7866; www.philalandmarks.org*

House of Dr. Philip Sung Physick, "father of American surgery," from 1815-1837. Restored Federal-style house with period furnishings; garden. Thursday-Sunday afternoons.

## PLEASE TOUCH MUSEUM FOR CHILDREN

*210 N. 21st St., Philadelphia, 215-581-3181; www.pleasetouchmuseum.org*

A group of artists, educators and parents conceived of this award-winning, interactive exploratory learning center for children of ages one to seven in 1976. The safe, hands-on learning laboratory has since become a model for children's museums nationwide. Story lovers will enjoy having tea with the Mad Hatter or hanging out with Max in the forest where the wild things are. Children who don't want to sit still can board the life-size bus or shop at the miniature supermarket. The ones who like to get their hands dirty can engage in science experiments. Creature lovers can interact with fuzzy human-made barnyard animals. And the entertainment-minded can see themselves on television or audition for a news anchor position. Daily.

## POWEL HOUSE

*244 S. Third St., Philadelphia, 215-627-0364; www.philalandmarks.org*

Georgian townhouse of Samuel Powel, last colonial mayor of Philadelphia and first mayor under the new republic. Period furnishings, silver and porcelain; garden. Tours. Thursday-Sunday afternoons.

## READING TERMINAL MARKET

*12th and Arch streets, Philadelphia, 215-922-2317; www.readingterminalmarket.org*

The nation's oldest continuously operating farmers market is alive—and thriving—in downtown Philadelphia. An indoor banquet for the senses, the market offers an exhilarating array of baked goods, meats, poultry, seafood, produce, flowers and Asian, Middle Eastern and Pennsylvania Dutch foods. Locals recommend the family-run stands, three of which are descendants of the original market. Monday-Saturday 8 a.m.-6 p.m., Sunday 9 a.m.-4 p.m.

**323**

**PENNSYLVANIA**

★
★
★
★
★

### RECONSTRUCTION OF LIBRARY COMPANY OF PHILADELPHIA

*221 South St., Philadelphia, 215-440-4242; www.laffhouse.com*

This humor hub located on the city's artsy and alternative South Street hosts comedy events all week.

### RITA'S WATER ICE

*239 South St., Philadelphia, 215-629-3910; www.ritasice.com*

The best water ice is not a solid and not quite a liquid, and visitors to Philadelphia will find it at Rita's. With locations throughout the city and surrounding area, Rita's is the city's favorite for frozen water ice, offering a changing selection of smooth, savory water ice, as well as ice cream and gelato. Daily.

### RITTENHOUSE SQUARE

*1800 Walnut St., Philadelphia; www.rittenhouserow.org*

In the blocks that surround this genteel urban square in Philadelphia's most fashionable section of town are exclusive shops, restaurants and cafes. Discover what's new at chic boutiques—Francis Jerome, Sophy Curson, Nicole Miller, Ralph Lauren—or experience department store shopping of old at the historic Wanamaker's building, which is now a Lord and Taylor outlet.

### RODIN MUSEUM

*22nd Street and Franklin Parkway, Philadelphia, 215-568-6026; www.rodinmuseum.org*

This museum, built in the Beaux Arts style, houses more than 200 sculptures created by Auguste Rodin and is considered the largest collection of his works outside his native France. "The Thinker," Rodin's most famous piece, greets visitors outside at the gateway to the museum. Tours available. Tuesday-Sunday 10 a.m.-5 p.m.

### SCHUYLKILL CENTER FOR ENVIRONMENTAL EDUCATION

*8480 Hagy's Mill Road, Philadelphia, 215-482-7300; www.schuylkillcenter.org*

A 500-acre natural area with more than seven miles of trails. Discovery room. Gift shop/bookstore. Daily.

### SESAME PLACE

*100 Sesame Road, Philadelphia, 215-752-7070; www.sesameplace.com*

The kids will love this wet and dry amusement park with attractions like Ernie's Bed Bounce and the Monster Maze. Elmo's world is also a popular spot. Daily; hours vary so check the web site.

### SHOPS AT THE BELLEVUE

*200 S. Broad St., Philadelphia, 215-875-8350; www.bellevuephiladelphia.com*

Beaux Arts architecture of the former Bellevue Stratford Hotel has been preserved and transformed; it now contains offices, a hotel and a four-level shopping area centered around an atrium court. Monday-Saturday 10 a.m.-5 p.m., Wednesday 10 a.m.-8 p.m.

### SOCIETY HILL AREA

*Seventh and Lombard streets, Philadelphia; www.ushistory.org/tour/tour_sochill.htm*

Secret parks, cobblestone walkways and diminutive alleys among beautifully restored brick colonial townhouses make this historic area a treasure for visitors. A popular, daily 30-minute walking tour will inspire history fans as well as architecture lovers.

★
★
★
★
★

Highlights along the way include a courtyard designed by I. M. Pei; gardens planted by the Daughters of the American Revolution; a sculpture of Robert Morris, one of the signers of the Declaration of Independence; Greek Revival-style architecture now home to the National Portrait Gallery; and the burial ground of Revolutionary War soldiers. In the summer months, the area hosts outdoor arts festivals in Headhouse Square. It's also home to some of Philadelphia's finest restaurants.

## SOUTH STREET DISTRICT

*South Street, Philadelphia, 215-413-3713; www.south-street.com*
On South Street, the young and hip will enjoy the search for thrift store finds and a fashion show of the pierced and tattooed sort. The rest can rifle through dusty rare books or cruise the art galleries. These blocks at the southern boundary of the city— as well as the numbered streets just off of it—are chock full of offbeat shops, cafés, street musicians and water ice stands, all within walking distance of Penn's Landing and Society Hill. For a Philadelphia signature treat, don't miss the cheesesteaks at Jim's Steaks.

## ST. PETER'S CHURCH

*Third and Pine streets, Philadelphia, 215-925-5968; www.stpetersphila.org*
Georgian colonial architecture; numerous famous people buried in churchyard.

## STENTON HOUSE

*4601 N. 18th St., Philadelphia, 215-329-7312; www.stenton.org*
Mansion built from 1723-1730 by James Logan, secretary to William Penn. Excellent example of Pennsylvania colonial architecture, furnished with 18th- and 19th-century antiques. General Washington spent August 23, 1777, here and General Sir William Howe headquartered here for the Battle of Germantown. Colonial barn, gardens, kitchen. April-December, Tuesday-Saturday afternoons; rest of year, by appointment.

## TEMPLE UNIVERSITY

*Cecil B. Moore Avenue and Broad Street, Philadelphia, 215-204-7000;*
*www.temple.edu*
Undergraduate, professional and research school of 34,000 students. Walking tours of campus, which was founded in 1884.

## THADDEUS KOSCIUSZKO NATIONAL MEMORIAL

*301 Pine St., Philadelphia, 215-597-9618; www.nps.gov/thko*
House of Polish patriot during his second visit to the United States. He was one of 18th century's greatest champions of American and Polish freedom and one of the first volunteers to come to the aid of the American Revolutionary Army. Exterior and second-floor bedroom have been restored. Wednesday-Sunday afternoons.

## TODD HOUSE

*Fourth and Walnut streets, Philadelphia; www.ushistory.org*
House of Dolley Payne Todd, who later married James Madison and became First Lady; 18th-century furnishings depict middle-class Quaker family life. Free tickets at park's Visitor Center. Admission by tour only.

**PENNSYLVANIA**

## THE TROCADERO THEATRE

*1003 Arch St., Philadelphia, 215-922-5483; www.thetroc.com*

This former 1870s opera house hosted vaudeville, burlesque and Chinese movies before it became the beautiful, contemporary live music venue that it is today. The theater now hosts many well-known rock and pop artists, as well as the annual eight-hour Philadelphia Pop Festival held in June, which highlights local bands. On Movie Mondays, the theater holds free screenings (on its original screen) of such classic movies as *Apocalypse Now* and *Escape from New York.*

## UNIVERSITY OF PENNSYLVANIA

*32nd and Walnut streets, Philadelphia, 215-898-5000; www.upenn.edu*

On campus are the restored Fisher Fine Arts Library (215-898-8325); Annenberg Center for performing arts (215-898-6791), University Museum of Archaeology and Anthropology and the Institute of Contemporary Art, located at 36th and Sansom streets. The university has 23,000 students.

## UNIVERSITY OF PENNSYLVANIA MUSEUM OF ARCHAEOLOGY AND ANTHROPOLOGY

*3260 South St., Philadelphia, 215-898-4000; www.museum.upenn.edu*

World-famous archaeological and ethnographic collections developed from the museum's own expeditions, gifts and purchases; features Chinese, Near Eastern, Greek, ancient Egyptian, African, Pacific and North, Middle and South American materials. Library. Restaurant. Shops. Tuesday-Sunday; closed Sunday in summer.

## U.S. MINT

*151 N. Independence Mall East, Philadelphia, 215-408-0110; www.usmint.gov*

Produces coins of all denominations. Gallery affords visitors an elevated view of the coinage operations. Medal-making may also be observed. Audiovisual, self-guided tours. Rittenhouse Room on the mezzanine contains historic coins, medals and other exhibits. Monday-Friday 9 a.m.-3 p.m.

## USS OLYMPIA

*Columbus Boulevard and Walnut Street, Philadelphia, 215-925-5439*

Commodore Dewey's flagship during Spanish-American War; restored. Naval museum has weapons, uniforms, ship models and naval relics of all periods. Also here is World War II submarine, *USS Becuna.* Daily.

## WAGNER FREE INSTITUTE OF SCIENCE

*1700 W. Montgomery Ave., Philadelphia, 215-763-6529; www.wagnerfreeinstitute.org*

Victorian science museum with more than 50,000 specimens illustrating the various branches of the natural sciences. Dinosaur bones, fossils, reptiles and rare species are all mounted in the Victorian style. Reference library and research archives. Tuesday-Friday.

## WALNUT STREET THEATRE

*825 Walnut St., Philadelphia, 215-574-3550; www.wstonline.org*

America's oldest theater. The Walnut Mainstage offers musicals, classical and contemporary plays. Two studio theaters provide a forum for new and avant-garde works.

## WASHINGTON SQUARE

*Walnut and Sixth streets, Philadelphia*

Site where hundreds of Revolutionary War soldiers and victims of the yellow fever epidemic are buried. Life-size statue of Washington has tomb of Revolutionary War's Unknown Soldier at its feet.

## WOK N' WALK TOURS OF PHILADELPHIA CHINATOWN

*1002 Chestnut St., Philadelphia, 215-928-9333; www.josephpoon.com*

Considered one of the best culinary tours in the country, Joseph Poon's Wok N' Walk Tour is rich with Chinese history and culture as well as calories. This two-and-a-half-hour tour begins at Poon's Asian restaurant. (Be sure to try Chef Poon's trademark potato carvings.) Walkers are treated to a tai chi demonstration, a peek at Poon's state-of-the-art kitchen and a vegetable carving lesson. Along the tour, you visit a Chinese herbal medicine expert, a fortune cookie factory and a Chinese noodle shop and best of all, snack on free samples from a Chinese bakery in one of the city's more vibrant ethnic communities. Daily.

## SPECIAL EVENTS

### ARMY-NAVY FOOTBALL GAME

*www.usna.edu*

First Saturday in December.

### THE BOOK AND THE COOK

*1528 Walnut St., Philadelphia, 215-545-5353; www.thebookandthecook.com*

Sample fine cuisine as world-famous cookbook authors team up with the city's most respected chefs to create culinary delights. Wine tastings. Market tours. Film festival. March.

### CORESTATES US PRO CYCLING CHAMPIONSHIP

*Broad and Walnut streets, Philadelphia*

At 156 miles, it's the longest single-day cycling event in the country. Mid-June.

### DELAWARE VALLEY FIRST FRIDAYS

*In the Old City, Second and Third streets, from Market to Race, Philadelphia; www.dvfirstfridays.com*

First Fridays is a citywide cultural event that takes place at rotating venues with alternating formats on the first Friday of every month, with socializing and networking as goals. Galleries, shops, theaters, restaurants and sidewalks in the Old City area along Second and Third Streets from Market to Race have hosted record label release parties, live concerts, comedy shows, children's festivals, fashion shows and vendor expositions. Proceeds go to African-American charitable organizations. First Friday of every month.

### ELFRETH'S ALLEY FETE DAYS

*126 Elfreth's Alley, Philadelphia, 215-574-0560; www.elfrethsalley.org*

Homes open to the public. Costumed guides. Demonstrations of colonial crafts. Food. Entertainment. Second weekend in June.

PENNSYLVANIA

★
★
★
★
★

### HEAD HOUSE OPEN AIR CRAFT MARKET

*Pine and Second streets, Philadelphia*

Crafts demonstrations. Children's workshops. June-August, Saturday and Sunday.

### HORSE RACING

*Philadelphia Park, 3001 Street Road, Bensalem, 215-639-9000;*
*www.philadelphiapark.com*

Flat racing at Philadelphia Park.

### MANN CENTER FOR THE PERFORMING ARTS

*Fairmount Park, 5201 Parkside Ave., Philadelphia, 215-546-7900; www.manncenter.org*

Orchestra performs late June-July, Monday, Wednesday and Thursday. Also popular music attractions. Late May-September.

### MUMMER'S PARADE

*Philadelphia, 215-336-3050; www.mummers.com*

The Mummers Parade is Philadelphia's version of New Orleans' Mardi Gras or Spain's Carnivale. It is an annual tradition to dress in outlandish costumes and noisily parade down the streets of Philadelphia on New Year's Day (the word "mummer" comes from an old French word that means to wear a mask). January 1.

### OPERA COMPANY OF PHILADELPHIA

*Academy of Music, Broad and Locust streets, Philadelphia, 215-893-3600;*
*www.operaphilly.com*

October-April, Monday-Friday 9 a.m.-5 p.m.

### PECO ENERGY JAZZ FESTIVAL

*2301 Market St., Philadelphia, 215-841-4000, 800-537-7676*

Jazz concerts around the city. Early-mid-February.

### PENN RELAYS

*Franklin Field, 235 S. 33rd St., Philadelphia, 215-898-6151; www.thepennrelays.com*

These races originally served as a way to dedicate Franklin Field to the University of Pennsylvania. That was in 1895. Today, the Penn Relays hold the record for being the longest uninterrupted amateur track meet in the country. Thousands of men and women, ranging in age from eight to 80, have competed. More than 400 races take place, one every five minutes. Last weekend in April.

### PHILADELPHIA FLOWER SHOW

*Pennsylvania Convention Center, 12th and Arch streets, Philadelphia, 215-988-8899;*
*www.theflowershow.com*

The country's first formal flower show took place here in 1829 in the city's Masonic Hall on Chestnut Street. More than 150 years later, exotic and rare flowers are still on display in the Pennsylvania Convention Center. Flower lovers will be dazzled by more than 275,000 flowers from Africa, Germany, Japan, England, France, Holland, Italy and Belgium. Early March. Sunday 8 a.m.-6 p.m., Monday-Friday 10 a.m.-9.30 p.m., Saturday 8 a.m.-9.30 p.m.

### PHILADELPHIA OPEN HOUSE

*325 Walnut St., Philadelphia, 215-869-4979*

House and garden tours in different neighborhoods. Distinguished selection of more than 150 private homes, gardens, historic sites. Many tours include lunches, candle-light dinners or high teas. Late April-early June.

### ROBIN HOOD DELL EAST

*Fairmount Park, 33rd and Ridge streets, Philadelphia, 215-685-9560; www.delleast.org*

Top stars in popular music stage outdoor concerts. July-August.

## HOTELS

### ★BEST WESTERN INDEPENDENCE PARK HOTEL

*235 Chestnut St., Philadelphia, 215-922-4443, 800-780-7234; www.independenceparkhotel.com*

36 rooms. Pets accepted; fee. Complimentary continental breakfast. High-speed Internet access. $$

### ★★COURTYARD BY MARRIOTT

*21 N. Juniper St., Philadelphia, 215-496-3200, 888-887-8130; www.courtyard.com*

498 rooms. Wireless Internet access. Pool. Fitness center. Airport transportation available. $$

### ★★DOUBLETREE HOTEL

*237 S. Broad St., Philadelphia, 215-893-1600, 800-222-8733; www.doubletree.com*

434 rooms. Pool. Fitness room. Airport transportation available. $

### ★★EMBASSY SUITES CENTER CITY

*1776 Benjamin Franklin Parkway, Philadelphia, 215-561-1776, 800-362-2779; www.embassysuites.com*

288 rooms, all suites. Complimentary full breakfast. High-speed Internet access. Airport transportation available. $$

### ★★★★FOUR SEASONS HOTEL PHILADELPHIA

*One Logan Square, Philadelphia, 215-963-1500, 866-516-1100; www.fourseasons.com/philadelphia*

Located on historic Logan Square, this hotel puts the city's museums, shops and businesses within easy reach. The eight-story Four Seasons is a Philadelphia institution in itself, from its dramatic Swann Fountain to its highly rated Fountain Restaurant, considered one of the better dining establishments in town. The rooms and suites are a celebration of Federalist décor, and some accommodations incorporate deep soaking tubs. City views of the Academy of Natural Science, Logan Square and the tree-lined Ben Franklin Parkway provide a sense of place for some guests, while other rooms offer tranquil views over the inner courtyard and gardens. The Four Seasons spa focuses on nourishing treatments, while the indoor pool resembles a tropical oasis with breezy palm trees and large skylights. 364 rooms. High-speed Internet access. Pool. Fitness room. Spa. Airport transportation available. $$$

**PENNSYLVANIA**

★
★
★
★
★

### ★★HILTON GARDEN INN PHILADELPHIA CENTER CITY

*1100 Arch St., Philadelphia, 215-923-0100, 877-782-9444; www.hiltongardeninn.com*

279 rooms. High-speed Internet access. Airport transportation available. $$

### ★★★THE HILTON INN AT PENN

*3600 Sansom St., Philadelphia, 215-222-0200, 800-774-1500; www.theinnatpenn.com*

Experience a distinctly collegiate environment at this hotel, located in the middle of the University of Pennsylvania's campus, not far from the city's central business district. Travelers find the Inn at Penn easily accessible from Interstate (I)-76, Amtrak's 30th Street Station, and the Philadelphia International Airport. The Penne Restaurant and Wine Bar features regional Italian cuisine with fresh pasta made daily, while the University Club at Penn serves up breakfast and brunch favorites daily. 238 rooms. High-speed Internet access. Restaurant. Bar. $$

### ★★★HYATT REGENCY PHILADELPHIA AT PENN'S LANDING

*201 S. Columbus Blvd., Philadelphia, 215-928-1234, 800-233-1234; www.hyatt.com*

Located in the Penn's Landing area of Philadelphia, this Hyatt property offers unobstructed views of the Delaware River. Major historic attractions and many shops and restaurants are within walking distance. Travelers can take advantage of the indoor pool and fitness center after a busy day of work or play; or head to the restaurant for a relaxing dinner. 345 rooms. High-speed Internet access. Restaurant. Bar. Fitness center. Pool. $$$

### ★★★THE LATHAM HOTEL

*135 S. 17th St., Philadelphia, 215-563-7474, 877-528-4261; www.lathamhotel.com*

This charming hotel is a favorite of guests looking for an intimate setting in downtown Philly. It is near Rittenhouse Square and close to Walnut Street, Philadelphia's main shopping area. 139 rooms. High-speed Internet access. Restaurant. Bar. Airport transportation available. $

### ★★★LOEWS PHILADELPHIA HOTEL

*1200 Market St., Philadelphia, 215-627-1200, 800-235-6397; www.loewshotels.com*

This 1930s National Historic Landmark building (formerly the Pennsylvania Savings Fund Society), is situated across from the Market East train station and the convention center. The modern, Art Deco guest rooms feel spacious with their 10-foot ceilings. Upscale amenities include 300-thread-count linens, Bloom toiletries (with natural plant and herb extracts), flat-screen televisions and large work areas with ergonomic chairs. There are three floors of Concierge-level rooms, which include entry to the private library and lounge. Guests can keep up with their workouts in the nicely equipped Balance Spa & Fitness center—a 15,000-square-foot-space, including a full-service spa, fitness room and heated indoor lap pool. 581 rooms. Children's activity center. $$$

### ★★★OMNI HOTEL AT INDEPENDENCE PARK

*401 Chestnut St., Philadelphia, 215-925-0000, 888-444-6664; www.omnihotels.com*

Situated in the downtown area, only 10 minutes from Philadelphia International Airport and just a stone's throw from historic sights like the Liberty Bell and Independence Hall, the Omni offers an ideal location for both business and leisure trips to Philadelphia. Each well-appointed guest room combines old-world elegance with modern day luxury. Feather pillows, comfortable bath robes, 27-inch TVs with cable, and executive desks are found in all rooms, while the ultra-plush penthouse suite features marble baths, Jacuzzi tubs and a parlor room with 20-foot cathedral ceilings, multiple sitting areas and a dining table. Kids feel welcome with the Omni Sensational Kids program. 150 rooms. Wireless Internet access. Restaurant. Fitness room. Spa. $$$

### ★★★PARK HYATT PHILADELPHIA

*200 S. Broad and Walnut streets, Philadelphia, 215-893-1234, 800-464-9288;*
*www.parkphiladelphia.hyatt.com*

This elegant hotel was built in 1904 and is listed on the National Historic Register. Beautiful, early 20th-century architecture reflects the building's history, yet guests are pampered with a number of modern amenities and comforts. Goose-down duvets are found in each guest room along with luxurious linens, large televisions, DVD players, minibars and plush bathrobes. 172 rooms. High-speed Internet access. Restaurant. $$$

### ★★★PENN'S VIEW HOTEL

*Front and Market streets, Philadelphia, 215-922-7600, 800-331-7634;*
*www.pennsviewhotel.com*

Located in historic Old City Philadelphia, near Penn's Landing and the Delaware River, Penn's View Hotel is on the National Historic Register. The décor here is European/Chippendale, but guest rooms have a slightly more modern feel. Guests looking for a smaller hotel with more personal touches will find this property especially appealing. 51 rooms. Complimentary continental breakfast. High-speed Internet access. Airport transportation available. $$

### ★★★PHILADELPHIA AIRPORT MARRIOTT

*1 Arrivals Road, Philadelphia, 215-492-9000, 800-682-4087; www.marriott.com*

This well-maintained Marriott property is situated within the Philadelphia Airport. It is physically connected to Terminal B, sharing the same parking garage. Sports complexes are close by, and historic and downtown Philadelphia are just a short drive away. 419 rooms. High-speed Internet access. Restaurant. Bar. $$

### ★★★PHILADELPHIA MARRIOTT DOWNTOWN

*1201 Market St., Philadelphia, 215-625-2900, 800-320-5744;*
*www.philadelphiamarriott.com*

Guests are assured a comfortable and relaxing stay at the Marriott Philadelphia Downtown. When not outdoors exploring nearby attractions like the Liberty Bell, Independence Park, the Franklin Institute and the waterfront area, guests can work out in the hotel's fitness center or take advantage of the indoor pool, whirlpool and sauna. There are also a number of dining options, from Steakhouse to Sushi. 1,408 rooms. Complimentary continental breakfast. High-speed Internet access. Restaurant. Airport transportation available. $$$

**PENNSYLVANIA**

★
★
★
★
★

### ★★★THE RADISSON PLAZA WARWICK HOTEL

*1701 Locust St., Philadelphia, 215-735-6000, 800-201-1718; www.radisson.com*
*www.radisson.com/philadelphia*

Just one block from Rittenhouse Park, this property is close to shops, restaurants, performing arts and museums. It is also convenient to the universities. Listed on the National Register of Historic Places, the 1926 hotel has an English Renaissance theme, with guest rooms providing a more contemporary feel. 301 rooms. Pets accepted. High-speed Internet access. Restaurant. Bar. Fitness center. $$

### ★★★THE RITTENHOUSE HOTEL AND CONDOMINIUM RESIDENCES

*210 W. Rittenhouse Square, Philadelphia, 215-546-9000, 800-635-1042;*
*www.rittenhousehotel.com*

This intimate hotel occupies a particularly enviable address across from the leafy Rittenhouse Square and is among the prestigious townhouses of this exclusive area. The accommodations are among the most spacious in the city and are decorated with a sophisticated flair. Guests at the Rittenhouse are treated to the highest levels of personalized service. From the mood-lifting décor of the gracious Cassatt Lounge and the striking contemporary style of Lacroix, to the rowing memorabilia of Boathouse Row Bar and the traditional steakhouse feel of Smith & Wollensky, the Rittenhouse Hotel also provides memorable dining experiences to match every taste. 98 rooms. Pets accepted; fee. High-speed Internet access. Restaurant. Whirlpool. Spa. Fitness room. $$$$

**PENNSYLVANIA**

★
★
★
★
★

### ★★★THE RITZ-CARLTON, PHILADELPHIA

*10 Avenue of the Arts, Philadelphia, 215-523-8000, 800-241-3333;*
*www.ritzcarlton.com*

This one-time home to Girard and ellon Banks was designed in the 1900s by the architectural firm of McKim, Mead and White, and was inspired by Rome's Pantheon. Marrying historic significance with trademark Ritz-Carlton style, this Philadelphia showpiece boasts handsome decor. Impressive marble columns dominate the lobby. The rooms and suites are luxurious, while Club-lvel accommodations offer private lounges filled with five food and beverage selections daily. Dedicated to exceeding visitors expectations, the Ritz-Carlton even offers a pillow menu, a bath butler and other unique services. Dining options are plentiful, and the Sunday jazz brunch is a local favorite. 300 rooms. Pets accepted; fee. Wireless Internet access. Restaurants. Spa. Golf. Airport transportation available. $$$

### ★★★SHERATON SOCIETY HILL

*1 Dock St., Philadelphia, 215-238-6000, 800-325-3535; www.sheraton.com/societyhill*

The Sheraton Society Hill offers affordable comfort in downtown Philadelphia, just steps from Independence Hall, Society Hill, the Liberty Bell, the Philadelphia Zoo and the Pennsylvania Convention Center. Wireless Internet access is available throughout the hotel. 365 rooms. Wireless Internet access. Restaurants. Indoor children's pool. Fitness center. Airport transportation available. $$

### ★★★SHERATON UNIVERSITY CITY

*36th and Chestnut streets, Philadelphia, 215-387-8000, 800-325-3535;*
*www.starwoodhotels.com*

Perfect for visitors to the University of Pennsylvania, this Sheraton is located in the midst of an eclectic university environment. The hotel's early American décor and lobby fireplace give it a cozy feel, and the friendly staff makes a stay here even more pleasant. A "pet suitcase," which includes a bed, bowls, mat, brush, toys and treat, is available for cats and dogs. 316 rooms. Wireless Internet access. Restaurants. Outdoor pool. Fitness room. **$$**

### ★★★SOFITEL PHILADELPHIA

*120 S. 17th St., Philadelphia, 215-569-8300, 800-763-4835; www.sofitel.com*

Modern French style permeates the Sofitel Philadelphia. This elegant hotel sits on the former site of the Philadelphia Stock Exchange, and its downtown Center City location makes it ideal for both business and leisure travelers. Warm and inviting, the accommodations welcome with a variety of thoughtful touches, such as fresh flowers and plush towels. Comfortable chic defines the lobby bar, La Bourse, while the bistro fare and unique setting of Chez Colette recall the romance of 1920s Paris. 306 rooms. Pets accepted. Wireless Internet access. Restaurant. Bar. Fitness center. **$$$**

## SPECIALTY LODGINGS

### ALEXANDER INN

*Spruce and 12th streets, Philadelphia, 215-923-3535, 877-253-9466;*
*www.alexanderinn.com*

48 rooms. Complimentary continental breakfast. Wireless Internet access. Fitness center. **$**

### RITTENHOUSE SQUARE BED AND BREAKFAST

*1715 Rittenhouse Square, Philadelphia, 215-546-6500, 877-791-6500;*
*www.rittenhouse1715.com*

This renovated 1900s carriage house affords guests a choice of 10 deluxe rooms in an ideal setting just off Rittenhouse Square, one of the city's most fashionable locations. Rooms feature marble bathrooms, telephone, cable TV and workstations with Internet access. Guests are made comfortable with 24-hour concierge service, nightly turndown service, a nightly complimentary wine and snack reception, and continental breakfast served in the café. 23 rooms. Internet access. Complimentary continental breakfast. Restaurant. **$$**

### THOMAS BOND HOUSE

*129 S. Second St., Philadelphia, 215-923-8523, 800-845-2663;*
*www.thomasbondhousebandb.com*

Perfect for history buffs and ideally situated in charming Old City Philadelphia, this beautiful bed and breakfast is actually a part of the Independence National Historic Park. The house, on the National Register of Historic Places, has a warm and inviting atmosphere and antique furnishings and is close to many important historical sites, great shopping and fine dining. 12 rooms. Complimentary continental breakfast. Whirlpool. Airport transportation available. **$**

**PENNSYLVANIA**

★
★
★
★
★

## RESTAURANTS

### ★★★AZALEA

*401 Chestnut St., Philadelphia, 215-925-0000; www.omnihotels.com*

Just a block from historic Independence Hall and the Liberty Bell, this restaurant at the Omni Hotel at Independence Park is a restful spot to enjoy a meal. The décor is stylishly eclectic, and the menus are rooted in classic French technique, featuring contemporary touches and international accents. Dishes range from comfortingly rich (house-made herb spaetzle baked with Gruyère and Emmental cheeses and assorted summer vegetables) to heart-healthy (mustard-glazed salmon over golden whipped potatoes with a sauce ver jus and baby bok choy). Sunday brunch is popular here, where live piano, harp or guitar music sets an elegant tone. Continental menu. Breakfast, lunch, dinner, Sunday brunch. Closed Monday. Bar. Children's menu. Business casual attire. Reservations recommended. Valet parking. $$$

### ★★★BISTRO ROMANO

*120 Lombard St., Philadelphia, 215-925-8880; www.bistroromano.com*

When you walk into this cozy Italian restaurant located in the Society Hill area, one of the first things you see is the majestic oak bar from the *City of Detroit III*, a 1912 side-wheel passenger steamer. There is also a beautiful painting from the ship, of a sea nymph, in the stairwell that leads downstairs to the romantic dining room. Besides the beautiful décor, Bistro Romano is well known for its tableside Caesar salad, homemade ravioli and award-winning tiramisù. Italian menu. Dinner. Bar. Children's menu. Business casual attire. Reservations recommended. $$

### ★★★BRASSERIE PERRIER

*1619 Walnut St., Philadelphia, 215-568-3000; www.brasserieperrier.com*

Brasserie Perrier, the laid-back, younger sibling of Le Bec-Fin, is a terrific spot for first-rate modern French fare with Italian and Asian influences. In traditional French brasserie style, you'll find plats du jour, steak frites, and frise aux lardons, among other perfectly prepared standards. The kitchen also departs from the traditional brasserie-style menu, offering creative takes on pasta and entrées painted with eclectic flavors from around the globe. If you love choucroute, make sure to call ahead and find out which day it is one of the plats du jours. The impressive wine list is mostly French but filled with offerings that will not only fit all budgets, but all tastes as well. French, Pacific-Rim/Pan-Asian menus. Lunch, dinner. Bar. Business casual attire. Reservations recommended. Valet parking. Outdoor seating. $$$

### ★★★BUDDAKAN

*325 Chestnut St., Philadelphia, 215-574-9440; www.buddakan.com*

Slick, sexy and spectacular, Buddakan is one of Philadelphia's hottest spots for dining, drinking and lounging. Whether you're seated in the shadow of the restaurant's 10-foot gilded Buddha at the elevated communal table or at one of the other more intimate tables for two in chairs backed with black-and-white photo portraits, you will never guess that this den of fabulousness was once a post office. If your mail carrier were feasting on Buddakan's brand of splashy Asian fusion fare, like lobster fried rice with Thai basil and saffron or crisp pizza topped with seared tuna and wasabi, you can be sure that the mail would never arrive on time. Entrées are meant for sharing. A nice way to kick off the evening is with the signature Buddalini, a sexy sipper made from

★
★
★
★
☆

Champagne, Cointreau and fresh mango juice. Pan-Asian menu. Lunch, dinner. Bar. Business casual attire. Reservations recommended. Valet parking. $$$

### ★★CAFÉ SPICE

*35 S. Second St., Philadelphia, 215-627-6273; www.cafespice.com*
Indian menu. Lunch, dinner, brunch. Bar. Casual attire. Reservations recommended. Outdoor seating. $$

### ★★★CHEZ COLETTE

*120 S. 17th St., Philadelphia, 215-569-8300; www.sofitel.com*
Black-and-white photos decorate the walls in this brasserie, jazz plays in the background, and the staff and menus are both bilingual—French and English. All the pastries, breads and desserts are made on premise. For breakfast, try the fruit sushi. French menu. Breakfast, lunch, dinner, Sunday brunch. Bar. Business casual attire. Reservations recommended. Valet parking. $$$

### ★★CITY TAVERN

*138 S. Second St., Philadelphia, 215-413-1443; www.citytavern.com*
American menu. Lunch, dinner. Closed Monday in January. Bar. Children's menu. Outdoor seating. $$$

### ★★DARK HORSE

*421 S. Second St., Philadelphia, 215-928-9307; www.darkhorsepub.com*
American menu. Lunch, dinner, Sunday brunch. Closed Monday. Bar. Children's menu. Casual attire. $$

### ★★★DEUX CHEMINEES

*1221 Locust St., Philadelphia, 215-790-0200*
Featuring classic and regional French cuisine in five beautifully appointed dining rooms, Deux Cheminees ("two fireplaces") is a testament to the fact that some traditions endure for good reason. Located in two 19th-century townhouses, the formal restaurant offers prix fixe, five-course menus and special value three-course dinners for early diners. This is the place for foie gras, pâtés, terrines, sweetbreads and escargot. The house specialty, rack of lamb for two, is roasted to order and served with truffle-filled Perigord sauce. French menu. Dinner. Closed Sunday-Monday. Business casual attire. Reservations recommended. $$$$

### ★FAMOUS FOURTH STREET DELICATESSEN

*700 S. Fourth St., Philadelphia, 215-922-3274; www.famouscookies.com*
Deli menu. Breakfast, lunch, dinner, brunch. Closed Rosh Hashanah, Yom Kippur. Casual attire. $$

### ★★FEZ

*620 S. Second St., Philadelphia, 215-925-5367; www.fezrestaurant.com*
Middle Eastern menu. Dinner. Casual attire. Reservations recommended. $$

**PENNSYLVANIA**

★
★
★
★
★

### ★★FORK
*306 Market St., Philadelphia, 215-625-9425; www.forkrestaurant.com*

American menu. Lunch, dinner, Sunday brunch. Bar. Business casual attire. Reservations recommended. Outdoor seating. $$$

### ★★★★FOUNTAIN RESTAURANT
*1 Logan Square, Philadelphia, 215-963-1500; www.fourseasons.com/philadelphia*

The Fountain is the stunning flagship restaurant of the Four Seasons Hotel Philadelphia. The wine list, which covers all of France as well as Germany, Italy, the United States, Australia, New Zealand and South America, is just one of the highlights of dining here. The kitchen often uses ingredients from local producers and includes the farms' names on the menu, so you'll know which farmer planted your baby greens and where your beets were picked. As you'll see here, the best ingredients really do make a difference. Vegetarian items are available on request, and the kitchen offers several selections that are marked nutritionally balanced, healthier fare. American, French menu. Breakfast, lunch, dinner, Sunday brunch. Bar. Children's menu. Jacket required. Reservations recommended. Valet parking. $$$

### ★GENO'S STEAKS
*1219 S. Ninth St., Philadelphia, 215-389-0659; www.genossteaks.com*

American menu. Breakfast, lunch, dinner. Late-night. Casual attire. Outdoor seating. $

### ★★ITALIAN BISTRO OF CENTER CITY
*211 S. Broad St., Philadelphia, 215-731-0700; www.italianbistro.com*

Italian menu. Lunch, dinner. Bar. Children's menu. Casual attire. Reservations recommended. $$

### ★★JACK'S FIREHOUSE
*2130 Fairmount Ave., Philadelphia, 215-232-9000; www.jacksfirehouse.com*

American menu. Lunch, dinner, Saturday-Sunday brunch. Bar. Children's menu. Casual attire. Outdoor seating. $$

### ★★★JAKE'S RESTAURANT
*4365 Main St., Philadelphia, 215-483-0444; www.jakesrestaurant.com*

Located in Manayunk, Philadelphia's funky, high-energy, artsy neighborhood, Jake's Restaurant is a lively spot to meet friends for drinks and stay for dinner. Chef/owner Bruce Cooper's chic regulars make a habit of staying all night, savoring his unique brand of stylish, regional American food. While at the bar, go for one of Jake's wild house cocktails or take a chance on a unique microbrew. The kitchen is in sync with its customers' desire for both fun and flavor in their food. For instance, on a recent visit, the prix fixe menu was titled Jake's Clam Bake, which featured a popular four-course clam bake-style shellfish menu paired with wine. American menu. Lunch, dinner, Sunday brunch. Bar. Business casual attire. Reservations recommended. Valet parking. Outdoor seating. $$$

### ★★JOSEPH POON
*1002 Arch St., Philadelphia, 215-500-9774; www.josephpoon.com*

Asian fusion menu. Lunch, dinner. Closed Monday and Chinese New Year. Bar. $$

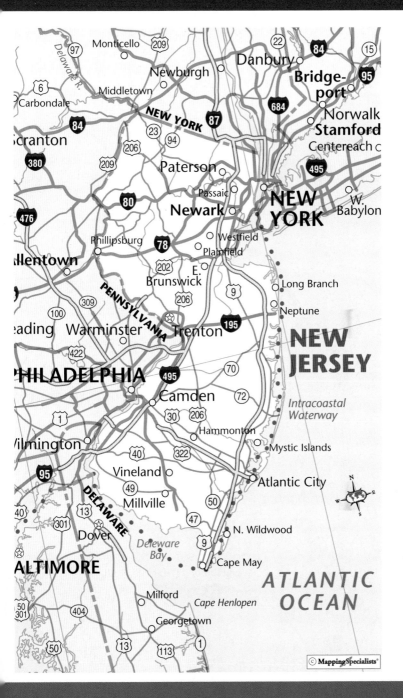

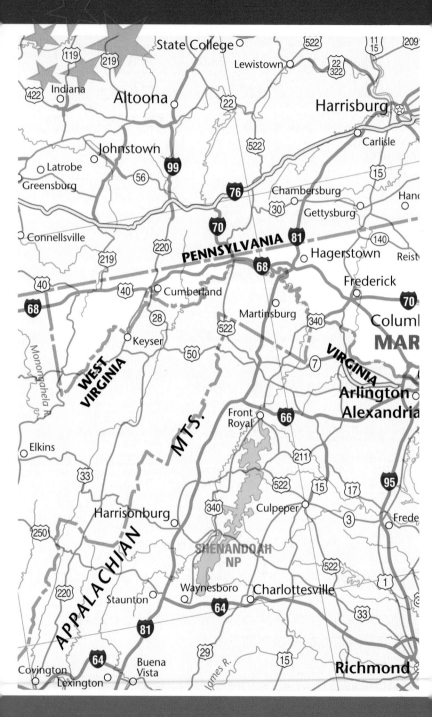

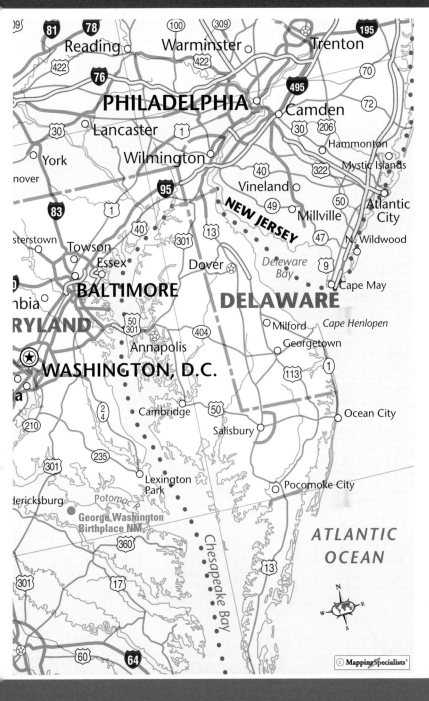

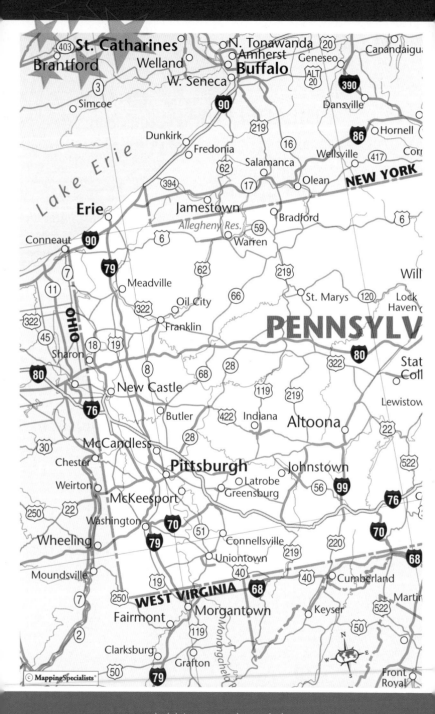

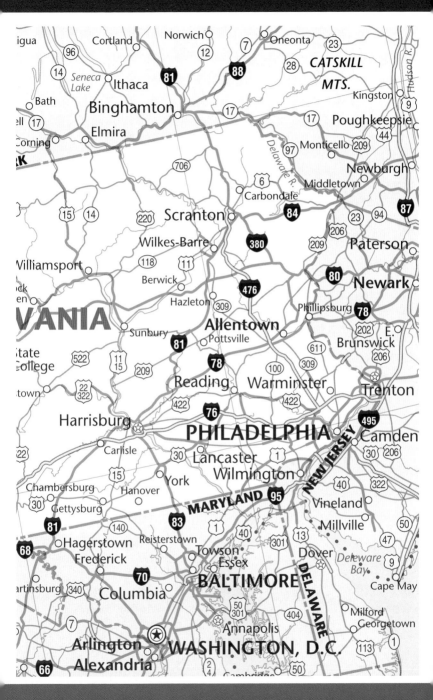

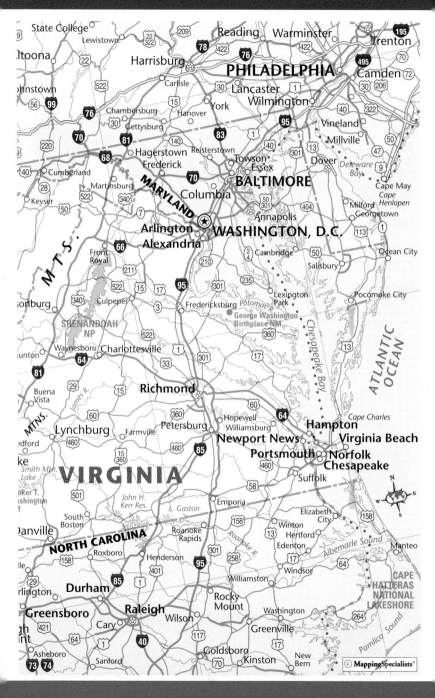

# *The* Center for Hospitality Research

Hospitality Leadership Through Learning

The Cornell School of Hotel Administration's world-class faculty explores new ways to refine the practice of hospitality management.

Our research drives better results.
Better strategy.
Better management.
Better operations.

See our work at:
www.chr.cornell.edu

537 Statler Hall • hosp_research@cornell.edu • 607.255.9780

Cornell University
School of Hotel Administration

#### ★★★★LACROIX AT THE RITTENHOUSE
*210 W. Rittenhouse Square, Philadelphia, 215-790-2533; www.rittenhousehotel.com*

Set in the stately Rittenhouse Hotel, Lacroix is a restaurant of understated elegance. The kitchen plays up fresh local ingredients with a delicate French hand, while guests dine in posh, sophisticated luxury and enjoy views of the charming Rittenhouse Square. While acclaimed chef Jean-Marie Lacroix has retired, the kitchen is still in able hands under the direction of Chef Matthew Levin. The flexible tasting menu is the best option here, where diners can choose three, four or five courses, and desserts are generously provided as a gift from the chef. The Sunday brunch (where the buffet is set up in the kitchen) is a particular Philadelphia favorite. French menu. Breakfast, lunch, dinner, Sunday brunch. Bar. Children's menu. Jacket required. Reservations recommended. Valet parking. $$$

#### ★★★LE BAR LYONNAIS
*1523 Walnut St., Philadelphia, 215-567-1000; www.lebecfin.com*

Since Georges Perrier added Le Bar Lyonnais to his internationally renowned Le Bec-Fin restaurant in 1990, the bar has achieved status as one of Philadelphia's best French bistros, winning kudos for its comfortable setting and accessible menu. The decor is subdued and casual, with dark wallpaper, dark woods, soft lighting and marble-topped tables. The bistro has featured dishes such as a cassolette of snails in champagne and hazelnut butter sauce, grilled Dover sole with herb gnocchi in beurre blanc and veal tenderloin with calves liver and onions. This lower-level bar is a great choice for diners who want to sample some of Le Bec-Fin's signature dishes without paying for a prix fixe menu. French bistro menu. Lunch, dinner. Closed Sunday. Bar. Business casual attire. Reservations recommended. Valet parking. $$$

#### LE BEC-FIN
*1523 Walnut St., Philadelphia, 215-567-1000; www.lebecfin.com*

Georges Perrier's Le Bec-Fin, which opened in 1970, remains a shining star for French cuisine, although the restaurant will be taking a more casual turn in 2009 (and will be re-rated accordingly in the future). The dining room at the restaurant now is a bastion of civility with fresh flowers, glass chandeliers, amber lighting and finely dressed tabletops. Perrier's talented team brings out the brilliance in classic dishes, while offering several new creations destined to be classics. Perrier's signature crab cake with haricot verts is divine and joins an exciting menu that leans on seasonal availability. French menu. Lunch, dinner. Closed Sunday. Bar. Jacket required. Reservations recommended. Valet parking. $$$$

#### ★★★LE CASTAGNE RISTORANTE
*1920 Chestnut St., Philadelphia, 215-751-9913; www.lecastagne.com*

This contemporary Italian restaurant offers a menu that concentrates on northern Italian dishes, and in season, a pretheater menu is offered. Everything is made in-house, including breads, pastas, sauces and desserts. Some dessert and fish selections are prepared tableside. Italian menu. Lunch, dinner. Closed Sunday. Bar. Business casual attire. Reservations recommended. Outdoor seating. $$$

**PENNSYLVANIA**

★
★
★
★
★

### ★MANAYUNK BREWERY AND RESTAURANT

*4120 Main St., Philadelphia, 215-482-8220; www.manayunkbrewery.com*

American menu. Lunch, dinner, late-night, Sunday brunch. Bar. Children's menu. Business casual attire. Reservations recommended. Valet parking. Outdoor seating. $$

### ★MANAYUNK DINER

*3720 Main St., Philadelphia, 215-483-4200*

American menu. Breakfast, lunch, dinner. Bar. Children's menu. Casual attire. Outdoor seating. $$

### ★★★MONTE CARLO LIVING ROOM

*150 South St., Philadelphia, 215-925-2220; www.montecarlolivingroom.com*

Chef Raymond Brown's weekly menus represent fine, contemporary Italian cuisine at its best. A starter duet of foie gras and sweetbreads is coupled with Firelli pears and aged balsamic vinegar, and the roasted lamb entrée is fragrant with sage and paired with cranberry beans and Barolo sauce. Cheese course selections are well thought out, and the desserts are creative. Italian menu. Dinner. Closed Sunday. Bar. Business casual attire. Reservations recommended. Valet parking. Outdoor seating. $$$

### ★★★MOONSTRUCK

*7955 Oxford Ave., Philadelphia, 215-725-6000; www.moonstruckrestaurant.com*

Formerly known as Ristorante DiLullo, this elegantly casual northern Italian gem has been doing business for more than 20 years. Menus let customers choose among a wide range of antipasti, primi piatti (pasta appetizers), secondi piatti (second courses) and piatti tradizionale (traditional classics). The latter menu section features one special dish per night, ranging from Friday's caciucco, a bouillabaisse of seafood and fish, to Tuesday's osso buco. Italian menu. Dinner. Bar. Children's menu. Business casual attire. Reservations recommended. $$$

### ★★★MORIMOTO

*723 Chestnut St., Philadelphia, 215-413-9070; www.morimotorestaurant.com*

Japanese fusion cuisine from Iron Chef Masaharu Morimoto of New York's Nobu fame (he was executive chef at Nobu Matsuhisa's restaurant for six years) pulsates with life and creativity. His Philadelphia outpost, stunningly shaped by local restaurant impresario Stephen Starr, is Morimoto's first restaurant in the United States. Ceilings undulate, booths change color and the sushi bar at the back never stops bustling. The best way to challenge your taste buds is to select one of Morimoto's omakase (multicourse tasting) menus. Japanese menu. Lunch, dinner. Bar. Business casual attire. Reservations recommended. $$$

### ★★★MOSHULU RESTAURANT

*401 S. Columbus Blvd., Philadelphia, 215-923-2500; www.moshulu.com*

Moshulu is a stunning South Seas-inspired restaurant housed in a 100-year-old, 394-foot, four-masted sailing ship. Its several dining rooms are elegantly decorated with rattan chairs, cane furniture, dark mahogany and Polynesian artwork. The kitchen, headed by Executive Chef Ralph Fernandez, churns out creative, delicious dishes that will keep you coming back for more. American menu. Lunch, dinner. Bar. Business casual attire. Reservations recommended. Valet parking. Outdoor seating. $$$

### ★★PALOMA

*6516 Castor Ave., Philadelphia, 215-533-0356*

French, Mexican menu. Dinner. Closed Sunday-Monday; last week of August-first week of September. Bar. Business casual attire. Reservations recommended. $$$

### ★★PHILADELPHIA FISH & CO

*207 Chestnut St., Philadelphia, 215-625-8605; www.philadelphiafish.com*

Seafood menu. Lunch, dinner. Bar. Children's menu. Business casual attire. Reservations recommended. Outdoor seating. $$$

### ★★THE PLOUGH & THE STARS

*Old City Philadelphia on Second Street, 215-733-0300; www.ploughstars.com*

Continental menu. Lunch, dinner, brunch, late-night. Bar. Children's menu. Business casual attire. Reservations recommended. Outdoor seating. $$$

### ★RANGOON BURMESE RESTAURANT

*112 N. Ninth St., Philadelphia, 215-829-8939; www.phillychinatown.com*

Burmese menu. Lunch, dinner. Casual attire. $$

### ★★★RISTORANTE PANORAMA

*Front and Market streets, Philadelphia, 215-922-7800; www.pennsviewhotel.com*

Panorama is part of the boutique-style Penn's View Hotel. The beautiful dining room features marble floors, a wall of windows and murals throughout. The cuisine is gutsy, old-world Italian, featuring dishes such as paillard of beef rolled in garlic, cheese, egg and herbs, slow-cooked in tomato sauce, and served with house-made gnocchi. But this place is known for its wine. Daily wine lists offer 22 to 26 different flights (five wines per flight), plus dozens of by-the-glass options. The quality, made possible by the restaurant's cruvinet preservation and dispensing system, is exceptional, earning Panorama numerous "Best Wines by the Glass" awards from national food magazines. Italian menu. Lunch, dinner. Bar. Business casual attire. Reservations recommended. Valet parking. $$$

### ★★★RUTH'S CHRIS STEAK HOUSE

*260 S. Broad St., Philadelphia, 215-790-1515, 800-544-0808; www.ruthschris.com*

Ruth's Chris is a top choice of many steak lovers. With a menu that highlights aged prime Midwestern beef that's broiled at 1800 degrees and drizzled with butter, how could it not be? Dark wood accents and comfortable leather booths give the room a club-like steakhouse feel. Steak menu. Dinner. Bar. $$$

### ★★★THE SALOON

*750 S. Seventh St., Philadelphia, 215-627-1811; www.saloonrestaurant.net*

Richard Santore has been operating this venerable establishment in Philadelphia's Bellavista neighborhood, bordering Center City and South Philly, for nearly 40 years. The food is classic Italian fare, served for lunch and dinner. Appetizers include poached pear and gorgonzola salad with roasted walnuts, baby greens and red onion with pear vinaigrette. Fettuccini Lobster Amatriciana is a toss of house-made fettuccini with lobster, bacon, onion, fresh tomato and pecorino cheese in tomato sauce. Daily dinner specials range from beef carpaccio drizzled with truffle essence and

339

**PENNSYLVANIA**

★
★
★
★

served with fava beans to a double veal chop marinated in white wine, pan seared and served with Yukon gold potatoes. Italian, steak menu. Lunch, dinner. Closed Sunday; also one week in early July. Bar. Business casual attire. Valet parking. No credit cards accepted. $$$

### ★★SERRANO

*20 S. Second St., Philadelphia, 215-928-0770; www.tinangel.com*

International menu. Dinner. Closed last week in August and first week in September. Bar. Business casual attire. Reservations recommended. $$

### ★SOUTH STREET DINER

*140 South St., Philadelphia, 215-627-5258*

American, Italian, Greek menu. Breakfast, lunch, dinner. Late-night. Children's menu. Casual attire. $$

### ★★★SUSANNA FOO

*1512 Walnut St., Philadelphia, 215-545-8800; www.susannafoo.com*

Thanks to the plethora of greasy Chinese takeout joints, Chinese food has been much maligned over the years. But at Susanna Foo, a Zen-like dining oasis, the delicious, traditional cuisine of China sheds its unfortunate reputation and gains the respect it deserves. For years, chef/owner Susanna Foo has been dressing up the dishes of her native land with sophisticated French flair and modern, global accents. Foo's dim sum can be a meal on their own. The entrées are equally mouthwatering, especially the famous tea-smoked Peking duck breast. You may never be able to order takeout again. Chinese, French menu. Lunch, dinner. Bar. Business casual attire. Reservations recommended. $$$

### ★★★SWANN CAFÉ

*1 Logan Square, Philadelphia, 215-963-1500, 866-516-1100;*
*www.fourseasons.com/philadelphia*

Named for the spectacular Logan Square fountain in front of the Four Seasons Hotel Philadelphia, Swann Café is the more accessible of the hotel's exceptional restaurants. Menus are overseen by Executive Chef Martin Hamann and range from light and lovely dishes, such as an appetizer ragout of forest mushrooms and asparagus tips, to a zesty sandwich of pulled osso buco with aged provolone and spicy pepper and onion relish on a stirato roll. American menu. Lunch, dinner, Sunday brunch. Bar. Children's menu. Casual attire. Reservations recommended. Valet parking. $$$

### ★★★TANGERINE

*232 Market St., Philadelphia, 215-627-5116; www.tangerinerestaurant.com*

This Middle Eastern-themed restaurant in the heart of Old City Philadelphia features a menu that blends flavors from the Mediterranean, France, Spain, Italy and Africa. An appetizer of harissa-spiced gnocchi is sweetened with dates and paired with celery root. Pistachio-crusted duck breast is served with creamy onions, seared foie gras and port-poached pear. Mediterranean menu. Dinner. Bar. Business casual attire. Reservations recommended. Valet parking. $$$

### ★★UMBRIA
*7131 Germantown Ave., Philadelphia, 215-242-6470*
International menu. Dinner. Closed Sunday-Tuesday. Business casual attire. Reservations recommended. $$

### ★★★VETRI
*1312 Spruce St., Philadelphia, 215-732-3478; www.vetriristorante.com*
Chef Mark Vetri learned to prepare rustic Italian cuisine (think: rabbit loin and sweetbreads wrapped in pancetta with morels or baby goat poached in milk and then oven roasted to crispness) from Italy's best chefs and then brought his skills home to Philly. Ensconced in the tiny, 35-seat space once occupied by other pinnacle establishments (Le Bec-Fin, Chanterelle), Vetri is intent on creating likewise legendary meals. The wine list has been nationally lauded, and the service is seamless. On Saturdays, indulge in Vetri's five- or seven-course prix fixe menus (not available during the summer). Italian menu. Dinner. Closed Sunday; two weeks in January and three weeks in August; Saturday in summer. Business casual attire. Reservations recommended. $$$$

### ★★WHITE DOG CAFÉ
*3420 Sansom St., Philadelphia, 215-386-9224; www.whitedog.com*
American, vegetarian menu. Lunch, dinner, brunch. Bar. Children's menu. Business casual attire. Reservations recommended. Outdoor seating. $$$

### ★★★XIX
*Park Hyatt Philadelphia, 200 S. Broad St., Philadelphia, 215-790-1919; www.nineteenrestaurant.com*
XIX (pronounced "nineteen") sits on the top 19th floor of the historic Bellevue Building (now the Park Hyatt), and exudes a level of opulence from a bygone era with two 36-foot-high grand rotundas, mosaic marble and a 19-foot-tall pearl chandelier. The fine dining experience is further enhanced by spectacular views of the city through floor-to-ceiling arched picture windows. The raw bar features a choice of 12 varieties of fresh oysters and a separate café offers its own menu and afternoon tea. American, French menu. Breakfast, lunch, dinner, Sunday brunch, late night. $$$

### ★★ZOCALO
*3600 Lancaster Ave., Philadelphia, 215-895-0139; www.zocalophilly.com*
Mexican menu. Lunch, dinner. Closed Sunday. Bar. Children's menu. Casual attire. Reservations recommended. Outdoor seating. $$

# PHOENIXVILLE

## RESTAURANT
### ★★SEVEN STARS INN
*23 Hoffecker Road, Phoenixville, 610-495-5205; www.sevenstarsinn.com*
Seafood menu. Dinner. Closed Monday; holidays. Bar. Children's menu. $$$

# PITTSBURGH
Pittsburgh has become one of the most spectacular civic redevelopments in America, with modern buildings, clean parks and community pride. The new Pittsburgh is a result of

★
★
★
★
★

a rare combination of capital-labor cooperation, public and private support, enlightened political leadership and imaginative, venturesome community planning. Its $1 billion international airport was designed to be the most user-friendly in the country.

After massive war production, Pittsburgh labored to eliminate the 1930s image of an unsophisticated mill town. During the 1950s and 1960s, Renaissance I began, a $500-million program to clean the city's air and develop new structures, such as Gateway Center, the Civic Arena and Point State Park. The late 1970s and early 1980s ushered in Renaissance II, a $3 billion expansion program deflecting the movement away from industry and toward high technology.

Today Pittsburgh has completed this dramatic shift from industry to a diversified base including high technology, health care, finance and education and continues its transition to a service-oriented city.

Pittsburgh's cultural personality is expressed by the Pittsburgh Symphony Orchestra, Pittsburgh Opera, Pittsburgh Ballet, Phipps Conservatory and the Carnegie Museums of Pittsburgh, which include the Museum of Natural History and the Museum of Art. The city has 25 parks, 45 "parklets," 60 recreation centers and 27 swimming pools.

Born of frontier warfare in the shadow of Fort Pitt, the city is named after the elder William Pitt, the great British statesman. Its strategic military position was an important commercial asset, and Pittsburgh soon became a busy river port and transit point for the western flow of pioneers.

Industry grew out of the West's need for manufactured goods; foundries and rolling mills were soon producing nails, axes, frying pans and shovels. The Civil War added tremendous impetus to industry, and by the end of the war, Pittsburgh was producing half the steel and one-third of the glass made in the country. Captains of industry and finance, such as Thomas Mellon, Andrew Carnegie and Henry Clay Frick, built their industrial empires in Pittsburgh. The American Federation of Labor was born here in 1881 because the city has been the scene of historic clashes between labor and management.

*Information: Greater Pittsburgh Convention & Visitors Bureau,*
*Liberty Avenue at Gateway Center, 425 Sixth Ave., Pittsburgh, 800-366-0093;*
*www.visitpittsburgh.com*

PENNSYLVANIA

★
★
★
★
☆

## WHAT TO SEE AND DO
### ALCOA BUILDING
*425 Sixth Ave., Pittsburgh*
Pioneer in aluminum for skyscraper construction, exterior work was done from inside; no scaffolding was required. Draped in aluminum waffle, 30 stories high; considered to be one of the country's most daring experiments in skyscraper design.

### ALLEGHENY COUNTY COURTHOUSE
*Grant Street and Fifth Avenue, Pittsburgh; www.alleghenycounty.us/directions*
One of the country's outstanding Romanesque buildings, the two-square city block structure was designed by Henry Hobson Richardson in 1884. Monday-Friday.

### ALLEGHENY OBSERVATORY
*159 Riverview Ave., Pittsburgh, 412-321-2400; www.pitt.edu*
Slides, tour of building. Maintained by University of Pittsburgh. Children under 12 years only with adult. Reservations recommended. April-October, Thursday-Friday.

## ANDY WARHOL MUSEUM

*117 Sandusky St., Pittsburgh, 412-237-8300; www.warhol.org*

The most comprehensive single-artist museum in the world. More than 500 works. Tuesday-Sunday 10 a.m.-5 p.m.

## BENEDUM CENTER FOR THE PERFORMING ARTS

*719 Liberty Ave., Pittsburgh, 412-456-6666; www.pgharts.org*

Expansion and restoration of the Stanley Theater, a movie palace built in 1928. Gilded plasterwork, a 500,000-piece-crystal chandelier and a nine-story addition to the backstage area make this an exceptional auditorium with one of the largest stages in the country. The center is home to Pittsburgh Ballet Theatre, the Pittsburgh Dance Council, the Pittsburgh Opera and Civic Light Opera. Free guided tours (by appointment).

## BLOCK HOUSE OF FORT PITT

*101 Commonwealth Place Pittsburgh, 412-281-9284; www.fortpittmuseum.com*

## CARNEGIE MELLON UNIVERSITY

*5000 Forbes Ave., Pittsburgh, 412-268-2000; www.cmu.edu*

Founded by Andrew Carnegie in 1900, this university is composed of seven colleges and is home to 7,900 students. Tours of campus.

## CARNEGIE MUSEUM OF ART

*4400 Forbes Ave., Pittsburgh, 412-622-3131; www.cmoa.org*

Possibly America's first modern art museum. Carnegie urged the gallery to exhibit works dated after 1896. Collection of Impressionist and Post-Impressionist paintings. Hall of Sculpture. Hall of Architecture. Films, videos.

## CARNEGIE MUSEUM OF NATURAL HISTORY

*412-622-3131; www.carnegiemnh.org*

Houses one of the most complete collections of dinosaur fossils. Exhibits include Dinosaur Hall, Polar World, Hillman Hall of Minerals and Gems and the Walton Hall of Ancient Egypt. changing exhibits. Tuesday-Saturday 10 a.m.-5 p.m., Thursday 10 a.m.-8 p.m., Sunday noon-5 p.m.; closed Monday.

## CARNEGIE MUSEUMS OF PITTSBURGH

*4400 Forbes Ave., Pittsburgh, 412-622-3360; www.carnegiemuseums.org*

Public complex built by industrialist Andrew Carnegie. Tuesday-Saturday 10 a.m.-5 p.m., Thursday 10 a.m.-8 p.m., Sunday noon-5 p.m

## CARNEGIE SCIENCE CENTER

*1 Allegheny Ave., Pittsburgh, 412-237-3400; www.carnegiesciencecenter.org*

Learning and entertainment complex has more than 40,000 square feet of exhibit galleries that demonstrate how human activities are affected by science and technology. U.S.S. Requin, moored in front of the center, is a World War II diesel electric submarine; 40 minute tours demonstrate the electronic, visual and voice communication devices on board. Henry Buhl Jr. Planetarium and Observatory is a technologically sophisticated interactive planetarium with control panels at every seat. Also here are the 350-seat Rangos Omnimax Theater and the Health Sciences Amphitheater. Restaurant. Gift shop. Sunday-Friday 10 a.m.-5 p.m., Saturday 10 a.m.-7 p.m.

**PENNSYLVANIA**

## CATHEDRAL OF LEARNING

*4200 Fifth Ave., Pittsburgh, 412-624-6000; www.tour.pitt.edu*

Unique skyscraper of classrooms built in 1935, stretching its Gothic-Modern architecture 42 floors high (535 feet). Vantage point on 36th floor. Surrounding a three-story Gothic commons room are an Early American Room and 24 Nationality Rooms, each reflecting the distinctive culture of the ethnic group that created and furnished it. Tours. Daily.

## CLAYTON, THE HENRY CLAY FRICK HOME

*7227 Reynolds St., Pittsburgh, 412-371-0600; www.frickart.org*

A restored four-story Victorian mansion with 23 rooms; only remaining house of area in East End once known as "Millionaire's Row." Some original décor and personal mementos of the Fricks' Tours. Reservations recommended.

## COUNTY PARKS

*Pittsburgh, 412-350-2455; www.alleghenycounty.us*

South Park, 12 miles South on Highway 88. North Park, 14 miles North on Highway 19. Boyce Park, 14 miles East on Interstate 376, Highway 22. Settler's Cabin Park, nine miles West on Interstate 279, Highway 22. Swimming, fishing, boating. Bicycling (rentals), ball fields, golf, tennis. Cross-country skiing, downhill skiing, ice skating (winter, daily). Picnicking. Parks open daily. Fees for activities. Attractions for each park vary.

## DUQUESNE INCLINE

*220 Grandview Ave., Pittsburgh, 412-381-1665; www.portauthority.org*

Built 1877. Restored and run by community effort. Observation deck. Free parking at lower station. Daily.

## FORT PITT MUSEUM

*101 Commonwealth Place Pittsburgh, 412-281-9284; www.fortpittmuseum.com*

Built on part of original fort. Exhibits on early Pittsburgh and Fort Pitt. Wednesday-Sunday 9 a.m.-5 p.m. Closed holidays.

## FRICK ART AND HISTORICAL CENTER

*7227 Reynolds St., Pittsburgh, 412-371-0600; www.frickart.org*

Museum complex built on grounds of estate once belonging to industrialist Henry Clay Frick; gardens, carriage house museum, greenhouse, café and restored children's playhouse that now serves as a visitor's center. Tuesday-Sunday 10 a.m.-5 p.m.; closed Monday.

## THE FRICK ART MUSEUM

*7227 Reynolds St., Pittsburgh, 412-371-0600; www.frickart.org*

Collection of Helen Clay Frick, daughter of Henry Clay Frick, includes Italian Renaissance, Flemish and French 18th-century paintings and decorative arts. Italian and French furniture, Renaissance bronzes, tapestries, Chinese porcelains. Also changing exhibits. Concerts, lectures. Tuesday-Sunday 10 a.m.-5 p.m.; closed Monday.

## FRICK PARK

*Beechwood Boulevard and English Lane, Pittsburgh, 412-422-6538;*
*www.pittsburghparks.org*

Covers 476 acres, largely in natural state. Nature trails wind through ravines and over hills. Also nature center (2005 Beechwood Blvd.), tennis courts, picnic areas, playgrounds. Daily.

## GATEWAY CENTER

*420 Fort Duquesne Blvd., Pittsburgh, 412-392-6000*

Complex includes four skyscrapers of Trizec Properties, Inc. Gateway Center Plaza, a two-acre open-air garden over underground parking garage, has lovely walks, three fountains, more than 90 types of trees and 100 varieties of shrubs and seasonal flowers. Monday-Friday.

## GUIDED BUS AND WALKING TOURS

*100 W. Station Square, Pittsburgh, 412-471-5808; www.phlf.org*

Offered through the Pittsburgh History and Landmarks Foundation.

## HARTWOOD ACRES

*200 Hartwood acres, Pittsburgh, 412-767-9200; www.alleghenycounty.us*

A 629-acre recreation of English country estate. Tudor mansion built in 1929 with many antiques. Formal gardens, stables. Tours (Tuesday-Sunday). Also music and theater events during summer. Monday-Friday 8 a.m.-4 p.m.

## HEINZ CHAPEL

*Fifth and Bellefield avenues, Pittsburgh, 412-624-4157; www.heinzchapel.pitt.edu*

Tall stained-glass windows. French Gothic architecture.

## HENRY CLAY FRICK FINE ARTS BUILDING

*Schenley Plaza, 104 Frick Fine Arts, Pittsburgh, 412-648-2400; www.haa.pitt.edu*

Glass-enclosed cloister; changing exhibits; art reference library. September-mid-June, daily; July-August, Monday-Friday; closed university holidays.

## JAMES L. KELSO BIBLE LANDS MUSEUM

*616 N. Highland Ave., Pittsburgh, 412-362-5610; www.pts.edu*

Artifacts and displays from the ancient Near East, especially Palestine. Monday-Saturday 10 a.m.-4 p.m.

## LIBRARY OF PITTSBURGH

*412-622-3114; www.clpgh.org*

Central branch contains more than 4½ million books. Houses first department of science and technology established in a U.S. public library.

## MELLON ARENA

*66 Mario Lemieux Place, Pittsburgh; www.mellonarena.com*

This $22-million all-weather amphitheater accommodates 17,500 people. Retractable roof can fold up within 2½ minutes.

**PENNSYLVANIA**

★
★
★
★

### MONONGAHELA INCLINE

*Pittsburgh, 412-442-2000*
Panoramic views from observation deck. Daily.

### MUSEUM OF PHOTOGRAPHIC HISTORY

*531 E. Ohio, Pittsburgh, 412-231-7881; www.photoantiquities.org*
Photo gallery and museum. Selections from 100,000 antique photographic images.
Wednesday-Saturday 10 a.m.-4 p.m.; closed Sunday-Tuesday.

### MUSIC HALL

*412-622-1906*
Home to Mendelssohn Choir, Pittsburgh Chamber Music Society and River City
Brass Band. Elaborate gilt and marble foyer. Walls of French eschallion, 24 pillars
made of green stone and a gold baroque ceiling.

### NATIONAL AVIARY

*700 Arch St., Allegheny Commons West, Pittsburgh, 412-323-7235; www.aviary.org*
The Aviary is home to one of the world's premier bird collections and is the only
indoor bird facility independent of a larger zoo in North America. Daily 10 a.m.-
5 p.m. Closed Christmas Day.

### PHIPPS CONSERVATORY

*700 Frank Curto Drive, Pittsburgh, 412-622-6914; www.conservatory.org*
Constantly changing array of flowers; tropical gardens; outstanding orchid collection.
Children's Discovery Garden with interactive learning opportunities. Seasonal flower
shows. Tuesday-Saturday evenings.

★
★
★
★
☆

### PITTSBURGH CHILDREN'S MUSEUM

*10 Children's Way, Pittsburgh, 412-322-5058; www.pittsburghkids.org*
Hands-on exhibits. Silkscreen studio. Storytelling, regularly scheduled puppet shows,
live performances. Two-story climber. Daily.

### PITTSBURGH PENGUINS (NHL)

*Mellon Arena, 66 Mario Lemieux Place, Pittsburgh, 412-323-1919;*
*www.penguins.nhl.com*
Professional hockey team.

### PITTSBURGH PIRATES (MLB)

*PNC Park, 115 Federal St., Pittsburgh, 412-323-5000; www.pittsburgh.pirates.mlb.com*
Professional baseball team.

### PITTSBURGH STEELERS (NFL)

*Heinz Field, 600 Stadium Circle, Pittsburgh, 412-432-7800; www.steelers.com*
Professional football team.

### PITTSBURGH ZOO & AQUARIUM

*1 Wild Place, Pittsburgh, 412-665-3640, 800-474-4966; www.pittsburghzoo.com*

More than 70 acres containing nearly 6,000 animals, children's farm (late May-October), discovery pavilion, reptile house, tropical and Asian forests, African savanna and aqua zoo. Merry-go-round and train rides (fee). Highland Park covers 75 acres and has tennis courts, picnic grounds, shelters (some require permit), twin reservoirs, swimming pool (fee). Daily.

### POINT STATE PARK

*101 Commonwealth Place Fort Duquesne and Fort Pitt boulevards, Pittsburgh, 412-471-0235; www.pointstatepark.com.*

Point where the Allegheny and Monongahela rivers meet to form the Ohio. A 150-foot fountain symbolizes the joining of the rivers. There are military drills with fifes, drums, muskets and cannon (May-Labor Day, some Sunday afternoons).

### PPG PLACE

*Market Square, Pittsburgh; www.ppgplace.com*

Designed by Philip Johnson, this is Pittsburgh's most popular Renaissance II building. PPG Place consists of six separate buildings designed in a postmodern, Gothic skyscraper style. Shopping and a food court can be found in Two PPG Place.

### RIVERVIEW PARK

*414 Grant St., Pittsburgh, 412-255-2135; www.city.pittsburgh.pa.us*

Swimming pool (mid-June-Labor Day, daily; fee). Tennis courts (April-November, daily). Picnic shelter (May-September, permit required). Also playgrounds, parklet. Nature, jogging trail. Fee for some activities.

### RODEF SHALOM BIBLICAL BOTANICAL GARDEN

*4905 Fifth Ave., Pittsburgh, 412-621-6566; www.rodefshalom.org/who/garden*

The natural world of ancient Israel is re-created here in settings that specialize in plants of the Bible. A waterfall, desert and stream all help simulate the areas of the Jordan, Lake Kineret and the Dead Sea. Tours (by appointment). Special programs and exhibits. June-mid-September, Sunday-Thursday 10 a.m.-2 p.m., Saturday noon-1 p.m.

### SANDCASTLE WATER PARK

*1000 Sandcastle Drive, Pittsburgh, 412-462-6666; www.sandcastlewaterpark.com*

The city's down-by-the-riverside water park has 15 slides, adult and kiddie pools; boardwalk and food. First Saturday in June-Labor Day, Daily 11 a.m.-6 p.m.

### SCHENLEY PARK

*5000 Forbes Ave., Pittsburgh, 412-687-1800; www.pittsburghparks.org*

Picnic areas, 18-hole golf course, lighted tennis courts. Swimming pool. Ice skating (winter). Softball fields, running track, nature trails; bandstand (summer; free). Fee for some activities. Daily.

### SENATOR JOHN HEINZ REGIONAL HISTORY CENTER

*1212 Smallman St., Pittsburgh, 412-454-6000; www.pghhistory.org*

In Chatauqua Ice Warehouse. Preserves 300 years of region's history with artifacts and extensive collection of archives, photos. Houses the Historical Society of Western Pennsylvania and Pittsburgh Sports Museum. Library. Tuesday-Saturday. Daily.

### SOLDIERS AND SAILORS MEMORIAL HALL AND MILITARY HISTORY MUSEUM

*At Bigelow Boulevard, 4141 Fifth Ave., Pittsburgh, 412-621-4253;*
*www.soldiersandsailorshall.org*

Auditorium has Lincoln's Gettysburg Address inscribed above stage; flags, weapons, uniforms, memorabilia from U.S. wars. Monday-Saturday 10 a.m.-4 p.m.

### STATION SQUARE

*125 W. Station Square, 450 Landmarks Building, Pittsburgh, 412-471-5808,*
*800-859-8959; www.stationsquare.com*

This 40-acre area features shopping, dining and entertainment in and among the historic buildings of the P and LE Railroad. Shopping in warehouses that once held loaded railroad boxcars. Monday-Saturday 10 a.m.-9 p.m., Sunday noon-5 p.m.

### STEPHEN FOSTER MEMORIAL

*4301 Forbes Ave., Pittsburgh, 412-624-4100*

Auditorium/theater. Collection of the Pittsburgh-born composer's music and memorabilia. Said to be one of the most elaborate memorials ever built to a musician. Monday-Saturday, Sunday afternoons.

### TOUR-ED MINE AND MUSEUM

*748 Bull Creek Road, Pittsburgh, 724-224-4720; www.tour-edmine.com*

Complete underground coal mining operation. Sawmill, furnished log house, old company store; historical mine museum, shelters. Playground. May-Labor Day week, daily 10 a.m.-4 p.m.; closed Tuesday.

**348**

★
★
★
★

### TWO MELLON BANK CENTER

*Grant Street and Fifth Avenue, Pittsburgh*

Formerly the Union Trust Building, its Flemish-Gothic style was modeled after a library in Louvain, Belgium. Interior has a glass rotunda.

### UNIVERSITY OF PITTSBURGH

*Fifth Avenue and Bigelow Boulevard, Pittsburgh, 412-624-4141; www.pitt.edu*

Founded in 1787, this city university has a student body numbering 33,000. Tours of Nationality Rooms in Cathedral of Learning. Campus of 70 buildings on 125 acres.

### U.S. STEEL TOWER

*Grant Street and Seventh Avenue, Pittsburgh*

The tallest building in Pittsburgh, and 35th tallest in the nation. 10 exposed triangular columns and an exterior paneling of steel make up its construction.

## SPECIAL EVENTS
### PHIPPS CONSERVATORY FLOWER SHOWS

*Schenley Park, 1 Schenley Drive, Pittsburgh, 412-622-6914;*
*www.phipps.conservatory.org*

Spring, summer, fall and holidays.

### PITTSBURGH IRISH FESTIVAL

*Chevrolet Amphitheatre, Station Square, 1 Station Square, Pittsburgh,*
*412-422-1113; www.pghirishfest.org*
Irish foods, dances and entertainment. Early or mid-September.

### PITTSBURGH PUBLIC THEATER

*621 Penn Ave., Pittsburgh, 412-316-1600; www.ppt.org*
City's largest resident professional company. September-June.

### PITTSBURGH SYMPHONY ORCHESTRA

*Heinz Hall for the Performing Arts, 600 Penn Ave., Pittsburgh, 412-392-4900;*
*www.pittsburghsymphony.org*
Classical, pop and family concerts. September-May, Monday-Friday 9 a.m.-8 p.m.,
Saturday noon-4 p.m.

### THREE RIVERS ARTS FESTIVAL

*937 Liberty Ave., Pittsburgh, 412-281-8723; www.artsfestival.net*
Juried, original works of local and national artists: paintings, photography, sculpture,
crafts and videos. Artists' market in outdoor plazas. Ongoing performances include
music, dance and performance art. Special art projects, film festival, food. Children's
activities. Early-mid-June.

### THREE RIVERS REGATTA

*412-427-4893; www.threeriversregatta.net*
Water, land and air events. Water shows and speedboat races. Last weekend in July
and first weekend in August.

## HOTELS

### ★★DOUBLETREE HOTEL

*One Bigelow Square, Pittsburgh, 412-281-5800, 800-222-8733; www.doubletree.com*
308 rooms. Complimentary continental breakfast. High-speed Internet access. Pool.
Fitness center. $

### ★★★HILTON PITTSBURGH

*600 Commonwealth Place, Pittsburgh, 412-391-4600; www.hilton.com*
713 rooms. Pets accepted. High-speed Internet access. Restaurant. Airport transportation available. $

### ★★★MARRIOTT PITTSBURGH CITY CENTER

*112 Washington Place, Pittsburgh, 412-471-4000, 888-456-6600; www.marriott.com*
Located across the street from Mellon Arena and the downtown business district, you
won't have to travel far to get a taste of the city. Guest rooms include luxury down
comforters, TVs and VCRs and free high-speed Internet access. 402 rooms. High-
speed Internet access. Restaurant. Pool. Fitness center. Spa. $$

**PENNSYLVANIA**

★
★
★
★
★

### ★★★OMNI WILLIAM PENN HOTEL

*530 William Penn Place, Pittsburgh, 412-281-7100, 888-444-6664;*
*www.omnihotels.com*

This hotel, built in 1916, fuses historic charm with modern luxury in the heart of downtown Pittsburgh. The rooms and suites are tastefully and elegantly appointed with a distinguished style. Executives on the go appreciate the hotel's complete business and fitness centers; families adore the Omni Kids Program; and leisure visitors enjoy the spa and salon services and proximity to the city's leading stores. The hotel offers a variety of convenient and tempting dining choices, from Starbucks to pub food at the Palm Court and Tap Room, to fine dining at the Terrace Room. 596 rooms. Pets accepted; fee. Wireless Internet access. Fitness center. Spa. Airport transportation available. $$

### ★QUALITY SUITES

*700 Mansfield Ave., Pittsburgh, 412-279-6300, 877-424-6423; www.choicehotels.com*
151 rooms. Complimentary full breakfast. High-speed Internet access. Fitness center. Airport transportation available. $

### ★★★RENAISSANCE PITTSBURGH HOTEL

*107 Sixth St., Pittsburgh, 412-562-1200, 800-468-3571; www.renaissancehotels.com*
Housed in the classic Fulton Building downtown, this hotel is an architectural stunner in the city's renowned Cultural District. Stroll across the Roberto Clemente Bridge to reach North Shore destinations. 300 rooms. Wireless Internet access. Restaurant. Spa. $$

### ★★★SHERATON STATION SQUARE HOTEL

*300 W. Station Square Drive, Pittsburgh, 412-261-2000, 800-255-7488;*
*www.sheraton.com*

In the heart of Station Square, a major nightlife destination, this riverfront hotel is convenient for sightseeing, North Shore destinations and the Gateway Clipper Fleet. 292 rooms. Wireless Internet access. Restaurant. Indoor pool. $$

### ★★★THE WESTIN CONVENTION CENTER PITTSBURGH

*1000 Penn Ave., Pittsburgh, 412-281-3700; www.westin.com*
The Westin Convention Center is located in the heart of Pittsburgh's business and cultural districts, and connected to the new David L. Lawrence Convention Center by a skywalk. 616 rooms. High-speed Internet access. Restaurant. Fitness center. Pool. $$

## SPECIALTY LODGINGS
### THE INN ON NEGLEY

*703 S. Negley Ave., Pittsburgh, 412-661-0631; www.innonnegley.com*
Historic building. 8 rooms. Children over 12 years only. Complimentary full breakfast. $$

### THE PRIORY INN

*614 Pressley St., Pittsburgh, 412-231-3338*
This European-style inn with a fountain and floral arrangements in the courtyard was previously a haven for Benedictine monks. 24 rooms. Complimentary continental breakfast. High-speed Internet access. Restaurant. Spa. $

★
★
★
★
★

# RESTAURANTS

### ★★1902 LANDMARK TAVERN

*24 Market Square, Pittsburgh, 412-471-1902*

Italian, American menu. Lunch, dinner. Closed Sunday. Bar. **$$**

### ★ABRUZZI'S RESTAURANT

*20 S. 10th St., Pittsburgh, 412-431-4511; www.abruzzis.net*

Italian menu. Lunch, dinner. Bar. Casual attire. **$$**

### ★★★CAFÉ ALLEGRO

*51 S. 12th St., Pittsburgh, 412-481-7788; www.cafeallegropittsburgh.com*

This restaurant's several intimate dining areas draw crowds for Mediterranean fare. Try uncomplicated dishes like fish cooked en papillote. Italian menu. Dinner. Bar. Valet parking. **$$**

### ★★CAFÉ AT THE FRICK

*7227 Reynolds St., Pittsburgh, 412-371-0600; www.frickart.org*

Lunch. Closed Monday. Outdoor seating. **$**

### ★★★CARLTON

*500 Grant St., Pittsburgh, 412-391-4099; www.thecarltonrestaurant.com*

American menu. Lunch, dinner. Closed Sunday. Bar. Children's menu. **$$$**

### ★★CASBAH

*229 S. Highland Ave, Pittsburgh, 412-661-5656; www.bigburrito.com/casbah*

Mediterranean menu. Lunch, dinner. Bar. Casual attire. Outdoor seating. **$$**

### ★★THE CHURCH BREW WORKS

*3525 Liberty Ave., Pittsburgh, 412-688-8200; www.churchbrew.com*

American menu. Dinner. Bar. Outdoor seating. **$$**

### ★★★COMMON PLEA

*310, Ross St., Pittsburgh, 412-697-3100; www.commonplea-restaurant.com*

With its dark paneling, glass wall and subdued lighting, this restaurant caters to the legal crowd. Seafood menu. Lunch, dinner. Bar. Valet parking (dinner only). **$$**

### ★★D'IMPERIO'S

*3412 William Penn Highway, Pittsburgh, 412-823-4800*

American, Italian menu. Lunch, dinner. Closed Sunday. Bar. Children's menu. **$$$**

### ★DAVE AND ANDY'S ICE CREAM PARLOR

*207 Atwood St., Pittsburgh, 412-681-9906; www.andrew.cmu.edu*

Dessert menu. **$**

### ★DEJA VU LOUNGE

*2106 Penn Ave., Pittsburgh, 412-434-1144; www.dejavulive.net*

American, Pan-Asian menu. Lunch, dinner, late-night. Closed Sunday. Bar. Casual attire. Outdoor seating. **$$**

★
★
★
★
★

### ★★GEORGETOWN INN

*1230 Grandview Ave., Pittsburgh, 412-481-4424; www.georgetowninn.com*
Seafood, steak menu. Lunch, dinner. Bar. $$$

### ★★★GRAND CONCOURSE

*1 Station Square, Pittsburgh, 412-261-1717; www.muer.com*
Converted railroad station on the river serves a legendary Sunday brunch. International menu. Lunch, dinner. Sunday brunch. Bar. Children's menu. Outdoor seating. $$$

### ★★INDIA GARDEN

*328 Atwood St., Pittsburgh, 412-682-3000; www.indiagarden.net*
Indian menu. Lunch, dinner. $

### ★★KAYA

*2000 Smallman St., Pittsburgh, 412-261-6565; www.bigburrito.com/kaya*
Caribbean menu. Dinner. Bar. Outdoor seating. $$$

### ★★LE MONT

*1114 Grandview Ave., Pittsburgh, 412-431-3100; www.lemontpittsburgh.com*
American menu. Dinner. Bar. Valet parking. $$$

### ★★★LE POMMIER

*2104 E. Carson St., Pittsburgh, 412-431-1901; www.lepommier.com*
Located in the oldest storefront in the area, Le Pommier serves French-American bistro entrées such as cauliflower sautéed in brown butter with a roasted cauliflower-gruyere sauce and fresh oregano in puff pastry. French menu. Lunch, dinner. Closed Sunday. Bar. Valet parking (Friday-Saturday). Outdoor seating. $$

### ★★MAX'S ALLEGHENY TAVERN

*537 Suismon St., Pittsburgh, 412-231-1899; www.maxsalleghenytavern.com*
German menu. Lunch, dinner. Bar. $$

### ★★MEZZANOTTE CAFÉ

*4621 Liberty Ave., Pittsburgh, 412-688-8070; www.mezzanottecafe.com*
Italian, Mediterranean menu. Lunch, dinner. Closed Sunday. Bar. Casual attire. $$

### ★★MONTEREY BAY FISH GROTTO

*1411 Grandview Ave., Pittsburgh, 412-481-4414; www.montereybayfishgrotto.com*
Lunch, dinner. Children's menu. $$$

### ★PENN BREWERY

*800 Vinial St., Troy Hill, Pittsburgh, 412-237-9402; www.pennbrew.com*
German menu. Lunch, dinner. Closed Sunday. Bar. Children's menu. Outdoor seating. $$

**PENNSYLVANIA**

★
★
★
★
★

## ★★PICCOLO MONDO

*661 Andersen Drive, Pittsburgh, 412-922-0920; www.piccolo-mondo.com*

Italian menu. Lunch, dinner. Closed Sunday. Bar. Children's menu. Jacket required. $$

## ★PRIMANTI BROTHERS

*46 18th St., Pittsburgh, 412-263-2142; www.primantibros.com*

American, Italian menu. Dinner. $

## ★★RICO'S

*One Rico Lane, Pittsburgh, 412-931-1989*

Italian, American menu. Lunch, dinner. Closed Sunday. Bar. Jacket required. Valet parking. $$$

## ★★SEVICHE

*930 Penn Ave., Pittsburgh, 412-697-3120; www.seviche.com*

Nuevo Latino tapas menu. Dinner. $$

## ★★★SOBA

*5847 Ellsworth Ave., Pittsburgh, 412-362-5656; www.bigburrito.com/soba*

A modern interior with a two-story waterfall, plush seating, tropical wood tones and mellow lighting serves as the perfect backdrop for Soba's sophisticated Asian fusion cuisine. Recent small-plate selections have included crispy tofu with lemongrass sauce and Vietnamese chicken spring rolls, while pad Thai, bacon-dusted sea scallops with sweet miso sake and scallion honey sauces, and filet mignon with chili-garlic mashed potatoes and wild mushroom ragout have been featured as large plate choices. A few soups, salads and bowls round out the menu. An ambitious wine list with selections that span the globe is also offered, along with a number of sakes, martinis and cocktails. Pan-Asian menu. Dinner. Bar. Outdoor seating. $$$

## ★★SONOMA GRILLE

*947 Penn Ave., Pittsburgh, 412-697-1336; www.thesonomagrille.com*

Californian, American menu. Lunch, dinner. $$

## ★★★STEELHEAD BRASSERIE AND WINE BAR

*112 Washington Place, Pittsburgh, 412-394-3474; www.thesteelhead.com*

This casual American brasserie features artistically prepared cuisine that highlights fresh seafood like Prince Edward Island mussels, seared ahi tuna and oysters. The menu also includes certified Angus beef strip steak, filet mignon and a porterhouse pork chop. On a daily basis, a special soup, pasta, pizza and grilled fresh fish dish are offered, all of which can be perfectly paired with a selection from the adventurous wine list. American, seafood menu. Lunch, dinner. Children's menu. $$$

## ★★SUSHI TWO

*2122 E. Carson St., Pittsburgh, 412-431-7874; www.eastwindsasianbistro.com*

Japanese menu. Lunch, dinner. Bar. $$$

★
★
★
★
★

### ★★TAMBELLINI

*860 Saw Mill Run Blvd., Pittsburgh, 412-481-1118; www.eatzucchini.com*

American menu. Lunch, dinner. Closed Sunday. Bar. Children's menu. Valet-parking dinner. **$$**

### ★★TESSARO'S

*4601 Liberty Ave., Pittsburgh, 412-682-6809*

American, Mexican menu. Lunch, dinner. Closed Sunday. Bar. **$$**

### ★★THAI PLACE

*5528 Walnut St., Pittsburgh, 412-687-8586; www.thaiplacepgh.com*

Thai menu. Lunch, dinner. Bar. Casual attire. **$$**

### ★★★TIN ANGEL

*1200 Grandview Ave., Pittsburgh, 412-381-1919; www.tinangel.com*

Located in a prime spot on Grandview Avenue, Tin Angel boasts wonderful views of downtown Pittsburgh in a candlelit setting. Signature items include the seven pepper meatloaf and the paella marinara with shrimp, mussels saffron and smoked paprika. Seafood, steak menu. Closed Sunday. Bar. **$$$**

# PITTSBURGH INTERNATIONAL AIRPORT AREA

★
★
★
★
★

## HOTELS

### ★HAMPTON INN

*8514 University Blvd., Coraopolis, 412-264-0020, 800-426-7866; www.hamptoninn.com*

129 rooms. Complimentary continental breakfast. Airport transportation available. **$**

### ★★★HYATT REGENCY PITTSBURGH INTERNATIONAL AIRPORT

*1111 Airport Blvd., Pittsburgh, 724-899-1234, 800-633-7313; www.hyatt.com*

Whether you're in town for the day and need a place to clean up or have an early flight in the morning, this Hyatt is connected to the airport terminals and offers soundproof windows so you're guaranteed a restful night. A 24-hour business center ensures that no matter what time you arrive, you'll be able to get to work. 336 rooms. High-speed Internet access. Fitness center. Pool. **$**

## RESTAURANT

### ★★★HYEHOLDE

*1516 Coraopolis Heights Road Moon Township, 412-264-3116; www.hyeholde.com*

Don a jacket and tie at this long-standing outpost of English-country elegance 20 minutes from downtown Pittsburgh. The game and seafood menu and manor-like setting of rich tapestries, exposed wood beams and candlelight are a popular choice for special events. International menu. Lunch, dinner. Closed Sunday. Valet parking. Outdoor seating. **$$$**

# POTTSTOWN

An iron forge operating in 1714 at Manatawny Creek, about three miles north of Pottstown, was the first industrial establishment in the state. The borough was established by John Potts, an ironmaster, on land William Penn had earlier deeded to his son, John. Today, the community is the commercial and cultural hub for an area with a population of 130,000. Nearly 200 modern industries are located here.

*Information: TriCounty Area Chamber of Commerce, 135 High St., Pottstown, 610-326-2900; www.tricopa.com*

## WHAT TO SEE AND DO

### POTTSGROVE MANOR

*West King Street and Highway 100, Pottstown, 610-326-4014; www.montcopa.org*

Built in 1752, this is the newly restored house of John Potts, 18th-century ironmaster and founder of Pottstown; outstanding example of early Georgian architecture and furniture. Includes recently discovered slave quarters and Potts's office. Slide orientation. Museum shop. Tuesday-Sunday.

### RINGING ROCKS ROLLER RINK

*1500 Ringing Rocks Park, Pottstown, 610-323-6560*

Roller skating (Friday-Sunday; fee); nature trails, picnicking, interesting rock formations. Daily.

## SPECIAL EVENT

### DURYEA DAY ANTIQUE & CLASSIC AUTO SHOW

*Boyertown Community Park, 28 Warwick St., Pottstown*

Antique autos, trucks and other vehicles; displays, arts and crafts, flea market with automotive memorabilia, activities. Pennsylvania Dutch food. Labor Day weekend.

## HOTELS

### ★BEST WESTERN POTTSTOWN INN

*1600 Industrial Highway, Pottstown, 610-327-3300; www.bestwestern.com*

122 rooms. Complimentary continental breakfast. High-speed Internet access. Fitness center. $

### ★COMFORT INN

*SR 100 & Shoemaker Road, Pottstown, 610-326-5000, 800-879-2477; www.choicehotels.com*

121 rooms. Complimentary continental breakfast. $

# QUAKERTOWN

Once a station on the Underground Railroad, Quakertown still retains some of its colonial appearance. In 1798, angered by what they considered an unfair federal tax, Quakertown housewives started greeting tax assessors with pans of hot water. The "hot water" rebellion cooled down when federal troops arrived, but the town switched political parties (from Federalist to Jeffersonian) almost en masse.

*Information: Upper Bucks County Chamber of Commerce, 2170 Portzer Road, Quakertown, 215-536-3211, or Bucks County Conference and Visitors Bureau, 152 Swamp Road, Doylestown, 215-345-4552, 800-836-2825; www.ubcc.org*

## RESTAURANT

### ★★BRICK TAVERN INN

*2460 Old Bethlehem Park, Quakertown, 215-529-6488; www.bricktavern.org*

American menu. Lunch, dinner. Bar. Casual attire. **$$**

# READING

A city of railroads and industry famous for its superb pretzels, Reading was the second community in the United States to vote a Socialist government into office; however, the city has not had such a government for many years. The characters of this unofficial capital of Pennsylvania Dutch land reflect the love of music and the thrift and vigor of the "Dutch."

William Penn purchased the land now occupied by Reading from the Lenni-Lenape Native Americans and settled his two sons, Thomas and Richard, on it. They named it Reading (fern meadow) for their home in England. During the Revolution, the citizens of Reading mustered troops for the Continental army, forged cannons and provided a depot for military supplies and a prison for Hessians and British. The hundreds of skilled German craftspeople, plus canal and railroad transportation, ignited Reading's industrial development.

*Information: Reading & Berks County Visitors Bureau, 352 Penn St., Reading,*
*610-375-4085, 800-443-6610; www.readingberkspa.com*

## WHAT TO SEE AND DO

### BERKS COUNTY HERITAGE CENTER

*2201 Tulpehocken Road, Reading, 610-374-8839; www.countyosderks.com/parks*

Here are the Gruber Wagon Works, where finely crafted wagons were produced for farm and industry; Wertz's Red Bridge, the longest single-span covered bridge in the state; Deppen Cemetery, with graves of Irish workers who died of "swamp fever" while building the Union Canal; C. Howard Hiester Canal-Center, with its collection of canal artifacts. Tours of wagon works and canal center; orientation slide program. May-October, Tuesday-Sunday.

### CONRAD WEISER HOMESTEAD

*28 Weiser Lane, Reading, 610-589-2934; www.conradweiserhomestead.org*

Originally built in 1729, this house is the restored and furnished house of colonial "ambassador" to the Iroquois nation; springhouse, gravesite, visitor center, picnicking in 26-acre park. Wednesday-Sunday.

### DANIEL BOONE HOMESTEAD

*400 Daniel Boone Road, Reading, 610-582-4900; www.danielboonehomestead.org*

Birthplace of Daniel Boone in 1734. Approximately 570 acres; includes Boone House, barn, blacksmith shop and sawmill. Picnicking. Nature trails. Youth camping. Visitors center. Tuesday-Saturday 9 a.m.-4:30 p.m., Sunday noon-4:30 p.m. Closed Monday.

### HISTORICAL SOCIETY OF BERKS COUNTY

*940 Centre Ave., Reading, 610-375-4376; www.berkhistory.org*

Local history exhibits; decorative arts, antiques, transportation displays. Tuesday-Saturday.

★
★
★
★
☆

### MID-ATLANTIC AIR MUSEUM

*11 Museum Drive, Reading, 610-372-7333; www.maam.org*

Aviation museum dedicated to the preservation of vintage aircraft; planes are restored to flying condition by volunteers. Collection of 40 airplanes and helicopters; 20 on public display, including Martin 4-0-4-airliners, B-25 bomber and others. Daily.

### OUTLET SHOPPING

*801 N. Ninth St., Reading, 610-375-4085, 800-443-6610*

More than 300 factory outlet stores can be found at five different shopping complexes.

### PLANETARIUM

*500 Museum Road, Reading, 610-371-5854; www.readingpublicmuseum.org*

Changing exhibits. Star and laser light shows.

### READING PUBLIC MUSEUM AND ART GALLERY

*500 Museum Road, Reading, 610-371-5850; www.readingpublicmuseum.org*

In 25-acre Museum Park with stream. Exhibits of art and science. Tuesday-Sunday.

## HOTELS

### ★★BEST WESTERN DUTCH COLONY INN & SUITES

*4635 Perkiomen Ave., Reading, 610-779-2345, 800-828-2830; www.bestwestern.com*

71 rooms. $

### ★COMFORT INN

*2200 Stacy Drive, Reading, 610-371-0500, 877-424-6423; www.choicehotels.com*

60 rooms. Complimentary continental breakfast. Wireless Internet access. Fitness center. Airport transportation available. $

## RESTAURANTS

### ★★ALPENHOF BAVARIAN

*903 Morgantown Road, Reading, 610-373-1624; www.restaurant.com/alpenhof*

American, German menu. Lunch, dinner. Bar. Outdoor seating. $$

### ★★★GREEN HILLS INN

*2444 Morgantown Road, Reading, 610-777-9611*

The owner of this small-town spot has big-city pedigree: He was a student of Georges Perrier, owner of Philadelpia's renowned La Bec-Fin. So it should came as no surprise that the kitchen churns out impeccable French fare including grilled moulard duck breast and chateaubriand. French, American menu. Dinner. Closed Sunday. $$$

# RENOVO

## WHAT TO SEE AND DO

### KETTLE CREEK

*Highway 62, Renovo, 570-923-6004*

Winds through beautiful valley developed as tourist area. Swimming beach, fishing, boating (mooring, launching); hunting, hiking, bridle trail, snowmobiling, sledding, ice skating, picnicking, playground, tent and trailer sites (electric hookups). Standard fees.

**PENNSYLVANIA**

★
★
★
★
★

## HOTEL

### ★★BEST WESTERN GRAND VICTORIAN INN

*255 Spring St., Sayre, 570-888-7711, 800-627-7972; www.bestwestern.com*

100 rooms. Pets accepted. Complimentary continental breakfast. High-speed Internet access. Pool. Fitness center. **$**

# SCRANTON

The first settlers here found a Monsey Native American village on the site. In 1840, George and Seldon Scranton built five iron furnaces using the revolutionary method of firing with anthracite coal instead of charcoal. Manufacture of iron and steel remained important industries until 1901, when the mills moved to Lake Erie to ease transportation problems.

After World War II, Scranton thoroughly revamped its economy when faced with depletion of the anthracite coal mines, which for more than a century had fired its forges. Scranton's redevelopment drew nationwide attention and served as a model for problem cities elsewhere. Today, Scranton is the home of electronic and printing industries and is host to several major trucking firm terminals.

*Information: Visitors Bureau Montage Mountain Road, Scranton, 570-963-6363, 800-229-3526; www.visitnepa.org*

## WHAT TO SEE AND DO

### ANTHRACITE HERITAGE MUSEUM

*Keyser Avenue and Bald Mountain Road, Scranton, 570-963-4804; www.anthracitemuseum.org*

History and culture of anthracite region. Other affiliated parts of the complex are the Iron Furnaces; Museum of Anthracite Mining, with emphasis on the technology of the industry, and the 19th-century miners' village of Eckley, near Hazleton. Daily.

### CATLIN HOUSE

*232 Monroe Ave., Scranton, 570-344-3841; www.lackawannahistory.org*

Originally built in 1912, this is the headquarters of Lackawanna Historical Society. Features period furnishings historic exhibits, antiques, research library (fee). Tours available (fee). Tuesday-Friday, Saturday afternoons.

### EVERHART MUSEUM

*1901 Mulberry St., Scranton, 570-346-7186; www.everhart-museum.org*

Permanent collections includes 19th- and 20th-century American art; Dorflinger glass; Native American, Asian and primitive art; natural history displays, including Dinosaur Hall. Gift shop. Tuesday-Sunday.

### HOUDINI MUSEUM

*1433 N. Main Ave., Scranton, 570-342-5555; www.houdini.org*

This museum is devoted to the career and life of the great magician Harry Houdini. Tours, films featuring Houdini himself and a magic show (with live animals) are all included. Daily.

★
★★
★★★
★★
★

## LACKAWANNA COAL MINE TOUR

*McDade Park, Keyser Ave., Scranton, 570-963-6463, 800-238-7245*

The tour of this underground coal mine provides a realistic glimpse of the working lives of anthracite miners in an earlier time. A five-minute ride in a coal-mine car takes you into the cool and damp mine, and the ensuing hour-long tour will enlighten you about the hazards and harsh conditions faced by miners, as well as the unfortunate pit ponies, who lived permanently in the mine. April-November, Daily.

## LACKAWANNA COUNTY STADIUM

*235 Montage Mountain Road, Scranton, 570-969-2255*

Open-air stadium/civic arena seats 11,000. Home of AAA baseball, high school and college football and marching band competitions. April-November.

## MONTAGE SKI AREA

*1000 Montage Mountain Road, Scranton, 570-969-7669; www.snomtn.com*

Quad, double, three triple chairlifts; school, rentals, snowmaking; bar, restaurant, lodge. Vertical drop 1,000 feet. Night skiing. More than 130 acres of trails set in 400 acres of mountainside. Early December-late March, daily, Summer activities include water slides, batting cages, amphitheater (June-Labor Day).

## NAY AUG PARK

*Arthur Avenue and Mulberry Street, Scranton, 570-348-4186*

More than 35 acres with memorials to pioneer days. Picnicking, swimming pool (fee), walking trail, refreshment stands, and the "Pioneer," a gravity railroad car dating back to 1850; weekend concerts (summer). Daily.

## SCRANTON IRON FURNACES

*159 Cedar Ave., Scranton, 570-963-3208; www.anthracitemuseum.org*

Partially restored site of four anthracite-fired iron furnaces built 1848-1857 and used until 1902. Visitor center, outdoor exhibits. Self-guided tours (daily). Guided tours. Late May-early September, Monday-Thursday.

## STEAMTOWN NATIONAL HISTORIC SITE

*Lackawanna and Cliff streets, Scranton, 888-693-9391; www.nps.gov/stea*

Site with large collection of steam locomotives and other memorabilia located in an authentic freight yard. Steam train ride through yard (Memorial Day-December, daily). 25-mile train excursion July 4-mid-October, Saturday-Sunday.

**PENNSYLVANIA**

★
★
★
★
★

## HOTELS

### ★★CLARION HOTEL

*300 Meadow Ave., Scranton, 570-344-9811, 800-347-1551; www.choicehotels.com*

135 rooms. Pets accepted. Complimentary continental breakfast. Wireless Internet access. Airport transportation available. **$**

### ★HAMPTON INN

*22 Montage Mountain Road, Scranton, 570-342-7002, 800-426-7866;*
*www.hamptoninn.com*

129 rooms. Complimentary continental breakfast. Wireless Internet access. Pool. Whirlpool. Airport transportation available. **$**

**★★RADISSON LACKAWANNA STATION HOTEL SCRANTON**

*700 Lackawanna Ave., Scranton, 570-342-8300; www.radisson.com*

146 rooms. High-speed Internet access. Fitness center. Airport transportation available. Located in the historic Lackawanna train station building. **$**

### RESTAURANT
**★COOPER'S SEAFOOD HOUSE**

*701 N. Washington Ave., Scranton, 570-346-6883; www.coopers-seafood.com*

American menu. Lunch, dinner. Bar. Children's menu. **$$**

# SELLERSVILLE

### RESTAURANT
**★★WASHINGTON HOUSE**

*136 N. Main St., Sellersville, 215-257-3000; www.washingtonhouse.net*

American menu. Lunch, dinner. Late-night. Bar. Children's menu. Casual attire. **$$**

# SHAWNEE ON DELAWARE

*Information: Pocono Mountains Vacation Bureau Inc., 1004 Main St., Stroudsburg, 717-424-6050, 800-762-6667; www.poconos.org*

### WHAT TO SEE AND DO
**SHAWNEE MOUNTAIN SKI AREA**

*Hollow Road, Shawnee on Delaware, 570-421-7231; www.shawneemt.com*

Quad, triple, seven double chairlifts; patrol, school, rentals, snowmaking; cafeteria, bar, nursery. 23 slopes and trails; longest run one mile; vertical drop 700 feet. Night skiing. Half-day rates. Late November-March, daily.

**SHAWNEE PLACE PLAY & WATER PARK**

*Hollow Road, Shawnee on Delaware, 570-421-7231; www.shawneemt.com*

Kids can jump in a pool of plastic balls, swing on a cable glide, climb on cargo nets, glide down water slides and splash in a wading pool. Magic shows, picnics, video games, snack bar. Mid-June-early September, daily; late May-mid-June weekends only.

### HOTEL
**★★SHAWNEE INN AND GOLF RESORT**

*1 River Road, Shawnee on Delaware, 570-424-4000, 800-742-9633; www.shawneeinn.com*

103 rooms. Children's activity center. **$$**

# SOMERSET

James Whitcomb Riley described the countryside in his poem "Mongst the Hills of Somerset," starting the poem by saying, "Mongst the Hills of Somerset, I wish I were a 'roamin' yet." The county offers fishing, swimming, boating, hiking, biking, camping, skiing and ice skating.

*Information: Somerset County Chamber of Commerce, 601 N. Center Ave., Somerset, 814-445-6431; www.shol.com/smrst/somrst.htm*

# WHAT TO SEE AND DO

### KOOSER STATE PARK

*943 Glades Pike, Somerset, 814-445-8673; www.dcnr.state.pa.us*

Approximately 220 acres, this park contains a four-acre lake with fishing and a swimming beach (Memorial Day-Labor Day). The park also offers cross-country skiing and sledding in winter and picnicking and camping in summer (tent and trailer sites, cabins).

### LAUREL HILL STATE PARK

*1454 Laurel Hill Park Road, Somerset, 814-445-7725; www.dcnr.state.pa.us*

Swimming beach, snack bar, boating (mooring, launching). Hiking, hunting; snowmobiling, ice fishing. Picnicking snack bar. Tent and trailer sites.

### MOUNT DAVIS

*Somerset, 724-238-9533*

Highest point in state (3,213 feet).

### SOMERSET HISTORICAL CENTER

*10649 Somerset Pike, Somerset, 814-445-6077; www.somersethistoricalcenter.org*

Museum exhibits on rural life; outdoor display includes log house, log barn, covered bridge, sugarhouse. Bus tour (fee). Tuesday-Saturday.

## SPECIAL EVENTS

### MAPLE FESTIVAL

*Festival Park, 120 Meyers Ave., 814-634-0213; Somerset, www.pamaplefestival.com*

A weeklong celebration with quilting contests, an auto show, a parade and tractor show. March-April.

### MOUNTAIN CRAFT DAYS

*Somerset Historical Center, 10649 Somerset Pike, Somerset, 814-445-6077;*
*www.somersethistoricalcenter.org*

More than 150 traditional craft demonstrations, antique exhibits; entertainment. Early September.

### SOMERFEST

*Laurel Arts/Phillip Dressler Center for the Arts, 214 S. Harrison Ave., Somerset,*
*814-443-2433; www.laurelarts.org*

German festival: dancing, competitions, entertainment, food, tours. Mid-July.

## HOTELS

### ★★★INN AT GEORGIAN PLACE

*800 Georgian Place Drive, Somerset, 814-443-1043; www.theinnatgeorgianplace.com*

This bed and breakfast overlooks Lake Somerset and is packed with antiques. The restaurant offers classic dishes wish seasonal ingredients including salmon filet served over crimson lentils and harvest apples. 11 rooms. Children over 5 only. Complimentary full breakfast. **$**

★
★
★
★
★

### ★QUALITY INN

*215 Ramada Road, Somerset, 814-443-4646, 877-424-6423; www.choicehotels.com*

146 rooms. Pets accepted. High-speed Internet access. Indoor pool. Fitness center. **$**

## RESTAURANTS

### ★★OAKHURST TEA ROOM

*2409 Glades Pike, Somerset, 814-443-2897; www.oakhursttearoom.com*

American menu. Lunch, dinner, Sunday brunch. Closed Monday. Bar. Children's menu. Outdoor seating. **$$**

### ★★PINE GRILL

*800 N. Center Ave., Somerset, 814-445-2102; www.pinegrill.com*

Breakfast, lunch, dinner. Bar. Children's menu. **$**

# SOUTH STERLING

## HOTELS

### ★★★FRENCH MANOR

*50 Huntington Road, South Sterling, 570-676-3244, 877-720-6090;*
*www.thefrenchmanor.com*

Each guest room in this elegant inn shines with personal touches and lots of space. But don't let the antique ambience foul you; modern amenities abound in the rooms including DVD players and free high-speed Internet access. The Great Hall has two floor-to-ceiling fireplaces. 9 rooms. Wireless Internet access. No children allowed. Restaurant. Airport transportation available. **$$**

### ★★★STERLING INN

*Highway 191, South Sterling, 570-676-3311, 800-523-8200; www.thesterlinginn*

Built in the 1850s, this country Inn is perfect for families ready to hit the nearby ski areas or antiques looking for a new piece of history. Guest rooms have quilts on the beds and personalized homey touches. 54 rooms. Airport transportation available. **$**

# SPRUCE CREEK

## WHAT TO SEE AND DO

### INDIAN CAVERNS

*Highway 45, Spruce Creek, 814-632-7578; www.indiancaverns.com*

Indian Caverns was first excavated by Harold and Leonore Wertz just before the beginning of the Great Depression. When their expedition uncovered arrowheads and human remains, it became clear the site belonged to the Mohawk and Algonquin peoples. Today, the site is preserved and includes areas used for rituals of fire and sacrifice, carvings hundreds of years old and even a former hideout for notorious criminal David Lewis. Still on some of the walls are examples of American Indian picture writing. April-May, September-November, Thursday-Sunday; June-August, daily.

# ST. MARY'S

## HOTEL
### ★★★TOWNE HOUSE INN
*138 Center St., Saint Mary's, 814-781-1556, 800-851-1180*
This historic townhouse has beautiful stained glass windows and loads of antiques. 57 rooms. Complimentary continental breakfast. **$**

# STATE COLLEGE
Not surprisingly, State College is the home of Pennsylvania State University. In the beautiful Nittany Valley, the borough is surrounded by farmland famous for its production of oats and swine. Iron ore was discovered just east of town in 1790, and many iron furnaces later sprang up.

*Information: Centre County Convention & Visitors Bureau, 800 E. Park Ave.,*
*State College, 814-231-1400, 800-358-5466; www.visitpennstate.org*

## WHAT TO SEE AND DO
### AG HILL, THE COLLEGE OF AGRICULTURE
*College and Atherton streets, State College, 334- 844-2345; www.ag.auburn.edu*
Showplace for state's dairy industry including the dairy center, off Park Road near stadium, with five herds of cows, automatic milking equipment (daily). The creamery, Curtain Road, has retail salesroom for cheeses, milk, cream, ice cream (daily). Also test flower gardens off Park Road near East Halls. July-September.

### EARTH AND MINERAL SCIENCES MUSEUM
*Steidle Building, Pollock Road, State College, 814-865-6427;*
*www.ems.psu.edu/museum*
Exhibitions of ores, gems and fossils; automated displays; art gallery. Monday-Friday.

### MOUNT NITTANY VINEYARD & WINERY
*350 Houser Road, State College, 814-466-6373; www.mtnittanywinery.com*
Stone-faced, chalet-style building nestled on southern slopes of Mount Nittany. Tasting room offers variety of wines and view of large pond, vineyard and mountains. Group tastings (by appointment). Friday-Sunday; closed January.

### OLD MAIN
*College and Atherton streets, State College, 814-865-2501*
Present building, on site of original Old Main, uses many of the original stones; topped by lofty bell tower. Here are Henry Varnum Poor's land grant frescoes. Monday-Friday.

### PENNSYLVANIA STATE UNIVERSITY
*College and Atherton streets, State College, 814-865-4700; www.psu.edu*
Founded in 1855, today this university is home to more than 40,000 students. There are approximately 760 major buildings on this 15,984-acre campus, which is the land grant institution of Pennsylvania.

★
★
★
★
★

## WHIPPLE DAM STATE PARK

*State College, 814-667-3808*

Approximately 250 acres. Swimming beach, fishing, hunting, boating (launching, mooring). Hiking, Snowmobiling, ice-skating, ice fishing. Picnicking, snack bar.

## SPECIAL EVENTS

### CENTRE COUNTY GRANGE FAIR

*Centre Hall, 169 Homan Lane, State College, 814-364- 9212; www.grangefair.net*

Exhibits, livestock show, rides, concessions, entertainment. Last week in August.

### CENTRAL PENNSYLVANIA FESTIVAL OF THE ARTS

*403 S. Allen St. 201, State College, 814-237-3682; www.arts-festival.com*

Open-air display of visual and performing arts, indoor exhibits, demonstrations of arts and crafts; food booths. Mid-July.

## HOTELS

### ★★★ATHERTON HOTEL

*125 S. Atherton St., State College, 814-231-2100, 800-832-0132;*
*www.athertonhotel.net*

This inn is located half a mile from Penn State. The Anthropology Museum, Historic Boalsburg Village and Palmer Museum of Art are also nearby. Guest rooms are roomy with large picture windows and work desks. 150 rooms. Fitness center. Airport transportation available. $

### ★★AUTOPORT MOTEL & RESTAURANT

*1405 S. Atherton St., State College, 814-237-7666, 800-932-7678;*
*www.autoport.statecollege.com*

86 rooms. $

### ★★★CARNEGIE HOUSE

*100 Cricklewood Drive, State College, 814-234-2424, 800-229-5033;*
*www.carnegiehouse.com*

When you've conquered the links, stow your golf gear in your cozy guest room, relax in a deep library chair and have a celebratory drink. Carnegie House offers packages for golf and Penn State football weekends. Guest rooms have dormer windows and floral bedspreads. 22 rooms. Complimentary continental breakfast. Restaurant. Airport transportation available. $

### ★★DAYS INN

*240 S. Pugh St., State College, 814-238-8454; www.daysinn.com*

184 rooms. Pets accepted. Complimentary continental breakfast. High-speed Internet access. Pool. Fitness center. Airport transportation available. $

### ★HAMPTON INN

*1101 E. College Ave., State College, 814-231-1590, 800-426-7866;*
*www.hamptoninn.com*

121 rooms. Complimentary continental breakfast. Pool. Fitness center. Business center. Airport transportation available. $

### ★★★THE NITTANY LION INN
*200 W. Park Ave., State College, 800- 233-7505; www.pshs.psu.edu*

Managed by the surrounding University, this hotel offers standard rooms with free high-speed Internet access, king-sized beds and coffee makers. 223 rooms. High-speed Internet access. Restaurant, bar. Airport transportation available. Located on the main campus of Penn State. **$**

### ★★★TOFTREES RESORT AND FOUR STAR GOLF CLUB
*1 Country Club Lane, State College, 814-234-8000, 800-458-3602; www.toftrees.com*

This "home among the trees" sits in 1,500 wooded acres and offers private patios and balconies from which guests can enjoy the view. 113 rooms. Fitness center. Business center. Airport transportation available. **$**

## RESTAURANT
### ★★TAVERN
*220 E. College Ave., State College, 814-238-6116; www.thetavern.com*

Seafood menu. Dinner. Bar. Children's menu. Reservations recommended. **$$**

# STRASBURG

## WHAT TO SEE AND DO
### CHOO-CHOO BARN, TRAINTOWN, USA
*Highway 741 East, Strasburg, 717-687-7911; www.choochoobarn.com*

A 1,700-square-foot layout of Lancaster County in miniature, featuring 22 operating trains and more than 150 animated and automated figures and vehicles. Gift shop. Picnicking. Mid-March-December, daily.

### MILL BRIDGE VILLAGE
*South Ronks and Soudersburg Roads, Strasburg, 717-687-8181, 800-645-2744; www.millbridge.com*

Restored historic colonial mill village with operating water-powered gristmill, covered bridge; country crafts include broom-making, quilting, candlemaking, blacksmithing; quilt log cabin; Amish kitchen exhibit; music boxes and nickelodeons; horse-drawn hay and carriage rides; 1890s playground; picnicking. Amish house and schoolhouse tour available. Oktoberfest (October weekends). Camp resort (early April-October, daily; fee). Village (early April-November, daily).

### NATIONAL TOY TRAIN MUSEUM
*300 Paradise Lane, Strasburg, 717-687-8976*

Trains from the 1880s to present; live operating layouts; movies; rare, unusual and specialty trains. May-October, daily; April and November-December, Saturday-Sunday.

### RAILROAD MUSEUM OF PENNSYLVANIA
*300 Gap Road, Strasburg, 717-687-8628; www.rrmuseumpa.org*

More than 50 locomotives, freight and passenger cars dating from 1825; audiovisual exhibits; railroading memorabilia. Picnicking. April-October, daily; November-March, Tuesday-Sunday.

**PENNSYLVANIA**

★
★
★
★
★

### STRASBURG RAILROAD

*Highway 741 East, Strasburg, 717-687-7522; www.strasburgrailroad.com*

Railroad runs 4½ miles to Paradise. Picnic stop. This 160-year-old line uses late 19th-century coaches, various steam locomotives. April-October, daily; winter, weekends.

## HOTEL

### ★★★NETHERLANDS INN & SPA

*1400 Historic Drive, Route 896, Strasburg, 717-687-7691*

Situated on 18 private acres, this inn gives you room to roam. Take a swim in the outdoor pool or go for a bike ride along the many trails. 102 rooms. Complimentary full breakfast. Wireless Internet access. Fitness center. Pool. $

# STROUDSBURG

*Information: Pocono Mountains Vacation Bureau, Inc., 1004 Main St., Stroudsburg, 570-424-6050, 800-762-6667; www.poconos.org*

## WHAT TO SEE AND DO

### CANOEING

*Stroudsburg, 570-421-0180*

Canoe trips on the Delaware River; equipment provided; also transportation to and from the river (May-October).

### DELAWARE WATER GAP KOA

*233 Hollow Road, East Stroudsburg, 570-223-8000, 800-562-0375; www.koa.com*

This KOA campground has both wooded and open sites. Electrical hook-ups, propane station. Laundry services, convenience store, outdoor pool, playground, game room, organized activities.

### QUIET VALLEY LIVING HISTORICAL FARM

*1000 Turkey Hill Road, Stroudsburg, 570-992-6161; www.quietvalley.org*

A log house built in 1765 with a kitchen and parlor added 1892; 12 other original or reconstructed buildings. Demonstrations of seasonal farm activities. Farm animals, garden, gift shop. Guided tours with costumed guides. Late June-Labor Day, Tuesday-Sunday.

### STROUD MANSION

*900 Main St., Stroudsburg, 570-421-7703*

Built by founder of city in the 18th century; houses Historical Society of Monroe County. Historical artifacts, genealogical records. Tours. Tuesday-Friday. Closed Sunday and Monday.

## HOTELS

### ★★BEST WESTERN POCONO INN

*700 Main St., Stroudsburg, 570-421-2200, 888-508-2378;*
*www.bestwesternpocono.com*

90 rooms. Complimentary continental breakfast. High-speed Internet access. Pool. $

## ★★CAESARS BROOKDALE

*Highway 611 and Brookdale Road, Scotrun, 570-839-8844, 800-233-4141;*
*www.caesarspoconoresorts.com*
119 rooms. Children's activity center. **$$**

## ★★SHANNON INN

*US Route 209 and State Route 447, Stroudsburg, 570-424-1951, 800-424-8052;*
*www.shannoninn.com*
120 rooms. Complimentary continental breakfast. Wireless Internet access. Pool.
Business center. **$**

### RESTAURANTS
### ★ARLINGTON DINER

*834 N. Ninth St., Stroudsburg, 570-421-2329*
American menu. Breakfast, lunch, dinner. Children's menu. Casual attire. **$$**

### ★BROWNIE'S IN THE BURG

*700 Main St., Stroudsburg, 570-421-2200; www.browniesintheburg.com*
American menu. Breakfast, lunch, dinner. Bar. Casual attire. **$$**

### ★SARAH STREET GRILL

*550 Quaker Alley, Stroudsburg, 570-424-9120; www.sarahstreetgrill.com*
American, sushi menu. Lunch, dinner. Bar. Children's menu. Casual attire. Outdoor
seating. **$$**

### ★★STONE BAR INN

*Highway 209, Stroudsburg, 570-992-6634; www.stonebar.com*
American menu. Dinner. Bar. Children's menu. Reservations recommended. Outdoor
seating. **$$**

# SWARTHMORE

### WHAT TO SEE AND DO
### SWARTHMORE COLLEGE

*500 College Ave., Swarthmore, 610-328-8000; www.swarthmore.edu*
Coeducational college of 1,320 students. Founded in 1864, the campus is located on
a wooded 357-acre campus and features Friends Historical Library and Peace Collec-
tion, an art gallery, concert hall, performing arts center, observatory, terraced grass
amphitheater, and more. Symposia, exhibits, music and dance programs are open to
the public.

# TITUSVILLE

Titusville spreads from the banks of Oil Creek, so called because of the oil that
appeared on its surface. Edwin L. Drake drilled the first successful oil well in the
world on August 27, 1859. Overnight, Titusville became the center of the worldwide
oil industry.
*Information: Titusville Area Chamber of Commerce, 202 W. Central Ave., Titusville,*
*814-827-2941; www.titusvillechamber.com*

★
★
★
★
★

## WHAT TO SEE AND DO
### DRAKE WELL MUSEUM
*205 Museum Lane, Titusville, 814-827-2797; www.drakewell.org*
Site of world's first oil well; operating replica of Drake derrick and engine house; picnic area. Museum contains dioramas, working models, life-size exhibits depicting history of oil. May-October, daily; November-April, Tuesday-Saturday, Sunday afternoons.

## HOTEL
### ★★CROSS CREEK RESORT
*Route 8 South, Titusville, 814-827-9611, 800-461-3173; www.crosscreekresort.com*
94 rooms. Restaurant. $

# TOWANDA
On the north branch of the Susquehanna River, Towanda takes its name from a Native American word meaning "where we bury the dead."

In 1793, the Asylum Company purchased 1,600 acres of these wild valleys as a refuge for Marie Antoinette of France, should she escape to America. "La Grande Maison" a queenly house, was built. French noblemen settled here and a thriving community (called Azilum) was planned. The colony was unsuccessful and most of its founders returned to France. Many of their descendants, however, still live in Bradford County.

*Information: Endless Mountains Visitors Bureau, 712 Route 6 East, Tunkhannock, 570-836-5431, 800-769-8999; www.endlessmountains.org*

★
★
★
★
★

## WHAT TO SEE AND DO
### DAVID WILMOT'S BURIAL PLACE
*Riverside Cemetery, William and Chestnut streets, Towanda*
Congressman, senator, leader of the Free Soil Party, Wilmot introduced the Wilmot Proviso in Congress, which would have required the U.S. to outlaw slavery in any lands purchased from Mexico. This was an important factor in the dissension between North and South that led to the Civil War.

### FRENCH AZILUM
*Route 456, Towanda, 570-265-3376; www.frenchazilum.com*
Site of colony for refugees from the French Revolution. Three cabins with crafts, tool exhibits; log cabin museum; Laporte House, built by son of one of colony's founders, reflects elegant French influence. Special events. Guided tours. June-August, Wednesday-Sunday; May, September-October, Saturday-Sunday.

# TUNKHANNOCK

## HOTEL
### ★★SHADOWBROOK INN AND RESORT
*615 Route 6 East, Tunkhannock, 570-836-2151, 800-955-0295;*
*www.shadowbrookresort.com*
73 rooms. Complimentary continental breakfast. Bar. Pool. Fitness center. $

## RESTAURANT
### ★FIREPLACE
*1111 PA 6 West, Tunkhannock, 570-836-9662; www.tunkhannock.com/thefireplace*
American menu. Lunch, dinner. Bar. Children's menu. $$

# UNIONTOWN
Coal and its byproducts made Uniontown prosperous, but with the decline in coal mining, the city has developed a more diverse economic base. First known as Union, this city has been the Fayette County seat since 1784. Uniontown was a hotbed of the Whiskey Rebellion, and federal troops were sent here in 1794.
*Information: Laurel Highlands Visitors Bureau, 120 E. Main St., Ligonier,*
*724-238-5661; www.laurelhighlands.org*

## WHAT TO SEE AND DO
### FORT NECESSITY NATIONAL BATTLEFIELD
*1 Washington Parkway, Farmington, 724-329-5512*
The site of Washington's first major battle and the opening battle of the French and Indian War. This land was known as the Great Meadows. A portion was later purchased by Washington, who owned it until his death. A replica of the original fort was built on the site following an archaeological survey in 1953. Picnic area (mid-spring-late fall).

### FRIENDSHIP HILL NATIONAL HISTORIC SITE
*1 Washington Parkway, Uniontown, 724-329-5512; www.nps.gov/frhi*
Preserves the restored home of Albert Gallatin, a Swiss immigrant who served his adopted country, in public and private life, for nearly seven decades. Gallatin made significant contributions to the young Republic in the fields of finance, politics, diplomacy and scholarship. He is best known as the Treasury Secretary under Jefferson and Madison. Exhibits, audiovisual program and audio tour provide information. Daily.

### JUMONVILLE GLEN
*200 Caverns Park Road, Uniontown*
Site of skirmish between British and French forces that led to the battle at Fort Necessity. Mid-April-mid-October.

### MOUNTAIN STREAMS & TRAILS OUTFITTERS
*Uniontown, 724-329-8810, 800-723-8669; www.mtstreams.com*
Also on the Youghiogheny, Big Sandy, Cheat and Tygart's Valley rivers. Also rentals of whitewater rafts, canoes, trail bikes.

### RIVER TOURS
Whitewater rafting on the Youghiogheny River; some of the wildest and most scenic in the eastern United States. Cost includes equipment and professional guides. Age limits are imposed because of level of difficulty.

### VISITOR CENTER
Exhibits on battle at Great Meadows; audiovisual program. Daily.

★
★
★
★
★

**WHITE WATER ADVENTURERS**

*6 Negley St., Uniontown, 800-992-7238; www.wwaraft.com*

**WILDERNESS VOYAGEURS**

*Uniontown, 800-272-4141; www.wilderness-voyageurs.com*

Trips on the lower and middle Youghiogheny. Also bicycle, canoe rentals; kayak and canoe lessons. Rafting, mountain biking.

## HOTEL
### ★★HOLIDAY INN

*700 W. Main St., Uniontown, 724-437-2816, 800-465-4329; www.hiuniontown.com*

179 rooms. High-speed Internet access. Restaurant. Pool. Fitness center. Business center. $

## SPECIALTY LODGING
### INNE AT WATSON'S CHOICE

*234 Balsinger Road, Uniontown, 724-437-4999, 888-820-5380; www.watsonschoice.com*

7 rooms. No children allowed. Complimentary full breakfast. $

## RESTAURANT
### ★★★COAL BARON

*7606 National Pike, Uniontown, 724-439-0111*

Small and intimate, this 20-year-old-restaurant offers a broad, continental menu. A painting of a coal tipple adorns the dining room wall, in honor of the establishment's name. American menu. Lunch, dinner. Closed Monday. Bar. Children's menu. Jacket required. Valet parking. $$

★
★★★
★★★★
★★★
★

# VALLEY FORGE NATIONAL HISTORICAL PARK

Two thousand soldiers died here from hunger, disease and cold, but General George Washington and his beleaguered army ultimately triumphed over the British in 1778. Today, Valley Forge has come to symbolize American perseverance and sacrifice on a lush, hilly, 3,600-acre expanse with rich historical significance and beautiful scenery. Visitors can tour the park by car or bus and see Washington's restored stone headquarters, log soldier huts, bronze statues and monuments, and weapons and equipment used during the American Revolution. You can even learn how Washington's soldiers were taught to load and fire their muskets. The visitor's center features exhibits, artifacts, a gift shop and an 18-minute film. Choose from a 16-mile walking trail, 10-mile horse trails, a bike path or a 10-mile self-guided tour. Picnic areas are available as well. Daily 9 a.m.-5 p.m.

*Information: 610-783-1077; www.nps.gov/vafo*

## WHAT TO SEE AND DO
### AUTO TAPE TOUR

*Valley Forge, 610-783-5788*

Self-guided tour dramatizes Washington's winter encampment. Bookstore (two-hour tape rental, May-October, daily).

## BUS TOUR

*Valley Forge, 610-783-5788*

Narrated tour includes stops at historic sites. Tours leave from Visitor Center. June-Labor Day, tour departures every half-hour; Labor Day-October, weekends only.

## NATIONAL MEMORIAL ARCH

Built in 1917 to commemorate Washington's army. Inscribed in the arch is a quote from General Washington: "Naked and starving as they are, we cannot enough admire the incomparable patience and fidelity of the soldiery."

## SOLDIER LIFE PROGRAM

Interpreters present programs detailing camp life of the Continental Army soldier (offered at various times during the year).

## VISITOR CENTER

*Highway 23 and Gulph Road, Valley Forge, 610-783-1077; www.valleyforge.org*

Information, exhibits, audiovisual program, tour maps. Bus tours depart from here. Daily.

## WASHINGTON HEADQUARTERS

Park staff will provide information about the house where Washington lived for six months and which served as military headquarters for the Continental Army during that time. Daily. Fee charged. April-November.

## WASHINGTON MEMORIAL CHAPEL

*Highway 23, Valley Forge, 610-783-0120; www.washingtonmemorialchapel.org*

Private property within park boundaries. Stained-glass windows depict the story of the New World, its discovery and development; hand-carved oak choir stalls, Pews of the Patriots and Roof of the Republic bearing the State Seal of all the states. Also part of the chapel is the 58 cast-bell Washington Memorial National Carillon, with bells honoring states and territories.

## RESTAURANT

### ★★★KENNEDY-SUPPLEE MANSION

*1100 W. Valley Forge Road, Valley Forge, 610-337-3777*

Enjoy classic American fare in one of eight dining rooms of this 1850s mansion. American menu. Lunch, dinner. Closed Sunday. Bar. Jacket required (dinner). Valet parking. $$$

# WARREN

At the junction of the Allegheny and Conewango rivers, Warren is the headquarters and gateway of the famous Allegheny National Forest. Named for General Joseph Warren, an American patriot killed in the Battle of Bunker Hill, the town was once the point where great flotillas of logs were formed for the journey to Pittsburgh or Cincinnati.

*Information: Warren County Chamber of Commerce, 308 Market St., Warren, 814-723-3050 or Travel Northern Alleghenies, 315 Second St., Warren, 814-726-1222; www.warrenpachamber.com*

**371**

**PENNSYLVANIA**

★
★
★
★
★

## WHAT TO SEE AND DO
### ALLEGHENY NATIONAL FOREST
*222 Liberty St., Warren, 814-723-5150*

More than 510,000 acres South and East on Highways 6, 62, located in Warren, Forest, McKean and Elk counties. Black bear, whitetail deer, wild turkey, a diversity of small birds and mammals; streams and reservoirs with trout, walleye, muskellunge, northern pike and bass; rugged hills, quiet valleys, open meadows, dense forest. These lures, plus swimming, boating, hiking, camping and picnicking facilities, draw more than 2 million visitors a year. Hundreds of campsites; fees are charged at some recreation sites.

### BUCKALOONS RECREATION AREA
*Klondike, Bradford, 814-362-4613*

Site of former Native American village on the banks of the Allegheny River. Boat launching, Picnicking, Camping (fee). Seneca Interpretive Trail.

### KINZUA DAM AND ALLEGHENY RESERVOIR
*1205 Kinzua Road, Warren, 814-726-0661*

Dam (179 feet high, 1,897 feet long) with 27-mile-long lake. Swimming, fishing, boating (ramps, rentals; fees). Picnicking, overlooks. Camping (fee). Kinzua Dam Visitor Center has displays. Kinzua Point-Information Center, 4 miles northeast of dam, 814-726-1291. Some fees. (It is possible that the Highway 59 bridge, 1½ miles east of Kinzua Dam, will be closed; phone ahead for information.)

# WASHINGTON

Originally a Native American village known as Catfish Camp, the village of Bassettown became Washington during the Revolution. During the Whiskey Rebellion, the town was a center of protest against the new federal government's tax. The arrival of federal troops quieted the rebellious farmers. Washington and Jefferson College is located here.
*Information: Washington County Tourism Promotion Agency, Franklin Mall,*
*1500 W. Chestnut St., Washington, 724-228-5520, 800-531-4114;*
*www.washpatourism.org*

## WHAT TO SEE AND DO
### DAVID BRADFORD HOUSE
*175 S. Main St., Washington, 724-222-3604; www.bradfordhouse.org*

Restored frontier home of a leader of the Whiskey Rebellion. April-mid-December, Wednesday-Saturday 11 a.m.-4 p.m., Thursday 2-7 p.m.; also Sunday afternoons.

### LEMOYNE HOUSE
*49 E. Maiden St., Washington, 724-225-6740; www.wchspa.org*

Abolitionist's home, built by the LeMoyne family, was a stop on the underground railroad; period furnishings, paintings, library; gardens; museum shop. Administered by Washington County Historical Society. January-February, Tuesday-Friday 11 a.m.-4 p.m.; March-December, Tuesday-Saturday.

### PENNSYLVANIA TROLLEY MUSEUM
*1 Museum Road, Washington, 724-228-9256; www.pa-trolley.org*

Museum displays include more than 35 trolley cars dating from 1894. Scenic trolley ride; car barn and trolley-restoration shop; visitor center and gift shop with exhibit, video presentation and picnic area. June-August, daily; April-May and September-December, weekends 11 a.m.-5 p.m.

## HOTEL
### ★★HOLIDAY INN
*340 Racetrack Road, Washington, 724-222-6200, 800-465-4329; www.holidayinn.com*
138 rooms. High-speed Internet access. Outdoor pool. Airport transportation available. $

# WASHINGTON CROSSING HISTORIC PARK
In a blinding snowstorm on Christmas night 1776, George Washington and 2,400 soldiers crossed the Delaware River from the Pennsylvania shore and marched to Trenton, surprising the celebrating Hessian mercenaries and capturing the city. Washington's feat was a turning point of the Revolutionary War. Tuesday-Sunday.
*Information: 215-493-4076; www.ushistory.org*

## WHAT TO SEE AND DO
### AREA OF EMBARKATION
Marked by a tall granite shaft supporting Washington's statue.

### BOWMAN'S HILL WILDFLOWER PRESERVE
*New Hope, 215-862-2924; www.bhwp.org*
Pennsylvania's native plants come into focus at this 134-acre preserve located 40 miles northeast of Philadelphia. Hike or walk along woodland, a meadow, a creek or an arboretum. Botanic enthusiasts will discover 1,000 species of trees, shrubs, ferns, vines and herbaceous wildflowers. There are many contemplative places for meditation and study, scenic picnic spots and several historic sites within hiking distance. Head five miles south to Washington Crossing Historic Park (215-493-4076), where George Washington crossed the Delaware River in 1776. Bowman's Hill Tower, a lookout commemorating the American Revolution, offers a view of the Delaware River and rolling countryside one mile on foot or by car (215-862-3155). Nearby is New Hope, a perfect place for antiquing, art gallery hopping, shopping, or taking a mule barge ride on the Delaware Canal. Daily.

### CONCENTRATION VALLEY
Where Washington assembled troops for raid on Trenton.

### MCCONKEY FERRY INN
This 1752 inn has been restored as an historic house. Sold in 1777 to Benjamin Taylor, whose descendents established the 19th-century village of Taylorsville.

### MEMORIAL BUILDING
*1112 River Road, Washington Crossing, 215-493-4076;*
*www.ushistory.org/washingtoncrossing*
Near Point of Embarkation. Houses copy of Emanuel Leutze's painting, "Washington Crossing the Delaware." Movie shown five times a day.

### MEMORIAL FLAGSTAFF
Bowman's Hill. Marks graves of unknown Continentals who died during encampment.

373

PENNSYLVANIA

★
★
★
★
★

## SPECIAL EVENT

### THE CROSSING

*1112 River Road, Washington Crossing, 215-493-4076*

Reenactment of Washington's crossing of the Delaware River, Christmas night in 1776. December.

## SPECIALTY LODGING

### INN TO THE WOODS

*150 Glenwood Drive, Washington Crossing, 215-493-1974, 800-574-1974;*
*www.inn-bucks.com*

6 rooms. Children over 12 years only. Complimentary full breakfast. **$$**

# WAYNE

## HOTELS

### ★★COURTYARD BY MARRIOTT

*1100 Drummers Lane, Wayne, 610-687-6700, 800-320-5748; www.courtyard.com*

150 rooms. Wireless Internet access. Pool. Whirlpool. Fitness center. **$**

### ★★★WAYNE HOTEL

*139 E. Lancaster Ave., Wayne, 610-687-5000, 800-962-5850; www.waynehotel.com*

Located 18 miles west of Philadelphia, this restored property reflects the elegance of a time past with its wraparound porch and antique reproduction furnishing. Individually decorated guest rooms feature voice mail, data ports and direct dial telephones. 38 rooms. Complimentary continental breakfast. Wireless Internet access. Airport transportation available. **$**

### ★★★WYNDHAM VALLEY FORGE HOTEL

*888 Chesterbrook Blvd., Wayne, 610-647-6700, 877-999-3223; www.vssuites.com*

229 rooms. Airport transportation available. **$$**

## RESTAURANTS

### ★★★TAQUET

*139 E. Lancaster Ave., Wayne, 610-687-5005; www.taquet.com*

This elegant Main Line restaurant prides itself on serving local products prepared with a French sensibility. Entrees include Norwegian salmon with tamarind barbeque glaze and vegetable couscous or Nebraska center-cut beef filet mignon with a cabernet wine reduction. French menu. Lunch, dinner. Closed Sunday. Bar. Outdoor seating. **$$**

### ★★TOWN AND COUNTRY GRILLE

*888 Chesterbrook Blvd., Wayne, 610-647-6700; www.wyndham.com*

Breakfast, lunch, dinner, Sunday brunch. Bar. Children's menu. **$$**

# WELLSBORO

Wellsboro is the gateway to Pennsylvania's "canyon country." Settled largely by New Englanders, the area yields coal, natural gas, hardwoods, maple syrup and farm products.

*Information: Wellsboro Area Chamber of Commerce, 114 Main St., Wellsboro,*
*570-724-1926; www.wellsboropa.com*

# WHAT TO SEE AND DO
## AUTO TOURS
There are more than a million acres of forests, mountains and streams to be explored. The Wellsboro Area Chamber of Commerce has published a map of three tours.

## RED ARROW TOUR
Follows Highway 660 southwest 10 miles from Wellsboro to Leonard Harrison State Park. Lookout Point, near the parking area, has large picnic area nearby. Path winds one mile from park to bottom of gorge, through shady glens, past waterfalls.

## ROBINSON HOUSE MUSEUM
*120 Main St., Wellsboro, 570-724-6116*
Built in 1820, this museum houses turn-of-the-century artifacts; genealogical library. Monday-Friday afternoons.

## SKI SAWMILL FAMILY RESORT
*383 Oregon Hill Road, Morris Wellsboro, 570-353-7521, 800-532-7669;*
*www.skisawmill.com*
Chairlift, three T-bars; patrol, school, rentals, snowmaking; cafeteria, restaurant, bar. Longest run 3,250 feet; vertical drop 515 feet. December-March, daily Year-round activities.

## WHITE ARROW TOUR
Leads from the Switchbacks (1½ miles west of Bradley Wales Park), three miles South to Leetonia, once a prosperous lumber village, now occupied by State Forest Rangers; then west and north to Cushman View, Wilson Point Road, Lee Fire Tower, Cedar Run Mountain Road and Highway 6; approximately 75 miles.

## YELLOW ARROW TOUR
Leads from Leonard Harrison State Park, back on Highway 660, northwest on Highway 362, then quarter mile west on Highway 6 to Colton Point Road for views of the canyon and Four Mile Run Country. At Colton Point State Park (observation points, picnic shelters, fireplaces) the arrows follow Pine Creek South on old lumbering railroad tracks, converted into roadways called the "Switchbacks," to Bradley Wales Park overlooking Tiadaghton, the next lookout point on Pine Creek. From here continue south on West Rim Road to Blackwell. From Blackwell, northeast on Highway 414 to Morris, then north on Highway 287 to Wellsboro—a circle of 65 miles.

# SPECIAL EVENT
## PENNSYLVANIA STATE LAUREL FESTIVAL
*114 Main St., Wellsboro*
Week-long event includes parade of floats, marching musical and precision units, antique cars, laurel queen contestants; crowning of the queen; arts and crafts; children's pet and hobby parade, exhibits and displays. Mid-June.

PENNSYLVANIA

★
★
★
★
★

## HOTELS

### ★CANYON MOTEL

*18 East Ave., Wellsboro, 570-724-1681, 800-255-2718; www.canyonmotel.com*
31 rooms. Complimentary continental breakfast. High-speed Internet access. Indoor pool. Fitness center. $

### KALTENBACH'S BED AND BREAKFAST

*Stony Fork Road, Wellsboro, 570-724-4954, 800-772-4954; www.kaltenbachsinn.com*
10 rooms. Complimentary full breakfast. $

### ★★PENN WELLS HOTEL & LODGE

*62 Main St., Wellsboro, 570-724-2111, 800-545-2446; www.pennwells.com*
73 rooms. Indoor pool. Fitness center. $

### ★SHERWOOD MOTEL

*2 Main St., Wellsboro, 570-724-3424, 800-626-5802; www.sherwoodmotel.org*
42 rooms. Wireless Internet access. Outdoor pool. $

# WEST CHESTER

In the heart of three Pennsylvania Revolutionary War historic sites—Brandywine, Paoli and Valley Forge—West Chester today is a university and residential community with fine examples of Greek Revival and Victorian architecture.
*Information: Chester County Tourist Bureau, 601 Westtown Road, West Chester, 610-344-6365, 800-228-9933; www.brandywinevalley.com*

## HOTEL

### ★★HOLIDAY INN

*943 S. High St., West Chester, 610-692-1900, 800-465-4329; www.holidayinn.com*
143 rooms. High-speed Internet access. Outdoor pool. Airport transportation available. $

## RESTAURANT

### ★★GILMORE'S

*133 E. Gay St., West Chester, 610-431-2800; www.gilmoresrestaurant.com*
French menu. Dinner. Closed Sunday, Monday; also one week in winter and one week in summer. $$$

# WEST CONSHOHOCKEN

## HOTEL

### ★★★MARRIOTT PHILADELPHIA WEST

*111 Crawford Ave., West Conshohocken, 610-941-5600, 800-237-3639; www.marriott.com*
This hotel is located just miles from the Valley Forge National Park, Philadelphia Zoo, Museum of Art and Franklin Institute, as well as many other local points of interest. Rooms are sizeable and well-appointed. 286 rooms. High-speed Internet access. Airport transportation available. $$

# WHITE HAVEN

*Information: Pocono Mountains Vacation Bureau, 1004 Main St., Stroudsburg,*
*570-424-6050, 800-762-6667; www.poconos.org*

## WHAT TO SEE AND DO
### HICKORY RUN STATE PARK

*Hickory Run, White Haven, 570-443-0400; www.visit.pa.park.com*

Approximately 15,500 acres of scenic area. Swimming beach, fishing, hunting; hiking; cross-country skiing, snowmobiling, sledding, ice skating, ice fishing. Picnicking, playground, snack bar, store. Tent and trailer sites. Standard fees.

## HOTELS
### ★COMFORT INN

*Highway 940, White Haven, 570-443-8461, 877-424-6423; www.choicehotels.com*

123 rooms. **$**

### ★★MOUNTAIN LAUREL RESORT AND SPA

*Interstate 80 at Pennsylvania Turnpike Northeast exit, White Haven, 570-443-8411;*
*www.mountainlaurelresort.com*

250 rooms. Children's activity center. Airport transportation available. **$$**

## RESTAURANT
### ★★★POWERHOUSE

*1 Powerhouse Road, White Haven, 570-443-4480; www.powerhouseeatery.net*

This restaurant is popular for its Italian-American menu. Its brick walls and exposed pipes and valves remind diners of its earlier function as a coal-fueled power plant. American, Italian menu. Lunch (Sunday), dinner. Bar. Reservations recommended (weekends). **$$**

# WILKES BARRE

Named in honor of two members of the British Parliament who championed individual rights and supported the colonies, Wilkes-Barre and the Wyoming Valley were settled by pioneers from Connecticut. Pennsylvania and Connecticut waged the Pennamite-Yankee War, the first phase ending in 1771 with Connecticut in control of the valley. It was later resumed until Connecticut relinquished its claims in 1800. Wilkes-Barre was burned by the Native Americans and Tories during the Revolution and again by Connecticut settlers protesting the Decree of Trenton, in which Congress favored Pennsylvania's claim to the territory. Discovery of anthracite coal in the valley sparked the town's growth after Judge Jesse Fell demonstrated that anthracite could be burned in a grate without forced draft.

*Information: Northeast Pennsylvania Convention & Visitors Bureau,*
*99 Glenmaura National Blvd., Scranton, 800-229-3526; www.visitnepa.org*

## HOTELS
### ★★BEST WESTERN EAST MOUNTAIN INN & SUITES

*2400 E. End Blvd., Wilkes Barre, 570-822-1011, 800-780-7234; www.bestwestern.com*

156 rooms. High-speed Internet access. Pool. Fitness center. Airport transportation available. **$**

### ★HAMPTON INN
*1063 Highway 315, Wilkes Barre, 570-825-3838, 800-426-7866; www.hamptoninn.com*
123 rooms. Complimentary continental breakfast. **$**

### ★★HOLIDAY INN
*880 Kidder St., Wilkes Barre, 570-824-8901, 888-466-9272; www.holidayinn.com*
120 rooms. Pets accepted. Complimentary continental breakfast. High-speed Internet access. Outdoor pool. **$**

### ★★★WOODLANDS INN & RESORT
*1073 Highway 315, Wilkes Barre, 570-824-9831, 800-762-2222;*
*www.thewoodlandsresort.com*
The Woodlands Inn & Resort offers urban warriors a chance to bask in the simple joys of nature. This wooded resort on 40 acres in the foothills of the Poconos is a perfect place to spend a vacation, a romantic getaway or even a corporate retreat. Golf and skiing are a short distance away, and the resort offers five nightclubs, bars and lounges, with live jazz and dancing. 179 rooms. Wireless Internet access. Pool. Airport transportation available. **$$$**

## RESTAURANT
### ★★SABER ROOM
*94 Butler St., Wilkes Barre, 570-829-5743; www.saberroom.com*
American menu. Lunch, dinner. Closed Sunday. Bar. Reservations recommended. **$$**

# WILLIAMSPORT

Now famous as the birthplace of Little League baseball, Williamsport was once known as the "lumber capital of the world." In 1870, a log boom extended seven miles up the Susquehanna River, and 300 million feet of sawed lumber were produced each year. When the timber was exhausted, the city developed diversified industry and remained prosperous. The historic district of Williamsport, known as "millionaire's row," includes homes of former lumber barons.

*Information: Lycoming County Tourist Promotion Agency, 454 Pine St., Williamsport, 800-358-9900; www.williamsportmd.gov*

## WHAT TO SEE AND DO
### "HIAWATHA"
*1500 W. Third St., Williamsport, 570-326-2500, 800-248-9287;*
*www.ridehiawatha.com*
Sightseeing trips down Susquehanna River aboard replica of an old-fashioned paddle-wheel riverboat. Public cruises May-October, Tuesday-Sunday.

### LITTLE LEAGUE BASEBALL INTERNATIONAL HEADQUARTERS
*Route 15, Williamsport, 570-326-1921; www.littleleague.org*
Summer baseball camp and Little League World Series Stadium are here. Monday-Friday.

### LITTLE LEAGUE BASEBALL MUSEUM
*Highway 15, Williamsport, 570-326-3607; www.littleleague.org*
Memorial Day-Labor Day, daily; rest of year, Monday, Thursday-Sunday.

### LITTLE PINE STATE PARK

*Williamsport, 570-753-6000; www.state.pa.us*

Approximately 2,000 acres. Swimming beach, fishing, boating (ramps, mooring); hunting; cross-country skiing, snowmobiling, sledding, ice skating, ice fishing. Picnicking, playground, store. Tent and trailer sites (electric hook-ups). Interpretive program.

### SHEMPP TOY TRAIN COLLECTION

Extensive toy train collection. More than 350 train sets on display, including the entire Lionel collection. Two detailed running displays allow visitors to start trains, blow whistles. Twelve unique trains include an American Flyer 3117 and Lionel "Super 381."

### THOMAS T. THABER MUSEUM OF THE LYCOMING COUNTY HISTORICAL SOCIETY

*858 W. Fourth St., Williamsport, 570-326-3326; www.lycominglineage.com*

Exhibits on regional history from 10,000 B.C. to present. Exhibits include Native American, frontier era; canals, steam fire engine and hose cart; military history; general store, blacksmith shop, woodworker's shop, gristmill, crafts and industry; Victorian parlor and furnished period rooms; wildlife, sports and Little League; lumber business. May-October, daily, November-April, Tuesday-Sunday.

## SPECIAL EVENTS

### LITTLE LEAGUE WORLD SERIES

Teams from all over the world compete. Third week in August.

### LYCOMING COUNTY FAIR

More than 50 acres of amusements, commercial displays, livestock judging, demolition derbies, grandstand entertainment, food. Mid-July.

### VICTORIAN SUNDAY

House tours, flower show, entertainment. Second Sunday in June.

## HOTELS

### ★★BEST WESTERN WILLIAMSPORT INN

*1840 E. Third St., Williamsport, 570-326-1981; www.bestwestern.com*

170 rooms. Pets accepted. High-speed Internet access. Pool. Fitness center. $

### ★★HOLIDAY INN

*100 Pine St., Williamsport, 570-327-8231, 800-315-2621; www.holidayinn.com*

148 rooms. High-speed Internet access. Indoor pool. Airport transportation available. $

### ★★GENETTI HOTEL & SUITES

*200 W. Fourth St., Williamsport, 570-326-6600, 800-321-1388; www.genetti.com*

206 rooms. Pets accepted. Wireless Internet access. Airport transportation available. $

**379**

**PENNSYLVANIA**

# WILLOW GROVE

## WHAT TO SEE AND DO
### BRYN ATHYN CATHEDRAL
*1000 Cathedral Road, Bryn Athyn, 215-947-0266; www.brynathyncathedral.org*
Outstanding example of Gothic architecture. Free guided tours April-November, Tuesday-Sunday.

## HOTELS
### ★★COURTYARD BY MARRIOTT
*2350 Easton Road, Willow Grove, 215-830-0550; www.courtyard.com*
149 rooms. High-speed Internet access. Indoor pool. Whirlpool. Fitness center. Airport transportation available. $

### ★HAMPTON INN
*1500 Easton Road, Willow Grove, 215-659-3535, 800-426-7866;*
*www.hamptoninn.com*
150 rooms. Complimentary continental breakfast. High-speed Internet access. Fitness center. Airport transportation available. $

# WYOMISSING

## HOTELS

### ★★INN AT READING
*1040 N. Park Road, Wyomissing, 610-372-7811, 800-383-9713; www.innatreading.com*
250 rooms. Complimentary full breakfast. Wireless Internet access. Airport transportation available. $

### ★★SHERATON READING HOTEL
*1741 W. Papermill Road, Wyomissing, 610-376-3811; www.sheratonreadingpa.com*
254 rooms. Airport transportation available. $

# YORK
York claims to be the first capital of the United States. The Continental Congress met here in 1777 and adopted the Articles of Confederation, using the phrase "United States of America" for the first time. The first Pennsylvania town founded west of the Susquehanna River, York was and is still based on an agricultural and industrial economy. The city is dotted with 17 historical markers and 35 brass or bronze tablets marking historical events or places. There are more than 10 recreation areas in the county.
*Information: Convention and Visitors Bureau, 1 Market Way East, York or*
*the Visitors Information Center, 1618 Toronita St., York, 717-843-6660; www.yorkpa.org*

## WHAT TO SEE AND DO
### BOB HOFFMAN WEIGHTLIFTING HALL OF FAME
*3300 Board Road, York, 717-767-6481, 800-358-9675 ext. 226; www.yorkbarbell.com*
Weightlifting section honors Olympic weightlifters, powerlifters, bodybuilders and strongmen; displays include samples of Iron Game artifacts, memorabilia and photos. Monday-Saturday.

PENNSYLVANIA

★
★
★
★
★

## CENTRAL MARKET HOUSE

*34 W. Philadelphia St., York, 717-848-2243*

Opened in March 1888. Over 70 vendors offer fresh produce, homemade baked goods, regional handcrafts and specialty items. Tuesday, Thursday, Saturday.

## FIRE MUSEUM OF YORK COUNTY

*757 W. Market St., York, 717-843-0464; www.yorkheritage.org/fire_museum.html*

Turn-of-the-century firehouse preserves two centuries of firefighting history; from leather bucket brigades to hand-drawn hose carts and pumps, horse-drawn equipment and finally to motorized equipment; artifacts and memorabilia; fire chief's office and firefighter's sleeping quarters are re-created, complete with brass slide pole. April-October, Saturday and second-Sunday every month; also by appointment.

## FRIENDS MEETING HOUSE

*135 W. Philadelphia St., York, 717-843-2285*

Original virgin pine paneling; restored. Regular meetings are still held here, by appointment.

## HARLEY-DAVIDSON, INC

*1425 Eden Road, York, 717-848-1177*

Guided tour through motorcycle assembly plant and the Rodney Gott Antique Motorcycle Museum. Children under 12 and cameras not permitted on plant tour. Plant and museum combination tour Monday-Friday. Museum tour Saturday.

## HISTORICAL SOCIETY OF YORK COUNTY

*250 E. Market St., York, 717-848-1587; www.yorkheritage.org*

Includes library with genealogical records (Tuesday-Saturday; fee for nonmembers). Museum features exhibits on the history of York County. Combination ticket for all historic sites maintained by the society. Daily. Sites include:

## BONHAM HOUSE

*152 E. Market St., York, 717-848-1587; www.yorkheritage.org/bonhamworkers.html*

Historic house reflects life in late 19th century, by appointment.

## GENERAL GATES' HOUSE

*157 W. Market St., York, 717-845-2951; www.yorkheritage.org/gatesplough.html*

It was here that Lafayette gave a toast to Washington, marking the end of a movement to replace him. Also here is Golden Plough Tavern, one of the earliest buildings in York, which reflects the Germanic background of many of the settlers in its furnishings and half-timber architecture, and the Bobb Log House, furnished with painted and grained furniture. Tuesday-Saturday 10 a.m.-4 p.m.

## WARRINGTON FRIENDS MEETING HOUSE

Fine example of early Quaker meetinghouse.

**PENNSYLVANIA**

### YORK COUNTY COLONIAL COURT HOUSE

*West Market Street and North Pershing Avenue, York, 717-848-1587;*
*www.yorkheritage.org*

Replica of 1754 original. Exhibits include multimedia presentation of Continental Congress's adoption of the Articles of Confederation, audiovisual story of 1777-1778 historic events; original printer's copy of Articles of Confederation, historic documents and artifacts. Tours. Daily.

## SPECIAL EVENT
### RIVER WALK ART FESTIVAL

*1 Market Way West, York*

Along Codorus Creek at York County Colonial Court House. Late August.

## HOTELS
### ★BEST WESTERN WESTGATE INN

*1415 Kenneth Road, York, 717-767-6931; www.bestwestern.com*

105 rooms. Complimentary continental breakfast. High-speed Internet access. Fitness center. $

### ★HAMPTON INN

*1550 Mount Zion Road, York, 717-840-1500, 800-426-7866; www.hamptoninn.com*

144 rooms. Complimentary continental breakfast. Wireless Internet access. Pool. Fitness center. $

### ★★HOLIDAY INN

*2000 Loucks Road, York, 717-846-9500, 800-465-4329; www.holidayinn.com*

181 rooms. Pets accepted. Pool, whirlpool. $

### ★★THE YORKTOWNE HOTEL

*48 E. Market St., York, 717-848-1111; www.yorktowne.com*

122 rooms. Wireless Internet access. Airport transportation available. $$

## RESTAURANTS
### ★★★ACCOMAC INN

*6330 S. River Drive, York, 717-252-1521; www.accomac.com*

This elegant country restaurant comes complete with white tablecloths and tableside preparation. French menu. Dinner, Sunday brunch. Bar. $$$

### ★★SAN CARLO'S

*333 Arsenal Road, U.S. 30, York, 717-854-2028; www.sancarlosrestaurant.com*

American menu. Dinner. Bar. $$

**PENNSYLVANIA**

★
★
★
★

# VIRGINIA

FROM VIENNA TO VIRGINIA BEACH AND RICHMOND TO ROANOKE, VIRGINIA REALLY IS FOR lovers—of nature, history, art, fine dining and family fun. The first of the Southern states stays true to its tourism slogan, "Virginia is for lovers," four words that just might be vague enough to encapsulate all that Virginia has to offer.

The state is best known for its prominent role in U.S. history, and strong ties to the past are readily apparent. More than 1,600 historical markers dot its 55,000 miles of paved roads. And over 100 historic buildings are open all year; hundreds more welcome visitors during the statewide Historic Garden Week (usually the last week in April).

Permanent English settlement of America began in Jamestown in 1607 and started a long line of Virginia "firsts:" the first legislative assembly in the Western Hemisphere (1619); the first armed rebellion against royal government (Bacon's Rebellion, 1676); the first stirring debates, in Williamsburg and Richmond, which left pre-Revolutionary America echoing Patrick Henry's inflammatory "Give me liberty, or give me death!" Records show that America's first Thanksgiving was held December 4, 1619, on the site of what is now Berkeley Plantation.

To Virginia the nation owes its most cherished documents: Thomas Jefferson's Declaration of Independence, George Mason's Bill of Rights and James Madison's Constitution. The Old Dominion was the birthplace of George Washington and seven other U.S. presidents.

Ironically, the state so passionately involved in creating a new nation was very nearly the means of its destruction. Virginia was the spiritual and physical capital of the Confederacy; the Army of Northern Virginia was the Confederacy's most powerful weapon, General Robert E. Lee its greatest commander. More than half the fighting of the Civil War took place in Virginia; and here, in the courthouse of the quaint little village of Appomattox, is where it finally came to an end.

When chartered in 1609, the Virginia territory included about one-tenth of what is now the United States; the present state ranks 36th in size, but the area is remarkably diverse. Tidewater Virginia—the coastal plain—is low, almost flat, arable land cut by rivers and bays into a magnificent system of natural harbors. Inland lies the gentle rolling Piedmont, Virginia's leading tobacco area, covering about half the state. The Piedmont also produces apples, corn, wheat, hay and dairy products. West of the Piedmont rise the Blue Ridge Mountains; high, rugged, upland plateaus occur to the south. Farther west is the Valley of Virginia, which is actually a series of valleys. The best known is the Shenandoah Valley, which contains some of the richest—and once bloodiest—land in the nation. Civil War fighting swept the valley for four years; Winchester changed hands 72 times. To the southwest are the Appalachian Plateaus, a rugged, forested region of coal mines.

For the vacationer today, the state offers colonial and Civil War history at every turn, seashore and mountain recreation year-round, caverns in the west, the Dismal Swamp in the southeast and the Skyline Drive, one of the loveliest scenic drives in the East.

*Information: www.virginia.org*

**383**

VIRGINIA

★
★
★
★
★

★ **FUN FACTS**

The Pentagon in Arlington is the largest office building in the world.

# ABINGDON

Daniel Boone passed through this area in 1760 and dubbed it "Wolf Hill" after a pack of wolves from a nearby cave disturbed his dogs. Wolf Hill had long been a crossing for buffalo and Native Americans; Boone later used it for his own family's westward migration. Later, Black's Fort was built here and the community adopted that name. Now known as Abingdon, this summer resort in the Virginia Highlands just north of Tennessee is Virginia's largest burley tobacco market and a livestock auction center.

*Information: Abingdon Convention & Visitors Bureau, 335 Cummings St., Abingdon, 800-435-3344; www.abingdon.com*

## WHAT TO SEE AND DO

### ABINGDON HISTORIC DISTRICT

*276-676-2282, 800-435-3440; www.virginia.org*

Listed on the National Register of Historic Places, this 20-block district features buildings that date from the 1700s. The historically significant structures aren't the only draw: The area has dozens of shops and galleries.

### CALLEBS COVE CAMPGROUND

*25136 Whitaker Hollow Road, Abingdon, 276-475-5222; www.callebscovecampground.com*

55 sites with full hook-ups.

### GRAYSON HIGHLANDS STATE PARK

*Abingdon, 276-579-7092, 800-933-7225; www.dcr.virginia.gov*

Within this 4,935-acre park are rugged peaks, some more than 5,000 feet high; alpine scenery. Hiking, horse trails, picnicking, camping, visitor center, interpretive programs, pioneer life displays (June-August). Adjacent to Mount Rogers National Recreation Area. Daily.

### RIVERSIDE CAMPGROUND

*18496 N. Fork River Road, Abingdon, 276-628-5333; www.holidayjunction.com*

Campers will enjoy the live music and bingo hall. 96 sites, full hook-ups; 68 sites, water and electric hook-ups. Pool, sports field, dump station.

### VIRGINIA CREEPER NATIONAL RECREATION TRAIL

*Virginia Creeper Trail Club, Abingdon, 276-676-2282, 800-435-3440; www.vacreepertrail.org*

Hikers, bicyclists, equestrians and anyone who wants to enjoy a good hike will find one on this 34-mile scenic railroad bed converted into a recreational facility. There are numerous shuttle and bike rental facilities nearby.

### WHITE'S MILL

*12291 White's Mill Road, Abingdon, 276-628-2960; www.whitesmill.org*

White's Mill is a still-functioning grist and flour mill built in 1790. Just 4½ miles from Abingdon, this Virginia Historic Landmark is one of the only water-powered mills in existence in southwestern Virginia. Watch as corn becomes cornmeal, and don't forget to take home a sample. Nearby is the working Blacksmith Shop. Wednesday-Sunday 10 a.m.-6 p.m.

★
★
★
★

**WOLF LAIR VILLAGE & CAMPGROUND**

*19091 County Park Road, Abingdon, 276-628-3680;*
*www.wolflairvillagecampground.com*

This campground is a half-mile from South Holston Lake and includes 48 sites, full hook-ups, 15/30-amp service. Pool. Water slide. Diving board. Miniature golf.

## SPECIAL EVENTS
### BARTER THEATRE

*127 W. Main St., Abingdon, 540-628-3991; www.bartertheatre.com*

America's oldest and longest-running professional repertory theater. Founded during the Depression on the theory that residents would barter their abundant crops for first-rate professional entertainment. Designated State Theatre of Virginia in 1946. Barter Players perform March-December. Children's theater June-August.

### VIRGINIA HIGHLANDS FESTIVAL

*208 W. Main St., Abingdon, 276-623-5266; www.vahighlandsfestival.org*

Exhibits, demonstrations of rustic handicrafts; plays, musical entertainment; historical reenactments and house tours, antique market. Early-mid-August.

## HOTELS
### ★COMFORT INN

*170 Old Jonesboro Road, Abingdon, 276-676-2222, 877-424-6423;*
*www.choicehotels.com*

80 rooms. Complimentary continental breakfast. Free local calls. Seasonal outdoor heated pool. $

### ★DAYS INN

*887 Empire Drive Southwest, Abingdon, 276-628-7131, 800-329-7466;*
*www.daysinn.com*

99 rooms. Free breakfast. Free high-speed Internet access. Business center. Pets accepted. Pool. Restaurant. $

### ★★★THE MARTHA WASHINGTON INN

*150 W. Main St., Abingdon, 276-628-3161, 888-888-5252;*
*www.marthawashingtoninn.com*

Experience Southern hospitality at its finest in this historic inn, built as a private residence for a Virginia general in 1832. The original architecture has been painstakingly maintained, with wood floors, crystal chandeliers and plaster detailing. Meals served in the Dining Room are innovative and well prepared. 62 rooms. Spa. Fitness center. Swimming pool. Wireless Internet access. Business center. Full breakfast daily. $$$

# ALEXANDRIA

A group of English and Scottish merchants established a tobacco warehouse at the junction of Hunting Creek and the "Potowmack" River in the 1740s. The little settlement prospered, and 17 years later surveyor John West, Jr., and his young assistant, George Washington, arrived and "laid off in streets and 84 half-acre lots" the town of Alexandria. Among the first buyers on the July morning in 1749 when the lots were offered for public sale were Lawrence Washington and his brother Augustus, William

Ramsay, the Honorable William Fairfax and John Carlyle. Erecting handsome town houses, these gentlemen soon brought a lively and cosmopolitan air to Alexandria with parties, balls and horse racing. George Washington made his home here, as did George Mason and Robert E. Lee.

In 1789, Virginia ceded Alexandria to the District of Columbia, but in 1846, the still Southern-oriented citizens asked to return to the Old Dominion, which Congress allowed.

During the Civil War, Alexandria was cut off from the Confederacy when Union troops occupied the town to protect Potomac River navigation. Safe behind Union lines, the city escaped the dreadful destruction experienced by many other Southern towns. Today, Alexandria has developed into a trade, commerce, transportation and science center. Free King Street Trolley 10 a.m.-10 p.m. Daily.

*Information: Convention/Visitors Association, 421 King St., Alexandria,*
*703-838-4200, 800-388-9119; www.funside.com*

## WHAT TO SEE AND DO

### ALEXANDRIA BLACK HISTORY RESOURCE CENTER

*638 N. Alfred St., Alexandria, 703-838-4356; www.oha.alexandriava.gov*
Photographs, letters, documents and artifacts relate the history of African-Americans in Alexandria. Tuesday-Saturday.

### ATHENAEUM

*201 Prince St., Alexandria, 703-548-0035; www.nvfaa.org*
Greek Revival structure built as a bank now houses the Fine Arts Association. Art shows, dance performances. Thursday, Friday and Sunday noon to 4 p.m., Saturday 1-4 p.m.

★
★
★
★
★

### ATLANTIC KAYAK

*1201 N. Royal St., Alexandria, 703-838-9072, 800-297-0066; www.atlantickayak.com*
See the capital's sights from a kayak on the Potomac. Atlantic Kayak runs short trips that include a brief lesson; all equipment is included and no experience is required. Sunset and moonlight tours are especially beautiful. Another outing takes you to the Dyke Marsh Wildlife area, where you'll see ospreys and great blue herons. On July 4, take a tour to view the fireworks. April-October, daily. Friday, Saturday and Sunday 10 a.m.-5 p.m.

### BOYHOOD HOME OF ROBERT E. LEE

*607 Oronoco St., Alexandria, 703-548-8454; www.leeboyhoodhome.com*
Federalist architecture. Famous guests include Washington and Lafayette.

### CARLYLE HOUSE

*121 N. Fairfax St., Alexandria, 703-549-2997; www.nvrpa.org*
This 1753 stately stone mansion built in Palladian style was the site of a 1755 meeting between General Edward Braddock and five British colonial governors to plan the early campaigns of the French and Indian War. Tuesday-Saturday 10 a.m.-4 p.m., Sunday noon-4 p.m.

# GEORGE WASHINGTON'S PLANTATIONS

Ask any historically knowledgeable American to name George Washington's home, and the answer you might get is Mount Vernon, just south of Alexandria, Va. This is only partly correct. In his youth, Washington lived on two other plantations, both of which, like Mount Vernon, now honor the country's first president.

Each unique home tells of a different aspect of his life. All three can be visited in a one-day, 170-mile round-trip. Make sure to get an early start, and begin in Alexandria, a Potomac River port long before the Capitol at Washington, D.C. was conceived. Paralleling the Potomac, the scenic Mount Vernon Parkway winds south for about 10 miles to Mount Vernon, a sprawling estate Washington inherited at the age of 20 from a half-brother. Here, you can tour his stately white mansion, enjoy the Potomac views, walk among the 18th-century farm fields and gardens, and pay homage at his and Martha's tombs. At Mount Vernon, you will learn about Washington the farmer, the soldier and the statesman. Plan to spend much of the morning at the estate.

Next, head south to Washington's two childhood homes. The first stop is Popes Creek Plantation, which is officially called the George Washington Birthplace National Monument. From Mount Vernon, take State Route 235 West to Highway 1 South and follow the signs to I-95 South to Fredericksburg, about 40 miles. In Fredericksburg, take State Route 3 east for about 36 miles. Make a left turn onto State Route 204, which ends at the plantation in about two miles. This is where Washington was born on February 22, 1732. Unlike Mount Vernon, nothing remains of the original house except a few foundation bricks and grand Potomac River views. And yet the 550-acre park—re-created in part as a colonial farm with fields, pastures and livestock—does a fine job of exploring Washington's origins. His great-grandfather, John, an English seaman, settled in the area in 1657, prospered and was eventually buried in the park. You can tour Memorial House, a Colonial-style farmhouse similar to one that might have stood on the property in 1732. Nearby are other reconstructed period farm buildings and a large herb garden. Walking trails trace the river's shoreline past a grove of towering cedars, and a shaded picnic area is provided. Packing a picnic is a good idea since the park has no food service.

Next head to Fredericksburg's Ferry Farm, where Washington's family moved when he was six. At the city outskirts, bear right onto Business Route 3. A sign to Ferry Farm will indicate a U-Turn at a stoplight. It is at Ferry Farm that Washington might have chopped down a cherry tree—wild cherries still grow on the property—and where he might have tossed a coin across the Rappahannock River. Archeological digs—sometimes open to visitors—are under way and a small museum describes Washington's childhood here. Return to Alexandria via Route 3 and I-95 North. Conclude your day there with dinner in early-American style at Gadsby's Tavern, built in 1792. *Approximately 170 miles.*

387

**VIRGINIA**

★
★
★
★
★

## CHRIST CHURCH

*118 N. Washington St., Alexandria, 703-549-1450; www.historicchristchurch.org*

Washington and Robert E. Lee were pewholders. Fine Palladian windows; interior balcony; wrought-brass and crystal chandelier brought from England. Structure is extensively restored but has changed little since it was built. Exhibit, gift shop at Columbus Street entrance. Monday-Saturday, also Sunday afternoons.

## DOORWAYS TO OLD VIRGINIA

*221 King St., Alexandria, 757-482-4848; www.chesapeakejubilee.org*

Offers guided walking tours of the historic district. March-October, Friday-Sunday evenings.

## FORT WARD MUSEUM AND HISTORIC SITE

*4301 W. Braddock Road, Alexandria, 703-838-4848; www.oha.alexandriava.gov*

Restored Union Fort from the Civil War; museum contains a Civil War collection. Museum. Tuesday-Sunday. Park, picnicking. Daily to sunset.

## GADSBY'S TAVERN MUSEUM

*134 N. Royal St., Alexandria, 703-838-4242; www.oha.alexandriava.gov*

Frequented by Washington and other patriots. Combines two 18th-century buildings; Tuesday-Sunday.

## GEORGE WASHINGTON MASONIC NATIONAL MEMORIAL

*101 Callahan Drive, Alexandria, 703-683-2007; www.gwmemorial.org*

American Freemasons' memorial to their most prominent member, this 333-foot-tall structure houses a large collection of objects that belonged to George Washington, which were collected by his family or the masonic lodge where he served as the first Master. Guided tours explore a replica of Alexandria Washington Lodge's first hall, a library, museum and an observation deck on the top floor. Daily 9 a.m.-4 p.m.

## KING STREET

This street is lined with trendy restaurants, shops and fine antique stores.

## LEE-FENDALL HOUSE

*614 Oronoco St., Alexandria, 703-548-1789; www.leefendallhouse.org*

Built by Phillip Richard Fendall in 1785 and occupied by the Lee family for 118 years. Both George Washington and Revolutionary War hero "Light Horse Harry" Lee were frequent visitors to the house. Remodeled in 1850, the house is furnished with Lee family belongings. Tuesday, Thursday-Saturday 10 a.m.-4 p.m., Wednesday and Sunday 1-4 p.m.

## THE LYCEUM

*201 S. Washington St., Alexandria, 703-838-4994; www.oha.alexandriava.gov*

Museum, exhibitions; Virginia travel information (limited). Daily.

## OLD PRESBYTERIAN MEETING HOUSE

*321 S. Fairfax St., Alexandria, 703-549-6670; www.opmh.org*

Tomb of the unknown soldier of the Revolution is in the churchyard. Monday-Friday.

★
★
★
★
★

### SIGHTSEEING BOAT TOURS

*Potomac Riverboat Company, Alexandria, 703-684-0580;*
*www.potomacriverboatco.com*

Tours of the Alexandria waterfront. Monday-Wednesday evenings: $47 per person, Thursday-Sunday evenings: $48 per person.

### STABLER-LEADBEATER APOTHECARY MUSEUM

*105-107 S. Fairfax St., Alexandria, 703-838-3852;*
*www.oha.alexandriava.gov/apothecary*

Largest collection of apothecary glass in its original setting in the country; more than 1,000 apothecary bottles. Original building is now a museum of early pharmacy; collection of old prescriptions, patent medicines, scales and other 18th-century pharmacy items. George Washington, Robert E. Lee, and John Calhoun were regular customers. Daily.

### TORPEDO FACTORY ARTS CENTER

*105 N. Union St., Alexandria, 703-838-4565; www.torpedofactory.org*

Renovated munitions plant houses an artists' center with more than 160 professional artists of various media. Studios, cooperative galleries, school. Also the home of Alexandria Archaeology offices, lab and museum; 703-838-4399. Daily 10 a.m.-5 p.m.

### WALKING TOUR OF HISTORIC SITES

*221 King St., Alexandria, 703-838-4200*

Start at the Visitor Center in Ramsay House (circa 1725), which is the oldest house in Alexandria and has been used as a tavern, grocery store and cigar factory. Here, you can obtain special events information and a free visitors' guide, and purchase block tickets good for reduced admission to three of the city's historic properties. Guided walking tours depart from here (spring-fall, weather permitting). The bureau also issues free parking permits, tour and highway maps, and hotel, dining and shopping information. Daily.

## SPECIAL EVENTS

### GEORGE WASHINGTON BIRTHDAY CELEBRATIONS

*1108 Jefferson St., Alexandria, 703-991-4474; www.washingtonbirthday.net*

Events include a race and a Revolutionary War re-enactment; climaxed by a birthday parade on the federal holiday. February.

### HOUSE TOURS

*221 King St., Alexandria, 703-838-4200*

Tours depart from the Ramsay House. Fine colonial and Federal-style houses are open to the public: Historic Garden Week (April); Hospital Auxiliary Tour of Historic Houses (September); Scottish Christmas Walk (December). Tickets, additional information at Alexandria Convention/Visitors Association.

### RED CROSS WATERFRONT FESTIVAL

*123 N. Alfred St., Alexandria, 703-549-8300; www.waterfrontfestival.org*

Commemorates Alexandria's maritime heritage. Features "tall ships," blessing of the fleet, river cruises, races, arts and crafts, exhibits, food, a variety of music and fireworks. June.

**389**

**VIRGINIA**

★
★
★
★

### SCOTTISH CHRISTMAS WALK

*Ramsay House, 221 King St., Alexandria, 703-548-0111, 800-388-9119;*
*www.scottishchristmaswalk.com*

Parade, house tour, concerts, greens and heather sales, and a dinner/dance to emphasize city's Scottish origins. First Saturday in December.

### VIRGINIA SCOTTISH GAMES

*Ramsay House, 221 King St., Alexandria, 703-838-4200; www.vascottishgames.org*

Athletic competition, Highland dance and music, antique cars, displays and food.
Fourth weekend in July.

## HOTELS

### ★BEST WESTERN OLD COLONY INN

*1101 N. Washington St., Alexandria, 703-739-2222, 800-780-7234;*
*www.bestwestern.com*

49 rooms. Complimentary full breakfast. Airport transportation available. **$**

### ★★CROWN PLAZA HOTEL

*901 N. Fairfax St., Alexandria, 703-683-6000, 800-111-000; www.crowneplaza.com*

258 rooms. Restaurant. Fitness center. Business center. Wireless Internet access. Swimming pool. Airport transportation available. **$**

### ★HAMPTON INN

*4800 Leesburg Pike, Alexandria, 703-671-4800; www.hamptoninn.com*

130 rooms. Complimentary continental breakfast. High-speed Internet access. Swimming pool. Business center. Fitness room. Pets accepted. **$**

### ★★★HILTON ALEXANDRIA MARK CENTER

*5000 Seminary Road, Alexandria, 703-845-1010; www.hilton.com*

The lakeside Hilton Alexandria Mark Center is situated near the central business district of Washington, D.C., and the shops and galleries of Old Town. This elegant atrium
hotel sits adjacent to a 43-acre botanical preserve and offers views of the Capitol.
Guests looking for onsite activities can work out in the 24-hour fitness center, take a
swim in the heated indoor/outdoor pool, or take in a game of tennis on one of the two
outdoor (lighted) tennis courts. 495 rooms. Airport transportation available. Wireless
Internet access. Swimming pool, whirlpool. Business center. Fitness room. Pets are
accepted. Breakfast. **$**

### ★HOTEL MONACO

*480 King St., Alexandria, 703-549-6080, 800-368-5047; www.monaco-alexandria.com*

241 rooms. Complimentary continental breakfast. Airport transportation available.
Wireless Internet access. Valet parking. Fitness center. Swimming pool. **$$**

### ★★★MORRISON HOUSE BOUTIQUE HOTEL

*116 S. Alfred St., Alexandria, 703-838-8000, 866-324-6628; www.morrisonhouse.com*

Just down the river from the Capitol, this Federal-style mansion presents visitors with
a peaceful alternative to the bustling city. Decorative fireplaces, four-poster mahogany
beds and silk sofas fill the guest rooms, all furnished in early American décor. But the

amenities are decidedly 21st century, with oversized marble bathrooms and luxurious Frette linens. The Grille attracts a smart, casual set with its clubby ambience and live piano music. Don't miss the exceptional Elysium, where menus are banished and the dishes are determined by the chef's conversations with each patron. 45 rooms. Complimentary newspaper. Wireless Internet access. Valet parking. Spa. **$$**

### ★★★SHERATON SUITES OLD TOWN ALEXANDRIA

*801 N. St. Asaph St., Alexandria, 703-836-4700, 800-325-3535; www.sheraton.com*
Just steps from the Potomac River, this hotel offers an easy commute from both Ronald Reagan Washington National Airport and D.C. 247 rooms, all suites. Airport transportation available. High-speed Internet access. Restaurant. **$$**

## RESTAURANTS
### ★★BILBO BAGGINS

*208 Queen St., Alexandria, 703-683-0300; www.bilbobaggins.net*
American menu. Lunch, dinner, Sunday brunch. Bar. Children's menu. **$$**

### ★★BISTROT LAF FAYETTE

*1118 King St., Alexandria, 703-548-2525; www.opentable.com*
French menu. Lunch, dinner. Closed Sunday. Bar. Casual attire. **$$$**

### ★★CHART HOUSE

*1 Cameron St., Alexandria, 703-684-5080; www.chart-house.com*
Seafood menu. Lunch, dinner, Sunday brunch. Bar. Children's menu. Outdoor seating. **$$$**

★
★★
★★
★

### ★★★CHEZ ANDREE

*10 E. Glebe Road, Alexandria, 703-836-1404; www.chezandree.com*
Chez Andree, family-owned for more than 40 years, offers country French cuisine in three different dining rooms. Originally a railroad bar that catered to the Potomac Yards, the restaurant now serves specials such as duck l'orange and rack of lamb to hungry diners. French menu. Lunch Monday-Friday, dinner. Closed Sunday. Bar. Reservations recommended. **$$**

### ★FACCIA LUNA

*823 S. Washington St., Alexandria, 703-838-5998; www.faccialuna.com*
American, Italian menu. Lunch Monday-Friday, dinner. Bar. Children's menu. Outdoor seating. **$**

### ★★FISH MARKET

*105 King St., Alexandria, 703-836-5676; www.fishmarketoldtown.com*
Seafood menu. Lunch, dinner. Bar. Children's menu. Casual attire. **$$**

### ★★GADSBY'S TAVERN

*138 N. Royal St., Alexandria, 703-548-1288; www.gadsbystavernrestaurant.com*
American menu. Lunch, dinner, Sunday brunch. Closed Christmas and New Year's day. Children's menu. Outdoor seating. Reservations recommended. **$$**

### ★★GERANIO

*722 King St., Alexandria, 703-548-0088; www.geranio.net*
Italian menu. Lunch Monday-Friday, dinner. Casual attire. **$$**

### ★★★THE GRILLE

*116 S. Alfred St., Alexandria, 703-838-8000, 800-367-0800;*
*www.morrisonhouse.com*
The Grille in the Morrison House Boutique Hotel lets diners create their very own flight of food based on what the chef has purchased from local markets and farmers that day. Instead of a dinner menu, you'll be presented with a wine list, followed by a personal visit from the chef to discuss what you're in the mood to eat. He'll give you the list of ingredients, and you work together to develop the menu. After dinner, a butler will escort you to the parlor for an after-dinner drink or an aromatic pot of special-blend loose tea made for the Morrison House Boutique Hotel. International menu. Breakfast, dinner. Bar. Children's menu. Casual attire. **$$$**

### ★★IL PORTO

*121 King St., Alexandria, 703-836-8833; www.ilportoristorante.com*
Italian menu. Lunch, dinner. Bar. Children's menu. Casual attire. Reservations recommended. **$$**

### ★★★LA BERGERIE

*218 N. Lee St., Alexandria, 703-683-1007; www.labergerie.com*
In a historic brick warehouse, La Bergerie serves up French dishes, including roasted wild rockfish on mussel and salmon caviar risotto with a saffron vanilla sauce, roasted wild boar chop with kimchi cabbage, burgundy carrots and a sweet and sour sauce, along with a daily prix fixe menu. French menu. Lunch, dinner. Closed Sunday except Mother's Day. Reservations recommended. Bar. **$$**

### ★★LANDINI BROTHERS

*115 King St., Alexandria, 703-836-8404; www.landinibrothers.com*
Italian menu. Lunch, dinner. Bar. Reservations recommended. **$**

### ★★LE GAULOIS

*1106 King St., Alexandria, 703-739-9494; www.legauloiscafe.com*
French menu. Lunch, dinner. Casual attire. Reservations recommended. Outdoor seating. **$$**

### ★★LE REFUGE

*127 N. Washington St., Alexandria, 703-548-4661; www.lerefugealexandria.com*
French menu. Lunch, dinner. Closed Sunday. Bar. Reservations recommended. **$$$**

### ★MANGO MIKE'S

*4580 Duke St., Alexandria, 703-370-3800; www.mangomikes.com*
Caribbean menu. Lunch, dinner, Sunday brunch. Bar. Children's menu. Outdoor seating. **$**

★
★
★
★
☆

## ★★MONROE'S
*1603 Commonwealth Ave., Alexandria, 703-548-5792; www.munroesrestaurant.com*
Italian menu. Dinner, Sunday brunch. Bar. Children's menu. Reservations recommended. Outdoor seating. **$$**

## ★★R. T.'S
*3804 Mount Vernon Ave., Alexandria, 703-684-6010; www.rtsrestaurant.net*
Cajun/Creole menu. Lunch, dinner. Bar. Children's menu. Reservations recommended. **$$**

## ★★TEMPO
*4231 Duke St., Alexandria, 703-370-7900; www.temporestaurant.com*
Italian, French menu. Lunch, dinner, Sunday brunch. Bar. Reservations recommended. Outdoor seating. **$**

## ★★THAI HUT
*408 S. Van Dorn St., Alexandria, 703-823-5357*
Thai menu. Lunch, dinner. **$**

## ★★UNION STREET PUBLIC HOUSE
*121 S. Union St., Alexandria, 703-548-1785; www.usphalexandria.com*
American menu. Lunch, dinner, Sunday brunch. Bar. Children's menu. **$$**

## ★★VILLA D'ESTE
*600 Montgomery St., Alexandria, 703-549-9477*
Italian menu. Lunch, dinner. Bar. Reservations recommended. **$$$**

## ★★THE WHARF
*119 King St., Alexandria, 703-836-2834; www.wharfrestaurant.com*
Seafood menu. Lunch, dinner. Bar. Children's menu. **$$**

# APPOMATTOX COURT HOUSE NATIONAL HISTORICAL PARK

★
★
★
★
★

The series of clashes between General Ulysses S. Grant and General Robert E. Lee that started with the Battle of the Wilderness May 5, 1864 finally ended here on Palm Sunday, April 9, 1865, in the little village of Appomattox.

A week earlier, Lee had evacuated besieged Petersburg and headed west in a desperate attempt to join forces with General Johnston in North Carolina. Ragged and exhausted, decimated by desertions, without supplies and beset by Union forces at every turn, the once-great Army of Northern Virginia launched its last attack April 9 at dawn. By 10 a.m., it was clear that further bloodshed was futile; after some difficulty in getting a message to Grant, the two met in the parlor of the McLean House. By 3 p.m., the generous surrender terms had been drafted and signed. The war was over. Three days later, 28,231 Confederate soldiers received their parole here.

The 1,743-acre park includes the village of Appomattox, restored and reconstructed to appear much as it did in 1865. Uniformed park rangers or interpreters in period dress answer questions about the residents and events. (Daily; closed holidays November-February.) Golden Eagle Passport accepted. Audiovisual programs, Braille guide folders, audio guide and large-print folder available for the hearing and visually impaired.

*Information: Superintendent, Highway 24, Appomattox, 434-352-8987; www.nps.gov/apco*

## WHAT TO SEE AND DO
### APPOMATTOX COURTHOUSE BUILDING
Reconstructed building houses visitor center, museum; audiovisual slide program (every half-hour, second floor). Self-guided tour of village begins here and includes:

### HOLLIDAY LAKE STATE PARK
*Route 2759, Appomattox, 434-248-6308; www.dcr.virginia.gov*
Approximately 250 acres in Buckingham-Appomattox State Forest. Swimming beach, bathhouse, fishing, boating (launch, rentals) on 150-acre lake; hiking trails, picnicking, concession, tent and trailer sites. Visitor center, interpretive programs. Standard fees. Park (daily); most activities, including camping (Memorial Day-Labor Day).

### MCLEAN HOUSE AND OUTBUILDINGS
Reconstruction of house where Generals Lee and Grant met on April 9, 1865.

### MEEK'S STORE AND MEEK'S STOREHOUSE
Period furnishings.

### STACKING OF ARMS
On the fourth anniversary of the firing on Fort Sumter, which triggered the outbreak of war, Confederate soldiers laid down their weapons here.

### WOODSON LAW OFFICE
Period furnishings.

# ARLINGTON COUNTY (RONALD REAGAN WASHINGTON-NATIONAL AIRPORT AREA)
*Information: www.mwaa.com/national/index.htm*

## WHAT TO SEE AND DO
### ARLINGTON FARMERS MARKET
*North Courthouse Road and North 14th Street, Arlington, 703-228-6423*
Irresistibly fresh berries, peaches and heirloom tomatoes are just some of the pleasures available at this lively market, which has been featuring the produce of farmers within 125 miles of Arlington since 1979. Don't miss the grass-fed meats, specialty goat cheeses and unusual varieties of familiar fruits and vegetables (one longtime vendor grows 35 different types of apples). Saturday.

### ARLINGTON HOUSE, THE ROBERT E. LEE MEMORIAL
*Arlington, 703-235-1530; www.nps.gov/arho*
National memorial to Robert E. Lee. Built between 1802 and 1818 by George Washington Parke Custis, Martha Washington's grandson and step-grandson/foster son of George Washington. In 1831 his daughter, Mary Anna Randolph Custis,

★
★
★
★
★

married Lieutenant Robert E. Lee; six of the seven Lee children were born here. As executor of the Custis estate, Lee took extended leave from the U.S. Army and devoted his time to managing and improving the estate. It was the Lee homestead for 30 years before the Civil War. On April 20, 1861, following the secession of Virginia, Lee made his decision to stay with Virginia. Within a month, the house was vacated. Some of the family possessions were moved for safekeeping, but most were stolen or destroyed when Union troops occupied the house during the Civil War. In 1864, when Mrs. Lee could not appear personally to pay property tax, the estate was confiscated by the federal government; a 200-acre section was set aside for a national cemetery. (There is some evidence that indicates this was done to ensure the Lee family could never again live on the estate.) G. W. Custis Lee, the general's son, later regained title to the property through a Supreme Court decision and sold it to the U.S. government in 1883 for $150,000. Restoration of the house to its 1861 appearance began in 1925. The Classic Revival house is furnished with authentic pieces of the period, including some Lee family originals. From the grand portico with its six massive, faux-marble Doric columns there is a panoramic view of Washington, D.C. Daily.

### ARLINGTON NATIONAL CEMETERY

*Arlington, 703-979-0690, 703-607-8000; www.arlingtoncemetery.org*

The solemn grounds of Arlington National Cemetery are a profoundly stirring sight. Gentle hills are studded as far as the eye can see with white stones marking the graves of more than 260,000 Americans who served in the nation's military, from the American Revolution to more recent conflicts. Many visitors stop at the Tomb of the Unknowns, which contains the unidentified remains of servicemen killed in the world wars and the Korean War, and provides quiet tribute to anonymous sacrifice. Most also pay their respects at the eternal flame that marks the granite-paved graves-ite of President John F. Kennedy and his wife, Jacqueline, as well as that of Robert F. Kennedy nearby.

★
★
★
★
★

### CRYSTAL CITY SHOPS

*Crystal Drive, Arlington, 703-922-4636; www.thecrystalcityshops.com*

Crystal City, a mixed-use residential and commercial development, has an under-ground shopping complex and a lot of street-level activity. It's currently being upgraded to provide more of a Main Street feel, with outdoor cafés as well as improved landscaping and opportunities for window-shopping. You will find jewelry and gift shops, men's and women's apparel, books and home furnishings, as well as a Japanese steakhouse, two American steakhouses, and a Legal Sea Foods. Daily. Monday-Friday 10 a.m.-7 p.m., Saturday 10 a.m.-6 p.m. Monday-Saturday 10 a.m.-6 p.m.

### FASHION CENTRE AT PENTAGON CITY

*1100 S. Hayes St., Arlington, 703-415-2400; www.fashioncentrepentagon.com*

The Ritz-Carlton Hotel's presence dictates a glamorous tone at this huge, glittering mall, anchored by Macy's and Nordstrom and home to more than 150 other tantalizing shops and restaurants. Women's fashion and accessories stores include Betsey Johnson and MAC Cosmetics. For home furnishings, check out Crate & Barrel and Williams-Sonoma. Daily. Sunday 11 a.m.-6 p.m., Monday-Saturday 10 a.m.-9:30 p.m.

### FREEDOM PARK

*1101 Wilson Blvd., Arlington, 703-284-3544*

Nearly 1,000 feet in length, the park occupies a never-used bridge. The park also features a memorial to the journalists killed in the line of duty and various icons of freedom.

### IWO JIMA STATUE

*On Arlington Boulevard, near Arlington National Cemetery*

Marine Corps War Memorial depicts raising of the flag on Mount Suribachi, Iwo Jima, February 23, 1945; this is the largest sculpture ever cast in bronze. Sunset Parade concert with performances by U.S. Marine Drum and Bugle Corps, U.S. Marine Corps Color Guard and the Silent Drill Team (late May-late August, Tuesday evenings).

### MEMORIAL AMPHITHEATRE

This impressive white marble edifice is used for ceremonies such as Memorial Day, Easter sunrise and Veterans Day services.

### NEWSEUM

*1101 Wilson Blvd., Arlington, 703-284-3700, 888-639-7386; www.newseum.org*

This 72,000-square-foot interactive museum of news takes visitors behind the scenes to see and experience how and why news is made. Be a reporter or newscaster; relive great news stories through multimedia exhibits; see today's news as it happens on a block-long video wall. Wednesday-Sunday.

### THE PENTAGON

*Jefferson Davis Highway, Washington Boulevard and I-395, Arlington, 703-695-1776; www.defenselink.mil*

With some 6 million square feet of floor area, this is one of the largest office buildings in the world. It houses the offices of the Department of Defense.

### TOMB OF THE UNKNOWNS

On November 11, 1921, the remains of an unknown American soldier of World War I were entombed here. A memorial was erected in 1932 with the inscription "Here rests in honored glory an American soldier known but to God." On Memorial Day 1958, an unknown warrior who died in World War II and another who died in the Korean War were laid beside him. On Memorial Day 1984, an unknown soldier from the Vietnam War was interred here. Sentries stand guard 24 hours a day; changing of the guard is every hour on the hour from October to March, and every 30 minutes April-September.

## SPECIAL EVENTS

### ARLINGTON COUNTY FAIR

*3308 S. Stafford St., Arlington, 703-920-4556; www.arlingtoncountyfair.com*

Countywide fair; arts, crafts, international foods, children's activities. August.

**ARMY 10-MILER**

*The Pentagon, Arlington, 202-685-3361; www.armytenmiler.com*

America's largest 10-mile road race, attracting thousands of military and civilian runners. Early October, Monday-Friday 9 a.m.-6 p.m.

**MARINE CORPS MARATHON**

*Route 110 and Marshall Drive, Arlington, 800-786-8762; www.marinemarathon.com*

Cheer on your favorite runner at the Marine Corps Marathon. The 26-mile, 385-yard route starts and ends near the Iwo Jima Memorial and winds through Arlington, Georgetown and D.C., passing the Capitol, the Pentagon and other inspiring sights along the way. The Marine Corps Marathon 5K race, organized in conjunction with the Special Olympics competition, starts at the Memorial at 9:10 a.m. Late October.

**MEMORIAL DAY SERVICE CEREMONY**

*Arlington National Cemetery, Arlington*

Wreaths placed at the Tomb of the Unknown Soldier. The National Symphony Orchestra gives a free concert later in the evening on the lawn of the Capitol. Memorial Day.

## HOTELS

### ★★ARLINGTON COURT HOTEL

*1200 N. Courthouse Road, Arlington, 703-524-4000; www.arlingtoncourthotel.com*

392 rooms. Complimentary dinner Monday-Wednesday. Complimentary hot breakfast. Wireless Internet access. Business center. Pets accepted. Fitness center. **$**

### ★★COURTYARD BY MARRIOTT

*2899 Jefferson Davis Highway, Arlington, 703-549-3434, 800-321-2211;*
*www.courtyard.com*

272 rooms. Airport transportation available. Airport. High-speed Internet access. Complimentary shuttle service. **$$**

### ★★★CROWNE PLAZA HOTEL

*1480 Crystal Drive, Arlington, 703-416-1600, 800-227-6963; www.cpnationalairport.com*

This Crowne Plaza Hotel is conveniently located near the attractions of Washington, D.C., Ronald Reagan National Airport and many businesses. Comfortable guest rooms feature two-line phones, 25-inch TVs and work desks. 308 rooms. Airport transportation available. High-speed Internet access. Complimentary breakfast. Business center. **$$**

### ★★EMBASSY SUITES

*1300 Jefferson Davis Highway, Arlington, 703-979-9799, 800-362-2779;*
*www.embassysuites.com*

267 rooms, all suites. Complimentary full breakfast. Airport transportation available. Business center. High-speed Internet access. Meeting rooms. Fitness room. Pool. Pets not accepted. **$$**

### ★HAMPTON INN

*2000 Jefferson Davis Highway, Arlington, 703-418-5901, 800-329-7466;*
*www.hamptoninn.com*

247 rooms. Airport transportation available. Business center. High-speed Internet access. Fitness room. Pool. Pets not accepted. Complimentary breakfast. **$**

### ★★★HILTON ARLINGTON

*950 N. Stafford St., Arlington, 703-528-6000, 800-695-7487; www.hiltonarlington.com*

This centrally located hotel is connected by a skybridge to the Ballston Common Mall and National Science Foundation Office Complex. The contemporary guest rooms feature Hilton's Serenity Bed and amenities such as Crabtree & Evelyn toiletries. 209 rooms. Complimentary breakfast. **$$**

### ★★★HYATT ARLINGTON

*1325 Wilson Blvd., Arlington, 703-525-1234, 800-233-1234; www.arlington.hyatt.com*

This hotel is located in the Rosslyn neighborhood across the bridge from Washington, D.C., and close to the Arlington National Cemetery. Sitting among businesses, shops and restaurants, the Hyatt Arlington is within walking distance of the Metro and Georgetown. 304 rooms. Airport transportation available. Fitness center. Complimentary wireless Internet access. Business center. Spa. **$$**

### ★★★MARRIOTT CRYSTAL CITY AT REAGAN NATIONAL AIRPORT

*1999 Jefferson Davis Highway, Arlington, 703-413-5500; www.crystalcitymarriott.com*

This conveniently located, boutique-style hotel has an underground walkway that gives guests access to the Metro system, the Crystal City shopping mall and the surrounding metropolitan area. A curved staircase in the lobby leads you to guest rooms that feature Revive, Marriott's new bed with 300 thread-count linens, and wireless Internet service. 343 rooms. Airport transportation available. Airport. Wireless Internet access. Pets not accepted. **$$**

### ★★★★THE RITZ-CARLTON, PENTAGON CITY

*1250 S. Hayes St., Arlington, 703-415-5000, 800-241-3333; www.ritzcarlton.com*

Five minutes from Washington National Airport, the Ritz-Carlton, Pentagon City offers tailored elegance with feather beds, Egyptian cotton linens, updated technology and luxurious club-level accommodations. Massages and personal fitness assessments are available at the fitness center. Afternoon tea takes on a whimsical edge with the Winnie the Pooh children's tea service in the Lobby Lounge, and The Grill never ceases to delight diners with its all-day dining. 366 rooms. Airport transportation available. Wireless Internet access. Complimentary breakfast. Business center. Pets accepted. **$$$**

### ★★★SHERATON CRYSTAL CITY HOTEL

*1800 Jefferson Davis Highway, Arlington, 703-486-1111, 800-862-7666;*
*www.sheraton.com/crystalcity*

Just across the river from Washington, D.C., the Sheraton Crystal City Hotel offers complimentary shuttle service to and from local businesses and Ronald Reagan Washington National Airport. 217 rooms. Airport transportation available. Free high-speed Internet access. Free local calls. **$$**

## RESTAURANTS

### ★★ALPINE

*4770 Lee Highway, Arlington, 703-528-7600; www.arlingtonsalpinerestaurant.com*

Italian menu. Lunch, dinner. Closed Monday. Bar. Business casual attire. Reservations recommended. Valet parking. $$$

### ★★BISTRO BISTRO

*4021 S. 28th St., Arlington, 703-379-0300; www.bistro-bistro.com*

French bistro menu. Lunch, dinner, Sunday brunch. Bar. Children's menu. Casual attire. Reservations recommended. Outdoor seating. $$

### ★CAFE DALAT

*3143 Wilson Blvd., Arlington, 703-276-0935; www.mytravelguide.com*

Vietnamese menu. Lunch, dinner. Closed Chinese New Year. Casual attire. Outdoor seating. $$

### ★★CARLYLE GRAND CAFE

*4000 S. 28th St., Arlington, 703-931-0777;*
*www.greatamericanrestaurants.com/carlyle/cm.htm*

American menu. Lunch, dinner, Sunday brunch. Bar. Children's menu. Casual attire. Outdoor seating. $$

### ★FACCIA LUNA

*2909 Wilson Blvd., Arlington, 703-276-3099; www.faccialuna.com*

Italian menu. Lunch, dinner. Bar. Children's menu. Casual attire. Outdoor seating. $$

### ★★★THE GRILL

*1250 S. Hayes St., Arlington, 703-415-5000; www.ritzcarlton.com*

The Grill at the Ritz-Carlton Pentagon City offers upscale American classics in a warm, clubby dining room decked out in mahogany wood. The seasonal menu features dishes such as lobster, filet mignon, foie gras, caviar and oysters. Weekends are busy for The Grill, as it houses one of the best brunches in the area. American menu. Breakfast, lunch, dinner, brunch. Bar. Children's menu. Casual attire. Reservations recommended. Valet parking. $$$

### ★★J. W.'S STEAKHOUSE

*1401 Lee Highway, Arlington, 703-524-6400; www.marriott.com*

Steak menu. Dinner, Sunday brunch. Bar. Business casual attire. Reservations recommended. $$$

### ★★LA COTE D'OR CAFE

*2201 W. Moreland St., Arlington, 703-538-3033; www.lacotedorcafe.com*

French menu. Lunch, dinner, Sunday brunch. Closed Monday. Bar. Business casual attire. Reservations recommended. Outdoor seating. $$$

### ★MATUBA

*2915 Columbia Pike, Arlington, 703-521-2811; www.matuba-sushi.com*

Japanese menu. Lunch, dinner. Closed Sunday. Casual attire. $$

★
★
★
★

### ★RED HOT AND BLUE

*1600 Wilson Blvd., Arlington, 703-276-7427; www.redhotandblue.com*

Barbecue menu. Lunch, dinner. Bar. Children's menu. Casual attire. **$$**

### ★SILVER DINER

*3200 Wilson Blvd., Arlington, 703-812-8600; www.silverdiner.com*

American menu. Breakfast, lunch, dinner, late-night. Children's menu. Casual attire. **$$**

### ★★★TIVOLI

*1700 Moore St., Arlington, 703-524-8900; www.tivolirestaurant.net*

This three-story northern Italian restaurant is named after the well-known cultural center in Rome. Located in a high-end indoor mall, it sits directly above the Rosslyn Metro Station. The décor features wood, marble and brass in the dining room. The large bar, which is located downstairs, is a great place for a drink before dinner. A prix fixe menu is offered every night, and entrées include cannelloni filled with grilled vegetables in a saffron sauce and sautéed filets of trout with jumbo lump crab meat. Italian menu. Lunch, dinner. Closed Sunday. Bar. Business casual attire. Reservations recommended. **$$$**

### ★VILLAGE BISTRO

*1723 Wilson Blvd., Arlington, 703-522-0284; www.villagebistro.com*

American, French menu. Lunch, dinner. Bar. Casual attire. Reservations recommended. Outdoor seating. **$$**

### ★★WOO LAE OAK

*1500 S. Joyce St., Arlington, 703-521-3706; www.woolaeoak.com*

Korean menu. Lunch, dinner. Casual attire. Reservations recommended. **$$$**

# ASHLAND

Ashland was founded when the president of the Richmond, Fredericksburg and Potomac Railroad bought land here. He dug a well, struck mineral water and started a health resort called Slash Cottage (wilderness acres were called "slashes"). A thriving village grew around it and was named after Henry Clay's Kentucky estate. In 1866, the railroad company gave land to the Methodist Church and induced the church to move Randolph-Macon College here. A section of early 1900s houses along the railroad tracks has been set aside as a historic district.

*Information: Ashland/Hanover Visitor Information Center, 112 N. Railroad Ave., Ashland, 804-752-6766, 800-897-1479; www.vatc.org*

## WHAT TO SEE AND DO

### AMERICAMPS RICHMOND NORTH

*11322 Air Park Road, Ashland, 804-798-5298, 800-628-2802; www.americamps.com*

Americamps is a wooded campground. 146 sites, 116 water and electrical hook-ups, 87 sewer hook-ups; 30 tent sites. Convenience store, pool, playground, game room.

### RANDOLPH-MACON COLLEGE

*204 Henry St., Ashland, 804-752-7305; www.rmc.edu*

Coeducational, liberal arts, Methodist-affiliated college (1,100 students). Historic buildings include Washington-Franklin Hall, Old Chapel and Pace Hall.

## SPECIALTY LODGING
### THE HENRY CLAY INN

*114 N. Railroad Ave., Ashland, 804-798-3100, 800-343-4565; www.henryclayinn.com*

This inn, an authentic reproduction of a Georgian Revival, is near the historic areas of Williamsburg, Charlottesville and Fredericksburg. 14 rooms. Complimentary continental breakfast. Restaurant. **$**

## RESTAURANT
### ★★IRONHORSE

*100 S. Railroad Ave., Ashland, 804-752-6410; www.ironhorserestaurant.com*

American, International menu. Lunch, dinner. Closed Sunday. Bar. Business casual attire. Reservations recommended. **$$**

# BASYE

## WHAT TO SEE AND DO
### BRYCE RESORT

*1982 Fairway Drive, Basye, 540-856-2121, 800-821-1444; www.bryceresort.com*

Bryce Resort sits in the Shenandoah Valley, with Stony Creek winding through its golf course, coming into play on seven different holes. This par-71 course is just a shade under 6,300 yards from the championship tees, and the challenging distance is never more evident than on the 575-yard opening hole. The course is played moderately, with about 30,000 rounds going off each year, but it's kept in great condition, and the teaching pros on staff are willing to help even the most inexperienced golfers. Swimming, tennis, golf, children's program, boating; horseback riding, hiking, grass skiing.

### BRYCE RESORT SKI AREA

*1982 Fairway Drive, Basye, 800-821-1444; www.bryceresort.com*

Day and night skiing. Two double chairlifts, three surface lifts; patrol, school, rentals, snowmaking; ski shop, restaurant, cafeteria, bar. Longest run 2,750 feet; vertical drop 500 feet. Mid-December-mid-March, daily. In summer: Fishing, swimming, boating; horseback riding, golf, tennis, hiking, grass skiing.

# BEAVERDAM

## WHAT TO SEE AND DO
### PATRICK HENRY HOME

*16120 Chiswell Lane, Beaverdam, 804-227-3500; www.redhill.org*

The 1719 Scotchtown was American Revolution-era hero Patrick Henry's home from 1771 to 1778. It was also the girlhood home of Dolly Madison. Fine colonial architecture. April-October, Thursday-Saturday 10 a.m.-4:30 p.m., Sunday 1:30-4:30 p.m.

★
★
★
★
★

# BIG STONE GAP

This rugged mountain country inspired author John Fox, Jr., to write *Trail of the Lonesome Pine* and *Little Shepherd of Kingdom Come*, best-selling novels of the early 1900s. The town lies at the junction of three forks of the Powell River, which cuts a pass through Stone Mountain.

*Information: Lonesome Pine Tourist Information Center, 619 Gilley Ave., Big Stone Gap, 276-523-2060; www.thelonesomepine.net*

## WHAT TO SEE AND DO
### JOHN FOX, JR., HOUSE & MUSEUM

*118 Shawnee Ave. E., Big Stone Gap, 276-523-2747; www.virginia.org*
Occupied from 1888 by John Fox, Jr. Memorabilia and original furnishings. Guided tours. June-September, Wednesday-Sunday.

### JUNE TOLLIVER HOUSE

*522 Clinton Ave. E., Big Stone Gap, 276-523-4707, 800-362-0149;*
*www.junetolliverhouse.org*
Heroine in *Trail of the Lonesome Pine* lived here; period furnishings; now an arts and crafts center; restored 1890 house. Daily.

### SOUTHWEST VIRGINIA MUSEUM

*10 W. First St., Big Stone Gap, 276-523-1322; www.swvamuseum.org*
Four-story mansion contains exhibits dealing with life in southwestern Virginia during original coal boom of the 1890s; also Native Americans of the area and early pioneers. Daily; closed Mondays Labor Day-Memorial Day.

## SPECIAL EVENT
### TRAIL OF THE LONESOME PINE

*Big Stone Gap, 540-523-1235; www.trailofthelonesomepine.org*
Outdoor musical drama. Late June-Labor Day, Thursday-Saturday.

# BLACKSBURG

The Washington and Jefferson national forests, which lie to the northwest, provide a colorful backdrop of azaleas, flowering dogwood and redbud in spring and brilliant hardwoods in fall. Virginia Polytechnic Institute and State University (Virginia Tech) is a source of employment for the town. The forests' Blacksburg Ranger District office is located here.

*Information: Blacksburg Regional Chamber of Commerce, 1995 S. Main St., Blacksburg, 540-522-4503, 800-288-4061; www.blacksburg-chamber.com*

## WHAT TO SEE AND DO
### MOUNTAIN LAKE

*110 Southpark Drive, Blacksburg*
A resort lake, particularly inviting in late June and early July, when azaleas and rhododendron are in bloom.

**SMITHFIELD PLANTATION**

*460 Bypass and Highway 314, Blacksburg, 540-231-3947;*
*www.smithfieldplantation.org*

Home of Colonel William Preston and three governors. Restored pre-Revolutionary house; original woodwork. Architectural link between Tidewater and Piedmont plantations of Virginia and those of the Mississippi Valley. Grounds restored by Garden Club of Virginia. April-November, daily; closed Wednesdays.

# BLUE RIDGE PARKWAY

Winding 469 mountainous miles between the Shenandoah and Great Smoky Mountains national parks (about 217 miles are in Virginia), the Blue Ridge Parkway represents a different concept in highway travel. It is not an express highway (speed limit 45 miles per hour) but a road intended for leisurely travel. All towns are bypassed. Travelers in a hurry would be wise to take state and U.S. routes, where speed limits are higher.

The parkway follows the Blue Ridge Mountains for about 355 miles, then winds through the Craggies, Pisgahs and Balsams to the Great Smokies. Overlooks, picnic and camp sites, visitor centers, nature trails, fishing streams and lakes, and points of interest are numerous and well-marked. Accommodations are plentiful in cities and towns along the way. Food availability is limited on the parkway.

The parkway is open all year, but the best time to drive it is between April and November. Some sections are closed by ice and snow for periods in winter and early spring. Fog may be present during wet weather. The higher sections west of Asheville to Great Smoky Mountains National Park and north of Asheville to Mount Mitchell may be closed January through March due to hazardous driving conditions.

*Information: 828-298-0398; www.nps.gov/blri*

## WHAT TO SEE AND DO

### CAMPING

Tent and trailer sites at Otter Creek, Peaks of Otter, Roanoke Mountain, Rocky Knob, Doughton Park, Julian Price Memorial Park, Linville Falls, Crabtree Meadows and Mount Pisgah. May-October. 14-day limit, June-Labor Day. No electricity; pets on leashes only; water shuts off at first freeze, usually late October. Primitive winter camping at Linville Falls when roads are passable.

### ELK RUN TRAIL

Mile 86. Forest, plant, animal community.

### FISHING

Rainbow, brook, brown trout and small-mouth bass in streams and lakes. State licenses required.

### GREENSTONE TRAIL

Mile 8.8. Of geologic interest.

### HUMPBACK ROCKS VISITOR CENTER

*Mile 5.8, Blue Ridge Parkway*
Pioneer mountain farm, park ranger.

**VIRGINIA**

★
★ ★
★ ★
★

### INTERPRETIVE PROGRAMS

*Miles 60.8, 86, 169, Blue Ridge Parkway*

Outdoor talks (mid-June-Labor Day) at Otter Creek (mile 60.8), Peaks of Otter (mile 86), Rocky Knob (mile 169). Obtain schedules at Parkway Visitor Centers.

### MABRY MILL

*Mile 176, Blue Ridge Parkway*

Old-time mountain industry, including tannery exhibits, picturesque mill, blacksmith shop.

### MABRY MILL TRAIL

*Mile 176, Blue Ridge Parkway*

Old-time mountain industry.

### MOUNTAIN FARM TRAIL

*Mile 5.8, Blue Ridge Parkway*

Typical mountain farm, reconstructed.

### PEAKS OF OTTER VISITOR CENTER

*Mile 86, Blue Ridge Parkway*

Wildlife exhibits, park ranger.

### ROCKY KNOB INFORMATION STATION

*Mile 169, Blue Ridge Parkway*

Information, exhibits, park ranger.

### ROCKY KNOB TRAIL

*Mile 168, Blue Ridge Parkway*

Leads to overlook of Rock Castle Gorge.

### TRAIL OF THE TREES

*Mile 63.6, Blue Ridge Parkway*

Leads to overlook of James River.

### VISITOR CENTERS

*Blue Ridge Parkway, Floyd, 828-259-0398, 800-727-5928; www.blueridgeparkway.org*

Exhibits, travel information, interpretive publications. Daily during peak travel season.

## HOTELS

### ★★DOE RUN LODGE RESORT AND CONFERENCE CENTER

*Mile Post 189, Blue Ridge Parkway, Fancy Gap, 276-398-2212, 800-325-6189*

47 rooms. **$**

### ★★PEAKS OF OTTER LODGE

*85554 Blue Ridge Parkway, Bedford, 540-586-1081, 800-542-5927;*
*www.peaksofotter.com*

60 rooms. Restaurant, bar. **$**

★
★★
★★★
★★★★
★★★★★

## BOOKER T. WASHINGTON NATIONAL MONUMENT

The 1861 property inventory of the Burroughs Plantation listed, along with household goods and farm implements, the entry "1 Negro boy (Booker)—$400." Freed in 1865, the boy and his family moved to Malden, West Virginia. There, while working at a salt furnace and in coal mines, the youngster learned the alphabet from *Webster's Blueback Spelling Book*. Later, by working at the salt furnace before school, then going to work at the mine after school, he got the rudiments of an education. When he realized that everyone else at the school roll call had two names, he chose Washington for his own.

At age 16 he started the 500-mile trip from Malden to Hampton Institute, where he earned his way. He taught at Malden for two years, attended Wayland Seminary, and returned to Hampton Institute to teach. In July 1881, he started Tuskegee Institute in Alabama with 30 pupils, two run-down buildings and $2,000 for salaries. When Washington died in 1915 the Institute had 107 buildings and more than 2,000 acres, and was assessed at more than $500,000.

The 224-acre monument includes most of the original plantation. A ¼-mile self-guided plantation trail passes reconstructed farm buildings, a slave cabin, crops and animals of the period; there is also a 1½-mile self-guided Jack-O-Lantern Branch nature trail. Picnic facilities. Visitor center has an audiovisual program, exhibits depicting his life. Daily. Information: 12130 Booker T. Washington Highway, Hardy, 540-721-2094; www.nps.gov/bowa

### RESTAURANT
#### ★★LAKE VIEW RESTAURANT
*85554 Blue Ridge Parkway, Bedford, 540-586-1081; www.peaksofotter.com*
American and seafood menu. Breakfast, lunch, dinner, Sunday brunch. Bar. Children's menu. Casual attire. **$$**

# BOYCE

### HOTEL
#### ★★★L'AUBERGE PROVENÇAL FRENCH COUNTRY INN
*13630 Lord Fairfax Highway, Boyce, 540-837-1375, 800-638-1702;*
*www.laubergeprovencale.com*
This French-style inn, decorated with Victorian and European antiques, is located in the heart of Virginia hunting country. 11 rooms. Children over 10 years only. Complimentary full breakfast. Restaurant. **$$**

### RESTAURANT
#### ★★★L'AUBERGE PROVENÇAL
*13630 Lord Fairfax Highway, Boyce, 540-837-1375, 800-638-1702;*
*www.laubergeprovencale.com*
This country inn has earned a reputation for fine cuisine served with detailed, personal attention. Innkeeper/chef Alain Borel, from Avignon, and his wife, Celeste,

**VIRGINIA**

★
★★
★★
★

provide an authentic, garden-inspired menu. French menu. Lunch (Sunday), dinner. Closed Monday-Tuesday. Bar. Outdoor seating. Jacket Required. Reservations recommended. **$$$**

# BREAKS INTERSTATE PARK

The "Grand Canyon of the South," where the Russell Fork of the Big Sandy river plunges through the mountains, is the major focus of this 4,600-acre park on the Kentucky-Virginia border. From the entrance, a paved road winds through an evergreen forest and then skirts the canyon rim. Overlooks provide a spectacular view of the "Towers," a huge pyramid of rocks. Within the park are extraordinary rock formations, caves, springs, a profusion of rhododendron and of course, the five-mile-long, 1,600-foot-deep gorge.

The visitor center houses historical and natural exhibits, including a coal exhibit (April-October, daily). Laurel Lake is stocked with bass and bluegill. Swimming pool, pedal boats; hiking, bridle and mountain bike trails, picnicking, playground, camping (April-October, fee); motor lodge, cottages (year-round), restaurant, gift shop. Park (daily); facilities (April-late December, daily).

*Information: 276-865-4413, 800-982-5122; www.breakspark.com*

# BRISTOL

Essentially a city in two states, Bristol is actually two cities—Bristol, Tenn., and Bristol, Va.—sharing the same main street and the same personality. Each has its own government and city services. Together they constitute a major shopping center. Named for the English industrial center, Bristol is an important factory town in its own right. These cities carry on the pioneer tradition of an ironworks established here about 1784, which made the first nails for use on the frontier. Bristol also has the distinction of being the "Official Birthplace of Country Music."

*Information: 423-989-4850; www.bristolchamber.org*

## WHAT TO SEE AND DO
### ANTIQUES
*State Street and Commonwealth Avenue, Bristol*
More than 20 large antiques shops are within a half-mile of these two perpendicular streets in downtown Bristol. Those searching for eclectic collectibles and furniture rave about the selection.

### BIRTHPLACE OF COUNTRY MUSIC ALLIANCE MUSEUM
*Bristol Mall, I-81, Exit 1, Bristol, 276-645-0111; www.birthplaceofcountrymusic.org*
Country music pioneers like Jimmie Rodgers, the Carter Family, Jim and Jesse, and Tennessee Ernie Ford all got their starts in Bristol. Every Thursday night, local pickers and singers gather to perform and produce a live radio show from the mall.

### BRISTOL WHITE SOX
*Devault Memorial Stadium, 1501 Euclid Ave., Bristol, 276-669-6859; www.bristolsox.com*
This minor league team is affiliated with the Chicago White Sox. June-August.

★
★
★
★
★

### ROCKY MOUNT HISTORIC SITE

*200 Hyder Hill Road, Bristol, 423-538-7396; www.rockymountmuseum.com*

Features the 2½-story log house that served from 1790 to 1792 as capital under William Blount, governor of the Territory of the United States South of the River Ohio. Restored to its original simplicity; 18th-century furniture. On grounds are restored log kitchen, slave cabin, barn, blacksmith shop and smokehouse. March-mid-December, Tuesday-Saturday 11 a.m.-5 p.m.

## HOTELS

### ★COMFORT INN

*2368 Lee Highway, Bristol, 276-466-3881, 877-424-6423; www.choicehotels.com*

87 rooms. Complimentary continental breakfast. Seasonal outdoor pool. Wireless Internet access. **$**

### ★★HOWARD JOHNSON BRISTOL

*2221 Euclid Ave., Bristol, 276-669-7171, 800-446-4656; www.hojo.com*

77 rooms. Free high-speed Internet access. Complimentary continental breakfast. Pool. **$**

### ★LA QUINTA INN

*1014 Old Airport Road, Bristol, 276-669-9353, 800-531-5900; www.laquinta.com*

123 rooms. Complimentary continental breakfast. Free high-speed Internet access. Outdoor swimming pool. Pets accepted. **$**

# BROOKNEAL

## WHAT TO SEE AND DO

### PATRICK HENRY NATIONAL MEMORIAL (RED HILL)

*1250 Red Hill Road, Brookneal, 434-376-2044; www.redhill.org*

Last home and burial place of Patrick Henry. Restoration of family cottage, cook's cabin, smokehouse, stable, kitchen. Patrick Henry's law office. Museum and gift shop on grounds. Interpretive video. Daily. Sunday 9 a.m.-5 p.m.

# CAPE CHARLES

The Chesapeake Bay Bridge-Tunnel (17.6 miles long) leads from Cape Charles (12 miles south of the town) to Virginia Beach/Norfolk. There is a scenic stop, gift shop, restaurant and fishing pier (bait available).

*Information: Chesapeake Bay Bridge & Tunnel District, Cape Charles, 757-331-2960, ext. 20; www.cbbt.com*

# CASANOVA

## HOTEL

### ★★★POPLAR SPRINGS

*9245 Rogues Road, Casanova, 540-788-4600, 800-490-7747;*
*www.poplarspringsinn.com*

This pretty inn is a lovely country getaway. Rooms are kitted out in colonial-style furnishings, but in case you don't want to enjoy lounging around in plush robes or

**VIRGINIA**

★
★
★
★
★

sleeping under luxe duvets, then take a calming walk around the 200 acres. 22 rooms. Complimentary continental breakfast. Restaurant. Spa. Pool, whirlpool. Fitness room. Tennis. $$$

# CENTREVILLE

## HOTEL

### ★★SPRINGHILL SUITES

*5920 Trinity Parkway, Centreville, 703-815-7800, 888-287-9400;*
*www.springhillsuites.com*

136 rooms, all suites. Complimentary continental breakfast. Free high-speed Internet access. Business center. Fitness center. Pets accepted. Pool. $

## RESTAURANT

### ★★SWEETWATER TAVERN

*14250 Sweetwater Lane, Centreville, 703-449-1100*

Lunch, dinner. Bar. Children's menu. $$

# CHANTILLY

## RESTAURANT

### ★★★PALM COURT

*14750 Conference Center Drive, Chantilly, 703-818-3522;*
*www.westfieldspalmcourt.com*

Housed in the Marriott Westfields Resort, this restaurant's menu is a throwback to the days of tableside dining. The buffet-style Sunday brunch is an extravaganza with tuxedo-clad waiters, mimosas and an unending array of sweets. American menu. Breakfast, lunch, dinner, Sunday brunch. Bar. Children's menu. Reservations recommended. Valet parking. $$$

# CHARLES CITY

## SPECIALTY LODGINGS

### EDGEWOOD BED AND BREAKFAST

*4800 John Tyler Memorial Highway, Charles City, 804-829-2962, 800-296-3343;*
*www.edgewoodplantation.com*

This Gothic home built in 1870 houses a collection of country primitives. It is famous for its ghost, which has been experienced by generations of occupants. The property includes a gristmill that once ground corn for both the Union and Confederate armies. Eight rooms. Children over 12 years only. Complimentary full breakfast. $$

### NORTH BEND PLANTATION BED AND BREAKFAST

*12200 Weyanoke Road, Charles City, 804-829-5176; www.northbendplantation.com*

Four rooms. Complimentary full breakfast. $

### PINEY GROVE AT SOUTHHALL'S PLANTATION

*16920 Southall Plantation Lane, Charles City, 804-829-2480; www.pineygrove.com*

Five rooms. Complimentary full breakfast. Two historic farmhouses circa 1800. $

## RESTAURANT

### ★★INDIAN FIELDS TAVERN

*9220 John Tyler Memorial Highway, Charles City, 804-829-5004*

American menu. Lunch, dinner. Closed Monday in January-February. Bar. Business casual attire. Reservations recommended. Outdoor seating. $$$

# CHARLOTTESVILLE

Popularly known as the number-one small city in the South, Charlottesville is famous as the home of Thomas Jefferson, the third president of the United States, and the University of Virginia, which Jefferson founded and designed.

Charlottesville offers much more than history. The downtown pedestrian mall streetscape at the center of the historic district is alive with more than 120 shops and 30 restaurants, outdoor cafés, theaters, bookstores and a skating rink. Charlottesville can also brag about its beautiful parks, top-notch museums, and award-winning wineries and outstanding entertainment.

The area's historic attractions include Monticello, Michie Tavern, Ash Lawn-Highland (James Monroe's home) and Montpelier. Constructed sculptures from the Art in Place program stand along the roadways. A myriad of scenic byways, hiking trails and river paths run throughout the area, as does the Blue Ridge Parkway, considered by some to be America's most beautiful drive.

*Information: Charlottesville/Albemarle Convention & Visitors Bureau, 600 College Drive, Charlottesville, 804-977-1783, 877-386-1102; www.pursuecharlottesville.com*

## WHAT TO SEE AND DO

### ALBEMARLE COUNTY COURTHOUSE

*Court Square, 501 E. Jefferson St., Charlottesville, 434-972-4083;*
*www.courts.state.va.us/courts/circuit/Albemarle/home.html*

North wing was used in 1820s as a "common temple" shared by Episcopalian, Methodist, Presbyterian and Baptist sects, one Sunday a month to each but with all who wished attending each week. Jefferson, Monroe and Madison worshipped here.

**VIRGINIA**

### ASH LAWN-HIGHLAND

*1000 James Monroe Parkway, Charlottesville, 434-293-9539;*
*www.ashlawnhighland.org*

Built on a site personally selected by Thomas Jefferson in 1799, this 535-acre estate was the home of President James Monroe from 1799 to1823. The estate is now owned by Monroe's alma mater, the College of William and Mary. This early 19th-century working plantation offers guided tours of the house with Monroe possessions, spinning and weaving demonstrations, old-boxwood gardens, peacocks, picnic spots. Daily.

★
★
★
★

### GEORGE ROGERS CLARK MEMORIAL

*West Main and Jefferson Park Avenue, Charlottesville*

Brother of William Clark and soldier on the frontier, this intrepid explorer who opened up the Northwest Territory was an Albemarle County native son.

### HISTORIC MICHIE TAVERN

*683 Thomas Jefferson Parkway, Charlottesville, 434-977-1234; www.michietavern.com*
Circa-1784 tavern located near Jefferson's Monticello. Visitors dine on hearty fare in the Tavern's Ordinary, where servers in period attire greet them. Afterwards, a tour of the original tavern features living history where guests participate in 18th-century activities, including a lively Virginia dance. Daily.

### LEWIS AND CLARK MONUMENT

*Midway Park, Ridge and Main streets, Charlottesville*
Memorial to Jefferson's secretary, Meriwether Lewis, who explored the Louisiana Territory with his friend William Clark.

### MONTICELLO

*931 Thomas Jefferson Parkway, Charlottesville, 434-984-9822; www.monticello.org*
Located on a mountaintop, Monticello is one of the most beautiful estates in Virginia and is considered a classic of American architecture. The house was designed by Thomas Jefferson and built over the course of 40 years, symbolizing the pleasure he found in "putting up and pulling down." Jefferson moved into the first completed outbuilding of his new home in 1771, although construction continued until 1809. Most of the interior furnishings are original. Tours of the restored orchard, vineyard, 1,000-foot-long vegetable garden, and Mulberry Row, once the site of plantation workshops. Jefferson died at Monticello on July 4, 1826, and was buried in the family cemetery. The Thomas Jefferson Memorial Foundation maintains the house and gardens. Daily.

**VIRGINIA**

★
★
★
★
★

### MONTICELLO VISITORS CENTER

*Highway 20 South and I-64, Charlottesville, 434-984-9822; www.monticello.org*
Personal and family memorabilia; architectural models and drawings; *Thomas Jefferson: The Pursuit of Liberty*, a 35-minute film, shown twice daily. Daily.

### ROBERT E. LEE MONUMENT

*First and Jefferson streets, Charlottesville*

### "STONEWALL JACKSON ON LITTLE SORREL"

*Adjacent to Courthouse, Charlottesville*

### UNIVERSITY OF VIRGINIA

*914 Emmet St. North, Charlottesville, 434-924-1019; www.virginia.edu*
Founded by Thomas Jefferson and built according to his plans. Handsome red brick buildings with white trim, striking vistas, smooth lawns, and ancient trees form the grounds of Jefferson's "academical village." The serpentine walls, one brick thick, which Jefferson designed for strength and beauty, are famous. Room 13, West Range, occupied by Edgar Allan Poe as a student, is displayed for the public. Walking tours start at the Rotunda. Daily; closed three weeks mid-December-early January.

### WALKING TOUR

*VA 20, Charlottesville, 434-293-6789; www.pursuecharlottesville.com*
The Charlottesville/Albemarle Information Center, located on Highway 20 S in the Monticello Visitors Center Building, has information for a walking tour of historic Charlottesville.

## SPECIAL EVENTS

### DOGWOOD FESTIVAL

*Charlottesville, 434-961-9824; www.charlottesvilledogwoodfestival.org*

Parade, lacrosse and golf tournaments, carnival. Nine days mid-April.

### FOUNDER'S DAY

*Charlottesville*

Jefferson's Birthday. Commemorative ceremonies. April 13.

### GARDEN WEEK

*Charlottesville, 804-644-7776; www.vagardenweek.org*

Some fine private homes and gardens in the area are open. Mid-late April.

## HOTELS

### ★BEST WESTERN CAVALIER INN

*105 N. Emmet St., Charlottesville, 434-296-8111, 800-987-8376;*
*www.bestwesterncavalierinn.com*

118 rooms. Complimentary continental breakfast. Airport transportation available. Reservations recommended. **$**

### ★★★BOAR'S HEAD INN

*200 Ednam Drive, Charlottesville, 434-296-2181, 800-476-1988;*
*www.boarsheadinn.com*

Located in the Blue Ridge Mountains, this resort welcomes guests to visit the past and enjoy the present. Guests can visit past presidential homes (a short drive away), stroll through local wineries or enjoy a panoramic view by hot-air balloon. 170 rooms. Spa. Three outdoor pools. Golf. Tennis. Four restaurants. Airport transportation available. Reservations recommended. **$$**

### ★★DOUBLETREE HOTEL

*990 Hilton Heights Road, Charlottesville, 434-973-2121, 800-222-8799;*
*www.charlottesville.doubletree.com*

240 rooms. Airport transportation available. High-speed Internet access. Free parking. Reservations recommended. **$**

### ★ENGLISH INN OF CHARLOTTESVILLE

*2000 Morton Drive, Charlottesville, 434-971-9900, 800-786-5400; www.wytestone.com*

88 rooms. Complimentary full breakfast. Airport transportation available. High-speed Internet access. Reservations recommended. **$**

### ★HAMPTON INN

*2035 India Road, Charlottesville, 434-978-7888, 800-426-7866; www.hamptoninn.com*

123 rooms. Complimentary continental breakfast. Airport transportation available. Reservations recommended. **$**

### ★★★OMNI CHARLOTTESVILLE HOTEL

*235 W. Main St., Charlottesville, 434-971-5500, 888-444-6664; www.omnihotels.com*

Located on a downtown pedestrian mall, the Omni Charlottesville Hotel is within walking distance of the government buildings. Guest rooms in this luxury hotel offers views of the Blue Ridge Mountains and historic Charlottesville. 211 rooms. Wireless Internet access. Reservations recommended. **$**

### ★★★SILVER THATCH INN

*3001 Hollymead Drive, Charlottesville, 434-978-4686, 800-261-0720; www.silverthatch.com*

Built in 1780, this clapboard home is full of history and is one of the oldest buildings in the area. Guest rooms are named for Virginia-born presidents. Seven rooms. Children over 14 years only. Complimentary full breakfast. Reservations recommended. **$$**

## SPECIALTY LODGINGS

### 200 SOUTH STREET INN

*200 W. South St., Charlottesville, 434-979-0200, 800-964-7008; www.southstreetinn.com*

19 rooms. Complimentary continental breakfast. Built 1856; antiques. Reservations recommended. **$$**

### INN AT MONTICELLO

*Route 20 South, 1188 Scottsville Road, Charlottesville, 434-979-3593, 877-735-2982; www.innatmonticello.com*

Guests can choose to relax by a fireplace in winter or sit on the porch in summer at this country manor house built in the mid-1800s. Guest rooms are decorated with period antiques and reproductions. Five rooms. Children over 12 years only. Complimentary full breakfast. Reservations recommended. **$$**

## RESTAURANTS

### ★★ABERDEEN BARN

*2018 Holiday Drive, Charlottesville, 434-296-4630; www.aberdeenbarn.com*

Steak menu. Dinner. Bar. Children's menu. Business casual attire. Reservations recommended. **$$**

### ★★C & O

*515 E. Water St., Charlottesville, 434-971-7044; www.candorestaurant.com*

French menu. Dinner, late-night. Closed one week after December 25 and one week at the end of summer. Bar. Children's menu. Business casual attire. Reservations recommended. Outdoor seating. **$$$**

### ★IVY INN

*2244 Old Ivy Road, Charlottesville, 434-977-1222; www.ivyinnrestaurant.com*

American menu. Dinner. Closed Sunday. Bar. Victorian-style house built in 1804; fireplaces. Business casual attire. Reservations recommended. Outdoor seating. **$$**

★
★★
★★
★

### ★★L'AVVENTURA

*220 W. Market St., Charlottesville, 434-977-1912; www.vinegarhilltheatre.com*

Italian menu. Dinner. Closed Sunday and Monday. Bar. Casual attire. Reservations recommended. Outdoor seating. $$

### ★★MAHARAJA

*139 Zan Road, Charlottesville, 434-973-1110; www.milan-indian-cuisine.com*

Indian menu. Lunch, dinner. Bar. Casual attire. Reservations recommended. Outdoor seating. $$

### ★★★OLD MILL ROOM

*200 Ednam Drive, Charlottesville, 434-972-2230, 800-476-1988;*
*www.boarsheadinn.com*

This dining room is located in the Boar's Head Inn at the University of Virginia. Dishes such as apple balsamic-glazed copper river salmon with cauliflower mousse and celeriac-apple salad are prepared with vegetables from the restaurant's garden. American menu. Breakfast, lunch, dinner. Bar. Valet parking. Outdoor seating. Children's menu. Business casual attire. Reservations recommended. $$$

### ★★★OXO

*215 W. Water St., Charlottesville, 434-977-8111; www.oxorestaurant.com*

Chef and co-owner John Haywood reinterprets French classics inside this airy restaurant. Try items such as braised pheasant breast with potato feuillette or pan-seared halibut, and don't leave without a sweet ending like chocolate souffle. French menu. Lunch, dinner. Bar. Business casual attire. Reservations recommended. Outdoor seating. $$$

413

# CHESAPEAKE

For beach lovers who seek a vacation off the beaten path, Chesapeake is an excellent choice. You'll be minutes away from 18th-century America, the oceanfront boardwalk of Virginia Beach, theme parks and more. The active Atlantic Intracoastal Waterway, home to a myriad of birds and wildlife, is complemented by the 49,000-acre Great Dismal Swamp National Wildlife Refuge managed by the Nature Conservancy. Bring your binoculars, your camera and your lifelong checklist of birds.

Farther up the coast, the Back Bay National Wildlife Refuge encompasses a series of barrier islands that feature large sand dunes, maritime forests, freshwater marshes and ponds populated with large flocks of wintering waterfowl. Move through the bay on the unique trolley designed not to disturb the wildlife, kayak on the waterway itself or stroll on the more than 19 miles of hiking trails at First Landing State Park.

*Information: Chesapeake Conventions & Tourism Bureau, 3815 Bainbridge Blvd.,*
*Chesapeake, 757-502-4898, 888-889-5551; www.visitchesapeake.com*

**VIRGINIA**

★
★
★
★

## WHAT TO SEE AND DO

### NORTHWEST RIVER PARK

*1733 Indian Creek Road, Chesapeake, 757-421-3145; www.chesapeake.va.us*

Approximately eight miles of hiking/nature trails wind through this 763-acre city park. Fishing, boating, canoeing (ramp, rentals); picnicking (shelters), playground, nine-hole miniature golf, camping, tent and trailer sites (April-December, daily; fee). Shuttle tram. Daily. Fragrance trail for the visually impaired.

## SPECIAL EVENT

### CHESAPEAKE JUBILEE

*City Park, 1500 Mount Pleasant Road, Chesapeake, 757-482-4848;*
*www.chesapeakejubilee.org*

National and regional entertainment, carnival, food booths, fireworks. Third weekend in May.

## HOTELS

### ★COMFORT SUITES

*1550 Crossways Blvd., Chesapeake, 757-420-1600, 877-424-6423;*
*www.choicehotels.com*

124 rooms. All suites. Complimentary continental breakfast. Reservations recommended. $

### ★★RED ROOF INN

*724 Woodlake Drive, Chesapeake, 757-523-1500, 800-733-7663; www.redroofinn.com*

229 rooms. Complimentary coffee. Free local calls. Wireless Internet access. Reservations recommended. $

## RESTAURANT

### ★★KYOTO

*1412 Greenbriar Parkway, Chesapeake, 757-420-0950; www.kyotochesapeake.com*

Japanese menu. Lunch, dinner. Bar. Children's menu. Casual attire. Reservations recommended. $$

# CHINCOTEAGUE

Oysters, wild ponies and good fishing are the stock in trade of this small island, connected with Chincoteague National Wildlife Refuge by a bridge and to the mainland by 10 miles of highway. The oysters, many of them grown on the hard sand bottoms off Chincoteague from seed or small oysters brought from natural beds elsewhere, are among the best in the East. Commercial fishing has always been the main occupation of the islanders, but now catering to those who fish for fun is also economically important.

Chincoteague's wild ponies are actually small horses, but when fully grown they are somewhat larger and more graceful than Shetlands. They are thought to be descended from horses that swam ashore from a wrecked Spanish galleon, their limited growth caused by generations of a marsh grass diet.

*Information: Chamber of Commerce, 6733 Maddox Blvd., Chincoteague,*
*757-336-6161; www.chincoteaguechamber.com*

## WHAT TO SEE AND DO

### ASSATEAGUE ISLAND

*8586 Beach Road, Chincoteague, 757-336-6577; www.nps.gov/asis*

A 37-mile barrier island, Assateague has stretches of ocean and sand dunes, forest and marshes that create a natural environment unusual on the East Coast. Sika deer, a variety of wildlife, and countless birds, including the peregrine falcon (autumn), can be found here, but wild ponies occasionally roaming the marshes offer the most exotic sight for visitors. Nature and auto trails; interpretive programs. Swimming (bathhouse), lifeguards in summer, surf fishing; camping, hike-in and canoe-in camp sites and day-use facilities. Picnicking permitted in designated areas; cars are limited to designated roads. Pets are not accepted. Obtain information at Toms Cove Visitor Center (spring-fall: daily) and at Chincoteague Refuge Visitor Center (daily). Access for the disabled to all facilities.

### CAPTAIN BARRY'S BACK BAY CRUISES & EXPEDITIONS

*6174 Landmark Plaza, Chincoteague, 757-336-6508; www.captainbarry.net*

Includes Bird Watch Cruise, Back Bay Expedition, Champagne Sunset Cruise, Moonlight Excursions and Fun Cruise. Trips vary from one to four hours. Reservations recommended.

### OYSTER AND MARITIME MUSEUM OF CHINCOTEAGUE

*7125 Maddox Blvd., Chincoteague, 757-336-6117; www.chincoteague.com*

Museum contains diorama, aquarium, shellfish industry interpretation. Also has the Wyle Maddox Library. May-August, daily; September-October, Saturday and Sunday.

### REFUGE WATERFOWL MUSEUM

*7059 Maddox Blvd., Chincoteague, 757-336-5800; www.chincoteaguechamber.com*

Rotating displays of antique decoys and hunting tools. Decoy making and waterfowl art. Call ahead for hours. Daily.

## SPECIAL EVENTS

### CHINCOTEAGUE POWER BOAT REGATTA

*Memorial Park, Chincoteague, 757-336-6161; www.chincoteague.com*

Late June.

### EASTER DECOY & ART FESTIVAL

*Chincoteague Combined School, 4586 Main St., Chincoteague, 757-336-6161; www.chincoteaguechamber.com*

Easter weekend.

### OYSTER FESTIVAL

*6733 Maddox Blvd., Chincoteague, www.chincoteaguechamber.com*

Columbus Day weekend.

**VIRGINIA**

## PONY PENNING

*Chincoteague, 757-336-6161; www.chincoteague.com*

The "wild" ponies are rounded up on Assateague Island, then swim the inlet to Chincoteague, where foals are sold at auction before the ponies swim back to Assateague. Carnival amusements. Last Wednesday and Thursday in July.

## WATERFOWL WEEK

*8231 Beach Road, Chincoteague*

National Wildlife Refuge open to vehicles during peak migratory waterfowl populations. Late November.

## HOTELS

### ★BEST WESTERN CHINCOTEAGUE ISLAND

*7105 Maddox Blvd., Chincoteague, 757-336-6557, 800-553-6117;*
*www.bestwestern.com*

52 rooms. Complimentary continental breakfast. At entrance to Assateague National Seashore. Wireless Internet access. Reservations recommended. $

### ★COMFORT SUITES CHINCOTEAGUE

*4195 Main St., Chincoteague, 757-336-3700, 877-424-6423; www.choicehotels.com*

87 rooms. Wireless Internet access. Free continental breakfast. Pets accepted. Reservations recommended. $

### ★★ISLAND MOTOR INN RESORT

*4391 Main St., Chincoteague, 757-336-3141; www.islandmotorinn.com*

60 rooms. Fitness center. Wireless Internet access. Reservations recommended. $

### ★REFUGE INN

*7058 Maddox Blvd., Chincoteague, 757-336-5511, 800-257-0034; www.refugeinn.com*

72 rooms. Children's activity center. Near wildlife refuge and national seashore. Chincoteague ponies on grounds. Free continental breakfast. Wireless Internet access. $

## SPECIALTY LODGINGS

### CEDAR GABLES SEASIDE INN

*6095 Hopkins Lane, Chincoteague, 757-336-6860, 888-491-2944;*
*www.cedargable.com*

This waterfront bed and breakfast inn overlooks Oyster Bay and the Chincoteague Wildlife Refuge. All rooms open to waterfront decks and offer breathtaking views of Assateague Island. The rooms have fireplaces and Jacuzzis. Guests can enjoy the nearby beach, wildlife refuge, fishing, biking and hiking. Four rooms. Closed one week in late December. Children over 14 years only. Complimentary full breakfast. $$

### MISS MOLLY'S INN

*4141 Main St., Chincoteague, 757-336-6686, 800-221-5620; www.missmollysinn.com*

Marguerite Henry stayed here while writing *Misty of Chincoteague*. The inn is a historic 1886 building with a library and sitting room. Seven rooms. Children over four years only. Complimentary full breakfast. $

★
★
★
★
★

**WATSON HOUSE**

*4240 Main St., Chincoteague, 757-336-1564, 800-336-6787; www.watsonhouse.com*

Five rooms. Children over 10 years only. Complimentary full breakfast. 1874 Victorian residence. **$**

## RESTAURANT

### ★DON'S SEAFOOD

*4113 Main St., Chincoteague Island, 757-336-5715; www.donsseafood.com*

Seafood menu. Lunch, dinner, late-night. Closed Sunday in fall and winter. Bar. Children's menu. Casual attire. **$$**

# CLARKSVILLE

*Information: Clarksville Lake Country Chamber of Commerce, 105 Second St., Clarksville, 434-374-2436, 800-557-5582; www.clarksvilleva.com*

## WHAT TO SEE AND DO

### OCCONEECHEE STATE PARK

*1192 Occoneechee Park Road, Clarksville, 434-374-2210; www.dcr.virginia.gov*

Approximately 2,700 acres under development; long shoreline on John H. Kerr Reservoir (Buggs Island Lake). Fishing, boat launching; hiking, picnic shelters, tent and trailer sites (hookups, season varies). Amphitheater; interpretive programs. Daily.

### PRESTWOULD

*429 Prestwould Drive, Clarksville, 434-374-8672*

Manor house built in 1795 by Sir Peyton Skipwith; rare French scenic wallpaper; original and period furnishings; restored gardens. Mid-April-October, daily; rest of year, by appointment.

## SPECIAL EVENTS

### NATIVE AMERICAN HERITAGE FESTIVAL AND POWWOW

*Occoneechee State Park, 105 Second St., Clarksville, 434-374-2210; www.clarksvilleva.com*

Native American music, dances, crafts. Second weekend in May.

### VIRGINIA LAKE FESTIVAL

*Occoneechee State Park, 105 Second St., Clarksville, 434-374-2210; www.clarksvilleva.com*

Juried arts and crafts show, beach music, dancers, gymnasts. Fun run, antique car show, sailboat race, hot-air balloons. Food vendors. Third weekend in July.

## HOTEL

### ★BEST WESTERN ON THE LAKE

*103 Second St., Clarksville, 434-374-5023; www.bestwestern.com*

70 rooms. Complimentary continental breakfast. Pool. Business center. High-speed Internet access. Reservations recommended. **$**

**VIRGINIA**

★
★
★
★
★

# CLIFTON

## RESTAURANTS

### ★★HEART-IN-HAND

*7145 Main St., Clifton, 703-830-4111; www.heartinhandrestaurant.com*

Lunch, dinner, Sunday brunch. Converted general store (circa 1870). Outdoor seating. Reservations recommended. $$

### ★★★HERMITAGE INN

*7134 Main St., Clifton, 703-266-1623; www.hermitageinnrestaurant.com*

A historic clapboard inn is the setting for an intimate dining experience. Mediterranean menu. Dinner, Sunday brunch. Closed Monday; July 14. $$$

# CLIFTON FORGE

The town, named after a tilt-hammer forge that operated profitably for almost 100 years, is at the southern tip of the Shenandoah Valley, just west of the Blue Ridge Parkway.
*Information: Alleghany Highlands Chamber of Commerce, 501 E. Ridgeway St., Clifton Forge, 540-862-4969, 888-430-5786; www.ahchamber.com*

## WHAT TO SEE AND DO

### C & O HISTORICAL SOCIETY ARCHIVES

*312 E. Ridgeway St., Clifton Forge, 540-862-2210; www.cohs.org*

Includes C & O Railroad artifacts, old blueprints for cars and engines, books, models, collection of photos. Monday-Saturday.

### DOUTHAT STATE PARK

*14239 Douthat State, Clifton Forge, 540-862-8100; www.dcr.virginia.gov*

Nearly 4,500 acres, high in the Allegheny Mountains, with 50-acre lake. Swimming beach, bathhouse, trout fishing (fee/day), boating (Memorial Day-Labor Day; rentals, some electric and water hook-ups, launching, electric motors only); hiking, self-guided trails, picnicking, restaurant, concession, camping (fee), tent and trailer sites (March-September; no hookups), cabins (all year). Visitor center, interpretive programs. Daily.

### IRON GATE GORGE

Perpendicular walls of rock rise from banks of Jackson River. James River Division of C & O Railroad and U.S. 220 pass through gorge. Restored chimney of old forge is here.

# COLONIAL NATIONAL HISTORICAL PARK

In its four independent areas—Cape Henry Memorial, the Colonial Parkway, Jamestown and Yorktown Battlefield—America as we know it began. Jamestown, Yorktown and Williamsburg (not a National Park Service area) are connected by the Colonial Parkway. Abundant in natural as well as historical wealth, the park boundaries enclose more than 9,000 acres of forest woodlands, marshes, shorelines, fields and a large variety of wildlife.
*Information: Route 17 and Goosley Road, Jamestown, 757-898-3400; www.nps.gov/colo*

★
★
★
★
★

# COVINGTON

Named for its oldest resident, Covington developed from a small village on the Jackson River. It is located in the western part of Virginia known as the Allegheny Highlands. The James River Ranger District office of the Washington and Jefferson national forests is located here.

*Information: Alleghany Highlands Chamber of Commerce, 501 E. Ridgeway St., Clifton Forge, 540-962-2178, 888-430-5786; www.ahchamber.com*

## WHAT TO SEE AND DO

### HUMPBACK BRIDGE

Erected in 1857, this 100-foot-long structure was made of hand-hewn oak held together with locust wood pins. In use until 1929, it is now maintained as part of a five-acre state highway wayside and is the only surviving curved-span covered bridge in the United States.

## HOTEL

### ★★BEST WESTERN MOUNTAIN VIEW

*820 E. Madison St., Covington, 540-962-4951, 800-937-8376; www.bestwestern.com*
76 rooms. Complimentary full breakfast. Pets are accepted with fee. Pool. Restaurant. High-speed Internet access. Free parking. Reservations recommended. $

# CULPEPER

Volunteers from Culpeper, Fauquier and Orange counties marched to Williamsburg in 1777 in answer to Governor Patrick Henry's call to arms. Their flag bore a coiled rattlesnake with the legends "Don't Tread on Me" and "Liberty or Death."

In the winter of 1862-1863, churches, homes and vacant buildings in Culpeper were turned into hospitals for the wounded from the battles of Cedar Mountain, Kelly's Ford and Brandy Station. Later, the Union Army had headquarters here.

Today, Culpeper is a light industry and trading center for a five-county area, with a healthy agriculture industry.

*Information: Chamber of Commerce, 109 S. Commerce St., Culpeper, 540-825-8628; www.culpepervachamber.com*

## WHAT TO SEE AND DO

### DOMINION WINE CELLARS

*1 Winery Ave., Culpeper, 540-825-8772*
Tours and tastings. Daily.

## HOTELS

### ★★BEST WESTERN CULPEPER INN

*791 James Madison Road South, Culpeper, 540-825-1253*
158 rooms. Complimentary breakfast. Fitness center. Restaurant. Pool. High-speed Internet access. Business center. Reservations recommended. $

### ★COMFORT INN

*890 Willis Lane, Culpeper, 540-825-4900, 877-424-6423; www.choicehotels.com*
49 rooms. Complimentary continental breakfast. Pets accepted. Reservations recommended. $

VIRGINIA

★
★★
★★
★

## SPECIALTY LODGING

### FOUNTAIN HALL BED AND BREAKFAST

*609 S. East St., Culpeper, 540-825-8200, 800-298-4748; www.fountainhall.com*

This charming bed and breakfast is located on the foothills of the Blue Ridge Mountains in historic downtown Culpeper. The 1859 Colonial Revival house was converted and now offers uniquely decorated rooms. Guests can relax in one of the spacious parlors or go off to discover the many historic sites and bike trails nearby. Six rooms. Complimentary full breakfast. Reservations recommended. **$**

# DANVILLE

This textile and tobacco center blends the leisurely pace of the Old South with the modern tempo of industry. It is one of the nation's largest brightleaf tobacco auction markets. Dan River Inc. houses the largest single-unit textile mill in the world. Nancy Langhorne, Viscountess Astor, the first woman to sit in the British House of Commons, was born in Danville in 1879.

*Information: Danville Welcome Center, 645 River Park Drive, Danville, 434-793-4636; www.visitdanville.com*

## WHAT TO SEE AND DO

### DANVILLE HISTORIC DISTRICT

*Ridge and High streets, Danville; www.visitdanville.com*

Take a self-guided walking tour of Danville's Historic District, including old tobacco buildings and Millionaires Row, with its eclectic mix of architectural styles dating from pre-Civil War times.

★
★
★
★
☆

### DANVILLE MUSEUM OF FINE ARTS AND HISTORY

*975 Main St., Danville, 434-793-5644; www.danvillemuseum.org*

Home of Major W. T. Sutherlin; built in 1857. President Jefferson Davis and his cabinet fled to Danville after receiving news of General Lee's retreat from Richmond. It was during this time that the Sutherlin mansion served as the last capital of the Confederacy. Victorian restoration in historical section of house (parlor, library and Davis bedroom). Rotating art exhibits by national and regional artists. Tuesday-Friday 10 a.m.-5 p.m., Saturday-Sunday 2-5 p.m.

### DANVILLE SCIENCE CENTER

*677 Craghead St., Danville, 434-791-5160; www.dsc.smv.org*

Hands-on museum for the entire family. Located in a restored Victorian train station. Daily.

### "WRECK OF THE OLD 97" MARKER

*Riverside Drive (Highway 58), Danville, between North Main and Locust Lane, Overpass*

Site of celebrated train wreck (September 27, 1903), made famous by a folk song.

## SPECIAL EVENTS

### DANVILLE HARVEST JUBILEE

*125 S. Floyd St., Danville, 434-799-5200*

Celebration of tobacco harvest season. Late-August-September.

### FESTIVAL IN THE PARK

*125 S. Floyd St., Danville, 434-793-4636*
Arts, crafts, entertainment. Third weekend in May.

## HOTELS

### ★HOLIDAY INN EXPRESS

*2121 Riverside Drive, Danville, 434-793-4000, 800-282-0244; www.hiexpress.com*
98 rooms. Complimentary continental breakfast. High-speed Internet access. Reservations recommended. **$**

### ★★STRATFORD INN

*2500 Riverside Drive, Danville, 434-793-2500, 800-326-8455; www.stratfordinn.com*
151 rooms. Complimentary full breakfast. Reservations recommended. **$**

# DUFFIELD

## WHAT TO SEE AND DO

### NATURAL TUNNEL STATE PARK

*Highway 871, Duffield, 276-940-2674; www.dcr.virginia.gov*
Consists of 648 acres. Giant hole chiseled through Purchase Ridge by Stock Creek; pinnacles or "chimneys." Railroad and stream are accommodated in this vast tunnel—100 feet or more in diameter, 850-feet long. Tunnel, visitor center with exhibits. Swimming, pool, fishing; hiking, picnicking, concession, camping, tent and trailer sites (Memorial Day-Labor Day). Interpretive programs. Chairlift. Park (daily); tunnel and most activities (Memorial Day-Labor Day, daily).

# DULLES INTERNATIONAL AIRPORT AREA

*Information: www.metwashairports.com/dulles*

## WHAT TO SEE AND DO

### RESTON TOWN CENTER

*11900 Market St., Reston, 703-689-4699; www.restontowncenter.com*
A 20-acre urban development incorporating elements of a traditional town square. Includes more than 50 retail shops and restaurants, movie theater complex, office space and hotel.

## SPECIAL EVENTS

### FOUNTAIN SQUARE HOLIDAY CELEBRATION

*Reston Town Center, Freedom Drive, Reston*
Choral groups, puppeteers, magicians, ice shows, dancers, parade. Thanksgiving-December 24.

### FOUNTAIN SQUARE ICE RINK

*Reston Town Center, 1830 Discovery St., Reston*
Outdoor public ice rink. Mid-November-mid-March.

### NORTHERN VIRGINIA FINE ARTS FESTIVAL

*Reston Town Center, 11921 Freedom Drive No. 980, Reston, 703-471-9242;*
*www.restonarts.org/festival*
Art sale, children's activity area, barbecue. Mid-May.

### OKTOBERFEST

*Reston Town Center, 11921 Freedom Drive, Reston; www.oktoberfestreston.com*
Biergarten with authentic German music, food. Mid-September.

### SUMMER CONCERTS

*Reston Town Center, 11921 Freedom Drive, Reston;*
*www.restontowncenter.com*
Saturday evenings June-August; also Thursday evenings in July.

## HOTELS

### ★COMFORT INN

*200 Elden St., Herndon, 703-437-7555, 800-228-5150; www.choicehotels.com*
103 rooms. Complimentary continental breakfast. Airport transportation available.
Reservations recommended. $

### ★★CROWNE PLAZA

*2200 Centreville Road, Herndon, 703-471-6700; www.cpdulles.com/herndon.html*
205 rooms. Complimentary continental breakfast. Airport transportation available.
Reservations recommended. $

### ★★HOLIDAY INN

*45425 Holiday Drive, Sterling, 703-471-7411, 800-465-4329; www.holidayinn.com*
296 rooms. Airport transportation available. Pool. Pets are accepted. Reservations
recommended. $$

### ★★★HYATT REGENCY RESTON

*1800 President's St., Reston, 703-709-1234, 800-633-7313; www.hyatt.com*
Located in the heart of Fairfax County's technology hub, this property offers a resort-
like ambience in a suburban setting. The oversized guest rooms offer flatscreen TVs,
ergonomic desk chairs and wireless Internet access. 514 rooms. Airport transporta-
tion available. Reservations recommended. $$

### ★★★MARRIOTT SUITES DULLES WORLDGATE

*13101 Worldgate Drive, Herndon, 703-709-0400, 800-228-9290; www.marriott.com*
This all-suite hotel located in the Dulles Technology Corridor is just minutes from
the airport and corporate offices. After a long day at the office or at play, guests can
relax in their spacious suites with high-speed Internet access and luxury bedding. The
hotel and surrounding area offer an indoor/outdoor pool, biking and jogging trails,
tennis, squash, bowling and miniature golf. There is also a Starbucks kiosk onsite.
253 rooms, all suites. Airport transportation available. Reservations recommended.
$$

★
★
★
★
★

### ★★★SHERATON RESTON HOTEL

*11810 Sunrise Valley Drive, Reston, 703-620-9000, 800-325-3535; www.sheraton.com*

Located just 20 minutes from Washington, D.C., and near shopping, various corporate headquarters and Reston Town Center, this contemporary hotel is a smart choice for both business and leisure travelers. Each spacious guest room features the famous Sheraton Sweet Sleeper Bed with a pillow-top mattress, individual climate control and a large work area. Golf lovers can get a game in at the adjacent Reston National Golf Course. 301 rooms. Business center. Fitness center. Pool. Pets accepted; fee. Reservations recommended. **$$**

### ★★★WESTFIELDS MARRIOTT WASHINGTON DULLES HOTEL

*14750 Conference Center Drive, Chantilly, 703-818-0300, 800-635-5666; www.marriott.com*

Located within 10 miles of the National Air and Space Museum and the Wolf Trap Center for Performing Arts, the Westfields Marriott Washington Dulles Hotel offers spacious accommodations and the Signature Fred Couples Golf Club. 340 rooms. Airport transportation available. Reservations recommended. **$$**

## RESTAURANTS

### ★★CLYDE'S

*11905 Market St., Reston, 703-787-6601; www.clydes.com*

American, seafood menu. Lunch, dinner, Sunday brunch. Bar. Outdoor seating. Reservations recommended. **$$**

### ★★FORTUNE

*1428 N. Point Village Center, Reston, 703-318-8898*

Chinese menu. Lunch, dinner. Reservations recommended. **$$**

### ★★★PALM COURT

*14750 Conference Center Drive, Chantilly, 703-818-3522; www.westfieldspalmcourt.com*

In the Westfields Marriott Hotel, this restaurant offers a buffet-style Sunday Brunch with tuxedo-clad waiters, mimosas and an unending array of sweets. American menu. Breakfast, lunch, dinner, Sunday brunch. Bar. Children's menu. Reservations recommended. Valet parking. **$$**

### ★★★RUSSIA HOUSE

*790 Station St., Herndon, 703-787-8880; www.russiahouserestaurant.com*

This contemporary restaurant features Russian artwork. The aristocratic dining experience includes dishes such as beef stroganoff or puff pastry with lamb, vegetables and tarragon sauce. Seafood menu. Lunch. Dinner. Reservations recommended.

### ★TORTILLA FACTORY

*648 Elden St., Herndon, 703-471-1156; www.thetortillafactory.com*

Mexican menu. Lunch, dinner. Children's menu. Homemade tortillas. Reservations recommended. **$$**

**VIRGINIA**

★
★
★
★
★

# FAIRFAX

Fairfax, nestled in northern Virginia in the shadow of Washington, D.C., is a quaint, historic town, which has become a government center, home to many major corporations and a thriving technology industry.

*Information: Fairfax County Convention & Visitors Bureau, 8300 Boone Blvd., 703-790-3329, 800-732-4732; www.visitfairfax.org*

## WHAT TO SEE AND DO

### ALGONKIAN

*47001 Fairway Drive, Fairfax, 703-450-4655; www.nvrpa.org*

An 800-acre park on the Potomac River; swimming (Memorial Day-Labor Day; fee); fishing, boating (ramp); golf, miniature golf, picnicking, vacation cottages, meeting and reception areas.

### BULL RUN

*7700 Bull Run Drive, Fairfax, 703-631-0550; www.nvrpa.org*

Consists of 1,500 acres. Themed swimming pool (Memorial Day-Labor Day, daily; fee); camping (one to four persons, fee; electricity available; reservations accepted, 703-631-0550); concession, picnicking, playground, miniature golf, public shooting center, nature trail. Mid-March-December.

### BURKE LAKE

*7315 Ox Road, Fairfax Station, 703-323-6601; www.fairfaxcounty.gov/parks/burkelake*

Consists of 888 acres. Fishing, boating (ramp, rentals); picnicking, playground, concession, miniature train, carousel (summer, daily; early May and late September, weekends), 18-hole and par-three golf, camping (May-September; seven-day limit). Beaver Cove Nature Trail; fitness trail. Fee for activities. Daily.

### COUNTY PARKS

*12055 Government Center Parkway, Fairfax, 703-324-8700; www.fairfaxcounty.gov/parks*

### GEORGE MASON UNIVERSITY

*4400 University Drive, Fairfax, 703-993-1000; www.gmu.edu*

This state-supported university (24,000 students.) started as a branch of the University of Virginia. Performing Arts Center features concerts, theater, dance; Fenwick Library maintains largest collection anywhere of material pertaining to Federal Theatre Project of the 1930s. Research Center for Federal Theatre Project contains 7,000 scripts, including unpublished works by Arthur Miller, sets and costume designs, and oral history collection of interviews with former Federal Theatre personnel. Monday-Friday.

### LAKE FAIRFAX

*1400 Lake Fairfax Drive, Reston, 703-471-5415; www.fairfaxcounty.gov*

Pool, boat rentals, fishing, excursion boat; picnicking, carousel, miniature train (late May-Labor Day, daily), camping (daily, closed Christmas; seven-day limit; electric additional fee). Fee for activities. Daily.

### REGIONAL PARKS

*5400 Ox Road, Fairfax Station, 703-352-5900; www.nvrpa.org*

### SULLY

*3601 Sully Road, Fairfax, 703-437-1794; www.fairfaxcounty.gov*

Restored 1794 house of Richard Bland Lee, brother of General "Light Horse Harry" Lee; some original furnishings; kitchen-washhouse, log house store, smokehouse on grounds. Guided tours. Monday, Wednesday-Sunday.

## SPECIAL EVENTS

### ANTIQUE CAR SHOW

*3601 Sully Road, Fairfax, 703-437-1794; www.fairfaxva.gov*

Four hundred antique cars, flea market and music. June.

### QUILT SHOW

*3601 Sully Road, Fairfax, 703-437-1794; www.fairfaxva.gov*

Quilts for sale, quilting demonstrations and antique quilts on display. September.

### TASTE OF THE TOWN

Selected restaurants offer sample-size specialties. Last weekend in June.

## HOTELS

### ★COMFORT INN UNIVERSITY CENTER

*11180 Fairfax Blvd., Fairfax, 703-591-5900, 877-424-6423; www.choicehotels.com*

205 rooms. Complimentary continental breakfast. Airport transportation available. Restaurant. Pets accepted. Reservations recommended. $

### ★★★HYATT FAIR LAKES

*12777 Fair Lakes Circle, Fairfax, 703-818-1234; www.hyatt.com*

Minutes from Washington Dulles Airport, this striking high-rise hotel in the wooded Fair Lakes Office Park offers large guest rooms. This property features a column-free ballroom and a towering atrium lobby. 316 rooms. Airport transportation available. High-speed Internet access. Fitness center. Pool. Reservations recommended. $$

## RESTAURANTS

### ★★ARTIE'S

*3260 Old Lee Highway, Fairfax, 703-273-7600; www.greatamericanrestaurants.com*

American menu. Lunch, dinner, late-night, Sunday brunch. Bar. Children's menu. Casual attire. $$

### ★BLUE OCEAN

*9440 Main St., Fairfax, 703-425-7555; www.izakayablueocean.com*

Japanese menu. Lunch, dinner. $$

### ★★BOMBAY BISTRO

*3570 Chain Bridge Road, Fairfax, 703-359-5810; www.bombaybistro.com*

Indian menu. Lunch, dinner, brunch. Bar. Outdoor seating. $$

★
★
★
★
★

### ★★★LARUE 123 AT THE BAILIWICK INN

*4023 Chain Bridge Road, Fairfax, 703-691-2266; www.larue123.com*

This Federal-style inn and restaurant, on the National Register of Historic Places, offers French-American cuisine in a quaint, romantic space. Visit for one of the seasonal wine dinners or for traditional English high tea in one of the intimate parlors. French, seafood menu. Lunch, dinner. Closed Monday, Tuesday. Reservations recommended. Outdoor seating. $$$

### ★P. J. SKIDOO'S

*9908 Lee Highway, Fairfax, 703-591-4515; www.pjskidoos.com*

American menu. Lunch, dinner, Sunday brunch. Bar. Children's menu. Outdoor seating. $$

# FALLS CHURCH

Falls Church is a pleasant, cosmopolitan suburb of Washington, D.C., just over the Arlington County line, graced with many interesting old houses. This was a crossover point between the North and the South through which pioneers, armies, adventurers and merchants passed.

*Information: Greater Falls Church Chamber of Commerce, 417 W. Broad St.,*
*Falls Church, 703-532-1050; www.fallschurchchamber.org*

## WHAT TO SEE AND DO

### THE FALLS CHURCH

*115 E. Fairfax St., Falls Church, 703-532-7600; www.thefallschurch.org*

This 1769 Episcopal building replaced the original wooden church built in 1732. Served as a recruiting station during the Revolutionary War; abandoned until 1830; used during the Civil War as a hospital and later as a stable for cavalry horses. Restored according to original plans with gallery additions in 1959. Monday-Friday, Sunday. Worship services: Wednesday noon and Sunday at 8 a.m. and noon.

### FOUNTAIN OF FAITH

*7400 Lee Highway, Falls Church*

Memorial dedicated to the four chaplains—two Protestant, one Jewish, one Catholic—who were aboard the *USS Dorchester* when it was torpedoed off Greenland in 1943. They gave their life jackets to four soldiers on deck who had none.

## HOTEL

### ★★★MARRIOTT FAIRVIEW PARK

*3111 Fairview Park Drive, Falls Church, 703-849-9400; www.marriott.com*

Sitting on a park-like setting, this property offers jogging paths through woods and around a lake. Guest rooms feature luxurious down pillows and comforters plus the Marriott's classic Revive beds. 394 rooms. Restaurant, bar. Pool. Fitness center. High-speed Internet access. Business center. Reservations recommended. $$

## RESTAURANTS

### ★★BANGKOK STEAKHOUSE

*926 W. Broad St., Falls Church, 703-534-0095;*
*www.fallschurchwebsite.com/BangkokSteakhouse.htm*

Thai, Laotian menu. Lunch, dinner. $$

### ★★★DUANGRAT'S

*5878 Leesburg Pike, Falls Church, 703-820-5775; www.duangrats.com*

This Thai restaurant has been a Virginia/Washington, D. C. area staple since its inception in 1980. Ignore its strip-mall location and dive into the vast menu; standouts include a spicy tom yum soup, flavorful bhram and the "grandma" duck dish. Thai menu. Lunch, dinner. Bar. **$$**

### ★★★HAANDI

*1222 W. Broad St., Falls Church, 703-533-3501; www.haandi.com*

The accolades are plentiful for this fine dining restaurant, renowned as one of the best in the region. The depth of flavor and unique spices found in each dish are unmatched. Entrées include kesar chicken korma, barbecued chunks of boneless chicken breast marinated in saffron and cooked in a creamy curry sauce. Indian menu. Lunch, dinner. **$$**

### ★★PEKING GOURMET INN

*6029 Leesburg Pike (Highway 7), Falls Church, 703-671-8088; www.pekinggourmet.com*

Chinese menu. Lunch, dinner. Reservations recommended. **$$**

### ★★PILIN THAI

*116 W. Broad St. (Highway 7), Falls Church, 703-241-5850; www.pilinthairestaurant.com*

Thai menu. Lunch, dinner. Bar. Reservations recommended. **$$**

# FARMVILLE

Longwood College's Jeffersonian buildings provide architectural interest in downtown Farmville.

## WHAT TO SEE AND DO
### TWIN LAKES STATE PARK

*Farmville, 434-392-3435; www.dcr.virginia.gov*

More than 250 acres of state forest; two lakes. Swimming, bathhouse, fishing, boating (rentals, launching electric motors only); hiking, bicycle and self-guided trails; picnicking, playground, concession, camping, hook-ups, tent and trailer sites, cabins (March-December); pavilion.

## HOTEL
### ★COMFORT INN

*2108 S. Main St., Farmville, 434-392-8163, 877-424-6423; www.choicehotels.com*

51 rooms. Complimentary continental breakfast. Pool. Tennis. Reservations recommended. **$**

# FREDERICKSBURG

One of the seeds of the American Revolution was planted here when a resolution declaring independence from Great Britain was passed on April 29, 1775. George Washington went to school in Fredericksburg, his sister Betty lived here and his mother, Mary Ball Washington, lived and died here. James Monroe practiced law in

**VIRGINIA**

★
★
★
★

town. Guns for the Revolution were manufactured here, and four of the most savage battles of the Civil War were fought nearby.

Captain John Smith visited the area in 1608 and gave glowing reports of its possibilities for settlement. In 1727, the General Assembly directed that 50 acres of "lease-land" be laid out and the town called Fredericksburg, after the Prince of Wales.

Ships from abroad sailed up the Rappahannock River to the harbor—ampler then than now—to exchange their goods for those brought from "upcountry" by the great road wagons and river carriers. The town prospered.

The Civil War left Fredericksburg ravaged. Situated midway between Richmond and Washington, it was a recurring objective of both sides; the city changed hands seven times and the casualties were high.

Even so, many buildings put up before 1775 still stand. Proudly aware of their town's place in the country's history, the townspeople keep Fredericksburg inviting with fresh paint, beautiful lawns and well-kept gardens.

*Information: Visitor Center, 706 Caroline St., Fredericksburg, 540-373-1776, 800-678-4748; www.fredericksburgva.com*

## FREDERICKSBURG'S PRESIDENTIAL LEGACY

Midway between Washington and Richmond, the old colonial river port of Fredericksburg earned the dubious nickname of battlefield city in the Civil War, as the site of four major battles between 1862 and 1864. As a result, many visitors overlook its colonial antecedents and its unique status as the hometown of both George Washington and James Monroe.

This one-hour, one-mile stroll down its quiet tree-shaded streets is an introduction to this presidential legacy. Begin by visiting the **Fredericksburg Visitor Center** at *706 Caroline St.* Walk north along Caroline Street, the Historic District's attractive main street, which is lined with interesting shops and cafes. At George Street, turn left one block to Charles Street, and then go right to *908 Charles,* the **James Monroe Museum.** As a young man, Monroe practiced law in an office on this site. The museum displays rich pieces of furniture he took with him to the White House as the country's fifth president.

Continue north on Charles Street to Lewis Street and turn left onto Washington Avenue. Turn right a half block to **Kenmore Plantation,** the lovely mansion and garden at *2101 Washington.* Built in 1752, it was the home of Betty Lewis, George Washington's sister, and her husband Fielding Lewis, a financier and gun manufacturer who aided the Revolutionary cause. The house is particularly noted for its richly decorated, hand-molded ceilings.

From Kenmore, retrace your steps on Lewis Street for three blocks to Charles Street. At *1200 Charles St.* stands the **Mary Washington House,** which George Washington bought for his mother in 1772 so she could be more easily looked after by daughter Betty. Though George, who lived 40 miles north at Mount Vernon, was a dutiful son, his mother often accused him of neglect, a story told at the museum.

Continue east on Lewis to Caroline Street, and turn north (left) to the **Rising Sun Tavern** at 1306, the tour's conclusion. Built in 1760 as a private home by Charles Washington, George's younger brother, it has been restored to the 18th-century tavern it became in 1792.

★
★
★
★
☆

## WHAT TO SEE AND DO

### BELMONT (THE GARI MELCHERS ESTATE AND MEMORIAL GALLERY)

*224 Washington St., Fredericksburg, 540-654-1015; www.umw.edu*

Residence from 1916 to 1932 of American-born artist Gari Melchers (1860-1932), best known for his portraits of the famous and wealthy, including Theodore Roosevelt, William Vanderbilt and Andrew Mellon and as an important impressionist artist of the period. The artist's studio comprises the nation's largest collection of his works, housing more than 1,800 paintings and drawings. The site is a registered National and State Historic Landmark and includes a 27-acre estate, frame house built in the late 18th century and enlarged over the years, and a stone studio built by Melchers. Owned by the state of Virginia, Belmont is administered by Mary Washington College. Daily.

### CONFEDERATE CEMETERY

*Willliam Street and Washington Avenue, Fredericksburg; 540-373-6122; www.nps.gov/frsp*

There are 2,640 Confederate Civil War soldiers buried here, some in graves marked "Unknown."

### FREDERICKSBURG AREA MUSEUM (TOWN HALL)

*907 Princess Anne St., Fredericksburg, 540-371-3037; www.famcc.org*

Former 1814 Town Hall is a Museum and cultural center that interprets the history of Fredericksburg area from its first settlers to the 20th century. Changing exhibits. Children's events. Daily.

### FREDERICKSBURG MASONIC LODGE NO. 4, AF AND AM

*803 Princess Anne and Hanover streets, Fredericksburg, 540-373-5885; www.masoniclodge4.com*

Washington was initiated into this Lodge November 4, 1752; the building, dating from 1812, contains relics of his initiation and membership; authentic Gilbert Stuart portrait; 300-year-old Bible on which Washington took his Masonic oath. Daily.

### GEORGE WASHINGTON'S FERRY FARM

*268 Kings Highway, Fredericksburg, 540-370-0732; www.kenmore.org*

The site of George Washington's boyhood home. Once a tobacco plantation, it now serves as an archaeological dig and a nature preserve. Guided tours. Daily.

### HUGH MERCER APOTHECARY SHOP

*1020 Charles St., Fredericksburg, 540-373-1776; www.apva.org*

This 18th-century medical office and pharmacy offers exhibits on the medicine and methods of treatment used by Dr. Hugh Mercer before he left to join the Revolutionary War as brigadier general. Authentic herbs and period medical instruments. Daily.

### JAMES MONROE MUSEUM

*908 Charles St., Fredericksburg, 540-654-1043; www.umw.edu*

As a young lawyer, James Monroe lived and worked in Fredericksburg from 1786 to 1789 and even served on Fredericksburg's City Council. This museum houses one of the nation's largest collections of Monroe memorabilia, articles and original documents. Included are the desk bought in France in 1794 during his years as ambassador and used in the White House for signing the Monroe Doctrine, formal attire worn at Court of Napoleon, and more than 40 books from Monroe's library; also garden. The site is a national historic landmark owned by the Commonwealth of Virginia and administered by Mary Washington College. Daily.

## KENMORE INN

*1201 Washington Ave., Fredericksburg, 540-373-3381; www.kenmore.org*
Considered one of finest restorations in Virginia; former home of Colonel Fielding Lewis, commissioner of Fredericksburg gunnery, who married George Washington's only sister, Betty. On an original grant of 863 acres, Lewis built a magnificent home in 1752; three rooms have full decorative molded plaster ceilings. Diorama of 18th-century Fredericksburg. Daily; closed January-February.

## MARY WASHINGTON COLLEGE

*1301 College Road, Fredericksburg, 540-654-1000, 800-468-5614; www.umw.edu*
Coeducational liberal arts and sciences institution (3,700 students.) that offers historic preservation, computer science, and business administration. College also includes 275 acres of open and wooded campus; red brick, white-pillared buildings. President of the college occupies Brompton (private), house built in 1830 on land sold to Fielding Lewis in 1760 and expanded by a later owner, Colonel John Lawrence Marye. Campus tours.

★
★
★
★
★

## MARY WASHINGTON HOUSE

*1200 Charles St., Fredericksburg, 540-373-1569; www.apva.org*
Bought by George for his mother in 1772; she lived here until her death in 1789. Here she was visited by General Lafayette. Some original furnishings. Boxwood garden. Daily.

## MARY WASHINGTON MONUMENT

*Washington Avenue and Pitt Street, Fredericksburg, www.kenmore.org*
Where Mrs. Washington often went to rest and pray, and where she is buried.

## MASONIC CEMETERY

*George and Charles streets, Fredericksburg; www.masoniclodge4.org*
One of nation's oldest Masonic burial grounds.

## OLD SLAVE BLOCK

*William and Charles streets, Fredericksburg*
Circular block of sandstone about three-feet high from which ladies mounted their horses and slaves were auctioned in antebellum days.

## PRESBYTERIAN CHURCH

*810 Princess Anne and George streets, Fredericksburg, 540-373-7057;*
*www.fredericksburgpc.org*
Cannonballs in the front pillar and other damages inflicted in 1862 bombardment. Pews were torn loose and made into coffins for soldiers. Clara Barton, founder of

the American Red Cross, is said to have nursed the wounded here. A plaque to her memory is in the churchyard. Open on request (Monday-Friday, Sunday).

## RISING SUN TAVERN

*1306 Caroline St., Fredericksburg, 540-371-1494; www.apva.org*

Washington's youngest brother Charles built this tavern around 1760, which became a social and political center and stagecoach stop. Restored and authentically refurnished as an 18th-century tavern; costumed tavern staff, English and American pewter collection. Daily.

## SAILOR'S CREEK BATTLEFIELD HISTORIC STATE PARK

*State Routes 307 N. and 17, Fredericksburg, 434-392-3435; www.dcr.virginia.gov*

The site of last major battle of the Civil War on April 6, 1865, preceding Lee's surrender at Appomattox by three days. Auto tour.

## ST. GEORGE'S EPISCOPAL CHURCH AND CHURCHYARD

*905 Princess Anne and George streets, Fredericksburg, 540-373-4133;*
*www.stgeorgesepiscopal.net*

Patrick Henry, uncle of the orator, was the third rector. Headstones in the churchyard bear the names of illustrious Virginians. Daily.

## ST. JAMES HOUSE

*1300 Charles St., Fredericksburg, 540-373-1569; www.apva.org*

Frame house built in 1760s, antique furnishings, porcelain and silver collections; landscaped gardens. Open Historic Garden Week in April and first week in October; other times by appointment.

## SPECIAL EVENTS

### CHRISTMAS CANDLELIGHT TOUR

*604 William St., Fredericksburg, 540-371-4504; www.hffi.org*

Historic homes open to the public; carriage rides; Christmas decorations and refreshments of the Colonial period. First weekend in December.

### HISTORIC GARDEN WEEK

Private homes open. Mid-late April.

### MARKET SQUARE FAIR

Entertainment, crafts demonstrations, food. Mid-May.

### QUILT SHOW

Exhibits at various locations. Demonstrations and sale of old and new quilts. September.

## HOTELS

### ★★HOLIDAY INN SELECT FREDERICKSBURG

*2801 Plank Road, Fredericksburg, 540-786-8321, 800-282-0244; www.holidayinn.com*

195 rooms. Airport transportation available. Reservations recommended. **$**

### ★★RAMADA INN SOUTH FREDERICKSBURG

*5324 Jefferson Davis Highway, Fredericksburg, 540-898-1102, 800-311-5192;*
*www.ramadainn.com*

195 rooms. Restaurant. Pool. Spa. Fitness center. Pets accepted. Reservations recommended. **$**

## SPECIALTY LODGINGS

### FREDERICKSBURG COLONIAL INN

*1707 Princess Anne St., Fredericksburg, 540-371-5666; www.fci1.com*

Located at the north end of Fredericksburg, this lodging is several blocks from the Rappahannock River and approximately seven blocks from the historic Olde Towne center. Guest rooms feature furnishings and décor that reflect the Civil War period. 27 rooms. Complimentary continental breakfast. Reservations recommended. **$**

### KENMORE INN

*1200 Princess Anne St., Fredericksburg, 540-371-7622; www.kenmoreinn.com*

This historic bed and breakfast, which dates to the early 19th century, is located at the northern end of Olde Towne Fredericksburg and several blocks from the Rappahannock River. The two-story white-brick building features a broad staircase leading to the guest rooms, which are uniquely furnished and decorated. Nine rooms. Complimentary full breakfast. Reservations recommended. **$$**

### RICHARD JOHNSTON INN

*711 Caroline St., Fredericksburg, 540-899-7606, 877-557-0770;*
*www.therichardjohnstoninn.com*

Easily accessible from Interstate 95, this historic inn is located in the heart of Fredericksburg's Olde Towne historic district. Each guest room is unique in décor and furnishings, with a mix of antiques and period reproductions. Nine rooms. Complimentary continental breakfast. Reservations recommended. **$**

## RESTAURANT

### ★★RENATO

*422 William St., Fredericksburg, 540-371-8228; www.ristoranterenato.com*

Italian menu. Lunch, dinner. Business casual attire. Reservations recommended. Valet parking. Outdoor seating. **$$$**

# FREDERICKSBURG AND SPOTSYLVANIA NATIONAL MILITARY PARK

## WHAT TO SEE AND DO

### CHANCELLORSVILLE VISITOR CENTER

*120 Chatham Lane, Fredericksburg and Spotsylvania National Military Park,*
*540-786-2880; www.nps.gov/frsp/chanville.htm*

Slide program, museum with exhibits; dioramas. Daily.

★
★
★
★
★

### CHATHAM MANOR

*120 Chatham Lane, Fredericksburg and Spotsylvania National Military Park,*
*540-371-0802; www.nps.gov/frsp/chatham.htm*

This Georgian brick manor house, owned by a wealthy planter, was converted to Union headquarters during two of the battles of Fredericksburg. The house was eventually used as a hospital where Clara Barton and Walt Whitman nursed the wounded. Daily.

### FREDERICKSBURG AND SPOTSYLVANIA NATIONAL MILITARY PARK

*Lafayette Boulevard and Sunken Road, Fredericksburg, 540-373-6122;*
*www.nps.gov/frsp*

Visitor Center on Old US 1.

### FREDERICKSBURG NATIONAL CEMETERY

*Lafayette Boulevard and Sunken Road, Fredericksburg*

More than 15,000 Federal interments; almost 13,000 unknown.

### FREDERICKSBURG VISITOR CENTER

*Lafayette Boulevard (Highway 1) and Sunken Road, Fredericksburg and*
*Spotsylvania National Military Park, Fredericksburg, 540-373-6122*

Information and directions for various parts of park. Tours should start here. Daily.

### MUSEUM

*1900 E. Kanawha, Fredericksburg*

Slide program, diorama, exhibits. Daily.

### OLD SALEM CHURCH

*Fredericksburg and Spotsylvania National Military Park, Fredericksburg*

Building used as a field hospital and refugee center. Scene of battle on May 3-4, 1863.

**VIRGINIA**

### STONEWALL JACKSON SHRINE

*120 Chatham Lane, Fredericksburg and Spotsylvania National Military Park,*
*804-633-6076; www.nps.gov/frsp*

Plantation office where, Confederate General Jackson, ill with pneumonia and with his shattered left arm amputated, murmured, "Let us cross over the river, and rest under the shade of the trees," and died on May 10, 1863. Mid-June-Labor Day, daily; April-mid-June, after Labor Day-October, Monday, Tuesday, Friday-Sunday; rest of year, Monday, Saturday-Sunday.

# FRONT ROYAL

Once known as "Hell Town" for all the wild and reckless spirits it attracted, Front Royal was a frontier stop on the way to eastern markets. The present name is supposed to have originated in the command, "Front the royal oak," given by an English officer to his untrained mountain militia recruits.

Belle Boyd, the Confederate spy, worked here extracting military secrets from Union officers. It is said that she once invited General Nathaniel Banks, whose regiment was occupying the town, and his officers to a ball. Later she raced on horseback to tell General Jackson what she had learned. The next morning (May 23, 1862), the

Confederates attacked and captured nearly all of the Union troops, providing Jackson one of his early victories in the famous Valley Campaign.

Front Royal was a quiet village until the entrance to Shenandoah National Park and the beginning of Skyline Drive opened in 1935, just one mile to the south. With millions of motorists passing through every year, the town has grown rapidly. The production of automotive finishes, limestone and cement contributes to the town's economy, but the tourism industry remains one of its largest.

*Information: Chamber of Commerce of Front Royal-Warren County, 104 E. Main St., Front Royal, 540-635-3185, 800-338-2576; www.frontroyalchamber.com*

## WHAT TO SEE AND DO

### JACKSON'S CHASE GOLF COURSE

*65 Jackson's Chase Drive, Front Royal, 540-635-7814; www.jacksonschase.com*

Jackson's Chase is built on a tract of land that was used by Confederate General "Stonewall" Jackson to chase Union forces through the Shenandoah Valley and into the eventual first Battle of Winchester. The course itself incorporates the area's rolling terrain into plateau fairways and holes lined with water. Holes three through eight surround a small area being developed for homes with one-acre lots, for those who wish to live in full view of history and the links.

### SHENANDOAH VALLEY GOLF CLUB

*134 Golf Club Circle, Front Royal, 540-636-4653; www.svgcgolf.com*

Nestled into the Blue Ridge Mountains, Shenandoah Valley offers 27 holes and has hosted such prestigious tournaments as the PGA Tour's Kemper Open. If you want to play, make sure to reserve a tee time at least a week in advance. The course is affordable and playable for most any golfer.

### SKY MEADOWS STATE PARK

*11012 Edmonds Lane, Front Royal, 540-592-3556; www.dcr.virginia.gov*

A 1,862-acre park. Fishing pond; hiking and bridle trails, picnicking, primitive walk-in camping. Visitor center; programs. Daily.

### SKYLINE CAVERNS

*10344 Stonewall Jackson Highway, Front Royal, 540-635-4545, 800-296-4545; www.skylinecaverns.com*

Extensive, rare, intricate flowerlike formations of calcite (anthodites); sound and light presentation; 37-foot waterfall; clear stream stocked with trout (observation only). Electrically lighted; 54 F year-round. Miniature train provides trip through surrounding wooded area. Snack bar; gift shop. Cavern tours start every few minutes. Monday-Friday: year round; daily. March-mid-November.

### WARREN RIFLES CONFEDERATE MUSEUM

*95 Chester St., Front Royal, 540-636-6982*

Historic relics and memorabilia of War between the States. Mid-April-October, daily; rest of year, by appointment.

★
★
★
☆
☆

### FESTIVAL OF LEAVES

*Main and Chester streets, Front Royal, 540-636-1446*

Arts and crafts, demonstrations; historic exhibits; parade. Second weekend in October.

### VIRGINIA MUSHROOM AND WINE FESTIVAL

Mushrooms, wine and cheese. Entertainment. Third Saturday in May.

### WARREN COUNTY FAIR

*540-635-5821; www.warrencountyfair.com*

Entertainment, livestock exhibits and sale, contests. First week in August.

### WARREN COUNTY GARDEN TOUR

Garden Club sponsors tours of historic houses and gardens. Mid-late April.

## HOTEL

### ★★QUALITY INN

*10 S. Commerce Ave., Front Royal, 540-635-3161, 877-424-6423;*
*www.choicehotels.com*

106 rooms. Free continental breakfast. Free wireless Internet access. Pets accepted. **$**

# GALAX

Galax is named for the pretty evergreen with heart-shaped leaves that florists use in various arrangements. It grows in the mountainous regions around Galax and is gathered to be sold all over the United States. Nearby are three mountain passes: Fancy Gap, Low Gap and Piper's Gap.

*Information: Galax-Carroll-Grayson Chamber of Commerce, 405 N. Main St., Galax, 276-236-2184; www.gcgchamber.com*

## WHAT TO SEE AND DO

### CLIFFVIEW TRADING POST

*442 Cliffview Road, Galax, 276-238-1530; www.merchantcircle.com*

Bike rentals (Tuesday-Saturday) and horse rentals (April-November, Tuesday-Saturday); trail rides in New River Trail State Park.

### JEFF MATTHEWS MEMORIAL MUSEUM

*606 W. Stuart Drive, Galax, 276-236-7874; www.jeffmatthewsmuseum.org*

Two authentically restored log cabins (1834 and 1860s). Relocated to present site and furnished with items used in the period in which the cabins were inhabited. Also house collection of photos of Civil War veterans, artifacts and memorabilia of the area; covered wagon; farm implements. One restored cabin used as a blacksmith's shop. Wednesday-Sunday.

### RECREATION

Swimming, boating, fishing on New River; hunting and hiking. Canoeing and other activities can be found.

435

**VIRGINIA**

★
★★
★
★

SPECIAL EVENT

**OLD FIDDLER'S CONVENTION**

*Felts Park, 276-236-8541; www.oldfiddlersconvention.com*

Folk songs, bands and dancing. Second week in August.

# GEORGE WASHINGTON BIRTHPLACE NATIONAL MONUMENT

George Washington, first child of Augustine and Mary Ball Washington, was born on February 22, 1732 (on the old-style calendar, February 11) at his father's estate on Popes Creek on the south shore of the Potomac. The family moved in 1735 to Little Hunting Creek Plantation (later called Mount Vernon), then in 1738 to Ferry Farm near Fredericksburg. The 538-acre monument includes much of the old plantation land. Daily.

*www.nps.gov/gewa*

## WHAT TO SEE AND DO

**COLONIAL FARM**

*1732 Popes Creek Road, George Washington Birthplace National Monument, 804-224-1732; www.nps.gov/gewa*

"Living" farm designed to show 18th-century Virginia plantation life; livestock, colonial garden, several farm buildings, furnished colonial kitchen, household slave quarters and spinning and weaving room.

**FAMILY BURIAL GROUND**

*1732 Popes Creek Road, George Washington Birthplace National Monument, 804-224-1732; www.nps.gov/archive/gewa*

Site of 1664 home of Colonel John Washington, first Washington in Virginia and great-grandfather of the first president. Washington's ancestors are buried here.

**MEMORIAL HOUSE**

*1732 Popes Creek Road, George Washington Birthplace National Monument, 804-224-1732; www.nps.gov/gewa*

Original house burned and was never rebuilt. The Memorial House is not a replica of the original; it represents a composite of a typical 18th-century Virginia plantation house. Bricks were handmade from nearby clay. Furnishings are typical of the time.

**PICNIC AREA**

*1732 Popes Creek Road, George Washington Birthplace National Monument, 804-224-1732; www.nps.gov/gewa*

**VISITOR CENTER**

*1732 Popes Creek Road, George Washington Birthplace National Monument, 804-224-1732; www.nps.gov*

Orientation film; museum exhibits.

436

VIRGINIA

# GLEN ALLEN

## HOTEL

### ★SPRINGHILL SUITES

*9701 Brook Road, Glen Allen, 804-266-9403, 800-287-9400; www.marriott.com/ricsh*
136 rooms. Complimentary continental breakfast. Pets not accepted. **$$**

# GLOUCESTER

In spring, acres of daffodil blooms make this area a treat for the traveler. This elm-shaded village is the commercial center of Gloucester (GLOSS-ter) County. There are many old landmarks and estates nearby, including the birthplace of Walter Reed, at the junction of Highways 614 and 616.

*Information: Chamber of Commerce, 6688 Main St., Gloucester, 804-693-2425; www.gloucestervacc.com*

## WHAT TO SEE AND DO

### COUNTY COURTHOUSE

*6489 Main St., Gloucester, 804-693-4042; www.gloucesterva.info*
Part of Gloucester Court House Circle Historic District. Portraits of native sons in the courtroom; plaques memorializing Nathaniel Bacon, leader in the rebellion of 1676, the first organized resistance to British authority, and Major Walter Reed, surgeon and conqueror of yellow fever. Monday-Friday.

### ROSEWELL HISTORIC RUINS

*6549 Main St., Gloucester, 804-693-2585; www.rosewell.org*
Three-story Georgian mansion's brickwork was put in place over 250 years ago. Majestic ruins hint at projecting pavilions, arched windows and stone-capped chimney stacks. Tours by appointment. April-October, Sunday; winter by appointment.

### VIRGINIA INSTITUTE OF MARINE SCIENCE, COLLEGE OF WILLIAM AND MARY

*1208 Greate Road, Gloucester Point, 804-684-7000; www.vims.edu*
Small marine aquarium and museum display local fish and invertebrates; marine science exhibits, bookstore. Monday-Friday.

**VIRGINIA**

★
★
★
★

# GREAT DISMAL SWAMP NATIONAL WILDLIFE REFUGE

Harriet Beecher Stowe found Virginia's Dismal Swamp a perfect setting for her anti-slavery novel *Dred* (1856); modern hunters, fishermen and naturalists find that the area fits their ambitions just as well. From its northern edge just southwest of Norfolk, the swamp stretches almost due south like a great ribbon, 25 miles long and 11 miles wide. Centuries of decaying organic matter have created layers of peat so deep that fire would sometimes smolder under the surface for weeks.

Creation of the refuge began in 1973 when the Union Camp Corporation donated 49,100 acres of land to the Nature Conservancy, which in turn conveyed it to the Department of Interior. The refuge was officially established through the Dismal Swamp Act of 1974 and is managed for the primary purpose of protecting and preserving a unique ecosystem. The refuge now consists of more than 107,000 acres of forested wetlands that have been greatly altered by drainage and logging operations.

Near the center is Lake Drummond, 3,100 acres of juniper water, which is water that combines the juices of gum, cypress and maple with a strong infusion of juniper or white cedar. The chemical mix added by the tree resins results in a water that remains sweet, or fresh, indefinitely. In the days of long sailing voyages, when ordinary water became foul after a few weeks, this "dark water" was highly valued.

The Great Dismal Swamp has also been commercially exploited for its timber, particularly cypress and cedar. A company organized by George Washington and several other businessmen bought a large piece of the swamp and used slave labor to dig the Dismal Swamp Canal, which both facilitated drainage of timber land and provided a transportation route in and out of the swamp.

Animal and bird life continues to abound in this eerie setting. There are white-tailed deer and rarely-observed black bears, foxes, bobcats and a large number of snakes, including copperheads, cottonmouths and rattlesnakes. Birding is popular in the swamp from April-June; the peak of spring migration is mid-April-mid-May.
*Information: Refuge Manager, 3100 Desert Road, Suffolk, 757-986-3705; www.fws.gov/northeast/greatdismalswamp*

# GREAT FALLS

## WHAT TO SEE AND DO

### COLVIN RUN MILL HISTORIC SITE
*10017 Colvin Run Road, Great Falls, 703-759-2771; www.fairfaxcounty.gov*
Tours of historical gristmill. General store, miller's house exhibit, barn and grounds. Closed Tuesday.

## RESTAURANTS

### ★★★DANTE
*1148 Walker Road, Great Falls, 703-759-3131; www.danterestaurant.com*
A historic Victorian home (previously a dairy farm and "lying-in" hospital) is the setting for this romantic restaurant. There are several small dining areas, each with its own unique décor, but all are charming—one room even has an entire wall displaying wine bottles. The authentic northern Italian menu offers items such as rabbit legs, osso buco and homemade ravioli. Don't leave without trying the layered chocolate cake (filled with a chocolate mousse) with a cup of espresso. Italian menu. Lunch, dinner. Bar. Business casual attire. Reservations recommended. Outdoor seating. $$$

### ★★★FIORE DI LUNA
*1025 Seneca Road, Great Falls, 703-444-4060; www.fiorediluna.com*
Fiore di Luna is a simple but elegant Northern Italian restaurant, serving dishes such as butternut squash gnocchi with a robiola cheese sauce, julienne celery, amaretti cookies and parmesan cheese or Grimaud farm-raised Muscovy duck breast with baby green and red Brussels sprouts, white polenta timbale and parsley purée. Italian menu. Lunch, dinner. Closed Monday. Bar. Business casual attire. Reservations recommended. Outdoor seating. $$$

★
★
★
★

### ★★★L'AUBERGE CHEZ FRANCOIS
*332 Springvale Road, Great Falls, 703-759-3800; www.laubergechezfrancois.com*

Rich, hearty dishes at this Alsatian-themed restaurant are served by dirndl-clad waitresses and waiters in red vests with gold buttons. Located outside the Great Falls area, this charming farmhouse restaurant is set along a winding, two-lane road. Outside, it is surrounded by flowers and an herb garden, a gazebo and fountains on the terrace. The inside is cozy with wood beams, wood burning fireplaces and stained glass panels. The Haeringer family focuses on traditional Alsatian French cuisine and offers a prix fixe menu. French menu. Dinner. Closed Monday. Children's menu. Business casual attire. Reservations recommended. Outdoor seating. $$$

### ★★★LE RELAIS
*1025-I Seneca Road, Great Falls, 703-444-4060*

French menu. Lunch, dinner. Closed Monday. Bar. Outdoor seating. $$$

### ★★★SERBIAN CROWN
*1141 Walker Road, Great Falls, 703-759-4150; www.serbiancrown.com*

Russian and French cuisines are fearlessly combined to create an elegant menu at this special-occasion restaurant. Beef stroganoff, stuffed cabbage rolls, marinated wild boar, and duck braised in sauerkraut are just a few of the items that keep diners coming back for more. Various live entertainments such as a violinist, Gypsy music and a singalong piano bar add to the unique ambience. French, international menu. Lunch, dinner, late-night. Bar. Business casual attire. Reservations recommended. $$$

# HAMPTON

Hampton is the oldest continuous English-speaking community in the United States (Jamestown, settled in 1607, is a national historical park, but not a town). The settlement began at a place then called Kecoughtan, with the building of Fort Algernourne as protection against the Spanish. In the late 1600s and early 1700s, pirates harassed the area. Finally in 1718, the notorious brigand Blackbeard was killed by Lieutenant Robert Maynard and organized piracy came to an end here.

Hampton was shelled in the Revolutionary War, sacked by the British in the War of 1812 and burned in 1861 by retreating Confederates to prevent its occupation by Union forces. Only the gutted walls of St. John's Church survived the fire. The town was rebuilt after the Civil War by its citizens and soldiers. Computer technology, manufacturing, aerospace research and commercial fishing are now big business here.

Langley Air Force Base, headquarters for the Air Combat Command, Fort Monroe, headquarters for the U.S. Army's Training and Doctrine Command, and the NASA Langley Research Center are all located here.

*Information: Hampton Visitor Center, 120 Old Hampton Lane, Hampton,*
*757-722-1222, 800-487-8778; www.hampton.va.us*

## WHAT TO SEE AND DO
### BLUEBIRD GAP FARM
*60 Pine Chapel Road, Hampton, 757-727-6739; www.virginia.org*

This 60-acre farm includes barnyard zoo; indigenous wildlife such as deer and wolves; antique and modern farm equipment and farmhouse artifacts. Picnicking, playground. Wednesday-Sunday.

**VIRGINIA**

## BUCKROE BEACH

*22 Lincoln St., Hampton, 757-850-5134; www.hampton.gov*

Swimming; public park, concerts. Lifeguards. Memorial Day-Labor Day. Hours: 8 a.m.-6 p.m.

## CASEMATE MUSEUM

*20 Bernard Road, Hampton, 757-788-3391; www.virginia.org*

Provides insight on heritage of the fort, Old Point Comfort and the Army Coast Artillery Corps. Museum offers access to a series of casemates and a walking tour of the fort. Jefferson Davis casemate contains a cell in which the Confederacy's president was confined on false charges of plotting to kill Abraham Lincoln. Museum features Civil War exhibits, military uniforms and assorted artwork, including three original Remington drawings, along with audiovisual programs. Scale models of coast artillery guns and dioramas represent the role of the coast artillery from 1901 to 1946. Daily.

## CHAPEL OF THE CENTURION

One of the oldest churches on the Virginia peninsula. Woodrow Wilson worshipped here occasionally.

## EMANCIPATION OAK

The Emancipation Proclamation was read here.

## FORT MONROE

First fort here was a stockade called Fort Algernourne; the second, Fort George, though built of brick, was destroyed by a hurricane in 1749; the present fort was completed about 1834.

## HAMPTON CAROUSEL

*602 Settlers Landing Road, Hampton, 757-727-6381; www.virginia.org*

Completely restored in 1991, this antique 1920 carousel is housed in its own pavilion and features 48 hand-carved horses. June-September, daily; October-November, Friday-Sunday; December-end of May, closed.

## HAMPTON UNIVERSITY

*Cemetery Road and Frissell Avenue, Hampton, 757-727-5253; www.hamptonu.edu*

Founded by Union Brigadier General Samuel Chapman Armstrong, chief of the Freedman's Bureau, to prepare the youth of the South, regardless of color, for the work of organizing and instructing schools in the Southern states; many blacks and Native Americans came to be educated. Now Virginia's only coeducational, nondenominational, four-year private college (6,100 students). The Hampton choir is famous. It "sang up" a building, Virginia-Cleveland Hall, in 1870 on a trip through New England and Canada, raising close to $100,000 at concerts.

## HAMPTON UNIVERSITY MUSEUM

*Huntington Building, Cemetery Road and Frissell Avenue, Hampton, 757-727-5308; www.museum.hamptonu.edu*

Collection of ethnic art; Native American and African artifacts; contemporary African-American works; paintings by renowned artists. Closed Sunday.

### MISS HAMPTON II HARBOR CRUISES

*764 Settlers Landing Road, Hampton, 757-722-9102, 888-757-2628;*
*www.misshamptoncruises.com*

Narrated three-hour cruise includes a stop at Fort Wool, a Civil War island fortress. April-October.

### SETTLERS LANDING MONUMENT

*Hampton*

Marks approximate site of first settlers' landing near Strawberry Banks in 1607. Painting by Sidney King depicts visit to Kecoughtan by colonists en route to Jamestown.

### ST. JOHN'S CHURCH AND PARISH MUSEUM

*W. Queens Way and Franklin Street, Hampton,*
*757-722-2567; www.stjohnshampton.org*

Fourth site of worship of Episcopal parish established in 1610. Bible dating from 1599; communion silver from 1618; Colonial Vestry Book; taped historical message. Daily.

### VIRGINIA AIR AND SPACE CENTER AND HAMPTON ROADS HISTORY CENTER

*600 Settlers Landing Road, Hampton, 757-727-0900, 800-296-0800; www.vasc.org*

Exhibits show the historical link between Hampton Roads' seafaring past and spacefaring future. Exhibits include 19 full-sized air- and spacecraft, the *Apollo 12* Command Module, a moon rock and rare NASA artifacts. Films shown in 283-seat IMAX theater. Daily.

## SPECIAL EVENTS
### HAMPTON BAY DAYS

*Hampton, 757-727-6122; www.baydays.com*

Arts and crafts, rides, science exhibits; entertainment. Mid-September.

### HAMPTON CUP REGATTA

*Mill Creek, Hampton, 800-800-2202; www.hamptoncupregatta.org*

Inboard hydroplane races. Mid-August.

### HAMPTON JAZZ FESTIVAL

*Hampton Coliseum, 1000 Coliseum Drive, Hampton, 757-838-4203;*
*www.hampton.gov/coliseum*

Three days late June.

## HOTELS
### ★QUALITY INN

*1813 W. Mercury Blvd., Hampton, 757-838-8484, 877-424-6423; www.qualityinn.com*

129 rooms. Complimentary continental breakfast. Airport transportation available. Free continental breakfast. Free high-speed Internet access. Pets not accepted. **$**

### ★★RADISSON HOTEL HAMPTON

*700 Settlers Landing Road, Hampton, 757-727-9700, 888-201-1718;*
*www.radisson.com/hamptonva*

172 rooms. Airport transportation available. On Hampton River. **$**

★
★
★
★
★

# HARRISONBURG

Originally named Rocktown for the limestone outcroppings prevalent in the area, Harrisonburg became the county seat of Rockingham County when Thomas Harrison won a race against Mr. Keezle of Keezletown, three miles east. They had raced on horseback to Richmond to file their respective towns for the new county seat.

Harrisonburg is noted for good hunting and fishing, recreational opportunities, beautiful scenery and turkeys. The annual production of more than five million turkeys, most of them processed and frozen, has made Rockingham County widely known. This is a college town with three four-year universities. Much of the Washington and Jefferson national forests are here.

*Information: Harrisonburg Tourism Center, 212 S. Main St., Harrisonburg, 540-432-8935; www.harrisonburgtourism.com*

## WHAT TO SEE AND DO

### CAVERNS
*888-430-2283; www.uvrpa.org.*
There are several caverns within 24 miles of Harrisonburg.

### EASTERN MENNONITE UNIVERSITY
*1200 Park Road, Harrisonburg, 540-432-4000; www.emu.edu*
Many Mennonites live in this area. On campus is an art gallery, planetarium (shows by appointment, free), natural history museum and the Menno Simons Historical Library, containing many 16th-century Mennonite volumes (school year, Monday-Saturday). Campus tours.

★
★
★
★
☆

### GRAND CAVERNS REGIONAL PARK
*Dogwood Avenue, Grottoes, 540-249-5705, 888-430-2283; www.uvrpa.org*
Known for its immense underground chambers and spectacular formations. Visited by Union and Confederate troops during the Civil War. Unique shield formations. Electrically lighted; 54 F. Park facilities include a swimming pool, tennis courts, miniature golf, picnic pavilions and hiking and bicycle trails. Guided tours. April-October, daily; November-March, weekends.

### JAMES MADISON UNIVERSITY
*800 S. Main St., Harrisonburg, www.jmu.edu*
Established in 1908, the university now has 15,000 students. Campus tours through Visitor Center, 540-568-5681.

### LINCOLN HOMESTEAD
Brick house, the rear wing of which was built by Abraham Lincoln's grandfather, and where his father was born. Main portion of the house was built about 1800 by Captain Jacob Lincoln. Private.

### MILLER HALL PLANETARIUM AND SAWHILL ART GALLERY
*800 S. Main, Harrisonburg, 540-568-3621*

### SHENANDOAH VALLEY FOLK ART AND HERITAGE CENTER

*115 Bowman Road, Harrisonburg, 540-879-2681; www.heritagecenter.com*

Featured is the Stonewall Jackson Electric Map that depicts his Valley Campaign of 1862. The 12-foot vertical relief map fills an entire wall and lets visitors see and hear the campaign, battle by battle. Also displays of Shenandoah Valley history, artifacts. Monday-Saturday.

### VIRGINIA QUILT MUSEUM

*301 S. Main St., Harrisonburg, 540-433-3818; www.vaquiltmuseum.org*

Resource center for the study of quilts and quilting. Thursday-Monday.

## SPECIAL EVENTS

### NATURAL CHIMNEYS JOUSTING TOURNAMENT

*Natural Chimneys Regional Park, 94 Natural Chimneys Lane, Harrisonburg; www.valleyarts.org/blog*

America's oldest continuous sporting event, held annually since 1821. "Knights" armed with lances charge down an 80-yard track and attempt to spear three small rings suspended from posts. Each knight is allowed three rides at the rings, thus a perfect score is nine rings. Ties are run off using successively smaller rings. Third Saturday in June and August.

### ROCKINGHAM COUNTY FAIR

*4808 S. Valley Pike, Harrisonburg*

Mid-August.

## HOTELS

### ★COMFORT INN

*1440 E. Market St., Harrisonburg, 540-433-6066, 800-424-6423; www.choicehotels.com*

102 rooms. Complimentary continental breakfast. Exercise room. Free wireless Internet access. **$**

### ★HAMPTON INN

*85 University Blvd., Harrisonburg, 540-432-1111, 800-426-7866; www.hamptoninn.com*

163 rooms. Complimentary continental breakfast. Fitness center. Business center. High-speed Internet access. **$**

### ★★THE VILLAGE INN

*4979 S. Valley Pike, Harrisonburg, 540-434-7355, 800-736-7355; www.thevillageinn.info*

37 rooms. Children's activity center. **$**

## RESTAURANT

### ★★VILLAGE INN RESTAURANT

*4979 South Valley Pike, Harrisonburg, 540-434-7355, 800-736-7355; www.thevillageinn.travel*

American menu. Breakfast, lunch, dinner. Closed Sunday. Children's menu. Casual attire. **$$**

# HOPEWELL

Hopewell, the second permanent English settlement in America, has been an important inland port since early times, with its 300-foot-wide, 28-foot-deep channel. It was the birthplace of statesman John Randolph of Roanoke. Edmund Ruffin, an early agricultural chemist who fired the first shot at Fort Sumter, was born near here.

"Cittie Point," at the junction of the James and Appomattox rivers, finally became one of Virginia's big cities during World War I when an E. I. du Pont de Nemours Company dynamite plant on Hopewell Farm supplied guncotton to the Allies.

*Information: Hopewell Area-Prince George Chamber of Commerce,*
*210 N. Second Ave., Hopewell, 804-458-5536*

## WHAT TO SEE AND DO

### CITY POINT UNIT OF PETERSBURG NATIONAL BATTLEFIELD

*Cedar Lane and Pecan Avenue, Hopewell, 804-458-9504; www.nps.gov/pete*
Grant's headquarters during the siege of Petersburg and largest Civil War supply depot. Includes Appomattox Manor, home to one family for 340 years; Grant's headquarters were on the front lawn. Many other buildings. Daily.

### FLOWERDEW HUNDRED

*1617 Flowerdew Hundred Road, Hopewell, 804-541-8897; www.flowerdew.org*
Outdoor museum on the site of an early English settlement on the south bank of the James River. Originally inhabited by Native Americans, settled by Governor George Yeardley in 1618. Thousands of artifacts dating from the prehistoric period through the present have been excavated and are on exhibit in the museum. A replicated 19th-century detached kitchen and working 17th-century-style windmill are open to visitors. Exhibits, interpretive tours. Picnicking. Monday-Friday.

### MERCHANT'S HOPE CHURCH

*1302 Merchant Hope Road, Hopewell, 804-458-6197*
Given the name of a plantation that was named for a barque plying between Virginia and England. The exterior has been called the most beautiful colonial brickwork in America. Oldest operating Protestant church in the country. Open by request.

## SPECIAL EVENTS

### HOORAY FOR HOPEWELL FESTIVAL

Arts and crafts, food, entertainment, children's rides. Third weekend in September.

### PRINCE GEORGE COUNTRY HERITAGE FAIR

Arts and crafts; educational exhibits and demonstrations; music, food, children's rides, hayrides. Last weekend in April.

## HOTEL

### ★QUALITY INN

*4911 Oaklawn Blvd., Hopewell, 804-458-1500, 877-424-6423; www.qualityinn.com*
115 rooms. Complimentary continental breakfast. Free wireless Internet access. $

VIRGINIA

★
★
★
★
★

# HOT SPRINGS

A Ranger District office of the Washington and Jefferson national forests is located here.

## WHAT TO SEE AND DO

### THE HOMESTEAD SKI AREA

*Highway 220, Hot Springs, 540-839-3860, 866-354-4653; www.thehomestead.com*

Double chairlift, T-bar, J-bar, baby rope tow; patrol, school, rentals, snowmaking; cafeteria, bar. Curling, ice skating rink. Thanksgiving-March.

## HOTELS

### ★★★THE HOMESTEAD

*Highway 220, Hot Springs, 540-839-1766, 866-354-4653; www.thehomestead.com*

Founded 10 years before the American Revolution, The Homestead is one of America's finest resorts. For more than two centuries, presidents and other notables have flocked to this idyllic mountain resort on 15,000 acres in the scenic Allegheny Mountains. From the fresh mountain air and natural hot springs to the legendary championship golf, this Georgian-style resort is the embodiment of a restorative retreat. A leading golf academy sharpens skills, while three courses challenge players. America's oldest continuously played tee is located here at the Old Course. Guests take to the waters as they have done for 200 years, while the spa incorporates advanced therapies for relaxation and rejuvenation. 483 rooms. Children's activity center. Ski in/ski out. Airport transportation available. **$$**

### ★★★THE HOMESTEAD SPA

*Highway 220, Hot Springs, 540-839-1766; www.thehomestead.com*

The Homestead Spa at the Homestead Resort grows out of a healing tradition nearly as old as the Allegheny Mountains themselves: taking the waters that bubble up from the ground in Hot Springs, Va. For thousands of years, natives and the Europeans who came later them have soaked in these mineral-rich waters, to ease aches and ailments. The Homestead is a National Historic Landmark, a spa since 1766. The octagonal wooden building atop the Hot Springs is even older, built in 1761 and essentially unchanged. Thomas Jefferson came to the Gentleman's Pool House to soak several times a day during his Homestead visit in 1818. Today, men can still retreat to the Jefferson Pools, while women have their own Ladies' Pool House atop another spring. Treatments have become more exotic over time, encompassing reflexology and Ayurvedic head massage, alpha-beta skin peels and banana-and-coconut hair therapy. The spa still values the time-tested mineral baths and salt scrubs of the past, often combined with fresh-picked flowers and herbs from the mountains that hug the Homestead. **$$**

**VIRGINIA**

★
★
★
★
★

## SPECIALTY LODGING

### VINE COTTAGE INNS

*7402 Sam Snead Highway, Hot Springs, 540-839-2422, 800-410-9755;*
*www.vinecottageinn.com*

15 rooms. Closed two weeks in March. Complimentary full breakfast. Built in 1894; family-oriented Victorian inn. **$**

## RESTAURANTS

### ★COUNTRY CAFÉ

*Route 220 S., Hot Springs, 540-839-2111*

American menu. Breakfast, lunch, dinner. Closed Monday. Children's menu. Casual attire. $$

### ★★SAM SNEAD'S TAVERN

*220 Main St., Hot Springs, 540-839-7666; www.thehomestead.com*

American menu. Dinner. Bar. Children's menu. Business casual attire. Reservations recommended. $$$

# IRVINGTON

## WHAT TO SEE AND DO

### CARTER RECEPTION CENTER

*420 Christ Church Road, Irvington*

Narrated video presentation; museum with artifacts from Corotoman, home of Robert Carter, and from the church construction; photographs of the restoration. Guides. April-November, daily.

### HISTORIC CHRIST CHURCH

*420 Christ Church Road, Irvington, 804-438-6855; www.christchurch1735.org*

Built by Robert Carter, ancestor of eight governors of Virginia, two presidents, three signers of the Declaration of Independence, a chief justice, and many others who served the country with distinction. Restored; original structure and furnishings, triple-decker pulpit. Built on site of earlier wooden church (1669); family tombs. Tours. Daily.

## HOTEL

### ★★★TIDES INN

*480 King Carter Drive, Irvington, 804-438-5000, 800-843-3746; www.tidesinn.com*

Water figures largely in the experience at this inn, which is Bordered by the Chesapeake Bay, Potomac River and Rappahannock River, and with views of gentle Carters Creek, A 64-slip marina is a boater's paradise. Golf, tennis, croquet, biking, blissing out in the spa and exploring the nearby historic sites are just some of the ways guests fill their days. Dining runs the gamut from the elegant setting at the dining room and dinner river cruises on the *Miss Ann* to the casual atmospheres of Commodores, Cap'n B's and the Chesapeake Club. 106 rooms. Closed January-mid-March. Children's activity center. $$

# JAMESTOWN (COLONIAL NATIONAL HISTORICAL PARK)

On May 13, 1607, in this unpromising setting, the first permanent English settlement in the New World was founded. From the beginning, characteristics of the early United States were established: self-government, industry, commerce, the plantation system and a diverse populace, originally made up of men of English, German, African, French, Italian, Polish and Irish descent.

Nothing of the 17th-century settlement remains above ground except the Old Church Tower. Since 1934, however, archaeological exploration by the National Park Service has made the outline of the town clear. Cooperative efforts by the Park Service and

★
★
★
★

the Association for the Preservation of Virginia Antiquities (which owns 22½ acres of the island, including the Old Church Tower) have exposed foundations and restored streets, property ditches, hedgerows, fences and the James Fort site from 1607. Markers, recorded messages, paintings and monuments are everywhere. Entrance station (daily). *Information: 757-229-1733; www.nps.gov/jame*

## WHAT TO SEE AND DO

### CONFEDERATE FORT
One of two Civil War fortifications on the island.

### DALE HOUSE
*1367 Colonial Parkway, Jamestown (Colonial National Historical Park)*
Archaeological laboratory. A viewing area is open to the public.

### FIRST LANDING SITE
*Colonial Historic Parkway and Jamestown Road,*
*Jamestown (Colonial National Historical Park)*
Fixed by tradition as point in river, about 200 yards from present seawall, upriver from Old Church Tower.

### GLASSHOUSE
*Colonial National Historic Parkway and Jamestown Road,*
*Jamestown (Colonial National Historical Park)*
Colonists produced glass here in 1608. Demonstration exhibits, glassblowing Daily.

### JAMES FORT SITE
*Colonial Historic Parkway and Jamestown Road, Jamestown*
Excavation of first fort can be viewed between seawall and Old Church Tower.

### MEMORIAL CHURCH
*Colonial National Historic Parkway and Jamestown Road,*
*Jamestown (Colonial National Historical Park)*
Built in 1907 by the National Society of the Colonial Dames of America over foundations of the original church. Within are two foundations alleged to be of earlier churches, one from 1617 that housed the first assembly.

### NEW TOWNE
*1367 Colonial Parkway, Jamestown (Colonial National Historical Park)*
Area where Jamestown expanded around 1620 may be toured along "Back Streete" and other original streets. Section includes reconstructed foundations indicating sites of Country House, Governor's House, homes of Richard Kemp, builder of one of the first brick houses in America, Henry Hartwell, a founder of the College of William & Mary, and Dr. John Pott and William Pierce, who led the "thrusting out" of Governor John Harvey in 1635.

### OLD CHURCH TOWER
Only standing ruin of the 17th-century town. Believed to be part of the first brick church. Has 3-foot-thick walls of handmade brick.

**447**

**VIRGINIA**

★
★
★
★

## COLONIAL PARKWAY

The Colonial Parkway is a 23-mile link between the three towns that formed the "cradle of the nation": Jamestown, Williamsburg and Yorktown. It starts at the Visitor Center at Jamestown, passes through Williamsburg (the Colonial Williamsburg Information Center is near the north underpass entrance) and ends at the Visitor Center in Yorktown.

At turnouts and overlooks along the route, information signs note historic spots such as Glebeland, Kingsmill, Indian Field Creek, Powhatan's Village, Fusilier's Redoubt and others. A free picnic area is provided during the summer at Ringfield Plantation, midway between Williamsburg and Yorktown. The parkway is free to private vehicles, and the speed limit is 45 miles per hour. There are no service stations along the way.

### TERCENTENARY MONUMENT

Erected by the United States in 1907 to commemorate the 300th Jamestown anniversary. Other monuments include Captain John Smith statue (by William Couper), Pocahontas Monument (by William Ordway Partridge), House of Burgesses Monument (listing members of first representative legislative body in America).

### TRAILS

Three- and five-mile auto drives provide access to entire area.

### VISITOR CENTER

*Colonial National Historic Parkway and Jamestown Road,*
*Jamestown (Colonial National Historical Park)*
Guide leaflets, introductory film and exhibits. Post office. Daily.

### SPECIAL EVENTS
#### FIRST ASSEMBLY DAY

Commemorates first legislative assembly in 1619. Late July.

#### JAMESTOWN WEEKEND

Commemorates arrival of first settlers in 1607; special tours and activities. Mid-May.

# KESWICK

### HOTEL
#### ★★★KESWICK HALL AT MONTICELLO

*701 Club Drive, Keswick, 434-979-3440, 800-274-5391; www.keswick.com*
Keswick Hall's 600-acre estate, set at the foot of the Blue Ridge Mountains, offers visitors individually designed guest rooms that reflect a modern interpretation of early American style, with overstuffed furniture, club chairs, Aubusson carpets and canopied four-poster beds. Views over the magnificent formal gardens are particularly coveted. The rolling hills of the Shenandoah Valley invite exploration and the historic halls of Monticello are only minutes away, but this resort also entices its guests with a variety of recreational opportunities. The members-only Keswick Hall, adjacent to the hotel, presents an exclusive opportunity for guests to enjoy its indoor/outdoor pool, tennis

courts, fitness facility, spa services and 18-hole Arnold Palmer golf course. 48 rooms. Children's activity center. Airport transportation available. $$$$

## RESTAURANT
### ★★★MAIN DINING ROOM
*701 Club Drive, Keswick, 434-979-3440; www.keswick.com*
"A feast for the eyes" best describes the chef's classically inspired culinary creations, most appropriate given the formal dining room's trompe l'oeil wall murals and expansive garden views. American menu. Breakfast, dinner. Bar. Children's menu. Casual attire. Reservations recommended. Valet parking. Outdoor seating. $$$

# LANCASTER
The family of Mary Ball Washington, mother of George Washington, were early settlers of this area. Washington's maternal ancestors are buried in the churchyard of St. Mary's Whitechapel Church five miles west of Lancaster.

## WHAT TO SEE AND DO
### LANCASTER COUNTY COURTHOUSE HISTORIC DISTRICT
Sycamore trees surround this area around the antebellum courthouse. Marble obelisk is one of the first monuments erected to Confederate soldiers.

### MARY BALL WASHINGTON MUSEUM AND LIBRARY COMPLEX
*8346 Mary Ball Road, Lancaster, 804-462-7280; www.mbwm.org*
Contains the Old Clerk's Office, the Old Jail, Lancaster House, the headquarters and main museum building. Also Virginia genealogical research center. Museum Tuesday-Friday; Library Wednesday-Saturday.

### ST. MARY'S WHITECHAPEL CHURCH
*5940 White Chapel Road, Warsaw, 804-462-5908; www.stmaryswhitechapel.org*
Church where Mary Ball and her family worshiped; many of the tombstones bear the Ball name.

## SPECIALTY LODGING
### INN AT LEVELFIELD
*10155 Mary Ball Road, Lancaster, 804-435-6887, 800-238-5578; www.innatlevelefields.com*
This 1857 antebellum landmark homestead is situated on 54 acres, with 12 acres of lawn and 42 acres of timberland. The building features a double-tiered portico and four massive chimneys, as well as a 1,000-foot driveway. Six rooms. Complimentary full breakfast. $

# LEESBURG
Originally named Georgetown for King George II of England, this town was later renamed Leesburg, probably after Francis Lightfoot Lee, a signer of the Declaration of Independence and a local landowner. Leesburg is located in a scenic area of rolling hills, picturesque rural towns and thoroughbred horse farms, where point-to-point racing and steeplechases are popular.
*Information: Loudoun County Visitors Center, 222 Catocin Circle S.E., Leesburg, 703-771-2170, 800-752-6118; www.visitloudoun.org*

VIRGINIA

★
★
★
★
★

## WHAT TO SEE AND DO

### BALL'S BLUFF BATTLEFIELD

*Ball Bluff Road, Leesburg, 703-737-7800; www.nvrpa.org*

One of the smallest national cemeteries in the U.S. marks the site of the third armed engagement of the Civil War. On October 21, 1861, four Union regiments suffered catastrophic losses while surrounded by Confederate forces; the Union commander, a U.S. senator and presidential confidant, was killed here along with half his troops, while attempting to recross the Potomac River. Oliver Wendell Holmes, Jr., later to become a U.S. Supreme Court justice, was wounded here.

### LOUDOUN MUSEUM

*16 Loudoun St. S.W., Leesburg, 703-777-7427; www.loudounmuseum.org*

Century-old restored building contains exhibits and memorabilia of the area; audio-visual presentation "A Special Look at Loudoun." Brochures, information about Loudoun County; walking tours; self-guided tour booklets (fee). Daily. Closed January.

### MORVEN PARK

*17263 Southern Planter Lane, Leesburg, 703-777-2414; www.morvenpark.org*

Originally the residence of Thomas Swann, early Maryland governor, the estate was expanded by Westmoreland Davis, governor of Virginia from 1918 to 1922. The 1,200-acre park includes a 28-room mansion, boxwood gardens, Winmill Carriage Museum with more than 70 horse-drawn vehicles, Museum of Hounds and Hunting with video presentation and artifacts depicting the history of fox hunting, and Morven Park International Equestrian Center. April-November, Friday-Monday afternoons.

### OATLANDS

*20850 Oatlands Plantation Lane, Leesburg, 703-777-3174; www.oatlands.org*

A 261-acre estate; Classical Revival mansion, built by George Carter, was the center of a 5,000-acre plantation; house was partially remodeled in 1827, which was when the front portico was added. Most of the building materials, including bricks and wood, came from or were made on the estate. Interior furnished with American, English and French antiques; reflects period between 1897 and 1965 when the house was owned by Mr. and Mrs. William Corcoran Eustis, prominent Washingtonians. Formal garden has some of the finest boxwood in U.S. Farm fields provide equestrian area for races and horse shows. April-December, daily.

### VINEYARD AND WINERY TOURS

*Loudon County Visitor Center, 222 Catoctin Circle, Leesburg,*
*703-771-2617, 800-752-6118; www.visitloudoun.org*

### WATERFORD

*15609 High St., Waterford, 504-882-3018; www.waterfordva.org*

Eighteenth-century Quaker village, designated a National Historic Landmark, has been restored as a residential community. An annual homes tour (first full weekend in October) has craft demonstrations, exhibits, traditional music. Waterford Foundation has brochures outlining self-guided walking tours.

450

VIRGINIA

★
★
★
★
★

## SPECIAL EVENTS

### AUGUST COURT DAYS

*108 South St. S.E., Leesburg, 703-777-2420*

Reenactment of the opening of the 18th-century judicial court. Festivities resemble a country fair with craft demonstrations, games and entertainers on the street. Third weekend in August.

### CHRISTMAS AT OATLANDS

*20850 Oatlands Plantation Lane, Leesburg, 703-777-3174; www.oatlands.org*

Candlelight tours, 1800s decorations, refreshments. Mid-November-December, Saturday evenings.

### HOMES AND GARDENS TOUR

*703-777-2420; www.vagardenweek.org/schedule*

Sponsored by Garden Club of Virginia. Mid-late April.

### LOUDOUN HUNT PONY CLUB HORSE TRIALS

*Morven Park International Equestrian Institute, 4173 Tutt Lane, Leesburg, 703-777-2890; www.loudenhunt.ponyclub.org*

Competition in combined training: dressage, cross-country and stadium jumping. Late March.

### OATLANDS SHEEP DOG TRIALS

*Oatlands, 20850 Oatlands Plantation Lane, Leesburg, 703-777-3174; www.oatlands.org*

Crafts, food and house and garden tours. May.

### WINE FESTIVAL

*Morven Park, 17263 Southern Planter Lane, Leesburg, 703-823-1868, 866-877-3343; www.virginiawinefestival.org*

Many wineries participate; includes seminar for home/commercial wine growers; grape-stomping, waiters' race, jousting tournament, music, wine tastings, awards presentations. September.

## HOTELS

### ★DAYS INN

*721 E. Market St., Leesburg, 703-777-6622, 800-329-7466; www.daysinn.com*

81 rooms. Complimentary continental breakfast. Free daybreak breakfast. Pets accepted. Free wireless Internet access. **$**

### ★★HOLIDAY INN

*1500 E. Market St., Leesburg, 703-771-9200, 800-282-0244; www.holidayinn.com*

124 rooms. Airport transportation available. Colonial circa-1773 mansion. **$**

### ★★★LANSDOWNE RESORT

*44050 Woodridge Parkway, Leesburg, 703-729-8400, 877-509-8400; www.lansdowneresort.com*

The stylishly streamlined Lansdowne Resort, which comprises a nine-story tower and two five-story wings, underwent a $55 million renovation. Guest rooms are reminiscent

★
★
★
★
★

of a country manor, elegant but casual, with lush woodland views. 296 rooms. Restaurant, bar. Fitness room. Pool. Golf. Tennis. Children's activity center. Airport transportation available. **$$**

### ★★★LEESBURG COLONIAL INN

*19 S. King St., Leesburg, 703-777-5000, 800-392-1332*

Bordered by the majestic Blue Ridge Mountains and the Potomac River, this circa-1830 inn is located in the heart of historic Leesburg (just 25 miles from Washington, D.C.) The inn is decorated in 18th-century American style. Each guest room features individual climate controls, antique poster beds, hardwood floors, fine rugs and period pieces. Some rooms also have whirlpool tubs and fireplaces. A complimentary full gourmet breakfast is offered each morning in the dining room. 10 rooms. Restaurant. Airport transportation available. **$**

## SPECIALTY LODGING

### NORRIS HOUSE INN

*108 Loudoun St. S.W., Leesburg, 703-777-1806, 800-644-1806; www.norrishouse.com*

Located in the historic district of Leesburg, this rambling colonial house dates back to 1760. Filled with antiques and plenty of charm, both the common rooms and guest rooms are comfortable and relaxing. The Stone House Tea Room serves an elegant afternoon tea. Six rooms. Complimentary full breakfast. Airport transportation available. **$**

## RESTAURANTS

### ★★GREEN TREE

*15 S. King St., Leesburg, 703-777-7246*

Lunch, dinner, Sunday brunch. Authentic 18th-century recipes. Windows open to street. **$$**

### ★★LEESBURG COLONIAL INN

*19 S. King St., Leesburg, 703-777-5000; www.leesburgcolonialinn.com*

American menu. Lunch, dinner. Bar. Children's menu. Outdoor seating. **$$**

# LEXINGTON

Lexington was home to two of the greatest Confederate heroes: Robert E. Lee and Thomas J. "Stonewall" Jackson. Both are buried here. Sam Houston, Cyrus McCormick and James Gibbs (inventor of the sewing machine) were born nearby.

Set in rolling country between the Blue Ridge and Allegheny mountains, this town is the seat of Rockbridge County. Lexington is known for attractive homes, trim farms, fine old mansions and two of the leading educational institutions in the Commonwealth: Washington and Lee University and Virginia Military Institute.

*Information: Visitors Bureau, 106 E. Washington St., Lexington,*
*540-463-3777, 877-453-9822; www.lexingtonvirginia.com*

## WHAT TO SEE AND DO

### GEORGE C. MARSHALL MUSEUM

*Virginia Military Institute Parade Ground, Lexington, 540-463-7103;*
*www.marshallfoundation.org*

Displays on life and career of the illustrious military figure and statesman (1880-1959); World War I electric map and recorded narration of World War II; Marshall Plan; gold medallion awarded with his Nobel Prize for Peace in 1953. Daily.

### GOSHEN PASS

Scenic mountain gorge formed by Maury River. Memorial to "the father of modern oceanography," Matthew Fontaine Maury is here.

### LEE CHAPEL AND MUSEUM

*Washington and Lee University campus, Lexington, 540-458-8768;*
*www.leechapel.wlu.edu*

Robert E. Lee is entombed here. Also houses Lee family crypt and museum, marble "recumbent statue" of Lee, portions of art collection of Washington and Lee families. Lee's office remains as he left it. Daily, closed late December.

### LEXINGTON CARRIAGE COMPANY

*106 E. Washington St., Lexington, 540-463-5647; www.lexcarriage.com*

Approximately 45-minute narrated horse-drawn carriage tours of historic Lexington. Groups of 10 or more by appointment only. April-October, daily, weather permitting.

### STONEWALL JACKSON HOUSE

**453**

*8 E. Washington St., Lexington, 540-463-2552; www.stonewalljackson.org*

Only home owned by Confederate General Thomas J. "Stonewall" Jackson, restored to its appearance in 1859-1861. Many of the furnishings were once owned by Jackson. Interpretive slide presentation and guided tours (½ hour). Restored gardens; shop. Daily.

### STONEWALL JACKSON MEMORIAL CEMETERY

*White and Main streets, Lexington; www.lexingtonvirginia.com/attractions.asp*

General Jackson and more than 100 other Confederate soldiers are buried here.

### VIRGINIA HORSE CENTER

*487 Maury River Road, Lexington, 540-464-2950*

Sprawling across nearly 400 acres, the Center provides a versatile site for numerous horse-related functions year-round: shows, clinics, auctions, festivals. Fees vary.

### VIRGINIA MILITARY INSTITUTE

*Letcher Avenue, Lexington, 540-464-7207; www.vmi.edu*

(1839) State military, engineering, sciences and arts college with 1,300 cadets. Coeducational since 1997. Stonewall Jackson taught here, as did Matthew Fontaine Maury, famed naval explorer and inventor. George Catlett Marshall, a general of the army and author of the Marshall Plan, was a graduate. Mementos of these men on display in VMI museum (daily). Dress parade (most Friday afternoons, weather permitting).

**VIRGINIA**

★
★
★
★
★

## WASHINGTON AND LEE UNIVERSITY

*West Washington Street, Lexington, 540-463-8400; www.wlu.edu*

Liberal arts university with 2,181 students situated on an attractive campus with white colonnaded buildings; also includes Washington and Lee Law School. Founded as Augusta Academy in 1749; became Liberty Hall in 1776; name changed to Washington Academy in 1798 after receiving 200 shares of James River Canal Company stock from George Washington, and then to Washington College. Gen. Robert E. Lee served as president from 1865-1870; soon after Lee's death in 1870, it became Washington and Lee University.

## SPECIAL EVENTS

### GARDEN WEEK IN HISTORIC LEXINGTON

*106 E. Washington St., Lexington, 804-644-7776; www.vagardenweek.org*

Tour of homes and gardens in the Lexington, Rockbridge County area. Mid-late April.

### HOLIDAYS IN LEXINGTON

*106 E. Washington St., Lexington, 540-463-3777; www.lexingtonvirginia.com*

Parade, plays, children's events. December.

### LIME KILN ARTS THEATER

*14 S. Randolph St., Lexington, 540-463-7088; www.theateratlimekiln.com*

Professional theatrical productions and concerts in outdoor theater, natural amphitheater and tent (during inclement weather). Memorial Day-Labor Day.

## HOTELS

### ★★BEST WESTERN INN AT HUNT RIDGE

*25 Willow Springs Road, Lexington, 540-464-1500, 800-780-7234; www.bestwestern.com*

100 rooms. Indoor, outdoor pool. High-speed Internet access. $

### ★COMFORT INN VIRGINIA HORSE CENTERS

*62 Comfort Way, Lexington, 540-463-7311, 877-424-6423; www.choicehotels.com*

80 rooms. Complimentary continental breakfast. Free wireless Internet access. Pets accepted. $

### ★HOLIDAY INN EXPRESS

*850 N. Lee Highway, Lexington, 540-463-7351, 800-282-0244; www.holidayinnexpress.com*

72 rooms. Complimentary continental breakfast. View of mountains. $

### ★★MAPLE HALL COUNTRY INN

*3111 N. Lee Higway, Lexington, 540-463-6693, 877-463-2044; www.lexingtonhistoricinns.com*

21 rooms. Complimentary continental breakfast. $

### ★REDWOOD FAMILY RESTAURANT

*898 N. Lee Highway, Lexington, 540-463-2168*
American menu. Breakfast, lunch, dinner, Sunday brunch. Children's menu. $

# LORTON

## WHAT TO SEE AND DO

### GUNSTON HALL PLANTATION

*10709 Gunston Road, Mason Neck, 703-550-9220; www.gunstonhall.org*
The 550-acre estate of George Mason, framer of the Constitution and father of the Bill of Rights. Restored 18th-century mansion with period furnishings; reconstructed outbuildings; boxwood gardens on grounds; nature trail. Picnic area, gift shop. Daily.

### POHICK BAY REGIONAL PARK

*6501 Pohick Bay Drive, Lorton, 703-339-6104; www.nvrpa.org/parks/pohickbay*
Activities in this 1,000-acre park include swimming (Memorial Day-Labor Day), boating (ramp, rentals, fee); 18-hole golf, miniature and Fribee golf, camping (7-day limit; electric hookups available; fee), picnicking. Park (all year). Fee charged for activities.

### POHICK EPISCOPAL CHURCH

*9301 Richmond Highway, Lorton, 703-339-6572; www.pohick.org*
(1774) The colonial parish church of Mount Vernon and Gunston Hall. Built under the supervision of George Mason and George Washington; original walls; interior fully restored. Daily.

**455**

# LURAY

This town's name is of French origin, and its fame comes from the caverns discovered here in 1878. Situated at the junction of Highways 211 and 340, Luray is nine miles away from—and within sight of—Shenandoah National Park and Skyline Drive. Park headquarters are located here. There are three developed recreation areas north and west of town in Washington and Jefferson national forests.
*Information: Page County Chamber of Commerce, 46 E. Main St., Luray,*
*540-743-3915, 888-743-3915; www.luraypage.com*

VIRGINIA

★
★
★
★
★

## WHAT TO SEE AND DO

### CAR AND CARRIAGE MUSEUM

Exhibits include 140 restored antique cars, carriages and coaches featuring the history of transportation from 1625.

### LURAY CAVERNS

*970 Highway 211 W., Luray, 540-743-6551; www.luraycaverns.org*
One of the largest caverns in the East. Huge underground rooms (one is 300-feet wide, 500-feet long, with a 140-foot ceiling) connected by natural corridors and paved walkways are encrusted with colorful rock formations, some delicate as lace, others massive. In one chamber is the world's only "stalacpipe" organ, which produces music of symphonic quality from stone formations. Indirect lighting permits taking

of color photos within caverns. The temperature is 54 F. One-hour guided tours start about every 20 minutes. Daily.

### LURAY SINGING TOWER
*970 Highway 211/340 W., Luray, 540-743-6551; www.virginia.org*
Houses 47-bell carillon; largest bell weighs 7,640 pounds. Features 45-minute recitals by celebrated carillonneur. June-August, Tuesday, Thursday and Sunday evenings; March-May and September-October, weekend afternoons. In park adjacent to caverns.

### LURAY ZOO
*1087 Highway 211 W., Luray, 540-743-4113; www.lurayzoo.com*
Features large reptile collection, exotic animals and tropical birds; petting zoo; live animal shows; life-sized dinosaur reproductions. Gift shop. Mid-April-October, daily.

### MASSANUTTEN ONE-ROOM SCHOOL
Restored and furnished as it was in the 1800s. Period displays and pictures. By appointment.

## SPECIAL EVENTS
### MAYFEST STREET FESTIVAL
*46 E. Main St., Luray*
Entertainment, crafts. Third Saturday in May.

### PAGE COUNTY HERITAGE FESTIVAL
Arts and crafts exhibits. Self-guided tour of churches and old homes. Columbus Day weekend.

## HOTELS
### ★★BIG MEADOWS LODGE
*Skyline Drive, Mile 51, Luray, 540-999-2221, 800-999-4714; www.visitshenandaoh.com*
97 rooms. Closed December-mid-May. Children's activity center. Panoramic view of Shenandoah Valley. $

### ★★DAYS INN
*138 Whispering Hill Road, Luray, 540-743-4521, 800-329-7466;*
*www.daysinn-luray.com*
100 rooms. Free daybreak breakfast. Free wireless Internet access. Exercise room. Outdoor pool. $

### ★LURAY CAVERNS MOTEL WEST
*1001 Highway 211 E., Luray, 540-743-4531*
20 rooms. Complimentary continental breakfast. Views of Blue Ridge Mountains. $

### ★★SKYLAND LODGE
*Skyline Drive, Luray, 540-999-2211, 800-999-4714*
177 rooms. Closed December-March. $

## SPECIALTY LODGINGS

### CABINS AT BROOKSIDE

*2978 Highway 211 E., Luray, 540-743-5698, 800-299-2655;*
*www.brooksidecabins.com*

This vacation development located 4½ miles from the entrance to Skyline Drive offers the privacy and seclusion of your own log cabin. The cabins have a plush country décor and front porches, and are set into the woods. A cozy restaurant on the property serves homestyle food. Nine rooms. **$**

### MAYNEVIEW BED AND BREAKFAST

*439 Mechanic St., Luray, 540-743-7921; www.mayneview.com*

This lovely inn sits in the heart of the Shenandoah Valley and has a wonderful wrap-around porch. Visitors can take day trips to the famous Luray Caverns, the New Market Battlefield and several antique shops. Five rooms. Complimentary full breakfast. Victorian building. **$**

### WOODRUFF HOUSE BED AND BREAKFAST

*330 Mechanic St., Luray, 540-743-1494, 866-937-3466; www.woodruffinns.com*

Three 1800s Victorian houses make up this bed and breakfast located near many local attractions including the Shenandoah National Park, Luray Caverns and the George Washington National Forest. 10 rooms. Complimentary full breakfast. **$$$**

## RESTAURANTS

### ★BROOKSIDE

*2978 Highway 211 E., Luray, 540-743-5698, 800-299-2655;*
*www.brooksidecabins.com*

American menu. Lunch, dinner, brunch. Closed four weeks in December. Children's menu. Casual attire. **$**

### ★PARKHURST

*2547 Highway 211 W., Luray, 540-743-6009; www.rainbow-hill.com*

American menu. Lunch, dinner. Casual attire. Outdoor seating. **$**

# LYNCHBURG

Lynchburg is perched on hills overlooking the James River, which was for many years the city's means of growth. Today, Lynchburg is home to more than 3,000 businesses and diversified industries. Educational institutions located here include Lynchburg College, Randolph-Macon Women's College and Liberty University.

One of the first buildings in the town was a ferry house built by John Lynch. The same enterprising young man later built a tobacco warehouse, probably the first one in the country. During the Civil War, Lynchburg was important as a supply base and hospital town. In June 1864, General Jubal A. Early successfully defended the town from an attack by Union forces. More than 2,200 Confederates are buried in the Confederate Cemetery, located within the Old City Cemetery.

*Information: Visitors Information Center, 12th and Church streets, Lynchburg,*
*434-522-9592, 800-732-5821; www.lynchburgchamber.org*

# WHAT TO SEE AND DO

## ANNE SPENCER HOUSE

*1313 Pierce St., Lynchburg, 434-845-1313; www.annespencermuseum.com*

House of the noted poet, the only black woman and only Virginian to be included in the *Norton Anthology of Modern American and British Poetry*. On grounds is Spencer's writing cottage Edan Kraal. Many dignitaries have visited here. Museum with artifacts, memorabilia, period antique furnishings; formal garden. House by appointment; gardens daily.

## BLACKWATER CREEK NATURAL AREA

Ruskin Freer Nature Preserve (115 acres) includes trails with plants; athletic area; bikeway winds past wildflower area and historical sites, ending downtown; Creekside Trunk Trail, natural grass trail with typical Piedmont species of plants, moist ravines, north-facing rocky bluffs. Daily.

## FORT EARLY

*Memorial and Fort avenues, Lynchburg; www.discoverlynchburg.org*

Defense earthwork for Lynchburg's closest battle during the Civil War. Confederates under General Jubal A. Early turned back forces under General David Hunter in 1864. Daily.

## MAIER MUSEUM OF ART AT RANDOLPH COLLEGE

*2500 Rivermont Ave., Lynchburg, 434-947-8136; www.randolphcollege.edu*

Collection is representative of 19th- and 20th-century American painting. Artists include Thomas Hart Benton, Edward Hicks, Winslow Homer, James McNeil Whistler, Mary Cassatt and Georgia O'Keeffe. Changing exhibits. Academic year: Tuesday-Sunday afternoons.

## OLD COURT HOUSE MUSEUM

*901 Court St., Lynchburg, 434-455-6226; www.lynchburgmuseum.org*

Restored to original 1855 Greek Revival appearance. Three galleries have exhibits on early history of the area, highlighting Quaker settlement and role of tobacco; restored mid-19th-century courtroom. Daily.

## PACKET BOAT "MARSHALL"

Mounted on a stone base, the boat carried the remains of Stonewall Jackson home to Lexington; for many years packets were the principal mode of transportation along the James River and Kanawha Canal.

## PEST HOUSE MEDICAL MUSEUM

*Old City Cemetery, Fourth and Taylor streets, Lynchburg, 434-847-1465;*
*www.gravegarden.org/pesthouse.htm*

The 1840s white-frame medical office of Quaker physician Dr. John Jay Terrell has been joined with Pest House quarantine hospital to typify the standard of medicine during the late 1800s. Original medical instruments include operating table, hypodermic needle, clinical thermometer and chloroform mask. Period furnishings on one side duplicate Dr. Terrell's office during the Civil War; other side represents quarantine hospital for Confederate soldiers in which Dr. Terrell volunteered to assume responsibility. Window displays with audio description. Tours (by appointment). Daily.

★
★
★
★
★

## POINT OF HONOR

*112 Cabell St., Lynchburg, 434-455-6226; www.pointofhonor.org*

(1815) Restored mansion on Daniel's Hill above the James River, built by Dr. George Cabell, Sr., physician to Patrick Henry. Federalist style with octagon bay façade and finely crafted interior woodwork; period furnishings; gardens and grounds being restored. Daily.

## RANDOLPH-MACON WOMEN'S COLLEGE

*2500 Rivermont Ave., Lynchburg, 434-947-8000; www.rmwc.edu*

(1891) (748 women) A 100-acre campus on historic Rivermont Avenue near James River. First college for women in the South that was granted a Phi Beta Kappa chapter. Campus has interesting mixture of architecture, including Vincent Kling design for Houston Chapel. Tours (by appointment).

## RIVERSIDE PARK

*2270 Rivermont Ave., Lynchburg*
Daily.

## SOUTH RIVER MEETING HOUSE

*5810 Fort Ave., Lynchburg, 434-239-2548; www.virginia.org/site*

Completed in 1798, the stone building remained the site of Quaker worship and activity until the 1840s. John Lynch, founder of Lynchburg, and other early leaders of community are buried in adjacent historic cemetery. Daily.

# HOTELS

### ★★HOLIDAY INN SELECT

*601 Main St., Lynchburg, 434-528-2500, 800-282-0244; www.hiselect.com/lynchburgva*
241 rooms. Airport transportation available. **$**

### ★HOLIDAY INN EXPRESS

*5600 Seminole Ave., Lynchburg, 434-237-7771, 800-282-0244; www.hiexpress.com*
102 rooms. Complimentary continental breakfast. Airport transportation available. Pets accepted. **$**

### ★★★RADISSON HOTEL LYNCHBURG

*2900 Candler's Mountain Road, Lynchburg, 434-237-6333, 800-333-3333; www.radisson.com*

Located at the foot of the Blue Ridge Mountains, this hotel sits on a unique, 10-acre, landscaped and wooded spread. The Natural Bridge, which some say is one of the seven natural wonders of the world, is easily accessible. 168 rooms. Airport transportation available. **$**

# RESTAURANTS

### ★★CROWN STERLING

*6120 Fort Ave., Lynchburg, 434-239-7744; www.thecrownsterling.com*
Steak menu. Dinner. Closed Sunday-Monday. Bar. Children's menu. Business casual attire. Reservations recommended. **$$$**

**VIRGINIA**

★
★
★
★
★

### ★★★SACHIKO'S PORTERHOUSE

*126 Old Graves Mill Road, Lynchburg, 434-237-5655*

Sachiko's Porterhouse has been in business for 25 years, serving beef, lamb, chicken and seafood dishes, as well as pastries fresh from their in-house bakery. American menu. Dinner. Closed Sunday; three weeks in January. Bar. Business casual attire. Reservations recommended. $$

# MANASSAS

The Native Americans who had occupied this area for thousands of years were driven out under a treaty in 1722. Afterwards, settlement remained concentrated along the Potomac River until the coming of the railroad in 1858. The Manassas rail junction was vital to the South, and many troops were stationed along this line of communication. Control of this junction led to two major battles nearby.

*Information: Prince William County/Manassas Conference & Visitors Bureau,*
*9431 W. St., Manassas, 703-361-6599, 800-432-1792; www.visitpwc.com*

## WHAT TO SEE AND DO

### THE MANASSAS MUSEUM

*9101 Prince William St., Manassas, 703-368-1873; www.manassascity.org*

Museum features collections dealing with Northern Virginia Piedmont history from prehistoric to modern times, with special emphasis on Civil War. Tuesday-Sunday.

## SPECIAL EVENT

### PRINCE WILLIAM COUNTY FAIR

*9101 Prince William St., Manassas, 703-368-0173; www.pwcfair.com*

Carnival, entertainment, tractor pull, exhibits, contests. Mid-August.

## HOTEL

### ★★HOTEL MANASSAS

*10800 Vandor Lane, Manassas, 703-335-0000; www.starwoodhotels.com*

158 rooms. Complimentary continental breakfast. Restaurant, bar. Near Manassas (Bull Run) Battlefield. $

## RESTAURANTS

### ★★★CARMELLO'S AND LITTLE PORTUGAL

*9108 Center St., Manassas, 703-368-5522; www.carmellos.com*

At Carmello's and Little Portugal, Italian and Portuguese cuisines are beautifully combined to create generous contemporary dishes. The restaurant's intimate atmosphere makes it a popular spot to celebrate special occasions. Italian, Spanish menu. Lunch, dinner. Bar. $$

### ★★JAKE'S

*9412 Main St., Manassas, 703-330-1534; www.jakesofmanassas.com*

American menu. Lunch, dinner. Bar. Outdoor seating. Closed Monday. $$

### ★★★PANINO

*9116 Mathis Ave., Manassas, 703-335-2566; www.panino-manassas.com*

Although off the beaten path, this chef-owned and operated restaurant has for the past decade offered perhaps the best regional Italian cuisine outside the Beltway.

Only the freshest ingredients are used. Italian menu. Lunch, dinner. Closed Sunday. Reservations recommended. $$

## NORTHERN VIRGINIA WINE COUNTRY

Virginia is home to more than 60 wineries, many of which produce award-winning vintages. Even California, home to some of America's most notable wines, cannot match everything done here: Several of Virginia's winemakers are producing new and different wines from grapes not yet grown on the West Coast.

In recent years, wine-tasting has become an inviting pastime for weekenders. Fortunately, many of the wineries are clustered conveniently to make a visit to three or four in half a day quite practical, though many visitors combine a sampling tour with a stay in a country inn that serves Virginia wines.

Part of the fun of visiting Virginia's wineries is that they tend to be located in out-of-the-way corners of the countryside. To get to them, drivers must negotiate winding back roads over which they might not otherwise travel. This one-day, 150-mile tour from Fairfax County (a Washington, D.C., suburb) traverses the scenic foothills of the Blue Ridge Mountains. Here and there it edges Shenandoah National Park, where a detour of a few miles will take you to one of the lofty overlooks along Skyline Drive, the famed ridge-top parkway. Begin the tour on Interstate 66 West just north of Fairfax City. Near Manassas, stop at the Visitor Information Center to pick up the latest edition of Virginia Wineries Festival and Tour Guide. It lists the operating hours of the tasting rooms, many of which are open daily; some only on weekends. If Civil War history interests you, stop briefly at Manassas National Battlefield Park, which commemorates the first major clash between the North and South.

At Gainesville, head south on Highway 29 past Culpeper to the village of Leon; the Prince Michel Vineyards will be on the right. Begin your visit with a self-guided tour of the winemaking facility. This French-owned facility produces a very nice Chardonnay. Its gourmet restaurant, serving lunch and dinner, overlooks acres of vineyards draped across rolling hills. From St. Michel, continue south on Highway 29 to Madison, and turn right onto State Route 231 North. For about 20 miles, this stretch of the road is a Virginia Scenic Byway. On your left, the high, forested ridge rising overhead is Shenandoah National Park. On both sides of the road, stately plantation homes carry descriptive names. Just south of Sperryville, pick up Highway 522 North. In Sperryville, browse the sprawling Sperryville Antiques Market. Continue north on Highway 522 toward Front Royal, turning right at Route 635. For about a mile, the road glides beneath towering tree; Oasis Winery is on the right, best known for its sparkling wines. After your visit, return to Highway 522 and continue north to Front Royal. Head east (right) on Route 55 to Linden. Turn right onto Route 638 and proceed two miles to Linden. Perched atop a small hill, its outdoor deck offers gorgeous Blue Ridge views. Linden is one of Virginia's finest wineries, and one of the prettiest. Linden's Seyval, a dry white wine, is popular with wine-loverslooking for something new. Return to Route 55 and turn west (left) one mile to the entrance to I-66. Take I-66 east back to Fairfax. Approximately 150 miles.

★
★
★
★
★

# MANASSAS (BULL RUN) NATIONAL BATTLEFIELD PARK

This 5,000-acre park was the scene of two major Civil War battles. More than 26,000 men were killed or wounded here in struggles for control of a strategically important railroad junction. The war's first major land battle was fought here on July 21, 1861, between poorly trained volunteer troops from both the North and South. The battle finally evolved into a struggle for Henry Hill, where "Stonewall" Jackson earned his nickname. With the outcome in doubt, Confederate reinforcements arrived by railroad from the Shenandoah Valley and turned the battle into a rout.

Thirteen months later (August 28-30, 1862) in the second battle of Manassas, General Robert E. Lee outmaneuvered and defeated Union General John Pope and cleared the way for a Confederate invasion of Maryland. Daily.

*Information: US 29 and Highway 234, Manassas, 703-361-1339; www.nps.gov/mana*

## WHAT TO SEE AND DO

### BATTLEFIELD MUSEUM

*6511 Sudley Road, Manassas (Bull Run) National Battlefield Park, 703-361-1339; www.nps.gov/mana*

Exhibits reflect incidents of battles; audiovisual presentations offer orientation. Daily.

### CHINN HOUSE RUINS

*6511 Sudley Road, Manassas (Bull Run) National Battlefield Park, 703-361-1339; www.nps.gov/mana*

The house served as a field hospital in both engagements and marked the left of the Confederate line at First Manassas; also the scene of Longstreet's counterattack at Second Manassas.

### DOGAN HOUSE

*6511 Sudley Road, Manassas (Bull Run) National Battlefield Park, 703-361-1339; www.nps.gov/mana*

An original structure at Groveton, a village around which the battle of Second Manassas was fought.

### STONE BRIDGE

*6511 Sudley Road, Manassas (Bull Run) National Battlefield Park, 703-361-1339; www.nps.gov/mana*

Where Union artillery opened the Battle of First Manassas; it afforded an avenue of escape for the Union troops after both First and Second Manassas.

### STONE HOUSE

*6511 Sudley Road, Manassas (Bull Run) National Battlefield Park, 703-361-1339; www.nps.gov/mana*

Originally a tavern (circa 1848); used as field hospital in both battles. Summer, daily.

### UNFINISHED RAILROAD

*6511 Sudley Road, Manassas (Bull Run) National Battlefield Park, 703-361-1339; www.nps.gov/mana*

Fully graded railroad bed, never completed, behind which Stonewall Jackson's men were positioned during the second battle.

*6511 Sudley Road, Manassas (Bull Run) National Battlefield Park, 703-361-1339;*
*www.nps.gov/mana*

A hill affords a look at much of the first battlefield. Information: Self-guided tours start here (walking tour of First Manassas, directions for driving tour of Second Manassas). Markers throughout park explain various aspects of battles. Ranger-conducted tours (summer).

# MARION

This popular vacation spot is surrounded by the George Washington and Jefferson national forests, abounding in game and birds and high enough to promise an invigorating climate. The seat of Smyth County, it was named for General Francis Marion, known during the American Revolution as the "Swamp Fox."

*Information: Smyth County Chamber of Commerce, 214 W. Main St., Marion,*
*276-783-3161; www.smythchamber.org*

## WHAT TO SEE AND DO

### HUNGRY MOTHER STATE PARK

*2854 Park Blvd., Marion, 276-781-7400; www.dcr.virginia.gov*

More than 2,180 acres amid the mountains with a 108-acre lake; panoramic views. Swimming beach, bathhouse, fishing, boating (rentals, launching, electric motors only); hiking, self-guided trails, picnicking, restaurant, concession, tent and trailer sites (electrical hookups, late March-December), cabins (year round). Hilltop visitor center, interpretive programs.

**463**

### MOUNT ROGERS NATIONAL RECREATION AREA

*3714 Highway 16, Marion, 276-783-5196;*
*www.stateparks.com/mount_rogers_smyth.html*

A 140,000-acre area includes Mount Rogers, the state's highest point (5,729 feet), mile-high open meadows known as "balds" and a great variety of animals and plants. Swimming, fishing; hunting, camping (fee at some areas), four visitor centers, approximately 400 miles of hiking, bicycle and bridle trails. Mount Rogers Scenic Byway (auto); Virginia Creeper Trail (hikers, bicycles, horses) follows an abandoned railroad grade through spectacular river gorges. Adjacent to New River Trails State Park. Visitor Center (daily all year). Mid-May-mid-September, daily; rest of year, Monday-Friday. Some fees.

**VIRGINIA**

★
★
★
★
☆

## SPECIAL EVENTS

### CHILHOWIE APPLE FESTIVAL

*www.chilhowieapplefestival.com*

Performances, shows, contests, crafts, parade, band competition. Mid-September.

### HUNGRY MOTHER ARTS AND CRAFTS FESTIVAL

*Hungry Mother State Park, 2854 Park Blvd., Marion, 276-781-7400;*
*www.hungrymotherfestival.com*

Mid-July.

### WHITETOP MOUNTAIN RAMP FESTIVAL

*www.virginia.org*

Arts and crafts, Ramp Eating Contest, Bluegrass music. Mid-May.

## HOTEL

### ★★ECONO LODGE MARION

*1420 N. Main St., Marion, 276-783-6031, 877-424-6423; www.choicehotels.com*

79 rooms. Complimentary continental breakfast. Pets accepted; fee. Free high-speed Internet. **$**

# MARTINSVILLE

Martinsville was named for Joseph Martin, a pioneer who settled here in 1773. Henry County takes its name from Patrick Henry, who lived here. When Henry County Court first opened in October 1776, 640 residents pledged an oath of allegiance to the United States; 40 refused to renounce allegiance to England. Located near the beautiful Blue Ridge Mountains, this community is home to Bassett Furniture and E. I. DuPont de Nemours.

*Information: Martinsville-Henry County Chamber of Commerce, 115 Broad St., Martinsville, 276-632-6401; www.martinsville.com*

## WHAT TO SEE AND DO

### PHILPOTT LAKE

*1058 Philpott Lake Road, Martinsville, 276-629-2703*

State's fourth-largest lake, formed by Philpott Dam, a U.S. Army Corps of Engineers project. Swimming, skin diving, waterskiing, boating, fishing; hunting, hiking, picnicking; four camping areas (April-October), one area free, some fees.

### VIRGINIA MUSEUM OF NATURAL HISTORY

*21 Starling Ave., Martinsville, 276-634-4141; www.vmnh.net*

Younger kids will appreciate this small museum, housed in an old school. They will enjoy exhibits featuring wild animals, butterflies, nature and science, along with a model of a giant sloth and a computer-activated, car-sized Triceratops. Monday-Saturday 10 a.m.-5 p.m., Sunday 1-5 p.m.

## SPECIAL EVENTS

### BLUE RIDGE FOLKLIFE FESTIVAL

*Blue Ridge Farm Museum, Highway 40, Martinsville, 540-365-4415; www.blueridgeinstitute.org*

Gospel, blues and string band music; traditional regional crafts; quilt show, antique autos, steam and gas-powered farm equipment, regional foods. Sports events include horse-pulling and log-skidding contests, coon dog swimming and treeing contests. Late October.

### STOCK CAR RACES

*Martinsville Speedway, Martinsville, 540-956-3151, 877-722-3849; www.stockcarracing.com*

Miller Genuine Draft 300, mid-March. Hanes 500, late April. Goody's 500, late September. Taco Bell 300, mid-October.

## HOTEL
### ★★BEST WESTERN MARTINSVILLE INN
*1755 Virginia Ave., Martinsville, 276-632-5611, 800-780-7234; www.bestwestern.com*
95 rooms. Complimentary breakfast. Free Internet access. Business center. Pets accepted. Pool. **$**

# MCLEAN
*Information: Fairfax County Convention & Visitors Bureau, 1961 Chain Bridge Road, Tyson's Corner, 703-752-9500, 800-732-4732; www.visitfairfax.org*

## WHAT TO SEE AND DO
### CLAUDE MOORE COLONIAL FARM
*6310 Georgetown Pike, McLean, 703-442-7557; www.1771.org*
Demonstration of 1770s low-income working farm; costumed interpreters work with crops and animals using 18th-century techniques. April-mid-December, Wednesday-Sunday (weather permitting). Wednesday-Sunday 10 a.m.-4.30 p.m. Admission: $3 for adults, $2 for children and senior citizens.

### GREAT FALLS PARK
*George Washington Memorial Parkway, McLean, 703-285-2965, 703-285-2513; www.nps.gov/grfa*
Spectacular natural beauty only 15 miles from the nation's capital at Great Falls Park, where the usually peaceful Potomac River narrows into a series of dramatically cascading rapids and 20-foot waterfalls before heading through Mather Gorge. Enjoy the view from a scenic overlook and then explore some of the park's 15 miles of trails, which take you past the remains of the Patowmack Canal, part of an 18th-century engineering project backed by George Washington, among others. Daily 7 a.m.-dark.

### TYSONS CORNER CENTER
*1961 Chain Bridge Road, McLean, 703-893-9400, 888-289-7667; www.shoptysons.com*
More than 250 stores, including Norstrom, Bloomingdale's and L.L.Bean. Restaurant. Monday-Saturday 10 a.m.-9:30 p.m., Sunday 11 a.m.-7 p.m.

## HOTELS
### ★★CROWNE PLAZA
*1960 Chain Bridge Road, McLean, 703-893-2100, 877-424-4225; www.crowneplaza.com*
316 rooms. Airport transportation available. Health and fitness center, High-speed Internet access. **$$**

### ★★★HILTON MCLEAN TYSONS CORNER
*7920 Jones Branch Drive, McLean, 703-847-5000, 800-445-8667; www.mclean.hilton.com*
Located close to the famous shopping area of Tyson Corners, this atrium-style hotel offers comfortable rooms, local shuttle service, a gift shop and live jazz Thursday-Saturday evenings. 458 rooms. Business center. Fitness center. Pets accepted. Wireless Internet access. Pool. **$$**

★
★
★
★
☆

#### ★★★★THE RITZ-CARLTON, TYSONS CORNER

*1700 Tysons Blvd., McLean, 703-506-4300, 800-241-3333; www.ritzcarlton.com*

Only 15 miles from Washington, D.C., this northern Virginia hotel is a luxurious retreat from the bustle of the city center. Guest rooms feature luxurious fabrics, flatscreen televisions and down duvet-covered beds. The Ritz-Carlton Day Spa offers unique treatments such as coffee anti-cellulite wrap or the bamboo lemongrass body scrub. The adjacent Tysons Galleria and Tysons Mall have more than 320 shops and a movie theater. 398 rooms. Pets accepted, restrictions. High-speed Internet access. Two restaurants, bar. Fitness room. Spa. Indoor pool, whirlpool. Complimentary newspaper. Complimentary overnight shoe shine. Pets accepted. Spa. **$$$$**

## RESTAURANTS

#### ★★CAFÉ OGGI

*6671 Old Dominion Drive, McLean, 703-442-7360; www.cafeoggi.com*

Italian menu. Lunch, dinner. Reservations recommended. **$$**

#### ★★CAFÉ TAJ

*1379 Beverly Road, McLean, 703-827-0444; www.mycafetaj.com*

Indian menu. Lunch (Monday-Saturday), dinner (daily). Bar. Outdoor seating. It also offers catering. **$$**

#### ★★DA DOMENICO

*1992 Chain Bridge Road, McLean, 703-790-9000; www.da-domenico.com*

Italian menu. Lunch (Monday-Sunday), dinner (Monday-Saturday). Closed Sunday. Bar. Reservations recommended. **$$**

#### ★★J GILBERT'S STEAKHOUSE

*6930 Old Dominion Drive, McLean, 703-893-1034; www.jgilberts.com*

Seafood, steak menu. Lunch, dinner, Sunday brunch. Bar. Children's menu. Outdoor seating. **$$**

#### ★★J. R.'S GOODTIMES

*8130 Watson St., McLean, 703-893-3390, 703-893-0546; www.jrsbeef.com*

Seafood menu. Lunch, dinner. Bar. Reservations recommended. **$$**

#### ★★KAZAN

*6813 Redmond Drive, McLean, 703-734-1960; www.kazanrestaurant.com*

Middle Eastern menu. Lunch (Monday-Friday), dinner (Monday-Saturday). Closed Sunday. Children's menu. **$$**

#### ★★PULCINELLA

*6852 Old Dominion Drive, McLean, 703-893-7777; www.pulcinellarestaurant.com*

Italian menu. Lunch, dinner. Bar. **$$**

#### ★★TACHIBANA

*6715 Lowell Ave., McLean, 703-847-1771; www.j-netusa.com/com/tachibana*

Japanese menu. Lunch, dinner. Circular dining room. **$$$**

# MIDDLETOWN

## WHAT TO SEE AND DO

### WAYSIDE THEATRE

*7853 Main St., Middletown, 540-869-1776; www.waysidetheatre.org*

Professional performances. Wednesday-Sunday. Reservations required. Late May-mid-October and December.

## SPECIAL EVENTS

### BATTLE OF CEDAR CREEK REENACTMENT

*Belle Grove, 8437 Valley Pike, Middletown, 540-869-2064, 888-628-1864;*
*www.cedarcreekbattlefield.org*

Demonstrations, tours, living history camps and full-scale battles. Mid-October.

### EAST COAST SURFING CHAMPIONSHIP

*Fourth Street, Ocean Front, 757-557-6140, 800-861-7873; www.surfecsc.com*

North America's oldest-running surfing competition. Skimboarding, volleyball, skateboarding, 5K. Fourth weekend in August.

### LEARNING WEEKEND

*8437 Valley Pike, Middletown*

Colonial Williamsburg. Family-oriented weekend of discovery on a single topic. March.

### WASHINGTON'S BIRTHDAY CELEBRATION

*Middletown*

President's Day weekend.

## HOTEL

### ★★★WAYSIDE INN

*7783 Main St., Middletown, 540-869-1797, 877-869-1797; www.alongthewayside.com*

Operating since 1797, this inn is located in the Shenandoah Valley at the foot of the Massanutten Mountains. Canopied beds, English, French and Oriental antiques, brocades, chintzes and silks decorate the property. Fresh cuisine is prepared and served in seven different dining rooms. 24 rooms. Complimentary continental breakfast. **$**

## RESTAURANT

### ★★WAYSIDE INN

*7783 E. Main St. (Highway 11), Middletown, 540-869-1797; www.alongthewayside.com*

American menu. Breakfast, lunch, dinner. Closed Monday-Tuesday in January and February. Bar. Children's menu. Sunday brunch. Casual attire. Reservations recommended. Outdoor seating. **$$**

# MIDLOTHIAN

## WHAT TO SEE AND DO

### SOUTHSIDE SPEEDWAY

*12800 Genito Road, Midlothian, 804-744-2700, 804-276-6913;*
*www.southside-speedway.com*

If you need to see some short-track action, this ⅓-mile asphalt oval is the ticket with Late Model Sportsman, Modified and Grand Stock racing on Friday nights. Heat races begin at 7 p.m. with the first feature at 8 p.m. Closed on NASCAR race weekends.

### RESTAURANT
#### ★★★RUTH'S CHRIS STEAK HOUSE
*11500 Huguenot Road, Midlothian, 804-378-0600; www.sizzlingsteak.com*
Located in the historic Bellgrade Plantation House, this restaurant offers fine dining with elegant Southern hospitality. Dine on the patio or in a private room with period furnishings and enjoy Ruth's Chris classic menu. Steak menu. Dinner. Bar. Business casual attire. Reservations recommended. Outdoor seating. **$$$**

# MONTEREY
*Highland County Chamber of Commerce, Monterey, 540-468-2550;*
*www.highlandcounty.org*

### SPECIAL EVENT
#### HIGHLAND COUNTY MAPLE FESTIVAL
*Highland County Chamber of Commerce, Monterey, 540-468-2550;*
*www.highlandcounty.org*
Tours of sugar camps producing maple syrup and maple sugar products. Juried craft show; food, entertainment. Mid-March.

### HOTEL
#### ★★★HIGHLAND INN
*68 W. Main St., Monterey, 540-468-2143, 888-466-4682; www.highland-inn.com*
Known for 75 years as the landmark Hotel Monterey, the Highland Inn maintains its traditional hospitality while offering upgraded amenities in the 1904 building. A detailed, double-decker porch graces the inn's façade, complete with rocking chairs from which guests can enjoy a view of the peaceful street. 18 rooms. Victorian building furnished with period antiques. Built in 1904. **$**

# MONTPELIER

### WHAT TO SEE AND DO
#### MONTPELIER
*11407 Constitution Highway, Montpelier Station, 540-672-2728; www.montpelier.org*
The former residence of James Madison, fourth president of the United States. Madison was the third generation of his family to live on this extensive plantation. He inherited Montpelier and expanded it twice. After his presidency, he and Dolley Madison retired to the estate, which Mrs. Madison sold after the president's death to pay off her son's gambling debts. In 1901, the estate was bought by William du Pont, who enlarged the house, added many outbuildings, including a private railroad station, built greenhouses and planted gardens. Today, under the stewardship of the National Trust for Historic Preservation, a long-term research and preservation project has begun. Self-guided tours of the arboretum, nature trails and formal garden. April-October, daily 9:30 a.m.-5:30 p.m.; November-March, daily 9:30 a.m.-4:30 p.m.; closed first Saturday in November.

# MONTROSS

## WHAT TO SEE AND DO

### STRATFORD HALL PLANTATION

*Highway 3 E. and Highway 214, Montross, 804-493-8038; www.stratfordhall.org*

Boyhood home of Richard Henry Lee and Francis Lightfoot Lee and birthplace of General Robert E. Lee. Center of restored, working plantation is a monumental Georgian house built circa 1735, famous for its uniquely grouped chimney stacks. Interiors span approximately a 100-year period and feature a Federal-era parlor and neoclassical paneling in the Great Hall. Flanking dependencies include kitchen, plantation office and gardener's house. Boxwood garden; 18th- and 19th-century carriages; working mill; visitor center with museum, video presentations. Plantation luncheon. Daily.

### WESTMORELAND STATE PARK

*1650 State Park Road, Highway 347, Montross, 804-493-8821;*
*www.dcr.virginia.gov/state_parks*

Approximately 1,300 acres on Potomac River. Sand beach, swimming pool, bathhouse, fishing, boating (ramp, rentals); hiking trails, picnicking, playground, concession, camping, tent and trailer sites (March-November; dump station, electrical hookups), cabins (March-December). Visitor center, evening programs. Standard fees. Pets accepted; fee.

# MOUNT JACKSON

## HOTEL

### ★★SUPER 8 MOTEL MOUNT JACKSON

*250 Conicville Blvd., Mount Jackson, 540-477-2911, 800-800-8000; www.super8.com*

92 rooms. Business center. Free continental breakfast. Free high-speed Internet access. Pets accepted. Pool. Restaurant. **$**

## SPECIALTY LODGING

### WIDOW KIP'S COUNTRY INN

*355 Orchard Drive, Mount Jackson, 540-477-2400, 800-478-8714;*
*www.widowkips.com*

This restored 1830 Victorian home is set on seven acres of rural countryside with a view of the Shenandoah River and the valley. Pets accepted. Seven rooms. Complimentary full breakfast. **$**

# MOUNT VERNON

## WHAT TO SEE AND DO

### FRANK LLOYD WRIGHT'S POPE-LEIGHEY HOUSE

*9000 Richmond Highway, Mount Vernon, 703-780-4000;*
*www.nationaltrust.org/woodlawn*

Erected in Falls Church in 1940, the house was disassembled due to the construction of a new highway and rebuilt at the present site in 1964. Built of cypress, brick and glass, the house is an example of Wright's "Usonian" structures, which he proposed as a prototype of affordable housing for Depression-era middle-income families; original Wright-designed furniture. March-December, Tuesday-Sunday. Combination ticket for both houses available.

### GRISTMILL

*Mount Vernon, 703-780-2000; www.mountvernon.org*
This mill was reconstructed in 1930 on the original foundation of a mill George Washington operated on the Dogue Run. Visitor center, programs. April-October, daily.

### MOUNT VERNON

*George Washington Parkway, Mount Vernon, 703-780-2000; www.mountvernon.org*
Touring Mount Vernon, George Washington's home for more than 45 years, gives visitors a fascinating glimpse of the world of landed gentry in 18th-century America, as well as the personal vision of the first U.S. president. Washington designed sections of the beautifully landscaped grounds himself, incorporating woods, meadows and serpentine walkways. He also added the red-roofed mansion's cupola, weather vane and two-story piazza, from which guests can enjoy an awe-inspiring view of the Potomac River. Explore the working areas of the estate, including the wash house, stable and kitchen: an audio tour describes the lives of some of the more than 300 slaves who lived and worked there. The house has been restored to its appearance in 1799, the year Washington died. He is buried on the estate with his wife, Martha. Daily; hours vary by season.

### WOODLAWN PLANTATION

*9000 Richmond Highway, Mount Vernon, Alexandria, 703-780-4000;*
*www.woodlawn1805.org*
(1800-1805) In 1799, George Washington gave 2,000 acres of land as a wedding present to Eleanor Parke Custis, his foster daughter, who married his nephew, Major Lawrence Lewis. Dr. William Thornton, first architect of the U.S. Capitol, then designed this mansion. The Lewises entertained such notables as Andrew Jackson, Henry Clay and the Marquis de Lafayette. The house was restored in the early 1900s and later became the residence of a U.S. senator; 19th-century period rooms; many original furnishings. Formal gardens. March-December, Tuesday-Sunday.

## RESTAURANT
### ★★MOUNT VERNON INN

*On the Grounds of Mount Vernon, Mount Vernon, 703-780-0011;*
*www.mountvernon.org*
Lunch, dinner. Bar. Children's menu. $$

# NATURAL BRIDGE

Native Americans worshipped at the stone bridge that nature formed across a deep gorge. The town and county were both named after it. The limestone arch, 215 feet high, 90 feet long and 150 feet wide in some places, attracted the interest of Thomas Jefferson, who purchased the bridge and 157 surrounding acres from King George III for 20 shillings, about $2.49, in 1774. Fully appreciative of this natural wonder, Jefferson built a cabin for visitors and installed caretakers. His guest book reads like

a colonial *Who's Who*. Surveyed by George Washington and painted by many famous artists, the bridge easily accommodates Highway 11. The Glenwood Ranger District of the Washington and Jefferson National Forests has its office in Natural Bridge.
*Information: Natural Bridge of Virginia, Highway 11 and Highway 130, Natural Bridge, 540-291-2121, 800-533-1410; www.naturalbridgeva.com*

## WHAT TO SEE AND DO
### CAVE MOUNTAIN LAKE RECREATION AREA
*811 Cave Mountain Lake Road, Natural Bridge, 540-291-2188; www.recreation.gov/camping*
Swimming; picnicking, camping (fee). May-October. Quitting hours: 10 p.m.-6 a.m.

### CAVERNS OF LANE NATURAL BRIDGE
*15 Appledorelane, Natural Bridge, 540-291-2121, 800-533-1410; www.naturalbridgeva.com/caverns.html*
More than 300 feet below ground on three levels; streams, hanging gardens of formations, flowstone cascade, totem pole, colossal dome and more. One-mile guided tour (one hour). March-November, daily; December-February, closed.

### "DRAMA OF CREATION"
*15 Appledore Lane, Natural Bridge, 540-291-2121, 800-533-1410; www.naturalbridgeva.com*
A musical presentation, viewed from beneath Natural Bridge, includes a light show cast under and across the arch. Nightly. April-October, daily. Winter, only on weekends.

### NATURAL BRIDGE
*15 Appledore Lane, Natural Bridge, 540-291-2121, 800-533-1410; www.naturalbridgeva.com*
Self-guided tours (one hour). Daily. Ticket includes entrance.

### NATURAL BRIDGE WAX MUSEUM
*70 Wert Faulkner Highway, Natural Bridge, 540-291-2426; www.visitnaturalbridge.com*
Wax figures depicting local history; self-guided factory tours. March-November, daily; December-February, weekends. Fees: adults $10, children $6.

### NATURAL BRIDGE ZOO
*5784 S. Lee Highway, Natural Bridge, 540-291-2420; www.naturalbridgezoo.com*
State's largest and most complete zoo with more than 400 reptiles, birds and mammals. Petting area; safari shop; picnic grounds. March-November, daily. Fee: adults $10, senior citizens $9, children $8, age 2 years and under free.

# NEW CHURCH

## HOTEL
### ★★★THE GARDEN AND THE SEA INN
*4188 Nelson Road, New Church, 757-824-0672, 800-824-0672; www.gardenandseainn.com*

★
★
★
★

This lovely Victorian inn offers romantically decorated rooms. The complimentary breakfast can be enjoyed in either the dining room overlooking the gardens or in the garden by the lily pond. Eight rooms. Closed late November-April. Pets accepted. Complimentary full breakfast. $

### RESTAURANT
#### ★★THE GARDEN AND THE SEA INN
*4188 Nelson Road, New Church, 757-824-0672, 800-824-0672;*
*www.gardenandseainn.com*
International menu. Dinner. Closed Monday-Wednesday; also Saturday after Thanksgiving-March. Business casual attire. Reservations recommended. $$

# NEW MARKET

New Market, situated in the Shenandoah Valley, gained its niche in Virginia history on May 15, 1864, when, in desperation, Confederate General Breckinridge ordered the cadets from Lexington's Virginia Military Institute to join the battle against the forces of General Franz Sigel. The oldest was just 20, but they entered the fray fearlessly, taking prisoners and capturing a battery. Their heroism inspired the Confederate defeat of Sigel's seasoned troops.

*Information: Shenandoah Valley Travel Association, New Market, 540-740-3132,*
*800-847-4878; www.visitshenandoah.org*

### WHAT TO SEE AND DO
#### BEDROOMS OF AMERICA
*9386 Congress St., New Market, 540-740-3512*
Authentic furnishings from William and Mary through the Art Deco period. Antique dolls. Gift shop. Daily.

#### ENDLESS CAVERNS
*1800 Endless Caverns Road, New Market, 540-896-2283, 800-544-2283;*
*www.endlesscaverns.com*
Lighted display of unusual rock formations; stalagmites and stalactites, columns, shields, flowstone and limestone pendants, presented in natural color. Temperature 55 degrees F summer and winter. Camping. Guided tours (75 minutes). Daily. Admission: adults $16, children $8.

#### NEW MARKET BATTLEFIELD MILITARY MUSEUM
*9500 George R. Collins Drive, New Market, 540-740-8065;*
*www4.vmi.edu/museum/nm/index.html*
Located on actual site of Battle of New Market, the museum houses a private collection of more than 2,000 military artifacts and genuine, personal artifacts of the American soldier from 1776 to the present. Includes uniforms, weapons, battlefield diaries, medals, mementos; film (30 minutes). Bookshop has more than 500 titles, some antique. Union and Confederate troop position markers are on museum grounds. Mid-March-November, daily.

★
★
★
★
★

### NEW MARKET BATTLEFIELD STATE HISTORICAL PARK

*8895 Collins Drive, New Market, 540-740-3101, 866-515-1864;*
*www.umi.edu/newmarket*

Site of Civil War Battle of New Market (May 15, 1864), in which 257 Virginia Military Institute cadets played a decisive role. Original Bushong farmhouse and outbuildings restored, period furnishings. Hall of Valor, exhibits, films. Scenic overlooks, walking tour. Daily.

### SHENANDOAH CAVERNS

*261 Caverns Road, New Market, 540-477-3115, 888-422-8376;*
*www.shenandoahcaverns.com*

Elevator lowers visitors 60 feet to large subterranean rooms, fascinating rock formations; snack bar, picnic areas. Interior a constant 54 degrees F. Daily.

## HOTELS

### ★BUDGET INN

*2192 Old Valley Pike, New Market, 540-740-3105, 800-296-6835; www.budgetinn.com*
14 rooms. $

### ★★SHENVALEE GOLF RESORT

*9660 Fairway Drive, New Market, 540-740-3181, 888-339-3181; www.shenvalee.com*
42 rooms. 27-hole PGA golf course. Pool. Restaurant. $

# NEWPORT NEWS

One of the three cities that make up the Port of Hampton Roads, Newport News has the world's largest shipbuilding company, Newport News Shipbuilding. During the two World Wars it was a vitally important point of embarkation and supply. The area still has many important defense establishments.

Newport News is located on the historic Virginia Peninsula between Williamsburg and Virginia Beach. The peninsula also contains Hampton, Yorktown and Jamestown, and it hosted some of the earliest landings in this country. The name "Newport News" is said to derive from the good "news" of the arrival of Captain Christopher Newport, who brought supplies and additional colonists to the settlement at Jamestown.

*Information: Visitor Center, 13560 Jefferson Ave., Newport News,*
*757-886-7777, 888-493-7386; www.newport-news.org*

## WHAT TO SEE AND DO

### FORT EUSTIS

*213 Calhoun St., Newport News, 757-878-4920; www.eustis.army.mil*
Headquarters of the U.S. Army Transportation Center. Self-guided auto tour available; brochures at Public Affairs Office (Building 213).

### HISTORIC HILTON VILLAGE

*Warwick Boulevard and Main Street, Newport News*
Listed on the National Register of Historic Places, this village was built between 1918 and 1920 to provide wartime housing for workers at Newport News Shipbuilding. Architecturally significant neighborhood features 500 English cottage-style homes and antique and specialty shops.

★
★
★
★
☆

### MARINERS' MUSEUM

*100 Museum Drive, Newport News, 757-596-2222; www.mariner.org*

Exhibits and displays represent international nautical history; ship models, figureheads, scrimshaw, paintings, decorative arts and small craft. The Age of Exploration Gallery chronicles advancements in shipbuilding, ocean navigation and cartography that led to early transoceanic exploration. The Chesapeake Bay Gallery exhibits Native American artifacts, workboats, racing shells, multimedia exhibits, a working steam engine and hundreds of artifacts and photos that tell the story of this body of water. Historical interpreters, research library; museum shop. A 550-acre park on the James River features five-mile Noland Trail with 14 pedestrian bridges; picnic area. Guided tours. Daily. Monday-Saturday 10 a.m.-5 p.m., Sunday noon-5 p.m. Closed Thanksgiving and Christmas.

### NEWPORT NEWS PARK

*13564 Jefferson Ave., Newport News, 757-886-7912, 800-203-8322; www.nnparks.com*

Facilities in this 8,065-acre park include freshwater fishing, canoes, paddleboats, boat rentals; history and nature trails, bicycle paths (rentals), archery, arboretum, discovery center, picnicking, Civil War earthworks, 188 campsites. All year. Some fees. Pets accepted.

### PENINSULA FINE ARTS CENTER

*101 Museum Drive, Newport News, 757-596-8175; www.pfac-va.org*

Changing bimonthly exhibits ranging from national traveling exhibitions to regional artists; classes, workshops and special events. Children's hands-on activity area; museum shop. Daily. Tuesday-Saturday 10 a.m.-8 p.m. Sunday 1-8 p.m.

### US ARMY TRANSPORTATION MUSEUM

*300 Washington Blvd., Besson Hall, Fort Eustis, 757-878-1115, 888-493-7386; www.transchool.eustis.army.mil/museum*

Depicts development of Army transportation from 1776 to the present; "flying saucer," amphibious vehicles, trucks, helicopters. Gift shop. Tuesday-Sunday. Museum opens 9 a.m.-4:30 p.m.

### VIRGINIA LIVING MUSEUM

*524 J. Clyde Morris Blvd., Newport News, 757-595-1900; www.thevlm.org*

Exhibits on natural science; native Virginia, wildlife living in natural habitats; indoor and outdoor aviaries; aquariums; wildflower gardens; planetarium with daily shows; observatory; children's hands-on Discovery Center. Daily. Admission: adults $15, children $12.

### VIRGINIA WAR MUSEUM

*9285 Warwick Blvd., Newport News, 757-247-8523; www.warmuseum.org*

More than 60,000 artifacts, including weapons, uniforms, vehicles, posters, insignias and accoutrements relating to every major U.S. military involvement from the Revolutionary War to the Vietnam War. Military history library and film collection. Civil War tours and educational programs available. Daily. Monday-Saturday 9 a.m.-5 p.m. and Sunday 1-5 p.m. Admission: adults $6, senior citizens $5, children $4, children under 4 years

★
★
★
★

free.

## HOTELS

### ★COMFORT INN

*12330 Jefferson Ave., Newport News, 757-249-0200, 877-424-6423;*
*www.newportnewscomfort.com*

124 rooms. Complimentary full breakfast. Airport transportation available. Free high-speed Internet access. Free cookies and popcorn. Seasonal outdoor pool. Pets accepted. **$**

### ★HAMPTON INN

*12251 Jefferson Ave., Newport News, 757-249-0001, 800-426-7866;*
*www.hamptoninn.com*

120 rooms. Complimentary full breakfast. Airport transportation available. Pool. Business center. Meeting room. Fitness center. Wireless Internet access. Pets not accepted. **$**

### ★★★OMNI NEWPORT NEWS HOTEL

*1000 Omni Blvd., Newport News, 757-873-6664, 800-843-6664; www.omnihotels.com*

Located minutes from historic Williamsburg. 182 rooms. High-speed Internet access. **$**

## RESTAURANTS

### ★★AL FRESCO

*11710 Jefferson Ave., Newport News, 757-873-0644;*
*www.alfrescoitalianrestaurant.com*

Italian menu. Lunch, dinner. Closed Sunday. Bar. Children's menu. Business casual attire. Reservations recommended. Outdoor seating. **$$**

### ★★DAS WALDCAFE

*12529 Warwick Blvd., Newport News, 757-930-1781*

German menu. Lunch, dinner. Closed Sunday. Bar. Casual attire. Reservations recommended. **$**

### ★★PORT ARTHUR

*11137 Warwick Blvd., Newport News, 757-599-6474*

Chinese menu. Lunch, dinner. Children's menu. Casual attire. Reservations recommended. **$**

# NORFOLK

This city is part of the Port of Hampton Roads, with a bustling trade center and many historic, cultural and resort areas nearby. Harbor tours depart from Norfolk's downtown waterfront.

In 1682, the General Assembly purchased 50 acres on the Elizabeth River from Nicholas Wise for "ten thousand pounds of tobacco and caske." By 1736, the town that developed was the largest in Virginia. On January 1, 1776, Norfolk was shelled by the British and later burned by the colonists to prevent a British takeover. The battle between the Merrimac and the Monitor in Hampton Roads in March 1862 was followed by the city's fall to Union forces in May of that year. In 1883, the first shipment of coal to the port by the Norfolk and Western Railway (now Norfolk Southern) began a new era of prosperity for the city.

Norfolk houses the largest naval facility in the world, and is headquarters for the United States Navy's Atlantic Fleet and NATO's Allied Command Atlantic. Norfolk has shipbuilding and ship-repair companies, consumer and industrial equipment manufacturers and food-processing plants. The city ships coal, tobacco, grain, seafood and vegetables. It is also the region's cultural center, home to the Virginia Opera, Virginia Symphony, Virginia Waterfront International Arts Festival and Virginia Stage Company.

Old Dominion University (1930), Virginia Wesleyan College (1967), Norfolk State University (1935) and Eastern Virginia Medical School (1973) are located in Norfolk. Within a 50-mile radius are ocean, bay, river and marsh fishing, as well as hunting. Nearby, there are 25 miles of beaches. The 17.6-mile-long Chesapeake Bay Bridge-Tunnel between Norfolk and the Delmarva Peninsula opened in 1964; toll for passenger cars is $10, including passengers.

*Information: Norfolk Convention and Visitors Bureau, 232 E. Main St., Norfolk, 757-441-1852, 800-368-3097; www.norfolkcvb.com*

## WHAT TO SEE AND DO
### AMERICAN ROVER
*Norfolk, 757-627-7245; www.americanrover.com*
This 135-foot, three-masted topsail passenger schooner cruises the "smooth waters" of Hampton Roads historical harbor; spacious sun decks, below-deck lounges, concessions. Tour passes historic forts, merchant and U.S. Navy ships. Some tours pass the naval base (inquire for tour schedule). April-October, 1½- and 2-hour tours daily.

### CARRIE B HARBOR TOURS
*Norfolk, 757-393-4735; www.carriebcruises.com*
Departs from the Waterside. Replica of 19th-century riverboat takes narrated 90-minute tour of naval shipyard and inner harbor (May-October, daily); narrated 2½-hour tour of naval base (May-October, daily); and 2½-hour sunset cruise to Hampton Roads and naval base. Daily.

### CHRYSLER MUSEUM OF ART
*245 W. Olney Road, Norfolk, 757-664-6200; www.chrysler.org*
Art treasures representing nearly every important culture, civilization and historical period of the past 4,000 years. Photography gallery; fine collection of Tiffany decorative arts and glass, includes the 8,000-piece Chrysler Institute of Glass. Wednesday-Sunday. Admission: adults $7, seniors, military $5. Children free.

### GENERAL DOUGLAS MACARTHUR MEMORIAL
*City Hall Avenue and Bank Street, Norfolk, 757-441-2965; www.macarthurmemorial.org*
Restored former city hall (1847) where MacArthur is buried. Nine galleries contain memorabilia of his life and military career. There are three other buildings on MacArthur Square: a theater where a film biography is shown, a gift shop and the

★
★
★
★

library/archives. Daily.

## HAMPTON ROADS NAVAL MUSEUM

*1 Waterside Drive, Norfolk, 757-322-2987; www.hrnm.navy.mil*

Interprets the extensive naval history of the Hampton Roads area, including detailed ship models, period photographs, archaeological artifacts, and a superior collection of naval prints and artwork. The museum is open daily from 9 a.m.-5 p.m. from Memorial Day-Labor Day. All other times of the year, Tuesday-Saturday 10 a.m.-5 p.m., Sunday noon-5 p.m. Closed Monday.

## HERMITAGE FOUNDATION MUSEUM

*7637 N. Shore Road, Norfolk, 757-423-2052; www.hermitagefoundation.org*

Guided tours of fine arts museum in Tudor-style mansion. Collections of tapestries, Chinese bronzes and jade, ancient glass. Monday, Tuesday and Thursday-Saturday 10 a.m.-5 p.m., Sunday 1-5 p.m. Closed Wednesday and major holidays.

## HUNTER HOUSE VICTORIAN MUSEUM

*240 W. Freemason St., Norfolk, 757-623-9814; www.hunterhousemuseum.org*

Built in 1894 and rich in architectural details, the house contains the Hunter family's collection of Victorian furnishings and decorative pieces, including a Renaissance Revival bedchamber suite, a nursery with children's playthings, an inglenook, and stained-glass windows; lavish period reproduction floor and wall coverings, lighting fixtures and drapery. Also exhibited is a collection of early-20th-century medical memorabilia. Tours begin every 30 minutes. April-December, Wednesday-Sunday. Admission: adults $5, senior citizens $4, children $1.

## MOSES MYERS HOUSE

*331 Bank St., Norfolk, 757-333-6283*

Excellent example of 1792 Georgian architecture; many pieces of original furniture, silver and china. Wednesday-Saturday.

## NAUTICUS-THE NATIONAL MARITIME CENTER

*1 Waterside Drive, Norfolk, 757-664-1000, 800-664-1080; www.nauticus.org*

Interprets aspects from marine biology and ecology to exploration, trade and shipbuilding. Interactive computer exhibits allow visitors to navigate a simulated ocean voyage, design a model ship, pilot a virtual reality submarine, and view actual researchers at work in two working marine laboratories. Active U.S. Navy ships and scientific research vessels periodically moor at Nauticus and open to visitors. Also 350-seat, 70 mm wide-screen theater; shark petting tank. Memorial Day-Labor Day, daily; rest of year, Tuesday-Sunday. Admission prices: adult $10.95, children ages 4-12 $8.50, military/seniors $9.95.

## NORFOLK BOTANICAL GARDEN

*6700 Azalea Garden Road, Norfolk, 757-441-5830; www.norfolkbotanicalgarden.org*

Azaleas, camellias, rhododendrons, roses (May-October), dogwoods and hollies on 155 acres. Japanese, Colonial, perennial and rose gardens; flowering arboretum; fragrance garden for the visually impaired; picnicking, restaurant and gift shop; tropical pavilion. Flowering displays best from early April-October. Gardens (daily; closed special events). Information center (daily). Narrated boat ride (30 minutes) and tram

**477**

VIRGINIA

tours (daily) open 9 a.m.-5 p.m. October 16-March. 9 a.m.-7 p.m. April-October 15. Admission: adults $7, seniors and military $6, children 3-18 $5.

### SPIRIT OF NORFOLK

*109 E. Main Road, Norfolk, 757-625-1748, 866-304-2469, 866-451-3866; www.spiritofnorfolk.com*

Departs from the Waterside. Harbor cruise aboard 600-passenger cruise ship. Captain's narration highlights the harbor's famous landmarks, including Waterside Festival Marketplace, Portsmouth Naval Hospital, Old Fort Norfolk, Blackbeard's hiding place, Norfolk Naval Base, and downtown area's dynamic skyline. Luncheon cruise (Tuesday-Sunday); evening dinner cruise (Tuesday-Sunday); moonlight party cruise (Friday-Saturday, in season).

### ST. PAUL'S EPISCOPAL CHURCH

*201 St. Paul's Blvd., Norfolk, 757-627-4353; www.saintpaulsnorfolk.com*

(1739) Only building to survive burning of Norfolk in 1776. Monday-Saturday. Also by appointment, Sunday 8 and 10:30 a.m.

### TOWN POINT PARK

*120 W. Main St., Norfolk, 757-441-2345; www.festeventsva.org*

Home to Norfolk Festevents, the park hosts more than 100 free outdoor concerts, parties, dances, movies and festivals each year.

### VIRGINIA ZOOLOGICAL PARK

*3500 Granby St., Norfolk, 757-441-2374; www.virginiazoo.org*

A combination zoo, park and conservatory. Playground, Tennis courts. Basketball courts; picnic area, concession. Daily. Hours 10 a.m.-5 p.m. Admission: adults $7, children 2-11 $5, senior citizens $6.

### WATERSIDE FESTIVAL MARKETPLACE

*333 Waterside Drive, Norfolk, 757-627-3300; www.watersidemarketplace.com*

A waterfront pavilion with more than 90 shops, restaurants. (Monday-Saturday 10 a.m.-9 p.m., Sunday noon-6 p.m.) Bordering the Waterside are the city's marina and dock areas, where harbor tour vessels take on passengers. Retail store. Night club.

### WILLOUGHBY-BAYLOR HOUSE

*601 E. Freemason St., Norfolk, 757-441-1526; www.chrysler.org*

Restored 1794 townhouse with period furnishings; herb and flower garden adjacent. By appointment; inquire at Moses Myers House. Closed on Monday and Tuesday. Wednesday-Saturday 10 a.m.-4 p.m., Sunday noon-4 p.m. Admission: adults $7; teachers, seniors and military $5; students and those under 18 years free.

## SPECIAL EVENTS

### HARBORFEST

*Town Point Park, 120 W. Main St., Norfolk, 757-441-2345; www.festeventsva.org*

Sailboat and speedboat races, tall ships, ship tours, waterskiing, military demonstrations, entertainment, children's activities, fireworks, seafood. First full weekend in June. Pets not accepted. No video recording. No open umbrellas during performances.

### INTERNATIONAL AZALEA FESTIVAL

*220 Boush St., Downtown and Norfolk Botanical Garden, Norfolk, 757-282-2801; www.azaleafestival.org*

A salute to NATO. Parade, coronation ceremony, air show (held at Norfolk Naval Air Station), events, concerts, fair, ball, entertainment. Late April.

### VIRGINIA CHILDREN'S FESTIVAL

*Town Point Park, 120 W. Main St., Norfolk, 757-441-2345; www.festeventsva.org*

More than 200 educational, creative and interactive activities; entertainment. Early October.

### VIRGINIA OPERA

*160 E. Virginia Beach Blvd., Norfolk, 757-627-9545, 866-673-7282; www.vaopera.org*

Harrison Opera House and other select locations. Statewide opera company; traditional and contemporary works. Features young American artists. October-April.

### VIRGINIA SYMPHONY

*861 Glenrock Road, Norfolk, 757-892-6366, 757-466-3060; www.virginiasymphony.org*

Chrysler Hall and other select locations. Five performance series. September-May.

### VIRGINIA WATERFRONT INTERNATIONAL ARTS FESTIVAL

*220 Boush St., Norfolk, 757-282-2800; www.virginiaartsfest.com*

Eighteen days of classical and contemporary music, dance, visual arts and theater performances. Late April-mid-May.

## HOTELS

### ★★BEST WESTERN CENTER INN

*235 N. Military Highway, Norfolk, 757-461-6600, 800-237-5517; www.norfolkcvb.com*

Near airport. 152 rooms. Complimentary continental breakfast. Airport transportation available. **$**

### ★BEST WESTERN HOLIDAY SANDS INN & SUITES

*1330 E. Oceanview Ave., Norfolk, 757-583-2621, 800-525-5156; www.bestwestern.com*

90 rooms. Complimentary continental breakfast. Airport transportation available. Free high-speed Internet access. Pool. **$**

### ★HAMPTON INN

*1450 N. Military Highway, Norfolk, 757-466-7474*

130 rooms. Complimentary full breakfast. Airport transportation available. **$**

### ★★★HILTON NORFOLK AIRPORT

*1500 N. Military Highway, Norfolk, 757-466-8000, 800-445-8667; www.norfolkhilton.com*

★
★
★
★
★

Conveniently located two miles from Norfolk International Airport, this hotel is ideal for those visiting the business district or military installations. 254 rooms. Airport transportation available. Pool. Fitness center. High-speed Internet access. Pets not accepted. $$

### ★★★MARRIOTT NORFOLK WATERSIDE

*235 E. Main St., Norfolk, 757-627-4200, 888-236-2427; www.marriott.com*

In Norfolk's historic district, the Marriott Norfolk Waterside offers well-appointed guest rooms and dining options such as Shula's 347 Steakhouse. 405 rooms. High-speed Internet access. $$

### PAGE HOUSE

*323 Fairfax Ave., Norfolk, 757-625-5033, 800-599-7659; www.pagehouseinn.com*

This 1898 Georgian Revival mansion, originally a family home and completely renovated in 1990, is located in the fashionable Ghent historic district. It offers distinctly decorated guest rooms. Restaurant. Fitness center. Complimentary candy, fresh fruit, beverages. Seven rooms. Children under 12 years only with reservation. $$

### ★QUALITY INN

*8051 Hampton Blvd., Norfolk, 757-451-0000, 877-424-6423; www.comfortinn.com*

119 rooms. Complimentary continental breakfast. Free high-speed Internet access. Heated indoor pool. $

### ★★★SHERATON NORFOLK WATERSIDE HOTEL

*777 Waterside Drive, Norfolk, 757-622-6664, 800-325-3535; www.sheraton.com*

Adjacent to Waterside Marketplace on the Elizabeth River, this landmark hotel affords great views of the harbor and downtown skyline. 445 rooms. High-speed Internet access. $

## RESTAURANTS

### ★★BAKER'S CRUST

*330 W. 21st St., Norfolk, 757-625-3600; www.bakerscrust.com*

Steak menu. Lunch, dinner. Bar. Children's menu. Casual attire. Outdoor seating. Daily. $$

### ★THE BANQUE

*1849 E. Little Creek Road, Norfolk, 757-480-3600; www.thebanque.com*

Dinner. Closed Monday. Bar. Western décor. $$

### ★FREEMASON ABBEY

*209 W. Freemason St., Norfolk, 757-622-3966; www.freemasonabbey.com*

American, seafood menu. Lunch, dinner, Sunday brunch. Bar. Children's menu. Casual attire. Renovated 1873 church many; antiques. Monday-Saturday 11 a.m. lunch; Sunday at 9:30 a.m. for brunch. $$

### ★★★LA GALLERIA

*120 College Place, Norfolk, 757-623-3939; www.lagalleriaristorante.com*

With its freestanding granite bar, live music and wood-burning oven, La Galleria is well equipped to serve authentic Italian cuisine with European flair. This Norfolk restaurant serves dishes such as buccatini carbonara, tortellini mac and cheese and ham marsala. Desserts are made in-house. Italian menu. Dinner. Closed Sunday and Monday. Bar. Business casual attire. Reservations recommended. Valet parking. **$$**

### ★★MONASTERY
*443 Granby St., Norfolk, 757-625-8193*
Czech, Eastern European menu. Dinner. Closed Mondays. Bar. Reservations recommended. **$$**

# ORANGE

Orange and Orange county were named for William of Orange in 1734. Located in the Piedmont (foothills) of the Blue Ridge Mountains, Orange was settled by Germans under the leadership of Alexander Spotswood between 1714 and 1719. This is riding and hunting country, drawing its livelihood from farming, livestock and light industry. The county boasts many antebellum houses.

## WHAT TO SEE AND DO
### JAMES MADISON MUSEUM
*129 Caroline St., Orange, 540-672-1776; www.jamesmadisonmus.org*
Exhibits commemorating Madison's life and his contributions to American history; also Orange County history and Hall of Agriculture that includes an 18th-century homestead. March-December, daily; rest of year, Monday-Friday 9 a.m.-5 p.m., Saturday 10 a.m.-5 p.m. Admission: adults $4, senior citizens $3, children $1.

## HOTELS
### GREENOCK HOUSE INN
*249 Caroline St., Orange, 540-672-3625, 800-841-1253; www.greenockhouse.com*
This inn is located close to Monticello, Montpelier and Skyline Drive and offers activities that include biking, hiking, antique shopping, boating and fishing. The inn comprises four buildings, including a century-old main house built by descendents of Thomas Jefferson. Verandas wrap around the building and look out over the wooded gardens. Five rooms. Closed late December-early January. Complimentary full breakfast. Pets not accepted. **$**

### HOLLADAY HOUSE
*155 W. Main St., Orange, 540-672-4893, 800-358-4422;*
*www.holladayhousebandb.com*
Six rooms. Children over 12 only. Complimentary full breakfast. Federal-style residence (circa 1830). Free wireless Internet access. Pets accepted. **$**

# PARIS

## HOTEL
### ★★★ASHBY INN

*692 Federal St., Paris, 540-592-3900, 866-336-0099; www.ashbyinn.com*

This restored 1829 inn is charming and elegant. Guests should certainly make a point to dine in the restaurant, which features seasonal fare. Nine rooms. Complimentary full breakfast. Restaurant. **$$**

## RESTAURANT
### ★★★ASHBY INN
*692 Federal St., Paris, 540-592-3900, 866-336-0099; www.ashbyinn.com*

Seasonal provisions inspire the simple, hearty menu that rivals those at trendy city restaurants. Look for garden-fresh tomatoes in the summer and wild game in the fall. Relax in a very warm, very country atmosphere. American menu. Dinner (reservation required), Sunday brunch. Closed Monday-Tuesday. Business casual attire. Reservations recommended. Outdoor seating. **$$$**

# PETERSBURG

This city, Lee's last stand before Appomattox (1864-1865), was settled in 1645 when the General Assembly authorized construction of Fort Henry at the falls of the Appomattox River. In 1784, three separate towns united to become the single city of Petersburg. Between the Revolutionary War and Civil War, the town was a popular stopping place with a social life that for a time eclipsed that of Richmond.

Physically untouched during the early years of the Civil War (though the town sent 17 companies to the front), Petersburg in 1864 was the scene of Lee's final struggle against Grant. In April 1865, when Lee's supply routes were finally cut and he was forced to evacuate the city, the Confederacy collapsed. A week later Lee surrendered at Appomattox.

The shattered city made a new start after the war, showing amazing recuperative powers. Petersburg added 20 more industries in 20 years, between 1850 and 1870. Today, besides being a storehouse of colonial and Civil War history, Petersburg is a thriving industrial city.

*Information: Petersburg Visitors Center, 425 Cockade Alley, Petersburg, 804-733-2402, 800-368-3595; www.petersburg-va.org*

## WHAT TO SEE AND DO
### APPOMATTOX RIVER PARK
*Petersburg, 804-733-2394*

A 137-acre park with canal for canoeing or fishing; access to rapids; picnic area. Mid-April-October, daily.

### BLANDFORD CHURCH AND CEMETERY
*321 S. Crater Road, Petersburg, 804-733-2396; www.petersburg-va.org/tourism*

Church (1735) and cemetery (1702); since 1901 a memorial to the Confederacy, has 15 Tiffany stained-glass windows. Daily. Admission: adults $5, seniors, military, children (7-12) $4, children under 7 free.

### CENTRE HILL MANSION
*1 Centre Hill Court, Petersburg, 804-733-2401; www.petersburg-va.org/tourism*

(1823) Federalist mansion visited by Presidents Tyler, Lincoln and Taft. Chandeliers,

★
★
★
★
★

finely detailed carvings; antiques, 1886 Knabe Art grand piano with hollywood inlaid on rosewood. Daily. 10 a.m.-5 p.m. Closed Christmas Eve, Christmas Day, Thanksgiving and New Year's Day. Admission: adults $5, seniors, military, children (7-12) $4, children under 7 free.

## FARMERS BANK

*19 Bollingbrook St., Petersburg, 804-733-2400; www.petersburg-va.com*
(1817) Banking memorabilia including original plates and press for printing Confederate currency. Tours depart from Visitor Center, Old Market Square. April-October, daily.

## FORT LEE

Army training center in World War I and World War II.

## LEE MEMORIAL PARK

*Petersburg, 804-733-2394*
Facilities of this 864-acre park include lake (launch fee), fishing (fee; license required); game fields and courts (fee), picnic area. Daily; lake facilities closed mid-October-mid-April.

## LEE'S RETREAT

*425 Cockade Alley, Petersburg, 800-673-8732; www.varetreat.com*
A 98-mile driving tour follows the route of General Robert E. Lee's retreat from Petersburg to Appomattox. Roadside pull-overs, signs and audio interpretation at important Civil War sites. For brochures and maps, contact the Petersburg Visitors Center.

★
★
★
★
★

## NATIONAL MUSEUM OF THE CIVIL WAR SOLDIER

*6125 Boydton Plank Road, Petersburg, 804-861-2408, 877-726-7546;*
*www.pamplinpark.org*
Exhibit on the Civil War's common soldier, one of the country's largest Civil War bookshops. Gift shop; restaurant.

## PAMPLIN PARK CIVIL WAR SITE

*6125 Boydton Plank Road, Petersburg, 804-861-2408, 877-726-7546;*
*www.pamplinpark.org*
Site of Gen. Ulysses S. Grant's decisive victory over Confederate forces in 1865. This 422-acre park includes battle trails, reconstructed soldier huts, plantation home. Interpretive Center and museum. Guided tours available. Daily. 9 a.m.-5 p.m. During summer 6 p.m.

## POPLAR GROVE (PETERSBURG) NATIONAL CEMETERY

On self-guided tour of Petersburg National Battlefield. Out of 6,315 graves, 4,110 are unidentified.

## SIEGE MUSEUM

*15 W. Bank St., Petersburg, 804-733-2404; www.petersburg-va.org/tourism*
Greek Revival building houses exhibits describing the 10-month Civil War siege of

Petersburg. The film *The Echoes Still Remain*, with Joseph Cotten, is shown every hour on the hour. Daily 10 a.m.-5 p.m. Closed Christmas Eve, Christmas Day, Thanksgiving, and New Year's Day. Admission: adults $5, seniors, military, children (7-12) $4, children under 7 free.

### ST. PAUL'S EPISCOPAL CHURCH

*110 N. Union, Petersburg, 804-733-3415; www.stpaulspetersburg.org*

(1856) Lee worshipped here during the siege of Petersburg (1864-1865). Open on request. Monday-Thursday.

### TRAPEZIUM HOUSE

*Market and High Street, Petersburg, 804-733-2400; www.petersburg-va.com*

(1817) Built by eccentric Irish bachelor Charles O'Hara in the form of a trapezium, with no right angles and no parallel sides. O'Hara is said to have believed the superstitions of his West Indian servant, who thought that ghosts and evil spirits inhabited right angles. Tours depart from Siege Museum. April-October, daily.

### U.S. ARMY QUARTERMASTER MUSEUM

*22nd St., Fort Lee, 804-734-4203; www.qmmuseum.lee.army.mil*

Uniforms, flags, weapons, equestrian equipment from 200 years of military service. Civil War and Memorial rooms. Tuesday-Friday 10 a.m.-5 p.m., Saturday-Sunday 11 a.m.-5 p.m.

## HOTELS

### ★★COMFORT INN PRINCE GEORGE

*5380 Oaklawn Blvd., Prince George, 804-452-0022; www.choicehotels.com*

125 rooms. Fitness center. High-speed Internet access. **$$**

### ★DAYS INN

*12208 S. Crater Road, Petersburg, 804-733-4400, 877-512-4400; www.daysinn.com*

155 rooms. Complimentary continental breakfast. Children's activity center. High-speed Internet. Pets accepted. Free local calls. Free newspaper. Restaurant. **$**

### ★★HOWARD JOHNSON

*12205 S. Crater Road, Petersburg, 804-733-0600, 800-446-4656; www.howardjohnson.com*

137 rooms. Children's activity center. High-speed Internet. Pets accepted. Pool. Tennis and Basketball courts. **$**

## RESTAURANT

### ★ALEXANDER'S

*101 W. Bank St., Petersburg, 804-733-7134*

American, Greek, Italian menu. Breakfast, lunch, dinner. Closed Saturday; week of July 4. Children's menu. In old town storefront. Casual attire. **$$**

# PETERSBURG NATIONAL BATTLEFIELD

At the price of 70,000 Union and Confederate casualties, the campaign that spelled doom for the Confederacy occurred in a huge, 40-mile semicircle around Richmond and Petersburg.

After his unsuccessful attempt to take Richmond by frontal assault (at Cold Harbor, June 3, 1864), General Grant withdrew and attacked Petersburg. After four days of fighting and failing to capture the city, Grant decided to lay siege. Petersburg was the rail center that funneled supplies to Lee and Richmond. The siege lasted 10 months, from June 15, 1864, to April 2, 1865, with the two armies in almost constant contact. When Petersburg finally fell, Lee's surrender was only a week away.

The park, at more than 2,700 acres, preserves Union and Confederate fortifications, trenches and gun pits. Another unit of the battlefield, Five Forks Unit, is located 23 miles to the west. Park (daily). Living history programs daily during summer. Access for the disabled includes several paved trails and ramps to the Visitor Center.
*Information: Superintendent, 1539 Hickory Hill Road, Petersburg, 804-732-3531; www.nps.gov/pete*

## WHAT TO SEE AND DO
### BATTERY 5
*Route 36 and I-95, Petersburg National Battlefield; www.civilwarbattlefields.us*
Strongest original Confederate position, captured on opening day of battle. From here "the Dictator," a Union mortar, shelled Petersburg, 2½ miles away. A similar mortar is displayed nearby.

### BATTERY 8
*Route 36 and I-95, Petersburg National Battlefield; www.civilwarbattlefields.us*
Confederate artillery position captured and used by Union as Fort Friend.

### BATTERY 9
*Route 36 and I-95, Petersburg National Battlefield; www.civilwarbattlefields.us*
Confederate position on original line. Site of reconstructed Union camp and living history programs.

### COLQUITT'S SALIENT
*www.civilwarbattlefields.us*
Section of Confederate defense line.

### THE CRATER
*www.civilwarbattlefields.us*
Hole remaining after Union troops tunneled beneath Confederate artillery position and exploded four tons of powder (July 30, 1864). The resulting breach in Confederate lines failed as a major breakthrough. Several special monuments in the vicinity.

### FIVE FORKS UNIT
*16302 White Oak Road, Petersburg National Battlefield, 804-265-8244; www.nps.gov*
(1,115 acres) This road junction, beyond Lee's extreme right flank, led to the only remaining Confederate supply line, the South Side Railroad. The Battle of Five Forks (April 1, 1865) saw Union forces under General Philip H. Sheridan smash Confederates commanded by General George Pickett and gain access to the tracks beyond. On April 2, Grant ordered an all-out assault, crumbling Lee's right flank. Only a heroic stand by Confederate forces at Fort Gregg held off the Union advance while

VIRGINIA

★
★
★
★
★

Lee evacuated Petersburg on the night of April 2. Visitor contact station (summer).

### FORT HASKELL
One of the points where Union troops stopped a desperate attempt by Lee to break the siege.

### FORT STEDMAN
Lee's "last grand offensive" concentrated here (March 25, 1865). The battle lasted four hours; the Confederates failed to hold their breakthrough.

### GRACIE'S DAM
Site of one of several Confederate dams intended to flood the area between lines.

### HARRISON'S CREEK
First Grant (June 1864), then Lee (March 1865) had advances checked here.

### SPRING GARDEN
Heaviest Union artillery concentration during Battle of Crater was along this ridge.

### VISITOR CENTER
Information, exhibits; maps for self-guided tours. Self-guided tour starts near center building.

# PORTSMOUTH

Connected to Norfolk by two bridge tunnels and a pedestrian ferry that cross the Elizabeth River, Portsmouth is part of the great Hampton Roads port, unrivaled for commercial shipping and shipbuilding activity. It is also the headquarters of the United States Coast Guard Atlantic Fleet.

In Gosport, long a part of Portsmouth, Scotsman Andrew Sprowle built a marine yard in 1767 that became a British naval repair station and after the Revolutionary War, a federal navy yard. Now called the Norfolk Naval Shipyard, it is the largest naval shipyard in the world. *The Chesapeake*, sister of the *USS Constitution* and one of the U.S. Navy's first warships, was built here. So was the *Merrimac*, which was seized by the Confederates, changed into an ironclad in 1861, and rechristened the *CSS Virginia*. The oldest dry dock (1831) here is still in use.

*Information: Portsmouth Convention and Visitors Bureau, 505 Crawford St., Portsmouth, 757-393-5327, 800-767-8782; www.portsmouth.va.us*

## WHAT TO SEE AND DO

### CHILDREN'S MUSEUM OF VIRGINIA
*221 High St., Portsmouth, 757-393-5258; www.childrensmuseumva.com*
More than 60 interactive activities in 12 areas; planetarium. Mid-June-Labor Day, Monday-Saturday, also Sunday afternoons. Admission $6

### COURTHOUSE GALLERIES
*420 High St., Portsmouth, 757-393-8543, 757-393-8393;*
*www.courthousegalleries.com*
Changing exhibits. Admission: adults $2, children age 2-17 $1, age under 2 free. No

registration required. Daily in summer. Closed Monday in winter.

## HILL HOUSE

*221 N. St., Portsmouth, 757-393-0241; www.portsmouthva.gov*
Headquarters of the Portsmouth Historical Association. Built in early 1820s, this four-story English basement-style (with a raised basement) house contains original furnishings collected by generations of the Hill family. In near-original condition, the house has undergone only limited renovation through the years. Garden restored. April-December, Wednesday, Saturday-Sunday.

## HISTORIC HOUSES

*6 Crawford Parkway, Portsmouth, 757-393-5111*
Portsmouth has over 300 years of history represented by more than 20 examples of colonial, Federal-style and antebellum houses. Among them is the circa-1730-50 Nivison-Ball House, (417 Middle St.), where Andrew Jackson and General Lafayette were entertained. These houses are private and may be viewed only from the exterior. Obtain Olde Towne Portsmouth walking tour brochures with map and descriptions of churches, homes and old buildings from the Visitor Center at High Street Landing.

## LIGHTSHIP MUSEUM

*London Slip and Water Street, Portsmouth, 757-393-8591;*
*www.portsnavalmuseums.com*
Built in 1915, commissioned in 1916 as "Lightship 101," it served 48 years in Virginia, Delaware and Massachusetts. Retired in 1964 and renamed Portsmouth. Admission: during summer $3, September-November, March-May adults $3, students, military $1.50, senior citizens' discount $0.50. Closed December-February.

## MONUMENTAL UNITED METHODIST CHURCH

*450 Dinwiddie St., Portsmouth, 757-397-1297; www.monumentalumc.org*
Oldest (1772) Methodist congregation in the South; history room. Guided tour Monday-Friday, by appointment.

## NAVAL SHIPYARD MUSEUM

*Second High St., Portsmouth, 757-393-8591; www.portsnavalmuseums.com*
Thousands of items of naval equipment, plus flags, uniforms, prints, maps and models, including models of the *CSS Virginia*; the U.S. Ship-of-the-line *Delaware,* built in Portsmouth; and the first ship drydocked in the U.S. Admission: during summer $3. September-November. March-May adults $3, students, military $1.50, senior citizens discount $0.50.

## THE PORTSMOUTH MUSEUMS

*221 High St., Portsmouth, 757-393-8983*
Located in a four-block radius, the museum complex has facilities housing artistic, educational and historic exhibits. Memorial Day-Labor Day, daily.

## TRINITY CHURCH

*500 Court St., Portsmouth, 757-393-0431; www.trinityportsmouth.org*
Oldest church building and parish in Portsmouth. Legend has it that the church bell cracked while ringing out news of Cornwallis' surrender; it was later recast. Confed-

erate Memorial window. Many colonial patriots are buried here. Open on request, Monday-Friday; office behind church in parish hall.

## HOTELS
### ★★HOLIDAY INN
*8 Crawford Parkway, Portsmouth, 757-393-2573, 800-282-0244; www.holidayinn.com*
219 rooms. **$**

### ★★HOLIDAY INN OLD TOWNE PORTSMOUTH
*8 Crawford Parkway, Portsmouth, 757-393-2573, 800-860-7109;*
*www.ichotelsgroup.com*
219 rooms. Fitness center. Outdoor pool. Restaurant. **$$**

### ★★★RENAISSANCE PORTSMOUTH HOTEL
*425 Water St., Portsmouth, 757-673-3000, 888-839-1775; www.marriott.com*
254 rooms. **$**

## RESTAURANTS
### ★★CAFÉ EUROPA
*319 High St., Portsmouth, 757-399-6652; www.portsmouthva.gov*
French, Italian menu. Lunch, dinner. Closed Sunday-Monday; also one week in spring. Bar. Business casual attire. Reservations recommended. Outdoor seating. **$$$**

### ★THE CIRCLE
*3010 High St., Portsmouth, 757-397-8196; www.thecirclerestaurant.com*
American, seafood menu. Lunch, dinner, brunch. Bar. Children's menu. Casual attire. Famous since 1947. Closed on Christmas. **$**

### ★★ISLAND GRILL
*8 Crawford Parkway, Portsmouth, 757-393-2573, 800-860-7109; www.holidayinn.com*
American. Breakfast, lunch, dinner. **$**

# RADFORD
*Information: Chamber of Commerce, 1126 Norwood St., Radford, 540-639-2202;*
*www.radfordchamber.com*

## WHAT TO SEE AND DO
### CLAYTOR LAKE STATE PARK
*4400 State Park Road, Radford, 540-643-2500; www.dcr.virginia.gov/state_parks*
Consists of 472 acres in wooded hills adjacent to 5,000-acre lake. Swimming, sand beach, bathhouse, fishing, boating (ramp, rentals, marina); hiking and bridle trails, picnicking, concession, tent and trailer sites (electrical hookups, April-September), cabins (March-early December). Visitor center, interpretive programs. Park office and visitor center in Howe House (1876-1879), built on land once settled by Dunkers (Dunkard Bretheren), a religious sect that fled persecution in Germany in the 1720s.

★
★
★
★
☆

Memorial Day-Labor Day: 8 a.m.-7 p.m.

## HOTEL
### ★★BEST WESTERN RADFORD INN
*1501 Tyler Ave., Radford, 540-639-3000, 800-628-1955; www.bestwestern.com*
104 rooms. Complimentary continental breakfast. High-speed Internet access. Pool. Pets accepted. **$**

# RICHMOND
Located at the falls of the James River, Richmond had to wait 170 years before becoming the state capital. Four hundred years later, with a history almost as old as Jamestown, the city blends its heritage with vibrant, contemporary commerce and trade. Its location, equidistant from the plantations of Tidewater Virginia and the Piedmont of central Virginia, gives the city a unique mix of heritage, culture and geography.

There have been few dull moments in Richmond's history. Native Americans and settlers fought over the ground on which it now stands. In 1775, Patrick Henry made his famous "liberty or death" speech in St. John's Church, and in 1780, the city was named capital of the state. British soldiers plundered it brutally during the Revolutionary War. And as the capital of the Confederacy from 1861 to 1865, it was constantly in danger. Finally, in 1865, the city was evacuated and retreating Confederate soldiers burned the government warehouse. A portion of the rest of the city also went up in flames. Richmond survived, and it now proudly exemplifies the modern South: industrially aggressive yet culturally aware, respectful of its own historical background yet receptive to new trends in architecture and modes of living.

Tobacco, paper, aluminum, chemicals, textiles, printing, publishing and machinery contribute to the city's economy. Richmond is also an educational hub; Virginia Commonwealth University, Virginia Union University and the University of Richmond are based here.

*Information: Convention and Visitors Bureau, 405 N. Third St., Richmond,*
*804-783-7450, 800-370-9004; www.visit.richmond.com*

**489**

**VIRGINIA**

## WHAT TO SEE AND DO
### 17TH STREET FARMERS' MARKET
*17th and Main Street, Richmond, 804-646-0477; www.17thstreetfarmersmarket.com*
This farmers' market is built at the site of a Native American trading village and features seasonal produce. April-December: Thursday, Saturday-Sunday.

### AGECROFT HALL
*4305 Sulgrave Road, Richmond, 804-353-4241; www.agecrofthall.com*
This half-timbered Tudor manor built in the late 15th century near Manchester, England was disassembled, brought here and rebuilt during the late 1920s in a spacious setting of formal gardens and grassy terraces overlooking the James River. It has English furnishings from 16th and 17th centuries. Tuesday-Saturday, 10 a.m.-4 p.m., Sunday 12:30-5 p.m. Closed Monday, national holidays.

### BILL "BOJANGLES" ROBINSON STATUE
*Leigh and Adams streets, Richmond*
Memorial to the famous dancer who was born at 915 N. Third St.

### BLACK HISTORY MUSEUM AND CULTURAL CENTER

*3 E. Clay St., Richmond, 804-780-9093; www.blackhistorymuseum.org*

Limited editions, prints, art, photographs; African memorabilia; Sam Gilliam collection. Tuesday-Saturday 10 a.m.-5 p.m. Closed Sunday-Monday, all major holidays.

### CANAL CLUB

*1545 E. Cary St., Richmond, 804-643-2582; www.thecanalclub.com*

Catch live music, especially blues and rock, or shoot a game of pool in Shockoe Bottom. A bonus: the interesting menu at The Under the Stage Café. Wednesday-Saturday.

### CANAL WALK

*Enter at S. Fifth, Seventh, 14th, 15th, or 17th streets*

The Canal Walk meanders 1¼ miles through downtown and features a pedestrian bridge to Brown's Island. Richmond Canal Cruisers (804-649-2800) depart on the

★
★★
★★★
★★★★
★★★★★

## RICHMOND'S HISTORICAL LEGACY

Once the Civil War capital of the Confederacy, Richmond is brimming with historical attractions. This two-mile walking tour of the city center will take you past many Civil War landmarks, as well as the city's less-troubling claims to historical fame.

Begin your walk at the Virginia State Capitol, designed in 1785 by Thomas Jefferson, himself a state governor, in the style of a classical temple. Surrounded by Capitol Square's expanse of well-tended lawn, it commands the eye despite the modern-day structures that surround it. Step inside the Rotunda to see the famous life-size statue of George Washington.

From Capitol Square, walk north (right) on Ninth Street across Broad Street to the neighborhood once known as Court End, which now bustles with students and faculty of the Medical College of Virginia. At 818 East Marshall Street (intersecting Ninth) stands the most important residence of Court End, the home of John Marshall, the distinguished chief justice of the U.S. Supreme Court from 1801 to 1835. Built in 1790, the two-story brick house where he lived for 45 years is a museum dedicated to his memory.

Although it's a seven-block detour, head west on Marshall Street to Second Street and turn north (right) two blocks to 110 East Leigh Street, the Maggie Walker National Historic Site. The modest two-story brick home on a quiet residential street honors a woman of impressive ability. Despite physical handicaps, Walker became America's first female bank president, establishing the Penny Savings Bank in 1903 as a way of helping local African Americans during the Jim Crow period.

Double back via Marshall Street past the John Marshall House to the Valentine Museum at 1015 East Clay Street. A small, innovative museum with a contemporary outlook, it focuses on the people and history of Richmond. Conclude the tour a block down the street at 12th and East Clay at the adjacent Museum of the Confederacy and the White House of the Confederacy. Not surprisingly, the museum emphasizes Southern leaders, featuring mementos of General Robert E. Lee. The White House, a neoclassical mansion built in 1818, recounts the home life during the Civil War of Confederate President Jefferson Davis and his wife, Varina.

hour from noon to 7 p.m. Wednesday to Saturday and from noon to 5 p.m. on Sunday from the Turning Basin between 14th and Virginia streets.

## CARYTOWN

*West Cary Street, between Boulevard Street and Thompson Street, Richmond;*
*www.carytown.org*

More than 300 shops and restaurants in this area include quirky clothing boutiques, antique shops, the city's best music store and collectibles ranging from Christmas decorations to glass and dolls. Monday-Saturday 10 a.m.-6 p.m. Some shops open on Sunday.

## CITY HALL OBSERVATION DECK

*901 E. Broad St., Richmond, 804-646-7000; www.ci.richmond.va.us*

Eighteenth-floor observation deck offers a panoramic view of the city, including the Capitol grounds, James River and Revolutionary and Civil War-era buildings contrasted with modern skyscrapers. Monday-Friday.

## CIVIL WAR VISITOR CENTER

*490 Tredegar St., Richmond, 804-780-1865; www.tredegar.org*

Begin your exploration of Richmond's Civil War heritage at the National Park Service Center at the restored Tredegar Iron Works near the James River. On the bottom floor, a continuously running film orients you to the 12 battlefields in the area. Park Service guides explain to kids how to fire the kind of cannon that Tredgar Iron Works made for the war. Daily.

## CHILDREN'S MUSEUM OF RICHMOND

*2626 W. Broad St., Richmond, 804-474-7000, 877-295-2667; www.c-mor.org*

A nice range of hands-on exhibits including the interactive James River Waterplay, which explores the hydrology and history of the James River. Labor Day-Memorial Day, Tuesday-Saturday 9:30 a.m.-5 p.m., Sunday noon-5 p.m.; Memorial Day-Labor Day, Monday-Saturday 9:30 a.m.-5 p.m., Sunday noon-5 p.m.

## CHURCH HILL HISTORIC AREA

*Main and 21st streets, bounded by Broad, 29th, Main, and 21st streets,*
*East of Capitol Square, Richmond*

Neighborhood of 19th-century houses, more than 70 of which predate Civil War. Some Church Hill houses are open for viewing during Historic Garden Week.

## EDGAR ALLAN POE MUSEUM

*1914-1916 E. Main St., Richmond, 804-648-5523, 888-213-2763;*
*www.poemuseum.org*

Old Stone House portion is thought to be oldest structure in Richmond dating back to 1737. Three additional buildings house Poe mementos; James Carling illustrations of "The Raven;" and a scale model of the Richmond of Poe's time. Guided tours. Tuesday-Saturday 10 a.m.-5 p.m., Sunday 11 a.m.-5 p.m. Closed Monday.

**VIRGINIA**

★
★
★
★
☆

## EQUESTRIAN STATUE OF WASHINGTON

*Ninth and Grace streets, Richmond*

Created by Thomas Crawford, this statue was cast in Munich over an 18-year period. The base features allegorical representations of six famous Revolutionary War figures from Virginia.

## THE FAN DISTRICT AND MONUMENT AVENUE

*Main and Belvidere streets, Richmond*

Named for the layout of streets that fan out from Monroe Park toward the western part of town, this historic neighborhood has restored antebellum and turn-of-the-century houses, museums, shops, restaurants and famed Monument Avenue. The fashionable Boulevard, between Lombard and Belmont streets, is dotted with imposing statues of Generals Lee, Stuart and Jackson.

## FEDERAL RESERVE MONEY MUSEUM

*701 E. Byrd St., Richmond, 804-697-8000; www.richmondfed.org*

Exhibits of currency include rare bills, gold and silver bars and other money-related artifacts. Monday-Friday 9:30 a.m.-3:30 p.m.

## GOVERNOR'S MANSION

*Ninth and Grace streets, Richmond, 804-371-8687; www.virginia.org*

This two-story Federal-style house was built after the capital was moved from Williamsburg in 1813. It is the oldest governor's mansion in the U.S. still in use as a governor's residence. Tours (by appointment).

## HISTORIC RICHMOND FOUNDATION

*4 E. Main St., Richmond, 804-643-7407; www.historicrichmond.com*

This non-profit organization saves and preserves historical properties within the city.

## HISTORIC RICHMOND TOURS

*1015 E. Clay St., Richmond, 804-649-0711; www.richmondhistorycenter.com*

The Valentine Richmond History center offers guided van tours with pickup at the Visitor Center and major hotels (daily); reservations required. They also provide guided walking tours (April-October, daily).

## HOLLYWOOD CEMETERY

*412 S. Cherry St., Richmond, 804-648-8501; www.hollywoodcemetery.org*

James Monroe, John Tyler, Jefferson Davis, and other notables and 18,000 Confederate soldiers are buried here. They offer an audiovisual program. Daily 8 a.m.-5 p.m.

## JACKSON WARD

*Broad and Belvidere streets, Richmond*

This historic downtown neighborhood was home to many famous black Richmonders, including Bill "Bojangles" Robinson. The area has numerous 19th-century, Greek Revival and Victorian buildings with ornamental ironwork that rivals the wrought iron of New Orleans.

## JAMES RIVER PARK

*West 22nd Street and Riverside Drive, Richmond, 804-646-8911;*
*www.jamesriverpark.org*

The James River drops 105 feet over a 7-mile stretch that passes through downtown Richmond and produces Class IV whitewater rapids. When the river is high enough—generally April through October—you can whitewater raft practically in the shadows of the city's skyline. Check with Richmond Raft Co., 800-540-7238; www.richmondraft.com; or Adventure Challenge, 804-276-7600; www.adventurechallenge.com/james.htm.

## JOHN MARSHALL HOUSE

*818 E. Marshall St., Richmond, 804-648-7998; www.apva.org/marshall*

The restored 1790 house of famous Supreme Court justice features original woodwork and paneling, family furnishings and mementos. Combination ticket available for Marshall House, Valentine Museum, Museum of the Confederacy, and White House of the Confederacy. Tuesday-Saturday 10 a.m.-4:30 p.m., Sunday noon-5 p.m.

## JOSEPH BRYAN PARK

*Bellevue Avenue and Hermitage Road, Richmond*

A 279-acre park, 20 acres of which are an azalea garden with more than 55,000 plants is best viewed late April-mid-May. Picnic facilities and tennis courts are available.

## KANAWHA CANAL LOCKS

*14th Street and Virginia Street, Richmond, 804-649-2800; www.venturerichmond.com*

These impressive stone locks were part of the nation's first canal system, planned by George Washington. A narrated audiovisual presentation explains the workings of the locks and canal. Picnic grounds available. Monday-Saturday.

## MAGGIE WALKER NATIONAL HISTORIC SITE

*3215 E. Broad St., Richmond, 804-771-2017*

This site commemorates the life and career of Maggie L. Walker, daughter of former slaves, who overcame great hardships to become successful in banking and insurance and was an early advocate for women's rights and racial equality. This two-story, red brick house was home to her family from 1904 to 1934. Monday-Saturday 9 a.m.-5 p.m. Closed Sunday.

## MAYMONT

*1700 Hampton St., Richmond, 804-358-7166; www.maymont.org*

The Dooley mansion, late Victorian in style, houses an art collection and decorative arts exhibits (Tuesday-Sunday). Also here are formal Japanese and Italian gardens, an arboretum, a nature center with a wildlife habitat for native species, an aviary, a children's farm and a working carriage collection. Daily.

## MEADOW FARM MUSEUM

*General Sheppard Crump Memorial Park, 3400 Mountain Road, Glen Allen,*
*804-501-5520; www.co.henrico.va.us/rec/current_programs/meadow_farm.html*

This is a living history farm museum depicting rural life in the 1860s, including an orientation center, farmhouse, barn, outbuildings, crop demonstration fields and 1860s doctor's office. There is also a 150-acre park with picnic shelters and a

VIRGINIA

★
★
★
★

playground. March-November, Tuesday-Sunday noon-4 p.m.; December-February, Saturday-Sunday noon-4 p.m.

## MONUMENTAL CHURCH
*1224 E. Broad St., Richmond*
Located on the Medical College of Virginia campus of Virginia Commonwealth University, this octagonal domed building was designed by Robert Mills, the architect of the Washington Monument. This commemorative structure was built in 1812 on the site where many prominent people, including the governor, perished in a theater fire in 1811. Interior closed; behind the church is the distinctive Egyptian Building.

## MUSEUM OF THE CONFEDERACY
*1201 E. Clay St., Richmond, 804-649-1861; www.moc.org*
The museum features the world's largest collection of Confederate artifacts: uniforms, weapons, tattered flags and daguerreotypes. Many of the exhibits feature artifacts from Confederate officers with descriptions of their demise. While it is comprehensive, the museum hasn't taken advantage of technology. You'll find yourself reading one typed description after another. Monday-Saturday 10 a.m.-5 p.m., Sunday noon-5 p.m.

## PARKS
*900 E. Broad St., Richmond, 804-646-5733; www.richmondgov.com*
For general information, contact the Department of Parks and Recreation.

## PLANTATION TOURS
*403 N. Third St., Richmond, 804-783-7450; www.richomndvisit.com*
The Richmond-Petersburg-Williamsburg area has many fine old mansions and estates. Some are open most of the year; others only during Historic Garden Week. The Metro Richmond Visitors Center has maps, information folders and suggestions.

## RICHMOND BRAVES
*The Diamond, 3001 N. Blvd., Richmond, 804-359-4444, 800-849-4627; www.rbraves.com*
The Richmond Braves are the AAA affiliate of the Atlanta Braves, playing their home games in a 12,134-seat stadium just off I-95.

## SCIENCE MUSEUM OF VIRGINIA
*2500 W. Broad St., Richmond, 804-864-1400; www.smv.org*
Located in the historic Broad Street Station (train tracks are still on the ground floor), this engaging museum will appeal to children with exhibits about space, flight, electricity, physics and the atom. Be sure to check out the laboratories and animal exhibits on the second floor. Daily 9:30 a.m.-5 p.m.

## SHOCKOE SLIP
*11 S. 12th St., Richmond*
Restored area of historic buildings and gaslit cobblestone streets including shopping, restaurants and galleries.

## SIXTH STREET MARKETPLACE

*Sixth St., between Coliseum and Grace streets, Downtown, Richmond*

Restored area of shops, restaurants and entertainment.

## STATE CAPITOL

*Ninth and Grace streets, Richmond, 804-698-1788; www.virginiacapitol.gov*

Modeled after La Maison Carre, an ancient Roman temple at Némes, France, the Capitol was designed by Thomas Jefferson. In this building, where America's oldest continuous English-speaking legislative bodies still meet, is the famous Houdon statue of Washington. The rotunda features the first interior dome in the United States. Monday-Saturday 8:30 a.m.-5 p.m., Sunday 1-4 p.m.

## ST. JOHN'S EPISCOPAL CHURCH

*2401 E. Broad St., at 24th St., Richmond, 804-648-5015, 877-915-1775;*
*www.historicstjohnschurch.org*

This is where Patrick Henry delivered his stirring "liberty or death" speech. The reenactment of the Second Virginia Convention occurs in late May-early September, Sunday. Guided tours. Daily.

## ST. PAUL'S CHURCH

*815 E. Grace St., Richmond, 804-643-3589; www.stpauls-episcopal.org*

Established in 1843, the Episcopal church survived the Civil War intact. It was here that Jefferson Davis received news of Robert E. Lee's retreat from Petersburg to Appomattox. Beginning in 1890, the church added many fine stained-glass windows, including eight from the Tiffany studios. Sanctuary ceiling features decorative plasterwork interweaving Greek, Hebrew and Christian motifs around a central panel. A Tiffany mosaic of da Vinci's "Last Supper" surmounts the altar. Daily.

**495**

**VIRGINIA**

★
★
★
★
★

## VALENTINE MUSEUM

*1015 E. Clay St., Richmond, 804-649-0711; www.valentinemuseum.com*

Tracing the history of Richmond, exhibits focus on city life, decorative arts, costumes and textiles and industrial and social history; and tours are offered of restored 1812 Wickham House. Lunch is served in a walled garden. Tuesday-Saturday 10 a.m.-5 p.m., Sunday noon-5 p.m. Closed Monday.

## VIRGINIA AVIATION MUSEUM

*5701 Huntsman Road, Richmond, 804-236-3622; www.vam.smv.org*

This museum offers exhibits and artifacts on the history of aviation, with an emphasis on Virginia pioneers. Daily.

## VIRGINIA HISTORICAL SOCIETY

*428 N. Blvd. St., Richmond, 804-358-4901; www.vahistorical.org*

The society has a comprehensive collection of Virginia history housed in its museum with permanent and changing exhibits, and the Library of Virginia History with historical and genealogical research facilities. Monday-Saturday 10 a.m.-5 p.m., Sunday 1-5 p.m.

## VIRGINIA MUSEUM OF FINE ARTS

*200 N. Blvd., Richmond, 804-340-1400; www.vmfa.state.va.us*

America's first state-supported museum of art has collections of paintings, prints and sculpture from major world cultures; Russian Imperial Easter eggs and jewels by Fabergé; decorative arts of the Art Nouveau and Art Deco movements; and a sculpture garden. Cafeteria. Wednesday-Sunday 11 a.m.-5 p.m.

## VIRGINIA STATE LIBRARY AND ARCHIVES

*800 E. Broad St., Richmond, 804-692-3888; www.lva.lib.va.us*

Outstanding collection of books, maps and manuscripts. Monday-Saturday 9 a.m.-5 p.m.

## VIRGINIA WAR MEMORIAL

*621 S. Belvidere St., Richmond, 804-786-2060; www.vawarmemorial.org*

Honors Virginians who died in World War II and the Korean and Vietnam wars. Mementos of battles; eternal flame; more than 12,000 names engraved on glass and marble walls. Monday-Saturday 9 a.m.-4 p.m., Sunday noon-4 p.m.

## WHITE HOUSE OF THE CONFEDERACY

*1201 E. Clay St., Richmond, 804-649-1861; www.moc.org*

Next door to the Museum of the Confederacy downtown, this Classical Revival house was used by Jefferson Davis as his official residence during the period when Richmond was the capital of the Confederacy. Abraham Lincoln met with troops here during the Union occupation of the city. It has been restored to its prewar appearance with many of its original furnishings. Monday-Saturday 10 a.m.-5 p.m., Sunday noon-5 p.m. Parking available.

★
★
★
★
★

## WILLIAM BYRD PARK

*224 S. Cherry St., Richmond, 804-643-2717; www.ci.richmond.va.us*

This park includes 287 acres of groves, artificial lakes, picnic areas, tennis courts, softball fields and a fitness course. The amphitheater is open June-August. Also at the park is the Carillon, Virginia's World War I memorial, a 240-foot, pink brick tower.

## WILTON HOUSE MUSEUM

*215 S. Wilton Road, Richmond, 804-282-5936; www.wiltonhousemuseum.org*

This Georgian mansion was built in 1753 by William Randolph III. It has fully paneled, authentic 18th-century furnishings and is the headquarters of the National Society of Colonial Dames in Virginia. Tuesday-Saturday 10 a.m.-4:30 p.m., Sunday 1:30-4:30 p.m. Open during Historic Garden Week.

## SPECIAL EVENTS

### HISTORIC GARDEN WEEK IN VIRGINIA

*12 E. Franklin St., Richmond, 804-643-4137; www.vagardenweek.org*

Many private houses and gardens of historic or artistic interest are opened for this event, which includes more than 200 houses and gardens throughout the state. Tours available. Mid-late April.

## JUNE JUBILEE
Performing and visual arts festival with ethnic foods, folk dances, music and crafts. First weekend in June.

## RICHMOND NEWSPAPERS MARATHON
Last Sunday in October.

## VIRGINIA STATE FAIR
*600 E. Laburnum Ave., Richmond, 804-228-3200; www.statefairva.org*
Animal and 4-H contests, music, horse show and carnival. Late September-early October.

## HOTELS
### ★★★THE BERKELEY HOTEL
*1200 E. Cary St., Richmond, 804-780-1300, 888-780-4422; www.berkeleyhotel.com*
This hotel opened in 1988 but its stylish look seems much more historic. The Berkeley Hotel is located at the crossroads of the business district and Historic Shockoe Slip. Dark wood paneling adorns the lobby and dining room. Dramatic windows to the ceiling give the hotel a European appearance. And diners at the hotel's restaurant get a view of the Slip's cobblestones and lamplights. 55 rooms. High-speed Internet access. **$$**

### ★★COURTYARD BY MARRIOTT
*6400 W. Broad St., Richmond, 804-282-1881, 800-321-2211; www.courtyard.com*
145 rooms. High-speed Internet access. **$**

### ★★★CROWNE PLAZA
*555 E. Canal St., Richmond, 804-788-0900, 877-424-4225; www.crowneplaza.com*
Just nine miles from Richmond International Airport, this hotel is situated in the heart of the historic district on the Canal Walk. Its higher floors have a spectacular view of the James River. The hotel is located minutes from area attractions such as Shockoe Slip, Sixth Street Market Place, museums, theaters and fine dining. Brown's Island, a concert and special-events venue, is located behind the hotel. Richmond Ballet is adjacent to the hotel, and ballet packages are available. 299 rooms. High-Speed Internet Access. Fitness Center. Indoor Pool. Whirlpool. Airport Transportation. **$**

### ★DAYS INN
*6910 Midlothian Turnpike, Richmond, 804-745-7100, 800-329-7466;*
*www.daysinnrichmond.com*
115 rooms. Complimentary continental breakfast. Complimentary Wireless Internet access. Outdoor pool. Free parking available. Pets accepted. **$**

### ★★DOUBLETREE HOTEL
*5501 Eubank Road, Sandston, 804-226-6400, 800-222-8733; www.doubletree.com*
160 rooms. Airport transportation available. Complimentary high-speed Internet access. Fitness center. **$**

VIRGINIA

★
★
★
★
★

## ★★EMBASSY SUITES

*2925 Emerywood Parkway, Richmond, 804-672-8585, 800-362-2779;*
*www.embassysuites.com*

226 rooms, all suites. Complimentary full breakfast. Airport transportation available. Complimentary Wireless Internet access. **$$**

## ★★★★★THE JEFFERSON HOTEL

*101 W. Franklin St., Richmond, 804-788-8000, 800-424-8014; www.jeffersonhotel.com*

The Jefferson Hotel is an institution in the heart of Richmond. A historic Beaux-Arts landmark dating back to 1895, the hotel offers elegant guest rooms furnished in a traditional style with antique reproductions and fine art. Pedigreed residents take afternoon tea here. TJ's provides a casual setting for fine dining with local dishes like oyster chowder and peanut soup, while the hotel's star restaurant, Lemaire, offers a sparkling ambience and a refined menu. Near the city's financial district, museums, shopping and the state capital. Complimentary car service transports guests to these and other destinations within a three-mile radius. 264 rooms. Wireless Internet access. Restaurant, bar. Airport transportation available. Fitness center. Indoor pool. Pets accepted. **$$$**

## ★★LINDEN ROW INN

*100 E. Franklin St., Richmond, 804-783-7000, 800-348-7424; www.lindenrowinn.com*

70 rooms. Complimentary continental breakfast. Restaurant (public by reservation). Complimentary high-speed Internet access. Valet parking. **$**

## ★★★MARRIOTT RICHMOND

*500 E. Broad St., Richmond, 804-643-3400, 800-228-9290; www.marriott.com/ricdt*

Attached to the Convention Center via skybridge, this high-rise hotel in the heart of the city is close to the Coliseum and both the historic and river districts. Business travelers will appreciate high-speed Internet access in their rooms, while families will love the spacious rooms, indoor pool and downtown location. The hotel offers complimentary shuttle service to Shockoe Slip, as well as to all major businesses within 3 miles. 401 rooms. High-speed Internet access. Valet parking. **$$**

## ★★★OMNI RICHMOND HOTEL

*100 S. 12th St., Richmond, 804-344-7000, 888-444-6664; www.omnihotels.com*

This contemporary hotel is conveniently located in the center of the financial and historic districts in the James Center and features scenic river views. It's across the street from the famous Tobacco Company restaurant, and a great place to stay if you intend to explore Shockoe Slip and Shockoe Bottom. 361 rooms. Wireless Internet access. Heated indoor and outdoor pool. **$**

## ★QUALITY INN

*8008 W. Broad St., Richmond, 804-346-0000, 877-424-6423; www.qualityinn.com*

190 rooms. Complimentary continental breakfast. Complimentary high-speed Internet access. Pets accepted. **$**

## ★★★SHERATON RICHMOND WEST HOTEL

*6624 W. Broad St., Richmond, 804-285-2000, 800-325-3535; www.sheraton.com*

With luxurious furnishings such as plush pillows and duvets on Sweet Sleeper beds, this upscale hotel offers its guests comfortable accommodations set in a richly landscaped business park just off the highway. With oversize writing desks and in-room WiFi, the hotel is geared toward the business traveler, but tourists and families will be just as comfortable here. 372 rooms. Wireless Internet access. Pets accepted. **$**

## RESTAURANTS

### ★★ACACIA
*2601 W. Cary St., Richmond, 804-354-6060; www.acaciarestaurant.com*
American menu. Lunch, dinner. Closed Sunday. Bar. Casual attire. Reservations recommended. Outdoor seating. **$$$**

### ★★AMICI
*3343 W. Cary St., Richmond, 804-353-4700; www.amiciristorante.net*
Italian menu. Lunch, dinner. Closed Sunday. Bar. Casual attire. Reservations recommended. Outdoor seating. **$$$**

### ★★BYRAM'S LOBSTER HOUSE
*3215 W. Broad St., Richmond, 804-355-9193; www.byrams.com*
American, seafood menu. Lunch, dinner. Bar. Children's menu. Casual attire. **$$**

### ★★★THE DINING ROOM AT THE BERKELEY HOTEL
*1200 E. Cary St., Richmond, 804-225-5105, 888-780-4422; www.berkeleyhotel.com*
Located in a European-style hotel, this handsomely decorated dining room serves elegant, impeccably prepared meals in a sophisticated and tranquil atmosphere. Entrée selections include seared rockfish with fried okra, sautéed spinach, Virginia spoon bread and lobster demi glace; and grilled black angus bistro steak with a sautéed zucchini medley and horseradish butter. American menu. Breakfast, lunch, dinner, Sunday brunch. Bar. Children's menu. Business casual attire. Reservations recommended. Valet parking. **$$$**

### ★★HALF WAY HOUSE
*10301 Jefferson Davis Highway, Richmond, 804-275-1760, 800-897-0848;*
*www.halfwayhouserestaurant.com*
American menu. Lunch, dinner. Business casual attire. Reservations recommended. **$$$**

### ★★HELEN'S
*2527 W. Main St., Richmond, 804-358-4370*
International menu. Dinner. Closed Monday. Bar. Reservations recommended. **$$**

### ★★KABUTO JAPANESE HOUSE OF STEAK
*8052 W. Broad St., Richmond, 804-747-9573; www.richmond.citysearch.com*
Japanese menu. Lunch, dinner. Bar. Business casual attire. Reservations recommended. **$$**

### ★★★LEMAIRE
*101 W. Franklin, Richmond, 804-788-8000, 800-424-8014; www.jeffersonhotel.com*
Old World fine dining comes to life at Lemaire, located in the historic Jefferson Hotel.

★
★
★
★
★

The restaurant is named for Etienne Lemaire, who served as maitre d' to President Jefferson and was widely credited for introducing the fine art of cooking with wines to America. His love of food and wine is continued at Lemaire, where contemporary Southern cooking goes upscale with French accents, homegrown herbs, featherweight sauces and seasonal ingredients. American menu. Breakfast, lunch, dinner. Bar. Children's menu. Business casual attire. Valet parking. Reservations recommended. **$$$**

### ★★★THE OLD ORIGINAL BOOKBINDER'S

*2306 E. Cary St., Richmond, 804-643-6900; www.bookbindersrichmond.com*
The first Bookbinder's to open outside of Philadelphia, this restaurant is located in a historic building that was once a Philip Morris manufacturing plant. Menu selections include high-quality seafood and homemade desserts. There is an outdoor courtyard area for alfresco dining. Seafood menu. Dinner. Bar. Children's menu. Business casual attire. Reservations recommended. Valet parking. Outdoor seating. **$$$**

### ★O'TOOLES

*4800 Forest Hill Ave., Richmond, 804-233-1781; www.otoolesrestaurant.com*
American menu. Lunch, dinner, brunch. Bar. Children's menu. Casual attire. Daily. **$$**

### ★★SAM MILLER'S OCEAN GRILL & OYSTER BAR

*1210 E. Cary St., Richmond, 804-644-5465; www.sammillers.com*
Seafood menu. Lunch, dinner. Bar. Business casual attire. Reservations recommended. **$$$**

### ★★SKILLIGALEE

*5416 Glenside Drive, Richmond, 804-672-6200*
Seafood menu. Lunch, dinner. Bar. Children's menu. Business casual attire. Reservations recommended. **$$**

### ★STRAWBERRY STREET CAFÉ

*421 N. Strawberry St., Richmond, 804-353-6860; www.strawberrystreetcafe.com*
American menu. Lunch, dinner, brunch. Bar. Children's menu. Casual attire. Reservations recommended. Daily. **$$**

### ★★★THE TOBACCO COMPANY

*1201 E. Cary St., Richmond, 804-782-9555; www.thetobaccocompany.com*
The Tobacco Company, the restaurant that helped pioneer the renaissance of Richmond's Shockoe Slip neighborhood, is carved from a former tobacco warehouse. Its centerpiece is a dramatic, skylit atrium with an antique cage elevator servicing three floors of dining. The menu is extensive if not inventive: steaks, prime rib, lobster, veal, shrimp, scallops, salmon, rainbow trout, chicken, crab, Virginia ham and pasta. Enjoy live music, a free buffet during happy hour (5-7 p.m., Wednesday-Friday) and cigars in the bar. American menu. Lunch, dinner, Sunday brunch. Bar. Business casual attire. Reservations recommended. **$$$**

### ★TRAK'S

*9115 Quioccasin Road, Richmond, 804-740-1700*
Greek, Italian menu. Lunch, dinner. Closed Sunday. Children's menu. Casual attire.

Reservations recommended. **$$**

**★YEN CHING**
*6601 Midlothian Turnpike, Richmond, 804-276-7430; www.yenchingdining.com*
Chinese menu. Lunch, dinner. Business casual attire. Reservations recommended. **$$**

# RICHMOND NATIONAL BATTLEFIELD PARK

The Union made a total of seven drives on Richmond, the symbol of secession, during the Civil War. Richmond National Battlefield Park, 770 acres in 10 different units, preserves sites of the two efforts that came close to success: McClellan's Peninsula Campaign of 1862 and Grant's attack in 1864.

Of McClellan's campaign, the park includes sites of the Seven Days' Battles at Chickahominy Bluffs, Beaver Dam Creek, Gaines' Mill (Watt House) and Malvern Hill. Grant's campaign is represented by the battlefield at Cold Harbor, where on June 3, 1864, Grant hurled his army at fortified Confederate positions, resulting in 7,000 casualties in less than one hour. Confederate Fort Harrison, Parker's Battery, Drewry's Bluff (Fort Darling) and Union-built Fort Brady are also included. Park (daily).
*Information: 3215 E. Broad St., Richmond, 804-226-1981; www.nps.gov/rich*

## WHAT TO SEE AND DO
### MAIN VISITOR CENTER
*3215 E. Broad St., Richmond, 804-226-1981*
Information, exhibits, film, slide program. Daily.

### OTHER VISITOR CENTERS
Cold Harbor, Highway 156 (daily, unstaffed) and Fort Harrison, Highway 5 and Battlefield Park Road, June-August, daily.

### SELF-GUIDED TOUR
*Richmond National Battlefield Park*
Auto drive (60 miles) with markers, maps, recorded messages providing background, detailed information for specific places. Visitors may select own route, including all or part of the drive.

# ROANOKE

The view from the top of Mill Mountain standing under the famous Roanoke Star (the world's largest man-made star) reveals the spectacular beauty and vastness of the Roanoke Valley, which seems to go on forever in every direction.

Tucked in the valley's center, the city itself evolved from a thriving, industrial railroading nexus in the late 1800s to a state-of-the-art destination. Over the years, Roanoke has become a sophisticated place, with a thriving arts community, a wealth of museums, and varied entertainment and theater offerings, which now share the stage with several world-class educational institutions. The hustle and bustle of the Norfolk and Southern Railroad has given way to health care, education, travel, conventions, industry and trade.
*Information: Roanoke Valley Convention & Visitors Bureau, 101 N.E. Shenandoah Ave.,*

**VIRGINIA**

★
★
★
★
☆

## WHAT TO SEE AND DO
### CENTER IN THE SQUARE
*1 Market Square, Roanoke, 540-342-5700; www.centerinthesquare.org*
Restored 20th-century furniture warehouse housing five independent cultural organizations: three museums, including Art Museum of Western Virginia, and two professional theater companies. Tuesday-Sunday.

### GEORGE WASHINGTON AND JEFFERSON NATIONAL FORESTS
*5162 Valleypointe Parkway, Roanoke, 540-265-5100;*
*www.southernregion.fs.fed.us/gwj*
The forests consist of approximately two million acres. Swimming; fishing for trout, bluegill and bass; hunting for deer, bear, wild turkey and small game; riding trails, camping and picnicking. Scenic drives past Crabtree Falls, hardwood forests and unusual geologic features. Overlooks of the Shenandoah Valley. Part of the Appalachian Trail crosses through the forest. Fees are charged at some recreation sites. Trails for the visually impaired.

### HISTORY MUSEUM OF WESTERN VIRGINIA
*1 Market Square S.E., Roanoke, 540-342-5760; www.artmuseumroanoke.org*
Permanent exhibits deal with Roanoke history from days of Native Americans to present. Archives, library (by appointment). Tuesday-Sunday 10 a.m.-5 p.m.

**502**

### MILL MOUNTAIN ZOOLOGICAL PARK
*Highway 220/I-581 and Blue Ridge Parkway, Roanoke, 540-343-3241;*
*www.mmzoo.org*
Zoo sits atop Mill Mountain; offers picnic areas with magnificent views of city and valley. Daily 10 a.m.-4:30 p.m.

### SCIENCE MUSEUM OF WESTERN VIRGINIA & HOPKINS PLANETARIUM
*1 Market Square, Roanoke, 540-342-5710; www.smwv.org*
Museum contains hands-on exhibits in the natural and physical sciences: animals of land and ocean, computers, TV weather station. Workshops, programs and classes for children and adults; special exhibits. Hopkins Planetarium shows films. Tuesday-Saturday 10 a.m.-5 p.m. Sunday 1-5 p.m.

### VIRGINIA MUSEUM OF TRANSPORTATION
*303 Norfolk Ave., Roanoke, 540-342-5670; www.vmt.org*
Vehicles from the past and present. Large steam, diesel and electric locomotive collection. Aviation exhibits; model of miniature traveling circus. Hands-on exhibits. March-December, daily; rest of year Monday-Saturday 10 a.m.-5 p.m., Sunday 1 p.m.-5 p.m.

### VIRGINIA'S EXPLORE PARK
*3900 Rutrough Road, S.E., Roanoke, 540-427-1800, 800-842-9163;*
*www.explorepark.org*

**VIRGINIA**

This 1,300-acre living history museum and nature center features re-created frontier settlement that depicts life in western Virginia in 1671, 1740 and 1850. Six miles of hiking trails. Picnic areas. May-mid-November, Wednesday-Sunday.

## SPECIAL EVENTS

### MILL MOUNTAIN THEATRE

*1 Market Square S.E., Roanoke, 540-342-5740; www.millmountain.org*

Center in the Square. Musicals, comedies, dramas. Nightly Tuesday-Sunday; Saturday-Sunday matinees. Regular season, October-August. Tuesday-Friday 10 a.m.-5:30 p.m. Saturday noon-4 p.m.

### VIRGINIA STATE CHAMPIONSHIP CHILI COOKOFF

*19 West Salem Ave., Roanoke, 540-342-4716*

Teams compete to represent Virginia in World Cook-off. Samples, entertainment. First Saturday in May 10 a.m.-5 p.m.

## HOTELS

### ★★DOUBLETREE HOTEL

*110 Shenandoah Ave., Roanoke, 540-985-5900, 800-222-8733; www.hotelroanoke.com*

332 rooms. Airport transportation available. High-speed Internet. Fitness center. Pools. **$**

### ★★HOLIDAY INN

*3315 Ordway Drive N.W., Roanoke, 540-362-4500, 800-282-0244; www.holidayinn.com*

153 rooms. Airport transportation available. Indoor pool. Pets accepted. Parking available. **$**

### ★★HOLIDAY INN

*4468 Starkey Road, Roanoke, 540-774-4400, 800-282-0244; www.holidayinn.com*

190 rooms. Airport transportation available. Pets accepted. Parking Available. Fitness Center. Outdoor pool. **$**

## RESTAURANTS

### ★★KABUKI JAPANESE STEAK HOUSE

*3503 Franklin Road S.W., Roanoke, 540-981-0222; www.kabukiva.com*

Japanese menu. Dinner. Bar. Children's menu. Casual attire. Reservations recommended. **$$**

### ★★★LIBRARY

*3117 Franklin Road, Roanoke, 540-985-0811*

Not only is this 1785 New England-style mansion a historic landmark, but it has served the likes of George Washington and a host of other presidents. French, American menu. Dinner. Closed Sunday. Business casual attire. Reservations recommended. **$$$**

# SALEM

Salem, part of the industrial complex of the Roanoke Valley, sits with Roanoke

★
★
★
★
★

between the Blue Ridge and Allegheny mountains. Historic markers throughout Salem indicate the city's colonial heritage.

*Information: Salem/Roanoke County Chamber of Commerce, 611 E. Main St., Salem, 540-387-0267; www.s-rcchamber.org*

## WHAT TO SEE AND DO
### DIXIE CAVERNS
*5753 W. Main St., Salem, 540-380-2085; www.dixiecaverns.com*
Stalactites in lofty chambers; modern lighting system makes the 45-minute tour comfortable as well as interesting. Pottery shop and mineral shop. Camping facilities. Daily 9:30 a.m.-6 p.m.

## HOTEL
### ★DAYS INN
*1535 E. Main St., Salem, 540-986-1000, 800-329-7466; www.daysinn.com*
70 rooms. Complimentary continental breakfast. Pets accepted. Complimentary high-speed Internet. $

# SHENANDOAH NATIONAL PARK

About 450 million years ago, the Blue Ridge was at the bottom of a sea. Today, it averages 2,000 feet above sea level, and some 300 square miles of the loveliest Blue Ridge area are included in Shenandoah National Park.

The park is 80 miles long and 2-13 miles wide. Running its full length is the 105-mile Skyline Drive. Main entrances are the North Entrance (Front Royal), from I-66, Highways 340, 522 and 55; Thornton Gap Entrance (31.5 miles south), from Highway 211; Swift Run Gap Entrance (65.7 miles south), from Highway 33; and the South Entrance (Rockfish Gap), from I-64, Highway 250, and the Blue Ridge Parkway. The drive, twisting and turning along the crest of the Blue Ridge, is one of the finest scenic trips in the East. Approximately 70 overlooks give views of the Blue Ridge, the Piedmont and to the west, the Shenandoah Valley and the Alleghenies.

The drive offers much, but the park offers more. Thousands of visitors explore on foot or on horseback. Most of the area is wooded, predominantly in white, red and chestnut oak, with hickory, birch, maple, hemlock, tulip poplar and nearly 100 other species. At the head of Whiteoak Canyon are 300-year-old hemlocks. The park, a sanctuary for deer, bears, foxes and bobcats, along with more than 200 varieties of birds, bursts with color in the fall, which makes this season particularly popular with visitors.

Accommodations are available in the park, with lodges, motel-type units and cabins at Big Meadows and Skyland, and housekeeping cabins at Lewis Mountain. For reservations and rates (which vary), contact ARA-MARK Virginia Sky-Line Company, Inc., P.O. Box 727, Luray, 22835-9051; 800-999-4714. Nearby communities provide a variety of accommodations. In the park, there are restaurants at Panorama, Skyland and Big Meadows; light lunches and groceries are available at Elkwallow, Big Meadows, Lewis Mountain and Loft Mountain waysides.

The park is open all year; lodge and cabin accommodations, usually March-December; phone ahead for the schedule. Skyline Drive is occasionally closed for short periods during November-March. As in all national parks, pets must be on a leash. The speed limit is 35 miles per hour. $15 per car per week, annual permit $30; Golden Age, Golden Access and Golden Eagle Passports are accepted.

Park Headquarters is five miles east of Luray on Highway 211. Detailed information and pamphlets may be obtained by contacting the Superintendent, Shenandoah National Park, 3655 Highway 211 E., Luray, 540-999-3500; www.nps.gov/shen

## WHAT TO SEE AND DO

### BIG MEADOWS

*Mile 51.1, Shenandoah*

Accommodations, restaurant; store, gas; tent and trailer sites; picnic grounds; nature trail. Usually April-November.

### BYRD VISITOR CENTER

*Mile 51, Shenandoah*

Exhibits, information, book sales, orientation programs, maps. Usually April-November, daily.

### DICKEY RIDGE VISITOR CENTER

*Mile 4.6, Shenandoah*

Exhibits, programs, information, book sales; picnic grounds. Usually April-November, daily.

### ELKWALLOW

*Mile 24.1, Shenandoah*

Picnic grounds; food, store. May-October, daily.

### LEWIS MOUNTAIN

*Mile 57.5, Shenandoah*

One- and two-bedroom cabins with heat; tent and trailer sites; picnic grounds, store. Usually May-October.

### LOFT MOUNTAIN

*Mile 79.5, Shenandoah*

Picnicking, camping; wayside facility; gas, store. May-October.

### LOFT MOUNTAIN INFORMATION CENTER

*Mile 79.5, Shenandoah*

Exhibits, information; programs, nature trail. Usually May-November.

### MARY'S ROCK TUNNEL

*Mile 32.4, Shenandoah*

Drive goes through 600 feet of rock (clearance 13 feet).

### PANORAMA

*Mile 31.5, at junction Highway, 211, Shenandoah*

Dining room. Gift shop. Trail to Mary's Rock. Closed in winter.

### PINNACLES

*Mile 36.7, Shenandoah*

**VIRGINIA**

★
★
★
★
★

Picnic grounds.

**SKYLAND**
*Mile 41.7, Shenandoah*
Accommodations; restaurant. Gift shop; guided trail rides; Stony Man Nature Trail.

**SOUTH RIVER**
*Mile 62.8, Shenandoah*
Picnic grounds, 2½-mile round-trip trail to falls.

# SPRINGFIELD

## HOTELS
### ★HAMPTON INN
*6550 Loisdale Court, Springfield, 703-924-9444, 800-426-7866; www.hamptoninn.com*
153 rooms. Complimentary continental breakfast. Fitness Room. Pool. Pets accepted. **$**

### ★★★HILTON SPRINGFIELD
*6550 Loisdale Road, Springfield, 703-971-8900, 800-445-8667; www.hilton.com*
The Hilton Springfield is located just 15 minutes from Washington, D.C., and offers complimentary shuttle service to the Springfield/Franconia Metro station. This modern, welcoming hotel puts every comfort at your fingertips. Accommodations are streamlined and stylish. Guest rooms feature complimentary wireless Internet access. The hotel's restaurant, Houlihan's, serves dishes such as grilled rosemary chicken and blackened center-cut pork medallions. 244 rooms. Complimentary Wireless Internet. Pets not accepted. **$**

## RESTAURANT
### ★★MIKE'S AMERICAN GRILL
*6210 Backlick Road, Springfield, 703-644-7100*
Steak menu. Lunch, dinner. Bar. **$$**

# STANLEY

## HOTEL
### ★★★JORDAN HOLLOW FARM INN
*326 Hawksbill Park Road, Stanley, 540-778-2285, 888-418-7000;*
*www.jordanhollow.com*
Find serene relaxation at this restored colonial horse farm. Some guest rooms feature beautiful vistas of the Blue Ridge Mountains. The Shenandoah Valley location offers many outdoor recreations, not the least of which is simply taking in the scenery. 15 rooms. Complimentary full breakfast. Pets accepted. **$$**

# STAUNTON

★
★
★
★
★

To historians, Staunton (STAN-ton) is known as the birthplace of Woodrow Wilson, and to students of government it is the place where the City Manager plan was first conceived and adopted. Set in fertile Shenandoah Valley fields and orchards between the Blue Ridge and Allegheny mountain ranges, the area around Staunton produces poultry, livestock and wool. Manufacturing firms in the city make air conditioners, razors, candy and clothing.

A Ranger District office of the George Washington and Jefferson national forests is located here.

*Information: Travel Information Center, 1250 Richmond Road, Staunton, 540-332-3972, 800-332-5219; www.visitstaunton.com*

## WHAT TO SEE AND DO

### FRONTIER CULTURE MUSEUM

*1290 Richmond Road, Staunton, 540-332-7850; www.frontiermuseum.org*

Living history museum consists of working farms brought together from England, Germany, Northern Ireland and an American farm. The European farms represent what America's early settlers left; the American farm, from the Valley of Virginia, reflects the blend of the various European influences. Visitors are able to see and take part in life as it was lived on these 17th-, 18th- and 19th-century farmsteads. Costumed interpreters demonstrate daily life at all four sites. Visitor center. Daily; closed first week in January. Regular hours: mid-March through December 1, 9 a.m.-5 p.m. Winter hours: December 1 through mid-March 10 a.m.-4 p.m.

### GYPSY HILL PARK

*Churchville and Thornrose avenues, Staunton, 540-332-3945; www.staunton.va.us*

Lake stocked with fish, swimming (late May-Labor Day); lighted softball field with concession stand, outdoor basketball courts, tennis, 18-hole golf, picnicking, miniature train ride, playgrounds, fairgrounds. Daily.

### TRINITY EPISCOPAL CHURCH

*214 W. Beverley St., Staunton, 540-886-9132; www.trinitystaunton.org*

Founded as Augusta Parish Church in 1746, the original building on this site served as Revolutionary capital of the state for 16 days in 1781. Open on request Monday-Friday 9 a.m.-5 p.m.

### WOODROW WILSON BIRTHPLACE AND PRESIDENTIAL MUSEUM

*24 N. Coalter St., Staunton, 540-885-0897; www.woodrowwilson.org*

Restored Greek Revival manse with period furnishings and Wilson family mementos from 1850s; museum building on grounds houses seven-gallery presidential exhibit, "The Life and Times of Woodrow Wilson," and his 1919 Pierce-Arrow limousine. Victorian gardens. November-February, Monday-Saturday 10 a.m.-4 p.m., Sunday, noon-4 p.m., March-October, Monday-Saturday 9 a.m.-5 p.m., Sunday noon-5 p.m.

## SPECIAL EVENT

### JAZZ IN THE PARK

*Gypsy Hill Park, 1000 Montgomery Ave., Staunton, 540-332-3945; www.stauentoen.va.us*

Thursday nights. July-August.

VIRGINIA

## HOTELS

### ★★★BELLE GRAE INN

*515 W. Frederick St., Staunton, 540-886-5151, 888-541-5151; www.bellegrae.com*

This century-old bed and breakfast offers carefully restored Victorian accommodations in four buildings. 14 rooms. Children over 12 years only. Complimentary full breakfast. Complimentary Wireless Internet access. **$$**

### ★BEST WESTERN STAUNTON INN

*92 Rowe Road, Staunton, 540-885-1112, 800-752-9471; www.dominionlodging.com*

80 rooms. Complimentary continental breakfast. Airport transportation available. Wireless Internet access. Pets accepted. **$**

### ★COMFORT INN

*1302 Richmond Ave., Staunton, 540-886-5000, 877-424-6423; www.comfortinn.com*

97 rooms. Complimentary continental breakfast. High-speed Internet access. Airport transportation available. Outdoor pool. Pets accepted. **$**

### ★★★FREDERICK HOUSE

*28 N. New St., Staunton, 540-885-4220, 800-334-5575; www.frederickhouse.com*

Built in 1809, the Frederick House's five restored buildings offer spacious rooms furnished with antiques and period furniture. 24 rooms. Complimentary full breakfast. Pets not accepted. **$**

### ★★HOLIDAY INN

*I-81, Highway 275, Staunton, 540-248-6020, 800-932-9061; www.histaunton.com*

114 rooms. Airport transportation available. Complimentary high-speed Internet access. **$**

## RESTAURANT

### ★MRS. ROWE'S RESTAURANT & BAKERY

*74 Rowe Road, Staunton, 540-886-1833; www.mrsrowes.com*

American menu. Breakfast, lunch, dinner. Children's menu. Casual attire. **$**

# STEPHENS CITY

## HOTELS

### ★COMFORT INN

*167 Town Run Lane, Stephens City, 540-869-6500, 877-424-6423; www.comfortinn.com*

60 rooms. Complimentary continental breakfast. Pets accepted. **$**

### ★★★THE INN AT VAUCLUSE SPRING

*231 Vaucluse Spring Lane, Stephens City, 540-869-0200, 800-869-0525; www.vauclusespring.com*

Located on 100 acres, this inn consists of four buildings: the Manor House, Chumley Homeplace, Gallery and Millhouse Studio. Visitors will enjoy the nearby wineries and scenic location. 15 rooms. Complimentary full breakfast. Restaurant. Reservations recommended. **$$**

# STRASBURG

Lying at the base of Massanutten Mountain and on the north fork of the Shenandoah River, Strasburg was founded in 1761 by German settlers. Prospering in the early 19th century as a center of trade and flour milling, the village later became identified with the manufacturing of high-quality pottery, earning the nickname "Pottown" after the Civil War. Strasburg played a pivotal role in Stonewall Jackson's Campaign of 1862 because of its location on the Manassas Gap Railroad and the Shenandoah Valley Turnpike. The first western Virginia town to be served by two railroads, Strasburg became a prominent railroad town, manufacturing center, and home of printing and publishing businesses after 1890.

Today Strasburg is located near the entrance to the Skyline Drive, attracting visitors with its antebellum and Victorian architecture and its burgeoning art community. The town calls itself the "antique capital of Virginia."

*Information: Chamber of Commerce, 160 E. King St., Strasburg, 540-465-3187; www.strasburgva.com*

## WHAT TO SEE AND DO

### BELLE GROVE
*336 Belle Grove Road, Strasburg, 540-869-2028; www.bellegrove.org*
This 1794 limestone mansion's design reflects Thomas Jefferson's influence. Used as Union headquarters during the Battle of Cedar Creek, October 19, 1864. Unusual interior woodwork; herb garden in rear. Guided tours. April-October, daily 10 a.m.-3 p.m.

### HUPP'S HILL BATTLEFIELD PARK AND STUDY CENTER
*33229 Old Valley Pike, Strasburg, 540-465-5884; www.waysideofva.com*
Former campsite for six different Civil War generals' troops, now a museum and hands-on interpretive center. Artifacts, documents, exhibits. Guided battlefield tours (by appointment). Daily.

### STRASBURG MUSEUM
*440 E. King St., Strasburg, 540-465-3175*
Blacksmith, cooper and potter shop collections; displays from colonial homes; relics from Civil War and railroad eras; Native American artifacts. Housed in Southern Railway Depot. May-October, daily 10 a.m.-4 p.m.

## SPECIAL EVENT

### MAYFEST
Celebration of town's German heritage with parade, entertainment and arts, crafts, antiques and foods fairs. Third weekend in May.

## HOTEL

### ★★HOTEL STRASBURG
*213 S. Holliday St., Strasburg, 540-465-9191, 800-348-8327; www.hotelstrasburg.com*
29 rooms. Complimentary continental breakfast. Victorian building. Reservations recommended. $

★
★
★
★

## RESTAURANT

### ★★★HOTEL STRASBURG

*213 S. Holliday St., Strasburg, 540-465-9191, 800-348-8327;*
*www.hotelstrasburg.com*

The inn's ornate Victorian lobby gives way to an invitingly cozy country restaurant, where locals and travelers alike dine on fine wines and elegant cuisine, including seasonal seafood dishes. Mediterranean menu. Lunch, dinner. Bar. Children's menu. Reservations recommended. **$$**

# STUART

## WHAT TO SEE AND DO

### FAIRY STONE STATE PARK

*Highway 346 North, Stuart, 276-930-2424; www.dcr.virginia.gov/state_parks/fai.shtml*

Located in the foothills of the Blue Ridge Mountains, the park features a number of cabins and campsites as well as swimming, a boathouse, boating (launch, rentals, electric motors only), hiking and biking trails, picnic facilities, and a concession stand. Fishing is allowed (license required), and a dump station and electrical hookups are available. The legendary fairy stones found in the park come from staurolite stones, a combination of silica, iron and aluminum.

# TAPPAHANNOCK

Bartholemew Hoskins patented the first land here in 1645. Following his lead, others came, and a small village soon sprang up, known at that time as Hobbes His Hole. Formally chartered in 1682 as New Plymouth, the town was to experience yet another name change. Built around the Rappahannock River, which means "running water," the town port became known as Tappahannock or "on the running water." Four hundred men gathered here in 1765 to protest the Stamp Act.

Today the area around Prince and Duke streets and Water Lane of Tappahannock has been declared a historic district. Highlights include the beautifully renovated Ritchie House, the Anderton House, once used for the prizing of tobacco into hogsheadsand Scot's Arms Tavern.

*Information: Chamber of Commerce, Tappahannock, 804-443-5241;*
*www.tappahannock-va.gov*

## HOTEL

### ★DAYS INN

*1414 Tappahannock Blvd., Route 17 Tappahannock Blvd., Tappahannock,*
*804-443-9200; www.daysinn.com*

60 rooms. Complimentary continental breakfast. Pets accepted. Fitness center. Pool. **$**

## RESTAURANT

### ★★LOWERY'S SEAFOOD RESTAURANT

*Route 17 and 360, Tappahannock, 804-443-2800; www.lowerysrestaurant.com*

Seafood menu, Breakfast, lunch, dinner. **$$**

# TREVILIANS

## HOTEL

### ★★★PROSPECT HILL PLANTATION INN

*2887 Poindexter Road, Trevilians, 540-967-0844, 800-277-0844; www.prospecthill.com*
This romantic 1732 manor house is set on 50 acres of lawn. 13 rooms. Reservations recommended. **$$$$**

# TRIANGLE

Quantico Marine Corps Base is three miles east of town.
*Information: Prince William County/Manassas Conference & Visitors Bureau,*
*8609 Sudley Road, 703-396-7130; www.visitpwc.com*

## WHAT TO SEE AND DO

### NATIONAL MUSEUM OF THE MARINE CORPS

*18900 Jefferson Davis Highway, Triangle, 703-640-7965, 800-397-7585;*
*www.usmcmuseum.org*
Chronological presentation of the Marine Corps Air-Ground Team's role in American history; artifacts on exhibit include aircraft, engines, armor, tracked and wheeled vehicles, artillery, small arms, uniforms, dioramas and photographs in pre-World War II aviation hangars. Daily 9 a.m.-5 p.m.

### PRINCE WILLIAM FOREST PARK

*18100 Park Headquarters Road, Triangle, 703-221-7181; www.nps.gov/prwi*
Consists of 18,000 acres. Hiking, bicycling, picnicking, camping (14-day limit; no hookups; fee; group cabins by reservations only), trailer campground off Highway 234 (fee; hookups, showers, laundry). Naturalist programs. Daily 9 a.m.-5 p.m.

# VIENNA

*Information: Vienna-Tysons Regional Chamber of Commerce, 513 Maple Ave. West,*
*Vienna, 703-281-1333; www.vtrcc.org*

## WHAT TO SEE AND DO

### BARNS OF WOLF TRAP

*1645 Trap Road, Vienna, 703-938-8463; www.wolf-trap.org*
A 350-seat theater with chamber music, recitals, mime, jazz, folk, theater and children's programs. For schedule contact the Barns. Late September-early May.

### MEADOWLARK BOTANICAL GARDENS

*9750 Meadowlark Gardens Court, Vienna, 703-255-3631;*
*www.nvrpa.org/parks/meadowlark*
Lilac, wildflower, herb, native plants, and landscaped gardens on 95 acres. Includes three ponds. Water garden. Gazebos. Trails. Visitor center. Daily. Children under 7 free.

**511**

**VIRGINIA**

★
★
★
★
★

## WOLF TRAP FARM PARK FOR THE PERFORMING ARTS

*1624 Trap Road, Vienna, 703-255-1900; www.wolf-trap.org*

Varied programs include ballet, musicals, opera, classical, jazz and folk music. Filene Center open theater seats 3,800 under cover and 3,000 on lawn. Picnicking on grounds, all year. Also free interpretive children's programs, July-August. Late May-September.

## HOTEL

### ★★★MARRIOTT TYSONS CORNER

*8028 Leesburg Pike, Vienna, 703-734-3200, 800-228-9790; www.marriott.com*

This property is located in the heart of Tysons corner, next to a major shopping mall. 390 rooms. Airport transportation available. High-speed Internet access. **$$**

## RESTAURANTS

### ★★AARATHI

*409 Maple Ave. East, Vienna, 703-938-0100; www.aditibistro.com*

Indian menu. Lunch, dinner. Reservations recommended. **$$**

### ★★BONAROTI

*428 Maple Ave. East, Vienna, 703-281-7550; www.bonarotirestaurant.com*

Italian menu. Lunch, dinner. Closed Sunday. Bar. Children's menu. Reservations recommended. **$$**

### ★★CLYDE'S

*8332 Leesburg Pike, Vienna, 703-734-1901; www.clydes.com*

American menu. Lunch, dinner, Sunday brunch. Bar. Business casual attire. Reservations recommended. **$$**

### ★★HUNAN LION

*2070 Chain Bridge Road, Vienna, 703-734-9828; www.hunanlion.com*

Chinese menu. Lunch, dinner. Bar. Reservations recommended. **$**

### ★★LA PROVENCE

*144 W. Maple Ave., Vienna, 703-242-3777*

French menu. Lunch, dinner. Closed Sunday. Bar. Reservations recommended. **$$**

### ★★★LE CANARD

*132 Branch Road, Vienna, 703-281-0070; www.le-canard.com*

The formal interior of dark red fabrics and mahogany wood sets the tone for an elegantly traditional dining experience. Rich, sumptuous dishes are followed by unique flaming specialty coffees. French menu. Lunch, dinner. Bar. Reservations recommended. **$$**

### ★★MARCO POLO

*245 Maple Ave. West, Vienna, 703-281-3922; www.marcopolorestaurant.com*

Italian, seafood menu. Lunch, dinner. Sunday brunch. Closed Monday-Tuesday. **$$**

★
★
★
★
★

### ★★★MORTON'S, THE STEAKHOUSE

*8075 Leesburg Pike, Vienna, 703-883-0800; www.mortons.com*

Consistent with expectations, this outlet serves the same famed entrées as its sister restaurants. The tableside menu presentation reveals generous portions and high-quality ingredients in the restaurant's warm, clublike atmosphere. Steak menu. Lunch, dinner. Bar. Jacket required. Reservations recommended. Valet parking. **$$$**

### ★★★NIZAM'S

*523 Maple Ave. West, Vienna, 703-938-8948*

Doner kebob, a forebear of the gyro, is the legendary mainstay of this refined Turkish restaurant. Thin, tender slices of marinated, spit-roasted lamb nestle inside soft pita bread in a dish that rivals anything Istanbul could turn out. Service is polished and attentive. Lunch, dinner. Closed Monday. Bar. Reservations recommended. **$$**

### ★★PANJSHIR II

*224 W. Maple Ave., Vienna, 703-281-4183*

Vegetarian menu. Lunch, dinner. Closed Monday. Bar. **$$**

### ★★TARA THAI

*226 Maple Ave. West, Vienna, 703-255-2467; www.tarathairichmond.com*

Thai menu. Lunch, dinner. Bar. Reservations recommended. **$$**

### ★★THAT'S AMORE

*150 Branch Road S.E., Vienna, 703-281-7777; www.thatsamore.com*

Italian menu. Lunch, dinner. Closed Labor Day. Bar. **$$$**

# VIRGINIA BEACH

Strolling down the expanded boardwalk, you can relive the pleasures of your youth and enjoy the buzz of entertainment, good food and people-watching at its finest.

The area's historical sites tie Virginia Beach to the first permanent English settlement over 400 years ago. In fact, First Landing State Park is where John Smith alighted before he went on to Jamestown. There are museums too, including the Virginia Marine Science Museum, voted one of the top ten marine science aquariums/museums in the United States.

Virginia Beach is also home to more than 106 square miles of wetlands and water, a 3,000-acre state park and two wildlife refuges. Amazingly, being this close to Virginia's largest city, the natural ecological areas surrounding Virginia Beach are among the most pristine and undiscovered areas along the mid-Atlantic. Even on a rainy day, the wildlife—native birds, whales and dolphins—are close enough for you to get a good look.

*Information: Visitor Information Center, 2100 Parks Ave., Virginia Beach,*
*757-437-4882, 800-822-3224; www.vbfun.com*

## WHAT TO SEE AND DO
### ADAM THOROUGHGOOD HOUSE

*1636 Parish Road, Virginia Beach, 757-460-7588; www.virginiabeachhistory.org*

One of the oldest remaining brick houses in U.S. (Circa 1680); restored, furnished; restored gardens. Closed Monday.

## ASSOCIATION FOR RESEARCH AND ENLIGHTENMENT

*67th Street and Atlantic Avenue, Virginia Beach, 757-428-3588; www.are-cayce.com*

Headquarters for study and research of work of psychic Edgar Cayce. Visitor Center has bookstore, library, displays, ESP-testing machine, movie and daily lectures. Daily.

## CONTEMPORARY ART CENTER OF VIRGINIA

*2200 Parks Ave., Virginia Beach, 757-425-0000; www.cacv.org*

This 32,000-square-foot facility is devoted to the presentation of 20th-century art through exhibitions, education, performing arts and special events. Daily.

## FIRST LANDING/SEASHORE STATE PARK

*2500 Shore, Virginia Beach, 757-412-2300; www.dcr.virginia.gov*

More than 2,700 acres with lagoons, cypress trees and sand dunes. Swimming at own risk, fishing, boating (ramp); hiking, bicycle and self-guided nature trails; picnicking, tent and trailer sites (March-November), 20 cabins (open year-round). Visitor center, interpretive programs. Access for disabled to nature trail. Daily.

## FISHING

*Linkhorn Bay and Rudee Inlet, Virginia Beach*

In the Lynnhaven and Rudee Inlets, look for channel bass, speckled trout, spots, croakers, flounder and whiting in season; in the Back Bay area, 18 miles South on Highway 615, for largemouth black bass, pickerel and perch. Pier fishing and surf casting from piers jutting into the Atlantic and piers in the Chesapeake Bay. Reef, deep-sea and Gulf Stream fishing from charter boats for sea bass, weakfish, flounder, cobia, bonito, tuna, marlin, false albacore, blue and dolphin. Lake and stream fishing at Lake Smith, Lake Christine, and the inland waterways of the Chesapeake and Albemarle Canal. Crabbing for blue crabs in Lynnhaven waters, Linkhorn Bay and Rudee Inlet. No license or closed season for saltwater fishing.

## FRANCIS LAND HOUSE HISTORIC SITE AND GARDENS

*3131 Virginia Beach Blvd., Virginia Beach, 757-431-4000; www.virginiabeachhistory.org*

Late 18th-century plantation home features period rooms, special exhibits, gardens and museum gift shop. Tuesday-Saturday 9 a.m.-5 p.m., Sunday 11 a.m.-5 p.m.

## LYNNHAVEN HOUSE

*4405 Wishart Road, Virginia Beach, 757-460-1688, 757-460-7109;*
*www.apva.org/lynnhaven*

This stately story-and-a-half masonry structure is a well-preserved example of 18th-century architecture and decorative arts. May and October, weekends only; June-September, Tuesday-Sunday.

## MOTOR WORLD

*700 S. Birdneck Road, Virginia Beach, 757-422-6419; www.vbmotorworld.com*

Park includes go-karts, arcade. Also a 36-hole miniature Shipwreck Golf Course, batting cages and large Children's Zone. May-early September, daily.

★
★ ★
★ ★
★

## NORWEGIAN LADY STATUE

*25th Street and Boardwalk, Virginia Beach; www.virginia.org*

A gift to Virginia Beach from the people of Moss, Norway. The statue commemorates the tragic wreck of the Norwegian bark *Dictator* off the shores of Virginia Beach in 1891.

## OCEAN BREEZE WATER PARK

*849 General Booth Blvd., Virginia Beach, 757-422-4444, 800-678-9453; www.oceanbreezewaterpark.com*

Slides, wave pool, rapids and children's water amusements. Mid-May-early September, daily.

## OLD CAPE HENRY LIGHTHOUSE AND MEMORIAL PARK

*583 Atlantic Ave., Fort Story, Virginia Beach, 757-422-9421; www.apva.org/capehenry*

On Fort Story, an active army base. First U.S. government-built lighthouse (circa 1791). Daily.

## OLD COAST GUARD STATION

*24th Street and Atlantic Avenue, Virginia Beach, 757-422-1587; www.oldcoastguardstation.com*

Former Coast Guard Station (1903); visual exhibits of numerous shipwrecks along the Virginia coastline tell of past bravery and disaster. "The War Years" exhibit relates United States Coast Guard efforts during World War I and World War II. Photographs, ship models, artifacts. Gift shop. Closed Monday.

## VIRGINIA MARINE SCIENCE MUSEUM

*717 General Booth Blvd., Virginia Beach, 757-385-3474; www.vmsm.com*

Live animals, interactive exhibits, six-story screen, 300-seat IMAX 3-D theater. Exhibits include ocean aquarium with sharks, large fish; sea turtle aquarium; seals and other habitats; aviary; salt marsh preserve; touch tank; river room; garden. Daily.

**VIRGINIA**

## SPECIAL EVENTS

### BOARDWALK ART SHOW

Works by more than 350 artists from U.S. and abroad. Mid-June.

### NEPTUNE FESTIVAL

*265 Kings Grant Road, Virginia Beach, 757-498-0215, 866-637-3378; www.neptunefestival.com*

Last two weeks in September.

### PUNGO STRAWBERRY FESTIVAL

*916 Princess Anne Road, Virginia Beach*

Saturday and Sunday of Memorial Day weekend.

### VIRGINIA SALTWATER FISHING TOURNAMENT

*968 S. Oriole Drive, Virginia Beach, 757-491-5160; www.mrc.virginia.gov*

The Commonwealth of Virginia sponsors this annual program. No entry fee or registration requirements; open to everyone who fishes in tournament waters and complies with tournament rules. March-December.

### WINTER WHALE-WATCHING BOAT TRIPS
*Virginia Beach, 757-385-4700, 800-822-3224; www.vbfun.com*
January-March, Monday, Wednesday, Friday-Sunday.

## HOTELS

### ★★★CROWNE PLAZA HOTEL VIRGINIA BEACH
*4453 Bonney Road, Virginia Beach, 757-473-1700, 877-424-4225;*
*www.cpvabeach.com*
Just off Interstate 264, this traditional hotel is conveniently located in the Town Center Business District with easy access to downtown Virginia Beach, Norfolk, Chesapeake and many corporate offices. Guests are treated to comfortable rooms, a 24-hour fitness center, indoor pool and whirlpool and sauna. Golf courses and tennis courts are nearby. 149 rooms. Airport transportation available. $$

### ★★DOUBLETREE HOTEL
*1900 Pavilion Drive, Virginia Beach, 757-422-8900, 800-222-8733;*
*www.doubletree.com*
292 rooms. $$

### ★★★FOUNDERS INN
*5641 Indian River Road, Virginia Beach, 757-424-5511, 800-926-4466;*
*www.foundersinn.com*
Sitting on 26 manicured acres, this Georgian-style inn has a southern-colonial décor and a unique combination of intimate charm and extensive meeting space. 240 rooms. Children's activity center. Airport transportation available. $

### ★★HOLIDAY INN
*2607 Atlantic Ave., Virginia Beach, 757-491-6900, 800-282-0244; www.holidayinn.com*
143 rooms. $$

### ★LA QUINTA INN AND SUITES
*2800 Pacific Ave., Virginia Beach, 757-428-2203; www.laquinta.com*
137 rooms. Complimentary full breakfast. $

### ★★WYNDHAM VIRGINIA BEACH OCEANFRONT
*5700 Atlantic Ave., Virginia Beach, 757-428-7025, 877-999-3223; www.wyndham.com*
216 rooms. Children's activity center. $$

## RESTAURANTS

### ★★ALDO'S
*1860 Laskin Road, Virginia Beach, 757-491-1111; www.aldosvb.com*
Italian menu. Lunch, dinner. Bar. Outdoor seating. $$

### ★★COASTAL GRILL
*1427 N. Great Neck Road, Virginia Beach, 757-496-3348; www.coastalgrill.com*
American menu. Dinner, late-night. Bar. Business casual attire. Reservations recommended. Outdoor seating. $$

### ★CUISINE AND COMPANY

*2648 Quality Court, Virginia Beach, 757-428-6700; www.cuisineandcompany.com*
California menu. Breakfast, lunch, dinner. **$**

### ★★IL GIARDINO

*910 Atlantic Ave., Virginia Beach, 757-422-6464; www.ilgiardino.com*
Italian menu. Dinner. Bar. Children's menu. Valet parking. Outdoor seating. **$$**

### ★★LUCKY STAR

*1608 Pleasure House Road, Virginia Beach, 757-363-8410;*
*www.theluckystarrestaurant.net*
American menu. Dinner. Closed Sunday. Bar. Business casual attire. Reservations recommended. **$$**

### ★★LYNNHAVEN FISH HOUSE

*2350 Starfish Road, Virginia Beach, 757-481-0003; www.lynnhavenfishhouse.net*
Seafood menu. Lunch, dinner, brunch. Bar. Children's menu. Casual attire. Reservations recommended. Valet parking. **$$**

### ★PUNGO GRILL

*1785 Princess Anne Road, Virginia Beach, 757-426-6655*
American menu. Lunch, dinner. Closed Monday; also winter. Bar. Children's menu. Casual attire. Reservations recommended. Outdoor seating. **$$**

### ★★RUDEE'S ON THE INLET

*227 Mediterranean Ave., Virginia Beach, 757-425-1777, 800-883-0850;*
*www.rudees.com*
Seafood, steak menu. Lunch, dinner, Sunday brunch. Bar. Children's menu. Casual attire. Valet parking (dinner). Outdoor seating. **$$**

# WALLOPS ISLAND

## WHAT TO SEE AND DO
### NASA VISITOR CENTER

*Wallops Island, 757-824-1344; www.sites.wff.nasa.gov*
Showcases world of past, present and future flight. Features moon rock brought from *Apollo 17* mission; scale models of space probes, satellites and aircraft; displays of current and future NASA projects; full-scale aircraft and rockets; films on space and aeronautics. Model rocket demonstrations (March-November, first Saturday; June-August also third Saturday, weather permitting). Picnic facilities. Gift shop. Thursday-Monday.

# WARM SPRINGS

Nestled at the foot of Little Mountain (3,100 feet), the spring wildflowers and groves of fall foliage make Warm Springs a very scenic spot for sightseeing, hiking and water activities. There are also walking tours to view the many historic buildings.

## HOTEL
### ★★★INN AT GRISTMILL SQUARE
*Highway 619, Warm Springs, 540-839-2231; www.gristmillsquare.com*

Wake up to the smell of fresh-baked muffins every morning at the Inn at Gristmill Square, a village-like collection of restored 19th-century buildings. Tucked into picturesque Warm Springs, the inn offers 17 guest rooms with comfortable, country décor. After exploring the area, end your day with a dinner of fresh local trout at the inn's restaurant in a converted mill. 17 rooms. Complimentary breakfast. $

## RESTAURANT
### ★★WATERWHEEL
*Route 619, Warm Springs, 540-839-2231; www.gristmillsquare.com*

American menu. Dinner, brunch. Bar. Reservations recommended. Outdoor seating. $$

# WARRENTON

Warrenton was named for General Joseph Warren, who fought at Bunker Hill in the Revolutionary War. The town is situated in the Piedmont Valley near the foothills of the Blue Ridge Mountains and is known for its cattle and thoroughbred horse farms. Many old buildings and houses provide for an interesting walking tour of the town.

*Information: Warrenton-Fauquier County Visitor Center, 33 N. Calhoun St., Warrenton, 540-341-0988, 800-820-1021; www.fauquierchamber.org*

## SPECIAL EVENT
### FLYING CIRCUS
*Morrisville Road and Brookes Store Drive, Warrenton, 540-439-8661;*
*www.flyingcircusairshow.com*

Flying shows of the barnstorming era, from comedy acts to precision and stunt flying. Rides, picnic area. May-October. Sunday.

## HOTEL
### ★COMFORT INN
*7379 Comfort Inn Drive, Warrenton, 540-349-8900, 877-424-6423;*
*www.comfortinn.com*

97 rooms. Complimentary continental breakfast. High-speed Internet access. $

## RESTAURANT
### ★★NAPOLEON'S
*67 Waterloo St., Warrenton, 540-347-1200; www.napoleonsrestaurant.com*

International menu. Lunch, dinner, brunch. Bar. Children's menu. Casual attire. Reservations recommended. Outdoor seating. $$$

# WASHINGTON

The oldest of more than 25 American towns to be named after the first president, this town was surveyed in 1749 by none other than George Washington himself. The streets remain laid out exactly as surveyed and still bear the names of families who owned the land on which the town was founded. It is rumored that Gay Street was named by the 17-year-old Washington after the lovely Gay Fairfax. The town is situated in the foothills of the Blue Ridge Mountains, which dominate the western horizon.

## HOTELS

### ★★★BLUE ROCK INN

*12567 Lee Highway, Washington, 540-987-3190; www.thebluerockinn.com*

The Blue Rock Inn, a turn-of-the-century restored farmhouse that now holds a dining room, a pub and five guest rooms, sits on 80 rolling acres, which guests can enjoy from their private balconies. 5 rooms. Complimentary full breakfast. $$

### ★★★★★THE INN AT LITTLE WASHINGTON

*309 Main St., Washington, 540-675-3800; www.theinnatlittlewashington.com*

Savvy epicureans book a room—and a table—at the Inn at Little Washington. Tucked away in the foothills of the Blue Ridge Mountains, the inn offers visitors a taste of the good life, complete with afternoon tea with scones and tartlets. Tempting as it may be to indulge, guests save their appetites for the evening's cuisine. Many make special trips just for the talented chef's award-winning meals, though lucky guests recount their memorable feasts while ensconcing themselves in one of the inn's lovely guest rooms. The surrounding area provides opportunities for hiking, fly-fishing, hot air ballooning, antiquing and wine tasting. 15 rooms. Closed Tuesday in January-March and July (and many in April & June; call ahead). Complimentary continental breakfast. Restaurant, bar. $$$$

## SPECIALTY LODGING

### MIDDLETON INN

*176 Main St., Washington, 540-675-2020, 800-816-8157; www.middletoninn.com*

This historic country estate was built in 1850 by Middleton Miller, who designed and manufactured the Confederate uniform of the Civil War. The inn faces the Blue Ridge Mountains, and the original slaves' quarters have been converted into a two-story guest cottage. 5 rooms. Children over 12 years only. Complimentary full breakfast. $$$

## RESTAURANTS

### ★★★BLUE ROCK INN

*12567 Lee Highway, Washington, 540-987-3190; www.thebluerockinn.com*

This country-inn farmhouse is located on 80 acres of rolling hillside overlooking the Blue Ridge Mountains and adjoining vineyards. It is a great place to stop between Harrisonburg and Washington, D.C. French menu. Dinner. Closed Monday-Tuesday. Bar. Business casual attire. Reservations recommended. Outdoor seating. $$$

### ★★★★★THE INN AT LITTLE WASHINGTON

*309 Main St., Washington, 540-675-3800; www.theinnatlittlewashington.com*

Chef Patrick O'Connell has amassed almost every culinary award in existence. Seasonal dishes include a crab cake "sandwich" with fried green tomatoes and tomato vinaigrette; sesame-crusted Chilean sea bass with baby shrimp, artichokes and grape tomatoes; rabbit braised in apple cider with wild mushrooms and garlic mashed potatoes; and for dessert, pistachio and white chocolate ice cream terrine with blackberry sauce. American menu. Dinner. Closed Tuesday (except in May and

★
★
★
★
☆

October). Bar. Business casual attire. Reservations recommended. Valet parking. $$$$

# WAYNESBORO

Waynesboro is at the southern end of the Skyline Drive and the northern end of the Blue Ridge Parkway.

*Information: Waynesboro Augusta County Chamber of Commerce, 301 W. Main St., Waynesboro, 540-942-6644, 866-253-1957; www.waynesboro.va.us*

## WHAT TO SEE AND DO

### P. BUCKLEY MOSS MUSEUM

*150 P. Buckley Moss Drive, Waynesboro, 540-949-6473, 800-343-8643; www.pbuckleymoss.com*

Museum's exhibits and programs examine the symbolism and aesthetic ideas of one of America's most notable living artists. Daily.

### SHENANDOAH VALLEY ART CENTER

*126 S. Wayne Ave., Waynesboro, 540-949-7662; www.svacart.com*

Art galleries, studios. Working artists; performing arts. Tuesday-Sunday.

### SHERANDO LAKE RECREATION AREA

*Waynesboro, 540-942-5965*

Facilities include 21-acre lake with sand beach and bathhouses, swimming, fishing; picnicking, camping (April-October, fee). Amphitheater, campfire programs. April-November, daily.

## SPECIAL EVENT

### FALL FOLIAGE FESTIVAL

*540-942-6644; www.fallfoliagefestival.com*

First and second weekends in October.

## HOTELS

### ★DAYS INN

*2060 Rosser Ave., Waynesboro, 540-943-1101, 800-329-7466; www.daysinn.com*

97 rooms. Complimentary continental breakfast. $

### IRIS INN

*191 Chinquapin Drive, Waynesboro, 540-943-1991, 888-585-9018; www.irisinn.com*

Overlooking the Shenandoah Valley, the Great Room at the Iris Inn features a 28-foot stone fireplace and a large mural of the wildlife in the mountains. A full and hearty breakfast is included, as is a "bottomless" cookie jar. 9 rooms. Complimentary full breakfast. Whirlpool. $$

# WILLIAMSBURG

After the Native American massacre of 1622, this Virginia colony built a palisade across the peninsula between the James and York rivers. The settlement that grew up around it was called Middle Plantation, now the site of Colonial Williamsburg.

Middle Plantation figured prominently in Bacon's Rebellion against Governor

Berkeley. Renamed in honor of William III of England, the new capital gradually became a town of about 200 houses and 1,500 residents. For 81 years, Williamsburg was the political, social and cultural capital of Virginia.

The colony's first successful printing press was established here by William Parks, and in 1736 he published Virginia's first newspaper. Williamsburg's capitol was the scene of stirring colonial events such as Patrick Henry's Stamp Act speech.

The First Continental Congress was called from here by the dissolved House of Burgesses in 1774. Two years later, the Second Continental Congress was boldly led by delegates from Virginia to declare independence; George Mason's Declaration of Rights, which became the basis for the Bill of Rights, was adopted here.

Williamsburg's exciting days came to an end in 1780 when the capital was moved to Richmond for greater safety and convenience during the Revolutionary War. For a century and a half it continued as a quiet college town, its tranquility interrupted briefly by the Civil War. In 1917, when a munitions factory was built near the town and cheap housing for the factory's 15,000 workers was hastily erected, Williamsburg seemed destined to blandly live out its days.

In 1926, however, John D. Rockefeller, Jr., and Dr. W. A. R. Goodwin, rector of Bruton Parish Church, who saw the town as a potential treasure-house of colonial history, joined forces for Williamsburg's restoration. For more than 30 years, Rockefeller devoted personal attention to the project and contributed funds to accomplish this nonprofit undertaking.

Today, after many years of archaeological and historical research, the project is near completion. The Historic Area, approximately a mile long and a half-mile wide, encompasses most of the 18th-century capital. Eighty-eight of the original buildings have been restored; 50 major buildings, houses and shops and many smaller outbuildings have been reconstructed on their original sites; 45 of the more historically significant buildings contain more than 200 exhibition rooms, furnished either with original pieces or reproductions, and are open to the public on regular seasonal schedules.

Visitors stroll Duke of Gloucester Street and mingle with people in 18th-century attire. Craftsmen at shops ply trades such as wig-making and blacksmithing, using materials, tools and techniques of pre-Revolutionary times. The Historic Area is closed to private motor vehicles 8 a.m.-10 p.m.

*Information: Chamber of Commerce, 421 N. Boundary Ave., Williamsburg, 757-229-6511, 800-211-7165; www.williamsburgcc.com*

**521**

**VIRGINIA**

## WHAT TO SEE AND DO
### 1700S SHOPPING
Superior wares typical of the 18th century are offered in nine restored or reconstructed stores and shops; items include silver, jewelery, herbs, candles, hats and books. Two craft houses sell approved reproductions of the antiques on display in the houses and museums.

### ABBY ALDRICH ROCKEFELLER FOLK ART CENTER
*307 S. England St., Williamsburg, 757-229-1000; www.colonialwilliamsburg.org*
An outstanding collection of American folk art. Items in this collection were created by artists not trained in studio techniques, but who faithfully recorded aspects of everyday life in paintings, sculpture, needlework, ceramics, toys and other media. Daily.

## AMERICA'S RAILROADS ON PARADE

*1915 Pocahontas Trail, Williamsburg, 757-220-8725*

More than 4,000 square feet of model train layouts, hands-on exhibits and a gift shop. Daily.

## BRUSH-EVERARD HOUSE

Home of an early mayor, with programs on slave life.

## BRUTON PARISH CHURCH

*331 Duke of Gloucester St., Williamsburg, 757-229-2891; www.brutonparish.org*

One of America's oldest Episcopalian churches, in continuous use since 1715. Organ recitals (March-December, Tuesday and Saturday). Daily; no tours during services.

## BUSCH GARDENS WILLIAMSBURG

*1 Busch Gardens Blvd., Williamsburg, 757-253-3000, 800-343-7946;*
*www.buschgardens.com*

This European-style theme park on 360 acres features recreated 17th-century German, English, French, Italian, Scottish and Canadian villages. Attractions include more than 30 thrill rides, including the Drachen Fire roller coaster, one of the nation's largest; the 3-D movie *Haunts of the Olde Country*, with in-theater special effects; live shows, an antique carousel, celebrity concerts, miniature of Le Mans racetrack, and rides for small children. Theme restaurants; shops. Transportation around the grounds by sky ride or steam train. A computer-operated monorail links the park with the Anheuser-Busch Hospitality Center, where visitors can take a brewery tour. Mid-April-August, daily; late March-mid-April and September-October, weekends.

★
★
★
★
☆

## THE CAPITOL

*Duke of Gloucester Street, Williamsburg*

The House of Burgesses met here (1704-1779); it was also the scene of Patrick Henry's speech against the Stamp Act.

## CARRIAGE AND WAGON RIDES

Take a ride through the Historic Area in a carriage or wagon driven by a costumed coachman. General admission ticket holders can make reservations on the day of the ride at the Lumber House ticket office. Daily, weather permitting.

## CHILDREN'S TOURS

Special programs, tours and experiences exclusively for children and families are offered in the summer.

## COLLEGE OF WILLIAM & MARY

*Richmond Road, Williamsburg, 757-221-4000; www.wm.edu*

Established in 1693, William & Mary is America's second-oldest college (only Harvard is older). It initiated an honor system, an elective system of studies, and schools of law and modern languages; it was the second to have a school of medicine (all in 1779). The prestigious Phi Beta Kappa Society was founded here in 1776. Today, there are 7,000 students.

## COLONIAL WILLIAMSBURG VISITOR CENTER

*102 Information Center Drive, Williamsburg, 757-220-7645, 800-246-2099;*
*www.colonialwilliamsburg.com*
An admission ticket is necessary to enjoy the full scope of Colonial Williamsburg. Daily.

## COURTHOUSE

*Duke of Gloucester Street, Williamsburg*
County and city business was conducted here from 1770 until 1932. The interior has been carefully restored to its original appearance. Visitors often participate in scheduled reenactments of court sessions.

## DEWITT WALLACE DECORATIVE MUSEUM

*Henry and Francis streets, Williamsburg, 757-220-7724, 800-447-8679*
Modern museum adjoining Public Hospital, features exhibits, lectures, films and related programs centering on British and American decorative arts of the 17th to early 19th centuries. Daily.

## DISABLED VISITOR INFORMATION

*Williamsburg, 800-246-2099*
Efforts are made to accommodate the disabled while still retaining the authenticity of colonial life. Many buildings have wheelchair access once inside, but it should be noted that most buildings are reached by steps. The Visitor Center has a list detailing accessibility of each building; wheelchair ramps may be made available at some buildings. In addition, there are wheelchair rentals and parking. A hands-on tour of several historic trades may be arranged for the visually impaired and sign language tours are available with advance notice.

## EVENING ENTERTAINMENT

Colonial Williamsburg presents "rollicking 18th-century plays" throughout the year; wide variety of cultural events, concerts and historical reenactments (fees vary). Chowning's Tavern offers colonial "gambols" (games), music, entertainment and light food and drink (evenings).

## FORD'S COLONY WILLIAMSBURG

*1 Ford's Colony Drive, Williamsburg, 800-334-6033; www.fordscolony.com*
This Dan Maples-designed course features 54 holes, comprising the par-72 Marsh Hawk Course, the par-71 Blackheath Course, and the par-72 Blue Heron Course. Ford's Colony was chosen as one of America's best golf courses by "Golf Week" Magazine. The course touts itself as a "player's course" that appeals to golfers of all levels.

## GO-KARTS PLUS

*6910 Richmond Road, Highway 60 W., Williamsburg, 757-564-7600;*
*www.gokartsplus.com*
This eight-acre park has four go-kart tracks that appeal to various ages and driving skills, as well as bumper cars and boats, a miniature golf course and an arcade. Admission is free; tickets must be purchased for activities. Memorial Day-Labor Day, daily. March-May and September-October, limited hours.

**523**

**VIRGINIA**

## GOVERNOR'S PALACE AND GARDENS

Residence of Royal Governor, one of the most elegant mansions in colonial America; set in 10-acre restored gardens.

## HAUNTED DINNER THEATER

*5363 Richmond Road, Williamsburg, 757-258-2500, 888-426-3746;*
*www.wmbgdinnertheatre.com*

Help unravel a murder mystery tame enough for little ones while feasting on a 71-item, all-you-can-eat dinner buffet at Capt. George's World Famous Restaurant. Performances are held Wednesday-Sunday evenings at 7 p.m.

## HISTORIC TRADES

Craftsmen in 18th-century costume pursue old trades of apothecary, printer, bookbinder, silversmith, wigmaker, shoemaker, blacksmith, harnessmaker, cabinetmaker, miller, milliner, gunsmith, wheelwright, basketmaker, cook, cooper and carpenter.

## JAMES GEDDY HOUSE

Once home of a prominent silversmith with working brass, bronze, silver and pewter foundry.

## JAMES RIVER STATE PARK

*Rte. 1, Williamsburg, 434-933-4355, 800-933-7275; www.dcr.state.va.us*

This 1,500-acre park has three fishing ponds and three miles of river frontage. An excellent spot is Pony Pasture, located on the south bank two miles downstream from the Huguenot Bridge on Riverside Drive. The area is also considered one of Richmond's best locations for bird-watching and inner-tubing. There are two boat launches at the park and a canoe launch at the Canoe Landing Campground at Dixon Landing. Belle Isle is directly under the Lee Bridge and may be reached on foot from the north side of the river via the pedestrian bridge suspended under the Lee Bridge. Excellent whitewater rapids are found at Belle Isle. Ancarrows Landing is a boat landing and fishing spot that is one of the areas most valuable historic sites. It is the place where William Byrd is believed to have established Richmond when he set up his trading post. Later, slave ships docked there in the 1700s and 1800s. It became known as Ancarrows Landing because it also was the home of Newton Ancarrows speedboat manufacturing company.

## JAMESTOWN SETTLEMENT

*Route 31 S. Jamestown Road, Williamsburg, 757-253-4838, 888-593-4682;*
*www.historyisfun.org*

Living history museum recreates the first permanent English settlement in the New World. Recalls early-17th-century Jamestown with full-scale reproductions of ships that arrived in 1607 and the triangular James Fort. The Powhatan Indian Village depicts Native American culture encountered by English colonists. Museum complex features an orientation film, changing gallery and three exhibit galleries focusing on the history of Jamestown and the Powhatan. Food service available. Combination ticket with Yorktown Victory Center available. Daily.

## LANTHORN TOUR

*Williamsburg, 800-246-2099*

A costumed interpreter conducts evening walking tour of selected shops that are illuminated by candlelight. March-December, daily.

## THE MAGAZINE

*Duke of Gloucester Street, Williamsburg*

Arsenal and military storehouse of Virginia Colony; authentic arms exhibited.

## MUSCARELLE MUSEUM OF ART

*Jamestown Road and Phi Beta Kappa Circle, Williamsburg, 757-221-2700; www.wm.edu/muscarelle*

Traveling displays and exhibitions from an extensive collection. Closed Monday.

## PEYTON RANDOLPH HOUSE

Home of president of First Continental Congress. Comte de Rochambeau's headquarters prior to Yorktown campaign.

## PLAY BOOTH THEATER

Scenes from 18th-century plays in open-air theater. Open to all Colonial Williamsburg ticket holders. Spring-fall, daily.

## PUBLIC GAOL

Where debtors, criminals and pirates (including Blackbeard's crew) were imprisoned.

## PUBLIC HOSPITAL

Reconstruction of first public institution in the English colonies devoted exclusively to treatment of mental illness.

## RALEIGH TAVERN

Frequent meeting place for Jefferson, Henry, and other Revolutionary patriots; a social center of the Virginia Colony.

## SHIRLEY PEWTER SHOP

*417 Duke of Gloucester St., Williamsburg, 757-229-5356, 800-550-5356; www.shirleypewter.com*

This shop features Williamsburg's own brand of pewter, Shirley Pewter. Items available include dinnerware, oil lamps and tableware. Many items can be engraved. Daily.

## SKATE PARK

*5301 Longhill Road, Williamsburg, 757-259-3200; www.james-city.va.us*

A great, safe place for inline skating, skateboarding and biking. The park is open to ages nine and up, and all skaters and bikers must wear protective gear. November-March, closed Monday, Tuesday, Thursday; rest of year, daily.

VIRGINIA

★ ★ ★ ★ ★

## SPECIAL FOCUS AND ORIENTATION TOURS

Orientation tours (30 minutes) for first-time visitors; special tours (90 minutes), called history walks, include African-American life, gardens, religion and women of Williamsburg. Reservations are available at any ticket sales location.

## WATER COUNTRY USA

*176 Water Country Parkway, Williamsburg, 757-253-3350, 800-343-7946; www.watercountryusa.com*

This park, the mid-Atlantic's largest water park, features water slides, thrill rides and live entertainment. If you're interested in visiting Busch Gardens as well, which is three miles from Water Country USA, a Bounce Pass gives admission to both parks. May, early-mid-September, weekends from 10 a.m.; June-August, daily from 10 a.m.

## WETHERBURN'S TAVERN

One of the most popular inns of the period.

## WILLIAMSBURG NATIONAL GOLF COURSE

*3700 Centerville, Williamsburg, 757-258-9738, 800-859-9182; www.wngc.com*

This 18-hole, par-72 public course is the only Jack Nicklaus-designed course in Virginia.

## WILLIAMSBURG WINERY

*5800 Wessex Hundred, Williamsburg, 757-229-0999; www.williamsburgwinery.com*

Founded in 1985, the winery carries on a Virginia tradition that began with the Jamestown settlers in 1607. Located two miles from the Historic Area, it has 50 acres of vineyards. Visitors can take 30-45 minute guided walking tours and tastings are available after the tour. Daily.

## WREN BUILDING

*Richmond Road and Duke of Gloucester Street, Williamsburg*

Oldest (1695-1699, restored 1928) academic building in America; designed by the great English architect Sir Christopher Wren. Tours. Daily.

## WYTHE HOUSE

Home of George Wythe, America's first law professor, teacher of Jefferson, Clay and Marshall. This was Washington's headquarters before siege of Yorktown.

## YORK RIVER STATE PARK

*5526 Riverview Road, Williamsburg, 757-566-3036; www.dcr.virginia.gov*

A 2,500-acre park along the York River and its related marshes. Includes the Taskinas Creek National Estuarine Research Reserve. Fishing, boating (launch), canoe trips; hiking and bridle trails, picnicking, interpretive center, programs, nature walks. Daily.

## SPECIAL EVENTS

### 18TH-CENTURY COMEDY

*Williamsburg Lodge Auditorium, 5363 Richmond Road, Williamsburg, 800-447-8679*
Saturday nights, March-December.

### ANTIQUES FORUM

*102 Information Center Drive, Williamsburg, 800-447-8679*
Colonial Williamsburg. Mid-February.

### COLONIAL WEEKENDS

*Williamsburg, 800-246-2099; www.bandbwilliamsburg.com*
Package weekends on 18th-century theme, features introductory lecture, guided tours, banquet at Colonial Williamsburg. January-early March.

### FIFE AND DRUM CORPS

*Carter's Grove and S. England Street, Williamsburg, 757-220-7453; www.fifedrum.org*
Colonial Williamsburg. Performances in the Historic Area. April-October, Saturday.

### GARDEN SYMPOSIUM

*102 Information Center Drive, Williamsburg, 800-447-8679*
Colonial Williamsburg. Lectures and clinics. Mid-late April.

### LIVING HISTORY PROGRAMS

*1340 S. Pleasant Valley Road, Williamsburg*
Colonial Williamsburg. Includes "An Assembly, Cross or Crown," and "Cry Witch!" Varying schedule weekly. Spring, summer and fall.

### MILITARY DRILL

*Market Square Green, Duke of Gloucester and Colonial streets, Williamsburg*
Costumed weekly drill by Williamsburg Independent Company. Mid-March-October.

### PRELUDE TO INDEPENDENCE

*102 Information Center Drive, Williamsburg, 800-447-8679*
Colonial Williamsburg. Mid-May.

### PUBLICK TIMES

*102 Information Center Drive, Williamsburg, 800-447-8679*
Colonial Williamsburg. Re-creation of colonial market days; contests, crafts, auctions, military encampment. Labor Day weekend.

### TRADITIONAL CHRISTMAS ACTIVITIES

*102 Information Center Drive, Williamsburg, 800-447-8679*
Colonial Williamsburg. Featuring grand illumination of city; fireworks. December.

**VIRGINIA**

★
★
★
☆
☆

## HOTELS

### BEST WESTERN HISTORIC AREA INN

*201 Bypass Road, Williamsburg, 757-220-0880, 800-289-0880;*
*www.bestwestern.com*

121 rooms. Complimentary full breakfast. Pool. Wireless Internet access. Fitness center. $

### ★★CROWNE PLAZA

*6945 Pocahontas Trail, Williamsburg, 757-220-2250, 877-424-4225;*
*www.cpwilliamsburghotel.com*

303 rooms. Indoor pool, outdoor pool, whirlpool. Fitness center. Tennis. Restaurant, bar. $

### ★★★KINGSMILL RESORT & SPA

*1010 Kingsmill Road, Williamsburg, 757-253-1703, 800-832-2665; www.kingsmill.com*

This playground for adults attracts golfers, tennis players and those seeking rest and relaxation to its 2,900 manicured acres along the James River. Three 18-hole golf courses and a nine-hole par-three course challenge players while the Golf Academy provides clinics and individual instruction. Tennis players take their pick from fast-drying clay, Deco-Turf and hydro courts at the state-of-the-art facility, while other racquet sports and a fitness center are available at the Sports Club. After a day filled with activities, hearty appetites are always satisfied at the resort's six restaurants and lounges. 425 rooms. Complimentary continental breakfast. Spa. Tennis. Golf. Restaurant. Children's activity center. Beach. Airport transportation available. $$$

### ★★★MARRIOTT WILLIAMSBURG

*50 Kingsmill Road, Williamsburg, 757-220-2500, 800-228-9290;*
*www.williamsburgmarriott.com*

The closest hotel to Busch Gardens, the Marriott Williamsburg is also conveniently located near Colonial Williamsburg, Jamestown and Yorktown, as well as shopping and outlet centers. After a busy day spent sightseeing, relax in the well-appointed guest rooms. 281 rooms. Children's activity center. $

### ★★★★WILLIAMSBURG INN

*136 E. Francis St., Williamsburg, 757-229-1000, 800-447-8679;*
*www.colonialwilliamsburg.com*

Furnished in English Regency style, the guest rooms have just the right amount of sophistication to appeal to adults while keeping children comfortable and satisfied. Blessed with a central location in the heart of this re-created 18th-century village, the inn is within a leisurely stroll of the blacksmith's shop, candlemaker and cobbler. After reliving history, guests reap the rewards of the inn's plentiful activities and play a round of golf, dive into the spring-fed pool, rally on the clay tennis courts, head to the fitness center to keep in shape, or spoil themselves at the spa or gourmet restaurant. 110 rooms. Complimentary full breakfast. $$$$

### ★★WILLIAMSBURG LODGE

*310 S. England St., Williamsburg, 757-220-7976, 800-447-8679;*
*www.colonialwilliamsburg.com*

261 rooms. Complimentary continental breakfast. Children's activity center. $$

★
★
★
★
☆

### ★★★WOODLANDS HOTEL AND SUITES

*105 Visitor Center Drive, Williamsburg, 757-220-7960, 800-447-8679, 757-253-2277;*
*www.colonialwilliamsburg.org*

One of Colonial Williamsburg's five resorts and inns, Woodlands Hotel and Suites is located on the grounds of the visitor center at the edge of a 40-acre pine forest. 300 rooms. Complimentary continental breakfast. $

## SPECIALTY LODGINGS

### COLONIAL CAPITAL BED AND BREAKFAST

*501 Richmond Road, Williamsburg, 757-229-0233, 800-776-0570; www.ccbb.com*

Five rooms. Children over 8 years only. Complimentary full breakfast. Built in 1926; antiques. $$

### COLONIAL GARDENS INN

*1109 Jamestown Road, Williamsburg, 757-220-8087, 800-886-9715;*
*www.colonial-gardens.com*

Four rooms. Children over 14 permitted. Complimentary full breakfast. Built in 1960. $$

### COLONIAL HOUSES-HISTORIC LODGING

*305 S. England St., Williamsburg, 757-220-7978, 757-253-2277, 800-447-8679;*
*www.colonialwilliamsburg.com*

These 18th-century historic buildings are very secluded, located on the 173 acres of Colonial Williamsburg. Guests can choose from a small house or a larger one with up to 16 rooms, each furnished with period reproductions. All are within walking distance of shops, museums and horse-drawn carriages. 74 rooms. $$

### LIBERTY ROSE BED AND BREAKFAST

*1025 Jamestown Road, Williamsburg, 757-253-1260, 800-545-1825;*
*www.libertyrose.com*

This restored house is decorated in a Victorian-style with European antiques and is located just one mile from Colonial Williamsburg's historic village. Four rooms. No children allowed. Complimentary full breakfast. $$

### WILLIAMSBURG SAMPLER BED AND BREAKFAST

*922 Jamestown Road, Williamsburg, 757-253-0398, 800-722-1169;*
*www.williamsburgsampler.com*

This 18th-century, plantation-style colonial home is located in the City of Williamsburg's Architectural Corridor Protection District. Four rooms. Complimentary full breakfast. $$

## RESTAURANTS

### ★★BERRET'S SEAFOOD RESTAURANT AND TAPHOUSE GRILL

*199 S. Boundary St., Williamsburg, 757-253-1847; www.berrets.com*

American menu. Lunch, dinner, late-night. Closed Monday in January and February. Bar. Children's menu. Casual attire. Reservations recommended. Outdoor seating. $$

**VIRGINIA**

### ★★★THE DINING ROOM AT FORD'S COLONY

*240 Ford's Colony Drive, Williamsburg, 757-258-4107; www.fordscolony.com*

Rich, imaginative American and European dishes are served in a quiet, elegant dining room. American menu. Dinner, Sunday brunch. Closed Sunday-Monday. Bar. Jacket required. Reservations recommended. Outdoor seating. **$$$**

### ★★GIUSEPPE'S

*5601 Richmond Road, Williamsburg, 757-565-1977; www.giuseppes.com*

Italian menu. Lunch, dinner. Closed Sunday. Children's menu. Casual attire. Reservations recommended. Outdoor seating. **$$**

### ★★KING'S ARMS TAVERN

*416 E. Duke of Glouchester St., Williamsburg, 757-229-2141, 800-828-3767; www.colonialwilliamsburg.com*

American menu. Lunch, dinner. Bar. Children's menu. Casual attire. Reservations recommended. Outdoor seating. **$$$**

### ★★LE YACA

*1915 Pocahontas Trail No. C10, Williamsburg, 757-220-3616; www.leyacawilliamsburg.com*

French menu. Lunch, dinner. Closed Sunday. Bar. Children's menu. Business casual attire. Reservations recommended. **$$$**

### ★OLD CHICKAHOMINY HOUSE

*1211 Jamestown Road, Williamsburg, 757-229-4689; www.visitwilliamsburg.com*

American menu. Breakfast, lunch. Casual attire. 18th-century stagecoach stop atmosphere. **$**

### ★★PEKING

*122 Waller Mill Road, Williamsburg, 757-229-2288; www.dining-reviews.com*

Chinese, Japanese menu. Lunch, dinner, brunch. Casual attire. Reservations recommended. **$**

★
★
★
★
★

### ★PIERCE'S PITT BAR-B-QUE

*447 E. Rochambeau Drive, Williamsburg, 757-565-2955; www.pierces.com*

American menu. Breakfast, lunch, dinner. **$**

### ★★★REGENCY DINING ROOM

*136 E. Francis St., Williamsburg, 757-229-2141, 800-828-3767; www.colonialwilliamsburg.com*

Set in the charming Williamsburg Inn, the Regency Dining Room offers diners a graceful setting in which to enjoy a leisurely dinner of contemporary Southern fare. The menu runs the gamut from modern dishes like tomato-rosemary ravioli with smoked duck and oxtail rillettes to tried-and-true classics like Chateaubriand and the signature Williamsburg Inn crab cake. Live music and dancing are offered on Friday and Saturday nights. American menu. Breakfast, lunch, dinner. Bar. Children's menu. Jacket required. Outdoor seating. **$$$**

### ★★RIVER'S INN RESTAURANT & CRAB DECK

*8109 Yacht Haven Drive, Gloucester Point, 804-642-9942, 888-780-2722;*
*www.riversinnrestaurant.com*

Seafood menu. Lunch, dinner. Closed Monday September-March. Bar. Children's menu. Casual attire. Outdoor seating. **$$**

### ★★SEASONS CAFÉ

*110 S. Henry, Williamsburg, 757-259-0018; www.seasonsofwilliamsburg.com*

International menu. Lunch, dinner, brunch. Bar. Children's menu. Casual attire. **$$**

### ★★★THE TRELLIS

*403 Duke of Gloucester St., Williamsburg, 757-229-8610; www.thetrellis.com*

Entrées include deep-dried catfish with vegetable slaw, screaming peanuts, watercress and cucumber mayonnaise; and grilled pork tenderloin with string beans and bourbon and honey-glazed sweet potatoes. American menu. Lunch, dinner, brunch. Bar. Casual attire. Outdoor seating. **$$$**

### ★★WHALING COMPANY

*494 McLaw Circle, Williamsburg, 757-229-0275; www.thewhalingcompany.com*

Seafood menu. Dinner. Bar. Children's menu. Casual attire. **$$**

### ★★YORKSHIRE STEAK AND SEAFOOD HOUSE

*700 York St., Williamsburg, 757-229-9790; www.theyorkshirerestaurant.com*

American menu. Dinner. Children's menu. Casual attire. Reservations recommended. In colonial-style building. **$$**

**531**

# WINCHESTER

Winchester is the oldest colonial city west of the Blue Ridge, a Civil War prize that changed hands 72 times (including 13 times in one day). Sometimes called the "apple capital of the world," it is located at the northern approach to the Shenandoah Valley.

George Washington, as a red-haired 16-year-old, headed for Winchester and his first surveying job in 1748, and began a decade of apprenticeship for the military and political responsibilities he would later assume as a national leader. During the French and Indian Wars, Colonel Washington made the city his defense headquarters while he built Fort Loudoun in Winchester. Washington was elected to his first political office as a representative from Frederick County to the House of Burgesses.

At the intersection of travel routes, both east-west and north-south, Winchester grew and prospered. By the time of the Civil War it was a major transportation and supply center, strategically located to control both Union approaches to Washington and Confederate supply lines through the Shenandoah Valley. More than 100 minor engagements and six battles took place in the vicinity. General Stonewall Jackson had his headquarters here during the winter of 1861-1862. From his headquarters in Winchester, Union General Philip Sheridan started his famous ride to rally his troops at Cedar Creek, 11 miles away, and turn a Confederate victory into a Union rout.

Approximately 3.5 million bushels of apples are harvested annually in Frederick County and are one of Winchester's economic mainstays. The world's largest apple cold storage plant and one of the world's largest apple processing plants are here.

*Information: Winchester-Frederick County Visitor Center, 1360 S. Pleasant Valley Road,*
*Winchester, 540-662-4135, 800-662-1360; www.visitwinchesterva.com*

VIRGINIA

★
★
★
★
★

## WHAT TO SEE AND DO
### ABRAM'S DELIGHT AND LOG CABIN
*1340 S. Pleasant Valley Ave., Winchester, 540-662-6519*
Oldest house in city, restored, furnished in 18th-century style; boxwood garden; log cabin, basement kitchen. (April-October, daily; rest of year, by appointment, weather permitting). Inquire about combination ticket.

### FIRST PRESBYTERIAN CHURCH OF WINCHESTER
*116 S. Loudoun St., Winchester, 540-662-3824; www.firstchurch-winchester.org*
Building has been used as a church, a stable by Union troops in Civil War, a public school, and an armory; restored in 1941. Daily.

### HANDLEY LIBRARY AND ARCHIVES
*100 W. Piccadilly St., Winchester, 540-662-9041; www.hrl.lib.state.va.us/handley*
Completed in 1913, the public library was designed in Beaux-Arts style. Rotunda is crowned on the outside with a copper-covered dome and on the inside by a dome of stained glass. Interesting interior features include wrought-iron staircases and glass floors. Historical archives are housed on lower level (nonresident fee). Monday-Saturday, Sunday (January-April, October-November).

### STONEWALL JACKSON'S HEADQUARTERS
*415 N. Braddock St., Winchester, 540-667-3242; www.winchesterhistory.org*
Jackson's headquarters November 1861-March 1862; now a museum housing Jackson memorabilia and other Confederate items of the war years. April-October, daily; rest of year, by appointment, weather permitting. Inquire about combination ticket.

### WASHINGTON'S OFFICE-MUSEUM
*Cork and Braddock streets, Winchester, 540-662-4412; www.fortedwards.org*
Building used by George Washington in 1755-1756 during construction of Fort Loudoun. Housed in this museum are French and Indian, Revolutionary and Civil War relics. April-October, daily; rest of year, by appointment, weather permitting.

## SPECIAL EVENTS
### APPLE HARVEST ARTS & CRAFTS
*Jim Barnett Park, Winchester*
Pie contests, apple-butter making, music, arts and crafts. Third weekend in September.

### HISTORIC GARDEN TOUR
*1340 S. Pleasant Valley Road, Winchester, 540-542-1326, 877-871-1326*
Open house and gardens in historic Winchester. Mid-late April.

### SHENANDOAH APPLE BLOSSOM FESTIVAL
*135 N. Cameron St., Winchester, 540-662-3863; www.thebloom.com*
Apple Blossom Queen, parades, arts and crafts, band contests, music, food and attractions. Late-April-early May.

## HOTELS
### ★HAMPTON INN
*1655 Apple Blossom Drive, Winchester, 540-667-8011, 800-426-7866;*
*www.hamptoninn.com*
103 rooms. Complimentary continental breakfast. $

### ★★HOLIDAY INN
*333 Front Royal Pike, Winchester, 540-667-3300, 800-282-0244;*
*www.holidayinn.com/winchesterva*
173 rooms. $

# WINTERGREEN

## WHAT TO SEE AND DO
### WINTERGREEN RESORT
*Highway 664, Wintergreen, 434-325-2200; www.wintergreenresort.com*
Quad, three triple, double chairlifts; patrol, school, rentals, snow making; lodge, nursery. Twenty runs; longest run 1½ miles; vertical drop 1,003 feet. December-March, daily. Night skiing. Summer activities include fishing, boating; golf, tennis, horseback riding.

## HOTEL
### ★★★WINTERGREEN RESORT
*Route 664, Wintergreen, 434-325-2200, 800-266-2444; www.wintergreenresort.com*
Wintergreen is a resort for all seasons: in the winter, guests can take advantage of its location in the Blue Ridge Mountains for prime skiing and snowboarding, while in summer, there are two golf courses to take tee time on. 300 rooms. Children's activity center. Ski in/ski out. Airport transportation available. $$

★
★
★
★
★

# WOODSTOCK
A German immigrant, Jacob Miller, received a land grant from Lord Fairfax and came here in 1752 with his wife and six children. A few years later, he set aside 1,200 acres for a town, first called Mllerstadt, later Woodstock. In January 1776 in a small log church here, John Peter Gabriel Mhlenberg preached his famous sermon based on Ecclesiastes 3:1-8: "There is a time to every purpose…a time to war and a time to peace," at the end of which he flung back his vestments to reveal the uniform of a Continental colonel and began to enroll his parishioners in the army that was to overthrow British rule. *The Shenandoah Valley-Herald*, a weekly newspaper established in 1817, is still published here.
*Information: Chamber of Commerce, 143 N. Main St., Woodstock, 540-459-2542*

## WHAT TO SEE AND DO
### SHENANDOAH COUNTY COURT HOUSE
*Main Street, Woodstock*
Oldest courthouse still in use west of the Blue Ridge Mountains; interior restored to original design. Monday-Friday.

### SHENANDOAH VINEYARDS

*3659 S. Ox Road, Woodstock, 540-984-8699; www.shentel.net/shenvine*
Valley's first winery. Premium wines; hand-picked and processed in the European style. Picnic area. Tours, free tastings available. Daily.

### WOODSTOCK TOWER

Panoramic view of seven horseshoe bends of the Shenandoah River.

## SPECIAL EVENTS

### SHENANDOAH COUNTY FAIR

*300 Fairgrounds Road, Woodstock, 540-459-3867; www.shencofair.com*
One of the oldest county fairs in the state. Harness racing last four days. Late August-early September.

### SHENANDOAH VALLEY MUSIC FESTIVAL

*102 N. Main St., Woodstock, 540-459-3396; www.musicfest.org*
Symphony pops, classical, folk, jazz, country and big band concerts. Pavilion and lawn seating. Outdoor pavilion on grounds of historic Orkney Springs Hotel in Orkney Springs. Four weekends, mid-July-Labor Day weekend.

## HOTELS

### ★★HOLIDAY INN EXPRESS

*1130 Motel Drive, Woodstock, 540-459-5000, 800-282-0244; www.holidayinn.com*
124 rooms. Airport transportation available. **$**

## SPECIALTY LODGING

### INN AT NARROW PASSAGE

*Route 11, 30 Chapman Landing Road, Woodstock, 540-459-8000, 800-459-8002;*
*www.narrowpassage.com*
This restored colonial wagon stop along the Old Valley Pike is located on the Shenandoah River. The guest rooms are decorated with Early American reproductions and antiques are available. The inn offers views of both the river and the Massanutten Mountains. 12 rooms. Complimentary full breakfast. **$**

# WYTHEVILLE

With lead mines and the only salt mine in the South nearby, Wytheville was a Union target during the Civil War. One story states that a detachment of Union cavalry attempted to take the town in July 1863, only to be thwarted by Molly Tynes, who rode 40 miles over the mountains from Rocky Dell to tell the countryside that the Yankees were coming. The alerted home guard turned them away. A transportation center today, Wytheville is also a vacationland nestled between the Blue Ridge and Allegheny mountains. Rural Retreat Lake is nearby. Wythe Ranger District office for the George Washington and Jefferson national forests is located here.
*Information: Wytheville-Wythe-Bland Chamber of Commerce, 150 E. Monroe St.,*
*Wytheville, 276-223-3365; chamber.wytheville.com*

★
★
★
★
☆

## WHAT TO SEE AND DO

### BIG WALKER LOOKOUT

*US 52 N., Wytheville, 276-228-4401, 276-663-4016; www.scenicbeauty-va.com*

A 120-foot observation tower at 3,405-foot elevation; swinging bridge. Gift shop; snack bar. April-late May, Thursday-Sunday; Memorial Day-mid-November, Tuesday-Sunday.

### WYTHEVILLE STATE FISH HATCHERY

*1260 Red Hollow Road, Wytheville, 804-367-1000; www.dgif.virgina.gov*

Approximately 150,000 pounds of rainbow trout produced annually. Five-tank aquarium; displays. Self-guided tours. Daily.

## SPECIAL EVENT

### CHAUTAUQUA FESTIVAL

*276-228-6855; www.wythevillefestival.org*

Held over a nine-day period. Includes parade, educational events, performing arts, art shows, children's activities, music, food, entertainment. Third week in June.

## HOTELS

### ★BEST WESTERN WYTHEVILLE INN

*355 Nye Road, Wytheville, 276-228-7300, 800-224-9172; www.bestwestern.com*

100 rooms. Complimentary continental breakfast. $

### ★★RED ROOF INN

*1900 E. Main St., Wytheville, 276-228-5483, 800-733-7663; www.redroof.com*

199 rooms. $

**535**

# YORKTOWN

Free land offered in 1630 to those adventurous enough "to seate and inhabit" the 50-foot bluffs on the south side of the York River brought about the beginning of settlement. When the Assembly authorized a port, started in 1691, the town slowly expanded and in the following years became a busy shipping center, its prosperity peaking around 1750. From then on, the port declined along with the Tidewater Virginia tobacco trade.

Yorktown's moment in history came in 1781. After raiding up and down Virginia with minimal resistance from the Marquis de Lafayette, British commander Cornwallis was sent here to establish a naval base in which supplies and reinforcements could be shipped to him. The Comte de Grasse's French fleet effectively blockaded the British, however, by controlling the mouth of the Chesapeake Bay. At the Battle of the Capes on September 5, 1781, a British fleet sent to investigate the French presence was defeated by the French. Cornwallis found himself bottled up in Yorktown by combined American and French forces under Washington, which arrived on September 28.

Shelling began October 9. The siege of Yorktown ended on October 17 with Cornwallis requesting terms of capitulation. On October 19, Cornwallis' troops marched out with flags and arms cased, their bands playing. Then they laid down their arms, bringing the last major battle of the Revolutionary War to a close.

**VIRGINIA**

★
★
★
★
★

Yorktown Battlefield, part of Colonial National Historical Park, surrounds the village. Though Yorktown itself is still an active community, many surviving and reconstructed colonial structures supply an 18th-century atmosphere.

*Information: Colonial National Historical Park, Yorktown, 757-898-3400; www.nps.gov/colo*

## WHAT TO SEE AND DO

### GRACE EPISCOPAL CHURCH

*111 Church St., Yorktown, 757-898-3261; www.gracechurchyorktown.com*

Walls of local marl (a mixture of clay, sand and limestone); damaged in 1781, gutted by fire in 1814. A 1649 communion service is still in use. Daily.

### MOORE HOUSE

*224 Ballard St., Yorktown, 757-898-3400; www.nps.gov/york*

In this 18th-century house the "Articles of Capitulation" were drafted. These were signed by General Washington in the captured British Redoubt No. 10 on October 19. Mid-June-mid-August, daily; spring and fall, weekends.

### NELSON HOUSE

*Nelson and Main streets, Yorktown, 757-898-2410; www.yorkcounty.gov*

Original restored mansion built by "Scotch Tom" Nelson in the early 1700s. Home of his grandson, Thomas Nelson, Jr., a signer of the Declaration of Independence. Impressive example of Georgian architecture. April-October, daily.

★
★
★
★
☆

### SELF-GUIDED BATTLEFIELD TOUR

Markers, displays aid in visualizing siege. Highlights include headquarters sites of Lafayette, von Steuben, Rochambeau, Washington; a key point is Surrender Field where British forces laid down their arms.

### VISITOR CENTER

*Colonial Parkway and Yorktown Visitor Center, Yorktown, 757-898-3400; www.nps.gov*

Information, special exhibits, General Washington's field tents. Daily.

### YORKTOWN BATTLEFIELD IN COLONIAL NATIONAL HISTORIC PARK

*Yorktown, 757-898-2410; www.nps.gov/yonb*

Surrounds and includes part of town. Remains of 1781 British fortifications, modified and strengthened by Confederate forces in Civil War. Reconstructed American and French lines lie beyond. Roads lead to headquarters, encampment areas of Americans, French. Admission fee includes access to Visitor Center, battlefield tour, Moore House and Nelson House. Golden Access, Age and Eagle passports honored. Daily.

### YORKTOWN NATIONAL CIVIL WAR CEMETERY

2,183 interments (1,436 unknown). Yorktown Victory Monument Elaborately ornamented 95-foot granite column memorializes American-French alliance in Revolutionary War.

### YORKTOWN VICTORY CENTER

*Route 1020, Williamsburg, 757-253-4838, 888-593-4682; www.visitwilliamsburg.com*

Museum of the Revolutionary War chronicles the struggle for independence from the beginning of colonial unrest to the new nation's formation. Exhibit galleries, living history Continental Army encampment and late-18th-century farm. Daily. Combination ticket with Jamestown Settlement available.

## SPECIAL EVENT
### YORKTOWN DAY

Observance of America's Revolutionary War victory at Yorktown in 1781. October 19.

## HOTEL
### ★DUKE OF YORK MOTOR HOTEL

*508 Water St., Yorktown, 757-898-3232; www.dukeofyorkmotel.com*

57 rooms. $

# WEST VIRGINIA

JOHN DENVER SAID IT BEST: WEST VIRGINIA IS ALMOST HEAVEN. FOR NATURE LOVERS AND outdoor sports enthusiasts, the Mountain State is a natural paradise of rugged mountains and lush, lyric-inspiring countryside.

With the highest total altitude of any state east of the Mississippi River, West Virginia's ski industry has opened several Alpine and Nordic ski areas. Outfitters offer excellent whitewater rafting on the state's many turbulent rivers. Rock climbing, caving and hiking are popular in the Monongahela National Forest. And West Virginia's state parks and areas for hunting and fishing are plentiful.

West Virginia is also a land of proud traditions, with many festivals held throughout the year as tributes to the state's rich heritage. These events include celebrations honoring the state's sternwheel riverboat legacy, its spectacular autumn foliage and even its strawberries, apples and black walnuts.

Archaeological evidence indicates that some of the area's very first settlers were the Mound Builders, a prehistoric Ohio Valley culture that left behind at least 300 conical earth mounds. Many have been worn away by erosion, but excavations in some have revealed elaborately adorned human skeletons and artifacts of amazing beauty and utility.

Centuries later, pioneers who ventured into western Virginia in the 18th century (West Virginia did not break away from Virginia until the Civil War) found fine vistas and forests, curative springs and beautiful rivers. George Washington and his family frequented the soothing mineral waters of Berkeley Springs, and White Sulfur Springs later became a popular resort among the colonists. But much of this area was still considered "the wild West" in those days, and life here was not easy.

The Commonwealth of Virginia largely ignored its western citizens—only one governor was elected from the western counties before 1860. When the western counties formed their own state during the Civil War, it was the result of many years of strained relations with the parent state. The war finally provided the opportunity the counties needed to break away. Although many sentiments in the new state remained pro-South, West Virginia's interests were best served by staying with the Union.

The war left West Virginia a new state, but like other war-ravaged areas, it had suffered heavy losses of life and property and the recovery took many years. West-Virginians eventually rebuilt their state. New industry was developed, railroads were built and resources like coal, oil and natural gas brought relative prosperity.

West Virginia continues to be an important source of bituminous coal and a major producer of building stone, timber, glass and chemicals. The state is also home to technological wonders such as the National Radio Astronomy Observatory, where scientists study the universe via radio telescopes, and the New River Gorge Bridge, the world's longest steel span bridge.

**FUN FACTS**

West Virginia was the first state to have sales tax. It became effective on July 1, 1921.

*Information: www.wv.gov*

# ANSTED

## WHAT TO SEE AND DO

### HAWK NEST STATE PARK

*WV Route 60, Ansted, 304-658-5212, 800-255-5982; www.hawksnestsp.com*

The former residence of Confederate Colonel George W. Imboden contains original woodwork, period furniture and a toy collection. Adjacent Fayette County Historical Society Museum features displays of Native American relics, local artifacts, Civil War items and a restored one-room schoolhouse. June-August, Monday-Saturday; September-May, by appointment.

### HAWK'S NEST STATE PARK

*177 W. Main St., Ansted, 304-658-5212, 800-225-5982; www.hawksnestsp.com*

Hawk's Nest is located on approximately 280 acres of Gauley Mountain with fine views of New River Gorge from rocks 585 feet above the river. A 600-foot aerial tramway carries passengers to the canyon floor. Features include a swimming pool, fishing, hiking trails, tennis, picnic area, playground, concessions, restaurant, lodge and log museum with early West Virginia artifacts. May-November, daily.

## HOTEL

### ★★HAWKS NEST STATE PARK LODGE

*177 W. Main St., Ansted, 304-658-5212, 800-225-5982; www.hawksnestsp.com*

31 rooms. Children's activity center. **$**

# AURORA

Located at the summit of Cheat Mountain, Aurora offers visitors clean air and high altitude.

## WHAT TO SEE AND DO

### CATHEDRAL STATE PARK

*Route 50, Aurora, 304-735-3771, 800-225-5982; www.cathedralstatepark.com*

Hiking trails through 132 acres of deep, virgin hemlock forest; cross-country skiing, picnicking.

# BECKLEY

The "smokeless coal capital of the world" is a center for more than 200 small mining and farming towns. Beckley is situated on a high plateau surrounded by fertile valleys. During the Civil War, the village was held at various times by both armies; Union troops shelled it in 1863. Coal was found here in 1774 but was not mined until 1890. Smokeless coal became the standard bunker fuel during World War I, and the demand continued for years thereafter. Beckley now serves as a commercial, medical and tourist center.

*Information: Southern West Virginia Convention & Visitors Bureau, 1406 Harper Road, Beckley, 304-252-2244, 800-847-4898; www.visitwv.org*

**WEST VIRGINIA**

# WHAT TO SEE AND DO

## BABCOCK STATE PARK

*HC 35, Clifftop, 304-438-3004, 800-225-5982; www.babcocksp.com*

More than 4,127 acres of rugged mountain scenery with a trout stream and waterfalls, views of New River Canyon, rhododendrons (May-July); restored operating gristmill. Swimming pool, lake and stream fishing, boating (rowboat, paddleboat rentals); hiking trails, horseback riding, game courts (equipment rentals), cross-country skiing, camping, 26 cabins (rentals, spring and fall). Nature and recreation programs (summer). Mid-April-October.

## BECKLEY EXHIBITION COAL MINE

*513 Ewart Ave., Beckley, 304-256-1747; www.beckleymine.com*

Riding tours in coal cars through 1,500 feet of underground passageways, constant 56 F; museum, coal company house, superintendent of coal mines' house, church, campground. April-October, daily.

## LAKE STEPHENS

*1400 Lake Stephens Road, Beckley, 304-934-5323; www.lakestephenswv.com*

A 303-acre lake with swimming, fishing and boating, plus trailer camping.

## PLUM ORCHARD LAKE WILDLIFE MANAGEMENT AREA

*Route 1, Scarbro, 304-469-9905; www.plumorchardlakewma.com*

More than 3,200 acres with rabbit, grouse and squirrel hunting. Also a 202-acre lake with more than six miles of shoreline; boating, fishing for bass, channel catfish, crappie and bluegill; picnicking, playground, camping.

## WHITEWATER RAFTING

*New River Park, Beckley, 304-252-2244, 800-847-4898; www.visitwv.com*

Many outfitters offer guided trips on the New and Gauley rivers.

## YOUTH MUSEUM OF SOUTHERN WEST VIRGINIA

*106 Adair St., Beckley, 304-252-3730, 800-718-1474; www.beckleymine.com*

Hands-on exhibits, planetarium, log house. May-Labor Day, daily; rest of year, Tuesday-Saturday.

# SPECIAL EVENT

## APPALACHIAN FESTIVAL

*200 Armory Drive, Beckley, 304-252-7328, 800-718-1474; www.appalachianfestival.net*

Exhibitions and demonstrations of native crafts; entertainment, food. August.

# HOTEL

## ★HAMPTON INN

*110 Harper Park Drive, Beckley, 304-252-2121; www.hamptoninn.com*

108 rooms. Complimentary continental breakfast. Pool. $

**WEST VIRGINIA**

★
★
★
★
★

**★★MACADO**

*3815 Robert C. Byrd Drive, Beckley, 304-256-3882; www.macados.net*

American, Italian menu. Lunch, dinner, late-night. Bar. Children's menu. Casual attire. **$$**

# BERKELEY SPRINGS

Popularized by George Washington, who surveyed the area for Lord Fairfax in 1748, Berkeley Springs is the oldest spa in the nation. Fairfax later granted the land around the springs to Virginia. The town is officially named Bath, for the famous watering place in England, but the post office is Berkeley Springs. The waters, which are piped throughout the town, are fresh and slightly sweet, without the medicinal flavor of most mineral springs. Washington and his family returned again and again.

The resort's popularity peaked after the Revolutionary War, becoming something of a summer capital for Washingtonians in the 1830s. But like all resort towns, Berkeley Springs declined as newer, more fashionable spas came into vogue. The Civil War completely destroyed the town's economy. Today, the town is again visited for its healthful waters, spas and charming downtown.

*Information: Berkeley Springs-Morgan County Chamber of Commerce,*

*127 Fairfax St., Berkeley Springs, 304-258-3738, 800-447-8797;*

*www.berkeleyspringschamber.com*

## WHAT TO SEE AND DO

### BERKELEY SPRINGS STATE PARK

*2 S. Washington St., Berkeley Springs, 304-258-2711; www.berkeleyspringssp.com*

Famous resort with health baths of all types (fees); five warm springs. Main bathhouse (daily). Roman bathhouse with second-floor museum (Memorial Day-mid-October, daily). Swimming pool (Memorial Day-Labor Day, daily).

### CACAPON RESORT STATE PARK

*818 Cacapon Lodge Drive, Berkeley Springs, 304-258-1022, 800-225-5328;*

*www.cacaponresort.com*

More than 6,100 acres with swimming, sand beach, fishing, boating (rowboat and paddleboat rentals); hiking and bridle trails, horseback riding, 18-hole golf course, tennis, game courts, cross-country skiing, picnicking, playground, concession, restaurant, lodge. Nature, recreation programs. Nature center.

### SLEEPY CREEK WILDLIFE MANAGEMENT AREA

*1910 Sleepy Creek Road, Berkeley Springs, 304-754-3855*

Approximately 23,000 acres of rugged forest offer wild turkey, deer, grouse and squirrel hunting; boating and bass fishing on 205-acre lake; primitive camping. Skiing. Also 70 miles of hiking trails crossing two mountains, several valleys.

### VIEW FROM PROSPECT PEAK

*Berkeley Springs*

Potomac River winds through what the National Geographic Society has called one of the nation's outstanding vistas.

**541**

**WEST VIRGINIA**

★
★
★
★
☆

# GEORGE WASHINGTON'S SPA AND BERKELEY SPRINGS

Tucked in a narrow, rock-shadowed valley along the Cacapon River, the little mountain community of Berkeley Springs has transformed itself into "Spa Town USA." A total of five separate spas employ more than 40 massage therapists—three times the number of practicing lawyers, town officials claim.

The town's clustering of so many spas is relatively new, but Berkeley Springs has a long heritage as a spa destination. Well before white settlers arrived, Native Americans sought out the warm, 74.3 degree mineral springs. Still bubbling forth from the base of Warm Springs Ridge at 2,000 gallons per minute, the water was believed to have curative powers. George Washington, who first visited the springs in 1748 as a 16-year-old surveyor, returned nearly a dozen times in later years seeking health benefits. In 1776, he and his prominent friends and family established the Town of Bath, intent on making it a popular spa, and the first bathhouses were built. Thus, Berkeley Springs claims to be "the country's first spa."

You can explore the town's spa heritage in a 30-minute, half-mile stroll in Berkeley Springs State Park, which doubles as the community's town square. One of America's most curious public parklands, the seven-acre Berkeley Springs State Park operates year-round as a very affordable, government-run spa. Begin a loop around the park at the large public swimming pool, which is fed by spring waters. Heading clockwise, take a peek inside the Main Bath House, where you can enjoy a private hot-tub soak and Swedish-style massage. Continue on to a stone-lined natural pool of flowing spring water, dubbed "George Washington's Bath Tub" in his honor. Move on to the Gentlemen's Spring House, where you are welcome to draw jugs of the famed drinking water for free. Conclude this plunge into historic bathing with a look into the Roman Bath House, where you can indulge in a private hot-tub soak without an accompanying massage.

## SPECIAL EVENT

### APPLE BUTTER FESTIVAL

*127 Fairfax St., Berkeley Springs, 800-447-8797; www.berkeleysprings.com/apple*

Crafts demonstrations, music, contests. Columbus Day weekend.

## HOTELS

### ★★CACAPON RESORT STATE PARK

*818 Cacapon Lodge Drive, Berkeley Springs, 304-258-1022, 800-225-5982; www.cacaponresort.com*

48 rooms. Children's activity center. Beach. $

### ★★COOLFONT RESORT

*3621 Cold Run Valley Road, Berkeley Springs, 304-258-4500, 800-888-8768; www.freemancompanies.com/coolfont.aspx*

19 rooms. Complimentary full breakfast. Children's activity center. $$

## ★★THE COUNTRY INN AT BERKELEY SPRINGS

*110 S. Washington St., Berkeley Springs, 304-258-2210, 866-458-2210;*
*www.thecountryinnatberkeleysprings.com*

68 rooms. Complimentary continental breakfast. Spa. Airport transportation available. **$**

## SPECIALTY LODGING

### HIGHLAWN INN

*171 Market St., Berkeley Springs, 304-258-5700, 888-290-4163;*
*www.highlawninn.com*

This Victorian-style manor, built in the late 1890s, has authentic furnishings and ornate fireplaces. The mineral bath waters of the area are an added feature. 12 rooms. Children over 14 years only. Complimentary full breakfast. **$**

# BETHANY

## WHAT TO SEE AND DO

### BETHANY COLLEGE

*1 Main St., Bethany, 304-829-7000; www.bethanywv.edu*

Founded in 1840 by Alexander Campbell, the leading influence in the 19th century religious movement that gave rise to the Disciples of Christ, Churches of Christ and Christian churches. Historic buildings on the 300-acre campus are home to 800 students and include Old Main, styled after the University of Glasgow in Scotland; Pendleton Heights, a 19th-century house used as the college president's residence; Old Bethany Meeting House and Delta Tau Delta Founder's House.

### CAMPBELL MANSION

*Historic Bethany, 304-829-4258; www.bethanywv.edu*

A 24-room house where Campbell lived; antique furnishings. On property are hexagonal brick study, one-room schoolhouse and smokehouse. The Campbell family cemetery, "God's Acre," is across from the mansion. April-October, Tuesday-Sunday; November-March, by appointment.

# BLUEFIELD

Named for the bluish chicory covering the nearby hills, Bluefield owes its existence to the Pocahontas Coal Field. The town came to life in the 1880s when the railroad came through to transport coal.

This commercial and industrial center of southern West Virginia is known as nature's "air-conditioned city" because of its altitude—one-half mile above sea level. Bluefield has a sister city by the same name in Virginia, directly across the state line.

*Information: Convention & Visitors Bureau, 704 Bland St., Bluefield, 304-325-8438,*
*800-221-3206; www.mccvb.com*

## WHAT TO SEE AND DO

### EASTERN REGIONAL COAL ARCHIVES

*Craft Memorial Library, 600 Commerce St., Bluefield, 304-325-3943;*
*craftmemorial.lib.wv.us*

This center highlights the history of West Virginia coal fields through exhibits, photographs, mining implements, films and research material. Monday-Friday afternoons.

★
★
★
★
★

### PANTHER STATE FOREST
*Bluefield, Panther, 304-938-2252; www.pantherstateforest.com*
More than 7,800 acres of rugged hills. Swimming pool (Memorial Day-Labor Day), fishing, hunting, hiking trails, picnicking, playground, concession, camping.

### PINNACLE ROCK STATE PARK
*Route 52 Bramwell, 304-248-8565; www.pinnaclerockstatepark.com*
Approximately 250-acre park contains a 15-acre lake and interesting sandstone formations, which resemble a giant cockscomb. Hiking, picnicking.

## HOTEL
### ★★HOLIDAY INN
*3350 Big Laurel Highway, Bluefield, 304-325-6170, 800-465-4329;*
*www.holidayinn.com/bluefieldwv*
120 rooms. $

# BUCKHANNON
*Information: Buckhannon-Upshur Chamber of Commerce, 16 S. Kanawha St.,*
*Buckhannon, 304-472-1722; www.buchamber.com*

## WHAT TO SEE AND DO
### AUDRA STATE PARK
*Route 4, Buckhannon, 304-457-1162, 800-225-5982; www.audrastatepark.com*
Approximately 360 acres offer swimming in a natural mountain stream surrounded by tall timber bathhouse. Hiking trails, picnicking, playground, concession, tent and trailer camping.

### WEST VIRGINIA WESLEYAN COLLEGE
*59 College Ave., Buckhannon, 304-473-8000; www.wvwc.edu*
Founded in 1890, this 80-acre campus is home to 1,600 students and features Georgian architecture. Wesley Chapel, the largest place of worship in the state, contains a Casavant organ with 1,474 pipes.

## SPECIAL EVENT
### WEST VIRGINIA STRAWBERRY FESTIVAL
*Buckhannon, 304-472-9036; www.wvstrawberryfestival.com*
Parades, dances, exhibits, air show, arts and crafts, other activities. Usually the week before Memorial Day.

## HOTELS
### ★BICENTENNIAL MOTEL
*90 E. Main St., Buckhannon, 304-472-5000, 800-762-5137;*
*www.veinotte.ca/us/24183.htm*
45 rooms. $

### ★HAMPTON INN BUCKHANNON
*1 Commerce Blvd., Buckhannon, 304-473-0900; www.hamptoninn.com*
62 rooms. Complimentary continental breakfast. $

# CHARLES TOWN

Charles Town is serene, aristocratic and full of tradition, with orderly, tree-shaded streets and 18th-century houses. It was named for George Washington's youngest brother, Charles, who laid out the town and named most of the streets after members of his family. Charles Washington's family lived here for many years. Charles Town is also known as the place where John Brown was jailed, tried and hanged in 1859 after his antislavery raid on Harpers Ferry.

*Information: Jefferson County Chamber of Commerce, 201 Frontage Road, Charles Town, 304-725-2055, 800-624-0577; www.jeffersoncounty.com*

## WHAT TO SEE AND DO

### CHARLES TOWN RACES AND GAMING
*Flowing Springs Road, Route 340 North, Charles Town, 304-725-7001, 800-795-7001; www.ctownraces.com*
Thoroughbred racing, clubhouse, video machines, dining room. Daily.

### JEFFERSON COUNTY COURTHOUSE
*100 E. Washington, Charles Town, 304-728-7713; www.nps.gov*
This red brick, Georgian colonial structure (1836) was the scene of John Brown's trial, one of three treason trials held in the U.S. before World War II. The courthouse was shelled during the Civil War but was later rebuilt; the original courtroom survived both the shelling and fires and is open to the public. In 1922, leaders of the miners' armed march on Logan City were tried here; one, Walter Allen, was convicted and sentenced to 10 years. Monday-Friday.

### JEFFERSON COUNTY MUSEUM
*200 E. Washington, Charles Town, 304-725-8628; www.jeffctywvmuseum.org*
Houses John Brown memorabilia, old guns, Civil War artifacts. April-November, Monday-Saturday.

### SITE OF JOHN BROWN GALLOWS
*S. Samuel and Hunter streets, Charles Town*
Marked by a pyramid of three stones supposedly taken from Brown's cell in Charles Town jail. At the execution, 1,500 troops were massed around the scaffold. Some were commanded by Thomas "Stonewall" Jackson; among them was John Wilkes Booth, Virginia militiaman.

### SPA MERCHANDISE
*Charles Town, 304-728-7713; www.riteaid.com*
Historical walking tours; candlelit tours of Jefferson County Courthouse (evenings); carriage rides. All tours by appointment.

### ZION EPISCOPAL CHURCH
*300 E. Congress St., Charles Town, 304-725-5312; www.zionepiscopal.net*
Buried in the cemetery around the church are about 75 members of the Washington family, as well as many Revolutionary War and Confederate soldiers. Interior, by appointment.

★
★
★
★
★

## SPECIAL EVENTS

### CHARLESTON VISITOR BUREAU

*Charles Town, 800-733-5469; www.charlestonwv.com*

Exhibits, performances, tours. First weekend in May.

### JEFFERSON COUNTY FAIR

*Fairgrounds, Charles Town, 304-728-7415*

Livestock show, entertainment, amusement rides, exhibits. Late August.

## HOTEL

### ★★TURF MOTEL

*741 E. Washington St., Charles Town, 304-725-2081, 800-422-8873; www.turfmotel.com*

67 rooms. Complimentary continental breakfast. Wireless Internet access. **$**

# CHARLESTON

Charleston, the state capital, is the trading hub for the Great Kanawha Valley, where deposits of coal, oil, natural gas and brine have greatly contributed to this region's national importance as a production center for chemicals and glass. Two institutions of higher learning, West Virginia State College and the University of Charleston, are located in the metropolitan area. Charleston is also the northern terminus of the spectacular West Virginia Turnpike.

Daniel Boone lived around Charleston until 1795. In 1789, during his residence in Charleston, he was appointed a lieutenant colonel in the county militia and was elected to the Virginia assembly. The area became important as a center of salt production in 1824, when steam engines were used to operate brine pumps. After Charleston became the capital of West Virginia in 1885, following a dispute with Wheeling, the town came into its own. During World War I, an increased demand for plate and bottle glass, as well as for high explosives, made Charleston and the nearby town of Nitro boom.

*Information: Convention & Visitors Bureau, Charleston Civic Center,*
*200 Civic Center Drive, Charleston, 304-344-5075, 800-733-5469;*
*www.charlestonwv.com*

## WHAT TO SEE AND DO

### COONSKIN PARK

*2000 Coonskin Drive, Charleston, 304-341-8000; www.kcprc.com*

Recreation area includes swimming, fishing for bass and catfish, pedal boating, hiking trails, 18-hole golf, miniature golf, tennis. Picnicking, playground, concession. (daily; some activities seasonal) Fees for activities.

### CULTURAL CENTER

*1900 E. Kanawha Blvd., Charleston, 304-558-0220;*
*www.wvculture.org/agency/cultcenter.html*

The Center houses the Division of Culture and History and Library Commission; archives library (Monday-Saturday); state museum; special events, changing exhibits. Daily.

★
★
★
★
☆

# CANYON COUNTRY-AROUND NEW RIVER GORGE

The New River has cut a deep and narrow gorge for more than 50 miles through the rugged mountains of southeastern West Virginia. Rafting enthusiasts consider this to be one of the best whitewater rivers in the nation. It's also very pretty to look at while standing on dry ground—albeit on a cliff's edge high above.

This two-day, 300-mile drive out of Charleston, which circles the gorge, provides plenty of scenic viewing opportunities. At the same time, the tour offers a look at the state's coal-mining heritage. At the turn of the century King Coal ruled the gorge, and at one time two dozen coal-mining towns prospered on the banks of the New River. Now, much of the gorge is protected as the New River Gorge National River.

From Charleston, head east on Highway 60, following the old Midland Trail up the Kanawha River. In the first few miles, the highway winds past industrial plants. The mountain scenery begins after about 30 miles at Gauley Bridge, where the New River flows into the Kanawha. Here, as the New River begins to display whitewater turbulence, the road climbs steeply and you spot the first of many waterfalls. One of finest gorge views is just ahead at Hawk's Nest State Park, which has a 31-room lodge at cliff's edge. A steep hiking trail down to the river provides a chance to stretch your legs.

About 25 minutes on, detour south on Highway 19 to the Canyon rim Visitor Center, which provides information about the park and the region. You also get a good look at the New River Gorge Bridge, one of the highest bridges in the country. Linking the north and south rims of the gorge, it has become famous for its once-a-year parachute jumps in October. Dozens of parachutists leap from its concrete safety barriers and float 876 feet to the river sandbar below. A stairway takes you partway down the cliff for more river and bridge views.

Continue east on Highway 60 to Route 41, where you again detour south (right) to Babcock State Park to see its old stone gristmill and to try its hiking trails. Back on Highway 60, head east to Route 20 south to Hinton, a picturesque riverfront town. A river-level road leads to a view of Sandstone Falls on the New River. You can stay in Hinton or continue south on Route 20 to Pipestem Resort State Park, a 4,000-acre preserve with a 113-room lodge and an 18-hole golf course.

From Pipestem, double back on Route 20 to Route 3 west to Highway 19 north to Beckley. Here you can ride a coal car deep into the Beckley Exhibition Coal Mine. From Beckley, take Route 61 north to Glen Jean and then head east on Route 25 to Thurmond, a former riverside mining boomtown. The still-active train tracks run down the main street next to the sidewalk. An Amtrak station doubles as a railroad museum. Return to Route 61 north to Interstate 64/Interstate 77 and back to Charleston. *Approximately 300 miles.*

WEST VIRGINIA

★
★
★
★
★

### ELK RIVER SCENIC DRIVE

*Charleston*

Beautiful drive along the Elk River from Charleston northeast to Sutton (approximately 60 miles). Begins just north of town; take Highway 119 northeast to Clendenin, then Highway 4 northeast to Highway 19 in Sutton.

### INFORMATION CENTER

*Shenandoah and High streets, Charleston, 304-535-6029; www.nps.gov/hafe*

Restored Federalist house built in 1859 by the U.S. government as a residence for the master armorer of the U.S. Armory. During the Civil War, it was used as headquarters by various commanding officers. Also on this street is the site of the U.S. Armory that John Brown attempted to seize; it was destroyed during the Civil War.

### KANAWHA STATE FOREST

*Loudendale Road, Route 2, Charleston, 304-558-3500, 800-225-5982; www.kanawhastateforest.com*

Approximately 9,300 acres with a swimming pool, bathhouse (Memorial Day-Labor Day), hunting, hiking, interpretive trail for the disabled, horseback riding, cross-country skiing, picnicking, playground, concession and camping.

### MOUNTAIN STAGE

*1900 Kanawha Blvd. E., Charleston, 304-342-5757; www.mountainstage.org*

Live public radio show heard on stations nationwide; features jazz, folk, blues and rock. Visitors may watch show; afternoon performances (Sunday).

### STATE CAPITOL

*1900 E. Kanawha Blvd., Charleston, 304-558-4839, 800-225-5982; www.wzculture.org*

One of America's most beautiful state capitols, the building was designed by Cass Gilbert in Italian Renaissance style and built in 1932. Within the gold-leaf dome, which rises 300 feet above the street, hangs a 10,080-piece, hand-cut imported chandelier weighing more than two tons. Guided tours available. Monday-Friday, Saturday afternoons.

### WHITEWATER RAFTING

*90 MacCorkle Ave. S.W., Charleston, 304-558-2200, 800-225-5982; www.wvriversports.com*

Many outfitters offer guided rafting, canoeing and fishing trips on the New and Gauley rivers.

## SPECIAL EVENTS

### STERNWHEEL REGATTA FESTIVAL

*Charleston, 304-348-6419; www.sternwheelregatta.com*

Sternwheeler and towboat races, parades, contests, hot-air balloon race, fireworks; nationally known entertainers nightly; arts and crafts. Late August-early September.

### VANDALIA GATHERING

*1900 Kanawha Blvd. E., Charleston, 304-558-0220; www.wvculture.org/vandalia*

A festival of traditional arts, craft demonstrations, clogging, gospel music, fiddling, banjo picking and special exhibits. Memorial Day weekend.

## HOTELS

### ★COMFORT SUITES CHARLESTON

*107 Alex Lane, Charleston, 304-925-1171, 800-424-6423; www.choicehotels.com*
67 rooms, all suites. Complimentary full breakfast. **$**

### ★COUNTRY INN & SUITES-CHARLESTON

*105 Alex Lane, Charleston, 304-925-4300, 800-456-4000; www.countryinns.com*
64 rooms. Complimentary continental breakfast. **$**

### ★★EMBASSY SUITES HOTEL CHARLESTON

*300 Court St., Charleston, 304-347-8700, 800-362-2779; www.embassysuites.com*
253 rooms, all suites. Complimentary full breakfast. Airport transportation available. **$**

### ★FAIRFIELD INN BY MARRIOTT CHARLESTON

*1000 Washington St. East, Charleston, 304-343-4661, 800-228-2800;*
*www.marriott.com*
136 rooms. Complimentary continental breakfast. **$**

### ★HAMPTON INN

*1 Preferred Place, Charleston, 304-746-4646, 800-426-7866; www.hamptoninn.com*
104 rooms. Complimentary continental breakfast. Airport transportation available. **$**

### ★★HOLIDAY INN

*600 Kanawha Blvd. East, Charleston, 304-344-4092, 888-465-4329;*
*www.holidayinn.com*
256 rooms. Airport transportation available. **$**

### ★HOLIDAY INN EXPRESS

*100 Civic Center Drive, Charleston, 304-345-0600, 800-315-2621; www.hiexpress.com*
196 rooms. Complimentary continental breakfast. Airport transportation available. **$**

### ★★★MARRIOTT CHARLESTON TOWN CENTER

*200 Lee St. East, Charleston, 304-345-6500, 800-228-9290;*
*www.charlestonmarriott.com*
This hotel, which is conveniently located just off the Interstate 77 and Interstate 64
interchange, sits adjacent to the Charleston Town Center and Civic Center in the heart
of downtown. Many services and amenities are offered here, and there are plenty of
recreational activities, restaurants and shops in the immediate area. Guest rooms are
attractively decorated in hues of green and terra-cotta. 352 rooms. High-speed Internet access. Airport transportation available. **$**

## RESTAURANTS

### ★★BLOSSOM DELI

*904 Quarrier St., Charleston, 304-345-2233; www.blossomdeli.com*
American menu. Breakfast, lunch, dinner. Closed Sunday. **$$**

★
★
★
★
☆

### ★★JOE FAZIO'S SPAGHETTI HOUSE

*1008 Bullitt St., Charleston, 304-344-3071; www.fazios.net*

Italian menu. Dinner. Closed Monday. Children's menu. $$

### ★★★LAURY'S

*350 MacCorkle Ave. Southeast, Charleston, 304-343-0055*

Located downtown near the Kanawha River in the old C&O Railroad Depot, this French-American Continental restaurant has welcomed diners since 1979. The dining room is an elegant space with dramatic high ceilings, floor-to-ceiling windows, oil paintings, mirrors in ornate gold frames, crystal chandeliers and fresh flowers. If you get the right table, you will be rewarded with an amazing view. American, French menu. Dinner. Closed Sunday; week of July 4. Bar. Business casual attire. Reservations recommended. $$

# CLARKSBURG

In the heart of the West Virginia hills, Clarksburg is the trading center for an area of grading lands, coal mines, and oil and gas fields. The Criminal Justice Information Services Division of the FBI is located here. During the Civil War, Clarksburg was an important supply base for Union troops. Famous Civil War general "Stonewall" Jackson was born in Clarksburg in 1824. His statue stands before the courthouse.

*Information: Greater Bridgeport Conference & Visitors Center, 164 W. Main St., Bridgeport, 304-842-7272, 800-368-4324; www.bridgeportwv.com*

## WHAT TO SEE AND DO

### STEALEY-GOFF-VANCE HOUSE

*123 W. Main St., Clarksburg, 304-622-2157*

House restored by Harrison County Historical Society as a museum with period rooms, antique furniture, tools and Native-American artifacts. May-September, Friday, limited hours.

## SPECIAL EVENT

### WEST VIRGINIA ITALIAN HERITAGE FESTIVAL

*340 W. Main St., Clarksburg, 304-622-7314; www.wvihf.com*

Italian arts, music, contests, entertainment. Labor Day weekend.

## HOTEL

### ★SUTTON INN

*250 Emily Drive, Clarksburg, 304-623-2600, 866-726-2322; www.suttoninn.com*

112 rooms. Complimentary continental breakfast. $

## RESTAURANT

### ★★MINARD'S SPAGHETTI INN

*813 E. Pike St., Clarksburg, 304-623-1711*

Italian menu. Lunch, dinner. Bar. Children's menu. Casual attire. $$

# CROSS LANES

## WHAT TO SEE AND DO

### TRI-STATE GREYHOUND PARK

*1 Greyhound Drive, Cross Lanes, 304-776-1000, 800-224-9683;*
*www.tristateracetrack.com*

Indoor grandstand, clubhouse, concessions. Monday-Saturday evenings. Matinees, Saturday-Sunday. Must be 18 to wager.

## HOTEL

### ★COMFORT INN

*102 Racer Drive, Cross Lanes, 304-776-8070, 800-798-7886; www.choicehotels.com*

112 rooms. Complimentary continental breakfast. Airport transportation available. **$**

# DAVIS

Davis, the highest town in the state, was founded by Henry Gassaway Davis, U.S. senator from 1871 to 1883. Senator Davis established the first night train in America in 1848. He and his son-in-law, Senator Stephen B. Elkins, became wealthy from coal, lumber and railroading.

*Information: West Virginia Mountain Highlands, Elkins, 304-636-8400, 800-982-6867;*
*www.mountainhighlands.com*

## WHAT TO SEE AND DO

### BLACKWATER FALLS STATE PARK

*County Route 29, Davis, 304-259-5216, 800-225-5892; www.blackwaterfalls.com*

This 1,688-acre park includes a deep river gorge with 66-foot falls of dark, amber-colored water. Swimming in lake (fee), bath houses (Memorial Day-Labor Day), fishing, boating (rowboat, paddleboat rentals), nature trails, horseback riding, cross-country ski trails, center (rentals, school), sledding, picnicking, playground, concession, lodge, cabins, tent and trailer campground. Nature, recreation programs and tours. Paved falls viewing area for the disabled.

### CANAAN VALLEY RESORT STATE PARK

*Davis, 304-866-4121, 800-662-4121; www.canaanresort.com*

Approximately 6,000 acres, including a valley 3,200 feet above sea level, which is surrounded by spectacular mountain peaks. Swimming pool, bathhouse, fishing, boating, hiking trails, 18-hole golf course, tennis courts, skiing, ice rink, playground, lodge, cabins, camping. Nature, recreation programs. Standard hours, fees.

### CANAAN VALLEY RESORT STATE PARK SKI AREA

*Highway 32, Davis, 304-866-4121, 800-622-4121; www.canaanresort.com*

Quad, two triple chairlifts, Pomalift; patrol, school, SKIwee program, rentals, snowmaking; restaurant, cafeteria, lodging, nursery; night skiing (Friday-Sunday). Twenty-two trails, 34 slopes; vertical drop 850 feet. December-March, daily. Eighteen miles of cross-country trails. Chairlift rides (early May-October, daily). Special programs for the disabled.

★
★
★
★
★

### TIMBERLINE FOUR SEASONS RESORT
*Highway 32, Davis, 304-866-4801, 800-766-9464; www.timberlineresort.com*
Triple, two double chairlifts; patrol, school, SKIwee program, rentals, snowmaking; restaurant, bar, nursery, lodging, night skiing and special events. Thirty-five slopes and trails; longest run two miles, vertical drop 1,000 feet (December-April, daily). Cross-country skiing. Chairlift rides (July-October, Saturday-Monday).

### WHITE GRASS TOURING CENTER
*Freeland Road, Davis, 304-866-4114; www.whitegrass.com*
Thirty-six miles of cross-country trails, some machine-groomed; patrol, school, rentals, snowfarming, telemark slopes; restaurant; guided tours. Late November-March, daily.

### WHITEWATER RAFTING
*200 Sycamore St., Davis, 800-225-5982; www.wvriversports.com*
Many outfitters offer guided trips on the Cheat River.

## SPECIAL EVENT
### TUCKER COUNTY ALPINE WINTER FESTIVAL
*William Avenue and Fourth Street, Davis, 304-866-4121; www.canaanresort.com*
Governor's Cup ski races. First weekend in March.

## HOTELS
### ★★ALPINE LODGE
*Williams Ave., Davis, 304-259-5245*

**552**

46 rooms. $

### ★★BLACKWATER LODGE
*County Route 29, Davis, 304-259-5216, 800-225-5982*
80 rooms. Children's activity center. $

### ★★CANAAN VALLEY RESORT AND CONFERENCE CENTER
*Highway 32, Davis, 304-866-4121, 800-622-4121; www.canaanresort.com*
256 rooms. Children's activity center. $

# DROOP

## WHAT TO SEE AND DO
### BEARTOWN STATE PARK
*Highway 219, Droop, 304-653-4254; www.beartownstatepark.com*
Approximately 110 acres of dense forest with unique rock formations created by erosion; a boardwalk with interpretive signs winds through the park.

### DROOP MOUNTAIN BATTLEFIELD STATE PARK
*Highway 219, Droop, 304-653-4254, 800-255-5982;*
*www.droopmountainbattlefield.com*
Encompasses approximately 285 acres where on November 6, 1863, Union forces under General William W. Averell defeated Confederates under General John Echols, destroying the last major rebel resistance in the state. Park features graves, breastworks and monuments. Hiking, picnic areas, playground. Museum. Battle reenactments (second week of October, every even year).

# ELKINS

Elkins was named for U.S. Senator Stephen B. Elkins, an aggressive politician and powerful industrial magnate who was secretary of war under Benjamin Harrison from 1888-1892. This town is in a coal and timber region and is also a railroad terminus and trade center. Some of the finest scenery in the state can be seen in and around Elkins.

*Information: Randolph County Convention & Visitors Bureau, 1035 N. Randolph Ave., Elkins, 304-636-2780, 800-422-3304; www.randolphcountywv.com*

## WHAT TO SEE AND DO

### BOWDEN NATIONAL FISH HATCHERY

*Route 33 (SR-55), Elkins, 304-637-0245; www.wvdnr.gov*

Produces brook, brown and rainbow trout for stocking in state and national forest streams; also striped bass for Chesapeake Bay restoration project. Hatchery (daily). Visitor center. Memorial Day-mid-October, daily.

## SENECA ROCKS

Serious rock climbers rate West Virginia's massive Seneca Rocks as one of the top East Coast destinations for their sport. More than 375 major mapped climbing routes ascend the sheer, slender rocks that thrust 900 feet above the North Fork River. On any nice day you are apt to see a half-dozen or more climbers laboriously pulling themselves, hand over hand, slowly up the wall. It might take them hours to get to the top. You can enjoy the same view from the summit, but without the effort.

A 1½ mile foot trail—rated only moderately difficult—zig-zags to the top. Heavily traveled and well-marked, it is a nonclimber's introduction to West Virginia's panoramic vistas. A notable West Virginia landmark, the dramatic rock formation is worth a visit simply as a scenic attraction. From the edge of the river, which tumbles in a fury of white water, a thickly forested ridge forms an imposing pedestal for the rocks. From this base, the twin towers form a rough, craggy wall with a knife's-edge point barely 15 feet wide.

Begin your ascent near the foot of the rocks at Seneca Rocks Discovery Center, a beautiful structure of stone and glass. Inside, exhibits detail the natural history of the rocks; outside, the deck is positioned for great views of the climbers. The hiker's trail to the top begins just across the river from the Discovery Center. It climbs steadily through shady woods. Sturdy benches are placed along the way if you need to rest. At several especially steep points, stone steps seem to stretch endlessly above, but that's only your imagination. From the summit overlooks, the view of the river-traced valley below is a generous reward for your pains. Give yourself an hour to reach the top, 30 minutes to enjoy your lofty perch, and another 30 minutes for the much easier descent. Afterward, cross the road for refreshments in the village of Seneca Rocks at Harper's Old Country Store, which looks much as it must have on its opening day in 1902.

**WEST VIRGINIA**

★
★
★
★
★

## SPRUCE KNOB/MONONGAHELA HIGH COUNTRY

In the big cities of the Mid-Atlantic, it's sometimes hard to believe that there is a vast and rugged mountain wilderness just to the west. You can find plenty of this unspoiled nature in West Virginia, where soaring mountain ridges stretch into the distance, interspersed with countless streams.

This one-day, 150-mile loop out of the pretty college town of Elkins takes you through some of the Mid-Atlantic's most scenic mountain terrain. The route crisscrosses 100,000-acre Spruce Knob-Seneca Rocks National Recreation Area in the Monongahela National Forest. From Elkins, take Highway 250 south through the national forest to Thornwood. Mile after mile, the road climbs and dips alongside splashing streams. At Thornwood, head north on Route 28 toward Riverton. Two miles south of Riverton, turn west (left) onto Forest Service Road 112 and follow the signs to Spruce Knob, about 15 miles. At an altitude of 4,861 feet, Spruce Knob is the state's loftiest mountain peak—although peak is not really an apt description. The summit is a broad plateau scattered with piles of age-smoothed rocks. A thin forest of red spruce, stunted by the strong and near-constant westerly winds, struggles for a foothold. This is one of the most remote and rugged areas of the Mid-Atlantic that can be reached in a passenger sedan. A rock-lined trail leads to the Observation Tower, a three-story stone structure that boosts sightseers above the trees for a majestic 360-degree panorama.

Return to Route 28 and continue north to Seneca Rocks, a slender 900-foot-high forested ridge favored by rock climbers. You can watch them from the Discovery Center or take the easier 1½-mile trail to the summit. Pause for snacks or lunch at Harper's Old Country Store. To continue, head west on Route 55 to Harmon and pick up Route 32 north to Davis. The road passes alongside 6,000-acre Canaan Valley Resort State Park, where you can stop to hike, bicycle or go for a swim in the outdoor pool. A year-round resort, the park operates a downhill skiing complex. In summer, the chairlift will carry you to the top for grand views. About 15 miles long and three miles wide, the valley is situated at an altitude of 3,200 feet, which all but guarantees moderate summer temperatures.

Just to the north, the town of Davis has become a major center for mountain biking, mostly on abandoned U.S. Forest Service roads. Outfitters offer rentals and maps. On the edge of Davis, turn left into Blackwater Falls State Park, a rumpled expanse of woodland ridges and valleys cut by the Blackwater River's impressively deep canyon. Motorists approach the park's 55-room lodge on a long, winding road that carries them deeper and deeper into the forest. Suddenly a clearing appears, revealing the lodge on the edge of the canyon. Visitors can view Blackwater Falls' 65-foot plunge from the canyon rim just upriver from the lodge or descend 214 steps to its base. In summer, the beach at little Pendleton Lake makes a refreshing rest stop. Continue north two miles to Thomas, an old mining town built in a double tier on a mountainside, and then return to Elkins on Highway 219 south, approximately 150 miles.

★
★
★
★
★

## SPECIAL EVENTS

### AUGUSTA FESTIVAL

*100 Campus Drive, Elkins, 304-637-1209; www.augustaheritage.com*

Celebration of traditional folk life and arts, featuring local and national performers, dances, juried craft fair, storytelling sessions, children's activities and homemade foods. Mid-August.

### MOUNTAIN STATE FOREST FESTIVAL

*101 Lough St., Elkins, 304-636-1824; www.forestfestival.com*

Queen Silvia is crowned; carnival, parades, entertainment, tilting at rings on horseback, sawing and wood-chopping contests, championship fiddle and banjo contest, juried craft fair and art exhibit. Late September-early October.

## HOTELS

### ★★ELKINS MOTOR LODGE

*830 Harrison Ave., Elkins, 304-636-1400, 877-636-1863; www.elkinsmotorlodge.com*

55 rooms. Airport transportation available. **$**

### ★SUPER 8

*350 Beverly Pike, Elkins, 304-636-6500, 800-800-8000;*
*www.super8.com*

44 rooms. Complimentary continental breakfast. **$**

## RESTAURANT

### ★★CHEAT RIVER INN

*Highway 33 East, Elkins, 304-636-2301; www.cheatriverlodge.com*

Dinner. Closed Monday. Bar. Children's menu. Outdoor seating. **$$**

# FAIRMONT

Fairmont was a Union supply depot plundered by Confederate cavalry in April 1863. General William Ezra Jones's division swept through town, took 260 prisoners, destroyed the $500,000 bridge across the Monongahela River and raided the governor's residence. After the war, resources in the region were developed and coal became the mainstay. Today, Fairmont manufactures aluminum, mine machinery and other products.

*Information: Convention & Visitors Bureau of Marion County, 110 Adams St., Fairmont, 304-368-1123, 800-834-7365; www.marioncvb.com*

## WHAT TO SEE AND DO

### FAIRMONT STATE COLLEGE

*1201 Locust Ave., Fairmont, 304-367-4892, 800-641-5678; www.fairmontstate.edu*

The college, which was founded in 1867 and is now home to 7,000 students, features on campus a one-room schoolhouse with original desks, books and other artifacts related to the early era of education. April-October, schedule varies.

### MARION COUNTY MUSEUM

*200 Jackson St., Fairmont, 304-367-5398; www.marionhistorical.org*

Displays of B & O china; five furnished rooms covering 1776-1920s; doll, train and toy collection. Monday-Friday 10 a.m.-2 p.m., Saturdays Memorial Day-Labor Day.

★
★
★
★
★

### PRICKETT'S FORT STATE PARK

*Route 3, Fairmont, 304-363-3030, 800-225-5982; www.prickettsforststatepark.com*

Approximately 200 acres with a reconstructed 18th-century log fort, colonial trade and lifestyle demonstrations by costumed interpreters, outdoor historical drama (July, Wednesday-Saturday). Boating (ramps); picnicking. Visitor center. Fort and museum (mid-April-October, daily). Museum (fee).

## SPECIAL EVENT
### THREE RIVERS FESTIVAL

*110 Adams St., Fairmont, 304-363-2625*

Entertainment, parade, Civil War re-enactment, carnival, games. Third weekend in May.

## HOTELS
### ★COMFORT INN

*1185 Airport Road, Fairmont, 304-367-1370, 877-424-6423; www.choicehotels.com*

85 rooms. Complimentary continental breakfast. $

### ★★HOLIDAY INN

*930 E. Grafton, Fairmont, 304-366-5500, 800-315-2621;*
*www.holidayinn.com/fairmontwv*

106 rooms. $

## RESTAURANT
### ★★MURIALE'S

*1742 Fairmont Ave., Fairmont, 304-363-3190; www.murialesrestaurant.com*

Italian menu. Lunch, dinner. Bar. Children's menu. Casual attire. Outdoor seating. $$

# FRANKLIN

*Information: Franklin Chamber of Commerce, Franklin, 304-358-7068;*
*www.visitpendleton.com*

## SPECIAL EVENT
### TREASURE MOUNTAIN FESTIVAL

*Franklin, 304-249-5117; www.tmf.squarespace.com*

Square dancing, clogging; parade, gospel and mountain music, drama; rifle-demonstration, cross-cut sawing contest; children's contests, games; trail rides craft exhibits, country food. Third weekend in September.

# GAULEY BRIDGE

This town, at the junction of the New and Gauley rivers, was the key to the Kanawha Valley during the Civil War. In November 1861, Union General W.S. Rosecrans defeated Confederate General John B. Floyd, a victory that assured Union control of western Virginia. Stone piers of the old bridge, which was destroyed by retreating Confederates in 1861, can be seen near the present bridge.

*Information: Upper Kanawha Valley Chamber of Commerce, Montgomery,*
*304-442-5756*

## WHAT TO SEE AND DO
### WHITEWATER RAFTING
*Gauley Bridge, 800-225-5982*
Many outfitters offer guided trips on the New and Gauley rivers.

## SPECIAL EVENT
### BRIDGE DAY
*Gauley Bridge, 304-465-5617, 800-928-0263; www.officialbridgeday.com*
Parachutists test their skills by jumping off the bridge and floating to the bottom of the gorge. Bridge is open to pedestrians. Third Saturday in October.

# GLEN JEAN

## WHAT TO SEE AND DO
### GAULEY RIVER NATIONAL RECREATION AREA
*104 Main St., Glen Jean, 304-465-0508; www.nps.gov/gari/index.htm*
Designated a federally protected area in October 1988, the 25-mile stretch of the Gauley from the Summersville Dam west to just above the town of Swiss is famous for whitewater rafting. There are no developed sites. Large tracts of land along the river are privately owned.

### GRANDVIEW UNIT OF NEW RIVER GORGE NATIONAL RIVER
*246 Glen Jean, 304-763-3715; www.4uth.gov*
Nearly 900 wooded acres at the northern end of the New River Gorge National River area; offers spectacular overlooks of New River Gorge and Horseshoe Bend; rhododendron gardens. Hiking trails, game courts (some fees), cross-country skiing, picnicking, playgrounds and concession. Outdoor dramas June-Labor Day, Tuesday-Sunday.

### NEW RIVER GORGE NATIONAL RIVER
*104 Main St., Glen Jean, 304-465-0508; www.nps.gov/neri*
One of the oldest rivers on the continent, the New River rushes northward through a deep canyon with spectacular scenery. The 52-mile section from Hinton to Fayetteville is popular among outdoor enthusiasts, especially whitewater rafters and hikers. The Hinton Visitor Center is located along the river at Highway 3 Bypass (Memorial Day-Labor Day, daily); 304-466-0417. A year-round visitor center is located on Highway 19 near the New River Gorge Bridge.

★
★
★
★
★

# GRAFTON
Mother's Day originated in Grafton in 1908 when Anna Jarvis observed the anniversary of her mother's death during a religious service. The idea caught on nationally, and in 1914 President Woodrow Wilson issued a proclamation urging nationwide observance. The International Shrine to Motherhood in the original Mother's Day church is located at 11 E. Main Street.

During the Civil War, Grafton was an important railroad center and 4,000 Union troops camped here before the Battle of Philippi in 1861. General McClellan also had his headquarters in the town. The first land soldier killed in the war, T. Bailey Brown, fell at Grafton and is buried in the Grafton National Cemetery.

*Information: Grafton-Taylor County Convention and Visitors Bureau,*
*214 W. Main St., Grafton, 304-265-1589, 800-225-5982;*
*www.graftonrecruitment.com*

## WHAT TO SEE AND DO
### TYGART LAKE STATE PARK
*Grafton, 304-265-3383, 800-225-5982; www.tygertlake.com*
This scenic 2,100-acre park contains one of the largest concrete dams east of the Mississippi (1,900 feet by 209 feet). Swimming, waterskiing, fishing, boating (ramp, rentals, marina); hiking, game courts, picnic area, playground, concession, lodge, tent and trailer camping, 10 cabins. Nature and recreation programs, dam tours (summer, 304-265-1760).

## SPECIAL EVENT
### TAYLOR COUNTY FAIR
*Fairgrounds, Highway 50, Grafton, 304-265-3303; www.taylorcountyfair.net*
Horse racing, livestock shows, auctions, carnival, crafts. Last week of July.

## HOTEL
### ★★TYGART LAKE STATE PARK LODGE
*Highway 1, Grafton, 304-265-6144, 800-225-5982; www.tygartlake.com*
20 rooms. Closed January-mid April. $

# HARPERS FERRY

**WEST VIRGINIA**

★
★★
★★★
★★★★
★★★★★

Scene of abolitionist John Brown's raid in 1859, Harpers Ferry is at the junction of the Shenandoah and Potomac rivers, where West Virginia, Virginia and Maryland meet. A U.S. armory and rifle factory made this an important town in early Virginia, and John Brown had this in mind when he began his insurrection. He and 16 other men seized the armory and arsenal the night of Oct. 16 and took refuge in the engine house when attacked by local militia. On the morning of Oct. 18, the engine house was stormed, and Brown was captured by 90 marines from Washington under Brevet Colonel Robert E. Lee and Lt. J.E.B. Stuart. Ten of Brown's men were killed, including two of his sons. He was hanged in nearby Charles Town for treason, murder and inciting slaves to rebellion.

When war broke out, Harpers Ferry was a strategic objective for the Confederacy, which considered it the key to Washington. The town changed hands many times in the war, during which many buildings were damaged. In 1944, Congress authorized a national monument here, setting aside 1,500 acres for that purpose. In 1963, the same area was designated a National Historical Park, now occupying more than 2,200 acres.

*Information: Jefferson County Chamber of Commerce, Box 426, Charles Town,*
*304-725-2055, 800-624-0577; www.jeffersoncounty.com/index.html*

## WHAT TO SEE AND DO
### CAMP HILL
*Shenandoah and High streets, Harpers Ferry*
Four restored, private houses built 1832-1850.

## HARPER HOUSE

*Shenandoah and High streets, Harpers Ferry*

Three-story stone house built between 1775 and 1782 by the founder of the town; both George Washington and Thomas Jefferson were entertained as overnight guests. Restored and furnished with period pieces.

## HARPERS FERRY NATIONAL HISTORICAL PARK

*Shenandoah and High streets, Harpers Ferry, 304-535-6029; www.nps.gov/hafe*

The old town has been restored to its 19th-century appearance; exhibits and interpretive presentations explore the park's relation to the water-power industry, the Civil War, abolitionist John Brown and Storer College, a school established for freed slaves after the war. A visitor center is located just off Highway 340. Visitors should park there, a bus will take them to Lower Town. Daily.

## JEFFERSON'S ROCK

*Harpers Ferry*

From here Thomas Jefferson, in 1783, pronounced the view to be "one of the most stupendous scenes in nature."

## JOHN BROWN WAX MUSEUM

*168 High St., Harpers Ferry, 304-535-6342; www.johnbrownwaxmuseum.com*

This museum contains an exhibit and film on John Brown, and a 10-minute slide presentation on the history of the park. To the right of the museum is High Street, which has two Civil War museums and two black history museums. Daily.

## JOHN BROWN'S FORT

*Shenandoah and High streets, Harpers Ferry*

Where John Brown made his last stand; rebuilt and moved near original site.

## LOCKWOOD HOUSE

*Harpers Ferry*

Greek Revival house built in 1848 was used as headquarters, barracks and stable during Civil War; later used as a classroom building by Storer College, which was founded to educate freed men after the war.

## RUINS OF ST. JOHN'S EPISCOPAL CHURCH

*Harpers Ferry*

Used as a guardhouse and hospital during the Civil War.

## THE POINT

*Shenandoah and High streets, Harpers Ferry*

Three states—West Virginia, Virginia and Maryland—and two rivers, the Shenandoah and Potomac, meet at the Blue Ridge Mountains.

## WHITEWATER RAFTING

*Harpers Ferry, 800-225-5982; www.wvtourism.com*

Many outfitters offer guided trips on the Shenandoah and Potomac rivers.

**WEST VIRGINIA**

★
★
★
★
★

## SPECIAL EVENTS

### ELECTION DAY 1860
*Shenandoah Street, Harpers Ferry, 304-535-6298; www.nps.gov*
More than 100 people in 19th-century attire reenact the 1860 presidential election. Second Saturday in October.

### MOUNTAIN HERITAGE ARTS AND CRAFTS FESTIVAL
*102 Frontage Road, Harpers Ferry, 304-725-2055, 800-624-0577;*
*www.jeffersoncounty.com*
More than 190 craftspeople and artisans demonstrate quilting, wool spinning, pottery throwing, vegetable dyeing and other crafts; concerts. Second full weekend in June and last full weekend in September.

### OLD TYME CHRISTMAS
*Harpers Ferry, 304-925-8019; www.historicharpersferry.com*
Caroling, musical programs, children's programs, taffy pull, candlelight walk. First two weekends in December.

## HOTEL

### ★COMFORT INN
*Route 340 and Union Street, Harpers Ferry, 304-535-6391, 877-424-6423;*
*www.comfortinn.com*
50 rooms. Complimentary continental breakfast. **$**

# HILLSBORO

Civil War troops marched through Hillsboro, and Confederates camped in town before the decisive Battle of Droop Mountain. Novelist Pearl S. Buck was born in her grandparents' house here while her parents, missionaries on leave from China, were visiting.
*Information: West Virginia Mountain Highlands, Elkins, 304-636-8400;*
*www.mountainhighlands.com*

## WHAT TO SEE AND DO

### PEARL S. BUCK BIRTHPLACE MUSEUM
*Route 219, Hillsboro, 304-653-4430; www.pearlsbuckbirthplace.com*
The Stulting House is the birthplace of the Pulitzer and Nobel Prize-winning novelist, restored to its 1892 appearance; original and period furniture; memorabilia. Sydenstricker House, home of Buck's father and his ancestors, was moved 40 miles from its original site and restored here. Guided tours. May-November, Monday-Saturday 9 a.m.-4 p.m.

### WATOGA STATE PARK
*HC 82, Marlinton, 304-799-4087, 800-225-5982; www.watoga.com*
More than 10,100 acres make this West Virginia's largest state park. Watoga, derived from the Cherokee term "watauga," means "river of islands." It aptly describes the Greenbrier River, which forms several miles of the park's boundary. Swimming pool, bathhouses, fishing, boating on 11-acre Watoga Lake (rentals); hiking and bridle trails, horseback riding, tennis, game courts, cross-country skiing, picnicking, playground, concession, restaurant (seasonal), tent and trailer camping, 33 cabins. Brooks Memorial Arboretum; nature, recreation programs (summer).

**CALVIN PRICE STATE FOREST**

*Highway 39 and Beaver's Creek Road, Hillsboro, 304-799-4087*

This vast, undeveloped forest has more than 9,400 acres for fishing; deer and small-game hunting, hiking and primitive camping (fee).

# HINTON

This railroad town on the banks of the New River is the seat of Summers County, where the Bluestone and Greenbrier rivers join the scenic and protected New River.

*Information: Summers County Chamber of Commerce, 200 Ballangee St., Hinton, 304-466-5332; www.summerscounty.net*

## WHAT TO SEE AND DO

### BLUESTONE STATE PARK

*Highway 20, HC 78, Box 3, Hinton, 304-466-2805; www.bluestonesp.com*

More than 2,100 acres on Bluestone Lake, which was created by the Bluestone Dam. Swimming pool (Memorial Day-Labor Day), wading pool, bathhouses, waterskiing, fishing, boating (ramps, marina nearby; canoe, rowboat and motorboat rentals); hiking trails, game courts, picnicking, playground, tent and trailer camping (dump station), 25 cabins. Nature, recreation programs (summer). Gift shop. Standard hours, fees.

### PIPESTEM RESORT STATE PARK

*Hinton, 304-466-1800, 800-225-5982; www.pipestemresort.com*

More than 4,000 acres with 3,600-foot aerial tramway to Bluestone River complex. Swimming, bathhouses, fishing, canoeing, paddle-boating; hiking trails, horseback-riding, 9- and 18-hole golf courses, miniature golf, tennis, archery, lighted game courts, cross-country skiing, sledding, playground, two lodges, four restaurants, tent and trailer camping (dump station), 25 cabins. Visitor center; nature, recreation programs. Aerial tramway, arboretum, observation tower. Amphitheater; dances.

## RESTAURANT

### ★KIRK'S

*215 Main St., Hinton, 304-466-4600*

American menu. Breakfast, lunch, dinner. Casual attire. Outdoor seating. $

# HUNTINGTON

The millionaire president of the Chesapeake and Ohio Railroad, Collis P. Huntington, founded this city and named it for himself. Originally a rail and river terminus, commerce and industry have made it the second-largest city in the state. Thoroughly planned and meticulously laid out, Huntington is protected from the Ohio River by an 11-mile floodwall equipped with 17 pumping stations and 45 gates. Glass, railroad products and metals are important city industries.

*Information: Cabell-Huntington Convention & Visitors Bureau, Huntington, 304-525-7333, 800-635-6329; www.wvvisit.org*

**WEST VIRGINIA**

★
★
★
★
★

## WHAT TO SEE AND DO

### BEECH FORK STATE PARK

*5601 Longbranch Road, Huntington, 304-528-5794, 800-225-5982;*
*www.beechforksp.com*

Nearly 4,000 acres on 720-acre Beech Fork Lake. Fishing, boating (ramp, marina); hiking trails, physical fitness trail, tennis, game courts, picnicking, camping. Store. Visitor center; nature, recreation programs (summer). Meeting rooms.

### CAMDEN PARK

*Highway 60 East, Huntington, 304-429-4231, 866-822-6336; www.camdenpark.com*

Amusement park with 27 rides, games, concessions; boat and train rides, log flume, miniature golf, roller rink, picnicking. Rides individually priced; also unlimited ride plan. Mid-April-Memorial Day, Saturday-Sunday; Memorial Day-Labor Day, Tuesday-Sunday.

### HERITAGE FARM MUSEUM & VILLAGE

*3300 Harvey Road, Huntington, 304-522-1244; www.heritagefarmmuseum.com*

Tours of Museum of Progress, Museum of Transportation and Country Store Museum. Restored Victorian B & O Railroad yard surrounding brick courtyard. Restaurant in original 1887 passenger station, restored Pullman car, shops in renovated freight and box cars, warehouses. Monday-Saturday.

### HUNTINGTON MUSEUM OF ART

*2033 McCoy Road, Huntington, 304-529-2701; www.hmoa.org*

Museum with American and European paintings, prints and sculpture; Herman P. Dean Firearms Collection; Georgian silver; Asian prayer rugs; pre-Columbian art; Appalachian folk art; Ohio Valley historical and contemporary glass. Complex includes exhibition galleries, library, studio workshops, amphitheater, auditorium, sculpture garden, observatory, art gallery for young people, nature trails.

## HOTEL

### ★DAYS INN

*5196 Route 60 East, Huntington, 304-733-4477; www.daysinn.com*

153 rooms. Complimentary continental breakfast. High-speed Internet access. $

# LEWISBURG

At the junction of two important Native American trails, the Seneca (now Highway 219) and the Kanawha (now Highway 60), Lewisburg was the site of colonial forts as well as a Civil War battle. The town's 236-acre historic district has more than 60 buildings from the 18th and 19th centuries in a variety of architectural styles.

*Information: Greenbrier County Convention & Visitors Center, 540 N. Jefferson St.,*
*Lewisburg, 304-645-1000, 800-833-2068; www.greenbrierwv.com*

## WHAT TO SEE AND DO

### LOST WORLD CAVERNS

*Fairview Road, Lewisburg, 304-645-6677, 866-228-3778; www.lostworldcaverns.com*

Scenic trail over subterranean rock mountain; prehistoric ocean floor; stalagmites, stalactites; flow stone, ribbons, hex stones. Self-guided tours (daily).

### NORTH HOUSE MUSEUM

*301 W. Washington St., Lewisburg, 304-645-3398*

Colonial and 19th-century objects and artifacts. Monday-Saturday.

### OLD STONE PRESBYTERIAN CHURCH

*200 Church St., Lewisburg, 304-645-2676; www.oldstonechurchwv.com*

Original log church was replaced by present native limestone structure. Daily.

## HOTELS

### ★★BRIER INN & CONFERENCE CENTER

*540 N. Jefferson St., Lewisburg, 304-645-7722; www.brierinn.com*

162 rooms. Complimentary full breakfast. Wireless Internet access. Airport transportation available. Pets accepted. $

### ★★★GENERAL LEWIS INN

*301 E. Washington St., Lewisburg, 304-645-2600, 800-628-4454;*
*www.generallewisinn.com*

Operating as a guest house since 1928, this bed and breakfast was built in the early 1800s. It is surrounded by flower gardens and lawns with a lily pond. Every room is furnished with antiques and crafts made by early settlers. 25 rooms. Children not allowed. Restaurant. $

# MARLINTON

Marlinton is the seat of Pocahontas County, an area known for its wide variety of outdoor recreational opportunities. A Ranger District office of the Monongahela National Forest is located in the town.

*Information: West Virginia Mountain Highlands, Elkins, 304-636-8400;*
*www.mountainhighlands.com*

## WHAT TO SEE AND DO

### CRANBERRY GLADES

*Highway 150 and Highway 39-55, Marlinton, 304-653-4826; www.fs.fed.us*

A USDA Forest Service botanical area. Approximately 750 acres featuring open bog fringed by forest and alder thicket. Boardwalk with interpretive signs. Guided tours leave from visitor center (June-Labor Day, weekends). Glades (year-round, weather permitting).

### CRANBERRY MOUNTAIN VISITOR CENTER-MONONGAHELA NATIONAL FOREST

*Highway 150 and Highway 39/55, Marlinton, 304-653-4826, 800-336-7009*

Exhibits, videos and publications on conservation and forest management. April-November, daily.

★
★
★
★
★

### GREENBRIER RIVER TRAIL

*Highway 39 and Beaver's Creek Road, Marlinton, 304-799-4087;*
*www.greenbrierrailtrailstatepark.com*

Part of the state park system, this 76-mile trail runs along the Greenbrier River from the town of Cass, on the north, through Marlinton to North Caldwell on the south; passes through small towns, over 35 bridges, and through two tunnels. Originally the trail was part of the Chesapeake & Ohio Railroad. Activities include backpacking, bicycling and cross-country skiing; trail also provides access for fishing and canoeing. No developed sites.

### POCAHONTAS COUNTY HISTORICAL MUSEUM

*810 Second Ave., Marlinton, 304-799-6659; www.pocahontas.org*

Displays on history of the county from its beginning to present. Extensive photo collection. Early June-Labor Day, daily.

### SENECA STATE FOREST

*Route 1, Dunmore, 304-799-6213, 800-255-5982; www.senecastateforest.com*

Approximately 12,000 acres with fishing and boating on a 4-acre lake; hunting, hiking trails, picnicking, playground. Camping, eight rustic cabins.

### SPECIAL EVENT
### PIONEER DAYS

*900 Ninth St., Marlinton, 304-799-4315, 800-336-7009*

Craft exhibits and demonstrations; horse-pulling contests, frog and turtle races; bluegrass and mountain music shows; 4 × 4 truck pulling; parade; antique car show. Early-mid-July.

# MARTINSBURG

Martinsburg is located in the center of an apple- and peach-producing region in the state's eastern panhandle. Because of its strategic location at the entrance to the Shenandoah Valley, the town was the site of several battles during the Civil War. The famous Confederate spy Belle Boyd was a resident. Officially chartered in 1778, Martinsburg is recognized for the preservation of its many 18th- and 19th-century houses, along with its mercantile and industrial buildings.

*Information: Martinsburg-Berkeley County Chamber of Commerce, 198 Viking Way,*
*Martinsburg, 304-267-4841, 800-332-9007; www.berkeleycounty.org*

## WHAT TO SEE AND DO
### GENERAL ADAM STEPHEN HOUSE

*309 E. John St., Martinsburg, 304-267-4434; www.museumsofwv.org*

Restored residence of Revolutionary War soldier and surgeon Adam Stephen, founder of Martinsburg. Period furnishings; restored smokehouse and log building. May-October, Saturday-Sunday limited hours; also by appointment.

### TRIPLE BRICK BUILDING

*309 E. John St., Martinsburg, 304-267-4434; www.martinsburg.com*

Completed in three sections just after the Civil War, the structure was used to house railroad employees. A museum of local history is located on the top two floors. May-October, Saturday-Sunday limited hours; also by appointment.

## MOUNTAIN STATE APPLE HARVEST FESTIVAL

*Martinsburg, 304-263-2500; www.msahf.com*

Parade, celebrity breakfast, contests, entertainment, Apple Queen coronation, square dancing, grand ball, arts and crafts show. Third weekend in October.

## HOTELS
### ★COMFORT INN AIKENS CENTER

*1872 Edwin Miller Blvd., Martinsburg, 304-263-6200, 877-424-6423;*
*www.choicehotels.com*

109 rooms. Complimentary continental breakfast. High-speed Internet access. Airport transportation available. **$**

### ★★HOLIDAY INN

*301 Foxcroft Ave., Martinsburg, 304-267-5500, 800-315-2621;*
*www.holidayinn.com/martinsburgwv*

120 rooms. Pets accepted. Indoor pool. **$**

# MATEWAN

This tiny hamlet was the site of the famous feud between the West Virginia Hatfields and the Kentucky McCoys. On Election Day, August 7, 1882, three McCoy sons stabbed and shot Ellison Hatfield. Devil Anse Hatfield avenged his brother by executing the three McCoys. Soon Kentucky bounty hunters made raids into West Virginia to capture the Hatfieds, who retaliated in 1888 by attacking a McCoy homestead. By 1890, the killings had ended but the feud continued to be sensationalized. In 1920, Matewan was the scene of a shootout between union organizers and coal company operators that left 10 dead, including the mayor.

*Tug Valley Chamber of Commerce, 304-235-5240; www.matewan.com*

# MORGANTOWN

Morgantown is both an educational and an industrial center. West Virginia University was founded here in 1867, and the Morgantown Female Collegiate Institute in 1839. Known internationally for its glass, Morgantown is home to a number of glass plants, which produce wares ranging from lamp parts to decorative paper weights and crystal tableware. The town is also home to a number of research laboratories maintained by the federal government.

*Information: Greater Morgantown Convention & Visitors Bureau, 68 Donley St.,*
*Morgantown, 800-458-7373; www.visitmorgantown.com*

## WHAT TO SEE AND DO
### COOPERS ROCK STATE FOREST

*Route 1, Morgantown, 304-594-1561; www.coopersrockstateforest.com*

More than 12,700 acres. Trout fishing; hunting, hiking trails to historical sites; Henry Clay iron furnace. Cross-country ski trails, picnicking, playground, concession, tent and trailer camping.

565

**WEST VIRGINIA**

★
★
★
★
★

### CHESTNUT RIDGE REGIONAL PARK

*Sand Springs Road, Bruceton Mills, 304-594-1773; www.chestnutridgepark.com*

Swimming beach, fishing; tent and trailer camping, rustic cabins, lodge (fees), hiking, picnicking, cross-country ski trails (December-February). Nature center. Park (daily).

### WEST VIRGINIA UNIVERSITY

*Visitors Resource Center, 1 Waterfront Place, Morgantown, 304-293-0111;*
*www.wvu.edu*

The university, which was founded in 1867, has more than 22,000 students attending its 15 colleges. Tours (Monday-Saturday; for reservations 304-293-3489). The Visitors Center in the Communications Building on Patterson Drive has touch-screen monitors and video presentations about the university and upcoming special events (304-293-6692 for 24-hour event information). Of special interest on the downtown campus are Stewart Hall and the university's original buildings, located on Woodburn Circle. In the Evansdale area of Morgantown are the Creative Arts Center, the 75-acre Core Arboretum and the 63,500-seat Coliseum.

### COOK-HAYMAN PHARMACY MUSEUM

*1 Medical Drive, Morgantown, 304-293-5101; www.hsc.wvu.edu*

Recreates pharmacy of yesteryear with old patent medicines. Monday-Friday; weekends by request.

### PERSONAL RAPID TRANSIT SYSTEM

*88 Beechhurst Ave., Morgantown, 304-293-5011*

A pioneering transit system, the PRT is the world's first totally automated system. Operating without conductors or ticket takers, computer-directed cars travel between university campuses and downtown Morgantown. Monday-Saturday; may not operate holidays and university breaks.

## SPECIAL EVENTS
### MASON-DIXON FESTIVAL

*Morgantown Riverfront Park, Morgantown, 304-599-1104; www.masondixonfestival.org*

River parade. Boat races. Arts and crafts. Concessions. Mid-September.

### MOUNTAINEER BALLOON FESTIVAL

*Morgantown Municipal Airport, 100 Hart Field Road, Morgantown, 304-296-8356;*
*www.mountaineerballoonfestival.com*

Hot air balloon races. Carnival. Music. Food. Mid-October.

## HOTELS
### ★CLARION HOTEL

*127 High St., Morgantown, 304-292-8200, 877-424-6423;*
*www.clarionhotelmorgan.com*

76 rooms. Complimentary continental breakfast. Fitness center. **$**

### ★COMFORT INN

*225 Comfort Inn Drive, Morgantown, 304-296-9364, 877-424-6423;*
*www.choicehotels.com*
80 rooms. Complimentary continental breakfast. High-speed Internet access. Pool. **$**

### ★HAMPTON INN

*1053 Van Voorhis Road, Morgantown, 304-599-1200, 800-486-7866;*
*www.hamptoninn.com*
107 rooms. Complimentary continental breakfast. High-speed Internet access. **$**

### ★★★LAKEVIEW GOLF RESORT & SPA

*1 Lakeview Drive, Morgantown, 304-594-1111, 800-624-8300;*
*www.lakeviewresort.com*
The Lakeview Golf Resort & Spa offers more than just driving ranges and putting greens. Located in the foothills of the Allegheny Mountains, this resort offers comfortable and well-sized guest rooms, conference and meeting space, event space, a fitness center and several dining and recreation options. There's also a spa on the premises. 187 rooms. Children's activity center. Airport transportation available. Tennis. Spa. Restaurant. **$**

### ★★QUALITY INN

*1400 Saratoga Ave., Morgantown, 304-599-1680, 877-424-6423;*
*www.choicehotels.com*
147 rooms.accepted. Complimentary continental breakfast. Pool. Pets accepted. **$**

## RESTAURANTS
### ★★BACK BAY

*1869 Mileground, Morgantown, 304-296-3027; www.backbay.com*
Seafood menu. Lunch, dinner. Bar. Children's menu. Casual attire. Outdoor seating. **$$**

### ★PUGLIONI'S

*1137 Van Voorhis Road, Morgantown, 304-599-7521*
Italian menu. Lunch, dinner. Bar. Children's menu. Casual attire. **$$**

# PARKERSBURG

After the Revolutionary War, Blennerhassett Island, in the Ohio River west of Parkersburg, was the scene of the alleged Burr-Blennerhassett plot. Harman Blennerhassett, a wealthy Irishman, built a lavish mansion on this island. After killing Alexander Hamilton in a duel, Aaron Burr came to the island, allegedly to seize the Southwest and set up an empire; Blennerhassett may have agreed to join him. On December 10, 1806, the plot was uncovered. Both men were acquitted of treason but ruined financially in the process. The Blennerhassett mansion burned in 1811 but was later rebuilt.

Today, Parkersburg is the center for many industries, including glass, chemicals, petrochemicals and ferrous and other metals. Fishing is popular in the area, especially below the Belleville and Willow Island locks and dams on the Ohio River.

*Information: Parkersburg/Wood Co. Convention & Visitor's Bureau, 350 Seventh St., Parkersburg, 304-428-1130, 800-752-4982; www.parkersburgcvb.org*

**WEST VIRGINIA**

## WHAT TO SEE AND DO
### ACTORS GUILD PLAYHOUSE
*724 Market St., Parkersburg, 304-485-1300; www.actorsguildonline.com*
Musical, comedic and dramatic performances. Friday-Sunday.

### BLENNERHASSETT ISLAND HISTORICAL STATE PARK
*137 Juliana St., Parkersburg, 304-420-4800, 800-225-5982;*
*www.blennerhassettislandpark.com*
A 500-acre island accessible only by sternwheeler. There are self-guided walking tours of the island, horse-drawn wagon rides and tours of the Blennerhassett mansion. Bicycle rentals, picnicking, concessions. Tickets are available for the boat ride at the Blennerhassett Museum. May-Labor Day, Tuesday-Sunday; September-October, Thursday-Sunday.

### BLENNERHASSETT MUSEUM
*Second and Juliana streets, Parkersburg, 304-420-4840;*
*www.blennerhassettislandpark.com*
Features archaeological and other exhibits relating to history of Blennerhassett Island and Parkersburg area; includes artifacts dating back 12,000 years. Theater with video presentation. May-October, Tuesday-Sunday; November-April, Saturday-Sunday.

### CITY PARK
*Park Avenue and 23rd Street, Parkersburg, 304-424-8400; parkersburg-wv.com*
A 55-acre wooded area with the Cooper Log Cabin Museum, which dates from 1804. Swimming pool, fishing, paddleboats; miniature golf, tennis, shelters and picnic facilities.

### NORTH BEND STATE PARK
*Route 1, Parkersburg, 304-643-2931, 800-225-5982; www.northbendsp.com*
Approximately 1,400 acres in the wide valley of the North Fork of the Hughes River; scenic overlooks of famous horseshoe bend. Swimming pool, bathhouse, fishing; miniature golf, tennis, game courts; hiking, bicycle and bridle trail; 71-mile North Bend Rail Trail. Picnicking, playground, concession, restaurant, lodge, tent and trailer camping, skiing, eight cabins. Nature, recreation programs. Nature trail for disabled.

### PARKERSBURG ART CENTER
*725 Market St., Parkersburg, 304-485-3859; parkersburgartcenter.org*
Changing exhibits. Wednesday-Saturday 10 a.m.-5 p.m.

### RUBLES STERNWHEELERS RIVERBOAT CRUISES
*Second and Ann streets, Parkersburg, 740-423-7268; www.greaterparkersburg.com*
Public and private riverboat cruises. May-October, daily.

## SPECIAL EVENTS
### PARKERSBURG HOMECOMING
*Point Park, Second and Avery streets, Parkersburg, 304-422-9970;*
*www.parkersburg-homecoming.com*
Riverfront celebration features entertainment, parade, sternwheeler races, waterskiing show, miniature car races, fireworks. Third weekend in August.

★
★ ★
★ ★ ★
★ ★
★

**WEST VIRGINIA HONEY FESTIVAL**

*4-H Grounds, Parkersburg, 304-424-1960*

Honey-related exhibits. Baking. Food. Arts and crafts. Mid-September.

## HOTELS

### ★★★BLENNERHASSETT HOTEL

*320 Market St., Parkersburg, 304-422-3131, 800-262-2536;*
*www.theblennerhassett.com*

This landmark hotel was built before the turn of the century in the "gaslight era" and was fully restored in 1986. The hotel's Victorian style is evident in the rich crown molding, authentic English doors, brass and leaded-glass chandeliers and antiques. 94 rooms. Pets accepted. High-speed Internet access. **$**

### ★ECONO LODGE PARKERSBURG

*1954 E. Seventh St., Parkersburg, 304-428-7500, 800-424-6423;*
*www.econolodge.com*

63 rooms. Pets accepted. Complimentary continental breakfast. **$**

### ★HAMPTON INN

*64 Elizabeth Drive, Parkersburg, 304-489-2900, 800-426-7866; www.hamptoninn.com*

68 rooms. Complimentary continental breakfast. High-speed Internet access. Pool. **$**

## RESTAURANTS

### ★MOUNTAINEER FAMILY RESTAURANT

*4006 E. Seventh St., Parkersburg, 304-422-0101*

American menu. Breakfast, lunch, dinner, late-night. Children's menu. Casual attire. **$**

### ★★★SPATS AT THE BLENNERHASSETT

*320 Market St., Parkersburg, 304-422-3131, 800-262-2536;*
*www.theblennerhassett.com*

Its downtown location makes Blennerhassett a great place to stop for a lunch break, and its continental menu makes it easy for everyone to find something to eat. The restaurant features dark wood ceilings, crown molding, wainscoting and leather arm-chairs. A charming garden patio area includes a bar, a dining area, a music stage and a large screen for sporting events. The restaurant also features a martini night, wine tastings and live music. Continental menu. Breakfast, lunch, dinner. Brunch bar. Children's menu. Business casual attire. Reservations recommended. Valet parking. Outdoor seating. **$$$**

# PETERSBURG

A Ranger District office of the Monongahela National Forest is located in Petersburg.
*Information: West Virginia Mountain Highlands, 1200 Harrison Ave., Elkins,*
*304-636-8400; www.mountainhighlands.com*

## WHAT TO SEE AND DO

### MONONGAHELA NATIONAL FOREST

*USDA Forest Service, Petersburg, 304-257-4488; www.fs.fed.us*

Recreation area is popular for canoeing, hiking and other outdoor sports. Camping (fee).

**WEST VIRGINIA**

★
★
★
★
★

## HOTEL
### ★★HERMITAGE MOTOR INN
*203 Virginia Ave., Petersburg, 304-257-1711, 800-437-6482; www.hermitageinn.net*
38 rooms. Complimentary continental breakfast. **$**

# PHILIPPI
The first land battle of the Civil War, a running rout of the Confederates known locally as the Philippi Races, was fought here on June 3, 1861. A historical marker on the campus of Alderson-Broaddus College marks the site. The Union attacked to protect the Baltimore & Ohio Railroad, whose main line between Washington and the West ran near the town.
*Information: Barbour County Chamber of Commerce, Philippi, 304-457-1958; www.barbourchamber.com*

## WHAT TO SEE AND DO
### BARBOUR COUNTY HISTORICAL SOCIETY MUSEUM
*146 N. Main St., Philippi, 304-457-4846; www.ohwy.com*
This B & O Railroad station was built in 1911 and used until 1956. It is now restored as a museum; also local arts and crafts. May-October, daily; November-April, by appointment.

### COVERED BRIDGE
*200 N. Main St., Philippi; www.philippi.org*
Spanning the Tygart River since 1852; restored in recent years; believed to be the only two-lane bridge of its type still in daily use on a federal highway (Highway 250).

## SPECIAL EVENTS
### BARBOUR COUNTY FAIR
*Fairgrounds, Highway 250 between Phillipi and Belington, 304-823-1328; www.barbourcountyfair.com*
Horse and antique car shows, quilt and livestock exhibits, carnival rides, nightly entertainment, parade and more. Week before Labor Day.

### BLUE & GRAY REUNION
*Philippi, 304-457-1958; www.philippi.org*
Commemorates the first land battle of the Civil War; reenactment, parade, crafts. First weekend in June.

## HOTEL
### ★PHILIPPI LODGING
*Highway 250 South, Route 4, Philippi, 304-457-5888*
39 rooms. **$**

## RESTAURANTS
### ★★BLUESTONE DINING ROOM
*Pipestem Resort, Pipestem, 304-466-1800*
American menu. Breakfast, lunch, dinner. Children's menu. Casual attire. **$$**

★
★
★
★

## ★★MOUNTAIN CREEK

*Pipestem Resort, Pipestem, 304-466-1800*

French, American menu. Dinner. Closed November-April. Bar. Children's menu. Casual attire. Dining room at 1,000-foot-deep gorge; accessible by tram only; park in Pipestem Resort State Park. **$$$**

## ★★OAK SUPPER CLUB

*Just North of Pipestem State Park entrance, Pipestem, 304-466-4800*

American menu. Dinner. Closed Sunday, Monday; also January-mid-February. Bar. Children's menu. Casual attire. **$$**

# POINT PLEASANT

On October 10, 1774, British-incited Shawnees under Chief Cornstalk fought a battle here against 1,100 frontiersmen. The colonists won and broke the Native American power in the Ohio Valley. Historians later argued that this, rather than the battle at Lexington, Massachusetts, was the first battle of the Revolutionary War. In 1908, the U.S. Senate rewrote history by recognizing this claim.

*Information: Mason County Area Chamber of Commerce, 305 Main St., Point Pleasant, 304-675-3844*

## WHAT TO SEE AND DO

### EAST LYNN WILDLIFE MANAGEMENT AREA

*McClintic Road, Point Pleasant, 304-675-0871*

Almost 23,000 acres used primarily by sportsmen; trails, primitive camping. Skiing.

### KRODEL PARK AND LAKE

*Highways 2 and 62, Point Pleasant, 304-675-1068; www.ptpleasantwv.org*

A 44-acre park with a 1775 replica of Fort Randolph. Fishing (license required), paddle boats (fee); miniature golf (fee), playground, camping. April-November.

### MANSION HOUSE

*1 Main St., Point Pleasant, 304-675-0869*

Oldest log building in Kanawha Valley, restored as a museum. May-October, daily.

### MCCLINTIC WILDLIFE MANAGEMENT AREA

*McClintic Road, Point Pleasant, 304-675-0871*

Approximately 2,800 acres with primitive camping (fee). Also fishing and hunting (licenses required).

### TU-ENDIE-WEI STATE PARK

*1 Main St., Point Pleasant, 304-675-0869, 800-225-5982;*
*www.wvparks.com/pointpleasant*

An 84-foot granite shaft was erected here in 1909 after the U.S. Senate agreed to a claim made by historians that the first battle of the Revolutionary War was fought

**571**

**WEST VIRGINIA**

★
★
★
★
★

here. The park also contains a marker where Joseph Celeron de Bienville buried a leaden plate in 1749, claiming the land for France, and the graves of Chief Cornstalk and "Mad Anne" Bailey, a noted pioneer scout.

### WEST VIRGINIA STATE FARM MUSEUM
*Highway 1, Point Pleasant, 304-675-5737; www.wvfarmmuseum.org*
Contains more than 30 farm buildings depicting early rural life, including a log church, one-room schoolhouse, kitchen, scale house and four-unit building. Barn contains mount of one of the largest horses in the world; also animals. April-November, Tuesday-Sunday.

### SPECIAL EVENT
### MASON COUNTY FAIR
*County Fairgrounds, Point Pleasant, 304-675-5463; masoncountyfairwv.org*
Livestock show, arts and crafts, contests, Nashville entertainers. Mid-August.

# ROANOKE

### HOTEL
#### ★★★STONEWALL RESORT
*940 Resort Drive, Roanoke, 304-269-7400, 888-278-8150; www.stonewallresort.com*
On the shore of Stonewall Jackson Lake, this resort offers accommodations in a lodge, private villa or waterfront home. The comfortable rooms come equipped with wireless Internet access and the resort features a signature Arnold Palmer golf course. 198 rooms. Children's activity center. Spa. Restaurant. Wireless Internet access. $

# SENECA ROCKS

### WHAT TO SEE AND DO
### SMOKE HOLE CAVERNS
*Highway 28 South, Seneca Rocks, 304-257-4442, 800-828-8478; www.smokehole.com*
These caverns were used centuries ago by the Seneca for shelter and the smoking of meat. During the Civil War, they were used by troops on both sides for storing ammunition. Later, they hid "moonshiners," illegal distillers of corn whiskey. It is claimed that the caverns contain the longest ribbon stalactite and the second highest cave room in the world. Guided tours. Large gift shop with wildlife exhibits; concessions. Daily 9 a.m.-5 p.m.

### HOTEL
#### ★SMOKE HOLE HOTEL & LOG CABINS
*Highway 28 South, Seneca Rocks, 304-257-4442, 800-828-8478; www.smokehole.com*
10 rooms. $

★
★★
★★★
★★★★

# SHEPHERDSTOWN

In 1787, Shepherdstown was the site of the first successful public launching of a steamboat. However, James Rumsey, inventor of the craft, died before he could exploit his success. Rival claims by John Fitch and Robert Fulton's commercial success with the "Clermont" 20 years later, have clouded Rumsey's achievement.

The state's first newspaper was published here in 1790, and Shepherdstown almost became the national capital. (George Washington considered it as a possible site, according to letters in the Library of Congress.) Shepherdstown is also the location of one of the early gristmills, which was most likely constructed around 1739. It finally ceased production in 1939. This is the oldest continuously settled town in the state.

*Information: Jefferson County Chamber of Commerce, 201 Frontage Road,*
*Charles Town, 304-725-2055, 800-624-0577; www.jeffersoncounty.com/chamber*

## WHAT TO SEE AND DO
### HISTORIC SHEPHERDSTOWN MUSEUM
*129 E. German St., Shepherdstown, 304-876-0910;*
*www.historicshepherdstown.com/museum.htm*
Artifacts dating to the 1700s, including many items concerning the founding of the town. Guided tours (by appointment). April-October, daily. Saturday 11 a.m.-5 p.m., Sunday 1 p.m.-4 p.m.

### GUIDED WALKING TOURS
*129 E. German St., Shepherdstown, 304-876-0910*
Historic sites in Shepherdstown.

## HOTEL
### ★★★BAVARIAN INN & LODGE
*164 Shepherd Grade Road, Shepherdstown, 304-876-2551;*
*www.bavarianinnwv.com*
This inn is decorated with Federal period reproductions and provides European-style hospitality. Four-poster mahogany beds, brass chandeliers and bathrooms with imported marble grace each room. 72 rooms. Restaurant. **$$**

## SPECIALTY LODGING
### THOMAS SHEPHERD INN
*300 W. German St., Shepherdstown, 304-876-3715, 888-889-8952, 304-260-5685;*
*www.thomasshepherdinn.com*
This cozy inn was built in 1868 in the Federal style of architecture. The guest rooms have been lovingly restored and feature the original floors and Oriental rugs. Six rooms. Complimentary full breakfast. **$**

## RESTAURANTS
### ★★★BAVARIAN INN AND LODGE
*164 Shepherd Grade Road, Shepherdstown, 304-876-2551;*
*www.bavarianinnwv.com*
Few places serve such authentic German fare. Seasonal entrees include pork tenderloin picatta on sautéed spatzle, wilted spinach and a Dijon mustard sauce; and seared grouper filet. Stone fireplaces and dark woods create a rustic yet elegant ambience. German menu. Breakfast, lunch, dinner. Bar. Children's menu. **$$$**

### ★★★YELLOW BRICK BANK RESTAURANT
*201 E. German St., Shepherdstown, 304-876-2208; www.yellowbrickbank.com*
Housed in a restored 19th-century bank building in a rural town near the upper Poto-

WEST VIRGINIA

★
★
★
★
★

mac, this surprisingly inventive restaurant serves creative cuisine in an airy, high-ceilinged dining room. Contemporary American menu. Lunch, dinner, Sunday brunch. Bar. $$

# SUMMERSVILLE

Twenty-year-old Nancy Hart led a surprise Confederate attack on Summersville in July 1861, captured a Union force and burned the town. She was captured, but her jail guard succumbed to her charms. The guard was then disarmed and killed by the young woman. She escaped to Lee's lines. After the war she returned to Summersville.

*Information: Chamber of Commerce, 411 Old Main Drive, Summersville,*
*304-872-1588, 800-760-6158; www.summersvillechamber.com*

## WHAT TO SEE AND DO

### CARNIFEX FERRY BATTLEFIELD STATE PARK

*1194 Carnifex Ferry Road, Summersville, 304-872-0825;*
*www.carnifexbattlefieldstatepark.com*

Here on September 10, 1861, 7,000 Union troops under General William S. Rosecrans fought and defeated a lesser number of Confederates under General John B. Floyd. The 156-acre park includes Patterson House Museum (Memorial Day-weekend after Labor Day, Saturday, Sunday, holidays). The museum displays Civil War relics. Hiking trails, picnicking, game courts, playgrounds, concession. Civil War reenactment (weekend after Labor Day). Park (May-early September, daily).

### SUMMERSVILLE LAKE

*Summersville, 304-872-3459*

A 2,700-acre lake. Swimming, waterskiing, fishing, boating; hiking, picnicking. Battle Run Campground is three miles West on Highway 129 (fee). May-October, daily. Fee for some activities.

## SPECIAL EVENTS

### NICHOLAS COUNTY FAIR

*616 Church St., Summersville, 304-872-1454*

Midway, flower show, agricultural and crafts exhibits. July.

### NICHOLAS COUNTY POTATO FESTIVAL

*411 Old Main Drive, Summersville, 304-872-1211*

Includes parades, entertainment, volleyball tournament, arts and crafts show, bed races. First full week in September.

## HOTELS

### ★BEST WESTERN SUMMERSVILLE LAKE MOTOR LODGE

*1203 Broad St., Summersville, 304-872-6900, 800-214-9551;*
*www.bestwestern.com*

57 rooms. Pets accepted. Complimentary continental breakfast. High-speed Internet access. $

## ★COMFORT INN

*903 Industrial Drive North, Summersville, 304-872-6500, 877-424-6423;*
*www.choicehotels.com*

99 rooms. Pets accepted. Complimentary continental breakfast. High-speed Internet access. **$**

# SUTTON

## WHAT TO SEE AND DO

### SUTTON LAKE

*South Stonewall St., Sutton, 304-765-2816*

Swimming in designated areas, boat launch (fee); camping (May-December; some electric hookups; fee) at Gerald R. Freeman Campground.

## HOTEL

### ★★DAYS INN

*2000 Sutton Lane, Sutton, 304-765-5055, 800-329-7466; www.daysinn.com*

201 rooms. High-speed Internet access. Fitness center. Pool. **$**

# VIENNA

## SPECIALTY LODGING

### WILLIAMS' HOUSE BED & BREAKFAST

*5406 Grand Central Ave., Vienna, 304-295-7212; www.wvbnbs.com/inns/65.html*

Built in 1920, this red brick home is a romantic getaway near the Ohio state line. Many antiques and family memorabilia, along with canopy and four-poster beds, add warmth and charm to this country home. Nearby attractions include the Grand Central Shopping Mall, Blennerhassett Island Historical Park, historical Marietta, Ohio and plenty of dining. Five rooms. Children over 12 years only. Complimentary full breakfast. **$**

# WEBSTER SPRINGS

Once a resort famed for its medicinal "lick" (a.k.a. spring) the town is now a trading center and meeting place for sportsmen.

*Information: Mayor's Office, 146 McGraw Ave., Webster Springs, 304-847-5411*

## WHAT TO SEE AND DO

### HOLLY RIVER STATE PARK

*Webster Springs, 304-493-6353; www.hollyriver.com*

More than 8,100 acres and the second largest state park in the state. Camping, cabins, picnicking, hiking. Standard fees.

### KUMBRABOW STATE FOREST

*Webster Springs, 304-335-2219; www.kumbrabow.com*

More than 9,400 acres of wild, rugged country with trout fishing; deer, turkey and grouse hunting; hiking trails, cross-country skiing, picnicking, playground, tent and trailer camping, five rustic cabins.

**WEST VIRGINIA**

★
★
★
★
★

## WEBSTER COUNTY FAIR

*Webster Springs, 304-226-3888; www.websterartists.com/local_attractions.html*
Rides, agricultural exhibits, entertainers, horse show. Labor Day week.

### WEBSTER SPRINGS WOODCHOPPING FESTIVAL

*Webster Springs, 304-847-7666; www.woodchoppingfestival.com*
Southeastern World Woodchopping Championships; state championship turkey calling contest, draft horse pull, horse show, fireman's rodeo. Arts and crafts. Music. Parades. Concessions. Memorial Day weekend.

# WEIRTON

Weirton has been a steel-producing town since its founding in 1910 by Ernest T. Weir, who also founded the Weirton Steel Company. In 1984, Weirton Steel became the largest employee-owned steel company in the world. Modern plants produce tin plate and hot-rolled, cold-rolled and galvanized steels for containers, automobiles, appliances and other products.

*Information: Chamber of Commerce, 3200 Maine St., Weirton, 304-748-7212; www.weirtonchamber.com*

## WHAT TO SEE AND DO

### TOMLINSON RUN STATE PARK

*Weirton, 304-564-3651; www.tomlinsonrunsp.com*
Approximately 1,400 acres. Swimming pool, bathhouse, fishing, boating on 27-acre lake (rowboat and paddleboat rentals); hiking trails, miniature golf, tennis, picnicking, playground, tent and trailer camping (dump station). Nature, recreation programs (summer).

### WEIRTON STEEL CORP AND HALF MOON INDUSTRIAL PARK

*400 Three Springs Drive, Weirton, 304-797-2828*
Tours of Alpo and others.

# WESTON

Surveyed originally by "Stonewall" Jackson's grandfather, Weston is a center for coal, oil and gas production, as well as the manufacture of glass products. The Weston State Hospital, completed in 1880 and said to be the largest hand-cut stone building in the nation, is located in town.

*Information: Lewis County Convention & Visitors Bureau, 499 U.S. Highway 33 East, Weston, 304-269-7328; www.stonewallcountry.com*

## WHAT TO SEE AND DO

### CEDAR CREEK STATE PARK

*2947 Cedar Creek Road, Weston, 304-462-7158; www.cedarcreeksp.com*
More than 2,400 acres. Swimming pool, bathhouse, fishing, boating (rentals); hiking trails, miniature golf, tennis, game courts, picnicking, playground, concession, tent and trailer camping (dump station). Park office in restored log cabin.

**576**

**WEST VIRGINIA**

★
★
★
★
★

### JACKSON'S MILL STATE 4-H CONFERENCE CENTER

*160 WVU Jackson Mill, Weston, 304-269-5100, 800-287-8206; www.wvu.edu*

First camp of its kind in the U.S.; 43 buildings, gardens, swimming pool, amphitheater, interfaith chapel. Picnicking.

### JACKSON'S MILL HISTORIC AREA

*Weston, 304-269-5100; www.wvu.edu*

Includes Blaker's Mill, an operating water-powered gristmill; blacksmith shop; McWharten cabin; Mary Conrad's cabin; and Jackson's Mill Museum, where "Stonewall" Jackson lived and worked as a boy. Museum represents grist and saw milling agriculture and home arts of the area as practiced 100 years ago. Memorial Day-Labor Day, Tuesday-Sunday; May and after Labor Day-mid-October, weekends only.

### STONEWALL JACKSON LAKE AND DAM

*Route 33 West, Weston, 304-269-4588*

Approximately 2,500-acre lake with over 82 miles of shoreline created by impounding the waters of the West Fork River. Swimming, scuba diving, waterskiing, fishing, boating (ramps, rentals, marinas); picnicking, camping. Visitor center.

### STONEWALL JACKSON LAKE STATE PARK

*Route 19, Weston, 304-269-0523, 888-278-8150;*
*www.stonewalljacksonsp.com*

Approximately 3,000 acres. Fishing, boating (launch, marina); nature and fitness trails, picnicking, playground, camping (hookups). Visitor center. Standard hours, fees.

**577**

## SPECIAL EVENTS
### HORSE SHOW

*Trefz Farm, Route 88 and National Road, Weston, 304-269-3257*

Saddle, walking, harness, pony, western and Arabian riding. Usually July.

### STONEWALL JACKSON HERITAGE ARTS & CRAFTS JUBILEE

*Weston, 304-269-1863; www.jubileewv.com*

Mountain crafts, music, dance and food. Labor Day weekend.

## HOTEL
### ★COMFORT INN

*Route 33 East and Interstate 79, Weston, 304-269-7000, 877-424-6423;*
*www.choicehotels.com*

70 rooms. Pets accepted. Complimentary continental breakfast. **$**

**WEST VIRGINIA**

★
★
★
★
★

# WHEELING

Wheeling stands on the site of Fort Henry, built in 1774 by Colonel Ebenezer Zane and his two brothers, who named the fort for Virginia's Governor Patrick Henry. In 1782 the fort was the scene of the Revolutionary War's final battle, a battle in which the valiant young pioneer Betty Zane was a heroine. The fort had withstood several Native American and British sieges during the war. However, during the last siege (after the war had officially ended), the fort's defenders ran out of powder. Betty Zane, sister of the colonel, volunteered to run through the gunfire to the outlying Zane cabin for more. With the powder gathered in her apron, she made the 150-yard trek back to the fort and saved the garrison. Zane Grey, a descendant of the Zanes, wrote a novel about Betty and her exploit.

Today, Wheeling is home to many industries, including producers of steel, iron, tin, chemical products, pottery, glass, paper, tobacco, plastics and coal.

*Information: Convention & Visitors Bureau, 1401 Main St., Wheeling, 304-233-7709, 800-828-3097; www.wheelingcvb.com*

## WHAT TO SEE AND DO
### ARTISAN CENTER
*1400 Main St., Wheeling, 304-232-1810; www.artisancenter.com*
Restored 1860s Victorian warehouse houses River City Ale Works, West Virginia's largest brew pub. "Made in Wheeling" crafts and exhibits; artisan demonstrations. Daily.

### JAMBOREE USA
*Capitol Music Hall, 1015 Main St., Wheeling, 304-234-0050, 800-624-5456; www.jamboreehills.com*
Live country music shows presented by WWVA Radio since 1933. Saturdays.

### KRUGER STREET TOY & TRAIN MUSEUM
*144 Kruger St., Wheeling, 304-242-8133, 877-242-8133; www.toyandtrain.com*
Collection of antique toys, games and playthings in a restored Victorian-era schoolhouse. Daily 10 a.m.-6 p.m.

### MANSION AND GLASS MUSEUM
*1330 National Road, Wheeling, 304-242-7272; www.museumsofwv.org*
Period rooms, exhibits trace history from 1835-present. Daily.

### OGLEBAY RESORT PARK
*Route 88 North, Wheeling, 304-243-4000, 800-624-6988; www.oglebay-resort.com*
A 1,650-acre municipal park. Indoor and outdoor swimming pools, fishing, paddle boating on three-acre Schenk Lake; three 18-hole golf courses, miniature golf, tennis courts, picnicking, restaurant, snack shop, cabins, lodge. Train ride; 65-acre Good Children's Zoo (fee) with animals in natural habitat. Benedum Natural Science Theater; garden center; arboretum with four miles of walking paths; greenhouses; observatory. Fee for most activities.

### SITE OF FORT HENRY
*11th and Main streets, Wheeling, 304-233-7709; www.wheelingcvb.com*
Bronze plaque marks the location of the fort that Betty Zane saved.

### WEST VIRGINIA INDEPENDENCE HALL
*1528 Market St., Wheeling, 304-238-1300; www.wvculture.org*
Site of the 1859 meeting at which Virginia's secession from the Union was declared unlawful, and the independent state of West Virginia was created. The building, used as a post office, custom office and federal court until 1912, has been restored. It

now houses, exhibits and events relating to the state's cultural heritage, including an interpretive film and rooms with period furniture. March-December, daily; January-February, Monday-Saturday.

## WHEELING PARK

*1801 National Road, Wheeling, 304-243-4085; www.wheeling-park.com*

Approximately 400 acres. Swimming pool, water slide, boating on Good Lake; golf, miniature golf, indoor/outdoor tennis, ice skating (rentals), picnicking, playground, refreshment area with video screen and lighted dance floor. Aviary. Fees for activities. Daily; some facilities seasonal.

## SPECIAL EVENTS

### JAMBOREE IN THE HILLS

*1015 Main St., Wheeling, 800-624-5456; www.jamboreeinthehills.com*

A four-day country music festival featuring more than 30 hours of music; top country stars. Camping available. Third weekend in July.

### OGLEBAYFEST

*Oglebay Resort Park, Route 88 North, Wheeling, 304-243-4000, 800-624-6988; www.oglebay-resort.com*

Country fair, artists' market, fireworks, parade, ethnic foods, contests, square and round dancing, entertainment. First weekend in October.

### WINTER FESTIVAL OF LIGHTS

*Oglebay Resort Park, Route 88 North, Wheeling, 304-243-4000, 800-624-6988*

A 350-acre holiday lighting display featuring lighted buildings and more than 500,000 lights, including 28-foot candy canes and giant swans on Schenk Lake. Winter Fantasy in Good Zoo. November-January.

## HOTELS

### ★HAMPTON INN

*795 National Road, Wheeling, 304-233-0440, 800-426-7866; www.hamptoninn.com*

104 rooms. Complimentary continental breakfast. Restaurant. **$**

### ★★OGLEBAY FAMILY RESORT

*Oglebay Park, Route 88 North, Wheeling, 304-243-4000, 800-624-6988; www.oglebay-resort.com*

212 rooms. Children's activity center. Airport transportation available. **$$**

## SPECIALTY LODGING

### WHEELING ISLAND

*1 S. Stone St., Wheeling, 877-943-3546; www.wheelingisland.com*

Greyhound racing has been a tradition in Wheeling since before the Civil War, and it continues to be so at Wheeling Island, where the downs have been augmented with casino action, three restaurants, a bar and a full-service hotel. 151 rooms. Restaurant, bar. **$$**

★
★
★
★
★

## RESTAURANT

### ★★★ERNIE'S ESQUIRE

*1015 E. Bethlehem Blvd., Wheeling, 304-242-2800*

A local landmark for nearly 50 years, this fine-dining restaurant serves a wide variety of options to suit any palate. Diners can enjoy the likes of tableside cooking and steaks cut to order. American menu. Lunch, dinner, late-night, Sunday brunch. Bar. Children's menu. Casual attire. Valet parking. $$$

# WHITE SULPHUR SPRINGS

In the 18th century, White Sulphur Springs became a fashionable destination for rich and famous colonists who came for the "curative" powers of the mineral waters. It has, for the most part, remained a popular resort ever since. A number of U.S. presidents summered in the town in the days before air-conditioning made Washington habitable in hot weather. The Tylers spent their honeymoon at the famous "Old White" Hotel. In 1913, the Old White Hotel gave way to the present Greenbrier Hotel, where President Wilson honeymooned with the second Mrs. Wilson. During World War II the hotel served as an internment camp for German and Japanese diplomats and later, as a hospital.

The first golf course in America was laid out near the town in 1884, but the first game was delayed when golf clubs, imported from Scotland, were held for three weeks by customs men who were suspicious of a game played with "such elongated blackjacks or implements of murder."

*Information: Chamber of Commerce, White Sulphur Springs, 304-536-2500; www.2chambers.com*

## WHAT TO SEE AND DO

### FISHING, SWIMMING, BOATING, CAMPING, HIKING

*White Sulphur Springs, 304-536-2144*

In Monongahela National Forest: Blue Bend Recreation Area, 6 miles North on WV 92, then 4 miles West on WV 16/21; Lake Sherwood Recreation Area, 23 miles North via WV 92, then 11 miles Northeast on WV 14.

### MEMORIAL PARK

*Greenbrier Avenue, White Sulphur Springs*

Swimming pool (Memorial Day-Labor Day; fee); tennis courts, ball fields, track, horseshoe pits, playground. Daily.

### NATIONAL FISH HATCHERY

*400 E. Main St., White Sulphur Springs, 304-536-1361*

Rainbow trout in raceways and ponds. Visitor center has display pool, aquariums and exhibits. Memorial Day-Labor Day, daily.

## SPECIAL EVENT

### DANDELION FESTIVAL

*White Sulphur Springs, 304-536-2323*

Entertainment. Exhibits. Arts and crafts. Memorial Day weekend.

## HOTEL
### ★★★★THE GREENBRIER
*300 W. Main St., White Sulphur Springs, 304-536-1110, 800-453-4858;*
*www.greenbrier.com*

Resting on a 6,500-acre estate in the picturesque Allegheny Mountains, The Greenbrier is one of America's oldest and finest resorts. The resort offers more than 50 recreational activities on its sprawling grounds. In addition to the three championship golf courses, the highly acclaimed Golf Digest Academy, tennis courts and fitness and spa facilities, guests are invited to partake in unique adventures like falconry, sporting clays and trap and skeet shooting. Consisting of rooms, suites, guest and estate houses, the accommodations reflect the resort's renowned tradition. The new Hemispheres restaurant serves up creative cuisine in a relaxed setting. 721 rooms. Children's activity center. Airport transportation available. Restaurant. Fitness center. Spa. **$$$**

## RESTAURANT
### ★★★THE GREENBRIER MAIN DINING ROOM
*300 W. Main St., White Sulphur Springs, 24986, 304-536-1110; 800-453-4858*
*www.greenbrier.com*

The breakfast menu changes with the seasons and the dinner menu changes daily at this elegant yet family-friendly resort, where diners can expect contemporary riffs on classic dishes along with a Southern-influenced continental style. The dinner menu offers lighter meals for those watching their intake, as well as a tempting dessert menu for those who are not. American, French menu. Breakfast, dinner. Children's menu. Jacket required. Reservations recommended. Valet parking. **$$$**

## SPA
### ★★★★THE GREENBRIER SPA
*300 W. Main St., White Sulphur Springs, 800-453-4858*

White Sulphur Springs has long drawn visitors to its waters for its purported healing powers. Modern-day wellness seekers visit the Greenbrier for its state-of-the-art spa facility. The spa's treatment menu draws on the history of the mineral springs, and guests are encouraged to enjoy one of the spa's famous hydrotherapy treatments, from mountain rain showers and sulphur soaks to detoxifying marine baths and mineral mountain baths. Mud, rose petal, mineral and marine wraps release toxins and revitalize skin, whereas black walnut and aromatherapy salt glows exfoliate and polish skin. Treatments designed for male guests, pregnant clients and teenagers round out this spa's comprehensive approach to well-being.

# WILLIAMSON

The center of the "billion-dollar coal field," Williamson is truly a coal town; the walls of the local Chamber of Commerce building, at the west corner of Courthouse Square, are made of coal.

*Information: Tug Valley Chamber of Commerce, 45 E. Second Ave., Williamson,*
*304-235-5240; www.2chambers.com*

★
★
★
★
★

## WHAT TO SEE AND DO

### CABWAYLINGO STATE FOREST

*Route 1, Williamson, 304-385-4255; www.cabwaylingo.com*

Approximately 8,100 acres. Swimming pool (Memorial Day-Labor Day), fishing; hunting, hiking trails, game courts, picnicking, playground, concession, tent and trailer camping (dump station), 13 cabins.

## SPECIAL EVENT

### KING COAL FESTIVAL

*28 Oak St., Williamson, 304-235-5560; www.kingcoalfestival.com*

Entertainment. Exhibits. Theatrical presentation. Country music. Square dancing. Mid-September.

# INDEX

**583**

**INDEX**

**584**

**INDEX**

★
★
★
★
★

**587**

**INDEX**

★
★
★
★
★

**591**

**INDEX**

★
★
★
★

**593**

**INDEX**

★
★
★
★
★

**INDEX**

**597**

**INDEX**

★
★
★
★
★

★
★
★
★
★

**599**

**INDEX**

★
★
★
★

**601**

**INDEX**

★
★
★
★

**603**

**INDEX**

★
★
★
★

**604**

**INDEX**

★
★
★
★

**605**

**INDEX**

★
★
★
★

**606**

**INDEX**

★
★
★
★

**607**

**INDEX**

**609**

**INDEX**

★
★
★
☆

**610**

**INDEX**

★
★
★
★

★
★
★
★
★

**613**

**INDEX**

★
★
★
★

★
★
★
★

**615**

**INDEX**

★
★
★
★

★
★
★
★

**620**

**INDEX**

★
★
★
★
★

**621**

**INDEX**

★
★
★

★
★
★
★
✦

INDEX

**625**

**INDEX**

★
★
★
★
★

Public Gaol (Williamsburg, VA), 525

Public Hospital (Williamsburg, VA), 525

Public Works Museum & Streetscape (Baltimore, MD), 96

Publick Times (Williamsburg, VA), 527

Pufferbelly (Erie, PA), 257

Puglioni's (Morgantown, WV), 567

Pulcinella (McLean, VA), 466

Pungo Grill (Virginia Beach, VA), 517

Pungo Strawberry Festival (Virginia Beach, VA), 515

The Putnam Sculptures (Princeton, NJ), 204

★
★
★
★

**Q**

Quality Inn & Suites (Erie, PA), 257

Quality Inn (Bedford, PA), 228

Quality Inn (Carlisle, PA), 241

Quality Inn (Chambersburg, PA), 243

Quality Inn (Danville, PA), 249

Quality Inn (Front Royal, VA), 435

Quality Inn (Gettysburg, PA), 265

Quality Inn (Hampton, VA), 441

Quality Inn (Hopewell, VA), 444

Quality Inn (Lebanon, PA), 294

Quality Inn (Morgantown, WV), 567

Quality Inn (Norfolk, VA), 480

Quality Inn (Ocean City, MD), 134

Quality Inn (Richmond, VA), 498

Quality Inn (Somerset, PA), 362

Quality Suites (Pittsburgh, PA), 350

The Queen Victoria Bed & Breakfast Inn (Cape May, NJ), 166

Queen's Hotel (Cape May, NJ), 166

Quiet Valley Living Historical Farm (Stroudsburg, PA), 366

Quilt Show (Fairfax, VA), 425

Quilt Show (Fredericksburg, VA), 431

**R**

R. T.'s (Alexandria, VA), 393

Rabbit's Ferry House (Lewes, DE), 62

Radisson Hotel Hampton (Hampton, VA), 441

Radisson Hotel Lynchburg (Lynchburg, VA), 459

Radisson Lackawanna Station Hotel Scranton (Scranton, PA), 360

Radisson Penn Harris Hotel & Convention Center (Camp Hill, PA), 273

The Radisson Plaza Warwick Hotel (Philadelphia, PA), 332

The Radnor Hotel (Saint Davids, PA), 285

Railfest (Altoona, PA), 226

Railroad Museum of Pennsylvania (Strasburg, PA), 365

Railroader's Memorial Museum (Altoona, PA), 225

Raku (Bethesda, MD), 107

Raku-An (Washington, DC), 51

Raleigh Tavern (Williamsburg, VA), 525

Ram's Head Inn (Galloway City, NJ), 176

Ramada (Lake Harmony, PA), 288

Ramada (Ligonier, PA), 297

Ramada Inn (Altoona, PA), 226

Ramada Inn (Hazleton, PA), 275

Ramada Inn (Salisbury, MD), 139

Ramada Inn (Toms River, NJ), 214

Ramada Inn Laurel (Laurel, MD), 131

Ramada Inn South Fredericksburg (Fredericksburg, VA), 432

Randolph-Macon College (Ashland, VA), 401

Randolph-Macon Women's College (Lynchburg, VA), 459

Rangoon Burmese Restaurant (Philadelphia, PA), 339

The Raven & the Peach (Fair Haven, NJ), 206

Reading Public Museum and Art Gallery (Reading, PA), 357

Reading Terminal Market (Philadelphia, PA), 323

River tours (Uniontown, PA), *369*

River Walk Art Festival (York, PA), *382*

River's Inn Restaurant & Crab Deck (Gloucester Point, VA), *531*

Riverfront Park, *272*

Riverside Campground (Abingdon, VA), *384*

Riverside Inn (Cambridge Springs, PA), *239*

Riverside Park (Lynchburg, VA), *459*

Riverview Park (Pittsburgh, PA), *347*

Robert E. Lee Monument (Charlottesville, VA), *410*

Robert Fulton Birthplace (Lancaster, PA), *291*

Robert Johnson House (Annapolis, MD), *85*

Robert Morris Inn (Oxford, MD), *118*

Roberto's Dolce Vita (Beach Haven Terrace, NJ), *156*

Robin Hood Dell East (Philadelphia, PA), *329*

Robinson House Museum (Wellsboro, PA), *375*

Rock Creek Park (Washington, DC), *27*

Rockingham County Fair (Harrisonburg, VA), *443*

Rockville Bridge (Harrisburg, PA), *272*

Rockwood Museum (Wilmington, DE), *73*

Rocky Gap Lodge & Golf Resort (Flintstone, MD), *120*

Rocky Gap State Park (Cumberland, MD), *116*

Rocky Grove fireman's Fair & parade (Franklin, PA), *261*

Rocky Knob Information Station, *404*

Rocky Knob Trail (Blue Ridge Parkway, VA), *404*

Rocky Mount Historic Site (Bristol, VA), *407*

Rod's Steak and Seafood Grille (Convent Station, NJ), *191*

Rodef Shalom Biblical Botanical Garden (Pittsburgh, PA), *347*

Rodin Museum (Philadelphia, PA), *324*

Roger Brooke Taney Home (Frederick, MD), *122*

Rose Festival, *298*

Rosewell Historic Ruins (Gloucester, VA), *437*

Round Valley State Park (Clinton, NJ), *170*

Roy's Place (Gaithersburg, MD), *125*

Rubles Sternwheelers Riverboat Cruises (Parkersburg, WV), *568*

Rudee's on the Inlet (Virginia Beach, VA), *517*

Ruins of St. John's Episcopal Church (Harpers Ferry WV), *559*

Russia House (Herndon, VA), *423*

The Rutgers Gardens (New Brunswick, NJ), *194*

Rutgers-The State University of New Jersey (New Brunswick, NJ), *194*

Ruth's Chris Steak House (Baltimore, MD), *103*

Ruth's Chris Steak House (Bethesda, MD), *107*

Ruth's Chris Steak House (Midlothian, VA), *468*

Ruth's Chris Steak House (Philadelphia, PA), *339*

The Ryland Inn (Whitehouse, NJ), *219*

## S

S. B. Elliott State Park (Clearfield, PA), *246*

Saber Room (Wilkes Barre, PA), *378*

Sachiko's Porterhouse (Lynchburg, VA), *460*

Sail Baltimore (Baltimore, MD), *96*

Sail into Summer Boat Show (Stone Harbor, NJ), *213*

Sailing Tours (Annapolis, MD), *82*

Sailor's Creek Battlefield Historic State Park (Fredericksburg, VA), *431*

Salisbury Zoological Park (Salisbury, MD), *139*

The Saloon (Philadelphia, PA), *339*

Sam and Harry's (Washington, DC), *52*

Sam Miller's Ocean Grill & Oyster Bar (Richmond, VA), *500*

Sam Snead's Tavern (Hot Springs, VA), *446*

Samuel C. Williams Library (Hoboken, NJ), *180*

San Carlo's (U.S. 30, York, PA), *382*

Sand Castle Bed and Breakfast (Barnegat Light, NJ), *186*

Sandcastle Water Park (Pittsburgh, PA), *347*

★
★
★
★

**629**

INDEX

**631**

**INDEX**

★
★
★
★

**633**

**INDEX**

★
★
★
★

**634**

**INDEX**

**635**

**INDEX**

★
★
★

★
★
★
★

**638**

**INDEX**

★
★
★
★

**INDEX**

★
★
★
★
★